When price elasticity is numerically	Demand is called	Thus if price changes	Quantity demanded changes (in opposite direction of price)	So that consumer
Greater than 1	Price-elastic	$P \uparrow$	More than in proportion	Fall
		$P \downarrow$	More than in proportion	Rise
Equal to 1	Unitary-elastic	$P \uparrow$	In proportion	Remain constant
		$P \downarrow$	In proportion	Remain constant
Less than 1	Price-inelastic	$P \uparrow$	Less than in proportion	Rise
		$P \downarrow$	Less than in proportion	Fall

Slutzky equation $\eta_t = \eta_s - k\iota$

Cross-price elasticity of demand $\eta_{xy} = \dfrac{\Delta q_x / q_x}{\Delta P_y / P_y} = \dfrac{\Delta q_x}{\Delta P_y} \cdot \dfrac{P_y}{q_x}$ or $\eta_{yx} = \dfrac{\Delta q_y / q_y}{\Delta P_x / P_x} = \dfrac{\Delta q_y}{\Delta P_x} \cdot \dfrac{P_x}{q_y}$

x and y are substitutes if $\eta_{xy} = \dfrac{\Delta q_x / q_x}{\Delta P_y / P_y}$

Quantity of x demanded increases} $\longrightarrow$
Price of y increases} $\longrightarrow$ $\dfrac{(+)/q_x}{(+)/P_y} = (+) = \eta_{xy}$

Quantity of x demanded decreases} $\longrightarrow$
Price of y decreases} $\longrightarrow$ $\dfrac{(-)/q_x}{(-)/P_y} = (+) = \eta_{xy}$

x and y are complements if

Quantity demanded of x increases} $\longrightarrow$
Price of y decreases} $\longrightarrow$ $\dfrac{(+)/q_x}{(-)/P_y} = (-) = \eta_{xy}$

Marginal revenue and price elasticity $MR = P\left(1 + \dfrac{1}{\eta}\right)$

Personal rate of discount
ρ = (marginal value an individual places on this year's goods in terms of foregone goods of next year) $- 1$

General formula for discounting $P_t = \dfrac{A}{(1 + r)^t}$

The relationship between marginal and average physical product
$MPP_L = APP_L + (\Delta APP_L)L$

The law of diminishing marginal returns
Holding technology and all inputs except one constant, as equal increments of the variable input are added, beyond a certain point the resulting rate of increase in output will decrease. Otherwise stated, after a certain point, the marginal physical product of the variable input will diminish.

INTERMEDIATE MICROECONOMICS: THEORY · ISSUES · APPLICATIONS

THIRD EDITION

INTERMEDIATE MICROECONOMICS
THEORY • ISSUES • APPLICATIONS

Roger LeRoy Miller
Department of Economics and
Center for Policy Studies
Clemson University

Roger E. Meiners
Department of Economics and
Center for Policy Studies
Clemson University

MCGRAW-HILL BOOK COMPANY

New York   St. Louis   San Francisco   Auckland   Bogotá   Hamburg
Johannesburg   London   Madrid   Mexico   Montreal   New Delhi
Panama   Paris   São Paulo   Singapore   Sydney   Tokyo   Toronto

INTERMEDIATE MICROECONOMICS: Theory · Issues · Applications

Copyright © 1986, 1982, 1978 by McGraw-Hill, Inc. All rights reserved.
Printed in the United States of America. Except as permitted under the
United States Copyright Act of 1976, no part of this publication may be
reproduced or distributed in any form or by any means, or stored in a data
base or retrieval system, without the prior written permission of the
publisher

1 2 3 4 5 6 7 8 9 0 HALHAL 89876

ISBN 0-07-042171-4

This book was set in Melior by J. M. Post Graphics, Corp.
The editors were Paul V. Short and Susan H. Ryf;
the designer was Gayle Jaeger;
the production supervisor was Phil Galea.
The drawings were done by Accurate Art, Inc.
Halliday Lithograph Corporation was printer and binder.

Library of Congress Cataloging-in-Publication Data

Miller, Roger LeRoy.
   Intermediate microeconomics.

   Includes bibliographies and index.
   1. Microeconomics.   I. Meiners, Roger E.   II. Title.
HB172.M64   1986   338.5   85-23183
ISBN 0-07-042171-4

53 5/1

ABOUT THE AUTHORS

ROGER LEROY MILLER earned his Ph.D. from the University of Chicago after his undergraduate studies at the University of California (Berkeley). Before coming to Clemson University, Miller taught at the University of Washington (Seattle) and at the University of Miami (Florida). He is one of the most prolific textbook authors in the history of economics. Fluent in French and Spanish, he enjoys travel to other nations and is an avid windsurfer in the summer and skier in the winter.

ROGER E. MEINERS received degrees in economics at Washington State University and the University of Arizona before obtaining the Ph.D. from Virginia Polytechnic Institute. He subsequently earned a law degree from the University of Miami, and taught at Texas A&M University, Emory University, and the University of Miami before becoming Professor of Economics at Clemson University. Reflecting his interests in law and economics, Meiners served as director of the Federal Trade Commission office in Atlanta. He has published a variety of books and articles that reflect broad interest in economic and legal policy. For relaxation he enjoys '50s and '60s rock and roll and supports the Clemson Tiger sports teams.

Contents

Preface

Microeconomics is exciting and relevant. A textbook for microeconomics should convey this excitement and this relevance. We have attempted in every way possible to do just that, while preserving completeness and thoroughness in the presentation of intermediate price theory.

Some have argued, and we concur, that microeconomics is the basis of virtually all economic analysis. It seems, therefore, especially imperative that students embarking upon a career in economics and/or business be conversant not only with the foundations of microeconomic theory but also with its application in the real world. At the end of each chapter, we have included a special Issues and Applications section which illustrates theory as a vehicle to clarify social issues and solve social problems. This serves two purposes: It reinforces the student's understanding of the theory and it demonstrates the theory's relevance. These special sections are inserted in such a way as to maintain the continuity of the text. Instructors can use them in a variety of ways or delete all or parts of them when desired.

Traditional materials included

In spite of the above-mentioned innovation, the organization of this book is traditional in nature. There is an introductory chapter; then there are chapters on the theory of consumer behavior, production and costs, the four product market organization possibilities, input markets, and general equilibrium and welfare economics. Thus, instructors used to a traditional text will feel at home with this one.

Before this book was published originally and before the publication of each new edition, decisions as to what to include were based in part on the results of extensive surveys undertaken by McGraw-Hill Book Company.

Detailed questionnaires have been sent to over a thousand professors who teach intermediate microeconomics. Each edition has, therefore, responded to the demands of the market to include more information on certain topics and less on other topics. Users of the previous edition—and nonusers—were asked to provide reviews of the text, so that the third edition reflects further refinements based on requested modifications and alterations.

Changes in the third edition

The first two editions of this text were written by Roger LeRoy Miller. For the third edition, Roger Meiners, who had authored one of the chapters in the original text, joined in the effort. We believe that this text had a reputation as being written clearly and in a user friendly manner. Nevertheless, we edited the text line-by-line to enhance its readability and to try to keep the vocabulary consistent with that of today's students.

The following is a partial list of the more significant changes made in the third edition.

1 Chapter One, often the most boring and useless chapter of a book, has been substantially revised to improve its usefulness and interest to students. Previously, it was the only chapter with no Issue and Applications section; it now has two topics on methodology that will be of interest to the instructor who discusses methodology.

2 The text now has a total of 56 topics in the Issues and Applications sections at the end of the chapters, an average of about three per chapter. One-half of these topics are new to this edition and many others have been revised. Consideration was given to integrating the topics into the text or to placing the topics in the text of the chapters, offset by a box or shaded pages, but we decided that this would distract the students as they concentrate on working through the theoretical tools being developed in the chapters. It also makes it easier for the instructor to eliminate issues of no interest.

3 The discussion of utility analysis and its applications has been expanded in Chapter 3. The discussion of "good goods" and "bad goods" expands the range of application of indifference analysis, as does the addition of some new topics in the Issues and Applications section.

4 Chapters 4 and 5 have been reorganized to make their flow seem more logical to the student. All of the derivations of elasticity measures are now in Chapter 5, so that those concepts, which are difficult to many students, are concentrated in one area to allow for comprehensive discussion. New topics include a review of Giffen's paradox and more examples of elasticity measurements.

5 Former Chapter 6, Time, Risk, Speculation and Hedging, has been divided into two chapters, 6 and 7, The Economics of Time: Planning for the Future, and Risk and Uncertainty in Decision Making. This allows for expansion of the discussion of issues that are being given more weight in intermediate microeconomics today. The discussion of risk and portfolio diversification has been expanded and the Issues and Applications section includes a review of Williamson's work on credible commitments.

6 Chapters 8 and 9 on the theory of the firm and production have new discussions of economies of scope and economies of scale, and a clearer explanation of multiplant production.

7 The chapter on linear programming has been moved to the back of the book as an appendix. It has not been reduced in coverage, but reviews indicate that many instructors do not use the chapter, and, of those who do, there was no agreement as to the proper location for the material. As an appendix, it can be assigned whenever the instructor thinks best.

8 Chapter 10, Competitive Pricing and Output, has been expanded to two chapters. New Chapter 11 covers Competitive Markets and the Role of Entrepreneurship. This allows for more discussion of competitive industries and the adjustment process in such industries. There is also a discussion of the expanding literature on market adjustment processes emphasized by the "Austrian school" of economics and a discussion of entrepreneurship, a popular topic with students today.

9 The two chapters on monopolies have been revised and new issues have been added, including a discussion of federal antitrust law, third-degree price discrimination, and profitability of regulated firms. As usual, such topics draw on articles published by leading economists in major journals.

10 The last edition had individual chapters on oligopoly and on monopolistic competition. The chapters have been shortened slightly and condensed into one chapter, in keeping with the general development in micro theory that devotes slightly less time to these subjects in favor of other topics now being given more attention.

11 Similarly, the two chapters from the last edition on input demand under competition and under monopoly have been condensed into one chapter. The major concepts are still covered, but, again, this appears to be in line with the general preference of the instructors.

12 Chapter 16 on Wages, Rents, and Income Differences has a clearer and more comprehensive discussion of economic rents and return to human capital. New Issues and Applications on discrimination in the labor force and on the economics of divorce have been added.

13 The chapter on welfare economics has been expanded to include a discussion of the meaning of social ethics in welfare economics and the importance of property rights or economic constitutions in determining the boundaries of economic inquiry.

14 An expanded explanation of game theory has been provided in an appendix, reviewing such concepts as the prisoners' dilemma.

The mathematics in this text

Students will find no mathematical "snow jobs" included herein. We have attempted to anticipate any difficult mathematical or analytical hurdles that students might encounter in understanding the development of a concept. We have, therefore, reduced the level of mathematics whenever this occurred or returned to very basic ideas and simple language in order to help the student understand what is going on. Thus, readers will find that any proofs given are fully explained, with no intermediate steps left out. There is no calculus anywhere, not even in the footnotes. The delta operator (Δ) is used extensively, though; students unfamiliar with the delta operator may consult the appendix to Chapter 3.

Key pedagogical aspects

There are a number of what we consider to be necessary features to this text to make it pedagogically more appealing to both instructors and students. Specifically, there are these features:

1   **Self-contained graphs.** All figures contain detailed legends which obviate the need to refer to the text to understand the graphs. This makes them easier to read the first time around and also allows the student to review more easily for examinations.

2   **Glossary of terms.** Each chapter presents new terms in **boldface** the first time they appear. They are again defined in a glossary section at the end of the chapter. Thus, the student finds reinforcement for new definitions while first reading the text and can also review terms at the end of each chapter. For further reference, an index of glossary terms is provided at the end of the book.

3   **Point-by-point chapter summaries.** These summaries serve as a brief refresher of the first reading of the chapter and also as a test of comprehension during review sessions with the book.

4   **Additional readings.** For those students who wish to do additional work in the area, appropriate references are provided.

5   **Problems.** Each chapter has problems; answers to even-numbered problems are given in the back of the book. Students can therefore test their understanding of the chapter materials by working through these problems. Professors can assign odd-numbered problems as homework or can use them in examinations. The problems never ask that the student do something the chapter has not prepared him or her to do.

6   **Endpapers.** The endpapers of this text contain a number of important theoretical notions that are developed throughout the book. They can be viewed as a quickie review/refresher/reference section for the student. After reading each chapter, students can glance at the endpapers to see which key theoretical points they should have mastered. They can also use the endpapers for quick reviews for examinations and quizzes.

7   **Supplementary materials.** This text is part of a complete package, which also includes a student's *Study Guide* and an *Instructor's Manual*. The *Study Guide*, prepared by our long-time associates, Ronald Reddall and William Lee, includes learning objectives, problems with answers, and other assorted materials which will greatly aid in the continued strengthening of the student's understanding of theoretical materials within each chapter.

The *Instructor's Manual* for this edition was prepared by Mark Mitchell, who wrote the manual while teaching the course using the text. The manual has been completely updated and includes a set of our random comments which can be integrated into lectures. These comments range from caveats in the analysis to more detailed theoretical points to areas in the theoretical development that may present problems for some students. There are also additional selected references relating to the theoretical and/or applications areas covered in each chapter. These references can be used as a basis for lecture preparation or can be given to more advanced students who wish to do further work in the specific areas under study.

Finally, and perhaps most importantly, the *Instructor's Manual* contains a test bank, with answers to all questions. Quizzes and examinations can be made up from the questions included in the test bank as well as the odd-numbered text problems, for which answers are provided in the manual.

An alternative short course

It is by no means necessary that the entire book be used in a one-term course. We suggest below the key chapters that might be used when sufficient time is not available for all materials to be covered:

Chapters 1–5
Chapter 8
Chapter 9
Chapter 10
Chapter 12
Chapters 15–16
Chapter 19

If, in a short course, the professor feels that he or she can cover more than this, then Chapters 14 and 18 can be added.

Acknowledgments to the first edition

There are a number of individuals who, at various stages of this project, offered careful and constructive criticism of the drafts of this manuscript. We list below in alphabetical order those individuals: Michael Behr (University of Wisconsin—Superior), Robert C. Bingham (Kent State University), Thomas Borcherding (Simon Fraser University), Louis De Alessi (University of Miami School of Law), William L. Holahan (University of Wisconsin—Milwaukee), Hugh Nourse (University of Missouri—St. Louis), Charles Shami (American Telephone and Telegraph), Eugene Silberberg (University of Washington), and Raburn Williams (University of Hawaii).

We would like to add a note of special thanks to Professor Robert C. Bingham, who helped out far in excess of the call of duty. His continued assistance aided appreciably in strengthening both the text and the supplementary materials.

Finally, we must express appreciation to our editors at McGraw-Hill Book Company, Stephen Dietrich and Michael Elia, both of whom worked more than they should have on this project.

Acknowledgments to the second edition

It would be impossible to list all the people who sent comments on the first edition. We give a partial list below of those people who provided extensive criticism: Roger Beck (University of Alberta—Canada), Thomas Borcherding (Simon Fraser University), Barry Field (University of Miami), Charles Holt (University of Minnesota), Curt Huttsell (Missouri Public Service Commission), Herbert Kessel (St. Michael's College), Nolin Masih (St. Cloud State University), Robert Puth (University of New Hampshire), Daniel Sullivan (ABT Associates), Fred Tank (University of Toledo), Roger Trenary (Kansas State University), and Edwin West (Carleton University—Canada).

We would like to thank Raymond P. H. Fishe (University of Miami) for his help in revising the chapter on linear programming and would also like to thank Robert Pulsinelli (Western Kentucky University) for his unfailing help at proofreading the galleys and page proofs.

Acknowledgments to the third edition

During the life of the last edition, many people wrote or called to point out specific errors or points that were less coherent than they should be. We thank everyone who was so kind as to take the time to provide such information. Detailed comments were provided by Jack Adams (University of Arkansas), Robert Cook (University of Richmond), Albert Danielson (University of Georgia), Charles Geiss (University of Missouri), Frank Maurer (Pace University), Bettina McConnell (Purdue University), James Moncur (University of Hawaii), Michael Morgan (College of Charleston), Marshall Nickles (Pepperdine University), Dorothy Siden (Salem State College), Stanley Stephenson (University of Hartford), and Rick Sullivan (University of Iowa).

Special thanks go to Craig Bolton of Emory University who provided comments on all aspects of the text.

ROGER LEROY MILLER
ROGER E. MEINERS

Introduction

One year we have a food surplus, and the next year Congress passes legislation giving farmers an incentive to produce more food. To fly from New York to Los Angeles, one person may pay $129 for a seat while the next person may pay $399 for an identical seat. The average annual salary of college professors probably is about $30,000, while major league baseball players consider striking because of "exploitation," even though their average salary is about $300,000 per year.

There are many more seeming paradoxes in the behavior of prices, markets, and individuals; the three just mentioned constitute only the tip of the iceberg. These problems also form the basis of a multitude of pressing social and economic issues that face us every day; if we don't notice them ourselves, the news media are sure to bring them to our attention. And if the media are not successful in that endeavor, politicians pick up these issues and use them in their campaigns.

How can an individual with some training in economics understand and, indeed, explain why paradoxes such as those mentioned above are not really paradoxes at all? How can one separate the real issues from the rhetoric when a politician speaks? For many such problems, a bare understanding of the so-called **budget constraint** is sufficient. When you realize that at any moment in time the total amount of resources is fixed, you are automatically faced with the fact that trade-offs must be made: When the politician asks for more of one thing, it usually means less of something else. But there are many issues which cannot be understood so simply. Rather, a more complete grasp of how markets work is necessary. The knowledge of and ability to apply basic microeconomic theory cannot fail to aid the inquisitive mind's attempt to understand how markets function. A microeconomic model can help give a better idea of how our entire economic system works and how it can be compared with other economic systems. It can even help predict what will happen in the world around us when parameters in our environment change.

THE CONCEPT OF SCARCITY

Why study microeconomics? The answer is the same as the answer to the broader question. Why study economics? The answer lies in the concept of **scarcity**. Scarcity is something that affects us all. Wouldn't you like to be able to study more and also have more time to watch TV or listen to music? Wouldn't you like to have more clothes without giving up any evenings "out on the town"? For most people, the answer to such questions is yes. Why can't we have more of everything? Because each of us individually and all of us collectively, as a society, are constrained by scarcity, the most basic concept in all of economics. Scarcity means that we do not have and cannot obtain enough income or wealth to satisfy every desire. We are referring to the way people feel: what they want, need, or desire *relative* to what is available at any moment in time.

SCARCITY AND CHOICE

Scarcity forces us to choose. You had to choose whether to go to college or instead get a job. You have to choose between jogging and studying during that same time period. Government policymakers must choose between using resources for the production of defense services or for the production of, say, educational services.

To be sure, the choices that we make are not constrained simply by economic resources. Choices also are constrained by political, legal, traditional, and moral forces. In this text, however, we will devote little space to the influence of such noneconomic forces on the choices that are made.

CLASSIFYING RESOURCES

We define "resources" as the inputs, or factors, used in the production of the things we desire.

Resources can be classified in a variety of ways. Every classification scheme is, to some extent, arbitrary. We can, nonetheless, consider natural resources, human resources, and capital resources as broad categories.

Natural resources: land and mineral deposits

Basically, when we think of land as a natural resource, we are considering the mineral deposits within the land. But there is also a natural resource on the surface and above the land: climate, topography, and fertility. Some land can grow phenomenal amounts of crops without the addition of much water or fertilizer; other land is incapable of growing anything without substantial alteration of its chemistry.

Human resources: labor

To produce the things we desire, human resources must be used. Those resources consist of the productive contributions of labor made by individuals when they work.

Capital resources

When labor is applied to land—to grow corn, for example—something else is used. Usually it is a plow or a tractor. That is to say, land and labor are combined with capital, or manufactured, resources to produce the things we desire. Capital consists of machines, buildings, and tools. Additionally, capital consists of improvements to natural resources, such as grading of land on which to build more factories.

Another human resource: entrepreneurship

There is, in effect, a fourth type of input used in production. It is a human resource, and it consists of entrepreneurial talents, or entrepreneurship. The way to understand entrepreneurship is to define what an entrepreneur does or is expected to do.

An entrepreneur can be defined as a person who does the following:

1 Takes the initiative in combining land, labor, and capital in order to produce a commodity
2 Makes the basic decisions that affect the destiny of a business
3 Takes risks, the reward for which is profit
4 Forms business organizations and introduces new products and new techniques

Without entrepreneurship virtually no large-scale business organization could function. Clearly, entrepreneurship as a human resource is scarce; not everyone is willing to take risks or has the ability to make correct business decisions.

ECONOMIC GOODS

Scarce resources are combined to produce what are called **economic goods,** the subject of our study throughout this book. Any good or service produced from scarce resources is also scarce. Because economic goods are scarce, we constantly face decisions about how to use them. After all, the quantity of goods demanded or desired, by definition, exceeds the amount that is directly available from nature at a zero price; this is implicit in our definition of economic goods.

However, not all goods are economic; some are free.

FREE GOODS

There are some things around that we call **free goods** as opposed to economic goods. No goods are really free; some simply have no market price at the present time, so they are treated as if they are free. Old economics textbooks called air a free good, but that is really no longer true; at least it is not true everywhere. In many cities, pollution makes the air "unfit to breathe." Clean air there is not a free good; there is a cost to making it clean. In many mountain areas, air is still clean and is a free good. You can have all that you want without sacrifice, and so can anybody else who manages to hike there. One needn't worry about how free goods, including air and running water in many wilderness areas, will be allocated among competing interests. There is a lot of air and water, and only a few want to use them. There is no scarcity involved.
There is no scarcity involved.

Who is interested in free goods, then? Certainly not economists. Perhaps physicists, hydrologists, biologists, and chemists are interested in free air and water. But the economist steps in only when the problem of scarcity arises, as it does in urban areas, where the allocation of scarce resources is at issue. We have seen throughout history that as population and production increase over time, many previously "free" goods have become "economic" goods, such as land for mining, water and air for industrial uses, and water for hydroelectric power. To the native American Indian population, tobacco leaves growing in the wild were a free good before Sir Walter Raleigh's arrival. The Indians could have all they wanted without sacrifice. Later, however, tobacco leaves became an economic good.

THE MARKET OR PRICE SYSTEM AS A FORM
OF SOCIAL ORGANIZATION

The subject matter of economics is the social **organization** of economic activity. There are numerous ways in which economic activity may be organized. When we refer to organization, we mean nothing more than the coordination of individuals, each doing different things, in the furtherance of one or more common ends. It does not take much reflection to realize that economic activities in our world are organized. The number of individuals who have contributed in many different ways to supplying the wants of even the poorest citizen in our country is immense. The type of social organization that we employ for this coordination of activities among individuals is predominantly a **market** or **price system.** In such a system, resources tend to flow where they yield the highest rate of return, or highest profit. Prices generate the signals that determine where the resources will flow; prices provide information cheaply and quickly; and prices affect incentives. These prices are determined in myriad markets for myriad goods and services that are bought and sold every day.

In brief, a market is a system of allocating resources and signaling information about their relative values. It is also a system that distributes income in proportion to the amount and market value of owned resources. The market system is one in which there is decentralized decision making. It involves, in essence, spontaneous coordination by millions of participants.

FIGURE 1-1
The circular flow of income
This highly simplified diagram shows the circular flow of resources and income within the economy. In this diagram we have left out the foreign sector and the credit and investment markets. What we do show, however, are the basic interrelationships that exist among the different sectors of the economy.

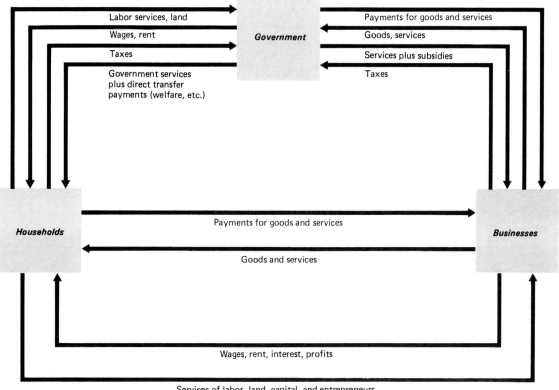

A market system is only one type of social organization for production and distribution. We could depict another social organization in which there was a dictatorship. This is sometimes called an extreme form of a **command economy.** In such a system, flows of goods and resources are not directed by prices; the flows are directed by whoever is in charge. In this text, we will concern ourselves with the determinants of flows within the market system of social organization.

Actually, within most countries a combination of market and command systems is used. This can be seen in the well-known circular flow of income diagram shown in Figure 1-1. In this simplified economic system, there are individuals, firms, and "government." The activities—i.e., the flows of goods and resources in the private (nongovernment) market sector of the economy—depend on voluntary exchanges. The flows of goods and resources to the government depend on the net result of political activity within the existing institutional framework of law, precedent, tradition, and custom.

THEORY AND MICROECONOMICS

The meaning of the term "microeconomic theory" can be inferred from the words themselves. Microeconomics—or price theory, as it is sometimes called—involves, at a minimum, the study of the behavior of individuals, households, firms, and the markets in which they operate. It is microeconomic as opposed to macroeconomic analysis; the latter involves the study of such economywide phenomena as inflation and unemployment. Microeconomic theory employs models which purport to explain and predict the behavior of consumers and producers.

Assumptions in microeconomics

Economists and other scientists utilize two types of assumptions in constructing their theories and explanations about the world around us. The first type of assumption is simply a stipulation of definitions for economic terms and a statement of the "rules of the game." This kind of assumption dictates how an "economic explanation" is to be constructed and what terms are to be used in an economic explanation. This kind of assumption places boundaries on what the economist can do, and it distinguishes economic theories and explanations from the competing theories of psychology or sociology.

The economic theory of consumer behavior, for instance, *assumes* that individuals attempt to maximize their satisfaction or utility in the choices they make. This **assumption** is not, in itself, a testable statement about how consumers consciously make choices. It is, rather, a rule for the economist to follow when constructing explanations of the particular choices which consumers have made or will make. The only possible "test" of the assumptions that define the boundaries of a field of study is an examination of the "fruitfulness" of the research program based on these assumptions.

The wider the range of things it can explain, and the more accurate its predictions about these things, the more fruitful the research program is. Sets of definitional assumptions (and their corresponding research programs) are never "true" or "false." They can only be more or less useful in finding the answers to particular problems.

The second type of assumptions made by economists are **empirical assumptions** that distinguish how the world actually functions from the many ways in which it might imaginably function. The assumption of a diminishing marginal rate of substitution in the theory of consumer behavior is an example of an empirical assumption. Another example is the assumption that purchases of a good by an individual consumer has no effect on market demand and relative prices. The most fundamental empirical assumptions are seldom directly testable. They should, however, have the property of simplicity, or freedom from excessive qualification, and they should imply many frequently tested propositions about real-world events.[1] The observation that we almost never see a consumer who specializes in the consumption of one particular good is, for instance, consistent with the assumption of a diminishing marginal rate of substitution.

We will consider other empirical assumptions that underlie economic analysis in later chapters. One of the strengths of economics is that there are a small number of such assumptions. By grasping these assumptions and by learning how to apply them consistently, you will be able to read, understand, and, ultimately, construct quite comprehensive and sophisticated explanations of why it is that things turn out the way they do in the various institutions and situations that surround us.

THE BROAD CLASS OF RATIONAL MODELS

Many microeconomic models are classified under the general heading of rational behavior models. We define **rational behavior** very simply: Alternatives are ranked systematically, and choices are made so as to maximize the individual's level of "satisfaction," all within real-world limitations. A rational behavior model is simply one that uses the assumption of rationality. The reason that economists have continued to use this type of model is that the assumption works in providing refutable implications which appear to be consistent with real-world social phenomena. Rational behavior is behavior which is purposive and systematic. Nonetheless, a rational behavior model is not necessarily deemed worthless if, when queried, individuals demonstrate thought processes which do not correspond to *our own* ideas

---

[1]Some economists would add that basic empirical assumptions should also be "intuitively appealing." Right intuition, like "common sense," is, however, all too uncommon. Intuitive statements are no more productive of scientific achievement than are those statements which are not so immediately obvious, such as Einstein's theory of the curvature of space.

of rational behavior. Our economic models are models of behavior rather than of thought processes.

Most important, even if specific individuals behave in an unsystematic manner, large groups of individuals taken together will demonstrate collective rationality, which predominates over the unsystematic elements of behavior within the group.

RATIONAL INDIVIDUALS AND RATIONAL ANALYSIS

It is useful here to make the distinction between rational individuals and rational analysis. We define rational analysis as a logically cohesive theory that enables us to derive empirically testable implications or predictions about the behavior of groups of people. If these predictions or implications are not refuted by experience, the rational theory has been found to be consistent with the real-world data, or at least has not been disproved. We make no statements about whether individuals really are rational; nothing in a rational theory is dependent upon the premise that individuals are logically consistent in their thought processes. A good example has been given by several researchers doing experiments in mental institutions. Such experiments demonstrate that rational theory, or analysis, works even for individuals who are not normally thought of as being "rational." Presumably individuals exhibiting severe mental illness do not *think* "rationally." Nonetheless, psychologists T. Allyon and N. H. Azrin found that the number of hours that psychotics in a study group were willing to work was a positive function of how much they were paid in the form of tokens which could be exchanged for clothing, toiletries, candy, cigarettes, and such additional hospital privileges as privacy. During one 20-day period, patients were rewarded with tokens when they completed their chosen jobs. In the following 20-day period, they were given tokens whether they completed their tasks or not. After about 5 days of the second 20-day period, the number of hours worked by the experimental group dropped to zero. When again they were paid only if their tasks were completed, the total number of hours worked per day jumped immediately.[2]

Therefore, even when dealing with individuals exhibiting severe mental illness, it would seem that we can use rational analysis. The results of the study just mentioned are consistent with analysis based on an assumption that the individuals acted *as if* they were rational. That is sufficient.

Note well, however, that the science of economics is not dependent now and forever upon the rationality postulate. If an alternative comes along that

---

[2]T. Allyon and N. H. Azrin, "The Measurement and Reinforcement of Behavior of Psychotics," *Journal of the Experimental Analysis of Behavior*, vol. 8, November 1965.

proves more usable in terms of explanatory and predictive capacity, that alternative undoubtedly will be adopted.

THE UNIT OF ANALYSIS: THE INDIVIDUAL

All theories developed in microeconomic analysis are based on propositions about individual behavior in response to changes in environment. Although the point may seem self-evident, many of us are rather loose in our discussions of "society" or "the public." If you were to tell me that the public has decided to clean up the nation's water because that is what is best for society, such a statement would sound somewhat unscientific. There is no such thing as an organized group called "the public" capable of making that decision. Moreover, an attribution to "society" is a reference to some sort of entity that presumably is capable of deciding what is good for itself. Individuals can determine whether they like the outcome of a particular economic change, and individuals can determine whether they are happy or sad. Society, however, cannot.

Perhaps a more appropriate way of making the same statement would be as follows: Politicians who expressed an interest in passing legislation to clean up the nation's waterways got voters to respond to them because of the increasing level of pollution in those waterways which caused harm to many individual voters. When a sufficiently large percentage of the electorate became concerned, those individuals in positions of political power made the decision to pass legislation to reduce the level of pollution.

It is worth noting that many individuals will be affected *adversely* by the cleanup of the nation's waterways. They are the ones who will incur the relatively high direct costs of the cleanup, e.g., polluting firms, their employees, shipowners, and the like. Thus, this fact is inconsistent with saying that the "public interest" has been served. What has been served are the dominant private interests, in this particular case, the interests of those who have the most concern for cleaner waterways.

Notice that the analysis here has been in terms of individual behavior. When we look at it this way, we see that the terms "public" and "society" are a bit too broad and vague to have much scientific meaning in rational discourse.

It should not seem very unusual that the basic unit of analysis in the science of economics is the individual. The physicist, for example, in the course of scientific investigation, may wish to describe the response of a "typical" molecule of gas when there is an increase in the temperature, even though the behavior of one *particular* molecule is unpredictable for all practical purposes. The economist may wish to predict the response of consumers in New York to a rise in the relative price of food, even though a particular individual living in a specific condominium near Central Park, perhaps in response to other stimuli, may actually buy more food when the price rises.

Although we treat the individual as the basic unit of analysis, we normally apply price theory to the behavior of individuals in groups. From a methodological point of view, we talk in terms of **individualism** because we obtain better predictions about group behavior by identifying and taking into account the diverse and often conflicting objections of the individuals who make up the group. Thus, our understanding of the behavior of groups is not dissimilar to the physicist's understanding of the behavior of a gas by considering the behavior of the molecules involved. In other words, we assert that more accurate predictions about group behavior are derivable from predictions about individual behavior.

SOME FINER POINTS IN MICROECONOMIC ANALYSIS

There are a number of points that can be brought out in this introductory chapter that will prevent the student of price theory from making simple analytical errors when applying economic analysis to real-world problems. Although the list below is not exhaustive, it does include some of the most common misunderstandings.

Prices

Much of economics revolves around prices. We talk about the law of demand, in which the quantity demanded is inversely related to price. We talk about the law of supply, in which the quantity supplied is directly related to the price. In short, we talk about prices a lot. But today we have to be careful, particularly when we are looking at quantities demanded and supplied in the real world and the prices of the commodities in question.

Relative versus absolute prices. Lunch in an average restaurant in Italy these days costs over 10,000 lira. Does that sound expensive? Not to Americans when they realize that is about $5. Price numbers—**absolute prices** or nominal prices—mean little by themselves. Occasionally you see projections that if the rate of inflation averages a said rate, then in the year 2020 a loaf of bread that now costs $1 will cost $5. What does that tell us? Not much since we don't know what will happen to income and other prices by that time. If average incomes are ten times higher in 2020 than today, then bread that costs $5 at that time may seem cheaper than it does now.

While absolute prices are important in the study of macroeconomics because of inflation, microeconomics is concerned with **relative** or **real prices**. Relative prices tell us what something costs *compared to other goods.* The greatest confusion about prices occurs during periods of inflation (or deflation), when the general price level is changing at the same time that relative prices are changing.

TABLE 1-1
Absolute and relative prices, 1967–1985

Good	Absolute price index 1967 = 100	Change in relative prices
All items	317	—
Fuel oil	628	+98%
Oranges	449	+42%
Taxi fares	315	− 1%
Household insurance	110	−65%
Televisions	92	−71%

Source: *Consumer Price Index, February 1985*

From 1967 to 1985 the general price level, as measured by the Consumer Price Index (CPI), rose 217 percent. Using an index stating that 1967 prices of all goods equalled 100, the government collects price information monthly to calculate the rate of inflation and to show what is happening to individual prices, so that we can measure change in the absolute price level and in relative prices. We see this in Table 1-1. The absolute price index rose from 100 in 1967 to 317 in 1985 for all items included in the price survey. Over the years, however, we see that relative prices changed at different rates (all were indexed at 100 in 1967). For example, fuel oil almost doubled in relative price. Taxi fares stayed about the same as the general price level, while the price of televisions fell by 71 percent. Not only did televisions fall in relative terms, they fell in absolute terms (from 100 to 92 on the index). Of course, these prices do not tell us everything, since changes in quality and other factors cannot be accurately measured.

Prices and information. A basic hypothesis of price theory is that individuals respond to relative prices rather than absolute prices. It is relative prices which are the conveyors of information in the marketplace. For the buyers, the relative price of a good indicates what the individual consumer must give up in terms of other goods in order to purchase that good. In certain cases, it also indicates the amount of resources given up to produce that good. Hence, when the relative price of a commodity goes up, that bit of information tells the buyer and the seller that the good is now relatively scarcer. Note that neither the producer nor the consumer has to know why that particular commodity has become relatively scarcer. It may not matter to you as a consumer whether the price of gasoline has gone up *because* of a restriction on imports or *because* of a new law which requires gasoline refineries to install more expensive pollution-abatement equipment. The only thing that does matter is the higher relative price, for that is the basis on which you normally will make a decision about the quantity to purchase. The message is transmitted by the higher relative price. Of course, how you respond to the message is impossible to predict on an individual basis, for the number of ways in which you can "conserve" on a relatively scarcer item is probably infinite.

Changes in relative prices convey this type of information to both buyers and sellers. Of course, buyers respond differently from sellers. Sellers may see a rise in the relative price of a particular commodity as an opportunity to increase profits, and eventually such information may be translated into a larger amount of resources going to the production of that now relatively higher-priced and at least temporarily more profitable product. It is in this manner that resources are allocated in a system that allows prices to convey the information about relative scarcities. *We call this a market system: Prices convey the information to the participants—buyers and sellers—in the marketplace.* There is no need for a central agency to produce information or allocate resources. This does not mean that problems will not arise and that certain economic activities could not be better handled by other than unrestricted market processes. We will treat such situations on different occasions in this book and in particular in Chapter 19.

Distinguishing between average and marginal

Since we have been talking about prices, it is important to realize that not everyone need be aware of the relative price of a particular commodity for microeconomic analysis to have meaning and usefulness.

Consider an experiment that was carried out in the 1960s. Customers of a large number of gas stations in a given geographic area were quizzed at the end of each purchase of gas. The customers were asked about the price of the gasoline they had just bought. It turned out that most customers did not know the cost of the gasoline. They were vaguely aware of the approximate price but not of the exact price, and they were not aware of the possibility of obtaining gasoline at a lower price elsewhere. This would suggest to the casual observer that prices have no meaning in an economic system and that consumers are "irrational" or, at the least, lazy shoppers.

However, at the same time this study was done, a close tab was kept on the quantity of gasoline sold at several gas stations in the area. Lo and behold, it turned out that those gas stations which sold gasoline at a lower price sold more. Now, how can these two facts be reconciled? They can be reconciled by making a distinction between the *average* consumer and the *marginal* consumer. The average consumer of gasoline was perhaps unaware of the price of gasoline. However, the fact that the gasoline stations selling gas at a lower price sold more made it clear that *some* consumers were aware. They are the people we call the marginal consumers, the ones who are just on the borderline between buying more and buying less. As the price of gas goes up in one gas station, these marginal consumers switch to a less costly station. They are indeed the determinants of the price of gasoline.[3] This situation shows that *information is conveyed by relative*

---

[3]Along with the suppliers, of course.

prices; but *for the price mechanism to work, that information does not need to be known with perfect accuracy by every individual acting in the marketplace.*

This is perhaps another reason why critics of the rationality model used in microeconomic theory go astray. They are confusing *average* with *marginal*. On the average, it may be true that consumers do not have much information about what they buy. (It may not pay them to search for better information.) But on the margin, there are consumers who do care. For example, purchasers of gasoline for, say, fleets of cars or delivery trucks certainly will take the time, effort, and energy to seek out a supplier offering gasoline at a relatively lower price. Whenever these marginal buyers find a better deal, they will switch suppliers. It is these marginal buyers who keep suppliers on their toes and tend to cause the price of a given commodity to be uniform within a given geographic area, correcting, of course, for differentials in transportation costs and in quality.

Constant-quality units

All the supply and demand analyses which follow, whether concerned with energy, the labor market, illegal activities, or what have you, must always be expressed in terms of **constant-quality units.** We know that all shoes are not alike and that all automobiles are not alike. Nonetheless, we talk about the market for shoes and the market for automobiles. We also talk about the law of demand as it applies to each of these markets. When we talk about the quantity demanded of these or any other commodities, we must be aware of the fact that we are talking about constant-quality units. Hence, the correct way to describe, say, the quantity of shoes demanded is to talk in terms of the *relative price* of shoes and of the quantity of shoes measured in *constant-quality units.* Now that's really a mouthful! Therefore, throughout the rest of this book, the word *"price" will be understood to mean the* relative price *of a commodity measured in constant-quality units.*

There is a direct relationship between quality and price per constant-quality unit. Often new restaurants start out with relatively high-quality food at a certain set of prices. If the restaurant is very successful, it is not uncommon to see (and experience) a decline in the quality of the food served at the same prices, or alternatively, it is not unusual to see the sizes of the servings get smaller. Thus, the price per constant-quality unit after the restaurant has become more successful rises because of this decline in the quality and/or portion size.

In this text, we don't have to worry about how we would actually measure the quantity demanded or supplied of a particular commodity in constant-quality units. That would be the job of the econometrician, that is, an economist trained in the application of mathematics and statistics to the verification of economic theories. Econometricians must worry about adjustments for quality variations in their statistical studies.

Stocks, flows, and the time dimension

Our last point is the distinction between stocks and flows. A **stock** is defined as a quantity of something that exists at a moment in time. One may have a stock of savings, an inventory stock of finished goods, a stock of boxes of Kleenex in the closet, and so on. These all essentially involve an instantaneous quantification of an amount available at a particular moment, say, right at this very instant. Much of microeconomic theory does not involve itself with stocks, however.

Rather, we are more inclined to develop theories about **flows** where flows are quantities received, used, or spent at a particular rate over a specified period. Defined thus, when we make reference to the law of demand, we are referring to the quantity of a commodity demanded at a particular relative price over a particular period. Suppose we say that at a price of $2 each, 10 million Big Macs will be purchased. That statement offers little information unless we specify a time period. Ten million Big Macs would represent a tremendous quantity demanded at that price if the time period is specified as 1 day. But it may not seem tremendous if the time period specified is 1 year. Thus, *for every statement about quantity demanded or supplied, we must also specify or imply a time period.*

The distinction between stocks and flows is perhaps best illustrated by considering a durable good such as an automobile. Let's say you purchase an automobile for $9,000. You then have a stock—one automobile—valued at $9,000. However, the automobile is generally not purchased for ownership of the stock per se. Rather, the automobile is usually purchased for the flow of services that the stock is expected to render over time. Thus, when we talk about the consumer demand for services from automobiles, it is generally best to talk in terms of the expected service flow from the stock of an automobile per unit time, or so much of a given quantity of automobile used per month or per year. This is true for all durable goods, including houses, laser-disc sound systems, and golf clubs. The analysis for an automobile can be done in terms of the *service flow per unit time* measured in, say, constant-quality miles per year. To handle the demand for a *stock* of a durable good, we refer to the services derived (flows) rather than stock.

Undoubtedly there are other "tricks" of analysis that you will pick up as you read through the theory in this book and apply it to issues other than those which have been chosen. And perhaps more important, you will see the importance of mastering the analytical fine points just mentioned by applying them to the statements you see in print or hear on the radio, on TV, or in conversation. That is where you may find the greatest reward from the study of microeconomic theory upon which you are embarking.

A FRAMEWORK FOR THE CHAPTERS TO FOLLOW

You have just been introduced to the way economists think about the world around them. The next step is to distinguish between economics and the economy. Once we do that, we can establish a framework for what this book and this course are all about. As you already know, economics is about "choices." We will be looking at "microeconomic" choices—consumer buying and selling decisions as well as producer buying and selling decisions—and how economists set up models to analyze and decide which is the best, or optimum, choice.

Economics versus the economy

Economics is a science, and, like any other science, it has its own particular set of tools for measuring and analyzing the world. The particular "world" measured and analyzed by economics is "the economy"—the activities and institutions of society that are related to satisfying material (and spiritual) wants. Thus, *economics* consists of tools of analysis and measurement. When you know how to use those tools, you can *describe,* *explain,* and *make predictions about* the economy.

Microeconomics and society's basic choices

Every society has three basic choices, at a minimum, which must be made:

1 The allocation of resources: Where do our limited resources flow? Which sectors of the economy will have more labor and materials, and what kinds? Which sectors will have less?
2 The level of production: How much capacity does the nation's economic system possess and how much will be used? How many hours will individuals work with the nation's land and capital? What will be the total amount of goods and services produced?
3 The pattern of activity over time: What will be the rate of economic growth?

Microeconomics is the portion of economics that focuses on the first of society's basic choices: the allocation of resources. Thus, in the chapters that follow, the tools of analysis and measurement you will learn about will be tools for understanding the allocation of resources within society.

Is economics a science?

In order to answer the question of whether economics is a science we must first have some notion of what distinguishes a science from other types of belief systems like theologies, ideologies, and philosophies. A science is a logically connected system of definitional and empirical premises, as described in this chapter. So are theologies, ideologies, and philosophies. The main thing which distinguishes a science from these other ways of analyzing the world is that a science has testable implications, which are tested, and which could be found to be a false description of the world as a result of these tests. In the language of methodology, a science has "falsifiable consequences." Other types of belief systems are explicitly or implicitly constructed in such a way that it is logically impossible for the results of a "test," or of any event in the world, to ever falsify a major tenet of the system.[4]

Critical or potentially falsifying tests of the major tenets of a science are ideally performed within controlled experimental situations. Other test conditions allow for greater ambiguity in the interpretation of the test results, for it is always possible to plead that uncontrolled circumstances caused the test to come out differently than it would have otherwise. Controlled experimental situations are usually repeatable, so that the effects of unwanted interfering influences can be eliminated or their effects on the outcome of the

experiment can be accurately estimated. That is, of course, not true of events which happen in the natural environment and are thus beyond the control of the scientist.

By these standards economics is a science, albeit an imperfect one. Microeconomics, as presented in this text, is a consistent and unified system of definitional and empirical assumptions with testable implications. (For some examples of such implications, see the issues and applications sections at the end of each chapter.) The tests of economic predictions and, to a lesser extent, the newer extensions of economic theory, are, however, far from ideal. Such tests frequently involve an explanation for empirical "results" derived from some data set which was itself collected by unspecified and unexplained methods.[5] While microeconomics often yields quite accurate *qualitative* (or directional) predictions about the consequences to be expected from particular changes in public policy, quantitative applications of microeconomics are much less successful in determining the *magnitudes* of predicted changes.

There are many reasons why the products of quantitative economics have remained at a crude level and why empirical economics as a whole has not become more rigorously scientific. The most obvious of these reasons is that it is difficult and expensive, although not impossible, to place economic actors in controlled experimental situations. Without a controlled experiment, however, repeatability of the "same" test is virtually impossible. The test results are thus always subject to varying interpretations, and it is difficult to

---

[4]This "line of demarcation" between science and the other ways of explaining reality is *roughly* that suggested by Karl Popper in his *Logic of Scientific Discovery* and other writings. Note that this classification scheme has nothing to do with the subject matter of the system being classified or the terms in which the explanations are constructed. Thus, an explanation of all observable phenomena in terms of the will of a supreme being could be a science if there were some way of performing a falsifying test of the system.

[5]A dated but still generally valid and insightful treatment of this problem is found in Oskar Morgenstern's *On The Accuracy of Economic Observations.*

obtain agreed-upon "experimental constants" for the values of the economic variables being tested.

Another problem faced by economic inquiry, which is not so prevalent in the physical sciences, is the influence of "ideological" preconceptions on the results of economic studies. Economics, unlike physics, has rather immediate consequences for the desirability of alternative public policies or for the determination of damages in certain civil court actions, to name but two examples. Although particular economists may be completely free from such bias, the system of rewards for coming to "correct" results tends to encourage "creative" empirical methods. Given the uncertainty about interpretation which exists in any nonexperimental and nonrepeatable "test," it is seldom difficult to discover some interpretation of the facts or data which will yield the desired conclusions.

While these observations should make the consumer of empirical economics cautious about basing his or her actions solely upon one study, they do not provide a good foundation for a more extensive cynicism about the achievements of the discipline. The abundance of empirical economic research cur-

rently underway[6] and the growing sophistication of econometric methods largely offset the inherent and environmental difficulties of empirical economics.

While there may still be considerable room for improvement in the empirical application of economics, the accomplishments of theoretical microeconomics are a matter of record. Over the past quarter-century, microeconomic theory, in its various branches, has become universally recognized as the most elegant and extensive engine of social analysis yet devised. The theory presented in this text is the recognized starting point for virtually all microeconomic analysis. It is what is held in common by microeconomists of all ideological orientations or academic specializations. While economics may not yet be the full scientific equal of physics, it is the nearest thing to such a science in the realm of social analysis.

---

[6]A recent survey of the journal literature in economics contained in the March 1984 *Journal of Economic Literature* lists 108 currently published economics journals, all of which contain some empirical research. This, of course, does not account for the multitude of empirical economic studies, which are commissioned daily by government agencies, businesses, and nonprofit educational foundations.

▬▬▬▬▬▬▬▬

Should economic models be realistic?

No model (theory) in any science, and therefore no microeconomic model (theory), is completely realistic in the sense that it captures every detail and interrelationship that exists. Not only is such a model impossible to build, it would also be impossible to work with. For example, no model of the solar system could possibly take account of all aspects of the entire system. The nature of scientific model

building is such that the model should capture the *essential* relationships that are sufficient to analyze or answer the particular questions at hand. For example, when we attempt to construct a model of consumer behavior in the face of changing prices for a particular commodity, there are at the very least a million determinants of how each consumer will respond to such changes in prices. However, most of those determinants are left out of our model. It is not that they are meaningless: rather, the model that we usually use, which includes the price of the particular commodity, the income of the consumer, the prices of substitutes for the commodity in question, and the prices of completeness for the commodity in question, seems to be adequate. That is, just taking into account the magnitudes of these four determinants of consumer demand works "well," even though the model is "unrealistic" because it does not capture *all* the various determinants of consumer demand.

Another way to regard the relationship between models and realism is to consider models as road maps. Sometimes we look at road maps that represent large geographic areas and are very general, showing only major highways. But we don't consider them "unrealistic." We use these maps because we expect to travel long distances and need to know only the major highways. Sometimes we look at road maps representing localities that show us many, if not all, of the minor streets because we are more interested in driving in the city. An economic model allows us to understand reality, even though not every "street" in the economy is included.

In sum, then, a microeconomic model cannot be faulted merely by stating that it is unrealistic vis-à-vis the real world, for that same model may be very realistic in terms of elucidating the *central* issue at hand on forces at work.

DECIDING ON THE USEFULNESS OF A MODEL

We generally do not attempt to determine the usefulness or "goodness" of a model merely by discussing its realism, i.e., the realism of its assumptions. Rather, if we use scientific methodology, we prefer and consider as successful the models that yield useful predictions and implications for the real world. The more implications, the better; the more implications not falsified by empirical, real-world facts, the better yet. The scientific approach to analysis of the world around us requires that we have a willingness to consider evidence. Evidence is used to test the usefulness of a model. Consider, for example, two competing models that concern themselves with the following phenomenon: Every time I leave paper currency on a table in the student union, it disappears. Why does it disappear? One model is based on several assumptions, including that of wealth maximization, or making oneself as well off as possible. This model predicts that if the cost of taking possession of the paper currency (which represents general purchasing power over all commodities) is low relative to the benefits obtainable from the paper currency, individuals will engage in this activity. The competing model uses a theory of magnetic attraction: Paper currency emits a magnetic force which causes people's hands to pick it up.

A testable, i.e., refutable, implication for the first model is that money will disappear faster the larger the denomination of the bills left. This is not an implication of the other competing model. We can run an experiment now to test the predictive capacity of these two models. On some days we randomly leave a dollar bill on a table at different intervals. Then we keep increasing the possible take, leaving next $5 at a time, then $10, then $50, then $100. If we observe that more individuals hang around the student union as the denomination of the bills gets larger, we have an observed fact that does not refute the implication or prediction of the first model. It does refute the second model, which would predict that $100 bills are not attracted to the students' hands any more than dollar bills, because denomination did not determine magnetic force. Therefore, we would choose the first model and tend to reject the second. Note here that we can never *prove* theories; we can only disprove them.

SIMPLICITY HAS ITS VIRTUES

We generally use the principle of Occam's Razor. If two models are competing with one another and each predicts equally well, the least complicated model will generally be chosen. For it was William of Occam who once said, "Essentia non sunt multiplicanda praeter necessitatem." In other words, essences shouldn't be multiplied beyond what we need for what we are studying. This is also known as the **principle of parsimony.**

The notion of simplicity in model building is worth one further comment. Often the goal of constructing a theory is to have a general model. The more simple the model, the more generalizable it is. The supposedly realistic model explains only a single special case and is therefore uninteresting.

SUMMARY

1 There are numerous possible organizations through which individuals coordinate their different activities in the furtherance of one or more common ends. Typically, we look at two such organizations for production and distribution: the market system and the command system.

2 Every economic system involves a circular flow of income among firms, households, the government, and other countries.

3 All models are based on assumptions that can never be perfectly realistic. Model building involves simplification by necessity.

4 In scientific methodology, the usefulness, or goodness, of a model depends on its predictive success record and the number of real-world implications that can be drawn from it.

5 Most economic models fall within the broad class of rationality models, which assume rational behavior. However, such models are not useful in analyzing individual thought processes.

6 It is important to distinguish between rational analysis and rationality: The former requires a logically consistent theory that allows us to derive empirically testable implications or predictions; the latter has to do with the logically consistent thought processes of individuals.

7 We use methodological individualism in our analysis of groups. In other words, our analyses are based on behavioral hypotheses about individuals.

8 It is important to distinguish between absolute and relative prices when doing microeconomic analysis. During a period of inflation, absolute prices may, for the most part, be rising. However, consumer and producer decisions are based on relative prices.

9 In a market system, prices convey information to buyers and sellers about the relative scarcities of commodities.

10 Prices are determined on the margin. The marginal buyer and the marginal seller determine the price in a market. The confusion between the average and the marginal buyer often leads to the erroneous

conclusion that price does not determine quantity demanded and is therefore unimportant.

11   Measurement of the quantities of commodities under study must be made in terms of constant-quality units so that we can talk meaningfully in terms of the relative price per constant-quality unit of the commodity in question.

12   Generally, in microeconomics we deal with flows, such as the rate of consumption per unit time, the rate of production per unit time, and so on. Hence, whenever we deal with a flow, we must specify a time period.

GLOSSARY

- **budget constraint** The resource constraint imposed on individual households, firms, and governments at any point in time. For at any point in time, the total amount of resources is fixed.
- **scarcity** A fact of nature. We cannot get the quantities desired or demanded at a zero price for all resources.
- **economic good** Any good that is scarce. The quantity demanded at a zero price is greater than the quantity supplied. By definition, all resources are economic goods.
- **free good** A good for which the quantity demanded at a zero price is less than the quantity supplied at a zero price.
- **organization** The coordination of individuals, each doing different things, in the furtherance of one or more common ends.
- **market or price system** A social system of organization in which prices direct the use of resources and in which prices are used to allocate resources.
- **command economy** A social system of organization in which the allocation of resources is carried out by way of centralized decision making.
- **assumption** A rule that defines the boundaries of a theory.
- **empirical assumption** A rule that defines the way the world works, that places limits on theories and makes them testable.
- **rational behavior** Individual actions commensurate with the achievement of explicit goals.
- **individualism** A particular type of scientific methodology in which we deduce our understanding of the behavior of groups from the behavior of individuals.
- **absolute prices** Prices expressed in terms of nominal (usually "money") units. Absolute prices are those prices which are given in a market at any point in time, to be contrasted with relative or real prices.
- **relative or real prices** Prices expressed in terms of how much of other goods must be given up to purchase a unit of the good in question. To establish relative prices, comparisons of nominal prices must be made.
- **constant-quality units** Units of commodities for which quality is held constant. To estimate price per constant-quality unit requires that all units of different qualities first be adjusted for differences in quality.

- **stock** A quantity of anything that exists at a moment in time, such as inventories, savings, houses, and automobiles.
- **flow** A quantity of anything measured, consumed, earned, produced, etc., per unit time, i.e., at a specific rate per unit time.
- **principle of parsimony** Sometimes called the principle of Occam's Razor. Given the choice between a less complicated and a more complicated model, the former will be chosen if it works (e.g., explains or predicts) at least as well as the latter.

QUESTIONS

(Answers to even-numbered questions are at back of text.)

1. What criteria are appropriate in evaluating a scientific model?
2. Does it matter whether all a model's assumptions are "realistic"? Why, or why not?
3. What is the problem with expressions such as "the health, safety, welfare, and morals of the public" and "the greatest good for the greatest number"?
4. Suppose that in 1974 a liter of beer cost 50¢, while the same quantity of tequila commanded $5. By 1982 the respective nominal prices had risen to 70¢ and $6.30. What happened to the real or relative price of tequila in relation to beer?
5. Continuing with question 4 above, suppose that the nominal prices of all other consumer goods and services rose by 70 percent over the same 8-year period so that, on the average, it cost $17 in 1982 to buy the same "market basket" of consumer goods and services that could have been bought for $10 in 1974. What has happened to the relative price of beer and of tequila in comparison to all other consumer goods and services?
6. Suppose that by 1988 the nominal price of electricity has doubled and that of natural gas has tripled? How would this affect consumer purchases of new refrigerators and clothes dryers? Explain.
7. Poorer nations typically use "primitive" methods to, say, construct a road. How would the concept of relative prices help to explain this? (*Hint:* The important relative prices to consider are those of labor and road-building equipment in poorer and wealthier nations.)
8. Suppose you met someone who insisted that "everyone he or she knew" went right on using sugar at the same rate while the price sextupled. How would you go about convincing that person of the unimportance of that observation?
9. It is not unlikely that the same person introduced in question 8 also knows a grower of sugar beets or sugarcane who invariably produces the same quantity of sugar each year without reference to changes in the expected wholesale price. What is your response?
10. "When I say *wheat*, I mean U.S. No. 1 Hard Red Winter Wheat." Why is it essential that in measuring quantities of goods, we must deal in constant-quality units?
11. Is the amount of water in a reservoir a stock or a flow? What units are commonly used to express the quantity? Is a city's consumption of water a stock or a flow? In what units might it be measured? Is rainfall a stock or a flow? How is it generally measured?

12 Express each of the following "stock" phenomena as an expected future flow: (a) a washing machine, (b) a Hobie Cat sailboat, (c) a 35-pound cooked turkey, (d) a share of common stock, (e) a fistful of dollars.

13 Actuaries are mathematicians who are commonly employed by insurance companies to, among other things, *predict* the frequency with which various groups of individuals will be involved in, say, traffic accidents. (a) To date, what are the factors which have been most widely used to predict "accident-proneness"? (b) Would a bigot make a good actuary? Why, or why not?

14 Suppose you have studied two phenomena, A and B, very carefully and have observed a very close correlation between them: Whenever A increases, B decreases, and vice versa. (a) Does it matter which one is the cause (independent variable) and which one the effect (dependent variable)? (b) What if they are both "effects" of some undetermined factor C?

15 Over the past decade, first-class mail rates have more than tripled, while prices of long-distance phone calls, CB radios, televisions, and sound systems have remained fairly stable. (After adjustments for improvements in quality are made, the prices of these latter items may have even declined.) Over a similar period, it has been reported that there has been a steady decline in the ability of high school graduates to communicate effectively in writing. Do you feel that this increase in the relative price of written communication is related to the alleged decline in writing ability? (For the sake of argument, assume that the latter has in fact occurred.) If so, what do you feel is the direction of causation? Which is causing which?

SELECTED REFERENCES

Boland, Lawrence, *The Foundation of Economic Method* (London: George Allen & Unwin, 1982).

Friedman, Milton, "The Methodology of Positive Economics," in *Essays in Positive Economics* (Chicago: University of Chicago Press, 1953), pp. 1–43.

Machlup, Fritz, "The Problem of Verification in Economics," *Southern Economic Journal*, vol. 22, 1955, pp. 1–25.

Robbins, Lionel, *An Essay on the Nature and Significance of Economic Science* (London: Macmillan, 1935).

Wicksteed, Philip H., "The Scope of Method of Political Economy," in G. J. Stigler and K. Boulding, eds., *Readings in Price Theory* (Homewood, Ill.: Irwin, 1952).

Demand and supply: a review

*T*he cornerstone of microeconomic analysis is the demand and supply model. Understanding what demand and supply are, as well as the relation between the two, is essential for understanding virtually all of economics. Much of what you will learn in an intermediate microeconomics course concerns a more detailed account of the factors underlying supply and demand and the application of these factors to an analysis of real-world situations. Demand and supply are two influences on the relative price of goods and services. Together they determine the market prices of goods.

MARKETS, MARKETPLACES, AND MARKET MECHANISMS

Economic activities take place through **markets.** In its broadest sense, a market is not necessarily a place but is an institution through which price-making forces operate. In other words, it is within markets that supply and demand operate.

On the other hand, **marketplaces** are geographic locations where exchanges occur, where the results of the interaction of supply and demand occur, and where the terms of exchange are registered.

Market mechanisms refer to the information network within and across markets (or marketplaces). For example, market mechanisms enable individuals to keep in touch with each other about the prices and availability of, say, cold-rolled steel or hard red winter wheat.

MARKET DEMAND AND SUPPLY

Even though all microeconomic analysis starts with the individual, it is not so simple to examine the basic concepts of supply and demand with respect to an individual, a task we reserve for later chapters in this text. It is simpler to examine the analytic framework of supply and demand with respect to entire markets: groups of actual and potential buyers and sellers. This is what we will do in this review.

THE LAW OF DEMAND

The **law of demand** can be stated in its simplest terms as follows:

- *At a higher price, a lesser quantity will be demanded than at a lower price, all other things being equal.*

Or, looked at another way:

- *At a lower price, a greater quantity will be demanded than at a higher price, all other things being equal.*

Thus, the law of demand tells us that the *quantity demanded* of any commodity is *inversely related* to that commodity's *price*, all other things being equal at all possible prices.

The phrase "all other things being equal" is part of the law of demand. Price is not the only thing that affects how much of a product people wish to buy. There are many other things that influence the amount purchased. One important "nonprice" influence is income. If, while the price of a good is changing, income also is changing, we would not know whether a change in the quantity bought and sold in the marketplace is due to the change in price or to a change in income. But if income is constant, as well as any other nonprice parameter, and only price changes, we would definitely know that the change in price has caused the change in quantity demanded.

THE DEMAND SCHEDULE

We now examine a hypothetical demand situation to observe the inverse relationship between price and quantity demanded. Let's consider the quantity of pizzas demanded per year by Americans. We have to specify a time period for quantity demanded because without it we wouldn't know whether we were talking about the quantity demanded per day, per month, or per decade. Another way of expressing the same concept is to say that demand (and supply) are flow concepts. That is, they refer to a rate of desired pur-

TABLE 2-1
Market demand schedule for pizzas

Price ($ per constant-quality pizza) (1)	Quantity demanded (constant-quality pizzas per year) (2)	Combination (see figure 2-1) (3)
4.10	100 million	E
4.20	80 million	D
4.30	60 million	C
4.40	40 million	B
4.50	20 million	A

chases or sales, rather than an absolute volume or stock. Consuming three pizzas per month is different from consuming three pizzas.

In Table 2-1 we see that at a price of $4.10, 100 million constant-quality pizzas are demanded per year (this is all hypothetical). Remember what we mean by the term "constant quality": We come up with a standard type of pizza in terms of taste, size, amount of cheese, amount of tomato sauce, etc., and then convert all pizzas demanded into this standard constant-quality pizza. That is, we "index" all pizzas to a comparable pizza standard. In any event, if the price is $4.50 per pizza, only 20 million will be bought. This reflects the law of demand. Table 2-1 is also called a **market demand schedule** because it gives a schedule of alternative quantities demanded per year at different possible prices. Here the term "schedule" refers to the quantities demanded at various possible prices. In a sense, it is similar to a schedule of freight rates for various distances and the price charged for each haul.

The market demand curve

Tabular data expressing a relationship between two variables can be represented in graphic terms. To do this, we need only construct a graph that portrays price per constant-quality pizza on the vertical axis and quantity of constant-quality pizzas per year on the horizontal axis. All we have to do is take combinations A, B, C, D, and E from Table 2-1 and plot those points in Figure 2-1. Now we connect these points with a smooth line, and we have a **market demand curve.**[1] The general definition of a market demand curve is the locus of points relating the various prices of a commodity and the associated quantity purchased at each price by all potential buyers.

[1]Even though economists frequently refer to any line within a graph as a "curve," for purposes of exposition we are drawing straight-line "curves" here. In some real-world situations, demand and supply "curves" may be nonlinear. To connect the points in Figure 2-1 with a smooth line, we assume that for all prices in between the ones shown, the quantities demanded will be found along that line.

FIGURE 2-1
*Graphic representation of market demand
schedule for pizzas: the market demand curve*
We take the price quantity combinations from
Table 2-1 and transfer them to this graph. The
result is a downward-sloping market demand
curve for pizzas.

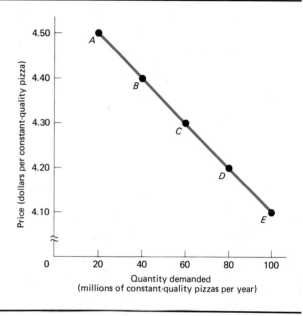

**The
determinants of
market demand**

There are several important things for you to remember about the market demand schedule, or market demand curve. For one, any particular demand schedule, or demand curve, represents a relation between the price of a good and the **quantity demanded,** that is to say, the quantity that will be demanded at that price, other things being constant. All other influences on the purchase, besides price, do not change and therefore do not affect the quantity demanded when we are examining a particular demand curve. What this means is that for movements along each particular demand curve, quantity demanded changes only in response to price and to nothing else. *The higher the price, the lesser will be the quantity demanded; the lower the price, the greater will be the quantity demanded.* All we have to remember here is that *any change in price results in a movement along a fixed, or given, market demand curve* and no other change will cause a movement along the curve.

Now, what happens when there are changes in one or more of the other nonprice determinants that affect purchases? Any change in a nonprice determinant will cause a "shift" in the market demand curve—that is, a **demand change.** To see what this means—that is, a *change in demand* rather than a *change in the quantity demanded*—let's take a look at several possible demand curves. In Figure 2-2 we have represented graphically market demand curves *DD, D'D',* and *D"D".* Note demand curve *DD.* A change in a nonprice determinant of demand will shift that demand curve either outward to the right or inward to the left. A change in price will not shift the demand curve *DD;* it will cause a movement *along* that demand curve. Demand curve

FIGURE 2-2
Shifts in the market demand curve
A nonprice determinant of demand that is
positively related to demand will cause it to
shift from DD to $D'D'$ if that nonprice
determinant increases and to $D''D''$ if it
decreases. For example, if demand is positively
related to changes in income and income
increases, demand will shift outward. If income
decreases, demand will shift inward.

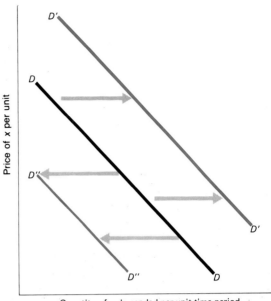

$D'D'$ shows an increase in demand; demand curve $D''D''$ shows a decrease
in demand as compared to the original demand curve, DD.

The position of any demand curve in the price-quantity graph will be a
function of other determinants of demand that are not measured on either
axis of the graph. Some of those determinants are (1) real income, (2) tastes
and preferences, (3) the price of related goods (substitutes and complements),
(4) changes in expectation of future relative prices, and (5) population. To
be sure, you can probably come up with other determinants of demand.

There are two main ideas for you to remember.

- *A change in price will lead to a movement along a given demand
curve, referred to as a change in the quantity demanded.*

- *Changes in variables other than price can shift the demand curve,
referred to as a change in demand.*

With those key ideas in mind, let us examine some of the nonprice factors
of demand.

Income. Typically, an increase in income will lead to an increase in
demand. Notice that the phrase is not "increase in quantity demanded" but
rather "increase in demand." That implies that the demand schedule has
shifted to the right, representing a greater quantity demanded at each and
every price. Thus, an increase in income will lead, for most goods, to a
rightward *shift* in the position of the demand curve from, say, DD to $D'D'$

in Figure 2-2.[2] The reader can avoid confusion about shifts in curves by always relating an *increase* in demand to a rightward shift in the demand curve. A decrease in demand refers to a leftward shift in the demand curve.

Tastes and preferences. Tastes and preferences—words often used synonymously—definitely do determine demand. Clearly, tastes are nonprice determinants of demand. If women's tastes change in favor of miniskirts, the demand curve for miniskirts will shift outward to the right (the demand for miniskirts will increase). If women's tastes for miniskirts decrease, that will be represented by a decrease in demand, or an inward shift to the left of the demand curve. We will talk more about tastes in Chapter 3, when we deal with consumer preferences.

Economists do not often use a change in taste as an explanation of a change in demand. Why? Because economists have little to say about what taste is and how it is determined. Indeed, simply stating that the world is the way it is because our tastes are what they are does not help much in predicting how human behavior will change in the future. It does not really tell us much about why behavior changed in the past, either. Additionally, we do not know how to measure alleged changes in taste. We do know how to measure changes in income, for example, and so we often talk about income changes causing a change in demand.

In sum, because of our difficulties in measurement and our lack of a theory about changes in taste, we usually assume that tastes are constant and look for other characteristics that may affect behavior.[3]

Prices of related goods: substitutes and complements. A demand schedule for a particular good is always represented graphically, with the prices of all other commodities given and constant. That is to say, *we assume that only the price of the good under study changes.* Actually, we normally concern ourselves only with making sure that the prices of *related* commodities remain constant when we draw a particular commodity's demand curve. For example, when we draw the demand curve for butter, we assume that the price of margarine is held constant. When we draw the demand curve for tennis rackets, we assume that the price of tennis balls is held constant. The general term "related goods" refers to any goods for which a change in price will change the demand for other goods.

There are two types of related goods: **substitutes** and **complements.** We can define and distinguish between substitutes and complements in terms of how the change in price of one commodity affects the demand for its related commodity.

Consider two goods, x and y, out of many possible goods, x, y, z, etc. If

---

[2]We will see later that in some instances an increase in income will cause the opposite to occur.

[3]It might seem that we cannot assume that tastes are constant if we want to analyze the introduction of new products into the marketplace. But it depends on whether tastes are defined for particular goods (such as word processors) or for general functions performed by these goods (producing a written document).

x and y are substitutes, when the price of y falls as the price of x remains unchanged, consumers will shift to more y and less x; the demand curve for x shifts to the left, indicating a decrease in demand for x. If the price of y rises, the demand curve for x will shift to the right, indicating an increase in the demand for x. Butter and margarine would be an example of such substitutes, as represented here by x and y. In other words, the relationship is positive: An increase in the price of y (butter) leads to an increase in the demand for x (margarine), and vice versa.

With complementary goods, the situation is reversed. If a decrease in the price of y leads to an increase in the demand for x, and an increase in the price of y leads to a decrease in the demand for x, x and y are said to be complementary. Tennis rackets and tennis balls would be an example of complementary goods. If the price of tennis balls rises, the demand for tennis rackets may fall. If the price of tennis balls falls, the demand for tennis rackets may increase.

Changes in expectations of future relative prices. Expectations about future relative prices play an important role in determining the position of the demand curve. If there is, all of a sudden, an expectation of a rise in the future *relative* price of eggs, we might predict, **ceteris paribus** (which means "all other things being equal, or held constant"), that the present demand curve will shift from DD to D′D′ in Figure 2-2. If, on the other hand, there is a new expectation of a future decrease in the price of eggs, the present demand curve will shift instead to D″D″ in Figure 2-2.

Note that we are talking about changes in expectations of future *relative* prices rather than *absolute prices*. If all prices are rising at 10 percent a year, year in and year out, and that situation is expected to continue, this fully anticipated inflation rate has no effect on the position of the demand curve for a particular commodity (if the price is measured in relative terms on the vertical axis). Consider, for example, what would happen to the demand curve for new automobiles if it were known that their price would rise by 10 percent next year. If it were anticipated that all prices would rise by 10 percent, the price of new cars relative to an average of all other prices would not be any different next year from what it is this year. Thus, the demand curve for new cars this year would not increase just because of the *anticipated* 10 percent price rise in their normal prices.

Such would not be the case if a group of investors, properly anticipating a secret shutdown of all South African gold mines for 10 years, anticipated an extraordinary rise in the market price of gold. They would be contemplating a rise in the relative price of a commodity. Presumably, their demand curve for gold today will shift outward to the right because of their anticipation of a higher relative price of gold tomorrow.

Population. Often an increase in the population in an economy (holding per capita income constant) shifts the *market* demand outward for most products. This is because an increase in population leads to an increase in the number of buyers in the market. Conversely, a reduction in the population will shift most demand curves inward because of the reduction in the number of buyers in the market. For example, as birthrates dropped in the United States, firms dealing in baby food started to diversify. They moved into other fields because of an anticipated inward shift in the market demand curve for their product.

DISTINGUISHING BETWEEN CHANGES IN DEMAND AND CHANGES IN QUANTITY DEMANDED: A RECAP

The term "demand" always relates to the position of the *entire* demand schedule, or curve. Demand, therefore, refers to a *schedule of planned purchase rates*. Demand—the demand curve, or schedule—depends on many nonprice determinants, such as those just discussed.

A *change in quantity demanded* occurs if and only if there has been a change in price; nothing else changes.

Look at Figure 2-3(a). We have drawn a market schedule, or curve, for good x. At a relatively low price, P_1, a relatively large quantity will be demanded, Q_1. This is shown as point A on the market demand curve, DD. On the other hand, at a relatively high price such as P_2, a relatively smaller quantity will be demanded, Q_2. We show this on the market demand curve as point B. *The idea to be remembered is that change in the* quantity demanded *is represented as a movement along a given market demand curve*. This movement is associated with a change in the price of the product.

In Figure 2-3(b), we have redrawn Figure 2-1 in order to demonstrate changes in quantity demanded with a specific numerical example. Let us assume that we start off with a price per constant-quality pizza of $4.30. If the price falls to $4.10, the quantity demanded will increase from 60 million pizzas per year to 100 million. You can see the arrow pointing down along the demand curve DD in Figure 2-3(b). The change from 60 million pizzas per year to 100 million represents a change in the *quantity demanded* because of a change in the price per pizza. We said nothing about a change in demand.

The ceteris paribus assumption and demand functions

As we have already seen, economists analyze the world by constructing thought experiments in which only one type of change occurs at any one time. In the case of market demand, where there are a number of people in the market willing and able to purchase a good, we call the good x, and we can write a mathematical function to express the demand:

$$Q_x = f(P_x, P_y, M, T, E) \tag{2-1}$$

FIGURE 2-3
Movement along a given market demand curve
In panel (*a*), we show the demand curve *DD* for hypothetical good *x*. If price is P_1, the quantity demanded will be Q_1; we will be at point *A*. If, on the other hand, the price is relatively high, P_2, the quantity demanded will be relatively small Q_2. We will be at point *B* on *DD*. In panel (*b*) we show with a numerical example that a change in relative price changes the quantity of a good demanded. It is a movement along a given market demand schedule. If, in our example, the relative price of pizzas falls from \$4.30 to \$4.10 per unit, the quantity demanded will increase from 60 million pizzas per year to 100 million.

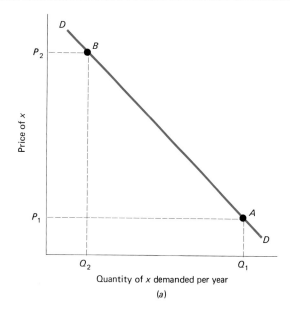

(*a*)

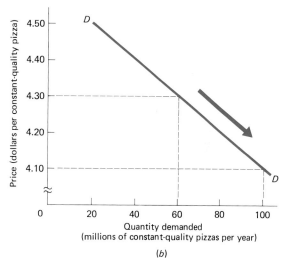

(*b*)

This means that the quantity Q of good x that can be sold is related to (is a function of *f*) the price P_x of x, the price P_y of some other good that has an impact on demand for x, consumers' money income M, consumers' tastes T, and consumers' expectations E about the future. Note two things: Each consumer is assumed to have a demand function for x, and any other variables that relate to the demand for x could be included in this equation. For simplicity's sake we tend to focus only on the variables that have the most significant impact on the demand for x.

On our usual demand graph, as in Figure 2-3, we are plotting the points that show the values of Q_x as P_x changes, *ceteris paribus*. That is, all of the other variables on the right-hand side of the function are held constant. This might be expressed as

$$Q_x = f(P_x, \overline{P_y}, \overline{M}, \overline{T}, \overline{E}) \tag{2-2}$$

We could, of course, vary another variable, such as M, while holding P_x and the other variables constant. Such a change would show up on our demand graph as a shift of the demand curve, as in Figure 2-2, because the axes of the graph are Q_x and P_x and the demand curve assumes that all variables other than Q_x and P_x are constant.

THE LAW OF SUPPLY

The **law of supply** can be stated as simply as we stated the law of demand.

■ *There is a direct, or positive, relation between the quantity supplied of a commodity and its price, other things held constant.*

When we refer to a direct, or positive, relation, we simply mean that when the commodity's price rises, the quantity supplied does also (it is more profitable to produce); and when the commodity's price falls, so does the quantity supplied (it is less profitable to produce).

Market supply schedule

Just as we were able to construct a market demand schedule, we can construct a **market supply schedule:** a table representing prices and the quantities that will be supplied at each alternative price. A market supply schedule is

TABLE 2-2
Market supply schedule for pizzas

At higher prices, suppliers will be willing to supply more pizzas. We see, for example, in column (1) that at a price per constant-quality unit of $4.10, only 20 million pizzas will be supplied; but at a price of $4.50 per unit, 100 million pizzas will be forthcoming from suppliers. We label these price-quantity combinations in column (3).

Price ($ per constant-quality pizza) (1)	Quantity supplied (constant-quality pizzas per year) (2)	Combination (see figure 2-4) (3)
4.10	20 million	F
4.20	40 million	G
4.30	60 million	H
4.40	80 million	I
4.50	100 million	J

a set of production *rates* that producers are willing and able to provide to the market depending on the price of the product. In Table 2-2, we show the supply schedule of pizzas per year.

Market supply curve

We can graphically represent the market supply schedule from Table 2-2 as a **market supply curve,** just as we earlier represented the market demand curve. All we do is take the price-quantity combinations from Table 2-2 and plot them, as shown in Figure 2-4. We have labeled these combinations *F* through *J*. Now we connect these points with a smooth line, and we have a "curve." It is upward-sloping to show the direct, or positive, relationship between price and the quantity supplied, other things being equal. Again, we must remember that we are referring to quantity supplied *per year*, measured in constant-quality units.

FIGURE 2-4

The market supply curve for pizzas

The horizontal axis measures the quantity of pizzas supplied expressed in constant-quality units per year. The vertical axis, as usual, measures price. We merely take the price-quantity combinations from Table 2-2 and plot them as points *F*, *G*, *H*, *I*, and *J*. Then we connect those points to find the market supply curve for pizzas. It is positively sloped, demonstrating the law of market supply. At higher relative prices, larger quantities will be forthcoming.

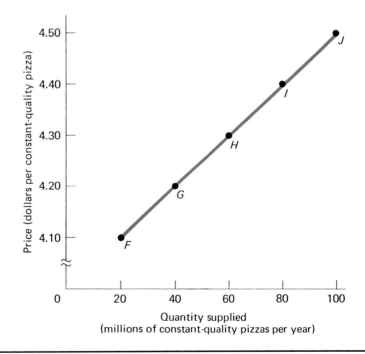

A movement along this supply curve occurs when the price changes. If the price goes up from $4.10 to $4.30, the quantity of pizzas supplied in constant-quality units goes up from 20 million per year to 60 million. If the price was originally $4.50 per pizza and falls to $4.30 per pizza, the quantity supplied will fall from 100 million units per year to 60 million.

A shift in the supply curve, or supply schedule

A change in the price of the commodity causes a movement along the market supply curve, as was just pointed out. A change in any nonprice variable that affects the quantity producers will supply affects the entire supply schedule, or supply curve, and will shift it. For example, a new method of cooking pizzas may reduce that particular cost by 50 percent. If this is the case, suppliers will supply more at each and every possible price, because their costs of supplying pizzas have fallen. Competition among sellers wishing to produce and sell more will shift the supply curve outward to the right. This is represented in the example given in Figure 2-5. A reduction in the cost of cooking pizzas will hypothetically shift the supply curve from SS to S'S'. Thus, at a price of $4.30 per pizza, the quantity supplied was originally 60 million per year but will now be 90 million.

Alternatively, let's assume that a new strain of harmful pests destroys

---

FIGURE 2-5
A shift in the supply schedule
If the price changes, we move along a given supply schedule. However, if, for example, the cost of production of pizzas were to fall, the supply schedule would shift outward from SS to S'S' so that at all prices a larger quantity would be forthcoming from suppliers. If the cost of production rose, the market supply curve would shift to S"S".

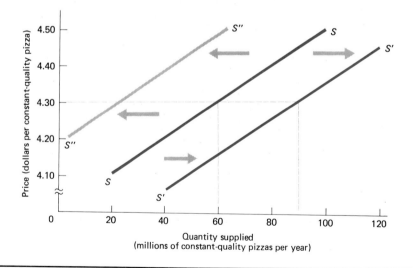

Quantity supplied
(millions of constant-quality pizzas per year)

most of the tomato crop. When pizza makers attempt to purchase the same amount of tomato sauce as they originally did, they will find that it costs more than before. All users of tomatoes will bid up the price of the now-scarcer supply. Ultimately, then, pizza makers will have to pay greatly increased prices for one of their ingredients. The market supply curve in Figure 2-5 will shift from SS to S″S″, which lies to the left of SS. Thus, at each and every price, the market quantity supplied will fall.

The determinants of supply in detail

The prices of resources used to produce the product. If one or more of the prices of the resources used (also called factors, or inputs) falls, the supply curve will shift outward to the right; that is, more will be supplied at each and every price. The opposite will be true if one or more productive inputs becomes more expensive; the SS curve will shift leftward.

Technology. Supply curves are drawn assuming a given technology, or "state of the art." Over time, the range of productive techniques available may change. If that change involves technology which is less costly in the short run, the supply curve will shift rightward. In other words, if a better production technique becomes available, the supply curve will shift to the right; a larger quantity will be forthcoming at each and every price.

Taxes and subsidies. It turns out that certain taxes, such as sales taxes, are effectively an addition to production costs because they must be paid in the production and marketing of the product. They therefore reduce the supply (*not* the quantity supplied). Consider the market supply curve SS in Figure 2-5. If a sales tax is added that did not exist before, that market supply curve will shift inward to the left to S″S″. A subsidy (negative tax) will do the opposite and shift the curve in Figure 2-5 rightward to S′S′.

Price expectations. Expectations of the future relative price of a product can affect producers' current willingness to supply, just as price expectations affect consumers' willingness to purchase. As an example, consider that some owners of natural gas wells may have kept them capped in anticipation that the federal government in the future will increase the legislated maximum price for natural gas. Farmers may withhold part of their current wheat crop from the market if they anticipate a higher wheat price in the future. In either case, the quantity currently being supplied at each and every price will decrease.

It should be noted that we are here referring to the entire chain of producers and marketers that ends in the product being sold to an ultimate consumer. Farmers themselves may sell their grain immediately after harvest. But grain dealers, if expecting a higher future price, may then buy and store some portion of that harvest. We will discuss the role of "middlepersons" and "dealers" in more detail in Chapter 7. For now, just remember that these groups are part of the group of producers responsible for supplying the market.

DEMAND AND SUPPLY INTERACTION

Table 2-3 is a composite of Tables 2-1 and 2-2. Column (1) lists prices, which are common to both supply and demand quantities. Column (2) is the quantity supplied per year, from Table 2-2. Column (3) is the quantity demanded per year, from Table 2-1. Column (4) is simply the difference between the quantity supplied and the quantity demanded per year. Column (5) characterizes in words the difference between quantity supplied and quantity demanded, that is, excess quantity supplied and excess quantity demanded at various prices. At a price above $4.30 per pizza, the quantity supplied exceeds the quantity demanded. Below a price of $4.30, the quantity demanded exceeds the quantity supplied.

Notice that there is something special about the price of $4.30 per constant-quality pizza. At that price, the market quantity supplied per year is 60 million pizzas and the market quantity demanded per year is 60 million pizzas. The difference between quantity supplied and quantity demanded is zero. There is neither an excess quantity demanded nor an excess quantity supplied. Hence, this price of $4.30 is called the **market-clearing price.** It clears the market of all excess market quantity supplied and all excess

TABLE 2-3
Putting market demand and market supply together

Here we combine Tables 2-1 and 2-2. Column (1) is the price per constant-quality unit. Column (2) is the quantity supplied, and column (3) is the quantity demanded, both on a per year basis. The difference between quantity supplied and quantity demanded is expressed in column (4). For the first two prices, we have a negative difference; that is, an excess quantity is demanded, as expressed in column (5). At the price of $4.40 or $4.50, we have a positive difference; that is, we have an excess quantity supplied. However, at a price of $4.30, the quantity supplied and the quantity demanded are equal, so that there is neither an excess quantity demanded nor an excess quantity supplied. We call this price the "equilibrium," or "market-clearing," price.

Price ($ per constant-quality pizza) (1)	Quantity supplied (constant-quality pizzas per year) (2)	Quantity demanded (constant-quality pizzas per year) (3)	Differences (2) − (3) (4)	Excesses (5)
4.10	20 million	100 million	−80 million	Excess quantity demanded
4.20	40 million	80 million	−40 million	Excess quantity demanded
4.30	60 million	60 million	0	Market-clearing price: equilibrium
4.40	80 million	40 million	40 million	Excess quantity supplied
4.50	100 million	20 million	80 million	Excess quantity supplied

market quantity demanded. There are no willing demanders who want to pay $4.30 but are turned away from pizza parlors, and there are no willing suppliers who want to provide pizza at $4.30 but cannot sell all they want at that price. *The market-clearing price is also called the* **equilibrium price,** or the price from which there is no tendency to change.

The demand and supply curves combined

If we can represent the supply and demand schedules together in a single table, as we did in Table 2-3, it seems that we can also represent on one graph the graphical representations of supply and demand curves.

In Figure 2-6 we have combined the demand curve from Figure 2-1 and the supply curve from Figure 2-4. The only difference between those figures and Figure 2-6 is that the horizontal axis measures both the market quantity supplied per year *and* the market quantity demanded per year. Everything else is the same. The demand curve is labeled *DD* and the supply curve *SS*. We have labeled the intersection of the market supply curve with the market demand curve as point *E*, for equilibrium. That corresponds to a price of $4.30, at which both quantity supplied and quantity demanded are equal to 60 million pizzas per year.

The meaning of equilibrium

The price of $4.30 is the equilibrium price in our example; the equilibrium quantity is 60 million pizzas per year.

Look at Figure 2-7. Here we show an equilibrium price of P_e. What if the price were P_1, which is more than P_e? The quantity supplied would

---

FIGURE 2-6
Supply and demand together: the curves
Here we combine Figures 2-1 and 2-4. Note that the intersection of the market supply and market demand curves is at *E*, occurring at a price of $4.30 per constant-quality unit of pizzas. At point *E* there is neither an excess quantity demanded nor an excess quantity supplied. At a price of $4.10 the quantity supplied will be only 20 million pizzas per year, but the quantity demanded will be 100 million. The difference is excess quantity demanded at a price of $4.10. There are forces that will cause the price to rise, and so we will move from point *A* up the market supply curve to point *E*, and from point *B* up the market demand curve to point *E*. At the other extreme, a price of $4.50 elicits a quantity supplied of 100 million, with a quantity demanded of 20 million. The difference is excess quantity supplied at a price of $4.50. Again, forces will cause the price to fall, and so we will move down the market demand and market supply curves to the equilibrium point *E*.

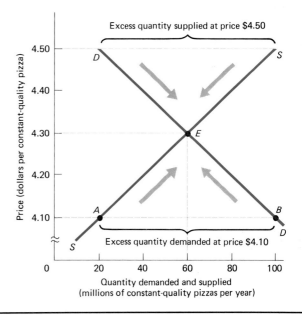

FIGURE 2-7

Equilibrium price, shortages, and surpluses
At a price of P_e, the quantity demanded equals
the quantity supplied. At price P_1, the quantity
supplied exceeds the quantity demanded. The
difference is the excess quantity supplied at
price P_1, sometimes called a *surplus*. At price
P_2, the quantity demanded exceeds the
quantity supplied. There is an excess quantity
demanded at P_2, sometimes called a *shortage*.
In both cases, forces will push the price toward
P_e.

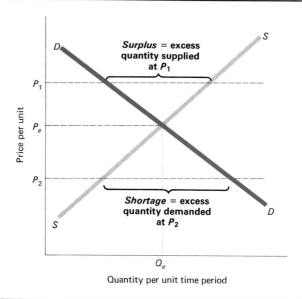

exceed the quantity demanded at that price. The result would be an excess
quantity supplied at price P_1, or a "surplus." However, given *DD* and *SS*,
there will be forces pushing the price back down toward P_e. Suppliers will
attempt to reduce their inventories by cutting prices, and producers, seeing
a lower price, will cut back on the quantity supplied. As the price falls,
demanders will offer to purchase more—that is, the quantity demanded will
increase. If not prevented from moving, the price will eventually reach its
equilibrium at P_e again.

What if the price is, for some reason, at P_2? At this below-equilibrium
price, the quantity demanded exceeds the quantity supplied. There is an
excess quantity demanded at P_2, or a "shortage." *Market forces will cause
the price to rise.* Demanders will bid up the price, and/or suppliers will raise
the price.

The point of this analysis is that any disequilibrium situation automatically brings into action correcting forces which will cause a movement back
toward equilibrium. The equilibrium price and quantity will be maintained
so long as demand and supply do not change.

When we refer to a *stable* equilibrium, we mean that if there is a movement away from the equilibrium price or quantity, there will be forces pushing price or quantity back to the equilibrium level or rate. An *unstable*
equilibrium is one in which, if there is a movement away from the equilibrium, there are forces that push price and/or quantity further away from
equilibrium (or at least do not push price and quantity back toward the
equilibrium level or rate). The difference between a stable and an unstable

equilibrium can be illustrated by looking at two balls, one made of hard rubber and the other made of soft, moist Play-Doh. If you were to squeeze the rubber ball out of shape, it would spring back to its original shape. However, if you were to squeeze the Play-Doh ball out of shape, it would remain out of shape. The former illustrates a stable and the latter an unstable equilibrium.

Boundary equilibria. We do not see any solid-gold Mercedes being produced. Is this an equilibrium situation? Yes, it is. It is a boundary equilibrium, which can be seen in panel (*a*) of Figure 2-8. The demand curve for solid-gold Mercedes is represented by *DD*. The supply curve is, however, somewhat different from what we are used to seeing. It is represented by *SS*. This supply curve starts at the origin, rises along the vertical axis to point P_2, and then takes on the familiar upward slope. The reason the supply curve has this shape is that no quantity of gold Mercedes will be forthcoming between the prices of 0 and P_2. However, the most that anyone would pay for a gold Mercedes is P_1, which is less than P_2. In a sense, we can say that the equilibrium quantity is 0 and the price is indefinite but lies somewhere in the range between P_1 and P_2. This is called a **boundary equilibrium;**

FIGURE 2-8
Boundary equilibria
In panel (*a*) the supply of solid-gold Mercedes is *SS* and is the vertical axis from 0 to price P_2 and then out along a normally sloped supply curve. The demand curve is *DD*, which actually coincides with the vertical axis at any price above price P_1. The equilibrium quantity of solid-gold Mercedes is 0 at an equilibrium price somewhere between P_2 and P_1. In panel (*b*) we show another boundary equilibrium for a good whose supply curve is *SS*. The equilibrium is at a zero price with quantity demanded of Q_D; the good is a free one; i.e., it is not scarce.

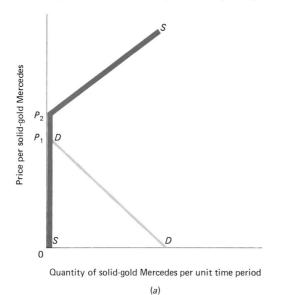

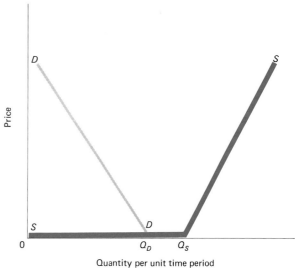

(*a*)

(*b*)

sometimes it is called a "corner solution." The equilibria that we have been shown prior to this diagram are called **interior equilibria** or **interior solutions.**

Another boundary situation occurs in panel (b) of Figure 2-8. The demand curve DD intersects the supply curve SS where the latter coincides with the horizontal axis. In other words, there is a supply Q_S forthcoming at a zero price. To obtain more than Q_S requires a positive price. However, the quantity demanded at a zero price is Q_D. The boundary equilibrium in this situation is at a zero price and quantity Q_D. Goods represented by these curves in panel (b) are generally called noneconomic resources—goods for which no market price currently exists.

MOVEMENTS IN PRICES AND QUANTITIES: THE COBWEB THEOREM

The prices and outputs of many commodities show cyclical movements over long periods of time. As prices move up and down in waves, quantities produced seem to move up and down in counterwaves. One explanation for such cycles in commodity prices and outputs is the so-called **cobweb theorem.** The name "cobweb" comes from the way the diagrams look. It turns out that the cobweb theorem is one of the simplest models of the dynamics of supply, demand, and price.

We divide the periods with which we are dealing into discrete units. For the sake of simplicity, they will be 1-year periods. We further assume that the quantity produced this year is a function of the price of the product last year, or

$$Q_{t+1}^S = f(P_t) \tag{2-3}$$

where the superscript S refers to supply and the subscript refers to the time period. Thus, the quantity supplied next year will be a function of this year's price, or alternatively, the quantity supplied this year is a function of last year's price. On the demand side, the quantity demanded this year is a function of the price this year, as always, or $Q_t^D = f(P_t)$. The equilibrium price in any one year is, of course, the price at which the quantity supplied equals the quantity demanded, or $Q_t^S = Q_t^D$. Finally, in any one year we assume that there is a perfectly inelastic supply which is equal to the quantity that has been produced. In the case of agricultural commodities, no more is forthcoming until after the next growing season.

We can see perpetually oscillating prices and quantities in panels (a) and (b) of Figure 2-9. Let us assume that the price in year 1 is P_1. Thus the quantity supplied in year 2 is going to be Q_2 in panel (a). But in order to sell Q_2 in year 2, the price that will be fetched in the marketplace is going to be P_2. In year 3, the quantity supplied will be a function of P_2 or Q_3, which will command a price P_1. This will continue. We see in panel (b) that price

FIGURE 2-9
A cobweb model
The quantity supplied next period is a function of this period's price. Assume that this year's price is P_1. The quantity supplied next year will be Q_2, but Q_2 can be sold only at price P_2. Thus, the quantity supplied the following year will be Q_3; however, that quantity can be sold at price P_1. In panel (b) we show the continuous oscillation of price and quantity.

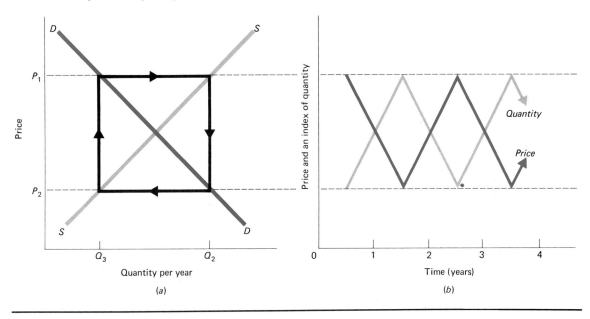

(a)   (b)

and quantity will oscillate between P_1 and P_2 and that quantity will oscillate between Q_2 and Q_3.

In the next example we see *damped* oscillation and the familiar cobweb appearance of the diagram. In a situation of damped oscillation, whatever is oscillating eventually "homes in" on some value rather than continuously moving up and down. A good example of damped oscillation is what happens when a perfectly balanced pendulum is pushed. The pendulum moves back and forth but eventually oscillates less and less until it ends up in its original position. Look at Figure 2-10. In panel (a), we have drawn the supply curve with a slope numerically greater than the slope of the demand curve.[4] We start out in year 1 with price P_1. That calls forth in year 2 the quantity Q_2, which is sold at a price P_2; but P_2 calls forth in year 3 a quantity of Q_3, which is sold at price P_3. This price calls forth in year 4 the quantity Q_4. We can see that eventually the oscillation will dampen to zero so that the price, year in and year out, will be P_0 at the intersection of DD and SS; and the quantity will be Q_0. In panel (b) we show that the oscillation damps over time. If we

[4]The absolute value of the slope of the supply curve is greater than the absolute value of the slope of the demand curve.

FIGURE 2-10

The cobweb model: damped oscillation

If the slope of the supply curve in panel (a) is numerically greater (in absolute value) than the slope of the demand curve, the cobweb model leads to damped oscillation, as shown in panel (b).

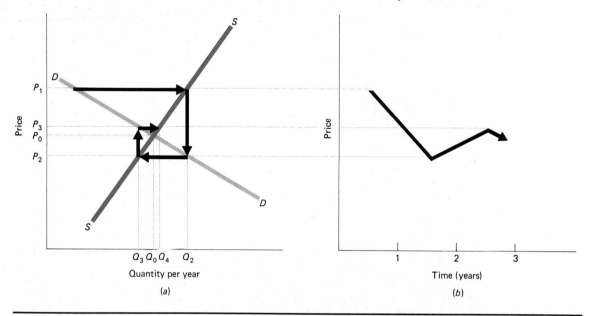

(a)

(b)

were to draw the demand curve with a slope numerically greater than the slope of the supply curve, we would get an explosive oscillation.

The real applicability of the cobweb model to commodities markets is dubious. Economic agents would eventually learn about these changes, anticipate them, and smooth them out through speculation. It might be, however, that the model somewhat better describes supply conditions in high-skill labor markets, if the workers in these markets require some significant amount of time to receive their initial education or training and the skills or knowledge learned are not highly transferable.

CHANGES IN DEMAND AND SUPPLY

Now that we have combined both market demand and market supply on one graph, we can analyze the effects of changes in supply and/or demand. In Figure 2-11 there are four panels. In panel (a), the market supply curve remains stable, but the market demand curve increases (shifts outward to the right) from DD to $D'D'$. Note that the result is both an increase in the market-clearing price from P_e to P'_e and an increase in the equilibrium quantity from Q_e to $2Q'_e$.

FIGURE 2-11
Shifts in market demand and market supply

In panel (a) the supply curve is stable at SS. The demand curve shifts out from DD to $D'D'$. The equilibrium price and quantities rise from P_e, Q_e to P'_e, Q'_e, respectively. In panel (b), again, the market supply curve remains stable at SS. The market demand curve, however, shifts inward to the left, showing a decrease in demand from DD to $D'D'$. Both equilibrium price and quantity fall. In panel (c) the market demand curve now remains stable at DD. Supply increase is shown by a movement outward to the right of the market supply curve from SS to $S'S'$. The equilibrium price falls from P_e to P'_e. The equilibrium quantity supplied increases, however, from Q_e to Q'_e. In panel (d) the market demand curve is stable at DD. The market supply curve decreases from SS to $S'S'$. The equilibrium price increases from P_e to P'_e. The equilibrium quantity decreases to Q'_e.

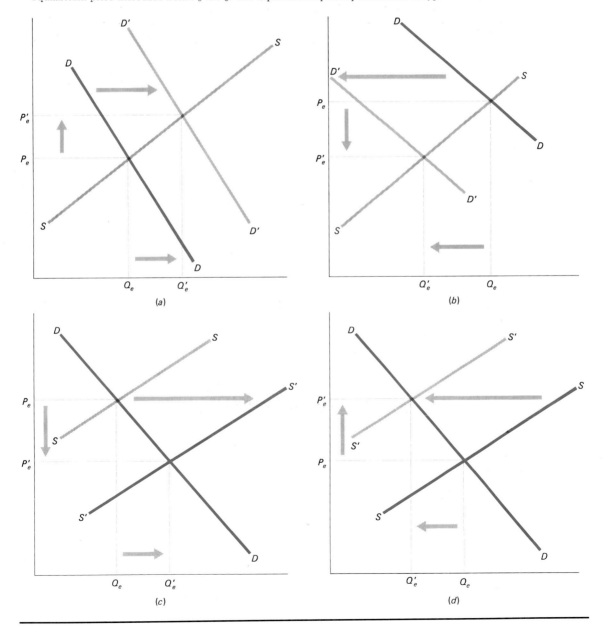

In panel (*b*), there is a decrease in market demand (a shift inward to the left) from *DD* to *D'D'*. This results in a decrease in both the market-clearing, or equilibrium, price of the good and the equilibrium quantity.

Panels (*c*) and (*d*) show the effects of a shift in the market supply curve while the market demand curve remains stable. In panel (*c*) the market supply curve has shifted out to the right—market supply increases. The equilibrium price of the product falls, whereas the equilibrium quantity increases. In panel (*d*) market supply has shifted inward to the left—there has been a market supply decrease. The equilibrium price increases, whereas the equilibrium quantity decreases.

WHERE TO?

Now that we have covered a brief review of supply and demand, their determinants, and how to analyze changes in supply and demand, we will look at several real-world issues and applications using these tools. Once you have mastered an understanding of how to conceptualize analytically the change in demand and/or supply, you should be able to predict what will happen to market (equilibrium) prices and market (equilibrium) quantities after some change in the economic environment has occurred.

ISSUES AND APPLICATIONS

The farm "problem" and price supports

Since the 1930s, the United States government has engaged in a number of agricultural programs to deal with the so-called farm problem. The farm problem, at least for politicians, was that farmers were not making high enough incomes. The political response to such a "problem" was to devise a method to keep the prices received by farmers higher than they would be in the absence of government intervention. One way that this was done was through a price-support program, which we will now explain.

Figure 2-12 presents the analysis of a price-support or minimum-price program. In an unrestricted market, the equilibrium price is P_e; the equilibrium quantity is Q_e. The government sets the support price for a particular commodity at P_{min}. This increases the quantity supplied to Q_S and decreases the quantity demanded to Q_D. The difference is the excess quantity supplied ($Q_S - Q_D$) at price P_{min}. This is called a surplus. The only way for the price P_{min} to continue is for the surplus to be continuously bought up by the government. For many years prior to 1973 (and for some commodities since then), the surplus, in effect,

FIGURE 2-12
The farm program: price supports

We show the analysis of the effects of price supports. The market-clearing price is P_e; the equilibrium quantity is Q_e. A price support greater than P_e is put on at P_{min}. The quantity demanded will now be Q_D; the quantity supplied Q_S. The difference between Q_D and Q_S is the excess quantity supplied at the support price.

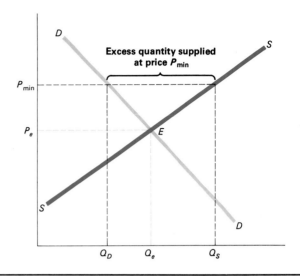

was purchased by the Commodity Credit Corporation (CCC). The CCC made nonrecourse loans at the support price for however much farmers wanted to "borrow." A nonrecourse loan works as follows: The farmer puts up as collateral some price-supported commodity, say, corn. The CCC lends the farmer a sum of money that is equal to the support price per unit times the number of units put up as collateral. At no time in the future is the farmer required to pay off the loan; this is the nonrecourse nature of the loan. The CCC will be stuck with the collateral so long as the equilibrium price stays below the support price.

Substitutes, or why unions want higher economywide minimum wages

We pointed out that one of the determinants of the position of a demand curve was the price of substitutes and complements. We defined substitutes as those commodities whose demand curves shift outward when the price of the related commodity rises. There is an interesting application of this analysis to the question of minimum wages. Ignoring for the moment the arguments concerning the desire for workers to earn "decent" or "living" wages—a topic which we will get to later in the text—why would we predict that unions would want legislation which raised the minimum wage?

First we must realize that union workers in virtually all industries and locations earn more (usually considerably more) than the minimum wage. Thus, when we talk about raising the minimum wage, we are really referring to raising the price of nonunion labor. Furthermore, we must understand that union workers and nonunion workers are substitutes. Thus, unions in their own self-interest will want to lobby to make their substitute, nonunion labor, more expensive. After all, more-expensive nonunion labor makes union labor *relatively* less expensive. Workers employed at the minimum wage are, by definition, substitutes for union workers. Unions can be expected, therefore, to lobby in favor of increases in the minimum wage.

This can be seen in Figure 2-13. The demand curve for union labor is *DD* when the price of the substitute—nonunion labor—is held constant at the minimum wage of $3.35 an hour. Now, if the minimum wage is raised to $4.50 an hour, the demand curve for union workers will shift to the right to *D'D'*. Thus, we can see in Figure 2-13 that for any given union wage rate, the quantity of union labor demanded per time period will be greater, the higher is the wage rate of the nonunion al-

ternative. In other words, more union labor will be hired.

It is not surprising that the record shows that union leaders and senators and members of Congress from heavily unionized states have been consistent advocates for raising minimum wages. Then-senator Jacob Javits of New York was reported in the *Congressional Record* of February 23, 1966, p. 2692, to have said:

> I point [out] to Senators from industrial states like my own that a minimum wage increase would also give industry in our states some measure of protection as we have too long suffered from the unfair competition based on substandard wages and other labor conditions in effect in certain areas of the country—primarily in the South.

In other words, the demand for industrial workers who are mostly unionized in the North is adversely affected by lower wages in the South; an increase in the legal minimum wage reduces the competition from the South. It shifts the demand schedule for union workers (primarily in the North) outward (to the right).

FIGURE 2-13
An increase in the demand for union labor resulting from an increase in the minimum wage
The demand curve for union labor is drawn with the price of substitutes held constant. It is first given as *DD* with the minimum hourly wage equal to $3.35. If legislation increases the minimum hourly wage to, say, $4.50, the demand curve for union labor will shift to the right to *D'D'*.

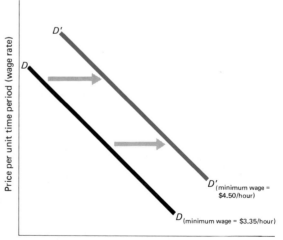

Queuing, waiting, and competition

A standard conclusion of supply and demand analysis is that competition will result in a price which causes the market to clear. Consumers willing and able to pay the market price should be able to purchase any amount of the good they want without paying any additional nonmarket price. Thus, when we see goods being allocated by queuing up (waiting in line), the most obvious conclusion is that the price in the market is being held below equilibrium by some noncompetitive force. That is not, however, always true.

Queuing may also arise when the demand characteristics of a market are subject to large or unpredictable fluctuations, and the additional costs to firms (and ultimately to consumers) of holding sufficient inventories or providing sufficient "excess" capacity to cover these peak demands are greater than the costs to consumers of waiting for the good. This is the usual case of waiting in line to purchase a "fast-food" lunch or to purchase a movie ticket a few minutes before the next show.

A similar situation exists when consumers can obtain a good at a lower price by agreeing to be placed on a list for future delivery. In this case the costs of waiting include no wasted time for the consumer. They are limited to the costs of deferring the utility gained from consuming the good and the chance that circumstances may change so as to make the good less valuable than originally anticipated when it is delivered. Even in the situation where a consumer is not obligated to actually accept the good once it becomes available, waiting lists may lower costs for producers. So long as the proportion of consumers who reject the good once it is offered is reasonably constant, producers can often lower their costs of estimating future demand by making their sales through waiting lists.[5]

[5]For a more extensive discussion of these topics see Cotton M. Lindsay and Bernard Feigenbaum, "Rationing by Waiting Lists," *American Economic Review* 74(3) (June 1984), pp. 404–417, and Arthur DeVany, "Uncertainty, Waiting Time and Capacity Utilization," *Journal of Political Economy* 84 (June 1976), pp. 523–542.

Controlling growth or making home owners rich?

During the late 1970s and early 1980s most areas of the nation saw housing prices rise substantially. It is generally agreed that the primary reason for the large price increases was inflation and the belief that many people had that inflation would continue at high rates. Land and housing appear to many people to be a good investment in times of uncertainty about high inflation, so people are willing to buy "more" house than they would otherwise because its investment value is greater than normal.

Adding to this incentive was the negative real interest rates many borrowers paid when they obtained mortgages in the late 1970s and early 1980s. The mortgage rates were high by historical standards but tended to be near the rate of inflation, which meant that the nominal rate was quite low. Most home owners obtain a tax saving by deducting the interest they pay on a mortgage, so that many borrowers faced a negative rate of interest. All of which increased the demand for housing and pushed up housing prices rapidly.

CALIFORNIA EXPERIENCE

While the housing price growth was high by historical standards almost everywhere in the U.S., the rates of increase in many California cities seemed astronomical. Clearly one factor in California was its above average population growth, which added to the price increase pressure. However, other areas of the nation experienced similar or greater increases in population but did not see as large an increase in average price as occurred in some cities in California, so other factors must have been at work there. For example, from 1972 to 1979, the average sale price of a house in the Santa Barbara area increased from $36,192 to $129,982—an increase of 260 percent (during the same time the general Consumer Price Index rose 75 percent).

WATER MORATORIUMS

Economists at the University of California at Santa Barbara have studied the impact on housing prices in that area due to water moratoriums.[6] They note that during the mid-1970s, various water districts in the Santa Barbara area imposed complete bans on new water hookups or severely limited the number of new water hookups, thereby reducing the number of new houses that could be built. There were various rationales expressed for these restrictions—the need to control growth, ecological degradation, and the increasing cost of providing new water supply. In any event, the homeowner groups that dominated the water district boards were responsible for a reduction in the number of new houses that were made available in the Santa Barbara area.

The impact of the partial water moratoriums over time can be seen on the stock and flow (sales) of houses in Figure 2-14. Looking

[6]Lloyd J. Mercer and W. Douglas Morgan, "An Estimate of Residential Growth Controls' Impact on House Prices," in *Resolving the Housing Crisis*, M. Bruce Johnson (ed.), Pacific Institute for Public Policy Research, 1982.

at panel (b) we see that at the time the water controls were first imposed the initial stock of houses in a given area was S_s. Without any controls, as demand increased over time from D_s to D'_s, more houses would have been added to the stock of houses, to S'_s. The equilibrium price for houses would have risen from A to B. However, with controls, the supply of new houses (the stock) was limited to S''_s, so that, given the same increase in demand, from D_s to D'_s, the equilibrium price rose to C. The same story is told in Figure 2-14(a) where we look at the flow of houses (sales). The equilibrium price may have moved from P to P' in the absence of controls, but with the restrictions on the supply of new houses, the market price of houses is pushed up toward P''.

The final equilibrium is impossible to know, but may be something like point D, corresponding with price P'''. The final supply curve may be to the left of the original supply curve because the flow of houses onto the market has been reduced over time. There are fewer new houses in the flow; most purchases must be resales of existing homes. The final demand may be reduced from D' to D'' as the overall growth of the area is reduced by the controls in housing growth. Since the area becomes more expensive to live in, fewer would-be residents choose to live there. In any event, the net effect of the controls on water hookups is clear—the price of existing homes has increased more than would have been the case without the controls

PRICE IMPACT OF CONTROLS

The economists from Santa Barbara estimated that from 1974 to 1979 approximately 27 percent of the real housing price increase was due to the growth controls. The result was a housing "crisis"—a lack of "affordable" housing for many new entrants into the area or for many lower-income residents who had hoped to be able to own a home. Existing homeowners appeared to have reaped a double benefit—their houses increased in value more than they would have without the controls and, because of the reduced growth, the increase in the cost of water was not as high as it might have been if there had been more growth.

FIGURE 2-14
Stock and flow of houses with and without controls

In panel (*a*) the original equilibrium is point *A*, corresponding to price *P* (the average price per house sold during a given time period). Over time, as the demand increases from *DD* to *D'D'*, supply increases from *SS* to *S'S'*, and new equilibrium *B* is established, corresponding to price *P'*. Panel (*b*) shows that this means that the stock of houses in this area would have increased from $S_s S_s$ to $S'_s S'_s$. However, because of the controls on growth, the stock of houses is allowed to increase only to $S''_s S''_s$, so that equilibrium is reached at point *C*. In a flow sense, in panel (*a*), we see that this may restrict the supply of houses at any given time to a lower level than existed originally, so that the flow shrinks to *S"S"*. If the high price of houses discourages entry into the area, demand may decline to *D"D"*, so that equilibrium level *D*, corresponding to price *P'''*, is reached at some point in time.

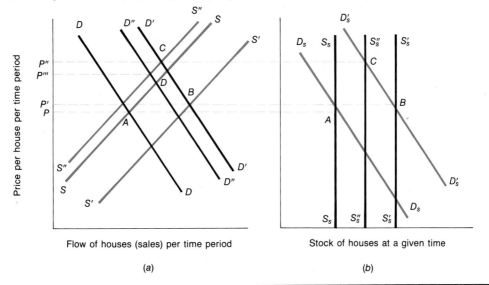

Flow of houses (sales) per time period

(a)

Stock of houses at a given time

(b)

SUMMARY

1   Economic activities take place in markets, which are institutions through which price-making forces operate.

2   There is an inverse relationship between the quantity demanded and price, holding all other things constant.

3   We can translate a numerical schedule of price-quantity pairs onto a diagram in which we observe a downward-sloping market demand curve.

4   It is important to distinguish between quantity demanded and demand. The only thing that can change quantity demanded is a change in price; all changes in the nonprice determinants of demand change demand only.

5   The position of the demand curve is a function of (*a*) income, (*b*) taste, (*c*) the prices of related goods, (*d*) changes in expectations of future relative prices, and (*e*) population.

6 Quantity supplied is directly related to price, holding all other things constant.

7 We can translate pairs of quantities and prices to a diagram to show an upward-sloping market supply curve.

8 A change in price causes a change in quantity supplied; a change in a nonprice determinant of supply shifts the entire market supply curve.

9 The determinants of supply are (a) the prices of resources used to produce the product, (b) technology, (c) taxes and subsidies, (d) price expectations, and (e) the number of firms in the industry.

10 At the intersection of the market demand curve and the market supply curve we will find the market-clearing, or equilibrium, price: the price from which there is no tendency to change.

11 At any price above the market-clearing price, there will be an excess quantity supplied; at any price below the market-clearing price, there will be an excess quantity demanded.

12 Equilibria can occur inside the price-quantity quadrant, in which case they are called interior equilibria, or on the axes, in which case they are called boundary equilibria. Generally, we are interested only in interior equilibria.

13 A cobweb model of dynamic adjustment has the quantity supplied in the current period as a function of the price in the previous period. If the supply curve has a numerically greater slope than the demand curve, we get damped oscillations that look like cobwebs on the demand and supply diagram.

GLOSSARY

- **market** The institution through which supply and demand operate.
- **marketplaces** Physical locations where exchanges take place and where the terms of exchange are registered.
- **market mechanisms** The information network within and across markets.
- **law of demand** Price and quantity demanded are inversely related, all other things held constant.
- **market demand schedule** Numerical pairs of prices and quantities showing planned purchase rates at different prices for the entire market.
- **market demand curve** A curve showing the quantities demanded for the entire market at different prices.
- **quantity demanded** The amount of a good desired by purchasers at various prices as reflected by points along a given demand curve.
- **demand change** A shift up or down in the amount of a good desired by purchasers caused by something other than a change in the price of the good itself; a movement of the demand curve.

- **substitute** A commodity whose demand varies directly, all other things held constant, with the price of another commodity.
- **complement** A commodity whose demand varies inversely, all other things held constant, with the price of another commodity.
- **ceteris paribus** Everything else held equal; to see the effect of one variable on another we hold all other variables constant.
- **law of supply** The quantity supplied is directly related to the price, all other things held constant.
- **market supply schedule** A numerical representation of pairs of prices and quantities, showing planned output rates at various prices, all other things held constant, for the entire market.
- **market supply curve** A curve showing the relationship between quantity supplied and price, other things held constant, for the entire market.
- **market-clearing, or equilibrium, price** The price that clears the market of all excess market quantity supplied and all excess market quantity demanded; the price from which there is no tendency to change.
- **boundary equilibrium** An equilibrium that occurs on the horizontal or the vertical axis; sometimes called a corner solution.
- **interior equilibrium** An equilibrium that occurs somewhere inside the price-quantity quadrant rather than on the axes; sometimes called an interior solution.
- **cobweb theorem** A simple dynamic model in which the quantities supplied in one period are a function of the price which prevailed in the previous period.

QUESTIONS

(Answers to even-numbered questions are at back of text.)

1 Explain the difference between a market and a marketplace.
2 Suppose an island economy exists in which there is no money; that is, there is no single agreed-upon *numeraire* in which prices of goods and services are expressed. Suppose further that every Sunday morning, at a certain location, hog farmers and cattle ranchers gather to exchange live pigs for cows. Is this a market, and if so, what do the supply and demand schedules/curves look like? Can you imagine any problems in arriving at terms of exchange?
3 Criticize the following statement: "Census data suggest that large numbers of men and women are now entering their twenties, a decade in which there is a high propensity to form new households. Aware of this fact, the construction, furniture, and appliances manufacturers are stepping up production to meet the anticipated increases in demand for their products."
4 What's wrong with the following assertion? "The demand has increased so much in response to our offering of a $500 rebate that our inventory of cars is now running very low."
5 Set this person straight: "Everybody knows that when people's incomes increase, they will go out to eat more frequently. This is bound to increase the demand for fast food."
6 How else might you explain a "spontaneous" increase in the demand for roller skating equipment rather than by merely asserting that there had been a change in "tastes"?

7 Suppose the leader of a major oil-exporting nation is interviewed live on *Face the Nation* and announces to the American audience that her nation's policy in the coming year will be to increase its oil production to maximum capacity, regardless of OPEC's disapproval. How might this influence the current demand for oil and why?

8 A supply schedule indicates the respective quantities which will be supplied at alternative possible prices. It could be argued that the suppliers are simultaneously demanders. What is it that they are demanding? Explain.

9 Where is the inaccuracy in the following statement? "In response to rising prices for our products, we have increased our supply by working overtime."

10 Below is a demand schedule and a supply schedule for lettuce:

Price ($ per crate)	Quantity demanded (crates per year)	Quantity supplied (crates per year)
1	100 million	0 million
2	90 million	10 million
3	70 million	30 million
4	50 million	50 million
5	20 million	80 million

What is the equilibrium price and equilibrium quantity? At a price of $2 per crate, what is the quantity demanded? The quantity supplied? What is the disequilibrium situation called? What is the *magnitude* of the disequilibrium, expressed in terms of quantities? Now answer the same questions for a price of $5 per crate.

11 Below is a demand schedule and a supply schedule for toaster ovens:

Price ($ toaster oven)	Quantity demanded (toaster ovens per year)	Quantity supplied (toaster ovens per year)
10	100,000	0
20	60,000	0
30	20,000	0
40	0	0
50	0	100,000
60	0	300,000
70	0	500,000

What is the equilibrium price and the equilibrium quantity? Explain.

12 Below is a supply schedule and a demand schedule for rainfall in an Amazon jungle settlement.

Price (cruzeiros per yearly centimeter of rain)	Quantity supplied* (centimeter of rain)	Quantity demanded (centimeters per year)
0	200	150
10	225	125
20	250	100
30	275	75
40	300	50
50	325	25
60	350	0
70	375	0
80	400	0

*We are assuming here that cloud seeding or other scientific techniques can be used to coax additional rainfall from the skies.

What is the equilibrium price and the equilibrium quantity? Explain.

13 Suppose federal legislation or action by a federal administrative agency banned a particular technique which was being widely used to slaughter livestock. How would this influence the supply of meat, and through which of the determinants of supply?

14 Criticize the following statement: "Federal farm price supports can never achieve their goals, since the above-equilibrium price floors which are established by Congress and the Department of Agriculture invariably create surpluses (quantities supplied in excess of quantities demanded), which in turn drive the price right back down toward equilibrium."

15 Suppose you have a given demand and supply for a commodity, and the market is presently clearing (the quantity demanded is equal to the quantity supplied at the current, equilibrium price). Now suppose that there was an increase in supply *and* a concurrent increase in demand. How would the new equilibrium price and quantity compare with the original? Explain.

SELECTED REFERENCES

Boulding, K. E., *Economic Analysis.* Vol. 1 *Microeconomics.* (New York: Harper & Row, 1966), chaps. 11 and 12.

Marshall, Alfred, *Principles of Economics,* 8th ed. (London: Macmillan, 1920), book III, chaps. 1, 2, and 3.

Working, E. E., "What Do Statistical 'Demand Curves' Show?" *Quarterly Journal of Economics,* vol. 41, 1927, pp. 212–235.

Preferences, utility, and consumer choice

*I*t is said that if you really understand supply and demand, you have mastered the essence of economics. While that statement is not completely accurate, it is true that an in-depth analysis of the influences that underlie demand and supply can tell us a lot about how markets operate.

Most of this intermediate microeconomics course is devoted to deepening our understanding of the underpinnings of demand and supply and to extending the insights from this process to a variety of real-world situations. In this chapter we consider the determinants of consumer decision making, what causes these decisions to change, and how the decisions of consumers create the demand for various goods. In Chapters 8 and 9 we will consider this same set of questions for the decisions of business firms and supply.

MARKET DEMAND

Market demand for a good is simply the sum of the individual demands by consumers in a particular market for a certain good. In Figure 3-1 we can see that when the price of pizza is $5 per unit, consumers A and B are the only buyers of that good. Market demand is thus the amount bought by A plus the amount bought by B at a price of $5 during a given time period. As we see in Figure 3-1, if the price should fall to $4 per unit, the consumers

FIGURE 3-1
Market demand curves are the sum of individual demand curves.
In this case the market consists of three people; by adding their individual demand curves together we construct the market demand curve for pizzas during a certain time period.

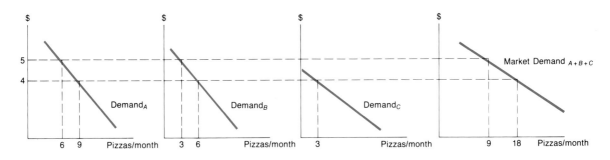

already purchasing pizza will buy more and another consumer, consumer C, will also join the market. The market demand then becomes the sum of the amounts bought by all three of these consumers.

From this information alone we can tell that market demand is downward sloping (the law of demand). We would like to know, however, whether each consumer's demand curve is also negatively sloped and what influences, besides price, determine a consumer's demand for (purchases of) a good. Are these other influences quantifiable and measurable, like price? Are they subject to systematic analysis or are they random and unpredictable? Those are the questions which we will seek to answer in this chapter.

UTILITY ANALYSIS

We begin with the observation that people have preferences for certain goods over others. That is, they prefer certain goods to other goods. A consumer's choices to purchase more or less of a good, or not to purchase some goods at all, are in part the result of preferences, as well as being a response to the relative prices (alternative costs) of the various goods available for purchase. Economists of the last century used the term **utility** to refer to a person's preferences, or to the satisfaction that a person receives from consuming particular units of a particular good.

Utility is a property common to all things that are desired. Some commodities are bought and sold; others, like love, are not exchanged in formal markets although they are certainly not lacking utility. Note, though, that utility is a purely subjective concept. There is no way that we, as economists, can measure the amount of utility that another person might be able to obtain from a particular commodity, for "having utility" *does not mean "useful" or "utilitarian" or "practical."* It refers only to what a particular consumer wants or desires. In this sense, there cannot be a scientific assessment of the utility that someone may receive by consuming a given quantity of a particular commodity.

Thus, in this analysis, illegal activities that many people may consider morally wrong can still be analyzed in terms of the utility that those activities generate for their consumers. Utility, it might be said, is in the perception of the consumer. It reflects what a person *wants*, not what someone thinks that person *should want*. Nonetheless, economists can analyze consumer choice in terms of utility, just as physicists have analyzed some of their problems in terms of force. No physicist has ever *seen* a unit of force. No economist has ever *seen* a unit of utility. In both cases, however, these constructs have proved useful for explaining certain aspects of the problems faced by physicists or economists in their analyses.

Cardinal versus ordinal utility

Utility theory was first developed in terms of a specific measurement of utility. The term "util" was used as the unit of measurement of satisfaction, or utility. Thus, the first chocolate bar might yield 4 utils of satisfaction, the first peanut cluster, 6 utils. Utility analysis using such definite numbers was called **cardinal utility analysis.** Numbers such as 1, 2, and 3 are cardinal. We know that 2 is exactly twice as many as 1; 3 is exactly three times as many as 1. This means that a cardinal measurement of utility implies a quantitative exactness to differences in utility.

However, economists soon found that it was not helpful in their analyses to make such stringent assumptions about the exactness of the measurement of utility. (This was particularly true in light of the fact that no one could conceive of how to measure cardinal utils.) Rather, it was found that the much weaker notion of merely *ordering* levels of utility was sufficient. Thus, **ordinal utility analysis** came into being. The term "ordinal" means ranked, or ordered. "First," "second," and "third" are ordinal numbers; they imply a rank, or order. Nothing can be said about the size relation of the ordinal numbers. We can only say something about their importance relative to one another.

Modern-day economics is based on assumptions about the ordering and consistency of choices and on observed facts about choices. It is not concerned with any psychological interpretation of such choices. What we call "utility" today therefore reflects only the *ranking* of preferences, as mentioned above. We will define utility as a variable whose *relative* magnitude indicates the order of preference. Therefore, when we refer to a "utility-maximizing model," we mean only that individuals make consistent choices and that they choose the alternatives that they *believe* will yield them the most utility (or satisfaction).

TABLE 3-1
Total and marginal utility measured in cardinal terms

Column (1) presents the number of movies viewed per month. Column (2) shows the total utility, using a cardinal measure, associated with each total quantity consumed. Marginal utility, represented in column (3), is defined as the difference—increase or decrease—in total utility due to a one-unit increase in the rate of consumption of movies. Notice that marginal utility falls to 0 and then becomes negative; this means that after five movies per month, the consumer finds an additional movie to be a nuisance (a "bad" rather than a good).

Quantity of good consumed (movies per month) (1)	Total utility from movies (utils per month) (2)	Marginal utility (utils per month) (3)
0	0	
		10
1	10	
		6
2	16	
		3
3	19	
		1
4	20	
		0
5	20	
		−2
6	18	

Total utility and marginal utility measured in cardinal terms

We now look at the relation between the quantity of a good consumed and the cardinal utility—or satisfaction—obtained from the quantity consumed. Look at Table 3-1, which relates total cardinal utility, in column (2), to various particular rates of movie consumption per month, in column (1). The measure of total utility is represented in utils since we are thinking in terms of cardinal utility. Total utility for each rate of consumption is graphically represented as the dashed-outlined vertical block in Figure 3-2(a). (Ignore the partially shaded areas for the moment; we will explain them shortly.) Notice that total utility increases as the rate of consumption increases up to the point where four movies are consumed per month. Total utility is 20 utils for four movies; it remains at 20 through the fifth movie, and then *falls* to 18 utils for the sixth movie. If we connect the tops of the total utility blocks with a smooth line, we come up with the total utility curve associated with the consumption of movies during a 1-month period. This is shown in Figure 3-3(a).

If you look carefully at both parts of Figure 3-2, the notion of marginal utility can be seen very clearly. In economic theory, "marginal" always refers to the *rate* at which a "total" is changing. In this case, the total happens to be total *utility*. Thus, marginal utility is the change in total utility per each additional movie consumed. In later sections of this book we will be using other marginal concepts—such as marginal cost, marginal revenue, etc.

Marginal utility is represented by the shaded portions of the blocks in Figure 3-2(a). We can transfer these shaded portions down to Figure 3-2(b) to construct a graphic representation of marginal utility. When we connect

FIGURE 3-2

Total and marginal utility in discrete units
In panel (a), the dashed outline indicates the total utility for each rate of consumption of movies per month. The shaded portion of each dashed box indicates the marginal utility for each additional movie. When we transfer the shaded boxes to panel (b), we have a diagram of discrete marginal utility.

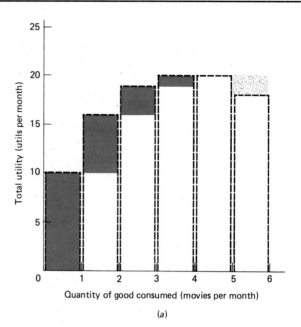

(a)

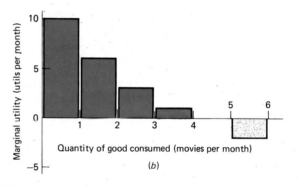

(b)

the tops of these marginal utility rectangles in Figure 3-3(b), we come up with a smooth, downward-sloping marginal utility curve that intersects the horizontal axis at the consumption rate of four movies per month.[1] The meaning of zero marginal utility is merely that the consumer has all he or she wants of the commodity in question. When marginal utility becomes negative, as it does in this example after the consumption of four movies per month, it means that the consumer gets disutility; the consumer is fed

---

[1]Note that because we are dealing with discrete changes our curves in Figure 3-3 are too smooth to be completely accurate. The curves actually have "steps" in them as in Figure 3-2.

FIGURE 3-3
Total and marginal utility
If we take the total cardinal utility units from column (2) in Table 3-1, we obtain rectangles like those presented in Figure 3-2(a). If we connect the tops of those rectangles with a smooth line, we come up with a total utility curve that peaks somewhere between four and five movies per month and then slowly declines [panel (a)]. Marginal utility is represented by the incremental change in total utility, shown as the shaded blocks in Figure 3-2(b). When these blocks are connected by a smooth line in panel (b), we obtain the marginal utility curve.

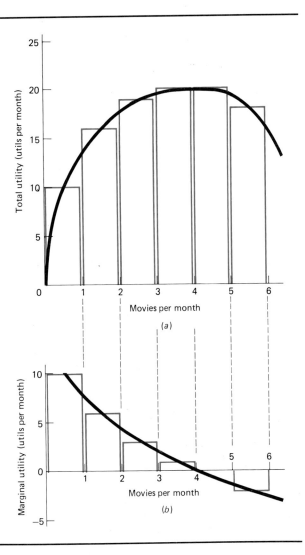

up with movies and would require some form of compensation to sit voluntarily through the sixth movie in 1 month.

Diminishing marginal utility

Notice that in Figure 3-3(b), marginal utility is continuously declining. This is because, although the total utility of Figure 3-3(b) increases, it increases by a smaller and smaller amount for each additional unit consumed. In other words, it is *increasing* at a *steadily decreasing rate*. When this occurs, we say that the individual in his or her consumption of a given commodity is experiencing **diminishing marginal utility.**

The law (?) of diminishing marginal utility

Most of us think that we "know" intuitively that the first unit consumed gives us more marginal satisfaction than the tenth unit consumed. Alternatively, we might consider that most goods have many uses. Therefore, marginal utility would appear to decline as more of a good is acquired, because additional units are put to successively less important uses. But these casual observations do not constitute a "proof" of the "law of diminishing marginal utility."

Since the law of diminishing marginal utility does not follow from any postulate about rational consumer decision making, no proof of it can be given. The proposition is, nonetheless, intuitively appealing. Both economists and laypersons for years have believed strongly in it, and that is why, even today, it is often called a "law."

ANALYSIS OF CONSUMER BEHAVIOR: THE MODERN APPROACH

We now turn from cardinal utility analysis to the more modern and justifiable approach, ordinal utility analysis. Let us first consider the assumptions relating to consumer preferences.

ASSUMPTIONS RELATING TO CONSUMER PREFERENCES

In order to make scientific statements about consumer choice, we have to start by making assumptions that define the basic hypotheses and definitions of our theory. The assumptions are straightforward and relate to choices of **commodities.** We define commodities as all goods and services. Commodities provide a flow of consumption services per unit of time. In our model of consumer behavior, people choose among the service flows from different commodities, not the commodities themselves.[2] That is, we own cars not just to look at them and not to consume them in one moment, but to get the benefits from the service a car provides over time. The assumptions of our model are as follows:

1   *The individual consumer, when faced with a choice between certain combinations of commodities, can decide which combination he or she prefers or that he or she is indifferent to certain combinations.* In other words, given any set of attainable combinations of satisfaction-yielding commodities, the consumer can determine which combination is preferable or which combinations yield equal satisfaction. Since the consumer knows the utility value of all possible choices, we say there is a *completeness* of preferences.

[2]We use the terms "commodities" and "goods" interchangeably. Both can refer to both tangible and intangible things that people want.

2   *The consumer is consistent in making choices among commodity combinations.* Thus, if the consumer first indicates a definite preference for Fords as opposed to Chevys, and then indicates a definite preference for Chevys as opposed to Toyotas, to be consistent, that consumer must also indicate a definite preference for Fords over Toyotas. The consumer's preferences are then said to be *transitive, or consistent.*

3   *More is preferred to less.* No individual is ever satisfied with all desired commodities, although he or she may become saturated with particular commodities. This is sometimes called the "assumption of nonsatiety" or "nonsatiation."

A simple way to remember these three assumptions is to label them as follows:

1   The assumption of *completeness*
2   The assumption of *consistency*
3   The assumption of *nonsatiation*

Go back and reread these three assumptions. You may find yourself disagreeing with one or more of them. Do we really consider all possible combinations of the goods available every time we make a choice? Aren't there some people who are not consistent in their consumer choices and others who can never make up their minds? Remember, assumptions are used to build models from which theories and predictions are derived. If the model we are building is insufficient to provide us with the predictions we want or is overwhelmingly refuted by the evidence, then the model has failed and another will replace it.

PREFERENCE ASSUMPTIONS LEAD TO INDIFFERENCE CURVES

Much of economic analysis lends itself well to graphic interpretation. That is fortunate because graphical analysis, at a very minimum, allows you to use a language for communicating theoretical analysis that economizes on words and clarifies ideas.

We can translate the three assumptions presented earlier into a geometric device that has been aptly labeled an **indifference curve.** An indifference curve is defined as a curve representing a constant level of satisfaction, or alternatively, as a locus of points representing combinations of two commodities (or baskets of commodities) between which the consumer is indifferent. (Such curves were first employed and named by a British economist, Francis Y. Edgeworth, 1845–1926.) Perhaps the easiest way to derive an indifference curve is to set up an example of an indifference schedule that shows the various combination of two commodities among which an individual feels indifferent. We see this in Table 3-2, where we have set up a

| **TABLE 3-2** | Movies | Concerts | Combination |
Indifference schedule: movies and concerts	per month	per month	(see Fig. 3-4)
This individual consumer has decided that he or she is indifferent between going to one movie and seven concerts per month, or going to three movies and four concerts per month. (Note that we express an explicit time period because we are dealing with a flow: consumption of goods and services per unit of time.)	1	7	A
	2	5	B
	3	4	C
	4	$3\frac{1}{2}$	D

hypothetical indifference schedule for a college student who likes both movies and concerts.

The indifference schedule

In Table 3-2, we look at a hypothetical indifference schedule that relates the different combinations of movies and concerts per month between which the consumer has declared indifference. Notice that we are talking about activities that occur over time, and therefore we specify a time period. The activities are the consumption of movies and concerts, and the time period specified is a month. If we were to specify a year, we would have to multiply both columns by 12.

The one thing that we see right away is that in order for the consumer to remain indifferent among various commodity combinations, if fewer units of one commodity are in a market basket, more of the other commodity must be included as compensation. The conclusion follows directly from assumption 3: More is preferred to less. Both of these commodities are goods that, by definition, give this consumer satisfaction. Therefore, if some of one commodity is given up, the only way that the consumer can remain equally satisfied is by being compensated with more of the other commodity.

The indifference curve

When we translate combinations A, B, C, and D from Table 3-2 onto a graph representing quantities of one commodity on the horizontal axis (movies per month) and quantities of the other commodity on the vertical axis (concerts per month)—a **commodity space**—we end up with an indifference curve. Because of nonsatiation (assumption 3), that indifference curve slopes downward and to the right. This means that more of one good must be obtained to compensate for the reduction in the amount of another good, if the consumer is to remain indifferent or to obtain a constant level of satisfaction from the combinations of the two goods plotted on the indifference curve. We plot A, B, C, and D in Figure 3-4.

Let's consider an upward-sloping curve for a moment. This curve implies that as consumers accepted less of x, they would also be quite willing to accept less of y. In Figure 3-5, point L would represent the same level of satisfaction as point N. But no consumer wants (by assumption) to give up

FIGURE 3-4
An indifference curve for movies and concerts
If we take combinations A, B, C, and D, plot them in the above commodity space, and then connect the points with a smooth line, we come up with an indifference curve for our hypothetical consumer. We note that the indifference curve is downward-sloping.

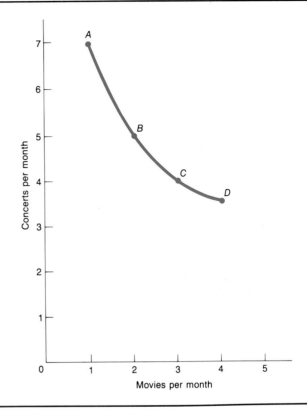

a higher level of total consumption for a lower level. That is why indifference curves always slope downward, not upward.

Another implicit assumption we have used in this consumer-choice model guarantees that there are an infinite number of indifference curves in the commodity space. After all, we have assumed that the consumer can compare any two bundles or commodities and decide that he or she has a preference for one over the other or is indifferent between the two. Then no matter what consumption level of movies and concerts per month we are talking about, a "higher" or "lower" indifference curve can be constructed. Higher curves—representing greater levels of satisfaction for the consumer—will lie to the northeast of ABCD in Figure 3-4. Lower curves—representing lesser levels of satisfaction for the consumer—will lie to the southwest of ABCD. This will be shown more completely in the following discussion.

Different people have different sets of preferences. We expect to see, therefore, different indifference curves. We show four possible indifference curves in Figure 3-6.

The last formal property of indifference curves arises from assumptions

■■■■■■
FIGURE 3-5
Implications of an upward-sloping indifference curve
If the curve in this diagram represented an individual's indifference curve, it would mean that the individual would accept less of *x* and less of *y* and still be indifferent. In other words, points *L* and *N* would give equal levels of satisfaction, even though *N* contains less of both *x* and *y*. This would violate assumption 3: more is preferred to less.

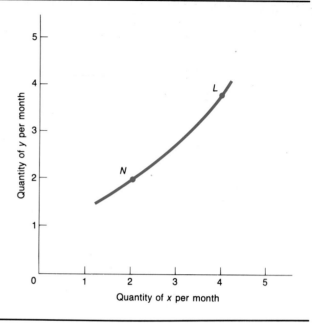

2 and 3. From these assumptions, we know logically that indifference curves cannot intersect. This can be easily seen by assuming the opposite and noting what results. Look at the intersecting indifference curves I and II in Figure 3-7. The indifference curve taken from Table 3-2 is again presented and labeled here as I. We now see another indifference curve that intersects curve I at point *B*. It is labeled II. Compare the two points *B* and *C*, both on curve I. The consumer is indifferent between these two combinations of movies and concerts; they yield equal levels of satisfaction. But if indifference curve II is also valid, the consumer is also indifferent to combination *B* and combination *H*; but by assumption 2—consistency—if our consumer is indifferent between *B* and *C* and also between *B* and *H*, that consumer must be indifferent between *C* and *H*. However, notice that point *H* represents both more movies per month and more concerts per month than does point *C*. Since we have also assumed that more is preferred to less, the consumer cannot be indifferent to combination *H* and combination *C*. Thus, it is logically impossible that indifference curves intersect, given our assumptions about consumer preferences.

Indifference curves summarized

We can now briefly present the properties of indifference curves.
1 They are negatively sloped.
2 There is an indifference curve that passes through each point in the commodity space.
3 They cannot intersect.

FIGURE 3-6
Indifference curves for different people
The four panels in this figure show four possible indifference curves for concerts and movies for four different individuals.

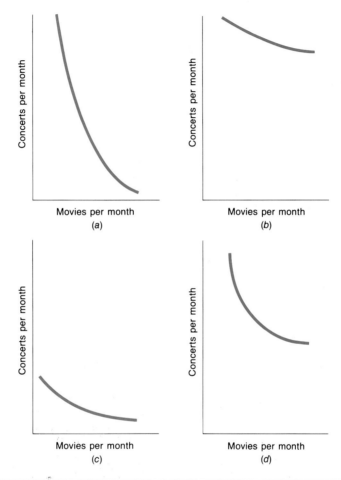

The above three properties of indifference curves have been derived using only the three assumptions that started our analysis: completeness, consistency, and nonsatiation. We now add a fourth assumption that relates directly to the shape of indifference curves.

The fourth assumption: convexity

The indifference curves we have been using in our examples have all had a particular shape: They have been convex to the origin of the graph. This property of indifference curves is one that we will assume. In other words, our fourth assumption is that all indifference curves will be convex. While

FIGURE 3-7

Intersecting indifference curves

Indifference curve I is taken from Figure 3-4. By definition, all combinations of movies and concerts are equally satisfactory along that indifference curve. Now we add indifference curve II, which intersects curve I at combination B. By definition, combinations B and C generate equal levels of satisfaction; i.e., the consumer is indifferent between them. Also by definition, since B and H lie on the same indifference curve, they are equally preferred, and the consumer is indifferent between them. The assumption of transitivity (consistency) requires, since the consumer is indifferent between B and C and indifferent between B and H, that the consumer must be indifferent between C and H. However, combination H involves both more movies and more concerts than does combination C. Because more is preferred to less, by assumption 3, it is logically impossible for the consumer to be indifferent between H and C. Hence, indifference curves cannot intersect.

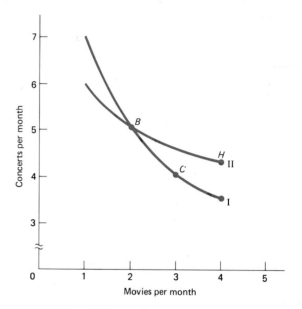

we cannot prove that this assumption is always true of all consumers, we will see that any other shapes for indifference curves imply very unusual things.

There are two ways to test whether a curve is convex:

1   If the curve lies above a tangent line drawn at any point on the curve, the curve is convex.
2   If a straight line connecting any two points on the curve (called a chord) lies above the curve, the curve is convex.

See Figure 3-8, which illustrates each test.

The assumption of the convexity of indifference curves is based upon, or is synonymous with, an assumption of diminishing marginal rate of substitution, a concept to which we now turn.

MARGINAL RATE OF SUBSTITUTION

Because the indifference curve shows something about the individual's subjective evaluations of two commodities, we should be able to learn something about the rate at which the consumer is willing to substitute one commodity for another by examining an indifference curve in detail. This rate of substitution is called the **marginal rate of substitution** of y for x, or MRS_{xy}. We can define it as follows:

FIGURE 3-8

Two tests for convexity

In panel (*a*) we demonstrate the first test for convexity: If a curve lies above a tangent line drawn at any point on the curve, the curve is convex to the origin of the graph. In panel (*b*) we show the other test for convexity: If a straight line connecting any two points on the curve lies above the curve, the curve is convex to the origin of the graph.

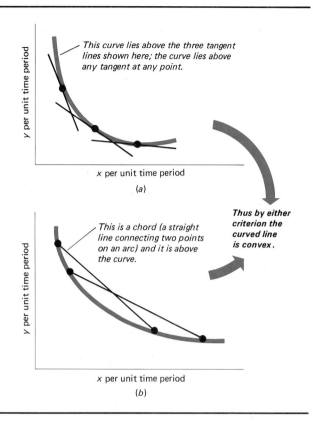

This curve lies above the three tangent lines shown here; the curve lies above any tangent at any point.

y per unit time period

x per unit time period

(*a*)

This is a chord (a straight line connecting two points on an arc) and it is above the curve.

y per unit time period

x per unit time period

(*b*)

Thus by either criterion the curved line is convex.

$$\text{MRS}_{xy} = \text{the number of units of commodity } y \text{ that must be given up per unit of commodity } x \text{ gained if the consumer is to feel indifferent or continue to obtain the same level of satisfaction}$$

If we take the example from Table 3-2, we can find the marginal rate of substitution of movies for concerts. We see this from the top part of Table 3-3. As we move in one-unit steps, for each movie gained per month, the consumer must first sacrifice two concerts per month, then one concert per month, then one-half a concert per month to remain indifferent. Thus, the marginal rate of substitution, as shown in the lower part of Table 3-3, is first 2:1, then 1:1, then $\frac{1}{2}$:1. This can be seen in Figure 3-9.

MRS at the limit

So far we have considered how to measure the MRS when the consumer's consumption of x and y changes by discrete amounts. That is, in Figure 3-9, changes between points *A* and *B* or *B* and *C* represent discrete changes in movies and concerts. If we want to consider only infinitesimally small changes in the consumption of one commodity, instead of measuring discrete changes in the consumption of x and y, a simple graphical technique can

TABLE 3-3
Marginal rate of substitution of concerts per movie

This table is merely Table 3-2 reproduced with an additional column showing the marginal rate of substitution of concerts per movie. The lower part presents the information verbally.

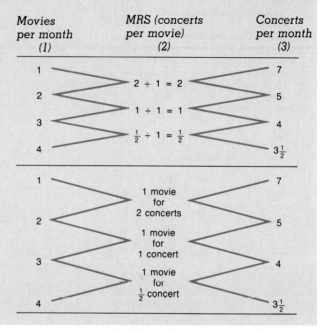

Movies per month (1)	MRS (concerts per movie) (2)	Concerts per month (3)
1		7
	$2 \div 1 = 2$	
2		5
	$1 \div 1 = 1$	
3		4
	$\frac{1}{2} \div 1 = \frac{1}{2}$	
4		$3\frac{1}{2}$
1		7
	1 movie for 2 concerts	
2		5
	1 movie for 1 concert	
3		4
	1 movie for $\frac{1}{2}$ concert	
4		$3\frac{1}{2}$

FIGURE 3-9
MRS graphically
Each time an additional movie per month is consumed, the individual must sacrifice something in order to remain at the same level of satisfaction. In this case, what is sacrificed is concerts or fractions of concerts per month. We see that, at first, the consumer is more willing to sacrifice concerts to get an additional movie when he or she is consuming fewer movies per month (and more concerts) than when consuming a large number of movies (and fewer concerts). MRS$_{movies,\ concerts}$ is a measure of concerts per movie; for example, MRS = 2 is read as "2 concerts per movie" and MRS = $\frac{1}{2}$ is "$\frac{1}{2}$ concert per movie." [For those students unfamiliar with the use of the delta (Δ) operator, it is discussed in the appendix to this chapter.]

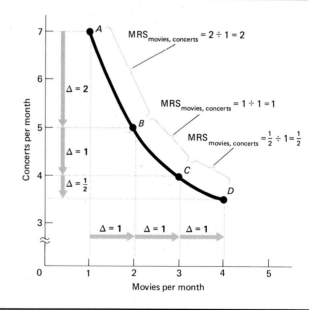

FIGURE 3-10
Measuring the slope of a curve
The slope at any point on the curve can be measured by drawing the tangent to that point and finding its slope. Slope is defined as the change in y divided by the change in x (where y is the variable measured on the vertical axis and x is the variable measured on the horizontal axis). Since the indifference curves that we are working with slope downward from left to right, the slope at point P is equal to $-\Delta y/\Delta x$. Since our definition of MRS requires a positive number, MRS at point P is equal to -1 times the slope at point P, or to $\Delta y/\Delta x$.

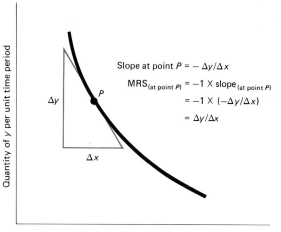

Slope at point $P = -\Delta y/\Delta x$

$MRS_{(\text{at point } P)} = -1 \times slope_{(\text{at point } P)}$

$= -1 \times (-\Delta y/\Delta x)$

$= \Delta y/\Delta x$

Quantity of y per unit time period

Quantity of x per unit time period

be used. The MRS at any point along an indifference curve is the value of the *slope* of the indifference curve at that point, as shown in Figure 3-10.[3]

All the indifference curves we will be working with will have slopes that get smaller as we move from left to right. Looking at Figure 3-11, we see that as successive tangents are drawn, moving rightward on the indifference curve, their (numerical) slope gets smaller; i.e., they become flatter.[4] Alternatively, the slope increases as we move leftward. This is a property of all indifference curves that are convex to the origin; hence, it is a property of the indifference curves that will be examined. This property is generally called the **diminishing marginal rate of substitution.**

[3]As demonstrated in Figure 3-10, this is given by the slope of the tangent drawn at the particular point in question. None of the indifference curves we consider has "sharp corners"— all are smoothly curved. Therefore, each point along each indifference curve has one and only one tangent to it. (Since MRS is a positive concept, we must do something to get the math to fit the concept, so we implicitly multiply the slope, which is negative, by -1.)

[4]Remember also that *along* an indifference curve

$$MRS_{xy} = \frac{\text{marginal evaluation of } x}{\text{marginal evaluation of } y} = \left| \frac{\Delta y}{\Delta x} \right|$$

In terms of *marginal utility analysis*, we know that along an indifference curve, when there is a change in x, the change in total satisfaction from having more or less x must equal the opposite change in satisfaction from having more or less y, or, along an indifference curve, $MU_x \cdot \Delta x = MU_y \cdot \Delta y$. Hence, along an indifference curve,

$$\frac{MU_x}{MU_y} = \left| \frac{\Delta y}{\Delta x} \right|$$

FIGURE 3-11
The changing slope along a convex indifference curve
All indifference curves that are convex to the origin exhibit the property that the slope becomes flatter and flatter as we move from left to right and closer to vertical as we move from right to left. This can be seen if we compare the changes in $\Delta y/\Delta x$ as we move down the indifference curve from point A to point B to point C. Note that its absolute value gets smaller and smaller.

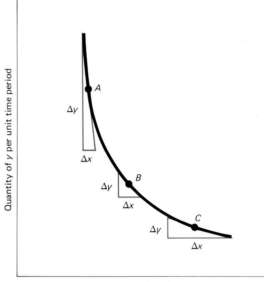

Diminishing MRS Notice in Table 3-3 that as more movies were consumed per month, the individual was willing to give up fewer and fewer concerts to obtain additional movies. As seen in column (2) of the top part of the table, the MRS or concerts given up for movies went from 2 to $\frac{1}{2}$. The same thing happens along all convex indifference curves because the property of the diminishing marginal rate of substitution is synonymous with the concept of the convexity of the indifference curve.

CONSUMER OPTIMUM: INDIFFERENCE CURVE ANALYSIS

While it is possible to develop a theory of consumer choice (decision making) using utility analysis, it is not necessary to do so once we understand ordinal preferences and indifference analysis. We can, however, use utility analysis when we talk of the position of indifference curves.

The position of indifference curves If we accept rank ordering of indifference curves, we can state that a higher total utility value must be given to all indifference curves that are above (to the northeast of) indifference curve I in Figure 3-12. Thus, indifference curves II and III are both preferred to indifference curve I. They generate a higher

FIGURE 3-12

Ordering of indifference curves

Higher indifference curves indicate a higher level of satisfaction or utility; thus, indifference curve III indicates a higher level of satisfaction than indifference curve II, which in turn is indicative of a higher level of satisfaction than indifference curve I.

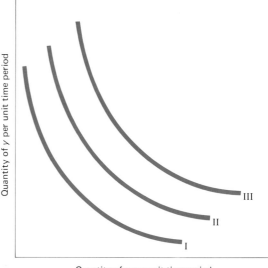

level of satisfaction or utility. Why? Merely because it is possible to consume more movies *and* more concerts as represented by points on higher indifference curves compared with points on lower indifference curves. Thus, with no strings attached (that is, no cost to higher consumption levels), a consumer in our model must prefer the combination of goods on higher indifference curves to those on lower indifference curves.

Facing reality: the budget constraint

We impose a constraint on the individual. That constraint has to do with scarcity. It is called the **budget constraint,** which is the amount of income M available to the consumer during the period being studied and the prices the consumer must pay to obtain various goods. More sophisticated models would include the amount of assets that the consumer could sell off to obtain additional income, the size of the gifts that the consumer would obtain from philanthropists, and the amounts that the consumer could borrow or steal. To simplify our analysis, we will ignore such possible additions to the consumer's available purchasing power.

We will continue to consider two goods: movies (x) and concerts (y). The nominal (current-dollar) prices of those two goods P_x and P_y are given as far as the individual consumer is concerned (the consumer cannot affect them), and they are assumed not to change during the time considered. Money income M will be some fixed amount per month. We let x equal the number of movies and y equal the number of concerts; furthermore, we assume that all income is spent.[5] The budget constraint will therefore be as follows:

$$M = \text{(quantity of movies/month} \times P_x)$$
$$+ \text{(quantity of concerts/month} \times P_y) \quad \text{(3-1)}$$

If we arbitrarily pick some numbers, we can easily see how to represent the budget constraint as a line drawn on the graph we call the commodity space. Assume that the market price of movies is $3 and the market price of concerts is $2. Assume further that the consumer in question has $30 per month of money income to spend. We draw the budget line in the commodity space given in Figure 3-13. The maximum quantity of concerts per month that can be purchased and consumed is equal to $30 ÷ $2, or 15. This is represented by point B. The maximum number of movies per month that can be consumed is $30 ÷ $3, or 10. This is represented by point B'. When we connect these two points with a straight line, we get the budget constraint BB'.

Let's generalize the equation above to any two commodities, y (plotted on the vertical axis) and x (plotted on the horizontal axis), priced at P_y and P_x, respectively. Again, M is the monthly money income available to spend on these commodities; therefore, *if all monthly income is spent,*

$$M = y \cdot P_y + x \cdot P_x \quad \text{(3-2)}$$

We solve Eq. (3-2) for y by dividing through by P_y, which results in

$$\frac{M}{P_y} = y + \frac{x \cdot P_x}{P_y} \quad \text{(3-2}a\text{)}$$

We subtract the term

$$\frac{x \cdot P_x}{P_y}$$

from both sides of Eq. (3-2a) to obtain

$$\frac{M}{P_y} - \frac{x \cdot P_x}{P_y} = y \quad \text{(3-2}b\text{)}$$

This equation is for the line drawn in Figure 3-13 that represents the budget constraint and is formally represented as

$$y = \frac{M}{P_y} - \frac{P_x}{P_y} \cdot x \quad \text{(3-3)}$$

The equation intersects the vertical axis (where x = 0) at the point M/P_y. In

---

[5]Although this assumption may seem unrealistic, it makes the analysis easier. The effects of allowing consumption and income to be shifted through time is examined in Chapter 6.

FIGURE 3-13
The budget constraint
When all the $30 money income is spent on concerts at $2 per concert, 15 concerts can be purchased per month. This gives us one point on the budget constraint, point B. When all the $30 of money income is spent on movies at $3 per movie, 10 movies can be purchased per month. This gives us point B'. Connecting B and B' gives us the budget constraint, or budget line. The right triangle formed by that line and the axes is called the budget space. It represents the set of combinations of movies and concerts per month attainable with a fixed money income of $30 per month when the price of each movie is $3 and the price of each concert is $2.

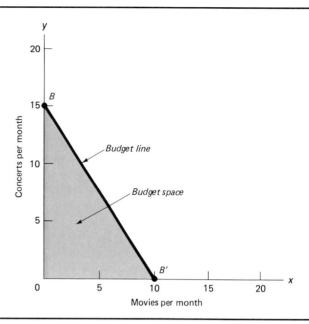

our example, that is the maximum number of concerts y per month (no movies), which is M divided by the price of concerts.

The marginal rate of market substitution

The slope of the budget constraint is the ratio of the prices of the two commodities under study. In our example, the ratio is $P_x/P_y = 3/2$. Since the budget constraint is negatively sloped, the slope of the budget constraint is the *negative* of the price ratio. Numerically, this slope represents the **marginal rate of market substitution** (MRMS) of the two goods. MRMS will be a constant in our discussions and the budget line will be straight, rather than curved, since prices are given to the consumer. MRMS is the *feasible* or market rate that the consumer *can* trade off x for y.

If we fill in the area between the axes and the budget constraint, or budget line, we get a graphic representation of the *budget space*. The budget line represents the maximum feasible combinations that can be purchased with the given income and prices.[6]

Now, to obtain the optimal combination of movies and concerts per month, we must somehow coordinate the *feasible* set of attainable combi-

---

[6]The budget constraint we use here completely exhausts income. We could use an inequality budget constraint such as the following: $P_x \cdot x + P_y \cdot y \leq M$. If we use this inequality as the budget constraint, it describes the entire shaded area—the budget space—in Figure 3-13 (including the x and y axes as well). Note also that if x and y are the only desired goods, we are excluding the possibility of saving, which can be defined as the purchase of future goods.

nations of x and y with the *subjectively preferred* combinations of x and y. In other words, we want to combine subjective marginal valuations (or marginal rates of substitution) represented by the slopes of points along indifference curves with the feasible rate of market substitution represented numerically by the slope of the budget constraint. Or, in still other words, we must impose the set of combinations allowed by prices and the consumer's money income on the consumer's preferred set of possibilities to obtain exactly the combination of x and y that the consumer will choose. The position of the budget constraint (its distance from the origin of the graph) imposes the other constraint on the consumer's behavior, for it gives a maximum amount that can be consumed.

Attaining an optimum for the consumer

We are assuming rational behavior. Individual decision making, therefore, consists of comparing *preferences* with *opportunities*. The rational individual arranges his or her affairs to best satisfy given preferences from available opportunities. If we wish to use the utility concept developed in this chapter, we say that the rational individual chooses a consumption basket, or combination, that maximizes his or her utility. The consumption basket that maximizes a consumer's satisfaction, therefore, is the *optimum* for the consumer. It is useful to point out here that the process of **optimization** applies to the *individual* economic agent's decision-making processes. In later chapters, we will deal with many individuals interacting in the marketplace. Then we will refer to the process of reaching an **equilibrium** in the marketplace. Generally speaking, equilibrium is a property of markets rather than of individual decision making. Here we can give a short definition of equilibrium as a situation in which the forces acting upon a system (generally a market) are balanced so that there is no net tendency to change.

A consumer optimum will occur whenever the consumer maximizes satisfaction, given his or her budget constraint. This can be viewed graphically by drawing the individual's set of indifference curves as in Figure 3-14. The consumer, by assumption, wishes to be on the highest indifference curve possible. However, there is a constraint. That constraint is determined by nominal prices and money income and is shown by *BB'*. The point at which the consumer maximizes satisfaction within this constraint is the point on the highest indifference curve attainable. In Figure 3-14, this is on indifference curve II. It is tangent to (just touches) the budget constraint *BB'* at point E. Such an equilibrium point is called an **interior solution**. Here, the consumer optimum occurs when the consumption rate is nine concerts per month and four movies per month. Point E is the point of consumer optimum:

■ *At the point of consumer optimum, the marginal rate of substitution is equal to the ratio of the price of* **x** *to the price of* **y**, *or*

$$\text{MRS}_{xy} = \frac{P_x}{P_y} = \text{MRMS}_{xy}$$

FIGURE 3-14
Consumer optimum
Utility maximization requires that the consumer attain the highest indifference curve possible. This occurs only when the rate at which the consumer is willing to substitute movies for concerts is equal to the rate at which the consumer can substitute movies for concerts (and where $M = x \cdot P_x + y \cdot P_y$). This occurs at point E on indifference curve II, where the highest attainable indifference curve is tangent to the budget constraint. This consumer purchases nine concerts and four movies per month.

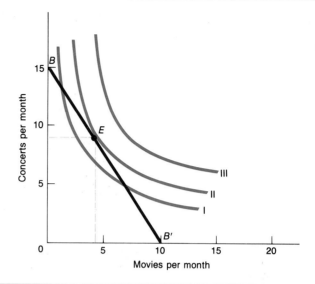

where MRS_{xy} is the marginal rate of (subjective) substitution and $MRMS_{xy}$ is the marginal rate of market substitution.

At the point of consumer optimum, the rate at which the consumer is just *willing* to substitute one commodity for the other is equal to the rate at which he or she *can* substitute one commodity for another; and the latter is determined by the prices of x and y.[7]

MAXIMIZING BEHAVIOR: THE EQUAL MARGINAL PRINCIPLE

Let's go back to our original model. The consumer is attempting to maximize satisfaction. He or she does this by optimally allocating a given income M over the various commodities that can be purchased. In our particular simple example, we consider only two goods, x and y.

If we think now in terms of cardinal utility functions, we can talk in terms of units of utils. The consumer-optimization problem is now quite simple. The consumer attempts to buy utils from the cheapest source.

Now we wish to come up with a mathematical representation or expression for consumer optimization.[8]

[7]And, of course, $M = x \cdot P_x + y \cdot P_y$.
[8]Equation (3-4) is derived from the constrained maximization of a utility function. It is a first-order condition only.

$$\frac{\text{Marginal utility of x}}{\text{Price of x}} = \frac{\text{marginal utility of y}}{\text{price of y}} \tag{3-4}$$

What does Eq. (3-4) mean? Simply that the marginal utility per last dollar spent on each commodity must be equal if maximum utility is to be achieved. In other words, the last dollar spent on x must yield the same satisfaction as the last dollar spent on y. If such were not the case, the consumer could increase total utility by shifting his or her consumption pattern. For example, assume that the marginal utility per last dollar spent was lower on x than on y.[9] This consumer could shift some income from expenditures on x to expenditures on y. The marginal utility of x would rise (as its consumption *fell*), and the marginal utility for the consumption of y would fall (as its consumption *rose*). Equation (3-4) eventually would be satisfied. Let's take a simple example. Suppose that the marginal utility of the last dollar spent on concerts was equal to 10 utils and that the marginal utility of the last dollar spent on movies was only 5 utils. By transferring $1 of income from movies to concerts, that individual would give up 5 units of utility from movies but gain 10 units of utility from concerts. Hence, total utility would increase by (approximately) 5 units of utility. Only when the marginal utility per dollar spent on both concerts and movies was equal would the consumer be obtaining maximum utility, given income and prices.

This optimal consumer situation is sometimes called the **law of equal marginal utilities per dollar** because utility per last dollar spent is equated on the margin for all goods consumed.[10] Another way of stating this "law" is

$$\frac{\text{Marginal utility of x}}{\text{Marginal utility of y}} = \frac{\text{price of x}^{11}}{\text{price of y}} \tag{3-5}$$

which is obtained by multiplying *both* sides of Eq. (3-4) by P_x/MU_y.

Thus, the equal marginal principle does not mean that each respective marginal utility should be equal to the others. Rather, it means that the marginal utilities *per last dollar* spent on each commodity should be equal. The marginal utility from owning a Mercedes Benz may be greater than that from owning a Ford, but the much higher price of the Mercedes may make the marginal utility per last dollar spent on the Ford higher. An individual with this evaluation would be inclined to buy the Ford instead of the Mercedes.

---

[9]We must further assume that the marginal utility of x does not depend on the marginal utility of y, or in other words, that there are no cross utility effects between consuming units of x and consuming units of y.

[10]Of course, we are only talking about an interior solution where both x and y are being consumed.

[11]Remember that MU_x/MU_y is an expression for MRS or the slope of an indifference curve. Since P_x/P_y is the slope of the budget constraint, whenever we are at an inferior solution in our indifference analysis, both Eqs. (3-4) and (3-5) are satisfied.

When equal-marginal principle does not hold true

We have already seen that the slope of an indifference curve is equal to the ratio of MU_x to MU_y, while the slope of the budget line is equal to the ratio of P_x to P_y. Since, by the rules of geometry, the slopes of two curves are the same at a point where the curves are tangent, the equal-marginal principle $MU_x/MU_y = P_x/P_y$ is an alternative mathematical expression for consumer equilibrium, as graphically represented by the tangency of the consumer's budget line with some "highest" indifference curve.

We have assumed the convexity of indifference curves. If we allowed for concave indifference curves, we would end up with optimization results that are contradicted by the real world. For this discussion to be meaningful, we must first define what a concave curve is, in the same manner that we defined a convex curve. The definition of concavity is the mirror image of the definition of convexity. Concavity can be determined if (1) the curve lies below a tangent line drawn at any point on the curve, and (2) a straight line connecting any two points on the curve (a chord) lies below the curve. If one or the other of these conditions is satisfied, the curve is concave. Figure 3-15 shows a concave curve.

Why indifference curves are convex

One way of illustrating that indifference curves are convex, rather than concave, to the origin is to observe the contradiction between the graphical (indifference curve–budget line) presentation of consumer equilibrium and the equal-marginal principle in the case of concave indifference curves. Figure 3-16 illustrates such a case. At point A the budget line BB' is tangent to indifference curve I. Therefore, at point A the equal-marginal principle is fulfilled. However, we can easily see from the graph that the consumer can reach higher indifference curves (those to the northeast or indifference curve I) by moving up or down BB' from point A. The highest indifference curve attainable along BB' is indifference curve III, at point D. When the consumer chooses D, however, he or she is ignoring an attainable point where

FIGURE 3-15

Concave indifference curve

The panel shows an indifference curve concave to the origin. (The curve is below its tangents and a chord is below the curve.)

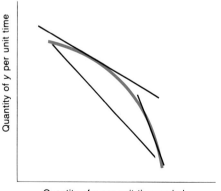

Quantity of y per unit time

Quantity of x per unit time period

FIGURE 3-16
Concave indifference curves
An interior solution to the consumer-optimization problem normally would be at a point such as A where the indifference curve is tangent to the budget line; however, point A represents a position that does not maximize satisfaction. At point A, the consumer is on indifference curve I. This consumer could increase satisfaction by moving to point D, which would put him or her on indifference curve III. Thus the concavity of indifference curves implies specialization in consumption because this consumer would optimize by consuming only good y.

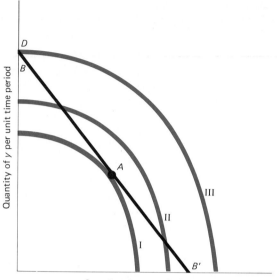

Quantity of x per unit time period

the equal-marginal principle would hold. In addition, the consumer has chosen to specialize in the consumption of y to the exclusion of x. In fact a consumer with concave indifference curves would *always* specialize in the consumption of a single good, and we never observe such consumers in the world around us.

Corner solutions. Does this mean that the equal-marginal principle must always hold in order for a consumer to be in equilibrium? No; as we will now see, the principle doesn't hold when a consumer is in equilibrium at a **corner solution**. In studying corner solutions, however, keep in mind that they differ from the case of concave indifference curves in that there is no point along the consumer's budget line where an equal-marginal position is attainable. As you will also see, corner solutions are an income-dependent phenomenon which do not imply that a consumer will *always* choose to specialize in consumption.

While corner solutions may be troublesome anomalies in the mathematics of consumer equilibrium, they do help to explain consumption behavior associated with so-called luxury goods. Some goods, such as expensive sports cars and designer-original clothing, might not be purchased at all by the typical lower- or middle-income consumer. Yet, these same goods may be accepted and popular marks of status among those in higher income brackets. We need not assume that these goods are necessarily inferior or superior, or that the indifference maps of consumers are in any way "skewed," in order to explain the phenomenon of luxury goods.

FIGURE 3-17
Convexity of indifference curves and corner solutions
The consumer attains his or her highest indifference curve, when income is at budget line *BB'*, at point *D*, a corner solution with no tangency and where none of good *x* is consumed. As income increases to *CC'* a new equilibrium is attained that happens to have a tangency equilibrium at point *E*.

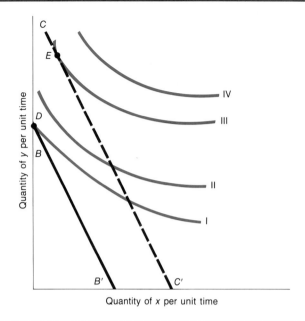

Assume an indifference map for a given consumer, such as the one shown in Figure 3-17. At an income level and price ratio shown by budget line *BB'*, the consumer will be in equilibrium at point *D*, corresponding to zero consumption of the "luxury" good. Now recall that we derived the indifference map by slicing out sections of a utility mountain at different "altitudes." This derivation implied that the indifference curves would become smaller circles as we approached the summit of the indifference mountain. It follows that if we move out into the indifference space along any line parallel to the vertical axis, we will hit indifference curves with progressively steeper slopes. If the consumer's income increases to a high enough level, with constant prices, the consumer will eventually reach a point where he or she is consuming some of the luxury good (that is, a point where the slope of some indifference curve will equal the slope of the budget line *interior to* the consumer's indifference map). Such a point is shown on Figure 3-17 along budget line *CC'*.

GOOD GOODS, BAD GOODS, AND INDIFFERENCE ANALYSIS

As we have seen, indifference curves and budget lines are used to analyze a consumer's choice between two scarce goods (commodities). A consumer can be made better off by consuming more of a good or less of a bad. What counts as a good or a bad for a given consumer often depends upon how much of the good he or she has consumed. That is, you may enjoy eating slices of pizza for lunch. If the price of the slices is zero, you would eat until the marginal utility from the last slice was zero. If you were forced to eat another slice the marginal utility would be negative—the good has become a bad.

There are scarce and free bads just as there are scarce and free goods. Just as a consumer will consume a free good to the point where the utility is zero from the last unit, a consumer will dispose of a free bad to the point where its marginal disutility (negative marginal utility) is zero. If you were stuffed full after five slices of pizza, and had five more free slices you could eat, you would dispose of them by refusing to eat them. Similarly, just as a consumer pays a positive price to acquire additional units of a scarce good, he or she must pay a negative price to dispose of a scarce bad.[12] Economists say that scarce bads have a positive disposal cost.

It is not difficult to extend the analysis of consumer choice that we have developed to include the existence of bads as well as goods. We proved that an indifference curve, showing the equal-utility trade-offs between two goods, must slope downward. As the consumer receives more of one good, he or she must give up some of the other good for total utility to remain the same. Similarly, as a person consumes more of a bad, he or she must receive more of a good in order for total utility to remain the same. As seen in Figure 3-18, we would expect the segment of a consumer's indifference curve showing the trade-off between a good and a bad to be upward-sloping.

It follows from our analysis that a consumer would be indifferent between consuming less of one bad and more of another bad at some rate of exchange. We would expect that the indifference curve between two bads would be downward-sloping, as in Figure 3-19.

Finally, we would expect that any commodity which a person consumes more and more of would at first, *ceteris paribus*, be a good, but eventually—when the last unit consumed has a negative marginal utility—would become a bad. We can connect together the indifference-curve segments from the graphs above to form a truly complete indifference map, as seen in Figure 3-20.

Notice that this person will become happier as he or she moves toward the center of the circle. Total utility would be highest at the center of the circle and would decline if the person had to accept more of the commodities than he or she would have at that point.

---

[12]"Negative price" refers to the amount of money a consumer would receive if he or she gave up a unit of a scarce bad. More commonly, the term refers to the amount a consumer must pay (or forgo) in order to dispose of a unit of a bad or, conversely, the amount a consumer would be paid (or would have to pay) if he or she consumed another unit of the bad. Remember that consuming less of a bad is equivalent to consuming more of a good, and consuming more of a bad is equivalent to consuming less of a good, so that the term "negative price" is applicable to both bads and goods.

FIGURE 3-18
The trade-off of a bad and a good
In panel (a), x is the good and y is the bad; to accept more y, one must be given more x at an increasing rate as the disutility from y increases with the additional units consumed. In panel (b) the goods reverse roles.

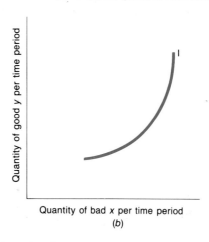

(a)   (b)

Equilibrium for a scarce good and a scarce bad

When a consumer has a limited money budget during a given period and must choose between two alternatives for increasing his or her utility—either disposing of units of a scarce bad or obtaining units of a scarce good—he or she will usually choose some combination of these two alternatives. The utility-maximization graph in this case will, as we see in Figure 3-21, look somewhat different from the maximization in the two-goods case of Figure 3-14.

FIGURE 3-19
The trade-off between two bads
One will accept more of another bad if one can trade away some of the other bad, but at greater prices as one becomes more saturated with one of the bads.

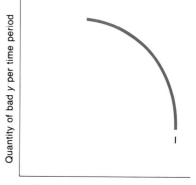

FIGURE 3-20
A complete indifference map for one level of utility for an individual during a given time period
Normally we operate only in the range on the curve where both commodities are goods.

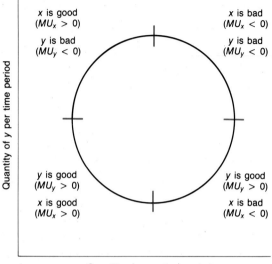

FIGURE 3-21
Utility maximization for a consumer when one commodity is a good and one is a bad
The budget line shows the highest amount of the good commodity the consumer may have if he or she consumes none of the bad commodity.

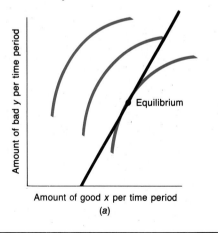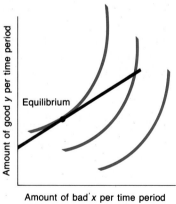

Note that the budget line in each case slopes upward. This is the result of our assumption that the bad in each case is scarce, so that the consumer must pay a negative price to dispose of it. Put in other words, the consumer can be paid for units of the bad he or she is willing to consume, allowing more consumption of the good commodity.

▬▬▬▬▬▬

Fringe benefits: Are they better than more money income?

We can analyze whether employees benefit to the fullest extent possible from fringe benefits offered by employers. Fringe benefits are goods and services made available to employees and paid for by employers. Many employees prefer fringe benefits to higher money income because such benefits rarely are subject to federal and state income taxation. We will ignore for the moment this aspect of the fringe benefit question. What we will do is analyze the offer of the fringe benefit called "dental care" to two representative workers. This is done in Figure 3-22.

The commodity space is now somewhat different from that with which we have been dealing. The vertical axis is labeled money income (dollars per month). The horizontal axis is dental services, or in-kind income per month. That is, we are looking at the trade-off of dental services against all other uses of income. Both workers' budget constraints are represented by BB'. We will look at preference patterns of two particular workers: worker 1 and worker 2. Worker 1 will reach consumer optimum at point E on indifference curve I_1. Worker 2 will reach consumer optimum at point F on indifference curve I_2. Worker 2 clearly prefers more dental services per month than does worker 1. In both cases, the worker must pay out of his or her pocket for all dental services purchased.

Now the employer offers both worker 1 and worker 2 fringe benefits in the form of dental services. The new budget constraint facing both of these workers is BCC'. The distance B to C or B' to C' represents the actual amount of additional dental services per month offered as higher fringe benefits. Worker 1 will move to his or her highest attainable indifference curve, which is II_1. It just touches the new budget constraint BCC' at point C. Worker 2, on the other hand, will reach a new optimum at point F'. His or her highest attainable indifference curve is represented by II_2. Worker 2 is clearly as well off as possible. That is, worker 2 would *not* acquire additional utility if he or she were given cash to equal the dental services income. This is not true for worker 1. Worker 1 is clearly affected by the constraint that all the additional income must be received in the form of dental services. If worker 1 were given the equivalent in additional money income, he or she would be better off. Worker 1, if given an increase of money income equal to $B'C'$ (or horizontal distance BC), could move to his or her indifference curve III_1. This would allow worker 1 to reach a consumer optimum at point E'.

Thus it would be possible, in principle, for the employer to make worker 1 better off by withholding the fringe benefit of increased dental care and offering in its place an increase in money income that is *less than* the amount of money that the employer has to

FIGURE 3-22
Fringe benefits versus additional take-home pay

In-kind income in the form of dental services is offered to all workers in this company. This moves the budget constraint over from *BB'* to *BCC'*. Worker 2 is definitely made better off by the full amount of the in-kind services offered. He or she shifts from indifference curve I_2 to II_2 and from consumer optimum *F* to *F'*. However, worker 1 could be made better off by offering him or her an equivalent increase in money income rather than in in-kind dental services, because while the dental services would put him or her on indifference curve II, an increase in money income could put him or her on indifference curve III_1.

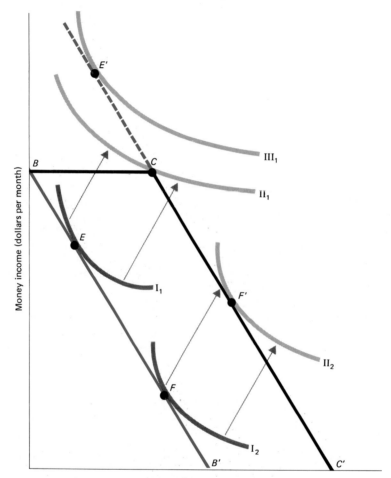

In-kind income (dental service per month)

spend to provide *BC* of dental care to worker 1. We can see that worker 1 would be just as happy to be at any point on indifference level II_1 as at point *C*. If the worker were given a cash increase in income that pushed budget line *BB'* outward until it was tangent to II_1, at a point to the northwest of point *C*, it would cost the employer less than *BC*, the cost of the dental plan. And, of course, worker 1 would be better off if he or she could attain any indifference curve higher than II_1, and that is possible without receiving the full cash equivalent of *BC*.

Again, we have a situation where waste seems to be appearing, even though there is voluntary exchange among individuals. However, by assumption, individuals know their own self-interest. Thus, workers, along with employers, will attempt to minimize such waste. This could help explain, to some extent, the homogeneity of work forces in small firms. If workers all have similar tastes, fringe benefit programs can be tailored to the average worker and not entail any, or very much, waste from the point of view of any of the individual workers in the firm.

A final point should be stressed. Fringe benefits are available for many workers. The reason is simple: Workers receive income in the form of additional fringe benefits but are not taxed on that income. On the other hand, the employer is able to deduct the cost of those fringe benefits from income before taxes are paid. This important tax consideration provides a reason for choosing the apparently wasteful alternative of "too many" fringe benefits, *particularly* to high-income, high-tax-bracket employees.

Paying for the good life: Sunshine isn't free

We all prefer good weather to bad weather. That statement is true, but what one person considers good weather another person may not. However, we have a lot of evidence that a clear, pollution free day of 75 degrees would be preferred by most people to a cloudy, smog filled day of 30 degrees. Evidence of this fact comes from casual observations about where people live or would like to live.

Revealing preferences

While for simplicity we often assume that all people have identical tastes and skills, we know that some people do have stronger preferences for certain things than do other people. For example, some people, call them type A, have a strong preference to live in cities with good weather, while type B people do not feel so strongly. The result will be that type A people will demand a wage premium to live in a city with worse weather, so that type B people will dominate the labor market in that city, while type A people will underbid type B people for jobs in a city with good weather. That is, type A people will pay a premium to live in a city with good weather.

Let's assume that people sort themselves into these two groups in choosing to live in city 1, which has W_1 (worse) weather compared to city 2, which has W_2 (better) weather. This is seen in Figure 3-23, where we measure the quality of weather on the horizontal axis and the average wage rate on the vertical axis. This tells us that we will expect to find, everything else the same, lower wages in the good weather city (or higher wages in the worse weather city). This would occur even if everyone had the same preferences (type A or B), but we see how different preferences by different people can accentuate the differences.

Paying for Sunshine

Economist Jennifer Roback used 1973 Census Bureau data for the 98 largest cities in the U.S. to measure the premiums that people pay for good weather by the lower wages they accept in good weather cities.[13] At that time, average annual earnings were $10,868 per worker. Accounting for other variables that affect the quality of life in a city (such as the crime rate, the unemployment rate, the pollution measurement, total population, population density, and population growth), she calculated

[13]"Wages, Rents, and the Quality of Life," *Journal of Political Economy*, December 1982, pp. 1257–1278.

FIGURE 3-23

Trading wages for better weather

There are two types of people, type A and type B. Type A people value good weather more than do type B people, so if we assume that the level of utility is the same for type A and type B people along I_A and I_B, we see that if there is a choice of living in city 1, where the average weather quality is W_1, or living in city 2, where the average weather quality is better, W_2, type A people will accept a lower wage to live in the better weather city than will type B people. Type A people would have to be paid a wage premium over type B people to live in city 1. Hence, we expect to see some self-sorting according to preferences for such things as weather.

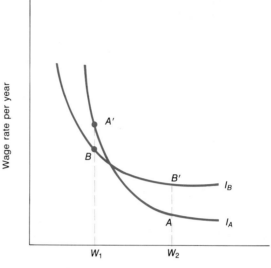

that the average worker would pay $69.55 per year for one additional clear day (or $78.25 to avoid an additional cloudy day), and would pay $7.30 to avoid an additional inch of snow. She also estimated that people would pay roughly $866 per year for the temperature to average 65 degrees.

Based on these factors, for 1973, she cal-culated that among the larger cities in the U.S., the three most desirable to live in were Los Angeles, Anaheim, and San Francisco. While additional factors can be added to such studies and lead to different rankings, it is clear that people are willing to pay a premium to live where (many people think) the weather is especially nice.

Property rights, incentives, and indifference analysis

One of several "simplifying assumptions" that we were implicitly making in this chapter was that the "goods" the consumer chooses are "completely disposable" by that consumer. To say that a consumer can "completely dis-pose" of a good is to say that the consumer can do anything he or she wants to do with that good. The consumer can destroy the good, transform its shape or character, or sell it at the prevailing market price. The con-sumer can put the good to its usual use or to any other use.

Such an assumption is sometimes untrue of particular goods or resources "owned" within the rules of particular legal systems. In most socialist economic systems, for instance, transactions for the purchase or sale of real estate cannot be made by individuals. Real estate can be "used" by the private individ-uals to whom it is assigned, but often only for certain purposes. In many jurisdictions in the U.S., goods which produce loud noises or large quantities of smoke can be used only under specific conditions. Thus, your ownership of a powerful stereo system does not give you the right to "crank it up" at 2 A.M. in your apartment building, nor does your ownership of the trees in your backyard automatically give you the right to burn the leaves which fall from the trees.

People who work for the government have certain ownership rights in their jobs, in that they must be accorded "due process" before being discharged. Those who work for private firms have no such rights (since they are employed "at will"), although they may have certain contractual claims to funds from retirement plans or other agreed upon benefits upon discharge.

As a general proposition, individuals value a good or asset less the fewer kinds of uses to which they are legally entitled to put that good or asset. Note that this does not mean that each individual wants to put each good or resource to the same use. Rather, it means that market demand for a particular good will be lower the more the restrictions placed on the use of that good. As an additional restriction is added, *some* individuals will find that the good no longer yields the service that they expected to obtain from it.

So long as we define goods or resources in terms of physical objects, the perceived tastes of consumers and producers for given goods or resources will shift with every change in the legal system which restricts or liberalizes the use of these goods or resources. A better technique is to define each productive characteristic of a physical object as a separate good or resource. Changes in the legal system then affect the constraints on choice (e.g., the slope of the consumer's budget line), not tastes or the physical productivity of resources.[14]

Property rights theory

This approach to an analysis of consumer and producer choice is known as *property rights analysis*. Property rights analysis proposes that goods and resources are best viewed as a *bundle of rights*. Each of these rights defines one way in which a given good or resource may or may not be used. Some of these rights may be time specific (e.g., playing your stereo between the hours of 1 A.M. and 7 A.M. or leasing an apartment for six months) and some rights may be use specific (e.g., the right to have a picnic on a public picnic table, without the right to sell or abuse the picnic table).

Property rights analysis is one way of making the microeconomic theory you are learning in this course applicable to the world around you. It states that in order to perform a microeconomic analysis of a situation you must identify the goods among which the decisonmaker can choose and the constraints on the number and size of such choices. As we will see later in the book, property rights analysis, as a way of translating the pure logic of choice into real world decisionmaking, is applicable in the areas of entrepreneurial choice and choice of leisure or income, as well as in the consumer choice.

[14]An informative survey of the literature of property rights analysis and a critical comparison of the property rights approach, of explaining differences in behavior through differences in constraints on choice, and in behavior through differences in tastes, is to be found in Louis De Alesi's "Property Rights, Transactions Costs, and X-Efficiency," *American Economic Review*, vol. 73 (March 1983) pp. 68–81. This comparison is also a useful exercise in applied economic methodology relevant to the issues which were discussed in Chapter 1.

SUMMARY

1 Cardinal utility analysis requires arithmetical measurement of levels of utility, or satisfaction obtained, from consumption. Ordinal utility analysis requires only a rank ordering.

2   If the cardinal total utility curve is increasing at a steadily decreasing rate, it has the property of diminishing marginal utility; however, it is impossible to prove diminishing marginal utility because we have no way to measure utility.

3   There are four assumptions in our model: (a) completeness—the consumer can determine which combinations of a commodity are preferable to other combinations and which combinations yield equal satisfaction, (b) consistency—preferences are transitive, (c) nonsatiation—more is preferred to less, and (d) convexity—all indifference curves are convex.

4   Indifference curves are negatively sloped, pass through each and every point in the commodity space, and cannot intersect.

5   Any tangent drawn on a convex-to-the-origin indifference curve lies below that curve at all points except, of course, the point of tangency.

6   Indifference curves that are convex to the origin have the property of a diminishing marginal rate of substitution of x for y. As more of x is consumed, the individual is willing to give up less of y in order to get one more unit of x; i.e., the person's marginal evaluation of x in terms of y falls.

7   A higher indifference curve indicates the consumption of more of both goods in the commodity space or the consumption of enough more of one good to more than compensate for the decreased consumption of the other. Hence, it is preferred to a lower indifference curve.

8   The slope of the budget line is equal to the negative of the ratio of the price of x to the price of y. It represents the feasible rate at which x can be exchanged for y.

9   The consumer optimum occurs when the highest indifference curve is tangent to the budget line. At this point, the marginal rate of substitution is equal to the marginal rate of market substitution; or, otherwise stated, the MRS_{xy} is equal to the ratio of the prices of x and y, or $MRS_{xy} = P_x/P_y = MRMS_{xy}$.

10 If indifference curves were concave to the origin, they would imply specialization rather than diversity in consumption. We use convex-to-the-origin indifference curves because they are consistent with observed nonspecialized consumption behavior while not being inconsistent with corner solutions.

11 Consumer optimum can also be viewed in marginal utility terms as the combination of commodities that yields equal marginal utility per last dollar spent on each. Otherwise stated, the marginal utility of any two commodities must be equal to the ratio of their prices.

GLOSSARY

- **market demand** The horizontal sum of all individual demands in a given market for a given good.
- **utility** The subjective pleasure, usefulness, or benefits that a person receives from any commodity consumed.
- **cardinal utility analysis** The use of cardinal numbers (1, 2, 3) which are quantitatively related to one another in order to measure and compare different levels of utility; such analysis requires the ability to measure levels of utility in discrete units that can be added to, or subtracted from, one another.
- **ordinal utility analysis** An analysis which uses rankings, or orderings, of utility levels rather than quantitative numbers on a cardinal scale. Ordinal utility analysis requires only a ranking (first, second, third) of preferences.
- **diminishing marginal utility** A property of cardinal total utility curves; whenever cardinal total utility increases at a steadily decreasing rate, diminishing marginal utility exists and can be interpreted to mean that the marginal utility derived falls as more units of a good are consumed.
- **commodities** A generic term including both tangible and intangible goods and services; synonymous with the economist's use of the term "goods."
- **indifference curve** The locus of points representing combinations of two commodities that all yield equal levels of satisfaction.
- **commodity space** The quadrant of a plane in which the horizontal and vertical axes are used to graphically represent all possible combinations of two commodities being considered.
- **marginal rate of substitution (MRS_{xy})** The number of units of y that must be given up per unit of x gained in order for a consumer to maintain a constant level of satisfaction.
- **diminishing marginal rate of substitution** MRS_{xy} declines as more of x and less of y is consumed; a property of convex-to-the-origin indifference curves.
- **budget constraint** The constraint imposed on consumer decision making by a combination of income and prices. Generally, this is defined as available money income per unit time period and prices in dollars per unit.
- **marginal rate of market substitution (MRMS_{xy})** The feasible rate at which the consumer can trade off y for x. This rate is usually given by the ratio of the prices of x and of y (= the negative of the slope of the budget line).
- **optimization** The individual economic agent's decision-making process which leads to a consumer optimum or maximum satisfaction position.
- **equilibrium** A property of markets, rather than individual decision making, in which forces acting upon a system are balanced so that there is no net tendency to change.
- **interior solution** A solution to either optimization or equilibrium problems that does not lie on either axis.
- **law of equal marginal utilities per dollar** A consumer optimum occurs when the marginal utility per dollar spent on a good is the same for all goods consumed.
- **corner solution** A solution to optimization or equilibrium problems that normally lies on either the x, or horizontal, axis or the y, or vertical, axis.

QUESTIONS

(Answers to even-numbered questions are at back of text.)

1   State the four assumptions which underlie our model of consumer choice.
2   What information is depicted by a single indifference curve?
3   What is the difference between total utility and marginal utility?
4   Suppose a consumer prefers A to B, and B to C, but insists that he or she also prefers C to A. Explain the logical problem here.
5   In the real world, information about alternatives available in the marketplace is a service, the provision of which requires resources which are not free. What does that say about the omniscience assumption?
6   Suppose you are indifferent among the following three combinations of food (f) and drink (d): 1f and 10d, 2f and 7d, 3f and 2d. Calculate the marginal rate of substitution (MRS) in consumption between the two goods. Does the substitution of the third f imply a greater sacrifice of d than did the second?
7   What is portrayed by (a) a vertical indifference curve, (b) a horizontal one, and (c) an upward-sloping one?
8   Explain why, if more is preferred to less, indifference curves cannot possibly intersect. In your answer, refer to Figure 3-7, adding a point D, directly above point C, to curve II.
9   Construct an indifference curve of the usual convex shape, representing coffee on the x axis and tea on the y axis. Now add a budget line just tangent to the indifference curve. Next rotate the budget line clockwise, keeping it tangent to the indifference curve as you do so. What do you observe happening, and what is its significance?
10   Construct a budget line from the following information: nominal income of $100 per week, price of beef P_b of $2 per pound, price of shelter P_S of $20 per week; all income is spent on beef and/or shelter. Suppose your money income remains constant, but the price of beef doubles to $4 per pound while that of housing falls to $10 per week. Draw the new budget line. Are you now better off or worse off? What do we need to know before deciding?
11   Start over again with the initial situation in question 10. Now indicate two separate ways to show an unambiguous decrease in real income (represented by an inward shift of the budget line without any change in its slope).
12   According to the law of diminishing marginal utility, the way to increase the marginal utility of a good is to consume less of it. Explain this seeming paradox.
13   Suppose you are paid your weekly income in kind; you get forty 3-pound chickens per week. Only one other good, avocados, is produced. There is no money at all; goods are bartered by persons not content with their holdings of chickens and avocados. What additional piece of information do you need in order to construct your budget constraint? (Remember, money is out of the picture.)
14   Draw an indifference map containing two indifference curves, I and II. How much better off is this consumer when consuming a combination of goods on curve II rather than on curve I? Can you tell? Why, or why not? Explain.
15   Suppose you are standing in the checkout line of a produce market. You have 10 pounds of tangerines and eight ears of corn. Tangerines cost 10¢ a pound; an ear

of corn is also a dime. Given the $1.80 which you have to spend, you are satisfied that you have reached the highest attainable level of indifference. Along comes your brother, who tries to convince you that you should put some of the ears of corn back and replace them with additional pounds of tangerines. From what you know about utility analysis, how would you explain the disagreement?

SELECTED REFERENCES

Alchian, Armen A., "The Meaning of Utility in Measurement," *American Economic Review*, March 1953, pp. 26–50.
Bowen, Howard R., *Toward Social Economy* (New York: Rinehart, 1948), chap. 19.
Hicks, John R., *Value and Capital*, 2d ed. (Oxford: Clarendon, 1946), chaps. 1 and 2.
Robertson, D. H., *Utility and All That* (New York: Macmillan, 1952), chap. 1.
Stigler, G., "The Development of Utility Theory," *Journal of Political Economy*, vol. 58, parts 1–2, August–October 1950, pp. 307–327, 373–396.

APPENDIX TO CHAPTER 3

THE USE OF THE Δ OPERATOR

In many places in this book, the formulations make use of the following proof. Let

$$A = B \cdot C \tag{A3-1}$$

Now increase B by a small amount equal to ΔB, and increase C by a small amount equal to ΔC. As a result A will increase by ΔA. We can write

$$(A + \Delta A) = (B + \Delta B)(C + \Delta C)$$
$$\text{or } A + \Delta A \tag{A3-2}$$
$$= BC + B\Delta C$$
$$+ C\Delta B + \Delta B\Delta C$$

From the left side of Eq. (A3-2), we may subtract the left side of Eq. (A3-1); and from the right side of (A3-2), we subtract the right side of Eq. (A3-1). We then have

$$\Delta A = B\Delta C + C\Delta B + \Delta B\Delta C \tag{A3-3}$$

The last term in Eq. (A3-3), $\Delta B\Delta C$, is assumed to be so small that we can ignore it (for

small Δ's). Equation (A3-3) is rewritten to express the approximate value of ΔA: the value of ΔA when we treat $\Delta B\Delta C$ as if it were 0.

$$\Delta A = B\Delta C + C\Delta B \tag{A3-4}$$

If we now divide both sides of Eq. (A3-4) by ΔB, we obtain

$$\frac{\Delta A}{\Delta B} = B\frac{\Delta C}{\Delta B} + C$$

or, rearranging the terms,

$$\frac{\Delta A}{\Delta B} = C + B\frac{\Delta C}{\Delta B} \tag{A3-5}$$

When we multiply the last term on the right side of Eq. (A3-5) by C/C (which is equal to 1) we find that

$$\frac{\Delta A}{\Delta B} = C + B\frac{\Delta C}{\Delta B} \cdot \frac{C}{C}$$

which may be written as

$$\frac{\Delta A}{\Delta B} = C\left(1 + \frac{B\Delta C}{C\Delta B}\right) \qquad \text{(A3-6)}$$

We will see Eq. (A3-6) in a number of different forms throughout the rest of this book.

To illustrate what we have done with the algebra above, suppose A is the area of a rectangle and B and C are the lengths of the sides of this rectangle. (The area of any rectangle A is equal to the product of the lengths of the sides, BC.)

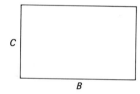

When we increase the lengths of the two sides by ΔB and ΔC, respectively, the area of the rectangle increases by ΔA.

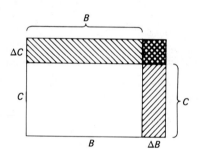

The area of the rectangle is now equal to $(B + \Delta B)(C + \Delta C)$, or—as we saw in Eq. (A3-2)—to $BC + B\Delta C + C\Delta B + \Delta B\Delta C$. But notice the little rectangle in the upper right portion of the larger rectangle above. Its area is equal to $\Delta B\Delta C$. If ΔB and ΔC are both very small, the area of this small rectangle is also very small. And if we wish to know the approximate value by which the area of the rectangle has increased when we increase the sides of the rectangle by ΔB and ΔC, we ignore this little rectangle. This approximate *increase* in A, which we have called ΔA, is equal to the small rectangle on the upper left,

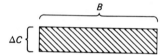

which has an area equal to $B\Delta C$, *plus* the small rectangle along the right side

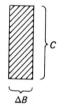

which has an area equal to $C\Delta B$. The change in A is close to $B\Delta C + C\Delta B$; and this is what Eq. (A3-4) told us.

Consumer demand

T he three main goals of this chapter are to extend the indifference curve analysis to find out more precisely how consumers react to changes in their money income; to find out how consumers react to changes in the relative price of a particular commodity, also using the indifference curve analysis; and to examine consumer decision making in the context of positive search and information costs.

The issues and applications treated in this chapter cover the following topics: measuring changes in living standards, the trade-off between labor and leisure, and a look at Irish potatoes, an alleged Giffen good.

CHANGES IN MONEY INCOME: DERIVING THE INCOME-CONSUMPTION CURVE

What happens when there is a change in money income available to the consumer for the purchase of goods x and y? Consider a doubling of money income, holding the prices of x and y, P_x and P_y, constant. Obviously, this will mean that twice as much of x and y can be purchased as before. An increase in money income, *ceteris paribus*, shifts the budget line away from the origin while it remains parallel to the original budget line. Similarly, a decrease in money income would shift the budget line toward the origin while it remains parallel to the original line. These shifts are shown in Figure 4-1.

The magnitude of changes in income in Figure 4-1 can be measured in terms of different goods, x or y, or in dollars. For example, if budget line

FIGURE 4-1
Changes in money income
If nominal prices stay the same, an increase in money income will shift the budget constraint *BB'* to the right and upward to *CC'*. These two budget lines are parallel. If money income decreases and nominal prices remain constant, the budget constraint would shift toward the origin, say, to *AA'*. This budget line is also parallel to the original budget line.

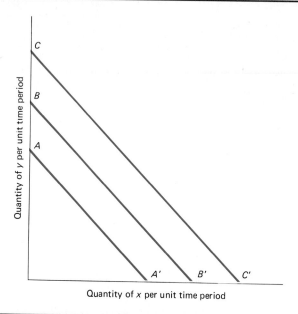

Quantity of *y* per unit time period

Quantity of *x* per unit time period

AA' represents $100 and x costs $1, the income, in terms of x, is equal to 100x. If income then increases such that we are on budget line *BB'*, and that represents $110, we can also say that there has been a 10x unit increase in income. We can do the same thing for y, at a given price of y. Remember that the slope of the budget line is equal to the negative of the ratio of the prices of the two commodities. Therefore, if those prices remain constant, the slope of the budget line will be the same no matter how much income increases.

Now we would like to find out how an individual consumer responds to successive increases in money income when nominal and relative prices are constant. We do this in Figure 4-2.

We start out with a money income of M and prices P_x and P_y for the commodities in question, x and y. In what follows, we will use x and y to signify any two desired commodities. The reader can, if he or she wishes, think in terms of movies and concerts from the example in Chapter 3 (or any other pair of goods, for that matter). Remember that the two extreme points of the budget line are found by dividing the nominal price of each commodity into a constant amount of money income. Thus, if all money income M were spent on y, an amount $M/P_y = B$ of y could be purchased. If it were all spent on x, $M/P_x = B'$ of x could be purchased. Consumer optimum is at point E, where the consumer attains his or her highest level of satisfaction on indifference curve I, given the budget constraint.

At point E, the rate at which the consumer *is willing* to substitute x for

▰▰▰

FIGURE 4-2

Deriving the income-consumption curve

Nominal and therefore relative prices are constant. Money income initially is M, yielding budget constraint BB'. The consumer optimum occurs at E, where indifference curve I is tangent to BB'. Then money income is increased first to M' and then to M''. New consumer optima are obtained at E' and E'', respectively. When we connect these and all other possible consumer optima, we have what is called an income-consumption curve.

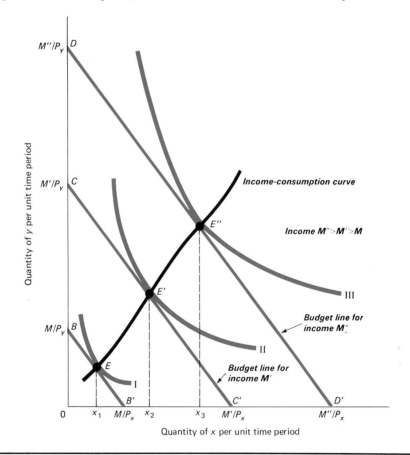

y (the slope of the indifference curve at that point) is equal to the rate at which the consumer *is able* to substitute x for y in the market (the slope of the budget line). Now let money income be increased from M to M'. The budget line shifts out to CC', which is parallel to BB', because relative prices have not changed. A new consumer optimum is established when the highest attainable indifference curve, II, is reached. That occurs when that indifference curve is tangent to the new budget line, at point E'. Let's assume that money income is again increased, to M''. A new consumer optimum is obtained at point E''.

If we connect the three consumer optimum points E, E', and E'', we have what is called an income-consumption curve. We define an **income-consumption curve** as the locus of the optimum consumption points that would occur if income for that consumer were increased continuously and the nominal and relative prices of the two goods in question remained constant.

NORMAL AND INFERIOR GOODS

We can classify commodities in terms of how consumers' purchases change when their incomes change. We portrayed a typical response to a change in income in Figure 4-2 when we drew the income-consumption curve. It shows the quantities of both x and y consumed as income changes. We can see that both the quantity of x and the quantity of y purchased went up as income increased. Whenever this occurs, we call x and y normal goods. We define a **normal good** as a good that an individual buys more of as his or her income increases and buys less of as his or her income decreases.[1]

Look at Figure 4-3. Here we have drawn the beginnings of a graph that would show an income-consumption curve. Income starts out at M; the prices are given and are equal to P_x and P_y. The consumer optimum is depicted by point E. Income is then increased to M'. The budget line shifts outward and parallel to the former budget line. We do not know where the consumer will end up unless we draw in additional indifference curves. We can, however, say something about whether x and/or y is a normal good. What if a second indifference curve is tangent to a new and higher budget line somewhere between points A and B on that new budget line? We know that if this happens, the consumer will purchase more of both x and y. In this situation, both x and y are normal goods.

However, if the consumer ends up at a point to the left of the vertical dashed line through A, we know that less x than x_1 will be purchased after this increase in income. In this situation, we call x an inferior good. An **inferior good** is defined as a good that a consumer purchases less of when his or her income rises and more of when his or her income falls. Pork hash or generic beer might be examples of inferior goods for most people. If the new point of consumer optimum is below the horizontal dashed line through B, less y than y_1 is purchased as income increases, and in this case, y is an inferior good. Notice that it is possible for both goods represented in the commodity space to be normal, but it is impossible for both of them to be inferior. (Why?)

---

[1] If the consumer buys the *same* amount of the good as income changes, like points A and B in Figure 4-3, it is a normal good.

FIGURE 4-3
Normal and inferior goods
If income increases to M', we can tell whether
x and/or y is normal or inferior by finding out
where the new point of consumer optimum lies.
If the new point of consumer optimum lies
between points A and B, both x and y are
normal goods because as income increases,
the optimal quantity of these two commodities
also increases. If the new point of consumer
optimum is to the left of the vertical dashed line
through point A, less of x is purchased as
income increases, and x is an inferior good. If
the point of consumer optimum lies below the
horizontal dashed line through point B on the
new budget line, y is an inferior good over that
income range.

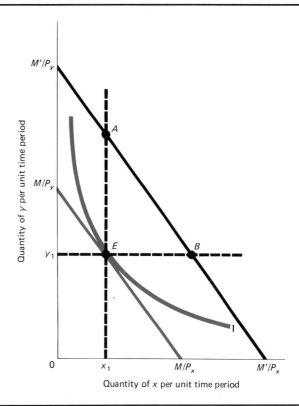

**No value
judgments made**

The use of the terms "normal" and "inferior" is arbitrary. No value judgments
are made about particular goods that are purchased either more or less as
income increases. These terms are only descriptive. A normal good for one
person may be an appalling commodity for someone else. Moreover, one
consumer may find a particular commodity to be an inferior good, and another may find it to be a normal good.

APPLYING THE INCOME-CONSUMPTION
CURVE: DERIVING ENGEL CURVES

We can use the income-consumption curve to derive the relation between
the level of income and the optimum quantity purchased of each good. A
nineteenth-century German economist, Ernst Engel, was the first to do empirical work relating expenditures on particular commodities to income. It
is fitting, therefore, that curves showing this relationship are named after

FIGURE 4-4

Deriving the Engel curve

We want to relate the optimum quantity of x purchased to various levels of income. We do this by plotting the combinations of money income and quantity of x purchased, holding the nominal and relative prices of x and y constant. Thus, point A is taken from Figure 4-1, where the quantity purchased is x_1 when income is M. Points B and C are obtained similarly. With higher income levels M' and M'', the quantities purchased are higher, equal to x_2 and x_3, respectively.

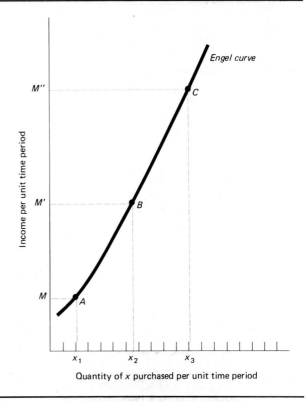

Engel. Here we start out using quantities purchased, rather than expendi-tures.[2]

Let's derive the **Engel curve** for commodity x. We do this by transferring the various combinations of income and quantity of x purchased from Figure 4-2 to Figure 4-4. Thus we get point A, representing income M and the optimal quantity purchased x_1 at that income; point B, representing income M' and optimal quantity purchased x_2 with income M'; and finally, point C, representing income M'' and optimal quantity purchased x_3. When we con-nect these three points, we construct an Engel curve. (Note that the nominal price P_x and relative price P_x/P_y of x remain constant throughout the analysis.) The income-consumption curve in Figure 4-2 and the Engel curve in Figure 4-4 appear similar in shape. However, they are not identical; the vertical axes on the two diagrams measure different variables. In Figure 4-2, the vertical axis measures the *quantity* of y purchased per unit time period; in Figure 4-4, the vertical axis measures *income* per unit time period.

---

[2]Economists call the relationship between the quantity of a good purchased and income an Engel curve, and the relationship between money *expenditures* on the good and income an *Engel expenditure curve*.

Possible shapes of Engel curves

In Figure 4-5, we present two broad categories of Engel curves. In panel (a), the quantity of commodity x purchased increases as income increases, but at a *decreasing rate*; that is, more of x is purchased for each incremental increase in money income but the percent of the increased income devoted to x declines. In panel (b), the quantity of x purchased also increases with increases in income, but at an *increasing* rate. Note that for the same amount of increase of money income from M to M', the increase in the quantity of x purchased is only $2\frac{1}{2}$ units in panel (a) but is 5 units in panel (b).

The Engel curve in panel (a) supposedly represents what happens to the quantity of groceries purchased as individual incomes rise. Basic foodstuffs, in this sense, are considered "necessities." A good such as the one represented in panel (b) might be a "luxury," such as gourmet restaurant dinners. (However, these labels should not be taken too seriously because they mean different things to different people.) At income M, you're probably already purchasing most of the food you think you "need"; increasing your income to M' won't cause you to buy much more food. But at income M, you probably don't buy too many gourmet dinners; if your income increased to M', you would probably consume gourmet dinners much more regularly.

FIGURE 4-5
Two general classes of Engel curves
In panel (a), the quantity of x purchased increases with income at a decreasing rate; but in panel (b), it does so at an increasing rate. Engel curves like the one in panel (a) are said to sometimes reflect "necessities," and those like the one in panel (b) reflect "luxuries."

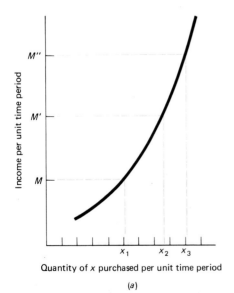

Engel curves and the classification of goods

We can consider one specific commodity and use the Engel curve to determine whether that commodity is an inferior or a normal good. Looking again at Figure 4-4, we can see that the Engel curve there is for a specific commodity, x, and that x clearly is a normal good because as income increases, quantity purchased increases. The same is true of x in both panel (a) and panel (b) of Figure 4-5. The quantity of x purchased increases as income increases in both cases; hence we are dealing with a normal good in both cases.

Now look at Figure 4-6. We have drawn a hypothetical Engel curve for the commodity x. We find that for increases in income up to income level M_1, the optimum quantity of x purchased per unit time period also increases. However, at income level M_1, the Engel curve starts to bend backward. Above income level M_1, the optimum quantity of x purchased per unit time period falls as income rises. Thus we say that for incomes from zero to M_1, good x is normal; for incomes above M_1, good x is inferior.

Real-world examples

It is not hard to find real-world examples of goods whose Engel curves can be represented by the one depicted in Figure 4-6. Consider how a family would react to a rise in income in terms of its purchases of macaroni dinners. If we assume that the family starts out at a very low level of income, we can be fairly confident that as the family's income increases, more macaroni

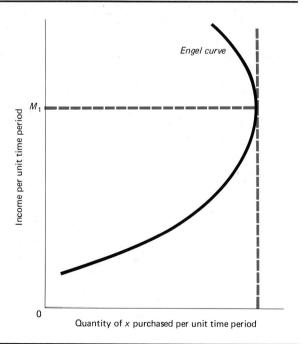

FIGURE 4-6
The Engel curve and classification of goods
Whenever the optimum quantity of x purchased increases as income increases, x is called a normal good. Thus, between income levels 0 and M_1, x is a normal good. However, above income level M_1, x becomes an inferior good because less is purchased as income rises.

dinners will be bought. However, at some point as income increases, meat will be introduced into the family's diet as a substitute for macaroni dinners, resulting in fewer and fewer of the latter being bought. Thus, the backward-bending Engel curve would seem appropriate.

Consider a student's purchase of relatively low-quality record albums recorded by unknown artists on "budget" labels. As the student's income increases, say due to an increase in part-time work or to an increase in stipends from the university, there will (probably) be an increase in the number of low-grade, low-quality, discounted record albums purchased. This type of record is a normal good over this income range. However, if for some reason the student suddenly has an increase in income of, say, $1,000 a month (perhaps an annuity from a rich uncle or aunt), we can imagine that the amount of low-quality records purchased will decrease and that higher-quality records by national recording artists may be substituted. Again, the backward-bending Engel curve in Figure 4-6 would be appropriate.

THE EFFECTS OF A CHANGE IN PRICE: DERIVING THE PRICE-CONSUMPTION CURVE

How do the actual or potential consumers of a commodity react to a change in the relative price of the commodity? In general, they purchase more when the relative price falls and purchase less when the relative price rises. This relationship can be derived by using indifference curve analysis.

The price-consumption curve

Let us hold money income, M, and P_y, the price of y, constant while we change the price of commodity x, P_x. This is done in Figure 4-7. What we do in Figure 4-7 is run an experiment in which the price of x falls as money income and the price of y remain constant. Remember that we can find the corner points, or axis intercepts, for the budget line (that is, points where the budget line cuts the x axis and the y axis) by asking how much of a commodity could be purchased at the existing price levels if none of the other commodity were purchased. Consider the horizontal axis. When the price of x is P_x, the amount that can be purchased is determined by dividing P_x into total money income M. The maximum amount of x is at quantity B. When the price of x falls to P_x', the maximum amount of x that can be purchased with total money income expands to B'; and it expands to B'' when the price falls further to P_x''. Thus, even though money income does not change, the amount of x that can be purchased increases. (Remember: $-P_x/P_y$ = slope of the budget line. The slope becomes "flatter" or smaller as P_x falls while P_y is constant.)

Each time the budget line changes, there will be a new point of consumer optimum. At first it is at point E, then point E', and then point E''. If we connect these three points, we obtain a **price-consumption curve.** That curve is defined as the locus of optimum combinations of x and y that result from

FIGURE 4-7

Deriving the price consumption curve

We start with budget line BB. Optimum consumption is at point E, where the indifference curve is tangent to the budget line. We now reduce the price of x to P'_x. The new budget line rotates out to BB', and the new optimum consumption is at point E'. We do this again by reducing the price of x further to P''_x. The new optimum consumption is at point E''. When we connect E, E', and E'', we have the locus of optimum combinations of x and y that would be purchased at different relative prices of x. This curve is called the price-consumption curve.

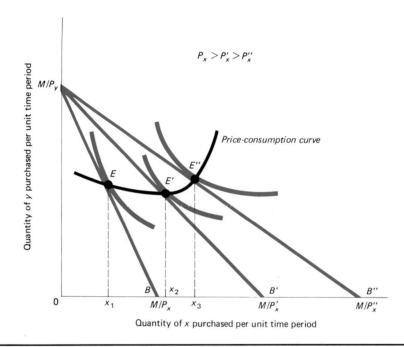

a change in relative prices, holding money income constant. We cannot say anything a priori about the shape or slope of the price-consumption curve.

Obtaining the demand curve from the price-consumption line

Given the way we have drawn our indifference curves, we can say something about the relation between the relative price of a particular commodity and the quantity purchased. We can similarly derive a relation between the optimum quantity of a good purchased and the relative price of that good by using the diagram showing the price-consumption curve in Figure 4-7. The resultant relationship forms the basis for the derivation of the demand curve. We see in Figure 4-7 that nominal income, M, the price of y, P_y, and the consumer's tastes are held constant. Realizing this, we plot the points representing the quantities of x demanded—x_1, x_2, and x_3—and the associated prices of x—P_x, P'_x, and P''_x. This gives us three points from which to construct the individual's demand curve shown in Figure 4-8.

FIGURE 4-8
Deriving the demand curve from the price-consumption curve
As we saw in Figure 4-7, holding M and P_y constant, we have three different relative prices: P_x, P'_x, and P''_x. Associated with these progressively lower prices of x are the progressively greater quantities demanded of x_1, x_2, and x_3. We transfer these pairs and obtain points A, B, and C. When these points are connected, they form a demand curve. (It should be noted that this is an individual's demand curve, not a market demand curve.)

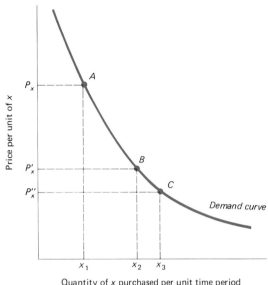

Quantity of x purchased per unit time period

The law of demand

The shape of the demand curve depicted in Figure 4-8 is important. It is a graphic representation of the law of demand, which was introduced in Chapter 2.

We can point out that a downward-sloping demand curve will almost always follow from convex indifference curves such as those drawn in Figure 4-7. Since the indifference curves are convex, when the budget line is rotated counterclockwise (as a result of a lower price of x, as in Figure 4-7), new tangency points will usually be to the right of the old tangency points. In other words, the new optimum E' in Figure 4-7 will not often be to the left of E if we use convex indifference curves. Remember that convex indifference curves follow from an assumption of diminishing marginal rates of substitution in consumption. It is important to realize from the above discussion that the law of demand is not implied by convexity.[3] We cannot prove that the law of demand (as in theory) has no exceptions. But clearly, as a general theory of consumer behavior, it has withstood the scrutiny of empirical testing.

[3]Later in this chapter we consider how to derive a demand curve that must be downward-sloping as long as indifference curves are convex. Deriving that kind of demand curve, we hold *real* income constant, whereas here we held *money* income constant.

MARKET DEMAND

The demand curve derived in Figure 4-8 was for an individual. As we discovered in Chapter 2, however, the market-clearing, or equilibrium, price is determined by the interaction of *market* demand and *market* supply. Hence, we must derive a market demand curve, a concept that we have already seen but not explored.

We derive a market demand curve by summing the individual demand curves. The individuals' demand curves are added together at each price, up to the price at which no more of the good is demanded by any of the consumers in that market. This is called a *horizontal* summation of individuals' demand curves. For example, let's assume that the good in Figure 4-8 is bottles of Coke. At *each price* we add together the corresponding quantities of Coke demanded by each individual in the market. Let's assume that in this market, during this time period, there are only two consumers

FIGURE 4-9
Deriving the market demand curve
Assume that there are only two individuals in the entire market. Individual 1's demand curve is given in panel (a); individual 2's demand curve is in panel (b). We obtain the market demand curve by horizontally summing d_1d_1 and d_2d_2. The result is given as *DD* in panel (c).

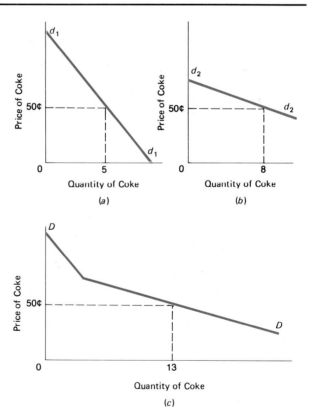

of Coke, individual 1 and individual 2. Their respective demand curves for bottles of Coke are shown as d_1d_1 in panel (*a*) of Figure 4-9 and d_2d_2 in panel (*b*) of Figure 4-9. The horizontal summation of the two demand curves is presented in panel (*c*). When the price is 50¢ per bottle, individual 1 buys five bottles and individual 2 buys eight bottles. The market thus demands a total quantity of 13 bottles at that price level. The aggregate, or market, demand curve is *DD*. The market demand curve presented in panel (*c*) is equal to individual 1's demand curve in panel (*a*), down to the price at which individual 2's demand curve intersects the vertical axis in panel (*b*). This is where the kink appears in the demand curve *DD* in panel (*c*).

A measurement of price responsiveness: the price elasticity of demand

Now we can develop a concept that relates the change in optimal quantity of a commodity demanded when its relative price changes. This concept is called the **price elasticity of demand.** We define it as:

■ *Coefficient of price elasticity of demand* = *percentage change in the quantity demanded of a good* ÷ *percentage change in the price of that good*

We will treat in detail the concept of price elasticity of demand and how to measure it in Chapter 5. At that time we will also see how to relate changes in quantity demanded to changes in income. For the moment, we wish to discover first the relation between price elasticity of demand and total expenditures on the particular good under study. Then we can find how to determine price elasticity of demand by observing the slope of the price-consumption curve.

The relation between price elasticity of demand and total expenditures on a good

We can make classifications according to the price elasticity of demand, and we do so in Table 4-1. In cases where price elasticity of demand is numerically greater (greater in absolute value) than 1, we call this **price-elastic demand.** When it is numerically equal to 1, we have a situation of **unitary price elasticity of demand.** In cases where it is numerically less than 1, we have a situation of **price-inelastic demand.**

Consider unitary price elasticity. A given percentage change in price elicits an identical percentage change in the quantity demanded in the opposite direction. For example, a 1 percent increase in price causes a 1 percent decrease in quantity demanded. Since the total expenditure on any product is equal to the number of units purchased times the price of each unit, consumer expenditures on a good whose price elasticity is numerically equal to 1 will remain constant as price changes in either direction. This is not the case when price elasticity is numerically greater or less than 1. When demand is price-elastic, for example, a reduction in price will lead to a more-than-proportionate increase in quantity demanded, and hence consumer ex-

TABLE 4-1
Price elasticities and changes in consumer expenditures

When price elasticity is numerically	Demand is called	Thus if price changes	Quantity demanded changes (in opposite direction)	So that consumer expenditures on the good ($P_x \cdot x$)
Greater than 1	Price-elastic	P ↑	More than in proportion	Fall
		P ↓	More than in proportion	Rise
Equal to 1	Unitary-elastic	P ↑	In proportion	Remain constant
		P ↓	In proportion	Remain constant
Less than 1	Price-inelastic	P ↑	Less than in proportion	Rise
		P ↓	Less than in proportion	Fall

penditures on that good will rise. You can work through the remaining examples in Table 4-1.[4]

We will return to a graphic treatment of price elasticity for movements along demand and supply curves in Chapter 5. Now, however, an examination of the relations between the total expenditure by a consumer on a product and the price elasticity of demand will allow us to use the slope of the price-consumption curve to tell us the price elasticity of demand.

Observing the elasticity of demand through the price-consumption curve

In Figure 4-10, we have drawn three different price-consumption curves. The commodity space in each of the panels is somewhat different from the one we have been using. The horizontal axis is the same as before. The difference is on the vertical axis, which designates "money for *all* other goods" rather than the quantity of another specific good. Thus if no x is purchased at all, M on the vertical axis represents money income available for all other goods. Hence, any purchase of x reduces money expenditures on all other goods (seen as a movement down along the vertical axis).

Now consider panel (a). Here we have drawn two budget constraints, one for a price of x, P_x, and another for a lower price P'_x. The two points of consumer optimum are E and E'. The price-consumption line connecting those two points is downward-sloping. Notice what happens when the price

[4]For a more mathematical presentation, go to the appendix at the end of Chapter 3 and let A = revenue, B = price, and C = quantity.

FIGURE 4-10
Price elasticity of demand and the slope of the price-consumption line
We can tell the price elasticity of demand by observing the slope of the price-consumption line. In these three commodity spaces, the vertical axis measures money for all other goods instead of good y. Thus, any time there is a reduction in money for all other goods, that implies an increase in expenditure on x. In panel (a), as the price of x falls, the amount of money available for all other goods falls, meaning that total expenditure on x increases; hence, the demand over the price range $P_x \rightarrow P'_x$ in panel (a) is price-elastic. In panel (b) the same thing occurs except that the amount of money available for all other goods remains constant. Hence, the demand over the price range $P_x \rightarrow P'_x$ in panel (b) is unit-elastic. Finally, in panel (c) the amount of money available for all other goods rises, and the demand over the price range $P_x \rightarrow P'_x$ is price-inelastic.

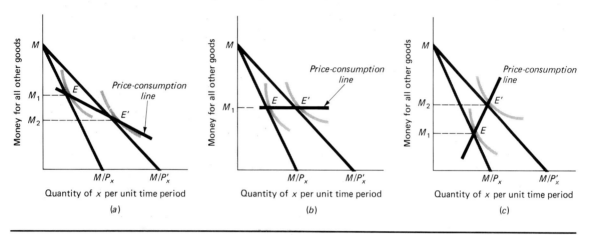

of x falls to P'_x. The quantity of x demanded goes up, but that is true in most cases when there is a price decrease. However, note that the amount of money available for all other goods has fallen from M_1 to M_2. This can mean only one thing: Total expenditures on x have gone up when the price of x has fallen. Because of the relationship between total expenditures and elasticity, we know that the demand for x over the price range P_x to P'_x, as presented in Figure 4-10 (a), is price-elastic.

Now look at panel (b). Here we show that after a reduction of P_x to P'_x, the amount of money left over for all other goods remains the same at M_1. Thus, because total expenditure on goods is constant, the demand for x over the price range P_x to P'_x represented in panel (b) must be of unit or unitary elasticity.

And finally, in panel (c), the demand is price-inelastic because as the price of x falls, the total amount of money left over for all other goods rises, and the total expenditures on x must have fallen. The increase in consumption of x was less than in proportion to the decrease in price.

In summary, the demand for x is:

1   *Price-elastic* when the price-consumption line is downward-sloping (a negative slope).

> **2** *Unitary-elastic* when the price-consumption line is horizontal (zero slope).
>
> **3** *Price-inelastic* when the price-consumption line is upward-sloping (a positive slope).

PRICE CHANGES, CHANGES IN REAL INCOME, AND THE LAW OF DEMAND

The law of demand states that as the price of a good declines the quantity demanded will increase, all other things being equal. We know from our discussion in Chapter 2 that the consumer's income is included among all other things that must remain equal or constant. But we now have a better-developed and broader idea of income than we had in Chapter 2.

By referring to the discussion of shifts in a consumer's budget line accompanying Figure 4-11, you can see that an increase in a consumer's income can result from an increase in the amount of money received during a period, with the money prices of goods constant, or it can result from a decrease in the money prices of goods purchased with a constant money income. We can thus define a consumer's *real income,* as opposed to money income, as a consumer's ability to demand or purchase a particular quantity of goods.

From this definition you can see that a consumer has more real income whenever the price of one of the goods in his or her consumption bundle falls, if prices of all other goods and money income remain constant.

Look at Figure 4-11. Here we show the now-familiar indifference curves I and II tangent to two separate budget lines, *BB'* and *BB''*. The area *OB'B''*, corresponding to a lower price for good x, includes all the consumption bundles contained in the area *BB'O,* plus the additional and "higher" bundles contained in the area *BB'B''*. As a result of the fall in the price of x, the consumer can increase his or her consumption of x without decreasing consumption of y, or increase consumption of y without decreasing consumption of x, or increase consumption of both x and y. The fall in the price of x has thus caused an increase in consumer income and utility.

We illustrate this effect of a price decrease in Figure 4-11. The consumer is originally consuming bundle A of x and y. With a decline in the price of x, the new bundle consumed is shown at point C. The movement from consumption of A to consumption of C is due to two changes in the consumer's condition. First, x is cheaper (in terms of the units of y that must be sacrificed for a unit of x) and y is more expensive (in terms of the units of x which must be sacrificed for a unit of y). Second, the consumer has more real income to purchase x and y after the decline in the price of x.

Income and substitution effects

Now we want to try to isolate each of the two effects that occur when there is a change in the relative price of the goods purchased by the consumer. One effect is due to the substitution of a good that becomes relatively less expensive for a good that becomes relatively more expensive. This is called

FIGURE 4-11
Substitution and income effect
The total effect of a lower price of *x* is composed of two effects: that is, the consumer buys more of *x* for two reasons: (1) substitution in favor of the relatively cheaper good and (2) an increase in real income (expressed in terms of good *x*). The total effect is given by the movement from x_1 to x_2. In order to derive a substitution effect, we hypothetically take away a sufficient amount of this consumer's income so that he or she is forced back to indifference curve I. What is taken away is represented by the vertical distance between *H* and *B*, or by the horizontal distance from *H'* to *B"*. In other words, we are confronting the consumer with the new relative prices represented by the slope of the new budget line *BB"*, but not allowing the consumer to have an increase in utility. There is no income effect here. The consumer substitutes *x* for *y* and moves from point *A* to point *D*, which in terms of good *x* is equivalent to the horizontal distance from x_1 to x_3. Now we give the consumer back the income that we took away and we find out how much more of *x* is purchased because of this increase in real income. This is represented by the movement from *D* to *C*, which in terms of good *x* is represented as the horizontal distance from x_3 to x_2. In this diagram, the income effect is positive, for we are dealing with a normal good.

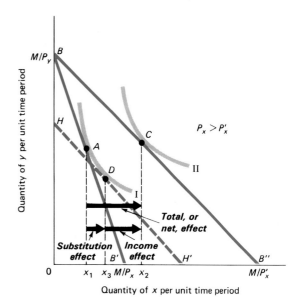

the **substitution effect**. The other effect is the result of the increase in the consumer's real income, expressed in terms of the now-cheaper good M/P_x, that comes about as that product becomes cheaper and money income remains unchanged. This is called the **income effect**. For normal goods, as income goes up, more is purchased. Therefore, the income effect is positive; i.e., the relationship between changes in income and in quantity demanded is a direct one. For inferior goods, the income effect is negative; i.e., the relationship between changes in income and in quantity demanded is an inverse one. We'll show these effects next.

Example for a reduction in price

Look at Figure 4-11 again. The position from which we start is money income *M* and prices P_y and P_x. The initial budget line is therefore *BB'*. The highest indifference curve attainable is I, which is tangent to that budget line at point *A*. The quantity of *x* demanded will be x_1. Now there is a reduction in the price of *x* to P_x'. The new budget line is *BB"*, where *B"* occurs at the point where money income *M* is divided by the new lower price of *x*, P_x'. The budget line has rotated outward to the right. The highest indifference curve attainable is II, which is tangent to *BB"* at point *C*. The new quantity of *x* purchased will be x_2. The horizontal distance from x_1 to x_2 is the total effect of a price change. It includes both substitution and income effects.

Now let's separate these two different effects. The way we can do so is by constructing a hypothetical budget line tangent to the initial indifference curve, curve I, but parallel to the higher budget line, BB''. In this manner, what we are doing is changing the relative prices facing the consumer so that he or she now sees the price ratio P_y/P_x' rather than P_y/P_x.

Another way of looking at this experiment is to consider imposing an imaginary lump-sum tax. The purpose of the lump-sum tax is to eliminate the income effect in order to isolate the substitution effect. Thus, relative prices have changed so that the new budget line is BB''. Keeping those same relative prices, we impose this imaginary lump-sum tax, which is just the right magnitude to put the consumer back on his or her original indifference curve, I. The size of the imaginary lump-sum tax in our diagram is either the vertical distance from B to H or the horizontal distance from B'' to H'.

We call the hypothetical budget line HH'; it is tangent to the original indifference curve at point D. Thus we can, in some sense, contend that the consumer still has the same level of satisfaction. That is, the consumer would still be on the original indifference curve I. In effect, then, in this experiment we are changing relative prices for the consumer such that x becomes cheaper. However, to prevent the consumer's utility from rising, we take away just enough income by the lump-sum tax so that the consumer moves from point C on indifference curve II back to point D on indifference curve I. In other words, we have taken away BH in income expressed in terms of good y, or what is the same thing, $B'' H'$, in income in terms of good x. Thus we are eliminating any possible income effect. The consumer's real income has not risen. What will the consumer do? Given the convexity of the indifference curve, the consumer will purchase a larger quantity of x and a lesser quantity of y. In fact, the optimum combination will shift from A to D. This is the substitution effect at work.

Now we allow the consumer to enjoy the increase in real income associated with the reduction in the price of x from P_x to P_x'. We give back the income we just took away in our experiment. Or, using the lump-sum tax analogy, we refund the imaginary tax. The consumer goes back to the new budget line BB'', and the new optimum is at C. The movement from x_3 to x_2 is the income effect because there has been an increase in income from H' to B'' as measured on the x axis in terms of the quantity of x. Since we are dealing with a normal good here, a change in income leads to a change in quantity demanded in the same direction. It leads to an even larger increase in the quantity purchased of x when P_x falls.[5]

Inferior goods   When there is an inferior good involved, the income effect is, by definition, negative: Changes in income are associated with changes in the opposite

---

[5]We will see alternative derivation of income and substitution effects later in this chapter.

FIGURE 4-12
Income and substitution effects: the case of an inferior good

We start off with relative prices and income such that the budget line is *BB'*. The optimum consumption is at point *A*, where indifference curve I is just tangent to *BB'*. The relative price of *x* falls from P_x to P'_x, so that the new budget line is *B''*. The new optimum consumption is at point *C*. In order to find the substitution effect, we hypothetically take away income until the consumer finds himself or herself back on the original indifference curve. This hypothetical budget line, then, is *HH'* and is parallel to *BB''*. Faced with constant utility and a lower price of *x*, the consumer moves from point *A* to point *D* on indifference curve I. The movement is the substitution effect, measured by the change in quantity consumed, from x_1 to x_3. Now we give back the income taken away from the consumer and move to the new optimum consumption on indifference curve II, at point *C*. The movement is the income effect. It is measured by the distance inward from x_3 to x_2. This is the case of an inferior good that has, by definition, a negative income elasticity of demand.

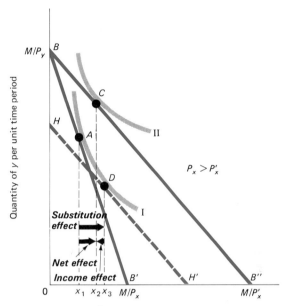

direction in quantity demanded. This can be seen in Figure 4-12, which is like Figure 4-11 except that the consumer's preference pattern is somewhat different. We start off at an optimum at point *A* in Figure 4-12, with a price of P_x and a quantity of x demanded, x_1. As in the prior case, when there is a reduction in the price from P_x to P'_x, there is an increase in the quantity demanded to x_2. Now we wish to sort out how much of that increase is due to the income effect and how much is due to the substitution effect.

First, we obtain the substitution effect by rotating the budget constraint *BB'* along the original indifference curve until it becomes *HH'*. That is, we rotate it to the point of tangency with the original indifference curve that reflects the new price ratio P_x/P'_y. We can see that the substitution effect always involves an inverse relationship between changes in a commodity's own price and the associated changes in quantity demanded. Therefore, at a lower price, quantity demanded increases; and at a higher price, quantity demanded decreases, *holding real income constant*. A reduction in the relative price of x leads to an increase in consumption of x, here from x_1 to x_3.

Now we find the income effect. We increase income by the amount *H'B''* as measured in terms of good x, or *HB* as measured in terms of good y. We end up at point *C*, the new point of consumer optimum on a higher indifference curve. Notice, however, that the movement from *D* to *C* is a negative one along the x axis—that is, a reduction in the quantity purchased of good x. The increase in real income has caused this consumer to purchase less of x by the distance x_3 to x_2. Thus, the income effect in this example is negative, or inverse; this is an inferior good. However, in this case the substitution effect is still larger than the negative income effect, and, consequently, the law of demand still holds.

Notice an important point. The substitution effect always requires an inverse relationship between a change in the price of a good and a change in the quantity demanded of that good. However, the income effect allows for either a direct or inverse relationship between changes in the consumer's *real income* and changes in the quantity demanded of that good (depending on whether the good is normal or inferior). When P_x falls, the consumer buys more x due to the substitution effect. However, the fall in P_x also increases real income. The consumer buys more x due to the increase in real income if x is normal, and less x if x is inferior. Thus, for all normal goods the income effect of a price change reinforces the substitution effect.

WHEN THE LAW OF DEMAND DOESN'T HOLD: GIFFEN'S PARADOX

When we are dealing with a strongly inferior good, it is conceivable—although unlikely—that the demand curve of an individual consumer for that good, called a **Giffen good**, will be positively sloped. This situation, illustrated by Figure 4-13, is due to the negative relationship between income and the quantity of inferior goods demanded. Assume that the price of x falls. This decline in the price of x will lower the alternative cost of x to consumers and raise the quantity demanded of x. However, the same price decrease will raise consumers' real incomes. If x is inferior, the increase in real income will lower the quantity demanded of x. It is possible that the decrease in x demanded due to the income effect may more than offset the increase in x demanded due to the substitution effect. Thus, on net, a decline in the price of x would lower the quantity of x demanded by this consumer.

This situation is unlikely in modern economies because it requires that expenditures on the Giffen good, as a good which follows this pattern is called, be a large proportion of the consumer's total budget and that the change in the price of this good be a large proportion of its original price. In any case, as we note in the following, what may be true for some particular consumers is seldom true for the market. The purported historical instances at the market level of this phenomenon, called "Giffen's paradox"—such as the famous Irish potato famine—are usually the result of bad statistics combined with worse reasoning.

Alternative concepts of demand curves

One way of eliminating Giffen's paradox as a theoretical possibility is to redefine demand in terms closer to our concept of real income. In our previous discussion, we discovered that there was a close relation between real

FIGURE 4-13

The case of the Giffen good

We start off in optimum consumption at point
A, where indifference curve I is just tangent to
the budget line BB', which is given for money
income M and prices P_y and P_x. We now
reduce the price of x to P'_x. The budget line
rotates out to BB''. In this case, the new
optimum consumption is at point C. The
quantity of x demanded has fallen from x_1 to x_2.
In order to ferret out the income and
substitution effects, we hypothetically take
away enough income to keep the consumer on
the original indifference curve I. This new
budget line is HH'. With the same utility or
"real income" and lower relative price of x, the
consumer increases his or her consumption of
x. The substitution effect is measured by the
movement from x_1 to x_3. Now we give back to
the consumer the income that we took away,
moving from point D to point C. The income
effect (x_3 to x_2) is strongly negative and
outweighs the substitution effect, such that the
net effect of a reduction in the price is a
decrease in the quantity demanded.

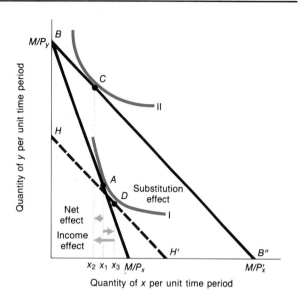

income and the consumer's attainable utility level. We used this insight in
constructing Figure 4-11, and we can now use it to arrive at a "real income
constant demand curve."[6]

In Figure 4-11, the total effect of the price change (given by the change
in the quantity of x demanded from point A to point C) corresponds to the
movement along the corresponding money income constant demand curve
for this price change. However, the substitution effect of this price change
(given by the change in the quantity of x demanded from point A to point
D), corresponds to the movement along the real income constant demand
curve for x. Starting out from some base price and quantity, like that given
by point A, the demand for x will be more elastic along the money income
constant demand curve than along the real income constant demand curve,
so long as x is a normal good, as we see in Figure 4-14(a).

If x is an inferior good, the change in the quantity of x demanded on a
real income constant basis will always be more than the change in the quantity of x demanded on a money income constant basis, as we see in Figure
4-14(b). This is because the income effect is negative for an inferior good
and the total effect is, thus, always smaller than the substitution effect.

[6]See Milton Friedman, "The Marshallian Demand Curve," *Journal of Political Economy*,
vol. 57, 1949, pp. 463–495; and Martin Bailey, "The Marshallian Demand Curve," *Journal of
Political Economy*, vol. 62, 1954, pp. 255–261, for a discussion of real income constant demand
curves and comparisons of price elasticity for a money income constant (Marshall), real income
constant (Hicks), and apparent real income constant (Slutsky) demand curves.

FIGURE 4-14
Money income constant and real income constant demand curves
Panel (a) illustrates the relationship between the two curves, starting from base point A, when x is a normal good. Panel (b) illustrates the relationship between the curves when x is an inferior good. These differences emerge, respectively, from the analysis developed in Figures 4-11 and 4-12.

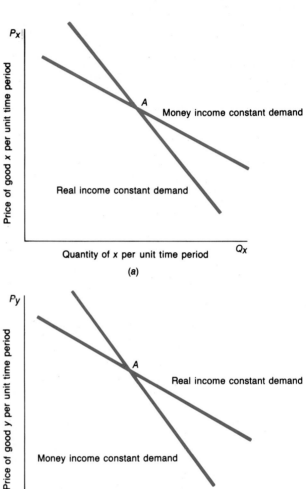

DERIVATION OF INCOME AND SUBSTITUTION
EFFECTS: AN ALTERNATIVE TECHNIQUE

To this point our derivation of substitution and income effects of a price change was based on altering the consumer's level of real income after the relative price change so that the consumer remains on the original indifference curve. This technique has been called the Hicksian approach, named after Sir John R. Hicks, an English economist. It has been criticized for its lack of real-world applicability because it is impossible to know by exactly how much income should be altered in order to keep the individual consumer on the original indifference curve. An alternative approach to analyzing the income effects and substitution effects has been developed. It involves hypothetically altering the consumer's income in such a way that the consumer could purchase the same bundle of commodities as was purchased before the price change. We impose an imaginary lump-sum tax to eliminate the income effect and isolate the substitution effect. Then we refund the tax to see the income effect. This is the so-called Slutsky technique, named after the Russian economist Eugene Slutsky (1880–1948).

This procedure for separating the income and substitution effects of a price change is presented in Figure 4-15. The diagram in many respects is the same as in Figure 4-11. The original budget line is BB' with prices P_y and P_x. The price of x falls to P'_x; the new budget line rotates counterclockwise to BB''. The consumer moves from optimum point A and consumption of x_1 to optimum point C and increased consumption of x_2.

To obtain the pure substitution effect, we have to find out how much more of x the consumer will buy strictly as a result of the new lower price which attracts him or her to give up some y (which hasn't changed in price) in order to buy more of x, which is now less expensive relative to y than it was. To do this, we must draw a hypothetical budget line that reflects the new relative price ratio P_y/P'_x in the consumer's original situation (where the price ratio was P_y/P_x) and see what happens there. In effect, what we will

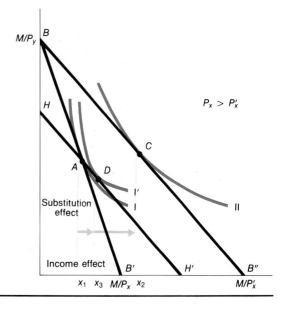

FIGURE 4-15
Income and substitution effect: the Slutsky method
This figure is essentially the same as Figure 4-11; however, instead of taking away income so as to keep the individual on the original indifference curve I, we take away just enough income to allow the consumer to purchase the original combination of x and y. Thus, we hypothetically reduce income after the relative price change so that a consumer is forced back to HH', which goes through point A, the original consumption optimum. Now the consumer faces the new relative price with constant purchasing power. The substitution effect is measured by the movement of quantity purchased from x_1 to x_3. Now we give back to the consumer the income that we took away, and we move from point D to point C, or from x_3 to x_2. This represents the income effect.

do with this hypothetical budget line is remove some of the consumer's new income.

Therefore, we draw the hypothetical budget line HH', which is exactly parallel to the new budget line BB'' and intersects point A, the original optimum point. Now we ask ourselves the following question: At its new relative price, how much of x would the consumer purchase? The answer isn't on the original indifference curve I because this hypothetical budget line cannot be tangent to that curve. The answer must be on a higher indifference curve. The answer is given by finding the point of tangency of the highest indifference curve to the new (Slutsky-compensated) budget line HH'. This is at point D. Thus the quantity of x represented by the horizontal distance from x_1 to x_3 represents the substitution effect. The income effect is given by the horizontal distance from x_3 to x_2.

For very small changes in prices, whether we use the Hicks technique or the Slutsky technique to derive the income and substitution effects makes little difference.

RELAXING THE ASSUMPTION OF FULL KNOWLEDGE

All the analysis so far has implicitly assumed that the consumer has full knowledge about the prices, availability, and qualities of the goods in question. When we relax the assumption of full knowledge, we have a slightly different situation.

Markets and transaction costs

As we pointed out in Chapter 2, economic activities take place in markets. Market mechanisms were defined as information networks that allow potential buyers and sellers to keep in touch with each other. Market mechanisms are often set up to minimize transactions costs.

But what are **transactions costs**? We can define them as all of the costs of enabling exchanges to take place. Transactions costs include the cost of being informed about the qualities of a particular product. The general nature of a product can include its price, availability, durability record, servicing facilities, degree of safety, warranties provided, and so on. Consider, for example, the transactions costs in shopping for a 10-speed bicycle. Such costs would include phone calls or actual visits to sellers in order to learn about product features and prices. These are transactions costs. In addition to these costs, we must include the costs of negotiating a sale. The specification and execution of any sales contract is thus included, and ultimately, transactions costs must include the cost of enforcing such contracts.

Without going into a full discussion of the theory of transactions costs, we can point out here that their relative magnitude is related to the following:

1 The number of distinct transactions per unit time period
2 The volume of goods traded per unit time period
3 The number of distinct parties involved in each transaction
4 The number of distinct goods per transaction

Information and price dispersion

Ignoring for the moment questions about the quality and availability of a product, let us dwell only on the fact of life that price dispersion exists even for homogeneous products, that is, products having similar qualities. Even if a product's attributes are well defined, it is often possible to purchase it at different prices from different sellers. Identical automobile models with exactly the same features may be sold at different prices by different dealers.

The relaxation of our assumption of full information, in the face of price dispersion, can be looked at as a situation of consumer choice with uncertainty. "Uncertainty," in this example, is uncertainty about where the product can be bought at the lowest price and about whether additional searching will find a lower price than we have already discovered. We now can define the term "information" in the context of price to mean a change in the consumer's knowledge of prices. Information generation is an active process. Acquiring information is therefore costly; it uses such resources as time and money income. As such, some **information costs** are transactions costs. However, Robinson Crusoe (before Friday's arrival on the scene) would have incurred information costs, but no transactions costs, because he was alone and therefore had no one with whom to exchange.

The optimal search process

Consider now a typical situation in which there is price dispersion and incomplete information about that dispersion. The consumer must engage in a search. But how much time should the consumer spend searching? Clearly not an infinite amount, because time is a scarce resource. Moreover, a consumer's search for a lower price must eventually run into what must be called "diminishing" marginal returns. Beyond some point, the expected reduction in unit price is less than the unit cost of the additional search time and effort. After a while, the consumer will find it more difficult to locate a seller who is going to sell the product at a price lower than the lowest price already quoted. Early search efforts are apt to turn up sellers whose prices lie considerably below the average price. After each successive lowest price is found, however, the consumer can expect to encounter more and more firms whose prices are higher. Thus, each time a lower price is found, it is less likely that the consumer in the next search period will encounter a still lower one.[7]

The rational consumer will continue to search for a lower price up to a

_____
[7]This follows from the law of diminishing returns, discussed in Chapter 8.

point at which the expected return from one more unit of search will not cover the cost of that activity.

Four propositions regarding the optimal amount of search to undertake can be made.[8]

1 The greater the price dispersion, the greater the optimal search time, *ceteris paribus.*
2 The greater the percentage of a consumer's total wealth that will be spent on the product in question, the greater the optimal search time. It may be worth an extended search for a new car bargain, but it is not worth the same time to search for a lower price of table salt.
3 The more repetitive the purchase in question, the greater the optimal search time (so long as differential prices among sellers persist).
4 The greater the value of the consumer's time, the smaller the optimal search will be, *ceteris paribus.* Other things being the same, the IBM executive will search less than the lower-salaried IBM filing clerk.

These propositions about search time can explain, for example, why big cities are not so expensive for residents as they are for tourists. Because tourists stay only for a relatively short period of time, it does not pay them to invest much of their relatively scarce time in learning about which are the cheapest-priced restaurants, bookstores, department stores, and so on. Rather, we can expect that rational tourists will frequent "tourist spots." The city resident, however, makes repeated purchases and hence will invest a larger amount of time searching for and acquiring information about where the prices of commodities are lowest.

The above argument may also explain the success of franchised fast-food and lodging chains. Although it may appear that the price to tourists is higher than the price to nontourists for "similar" commodities, such may not be the case. The services offered to tourists may be different. There may be more advertising and use of nationally standardized products, both of which are costly. The tourist's time is more valuable, in a sense, than the nontourist's time in any particular city the tourist is visiting. The tourist just doesn't have the time for shopping that the nontourist does. The tourist ends up at the Hilton or the Holiday Inn and pays for advertising, cleanliness, and the assurance of a standardized product. In other words, the information about the expected quality of the product has a value for the tourist, and the tourist is often willing to pay for it in order to avoid searching and to reduce risk.

We conclude by stating that the full price paid for a commodity is the money price plus the transactions costs.

---

[8]A detailed discussion can be found in G. Stigler, "The Economics of Information," *Journal of Political Economy,* vol. 69, no. 3, June 1961.

Can we measure a change in living standards?

We live in a dynamic world. Prices change, and so do the consumption combinations that individuals purchase. We often attempt to make comparisons between two time periods. One frequent question is, Has our standard of living increased? In this application of theory, we make an attempt at showing when we can definitely say that the consumer is better off and when we cannot.

EXAMINING THE COMMODITY SPACE: NO KNOWLEDGE OF CONSUMER'S INDIFFERENCE CURVES ASSUMED

Let us go back to a commodity space where good x is on the horizontal axis and good y is on the vertical axis. We have no knowledge of the individual consumer's preference map. All we assume is that the consumer makes rational choices: The consumer chooses an optimum combination of goods x and y for his or her income and the prices that must be paid in each period.

Look at Figure 4-16. Here we start off in period 1 with budget line BB'. The consumer has revealed his or her optimum combination of x and y to be at point A_1. Since we are talking about commodities, we know that any combination that yields more of both x and y would be preferred to combination A_1. Now consider the situation in which the period 2 budget line has greater intercepts on both the x and y axes than does the original budget line. The individual consumer's purchasing power over both commodity x and commodity y has increased. The consumer's revealed optimum, shown in Figure 4-16, is at combination A_2 on the new budget line CC'. In this case, the consumer is able to (and does) buy more of x and more of y. The consumer is unquestionably better off.

If the new budget line *intersects* the old budget line, it is more difficult to say whether the consumer is better off, i.e., has a higher level of material welfare. However, in *some* situations we can be certain that the consumer is unambiguously better off, even though the new and the old budget lines intersect. This is shown in Figure 4-17. Here we show the period 1 budget line to be, again, BB'. The consumer optimum is at combination A_1. Now the budget line changes to CC' in time period 2. The preferred consumer optimum is revealed to be at combination A_2. Since A_2 lies within the quadrant shown within the shaded area, every point of which is above combination A_1, we know that the consumer is unambiguously better off in period 2 because both good x and good y are being consumed in greater quantities. The consumer has attained a consumption basket A_2 that *dominates* the consumption basket A_1.

Consider the situation in Figure 4-18. In period 2, the optimum consumption combination is not within the quadrant shown by the dashed lines immediately above and to the right of first-period consumer optimum combination A_1. Here we do not have a situation in which the second-period optimum consumption basket of goods completely dominates the basket of goods chosen in period 1. The outside observer who does not have knowledge of the individual consumer's indifference map cannot draw a conclusion from the observation of points A_1 and A_2. In other words, without knowing the indifference curves, one does not know whether A_2 is on a higher or a lower indifference curve than A_1.

In some situations, at first glance it does

FIGURE 4-16
Increase in standard of living:
the dominant case

Assume that the consumer starts with combination A_1 on budget line BB'. Any point within the area immediately above and to the right of point A_1 is definitely preferred because it includes at least as much of both goods and more of at least one of the two goods. If income and prices change so that the new budget line is CC' and the consumer's revealed preferred position is at point A_2, we can unambiguously state that the consumer is better off. (Any point on CC' has to represent an increase in welfare because the consumer can still buy combination A_1 if he or she chooses, but only in the shaded box can we express the dominant case, in which at least as much of one good is available and more of the other is also available.) Even if the individual doesn't buy a bundle in the shaded area, the CC' case is still dominant. The reasoning is as follows: A_2 is preferred to A_1 by the nonsatiation assumption. If the individual buys any bundle on the CC' budget not in the shaded area (call it A_3), A_3 is at worst indifferent to A_2, and more likely is preferred to A_2. By the transitivity assumption, A_3 must be preferred to A_1.

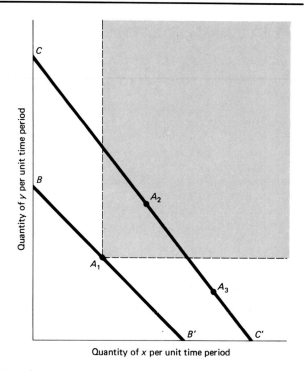

FIGURE 4-17
Increase in standard of living:
the nondominant case

The consumer starts with combination A_1. Relative prices and income change so that the new budget line CC' intersects the old budget line. However, if by his or her revealed preference the consumer chooses point A_2, we can unambiguously say that the consumer is better off because that point occurs within the quadrant bounded by lines immediately above and immediately to the right of point A_1.

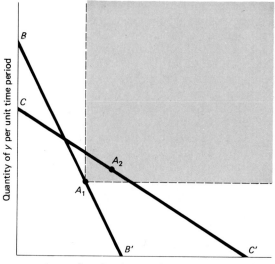

FIGURE 4-18
*Assessing a standard-of-living change:
the ambiguous case*
We start off with budget line *BB'*. The consumer
places himself or herself at point A_1. Now
prices and income change so that the
consumer faces budget line *CC'*. The consumer
then chooses point A_2. Without knowledge of
the consumer's preferences, we cannot
unambiguously state that the consumer is
better off. Only in situations in which A_2 lies
within the quadrant immediately to the right of
and immediately above A_1 can we be sure that
the combination in the second period
dominates the combination in the first period.

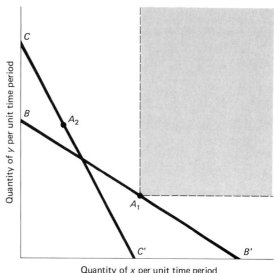

not seem that we can unambiguously state
whether the consumer is better off or worse
off after a change in income and in the relative
prices of x and y. Nonetheless, we can make
an unambiguous statement if we are willing
to make inferences from the consumer's behavior. Look at Figure 4-19. We start off in
period 1, as before, with budget line *BB'*. The
consumer chooses bundle of goods A_1. Note
that the consumer could have chosen any other
bundle of goods along the budget line *BB'* or
anywhere within the entire budget constraint
that is the dotted area below *BB'* in Figure 4-
19. But since the consumer did not choose any
other bundle of goods, it is clear that the consumer is best off with the combination A_1. Now,
in period 2, the budget line moves to *CC'*. The
consumer chooses combination A_2. A_2 clearly
does not lie within the quadrant immediately
above and to the right of A_1, as it did not in
the previous figure, Figure 4-18. However, A_2
lies within the period 1 budget constraint. Since
A_2 was not chosen in period 1, we infer that
it is inferior to combination A_1. Hence we can
state by inference that if preferences have not
changed, the standard of living of this con-

sumer must have *fallen* between period 1 and
period 2 as a result of the income and price
changes. This can be inferred without any
knowledge of the indifference curves of the
consumer.

A similar analysis can be applied to show
that there has been an unequivocal rise in the
standard of living of the consumer, even though
we are not in the dominant situation. Look at
Figure 4-20. In period 1, the preferred combination is A_1. In period 2, the preferred combination is A_2. Clearly, A_2 does not lie within
the quadrant immediately above and to the
right of first-period combination A_1. Thus we
cannot state unambiguously that the period 2
combination dominates the period 1 combination. However, we do know that in period
2 the budget constraint includes the entire
shaded area under budget line *CC'*. Combination A_1 is therefore possible in period 2.
However, by the consumer's revealed preference, we know that combination A_2 is preferred. Thus, we can infer that there has been
an increase in the consumer's standard of
living.

Not all implications of indifference anal-

FIGURE 4-19
An unambiguous reduction in the standard of living: the nondominant case

The consumer starts off at point A_1. Anywhere within the dotted area is feasible in period 1 because it is to the left of the budget line BB'. Prices and income change so that in period 2 the consumer faces budget line CC'. The consumer chooses bundle A_2. It does not lie within the dominant area immediately above and to the right of point A_1. Moreover, it was not chosen in period 1 even though it could have been; therefore, it must be inferior to bundle A_1 and the standard of living must have fallen.

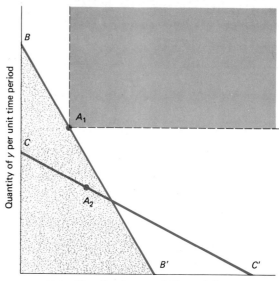

FIGURE 4-20
A rise in the standard of living: the nondominant case

In period 1 the consumer is at point A_1. Anywhere above and to the right of that point represents more of at least one of the goods and is therefore in the dominant area. In period 2, money income and prices change so that the budget line facing the consumer is CC'. The consumer chooses point A_2, which is not in the dominant area. However, in period 2 the consumer could have chosen any point within the dotted area below and to the left of budget line CC'; however, the consumer did not choose A_1. Therefore, the consumer must have preferred A_2 to A_1 and is therefore better off. We infer that the consumer has experienced a rise in his or her standard of living.

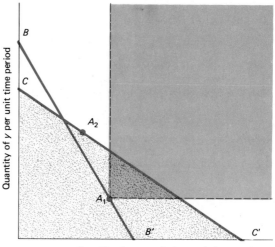

ysis are as intuitive as you might at first believe. One such surprising implication of indifference analysis is the effect on a consumer's
utility level of a change in prices when the
consumer is left with the same apparent purchasing power before and after the price
change.

Assume that the consumer is initially consuming at point A along budget line BB' in
Figure 4-21. After a change in the relative prices
of x and y, the new budget line, CC', crosses
BB' at point A. Since the consumer can purchase A before and after the price change, he
or she has the same "apparent" real income.

Will this change in relative prices make
the consumer better or worse off, or will it
have no effect on the consumer's utility level?
Our intuition might tell us that the consumer
will be unaffected by the change or that the
effect will be indeterminant, but that intuition
is wrong. If the consumer's indifference curves
are normally shaped (convex to the origin and
continuous), the consumer will necessarily
benefit by the price change.

The graphics of this case are straightfor-

ward. After the price change, the new budget
line (labeled CC' in Figure 4-21) necessarily
cuts the consumer's original indifference curve,
curve I, *in such a way that some portion of the
new budget line is above indifference curve
I.* The consumer can move into this portion of
the new budget line and thus reach a higher
indifference curve than before. In Figure 4-21
the price change involved a decrease in the
price of good x and a corresponding increase
in the price of good y. We can see the same
result, however, if the price change was in
the opposite direction. In Figure 4-22 the price
of good x increases and the price of good y
falls.

Although the reasons for this result may
seem somewhat mysterious, the result actually follows from some of our basic assumptions. Of all the combinations of goods
x and y available to the consumer before the
price change, the bundle shown by point A
was chosen. Since this bundle is still available after the price change, the consumer cannot be any worse off, although he or she can
no longer choose to consume any of the bun-

FIGURE 4-21

Apparent real income constant
The consumer is originally at point A along
budget constraint BB'. The relative prices of
goods x and y change, shifting the budget
constraint to CC'. Since y has become more
expensive relative to x, the consumer shifts
consumption to point H, which produces a
higher level of satisfaction than the consumer
had before. Although at point A the apparent
real income is constant for the old and new
price levels, the change in prices has left this
consumer at a higher utility.

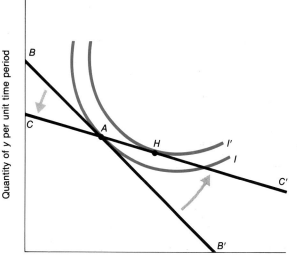

Quantity of x per unit time period

FIGURE 4-22
Apparent real income constant
The consumer is originally at point A. The price of y falls relative to price x, shifting the budget constraint from BB' to CC'. The consumer moves form point A to point H, a higher utility in relative prices, since the consumer can still purchase the quantities at point A, the price change cannot make the consumer worse off.

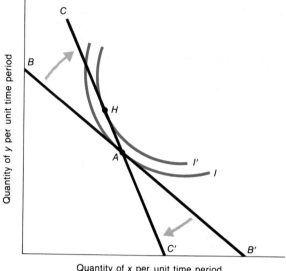

Quantity of x per unit time period

dles in triangles CBA and C'B'A in Figures 4-21 and 4-22. The consumer can, however, choose from a variety of new bundles of x and y after the price change, as shown by the new choice areas B'AC' and BAC, respectively on the graphs. Since more choices are now available, it seems reasonable to expect that one

or more of them may be preferred to the previous alter natives.

The kind of apparent real income constant change in relative prices just described is useful in distinguishing the impact of real and money income changes in statistical demand studies.

Irish potatoes and Giffen's paradox

Giffen's paradox of upward-sloping demand may sometimes characterize the behavior of individual consumers, but there is little evidence to indicate that it has ever held true at the market level.

The Irish potato famine of 1845–46 is a widely cited situation that supposedly illustrates a real-world Giffen good. In 1845, a fungus infection destroyed about one-half of the potato crop in Ireland, and in 1846 the same

fungus destroyed about 90 percent of the potato crop. Potatoes were widely consumed in Ireland and formed a large portion of the diet and expenditures of the typical Irish peasant. The cultivation and marketing of potatoes also accounted for a significant portion of peasant income. Ireland was essentially a closed market in potatoes, growing most of what was consumed and selling little to other countries. Available data indicate that the market price

FIGURE 4-23
Market behavior under Giffen's paradox
For the paradox to hold, the demand curve
must be upward-sloping, so that as the supply
falls the market price falls. Even stranger, if
demand increases, market price falls. There is
no evidence of a market ever operating like
this.

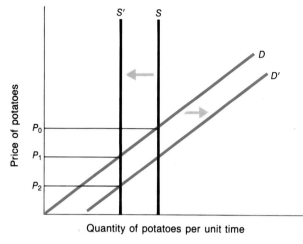

Market behaving according to Giffen's paradox

FIGURE 4-24
Individual behavior under Giffen's paradox
We may observe for some individuals that as the price of the good rises the quantity they demand rises, giving
them an upward-sloping demand curve during a particular time period.

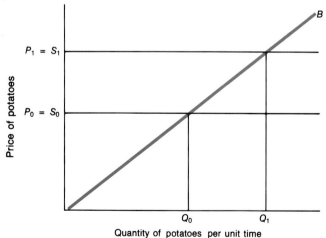

Individual behaving according to Giffen's paradox

of potatoes rose in Ireland during the years of the famine and remained "high" for several years thereafter. How can we analyze this situation?

First of all, it is clear that market demand could not be upward-sloping, as Giffen's paradox would require. If demand is constant and upward-sloping, then, as market supply falls, market price will also fall (from P_0 to P_1 in Figure 4-23). Price would fall even further (from P_1 to P_2) if we assume, as is likely, that po-

tatoes are an inferior good and that consumer money income decreased during the years of the famine. Yet the market price of potatoes in Ireland increased, rather than decreased, during the famine years.

While it is possible that some individual, competitive consumers increased rather than decreased their purchases of potatoes as the price rose (see Figure 4-24), they must have represented a small portion of total market demand.

The effect of income taxes on work effort: What is the supply curve of labor?

We can use indifference curve analysis to analyze the effect of an income tax on the quantity of work effort supplied. At the same time we can also determine the income and substitution effects of a change in the rate of income taxation.

We will make some simplifying assumptions for this issue: (1) We will assume that we start out in a situation where there are no income taxes. (2) We will assume that the income tax imposed is a proportional one, that is, a constant percentage levied on every dollar earned. (3) We will assume that there are only two goods, leisure and "all other goods," where all other goods refers to money income derived from working.

Look at Figure 4-25. We measure leisure per unit time period on the horizontal axis and all other goods on the vertical axis. The maximum amount of leisure possible is some fixed quantity L. It really doesn't matter at what time period we are looking because we are still faced with a specified physical maximum of leisure that an individual can take. Assuming that the individual lumps together all activities other than work under the heading of leisure, if our time period is a day, L equals

24 hours per day. Given that the maximum amount of leisure available is fixed, any reduction in leisure means an increase in work and vice versa.

On the vertical axis we measure "all other goods." But what are all other goods? They are everything besides leisure; in other words, they are all the things that money income can buy. We could alternatively label the vertical axis "money income." The maximum amount of all other goods possible is equal to the total amount of money income that could be earned if zero leisure were consumed. This is the vertical distance $0Y$. We now have two extreme points that define the budget constraint in our rather peculiar commodity space in Figure 4-25. If only "all other goods" are purchased, the maximum amount that can be purchased is $0Y$. If only leisure is purchased, the maximum amount available is $0L$. When we connect these two points, we get the budget line labeled WW'. Notice that the negative of the slope of this budget line—(Δ money income/Δ leisure)—is the wage rate. After all, what is the "price" of obtaining one more unit of leisure? It is the wage rate for that time period that has been sacrificed or forgone. Since the

FIGURE 4-25
The labor-leisure budget constaint
On the horizontal axis we measure the quantity of leisure per unit time period. The maximum amount is some time period such as 24 hours per day. On the vertical axis, we measure all other goods per unit time period. This is equivalent to money income earned by working. If there is no leisure, then the maximum amount of income that can be earned is Y. This gives us two points on a labor-leisure budget line that is labeled WW'. If leisure is decreased by 1 hour, the increase in money income or income available to purchase all other goods goes up by the wage rate per hour, the negative of the slope of the budget line WW'.

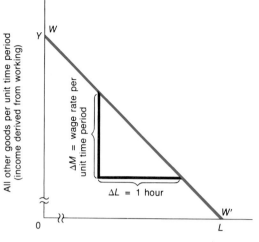

wage rate is positive, the slope of the budget line is equal to the negative of the wage rate, or $-w$.

In Figure 4-26 the initial budget line facing the worker is WL. Given the worker's indifference curve II, the quantity of leisure demanded will be L_2, which is determined at point A, where curve II is tangent to the budget line. Note that if the worker took no leisure and devoted all his or her time to working during the time period, the take-home income would be $0W$.

Now we impose an income tax. What does the income tax do? To answer that, let's first consider that price of leisure is the opportunity cost of not working. Without a tax, the opportunity cost of not working is exactly equal to a worker's total wages for the period (assuming that there are no deductions for other things, e.g., pension, Social Security, etc.). With an income tax, the cost of not working is equal to the net (after-tax), or take-home, wages. Since the income tax reduces the take-home pay, the opportunity cost of not working is lower; this is the same as saying that the

income tax lowers the relative price of leisure. Now, if the worker took no leisure and devoted all his or her time to working during the time period, the take-home income would be $0W'$, which is less than $0W$ by the amount of the tax deducted from income. This rotates the budget line WL counterclockwise to $W'L$, the taxed budget line. Effectively, this means that income taxes reduce the price of leisure with respect to all other goods (income for the period).[9]

What happens when the consumer is faced with a proportional income tax? In our particular example, this consumer will go to a new optimum at point B, where he or she consumes a new quantity of leisure L_1. Since leisure is measured on the horizontal axis, L_1 represents a reduction in the quantity of leisure demanded and therefore an increase in the total

[9]However, it has been shown that the wage rate is biased upward as a measure of the cost of leisure. We say this because, in general, there is disutility associated with work but not with leisure. See M. Bruce Johnson, "Travel Time and the Price of Leisure," *Western Economic Journal,* Spring 1966, pp. 135–145.

FIGURE 4-26
The effects of a proportionate income tax on work effort

The consumer starts out with quantity of leisure demanded L_2 at the consumption optimum point A. A proportionate income tax reduces the amount of money income that is earned per hour of work. If no leisure were consumed, i.e., the individual worked all the time, instead of being able to buy $W0$ of all other goods, the consumer now could buy only $W'0$ of all other goods. The budget line rotates counterclockwise to $W'L$. The new consumption optimum is at point B. The quantity of leisure demanded has fallen from L_2 to L_1. Even though the price of leisure is lower because the take-home pay is lower, the consumer works more to make up for the lost income. To derive the substitution and income effects, we hypothetically increase the consumer's income so that he or she is on the old indifference curve II. The hypothetical budget line facing the consumer is now NN'. With the lower price of leisure, the consumer moves from point A to point C and the substitution effect is negative. Now we take away the income that we hypothetically gave the consumer. The consumer moves from point C to point B. The distance from L_3 to L_1 is the income effect.

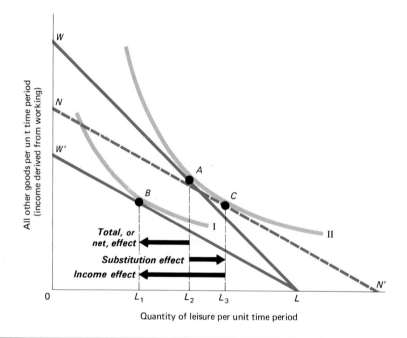

number of hours worked. Why does this consumer work more? Because the income effect outweighed the substitution effect. In other words, the income tax reduced the consumer's income by so much that, even though leisure had become cheaper in this case, the consumer worked more to try to make up some of the lost income that went into taxes.

We can find the substitution effect by drawing in a hypothetical budget constraint that leaves the worker on the same indifference curve II but presents him or her with the new lower relative price of leisure. This is the hypothetical budget line NN', which has the same slope as $W'L$ and is tangent to indifference curve II. Along this hypothetical budget line, the consumer optimum is at C. A larger quantity of leisure L_3 would be bought. The substitution effect is always negative. The lower price of leisure has to lead to a larger quantity demanded; it costs less *not* to work. However, the income effect is measured by the horizontal displacement from C to B, which is the reduction in leisure from L_3 to L_1. It is highly positive because a reduction in income has led to a dramatic reduction in the quantity of leisure demanded. In other words, leisure is clearly a normal good. The normal nature of leisure is verified by experience. For example, windfall gains, such as those acquired by winning the Irish Sweepstakes or the New York State lottery, usually result in more rather than less leisure consumed.

We can turn the analysis around and ask what will happen as the take-home wage rate is increased. In other words, what happens to the quantity of work effort, or the quantity of labor supplied, as wage rates rise? One hypothetical example is given in Figure 4-27. We keep raising the take-home wage rate—represented by the slope of the budget line—so that the budget constraint rotates upward from

---

FIGURE 4-27

Derivation of a labor supply curve

In panel (a) we progressively increase the wage rate—the slope of the budget line—so that the budget line rotates clockwise from $L'L$ to $L''L$ to $L'''L$. The consumer moves to successively high indifference curves, from I to II to III. The optimum consumption moves from E to E' to E''. At first, the amount of leisure consumed falls because the substitution effect overrides the income effect; later the quantity of leisure demanded rises as income rises because the income effect overrides the substitution effect. The result, shown in panel (b), is a backward-bending supply curve for labor. Above the wage rate where SS starts to turn backward, the income effect is overriding the substitution effect— the individual is so much richer that he or she purchases more leisure in spite of its much higher relative price.

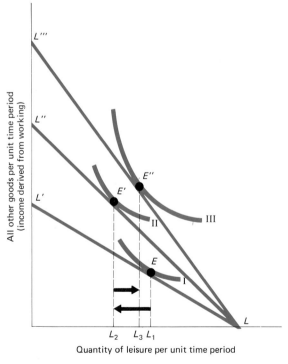

(a)

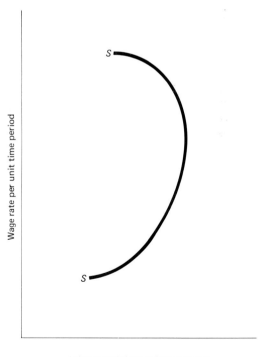

(b)

$L'L$ to $L''L$ and finally to $L'''L$. The indifference curves are tangent to these various budget constraints at E, E', and E''. An increase in wage rates which causes the budget constraint to move from $L'L$ to $L''L$ leads to a reduction in the quantity of leisure demanded from L_1 to L_2. In this case, the substitution effect overrides the income effect. Even though workers are richer, i.e., have more income to spend on all goods, including leisure, they purchase less leisure because the opportunity cost of leisure has risen so much. However, when wage rates rise so that the new budget constraint is LL''', the situation is similar to the one presented in Figure 4-26 (but in the opposite direction). The new point of consumer optimum is at E''. The new quantity of leisure purchased is L_3. In other words, more leisure is purchased, even though its opportunity cost, or price, has gone up. In *this* case, the income effect overrides the substitution effect.

If we take the various rates and quantity of work effort and plot them on a separate diagram in panel (b) of Figure 4-27, we get a supply curve for labor SS that shows the relation between the wage rate and the quantity of labor forthcoming per unit time period. [The wage rate can be obtained from panel (a) by measuring the negative of the slope of the budget constraint.] Note that the supply curve SS is backward-bending. At some point, higher wage rates lead the individual worker to work less rather than more. This begins the point at which the income effect begins to override the substitution effect. Although a backward-bending supply curve for labor is impossible in the aggregate,[10] we would expect any particular worker to respond to unanticipated changes in the wage rate as shown in Figure 4-27 (a) and (b). If you study macroeconomics in another course, you will see this concept again in the "permanent-income hypothesis."

---

[10]In the aggregate, there is no net income effect when we hold community opportunities as given or constant. Higher wage rates mean less return to other nonhuman assets. In turn, this means that an income-compensated supply curve of labor must be of the normal sort—i.e., as the wage rate rises, more labor is offered. See Yoram Barzel and Richard J. McDonald, "Assets, Subsistence, and the Supply Curve of Labor," *The American Economic Review*, vol. 63, no. 4, September 1973, pp. 621–633.

SUMMARY

1   If we hold relative and nominal prices constant and increase money income, we shift the budget line outward. If we connect the tangency points between the indifference curves and the budget lines, we derive the income-consumption curve, which shows the combinations of x and y that will be chosen as income changes.

2   A normal good is one that an individual buys more of as his or her income increases and buys less of as income decreases. An inferior good is a good that a consumer buys less of as income increases and more of as income decreases.

3   It is important to remember that the terms "normal" and "inferior" carry with them no value judgment; i.e., they are *not* descriptive of some subjective feeling that all consumers have about a particular commodity.

4   Engel curves are derived by considering the change in the quantity purchased of only one commodity as relative prices remain constant and

income changes. In a diagram with x on the horizontal axis and income on the vertical axis, an upward curvature indicates less than a one-for-one increase in quantity demanded as income goes up; a downward curvature indicates the opposite.

5 When the Engel curve slopes backward, or has a negative slope, the good is inferior.

6 Since the consumer faces a budget constraint, the separate Engel curves for all the commodities in the consumer's market basket of commodities purchased are not independent.

7 We derive the price-consumption curve by connecting the optimum consumption points when the relative price of one good is changed, while holding the price of the other good and money income constant.

8 We can derive a downward-sloping demand curve from the price-consumption curve by reading off the price-quantity pairs from the latter curve. That demand curve will be downward-sloping in all cases, except the one in which we have extremely strong inferior goods.

9 Whenever demand is price-elastic, consumer expenditures $(P_x \cdot q_x)$ will change in the opposite direction of a price change. When demand is unitary-elastic, consumer expenditures will remain constant for any small change in price. Finally, when demand is price-inelastic, consumer expenditures will change in the direction of a change in price.

10 If we use a diagram with x on the horizontal axis and money income for all other goods on the vertical axis, we can determine price elasticity of demand by the slope of the price-consumption line. When it slopes down, demand for good x is price-elastic; when it is horizontal, demand is unit-elastic; and when it is positively sloped, demand is price-inelastic.

11 Whenever there is a change in the relative price of a commodity, there is also a change in real income, defined as purchasing power. The larger the fraction of the total budget spent on the good whose price fell, the greater the increase in real income, and vice versa.

12 When there is a relative price change, we can separate the two parts of the total effect of that price change: the substitution effect and the income effect. We do this by running an experiment in which we change relative prices and then alter income so as to eliminate the income effect. We can then see the substitution effect that is due to the price change. When we reinstate the individual's original income, we find out what the income effect is.

13 For all normal goods, the income effect reinforces the substitution effect.

14 Only when the income effect is highly negative—the case of a strongly inferior good—is it possible for the income effect to outweigh the

substitution effect and, therefore, for the law of demand not to hold. This is called a Giffen good.

15 Transactions costs are a function of (a) the number of distinct transactions per time period, (b) the volume of goods traded per time period, (c) the number of distinct parties involved, and (d) the number of distinct goods per transaction.

16 The optimal amount of search to undertake depends on (a) the degree of price dispersion, (b) the percentage of the consumer's budget spent on the product, (c) the more repetitive the purchase, and (d) the greater the opportunity cost of the consumer's time.

GLOSSARY

- **income-consumption curve** The locus of optimum consumption points that would occur if income were successively increased, nominal and relative prices remaining constant. In other words, it represents the optimum quantities of goods x and y that would be purchased at various levels of income.
- **normal good** A good of which the consumer purchases more as income increases and whose income elasticity is greater than 0.
- **inferior good** A good of which a consumer purchases less as income increases and whose income elasticity of demand is negative.
- **Engel curve** The locus of points showing the various quantities of a commodity purchased at different levels of income. It is not to be confused with the income-consumption curve, which shows the various combinations of two goods purchased at different levels of income.
- **price-consumption curve** The locus of optimum consumption combinations of goods x and y that the consumer would choose as the relative price of the goods changed while money income remained constant.
- **price elasticity of demand** The responsiveness of quantity demanded to changes in relative price; defined as the proportional change in the quantity demanded divided by the proportional change in the relative price.
- **price-elastic demand** A property of the demand curve; the quantity demanded changes more than in proportion to the change in price. $(\% \Delta Q_x \times 1\% \Delta P_x) > 1$.
- **unitary price elasticity of demand** A property of the demand curve; the quantity demanded changes exactly in proportion to the change in price. $(\% \Delta Q_x \times 1\% \Delta P_x) = 1$.
- **price-inelastic demand** A property of the demand curve; the quantity demanded changes less than in proportion to the change in price. $(\% \Delta Q_x \times 1\% \Delta P_x) < 1$.
- **substitution effect** Relates to the change in the quantity demanded as one good becomes relatively cheaper and the other good becomes relatively more expensive while real income is held constant.
- **income effect** Change in the quantity demanded of a good due to a change in real income while relative prices are held constant.
- **Giffen good** A good that is so strongly inferior that a fall in price induces a reduction in the quantity demanded; i.e., the demand curve slopes upward.

- **transactions costs** All the costs associated with exchange, which include the costs of contracting, the costs of enforcing contracts, and the costs of obtaining information.
- **information costs** Transactions costs, which include the cost of obtaining information on prices, qualities, availability, and the service record in the case of durable goods.

QUESTIONS

(Answers to even-numbered questions are at back of text.)

1   What is the significance of the point at which an indifference curve is tangent to a budget constraint? Explain.
2   Define an inferior and a normal good. Can a good be both? How?
3   In deriving a price-consumption curve, which variables are held constant and which are allowed to change?
4   How is a demand curve derived from a price-consumption curve?
5   Suppose your money income tripled and so did the prices of both of the goods in your two-good world. Does this situation give you data revealing an additional point on your income-consumption curve? Why or why not?
6   Suppose that as nominal money income changes, the nominal price of one of the goods also changes. Why will your efforts to trace out the income-consumption curve be thwarted?
7   Since it is possible for all goods in a consumer's budget to be normal, why can't they all be inferior?
8   Suppose you were determined to buy a business, and you also expected an economic recession (a decline in real national income) to befall the country. Suppose further that you are the only person on the planet who is bearish (pessimistic) on the nation's economic future. What type of business would you buy: one producing an inferior good or a normal good? Why?
9   Is it possible that the demand for a particular good could be both price-inelastic and price-elastic? Explain.
10   When a good's price changes, there are two effects: substitution effect and income effect. Under what circumstances might one be justified in ignoring the income effect of a change in price? Why?
11   "Rice in Asia" is often asserted to be an example of a Giffen good which defies the "law" of demand. Assuming for the moment that the assertion is correct, what is the reasoning underlying it?
12   In light of the fact that information is a scarce commodity, one must decide how much of it to "consume" (generate) before making a decision. Concerning the purchase of a new car, would you expect a movie star to spend more or less time searching than a police officer? Why?
13   Suppose that last year you spent half your income on food and half on rent. This year your nominal income has gone up 10 percent, the price of food has increased 20 percent, and rental rates have not changed. Are you able to determine whether your real income has gone up, has gone down, or has remained unchanged? Why, or why not? Explain.

14 Compare the following three systems of welfare payments:

System 1: $100 per family per week, regardless of whether any family members earn any income on their own.
System 2: $100 per family per week, reduced by $1 for every $3 earned by family members on their own.
System 3: $100 per family per week, reduced by $1 for every $1 earned by family members on their own.

At what level of weekly earnings would a family get off welfare under each of the three systems? Which system appears to have greater incentives for a family to work and to become at least partially self-supporting?

SELECTED REFERENCES

Ferguson, C.E., "Substitution Effect in Value Theory: A Pedagogical Note," *Southern Economic Journal,* vol. 24, 1960, pp. 310–314.
Prais, S.J., and H.S. Houthakker, *The Analysis of Family Budgets* (Cambridge: Cambridge University Press, 1955).
Robbins, Lionel, "On the Elasticity of Demand for Income in Terms of Effort," *Economica,* new ser., vol. 10, November 1930, pp. 245–258; also in American Economic Association, *Readings in the Theory of Income Distribution* (Philadelphia: Blakiston, 1946).
Stigler, George, "The Economics of Information," *Journal of Political Economy,* vol. 69, June 1961, pp. 213–225.
———, "Notes on the History of Giffen Paradox," *Journal of Political Economy,* vol. 40, April 1947.

APPENDIX TO CHAPTER 4

THE SLUTSKY EFFECT MATHEMATICALLY PRESENTED

The income effect can be negative or positive, depending on whether the good is inferior or normal. Since price elasticity of demand relates the change in the quantity demanded to the change in price, it would seem to follow that there is some relation between price elasticity of demand and income elasticity of demand.

Remember that the definition of income elasticity of demand (μ) is the percentage change in the quantity demanded divided by the per- centage change in income. Let us be specific here and refer to *real income.* Thus the coefficient of real income elasticity of demand is defined as

$$\iota = \frac{\Delta q/q}{\Delta R/R} = \frac{\Delta q}{\Delta R} \cdot \frac{R}{q} \qquad (A4\text{-}1)$$

where ι is the Greek *iota* and R is real income (defined as money income divided by the price level, or M/P).

Now let us divide up the change in the quantity demanded due to a change in the relative price of x into its two parts, the substitution effect and the income effect. Thus we will have

$$\Delta q_t = \Delta q_s + \Delta q_i \qquad \text{(A4-2)}$$

where the subscript t refers to the total effect, the subscript s refers to the substitution effect, and the subscript i refers to the real income effect. Thus the total change in the quantity demanded is equal to the change due to the substitution effect (the relative price of x has fallen) plus the income effect (due to a change in real income). Note that real income rises, even though money income doesn't, when the relative price of one good in the market basket of goods falls. After all, if the nominal and relative price of one particular good that is being purchased falls, no other prices change, and money income is constant, it becomes possible to buy more of the now-cheaper good and still purchase the same quantity of all other goods. Hence, real income goes up.

We maintain the equality of the relation given by Eq. (A4-2) when we divide both sides of it by ΔP, which gives us

$$\frac{\Delta q_t}{\Delta P} = \frac{\Delta q_s}{\Delta P} + \frac{\Delta q_i}{\Delta P} \qquad \text{(A4-3)}$$

Now we multiply the last term in Eq. (A4-3) by the quantity $\Delta R/\Delta R \cdot R/R$ (which is equal to 1). When we do this, we obtain

$$\frac{\Delta q_t}{\Delta P} = \frac{\Delta q_s}{\Delta P} + \frac{\Delta q_i}{\Delta P} \cdot \frac{\Delta R}{\Delta R} \cdot \frac{R}{R} \qquad \text{(A4-4)}$$

Now we multiply both sides of Eq. (A4-4) by the same quantity P/q. This does not alter the equality, and we obtain

$$\frac{\Delta q_t}{\Delta P} \cdot \frac{P}{q} = \frac{\Delta q_s}{\Delta P} \cdot \frac{P}{q}$$
$$+ \frac{\Delta q_i}{\Delta P} \cdot \frac{\Delta R}{\Delta R} \cdot \frac{R}{R} \cdot \frac{P}{q} \qquad \text{(A4-5)}$$

In order to simplify this rather messy equation, we have to find an equivalent expression for ΔR, the change in real income. It turns out that

$$\Delta R = -q\Delta P \qquad \text{(A4-6)}$$

Why? Because the change in real income is equal to the amount of income that is released for the purchase of other goods when the relative price of the commodity in question falls and the nominal price of all other goods remains constant.

If, for example, a consumer were buying 100 Big Macs a year at $1 apiece and their price fell by 10¢, that consumer could still buy 100 a year and pay only $90. The increase in real income, or money income, released for the purchase of other goods, is $10 {or $[-100 \cdot (-\$0.10)] = +\$10$}.

Now by substituting the right side of this identity for ΔR in the numerator of the last term in Eq. (A4-5), we obtain

$$\frac{\Delta q_t}{\Delta P} \cdot \frac{P}{q} = \frac{\Delta q_s}{\Delta P} \cdot \frac{P}{q}$$
$$+ \frac{\Delta q_i}{\Delta P} \cdot \frac{(-q\Delta P)}{\Delta R} \cdot \frac{R}{R} \cdot \frac{P}{q} \qquad \text{(A4-7)}$$

In the last term we can "cancel out" the ΔP's and rearrange the terms so that the equation becomes

$$\frac{\Delta q_t/q}{\Delta P/P} = \frac{\Delta q_s/q}{\Delta P/P} - \left(\frac{Pq}{R}\right)\left(\frac{\Delta q_i/q}{\Delta R/R}\right) \qquad \text{(A4-8)}$$

Now we can define two different price elasticities of demand.

The normally defined price elasticity of demand (that is, what we will call the "total price elasticity of demand"), we will denote with the symbol η_t. The total price elasticity of demand is computed with a constant money income but a changed real income. Thus, the left-hand term of Eq. (A4-8) is the total price elasticity of demand η_t.

The price elasticity of demand associated with the substitution effect is computed by holding real income constant. We will denote the price elasticity of demand associated with the substitution effect as η_s. The first term on the right-hand side is the substitution effect price elasticity of demand η_s; and the second parenthetical term on the right is the percentage of real income[1] originally spent on the commodity. The second expression in the second term on the right-hand side of the equation is our definition of the coefficient of the real income elasticity of demand ι. Hence, Eq. (A4-8) can be written as follows:

$$\eta_t = \eta_s - k_\iota \qquad \text{(A4-9)}$$

where we denote the percentage of income spent on the commodity as $k \, (= Pq/R)$.

This equation (due to E. E. Slutsky) indicates that the price elasticity of demand, as normally measured, is a combination of two things: the price elasticity of demand with respect only to a relative price change, plus some fraction of the income elasticity of demand. That fraction is the share of total expenditures taken up by the good in question.

IMPLICATIONS OF THE SLUTSKY EQUATION

Equation (A4-9) allows us to generate some hypotheses about price elasticities of demand. First, we repeat that the substitution effect η_s is al-

ways negative (inverse) because it follows the law of demand. Similarly, k is always positive (direct) because it represents the percentage of income spent on the commodity. We can now determine that when the good in question is a normal good (i.e., η is positive), then (1) the total price elasticity of demand η_t will be negative and (2) η_t will be larger in absolute value (numerically) than η_s.[2] This means that the income effect reinforces the substitution effect.

When x is an inferior (but not Giffen) good, the income elasticity of demand ι is negative. The income effect works counter to the substitution effect; η_t will be smaller numerically than η_s. In the case of a Giffen good, the second term on the right-hand side of Eq. (A4-9) is larger than the first term; the total price elasticity of demand η_t is a positive number; and the demand curve slopes upward.

---

[1] And money income, too, since the initial situation is our base period.

[2] When we refer to the absolute or numerical value of a number, we disregard the sign. Thus, if $\eta_1 = -100$ and $\eta_2 = -10$, then the former is greater numerically than the latter, i.e., η_1 is greater in absolute value than η_2, or $|\eta_1| > |\eta_2|$ since 100 is a larger number than 10. Of course, in real values $\eta_1 < \eta_2$ since -100 is less than -10.

Investigation of elasticity concepts

W e introduced the concept of the price elasticity of demand in Chapter 4. We saw that elasticity was related to changes in total expenditures and that the price elasticity of demand could be gleaned from the slope of the price-consumption curve. In this chapter, we want to look at how the price elasticities of demand and of supply are computed, at changes in price elasticity along a straight-line demand curve, and at the difference between slope of a demand curve and elasticity of demand; we'll also look at slope and elasticity for supply. Additionally, we will examine the relation between revenues and elasticity, the determinants of the price elasticity of demand and of supply, the definitions and uses of cross elasticity and income elasticity, and finally, real-world examples of price elasticities. The Issues and Applications section of this chapter will cover the demand for fuel economy in automobiles and that for physiologically addicting drugs. It also reviews various estimates of the elasticity of demand for transportation services and considers the impact of additional referees on the supply of fouls in basketball games.

DEFINITION OF PRICE ELASTICITY

We formally defined price elasticity of demand as

$$\text{Price elasticity of demand} = \frac{\text{relative change in quantity demanded}}{\text{relative change in price}} \qquad (5\text{-}1)$$

Price elasticity of demand is a measure of the relative responsiveness of the quantity demanded to a change in price (Figure 5-1). The term "relative" is important in this definition. A more concrete way of thinking about relative changes is to define them in terms of percentage changes. The definition would become (denoting price elasticity with the Greek letter η, or eta):

FIGURE 5-1

Price elasticities of demand

These graphs represent the general idea of inelastic, unitary elastic, and elastic price elasticity of demand. Elasticity changes as we move along a demand curve, so we cannot say, without numerical computation, whether a given point on a demand curve is relatively elastic or relatively inelastic. Furthermore, the slope of a demand curve is not the same as price elasticity of demand. Hence, what we see in these graphs is only for purposes of defining and summarizing the categories of elasticity.

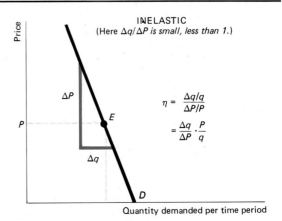

INELASTIC
(Here $\Delta q/\Delta P$ is small, less than 1.)

$$\eta = \frac{\Delta q/q}{\Delta P/P}$$

$$= \frac{\Delta q}{\Delta P} \cdot \frac{P}{q}$$

Quantity demanded per time period

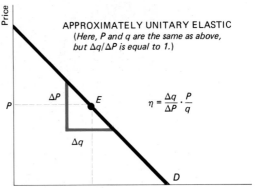

APPROXIMATELY UNITARY ELASTIC
(Here, P and q are the same as above, but $\Delta q/\Delta P$ is equal to 1.)

$$\eta = \frac{\Delta q}{\Delta P} \cdot \frac{P}{q}$$

Quantity demanded per time period

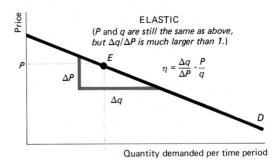

ELASTIC
(P and q are still the same as above, but $\Delta q/\Delta P$ is much larger than 1.)

$$\eta = \frac{\Delta q}{\Delta P} \cdot \frac{P}{q}$$

Quantity demanded per time period

$$\eta = \frac{\text{percentage change in quantity demanded}}{\text{percentage change in price}} \qquad (5\text{-}2)$$

When we assume that the changes both in the quantity demanded and in the price are quite small, we can define the price elasticity of demand as

$$\eta = \frac{\Delta q/q}{\Delta P/P} = \frac{\Delta q}{\Delta P} \cdot \frac{P}{q} \qquad (5\text{-}3)$$

As stated before, the Greek letter *delta* (Δ) signifies a small change; P is price and q is quantity.

We have stated the law of demand a number of times; there is an inverse relationship between a change in the price of a commodity and the resulting change in the quantity demanded of that commodity. Price elasticity of demand, η, will therefore *always* be a negative number. In our use of Eq. (5-3) we allow small changes in price and quantity, ΔP and Δq, to be either positive or negative. We know, therefore, that when ΔP is positive, Δq will be negative, and vice versa. Hence, the resultant η will invariably be negative.

This definition of price elasticity of demand leads to a measure which is completely independent of the units in which quantities and prices are measured. Elasticity is a pure number. This makes it easy for us to compare the price elasticities of various commodities or of the same commodity at two different times or places, priced in different currencies or measured in different physical units. Consider a purely hypothetical example for wheat

where P = \$5/bushel

q = 100 bushels per unit time period

ΔP = \$1/bushel (\$1 increase in price per bushel)

Δq = -5 bushels (a decrease of 5 bushels demanded)

Then Eq. (5-3) becomes

$$\frac{\dfrac{-5 \text{ bushels}}{100 \text{ bushels}}}{\dfrac{\$1/\text{bushel}}{\$5/\text{bushel}}} = \frac{-0.05}{0.20} = -0.25$$

This number has no physical or valuative dimensions; they all were canceled out. The dimension of bushels was canceled out in the numerator, and the dimension of dollars per bushel was canceled out in the denominator.

A conceptual discussion

It is possible to get so totally involved in the algebra of elasticity that we lose sight of what the concept is all about. In rereading the preceding section and then doing the remaining analysis in this chapter, you must continuously be aware of the fact that elasticity is used as a way to describe a particular aspect of demand. It tells us something about the demand curve, or demand schedule. What it tells us is how responsive consumers are to any given change in price. Thus, the definition in Eqs. (5-1) and (5-2) uses the percentage change in quantity demanded as the numerator and the percentage change in price per unit as the denominator. The percentage change in quantity demanded is the dependent variable, and the percentage change in price per unit is the independent variable. A change in price causes a specific change in quantity demanded, in the opposite direction. How much of a change in quantity demanded? We don't know until we know the price elasticity of demand. As we will see later in the chapter, other elasticity measures can be used to talk about the income or related-goods aspects of demand.

In addition, as you will see in greater detail later, looking at a demand curve will not tell you the relevant elasticity. For example, all you can tell about a straight-line demand curve by looking at it is its slope. To understand why, look at the right-hand side of Eq. (5-3). The slope of the demand curve is related only to the *first* part of the definition of elasticity.

Slope does not equal elasticity

The last statement should suggest to you the inadvisability of looking at the slope of a linear demand curve as being indicative of its elasticity. Let's go back to our original mathematical expression for price elasticity of demand

$$\eta = \frac{\Delta q}{\Delta P} \cdot \frac{P}{q} \tag{5-4}$$

We know that $\Delta q/\Delta P$ is the reciprocal of the slope, and we also know that P/q is the ratio of the price to the quantity. The slope of a demand curve, i.e., its flatness or steepness, is based on the *absolute* changes in price and quantity; in other words

$$\text{Slope} = \frac{\Delta P}{\Delta q} = \frac{1}{\Delta q/\Delta P}$$

However, price elasticity of demand has to do with *relative* changes in price and quantity, that is, the change in quantity relative to the original quantity and the change in price relative to the original price; or, in other words

$$\eta = \frac{\Delta q/q}{\Delta P/P}$$

Therefore, the reason the slope of the demand curve does not equal price elasticity of demand is that the elasticity contains a weighting factor given by the ratio P/q. That is, elasticity equals 1/slope of demand $\cdot P/q$. Furthermore, by definition, the slope of a straight-line or linear demand curve, such as the one presented later on in Figure 5-6, is constant, whereas the price elasticity of demand varies from $-\infty$ to 0. It is important, therefore, that you not confuse flatness or steepness in a demand curve with its price elasticity. This caveat can be illustrated by comparing the price elasticities of two or more demand curves.

DETERMINANTS OF THE PRICE ELASTICITY OF DEMAND

In Chapter 2, we gave five determinants of the position of the demand schedule. It is also possible for us to come up with a list of the determinants of the price elasticity of demand. The price elasticity of demand depends on:

1 The existence and closeness of substitutes
2 The "importance" of the commodity in the total budget of the consumer
3 The length of time allowed for adjustment to changes in price

Existence of substitutes

The strongest statement we can make about what determines the price elasticity of demand is that the more substitutes there are, the greater (numerically) η will be. In the limit, if there is a perfect substitute—if indifference curves are straight lines—the price elasticity of demand for the commodity will be $-\infty$. We're really talking about two goods that the consumer believes are exactly alike and desirable, such as a half-dollar and two quarters. We can predict that the more narrowly and more specifically a commodity is defined, the more close substitutes there will be for that commodity and hence the more price-elastic will be the demand. Thus, the price elasticity of demand for a particular brand of tea will be greater (numerically) than the price elasticity of demand for all tea. In turn, the price elasticity of demand for all tea will be (numerically) greater than the price elasticity of demand for all beverages.

The importance of the commodity in the consumer's budget

If we mean by "importance" the percentage of total expenditures that the individual allocates to a particular commodity, we can speculate that the greater the percentage of total real income spent on the commodity, the greater the person's price elasticity of demand for that commodity.[1]

This argument, however, is not totally compelling. To be sure, if a commodity constitutes a large fraction of the consumer's total expenditures, a drop in the price of that commodity will entail a relatively large increase in real income, and thus for all normal commodities there will be an increase

---

[1]There is an alternative argument about why the "importance" of the good contributes to its price elasticity of demand. If search costs are independent of "importance," whenever there is price dispersion, an individual seller of an "important" good faces a demand that is more price-elastic than that faced by an individual seller of an "unimportant" good. Why? Because information costs about alternative prices are relatively "too high" to justify consumer search in the case of "unimportant" goods.

in purchases. Here we mean an *absolute* increase in the purchase of the commodity in question due to the increase in real income resulting from a drop in that commodity's price. When we refer to the notion of elasticity, however, we are talking about *relative* changes in consumption. If the absolute quantity of the good in question is already large, there is no reason to think that the relative increase in the quantity demanded of the commodity will be greater because of any given drop in its price, just because it constitutes a large portion of the budget. In the extreme case, when the commodity in question constitutes 100 percent of the budget, the total price elasticity of demand η_t cannot be large. It must, in fact, be exactly equal to -1. (Why?)

The time for adjustment in rate of purchase
When the price of a commodity changes, the longer that price change persists, the greater will be the information flow about that price change; i.e., more people will learn about it. Second, consumers will be better able to revise their consumption patterns, the longer the time they have to do so. In fact, the longer the time they do take, the less costly it will be for them to engage in this revision of consumption patterns. Consider a price decrease. The longer the time that that price decrease persists, the greater will be the number of new *uses* that consumers will "discover" for the particular commodity, and the greater will be the number of new *users* of that particular commodity. Similarly, the longer a price increase is sustained, the more

FIGURE 5-2
Long- and short-run price elasticity of demand
The longer the time allowed for adjustment, the greater the price elasticity of demand. We have, therefore, a whole family of demand curves depending on the time allowed for adjustment. D_1D_1 is a demand curve for a zero adjustment period.

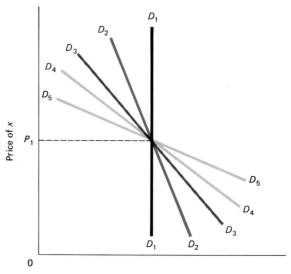

goods or activities will be discovered to substitute for the good that is now higher priced.

It is possible to make a very strong statement about the relationship between the price elasticity of demand and the time allowed for adjustment: *The longer any price change persists, the greater (numerically) the price elasticity of demand.* Otherwise stated, price elasticity of demand is greater in the long run than in the short run.

We can think of an entire family of demand curves, such as those depicted in Figure 5-2. The immediate-run (or market period) demand curve may be D_1D_1. The immediate period, or market period, is defined as one in which there is *no* time for adjustment. As more time is allowed, the demand curve becomes flatter, going first to D_2D_2 and then all the way to D_5D_5. We know that the flatness or steepness of a demand curve is not an indication of its elasticity. However, if we are comparing straight-line demand curves that intersect at a particular price, we know from the vertical axis formula for calculating the price elasticity of demand that those curves which intersect the vertical axis at lower and lower levels are more and more elastic.

THE NUMERICAL COMPUTATION OF PRICE ELASTICITY OF DEMAND

Equation (5-2) gives us a definition of the coefficient of the price elasticity of demand. However, it is given in terms of small, but discrete, changes in both price and quantity. That is not what the real world presents to us. Rather, we observe discrete changes that are sometimes rather large. Even if we think in terms of percentage changes in both price and quantity, we still have trouble.

Point elasticity

Inherent in the definition given in Eq. (5-3) is the notion that elasticity is measured around or "in the neighborhood of" a *point* along the demand curve. This is so because we are talking about a ratio of a very small relative change in quantity to a very small relative change in price. When the price range is made as small as possible, that is, shrunk to a point, the relative changes must also be made as small as possible. We get the term **point elasticity** when we use a formula such as the one in Eq. (5-3).

Arc elasticity

If, instead of trying to measure price elasticity of demand at a point on the demand curve, we measure it over a price range, or arc, we can come up with a workable definition of price elasticity that actually allows us to approximate it numerically. However, there are problems.

It's not enough just to say that we will measure **arc** price **elasticity** of demand by comparing percentage changes in price. The percentage change in price, for example, will depend critically on whether we are talking about an increase or a decrease in the price. For example, consider the percentage change associated with a price change of 25¢, or $\Delta P = 25¢$. If we start off with $1 as the initial price and reduce it by 25¢, the percentage change is -25 percent. However, if we consider an increase in the price by the same amount (25¢), from 75¢ to $1, the percentage price change is $+33\frac{1}{3}$ percent. Clearly, then, the percentage change in price will depend upon whether we talk about an increase or a decrease in price and on the resulting base price that we are using in our computations. You can easily verify this for yourself by taking a couple of numerical examples.

Using average values

One way out of this difficulty is to take the average of the two prices and of the two quantities. In this manner, the estimate of price elasticity of demand is at the midpoint of the arc on the demand curve. The formula for computing arc elasticity then becomes

$$\eta = \frac{\Delta q / [\frac{1}{2}(q_1 + q_2)]}{\Delta P / [\frac{1}{2}(P_1 + P_2)]} \tag{5-5}$$

where the subscripts refer to the quantities and prices which establish the dimensions of the "arc" in question. We see the meaning of the midpoint

---

FIGURE 5-3
Using the midpoint formula for arc elasticity
The percentage change in both price and quantity will be different if we go from point A to point B on the demand curve than if we go from point B to point A. As a compromise, we compute an average price elasticity of demand calculated at the midpoint of a straight line between points A and B. Our formula is then

$$\eta = \frac{\Delta q / [\frac{1}{2}(q_1 + q_2)]}{\Delta P / [\frac{1}{2}(P_1 + P_2)]}$$

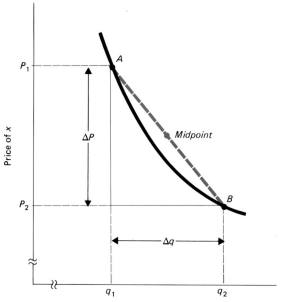

formula in Figure 5-3. This formula can be simplified by eliminating or canceling the $\frac{1}{2}$, so the formula becomes

$$\eta = \frac{\Delta q/(q_1 + q_2)}{\Delta P/(P_1 + P_2)}$$

THE GEOMETRIC COMPUTATION OF ELASTICITY

It is possible to obtain a geometric counterpart for the point price elasticity of demand. It turns out that there are two ways of doing this. There is a horizontal axis formula and a vertical axis formula. Both were developed by Alfred Marshall, a British economist who lived during the late nineteenth and early twentieth centuries.

Horizontal axis formula

Look back at Eq. (5-3). It consists of two parts, $\Delta q/\Delta P$ and P/q. The first part of the formula for price elasticity of demand ($\Delta q/\Delta P$) is approximately equal to the reciprocal of the slope $\Delta P/\Delta q$ of a demand curve for small changes in P around some price.[2] We already know P and q since they are represented by the point along the demand curve that we are examining. Hence, the formula for price elasticity consists of the reciprocal of the slope of the demand curve multiplied by the ratio P/q.

Look at the straight-line curve AB in Figure 5-4. Let us see whether we can translate our price elasticity of demand formula, Eq. (5-3), into geometric terms. Starting from point B, the slope at point E on the demand curve AB is equal to CE/CB:

$$\frac{\Delta P}{\Delta q} = \frac{CE}{CB} \tag{5-6}$$

We can invert this to CB/CE and obtain the first part of the expression in Eq. (5-3). The second part is just price and quantity; but price is equal to the vertical distance of CE, and the quantity is equal to $0C$. Thus

$$\eta = \left(\frac{\Delta q}{\Delta P} \cdot \frac{P}{q}\right) = \left(\frac{CB}{CE} \cdot \frac{CE}{0C}\right) = \frac{CB}{0C} \tag{5-7}$$

This horizontal axis formula for the price elasticity of demand tells us that to compute price elasticity of demand for a straight-line or linear demand curve, we drop a line from the point we are interested in perpendicular to the horizontal axis. The ratio of distance from that point to the intersection of the demand curve with the horizontal axis and the distance from the

---

[2] $\Delta q/\Delta P$ is equal to the *reciprocal* of the slope of the demand curve because economists put quantity on the horizontal axis instead of on the vertical axis.

FIGURE 5-4
Geometric computation of price elasticity of demand
We wish to measure price elasticity of demand at point E on demand curve AB. The slope of AB is equal to $\Delta P/\Delta q$. To derive the horizontal axis formula, consider the slope at point E. $\Delta P/\Delta q$ is equal to CE/CB. If we insert this into the formula $\eta = (\Delta q/\Delta \cdot p)$ (p/q), then we obtain $(CB/CE)(CE/0C)$, which is equal to $CB/0C$. We can derive the vertical axis formula similarly. It is equal to $0D/DA$.

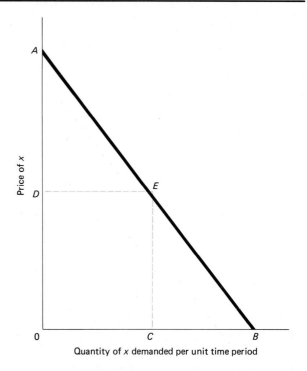

Price of x

Quantity of x demanded per unit time period

origin to the point where the perpendicular hits the horizontal axis gives us the price elasticity of demand.

Vertical axis formula

A similar formula for η can be derived involving the ratio of the two distances on the vertical axis. We do this by obtaining another expression of the slope of the demand curve AB. Starting from point A, $\Delta P/\Delta q$ is equal to DA/DE. Hence our formula becomes

$$\eta = \left(\frac{\Delta q}{\Delta P} \cdot \frac{P}{q}\right) = \left(\frac{DE}{DA} \cdot \frac{0D}{DE}\right) = \frac{0D}{DA} \tag{5-8}$$

Point elasticity for a nonlinear demand curve

We can apply either the horizontal or the vertical axis formula to obtain the point elasticity of demand for a nonlinear demand curve, such as the one shown in Figure 5-5. Our task is to compute the price elasticity of demand for point E. This is easily done by drawing the tangent line AB to point E. Then we construct a perpendicular to either the horizontal axis or the vertical axis. When we have done this, we can compute the price elasticity of demand.

Using the horizontal axis formula, Eq. (5-3), price elasticity of demand at point E in Figure 5-5 is $\eta = CB/0C$; using the vertical axis formula from Eq. (5-8), the price elasticity of demand is $\eta = 0D/DA$.

FIGURE 5-5
Point elasticity of demand for a nonlinear curve
If we wish to derive the price elasticity of demand at point E on the nonlinear demand curve shown above, we draw the tangent at that point and extend it to both the horizontal and vertical axes. That tangent is labeled AB. We can then apply either the horizontal or the vertical axis formula.

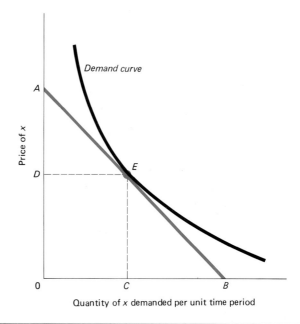

ELASTICITY AND THE CLASS OF LINEAR DEMAND CURVES

We can use either the horizontal or the vertical axis formula to demonstrate that the price elasticity of demand changes continuously along any straight-line or linear demand curve.

We can find, first of all, the price at which the elasticity of demand is -1. This is where the perpendicular, dropped from a point on the demand curve, bisects (cuts in half) the distance $0B$ in Figure 5-6. The horizontal axis formula will give us elasticity $\eta = CB/0C$, and since those two distances are equal, the result will be 1. Since we are accepting the law of demand, which asserts an inverse relationship between P and q, we must introduce the negative sign. Negative changes in price are associated with positive changes in quantity demanded and vice versa. The negative sign is labeled accordingly in Figure 5-6. Above price P_1, the midpoint on demand curve AB in Figure 5-6, price elasticity of demand is numerically greater than 1 ("elastic"). For prices less than P_1, it is numerically less than 1 ("inelastic"). Thus, we have two ranges on a straight-line, downward-sloping demand curve: above price P_1, where demand is elastic; and below price P_1, where demand is inelastic. At price P_1 there is unitary elasticity.

The two extremes are price $0A$ and quantity $0B$. At price $0A$ ($q = 0$), demand is infinitely elastic. At quantity $0B$ ($P = 0$), demand has zero elas-

FIGURE 5-6
Changing price elasticity of demand along a linear demand curve
We draw a perpendicular line midway between the origin and where the demand curve *AB* intersects the horizontal axis. We will hit point *E* on the demand curve *AB* where $\eta = -1$. At prices above P_1, price elasticity of demand is numerically greater than 1; at prices below P_1, it is numerically less than 1. At point *A*, it is equal to $-\infty$, and at point *B*, it is equal to 0.

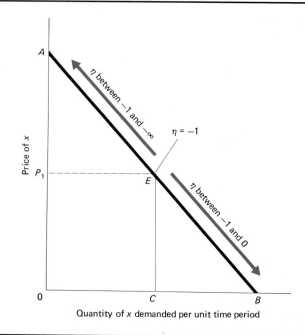

In sum, a straight-line demand curve has a price elasticity of demand that ranges from $-\infty$ to 0 as we move down the curve.

Comparing elasticities of demand curves

In Figure 5-7, we have drawn two demand curves, *AB* and *A'B'*. If you were asked to figure out, just by inspection, which demand curve was more elastic than the other, you probably would say *A'B'*. After all, it is flatter, and so it *looks* more price-responsive. But you would be wrong.

In the first place, as we have already pointed out, elasticity ranges from 0 to $-\infty$ along *every* straight-line, downward-sloping demand curve that touches both axes. Thus, we can make reference to a comparison of price elasticities only at a particular price, over a given price range. A question about comparing the elasticity of two different demand curves is meaningless.

Slope of a demand curve as a proxy for elasticity of demand

Now consider the vertical axis expression for price elasticity of demand. According to this expression, price elasticity of demand is equal to the ratio of the vertical distance from the origin to a horizontal price line drawn from the point on the demand curve where elasticity is to be measured to the vertical distance from that point to where the demand curve intersects the vertical axis. Take any particular price, say price *D*, where we wish to compare the elasticities of the two demand curves in Figure 5-7. This will be at

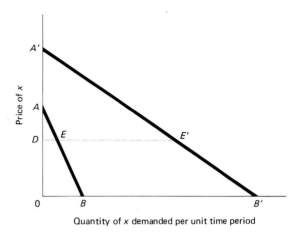

FIGURE 5-7
Comparing the price elasticity of demand of two demand curves
Even though demand curve *AB* is steeper than demand curve *A'B'*, at most prices it is more price-elastic. You can prove this by using the vertical axis formula where $\eta = 0D/DA$ at price *D*, corresponding to point *E* on demand curve *AB*. Elasticity is numerically greater than 1 at that point for demand curve *AB*; however, using the same formula but substituting *DA'* for the denominator, we see, by inspection, that price elasticity of demand is numerically less than 1 at price *D*, corresponding to point *E'* on demand curve *A'B'*.

points *E* and *E'*. The dashed line drawn from *E'* goes through *E* to *D* on the vertical axis. The price elasticity of demand for the steeper demand curve, *AB*, at price *D* is (0D/DA), which is, by inspection, numerically greater than unity. However, the price elasticity of demand for the flatter demand curve *A'B'* at price *D* is (0D/DA') and is observably numerically less than unity. Hence, at price *D* (and all other prices as well), demand curve *AB* is relatively more elastic than demand curve *A'B'*. The moral of the story? You usually can't look at the slope of two demand curves to determine which is more elastic.

However, when *P* and *q* are identical, you can look at the relative flatness or steepness of the two intersecting demand curves to determine which one is less or more elastic at that point. Can you tell why by examining the price elasticity formula? This can be seen in Figure 5-8. Here we show two demand curves, *AB* and *A'B'*, which intersect at point *E*. If we wish to make a statement about the relative price elasticities of demand of the two different curves at price P_1, where they intersect, we can unambiguously state that the flatter curve is the more elastic one. In other words, if we rotate a demand curve at a point, as that demand curve gets flatter, its elasticity increases at that particular price around which the curve is being rotated. This can be understood by remembering Eq. (5-3). Elasticity is the reciprocal of the slope of the demand curve times *P/q*. If we are rotating the demand curve at a particular point, *P* and *q* do not change; however, the slope of the demand curve does. Therefore

$$\eta = \frac{\Delta q}{\Delta P} \cdot \left(\frac{P}{q}\right)$$

where (*P/q*) equals a constant number, *k*. Or

FIGURE 5-8

Comparing elasticities at a price where two demand curves intersect

It is possible to deduce the relative price elasticities of two demand curves at the price where they intersect by their relative steepness or flatness. Demand curve AB is more elastic at a price P_1 (point E) than is demand curve $A''B'$. You can prove this using the vertical axis formula. Whichever demand curve intersects the vertical axis closest to the origin is more elastic at each and every price.

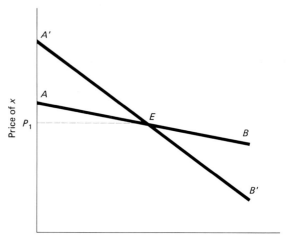

$$\eta = \frac{\Delta q}{\Delta P} \cdot k$$

in which case η is a function solely of the slope.

As the demand curve gets flatter, the slope decreases. Therefore, the reciprocal of the slope, or $\Delta q/\Delta P$, becomes greater. Thus the elasticity becomes greater in numerical terms.

FIGURE 5-9

Price elasticity of demand for parallel demand curves

Demand curve AB and demand curve $A'B'$ are parallel; they have exactly the same slope. However, demand curve AB is more elastic than demand curve $A'B'$ at any given price. Use the vertical or horizontal axis formula to show why.

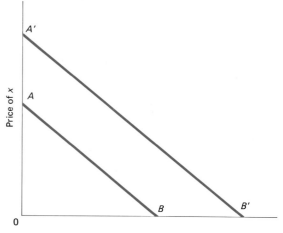

FIGURE 5-10
Comparing price elasticities again
Even though demand curve AB' is considerably
flatter than demand curve AB at each and
every price, they have exactly the same price
elasticity of demand because they intersect the
vertical axis at the same point A.

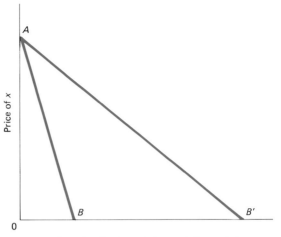

Another way of proving that the flatter demand curve is more elastic at
price P_1 in Figure 5-8 is by remembering the vertical axis formula. In fact,
we can make a general statement: *Whichever linear demand curve intersects
the vertical axis closer to the origin will be more elastic than the other at
any given price.*

Even two parallel demand curves will have different relative elasticities
at each and every price. In Figure 5-9, the one closer to the origin will be
the more elastic of the two.

Finally, you should be able to see immediately from the vertical axis
formula, Eq. (5-8), that demand curves AB and AB' in Figure 5-10 have
exactly equal elasticities at every single price!

THE SELLERS' SIDE OF THE STORY: THE
RELATION BETWEEN PRICE ELASTICITY OF
DEMAND AND REVENUES

When we introduced elasticity, we noticed a relation between price elasticity
of demand and the total expenditures of buyers. Briefly, total consumer
expenditures vary inversely with price changes when demand is elastic and
directly with price changes when demand is inelastic; they are invariant to
small price changes when demand is unit-elastic. It turns out that if we look
at the seller's side of the picture, we find the same relation between price
elasticity of demand and the total revenues of the sellers of the product.
Their revenues are the mirror image of buyers' expenditures.

Computing total, average, and marginal revenue

We define **total revenue** TR as price per unit times quantity demanded because that is the amount of revenue received by any seller of a product who charges a single price, P, for all Q units sold. **Marginal revenue** MR is defined as the change in total revenue associated with a one-unit change in the quantity sold. **Average revenue** AR is defined as total revenue divided by quantity demanded:

$$MR = \frac{\Delta TR}{\Delta Q} \tag{5-9}$$

$$AR = \frac{TR}{Q} = \frac{P \times Q}{Q} = P \tag{5-10}$$

assuming that the same price is charged to everyone. And in fact, the demand curve is sometimes called the average revenue curve because any point on the demand curve gives the average revenue realizable from the sale of that particular quantity per unit time period (again, assuming that a single price is charged for all units sold).

Look at Table 5-1. Here we have shown a hypothetical demand schedule. In column (1) is the price of x. In column (2) is the number of units demanded. Thus, columns (1) and (2) constitute the demand schedule of product x. Column (3) is total revenue, or the price of x times the quantity demanded. Column (4) is marginal revenue, defined as the change in total revenues due to a one-unit change in the quantity sold. Marginal revenue is equal to the difference in the total revenue between row entries (as long as $\Delta Q = 1$).

Note that total revenue reaches its maximum at 5 units sold, stays constant for one more unit, and then starts to fall. Marginal revenue, therefore, becomes 0 for quantities between 5 and 6 and thereafter becomes negative. We can plot all the information in the four columns in Table 5-1 on two diagrams in Figure 5-11. The top of the figure shows total revenue. It starts at 0, peaks at 5 units, remains constant at $30 through the sixth unit, and falls thereafter. The bottom diagram in Figure 5-11 shows the demand curve, or average revenue curve, plotted as DD. It represents the price-quantity pairs of columns (1) and (2) in Table 5-1. Marginal revenue is a stepladder-type function because we are dealing in discrete units. The marginal revenue curve, if we can call it a curve, starts at $10 and falls to 0 at 5 units and then becomes negative after 6 units sold.

Notice that there is a relation between marginal revenue and total revenue. Marginal revenue becomes 0 when total revenue reaches its maximum. This is shown by the shaded area between 5 and 6 units. Beyond 6 units, MR becomes negative.

The marginal revenue curve always lies below downward-sloping market demand curves. This is because price, which is identically equal to average revenue, is greater than marginal revenue after the first unit sold. Marginal

TABLE 5-1 Calculating total revenue and marginal revenue	Price of x ($/unit) (1)	Quantity demanded (units/time period) (2)	Total revenue $TR = P_x \cdot Q$ [(1) × (2)] ($/time period) (3)	Marginal revenue $MR = \Delta TR$* ($/unit) (4)
*For marginal revenue, $MR = \Delta TR/\Delta Q = \Delta TR/1$, and therefore $MR = \Delta TR$.	11	0	0	
				$10
	10	1	$10	
				8
	9	2	18	
				6
	8	3	24	
				4
	7	4	28	
				2
	6	5	30	
				0
	5	6	30	
				-2
	4	7	28	
				-4
	3	8	24	
				-6
	2	9	18	
				-8
	1	10	10	

revenue is always less than price for a downward-sloping market demand curve. This can perhaps be better understood by looking at Figure 5-12. Here we show a unit increase in sales due to a reduction in the price of product x from P_1 to P_2. After all, the only way that sales can increase for a given downward-sloping demand curve is for price to fall. The price P_2 is the price received for the last unit, $Q + 1$. Thus that price P_2 times the last unit sold represents what is received from the last unit sold. That would be equal to the horizontally gridded column showing the effects of a one-unit increase in sales. The area of that horizontally gridded column is one unit wide times P_2 high.

But the price times that last unit sold is not the addition to total revenues received from selling that last unit. Why? Because price was reduced on all other units sold (0Q) in order to sell the larger quantity (0Q + 1). The reduction in price is represented by the vertical distance from P_1 to P_2 on the

FIGURE 5-11
Total and marginal revenue curves
Data from Table 5-1 are transferred to this figure. The top diagram shows the total revenue curve; the bottom diagram shows the marginal revenue curve, which is the change in total revenue resulting from a unit change in output. Note that when total revenue reaches its maximum between five and six units, marginal revenue is equal to zero. Thereafter, it becomes negative.

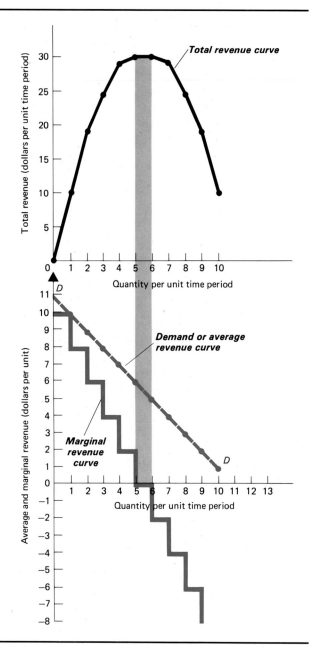

FIGURE 5-12
*Marginal revenue is always less than price for
downward-sloping market demand curves*
The only way to sell one more unit when facing
a downward-sloping market demand curve is
by lowering the price. The price received for
the last unit is equal to P_2. The revenues
received from selling this last unit are equal to
P_2 times one unit, or the area of the
horizontally crosshatched vertical column.
However, if a single price is being charged for
all units, total revenues do not go up by the
amount of the area represented by that
column. The price had to be reduced on all the
previous $0Q$ units which could still have been
sold at price P_1. Thus, we must subtract the
vertically lined area from the horizontally lined
area in order to derive marginal revenue.
Marginal revenue is, therefore, always less
than price.

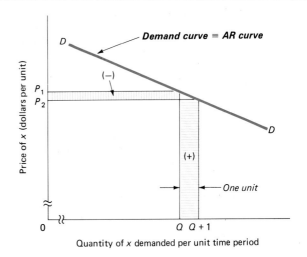

vertical axis. We must subtract, therefore, the vertically gridded row from
the horizontally gridded column in order to come up with the *net change*
in total revenues due to a one-unit increase in sales. Clearly, the change in
total revenues, i.e., marginal revenue must be less than price because marginal revenue is always the difference between the two gridded areas in
Figure 5-12.

**The relation
between
marginal
revenue and
price elasticity**

There is a definite relation between marginal revenue and the price elasticity
of demand. If we look at the definition of marginal revenue, we can find this
relation. Marginal revenue is equal to the change in total revenue due to a
one-unit change in sales. In the case of a price decrease, it is identical,
therefore, to the lower price at the higher unit-sales rate minus the change
in price times all the initial quantity sold. To see this, consider Figure 5-12
again. To make the proof easier, let the inifial quantity Q be called Q_1 and
the other quantity $(Q_1 + 1)$ be called Q_2. Then

Total revenue at price $P_1 = \text{TR}_1 = P_1 \cdot Q_1$

Total revenue at price $P_2 = \text{TR}_2 = P_2 \cdot Q_2$

Marginal revenue from selling Q_2 is then

$\text{MR}_{1\text{-}2} = \text{TR}_2 - \text{TR}_1$

$= P_2 Q_2 - P_1 Q_1$

But we let $Q_1 + 1 = Q_2$, and so if we substitute, we get

$$MR_{1-2} = P_2(Q_1 + 1) - P_1Q_1$$

$$= P_2Q_1 + (P_2 \cdot 1) - P_1Q_1$$

$$= (P_2 \cdot 1) + Q_1(P_2 - P_1)$$

This is exactly what we see in Figure 5-12. P_2 is less than P_1, and so $(P_2 - P_1)$ is a negative number. Hence, MR_{1-2} will be the new lower price P_2 minus some number; ergo, $MR_{1-2} < P_2$.

We can generalize the above:

$$MR = P - (\Delta P \cdot q) \text{ for price increases} \qquad (5\text{-}11)$$

$$MR = P + (\Delta P \cdot q) \text{ for price decreases} \qquad (5\text{-}12)$$

Here we are dealing with *one-unit* discrete changes in q, and when we consider other arbitrary changes in q in the amount of Δq, we must write as a general statement[3]

$$MR = P + \frac{\Delta P \cdot q}{\Delta q} \qquad (5\text{-}13)$$

Now we do a little algebraic manipulation. We multiply the right-hand term of Eq. (5-13) by P/P, which does not change the equality. This gives us

$$MR = P + \left(\frac{\Delta P}{\Delta q}\right)\left(\frac{q}{P}\right)\left(\frac{P}{1}\right) \qquad (5\text{-}14)$$

Now we factor out P:

$$MR = P\left(1 + \frac{\Delta P}{\Delta q} \cdot \frac{q}{P}\right) \qquad (5\text{-}15)$$

But the second term in the parentheses is merely the reciprocal of the elasticity of demand so that

$$MR = P\left(1 + \frac{1}{\eta}\right) \qquad (5\text{-}16)$$

Since we are always dealing with downward-sloping demand curves, the price elasticity of demand η will always be negative. Hence, Eq. (5-16) is consistent with the notion that marginal revenue is always less than price, since as long as the term $1/\eta$ does not equal 0, the term will be negative and therefore require that the entire quantity in parentheses in Eq. (5-16) be less than unity.

Using Eq. (5-16), we see that when η is numerically greater than 1, MR

---

[3]Actually, Eq. (5-13) holds only at the limit ($\Delta q \to 0$ and $\Delta P \to 0$).

must be positive; when η is numerically less than 1, MR must be negative. (Why?)

From Eq. (5-16) we can find out the geometric relationship between marginal revenue and the demand curve.

Deriving the marginal revenue curve

Look at the demand curve AB in Figure 5-13. It is a linear demand curve, and therefore we can use the horizontal axis formula to find out where along that curve the elasticity of demand is unitary (technically, -1). All we have to do is find the midpoint of the distance $0B$. That midpoint is at C. If we draw a perpendicular line from C up to the demand curve, it intersects at point E, and we know that at point E, $\eta = -1$. We have some information about point E in terms of marginal revenue. Substitute -1 for η in Eq. (5-16). Marginal revenue then becomes equal to 0 for the quantity-price combination denoted by E on the demand curve AB. Thus, where demand is unitary-elastic at point E, marginal revenue is equal to 0.

Let's see whether we can find another point. We do this by using the vertical axis formula for price elasticity of demand. Using the vertical axis formula, we know that where the demand curve cuts the vertical axis, the price elasticity of demand is $-\infty$. (Why?) Thus we have some information about the marginal revenue at price A. From Eq. (5-16), marginal revenue $= P(1 + 1/-\infty)$. Since anything divided by infinity is equal to 0, marginal rev-

---

FIGURE 5-13

Deriving the marginal revenue curve
By using the formula $M = P(1 + 1/\eta)$, we know that marginal revenue will equal zero only when $\eta = -1$. But this is exactly at the midpoint between the origin and where the demand curve AB intersects the horizontal axis at point B. This gives us point C below E on demand curve AB. Using the same formula, we know that $MR = P$ when $\eta = -\infty$. This gives us point A. We now have two points and can draw the marginal revenue curve, which always bisects a line drawn parallel to the horizontal axis from the vertical axis outward to any linear demand curve.

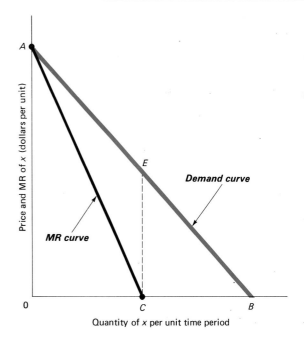

TABLE 5-2 *The effect of a price change on total revenue* *depends on price elasticity of demand*		*Price- elastic demand*	*Unitary price elasticity*	*Price- inelastic demand*
	Price decrease	TR ↑	TR constant	TR ↓
	Price increase	TR ↓	TR constant	TR ↑

enue equals price (MR = P) where the linear demand curve *AB* cuts the vertical axis. Thus marginal revenue equals price A. We now have two points to connect for our marginal revenue curve. Those two points are A and C, and we have therefore defined that linear curve.

All straight-line demand curves have straight-line marginal revenue curves which coincide with the demand curve at its vertical axis intercept and bisect the horizontal axis between the origin and where the demand curve intercepts the horizontal axis. In fact, any point on the marginal revenue curve always bisects any horizontal line (parallel to the horizontal axis) drawn through it from the vertical axis to the demand curve.

The relation between price elasticity and total revenue

There is a relation between price elasticity of demand and total revenue that should be quite clear by now. It is a relation similar to the one we discussed in Chapter 4, when we talked about total expenditures. This relation is shown in Table 5-2. We note that an elastic demand implies a negative relation

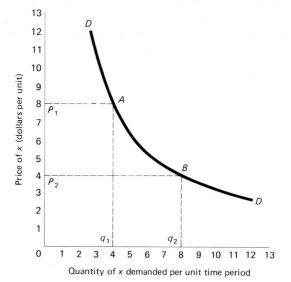

FIGURE 5-14
A rectangular hyperbola demand curve
DD is a rectangular hyperbola. At any point along it, price elasticity of demand equals −1. You can prove this by finding out total revenues at point *A* and at point *B*. In other words $(P_1q_1) = (P_2q_2)$.

between changes in price and total revenue and that an inelastic demand yields a positive relation. When demand is of unitary elasticity, total revenue is invariant to price changes.

One type of nonlinear demand curve you will sometimes see has the shape of a rectangular hyperbola, shown in Figure 5-14. Note that the general algebraic expression for a rectangular hyperbola is $x \cdot y$ = constant, or in our case, the prices and quantities, $P \cdot q$ = constant, so that total revenue is constant, regardless of price. The demand curve, *DD*, is a rectangular hyperbola. It has the property that at any point along the curve, the area enclosed by the rectangle, formed by the lines to the vertical and horizontal axes, always has the same value. This area is, of course, total revenue.

Take A. Here the price is P_1 and the quantity demanded is q_1. Total revenues are $P_1 \cdot q_1$, or \$8 per unit times 4 units = \$32. At *B*, the total revenues are $P_2 \cdot q_2$, or \$4 per unit times 8 units, which again equals \$32.

THE ESTIMATION OF ELASTICITIES

When physicists want to find out the relation between two variables, they can often construct experiments to measure it. Chemists can do so as well. However, economists generally cannot run similar types of experiments. If an economist wants to find out the price responsiveness that one or more consumers exhibit for a particular commodity, it is generally not possible to set up an experiment in which a set of consumers are faced with different prices for the same commodity and are asked to purchase accordingly. Moreover, it is generally useless to engage in interviews to ask individuals how much they would buy of a particular commodity at various prices because consumers typically are not sure just how much they will buy until actually faced with the prices. Of course, this is not to say that some researchers have not gone this route. For example, in one study a group of duck hunters were sent a detailed questionnaire in which each was asked to indicate how many ducks he or she should want to shoot each hunting season at various prices charged per bagged bird.

Such interview techniques cannot guarantee satisfactory estimates of the price responsiveness of an individual for a particular commodity. We do not find out how consumers *will* react to something by asking them how they think they *would* react. We have to have some evidence of what they actually do in a real-world situation. Consumers can be fickle individuals. It is generally safest to infer their preferences from their actual buying behavior.

What the economic researcher has to do to estimate price elasticities of demand is look at what consumers did when relative prices changed. However, we know that price is not the only thing that determines the demand curve for a commodity. In our particular model, price has generally been the only determining variable shown on the diagrams. We did point out, however, that there were other determinants of change in demand. These were changes in such things as real income, tastes and preferences, the prices of related goods, expectations of future price changes, and population. Thus we know that if we were to attribute changes in quantity demanded solely to changes in the relative price of that particular good, we would probably be introducing a serious error into our estimates of price elasticity of demand. The error would be due to the fact that we had not held constant the other variables that affect the position of the demand curve.

By using what are called multiple-regression econometric techniques, it is possible to hold constant, in effect, these other important demand-determining variables. In multiple-regression analysis, equations are set up relating the quantity demanded to the relative price, real income, the price of related commodities—complements and substitutes—and so on. Data are collected on all these variables over a certain period of time during which the relative price for the commodity in question changed often enough to generate statistically significant estimates of the price elasticity of demand.

Other elasticities of demand

As just noted, so far we have concentrated on the relation between a percentage change in price and in quantity demanded. However, demand is a relation or function in which the price of a good itself, the prices of substitute or complementary goods, the consumer's income, and a variety of other influences affect the quantity demanded. Functionally, $Q_x = f(P_x, P_y, M,$ tastes, etc.$)$. As always, we examine changes in each of the "independent variables" (the variables on the right side of the equation) one at a time, according to our rule of *ceteris paribus*. When we were varying P_x in our discussion of price elasticity, we held P_y, M, tastes, and all other variables constant. We can also define elasticities for changes in each of the other independent variables in the demand function. We now turn to a discussion of two of these: income elasticity of demand and cross-price elasticity of demand.

RELATING CHANGES IN THE QUANTITY DEMANDED TO CHANGES IN INCOME: INCOME ELASTICITY OF DEMAND

For any good there is a straightforward way for us to relate the quantity demanded to changes in money income (if we assume that the nominal and relative price of that good is held constant). This measure of responsiveness to income changes is called income elasticity. We define it as follows:

■ *Income elasticity of demand = the percentage change in the amount of a commodity purchased ÷ the percentage change in money income*

TABLE 5-3	Time period	Income per month	Quantity of record albums demanded per month
	Period 1	$200	6
	Period 2	$300	8

Income elasticity of demand can be represented mathematically by the following ratio:[4]

Income elasticity of demand $= \mu$

$$= \frac{\text{percentage change in optimal amount purchased}}{\text{percentage change in income}} \qquad (5\text{-}17)$$

where μ is the Greek letter *mu*, which we'll use to represent income elasticity of demand.

Sometimes it is useful to define income elasticity of demand in terms of the responsiveness of optimal quantity purchased to changes in *real* income as opposed to *money* income or *nominal* income. This is particularly relevant when the percentage of total expenditures going to the commodity in question is relatively large so that any change in that commodity's price will greatly affect real income.

Computing income elasticity

A simple example will demonstrate how income elasticity of demand can be computed. In Table 5-3 we give the relevant data. The product in question is stereo records. We assume that the price of stereo records remains constant relative to other prices. In period 1, six records per month are purchased, and income per month is $200. In period 2, monthly income is increased to $300 and the quantity of records purchased per month is increased to eight. We can apply Eq. (5-17) to calculate

Income elasticity of demand $= \mu$

$$= \frac{(8 - 6)/6}{(300 - 200)/200} = \frac{\frac{1}{3}}{\frac{1}{2}} = 0.667 \qquad (5\text{-}18)$$

[4]Empirical estimates of the income elasticity of demand often use expenditures on a product rather than quantity purchased. Alternatively, these estimates are derived using expenditures on the product divided by a price index.

Hence, measured income elasticity of demand for record albums for the individual represented in this example is 0.667. In other words for every 1 percent change in income (between $200 and $300), there is a corresponding two-thirds of a percent change in the same direction in purchases of records. Note that this holds only for the move from six records to eight records per month. If income fell from $300 to $200 and the consumer cut purchases from eight to six records per month, the income elasticity in Eq. (5-18) becomes

$$\frac{(6 - 8)/8}{(200 - 300)/300} = \frac{-\frac{1}{4}}{-\frac{1}{3}} = 0.75$$

with the result that the measured income elasticity of demand is 0.75.

There is a way to calculate μ that is an approximation of the true income elasticity of demand. This approximation method is independent of whether μ is calculated for increases or decreases in income. In other words, it is independent of the starting point because it measures the arc of change. It is as follows:

$$\mu = \frac{\Delta x/(x_1 + x_2)}{\Delta M/(M_1 + M_2)} \tag{5-19}$$

where x_1 = purchases of x in period 1

x_2 = purchases of x in period 2

M_1 = income in period 1

M_2 = income in period 2

Δx = change in x and can be either negative or positive

ΔM = change in income and can be either negative or positive

Inserting the values from Table 5-3 into Eq. (5-19), the income elasticity is

$$\frac{2/(6 + 8)}{100/(200 + 300)} = \frac{\frac{1}{7}}{\frac{1}{5}} = 0.71$$

Point and arc income elasticity   Perhaps the fact that we can obtain different values for income elasticity from the same definition needs a bit of explanation. Basically, Eq. (5-17) is valid for measurement taken at a *point*. When we are forced to measure it over a discrete range of incomes, as opposed to an infinitely small change, the income elasticity of demand will vary depending on whether it is calculated for the beginning point, for the ending point, or as an average over the arc of change. We ran into exactly the same phenomenon when we examined how to measure price elasticity of demand.

Normal and inferior goods

Now we can classify goods according to their income elasticity, as we do in Table 5-4. We have already defined an inferior good as one whose quantity demanded goes down as income goes up, and vice versa. Clearly then, the income elasticity of demand of an inferior good will be negative. Hence we define all goods whose income elasticity of demand is less than 0 as inferior goods. (Typically, our examples of inferior goods have been ones which become inferior after a certain higher income level is reached; that is, the income elasticity of demand becomes negative above a certain income level.)

Similarly, we know that a normal good is a good whose quantity demanded rises as income rises. Hence, all goods whose income elasticity of demand is greater than 0 are normal goods.

Empirical estimates of income elasticities

It is interesting to look at some of the estimated income elasticities of demand for certain groups of commodities that are commonly purchased. In Table 5-5, we do just that. According to our definition of inferior and normal goods, we can say that if these estimates are correct, all goods on the list, at least over the income ranges studied, are normal goods. Note that the categories are broad and that both "low-quality" and "high-quality" items have been lumped together.

The relation between income elasticities of demand for several commodities

Given a change in the budget constraint, a more-than-proportionate change in the consumption of one commodity implies a less-than-proportionate change in the consumption of at least one other commodity. Thus, the income elasticity of demand of several commodities in a consumer's expenditure pattern are related because of the budget constraint. By implication, then, it turns out that there is a relation among the separate Engel curves for the different commodities that a consumer purchases.

The Engel curves for each of the goods in any particular consumer's market basket are not independent of each other. This becomes clearer if we look at the proposition that not all Engel curves can have a negative slope

---

TABLE 5-4
Classification of income elasticities

	Income elasticity of demand	Classification
	$\mu < 0$	Inferior
	$\mu > 0$	Normal

TABLE 5-5
Estimated coefficients of income elasticity of demand

Here we find the estimated income elasticities for selected groups of commodities. Notice that none of them was estimated to be an inferior good.

Source: H. S. Houthakker and L. D. Taylor, Consumer Demand in the United States: Analyses and Projections (Cambridge, Mass.: Harvard University Press, 1970), pp. 260–263, table 6.5.

Categories of commodities	Coefficient of income elasticity of demand
Alcoholic beverages	1.54
Food	0.51
Tobacco	0.63
Clothing	1.02
Housing	1.04
Furniture	1.48
Electricity, gas	0.50
Fuel	0.38
Drugs (health-oriented)	0.61
Physicians' services	0.75
Dentists' services	1.41
New cars	2.45
Books	1.44
Private education	2.46

at the same income level. After all, not all commodities can be inferior goods at the same time. This was seen in the two-commodity case in Figure 4-3. Thus we know that *all income elasticities of demand cannot be negative.* Furthermore, we will see that the (weighted) average income elasticity of demand of all goods taken together must be 1, and this leads to some very interesting implications when we describe a particular good as being strongly inferior. Before we get to the implications, though, we have to prove that separate Engel curves are interrelated.

We do this by first assuming that all money income is spent on the two goods in our two-commodity world and that prices are constant. Hence

$$M = (P_x \cdot x) + (P_y \cdot y) \tag{5-20}$$

Now, consider an increase in money income of some small amount. Given our assumption that all money income is spent, an increase in money income by ΔM will lead to a change in the consumption of x by the amount Δx and a change in the consumption of y by the amount Δy. Hence, the increase in income is spent according to the following:

$$\Delta M = P_x \Delta x + P_y \Delta y \tag{5-21}$$

Since an equation is unchanged if both the right-hand and the left-hand sides are multiplied or divided by the same quantity, let us divide both sides of Eq. (5-21) by the change in money income ΔM:

$$\frac{\Delta M}{\Delta M} = P_x \cdot \frac{\Delta x}{\Delta M} + P_y \cdot \frac{\Delta y}{\Delta M} \tag{5-22}$$

We can also multiply either side (or any term, for that matter) by 1. What we do here is multiply the first term in the right-hand side of Eq. (5-22) by x/x and M/M, both of which equal 1. We then multiply the second term by y/y and again by M/M, both of which equal 1. The result is

$$1 = \left[P_x \cdot \frac{\Delta x}{\Delta M} \cdot \frac{x}{x} \cdot \frac{M}{M} \right] + \left[P_y \cdot \frac{\Delta y}{\Delta M} \cdot \frac{y}{y} \cdot \frac{M}{M} \right] \tag{5-23}$$

Now, if we rearrange the terms in Eq. (5-23), we come up with a somewhat more interesting equation:

$$1 = \frac{P_x x}{M} \cdot \left(\frac{\Delta x/x}{\Delta M/M} \right) + \frac{P_y y}{M} \cdot \left(\frac{\Delta y/y}{\Delta M/M} \right) \tag{5-24}$$

We can make some sense out of Eq. (5-24) by realizing two things:

1 The term $P_x x/M$ is the relative share of income and thus of total expenditures spent on good x; similarly, $P_y y/M$ is the relative share of income and thus of total expenditures spent on good y. Remember that the sum of these two relative shares must equal 1.

2 The expressions in parentheses are merely another way of stating the calculations for the coefficients of income elasticity of demand for x and y. Rather than stating percentage changes, we have merely indicated discrete, small changes by Δ.

Now let's represent the relative shares of income spent for each good as

$$k_x = \frac{P_x x}{M} \tag{5-25a}$$

$$k_y = \frac{P_y y}{M} \tag{5-25b}$$

And let's represent the income elasticity of demand for x and y as

$$\mu_x = \frac{\Delta x/x}{\Delta M/M} \tag{5-26a}$$

$$\mu_y = \frac{\Delta y/y}{\Delta M/M} \tag{5-26b}$$

Then Eq. (5-24) becomes

$$1 = k_x \mu_x + k_y \mu_y \tag{5-27}$$

Equation (5-27) states that the *weighted* average of income elasticities of demand (μ_x and μ_y) for all commodities purchased by an individual consumer at a given level of income must be equal to a positive 1 where the weights are the k's. The respective weights—that is, the k's—are the relative shares of money income spent on each good. The weights must themselves add up to 1.

We can see that Eq. (5-27) makes sense. If we assume that all income is spent, then *on average*, a 1 percent increase in income will yield a 1 percent increase in purchases. To get the appropriate "average," we weight the income elasticity by the share of total money income spent on each good. In this case, we consider only two goods, x and y. In the more general case, we would consider the entire array of goods and services that the consumer purchases. Equation (5-27) would become quite long, but the implication would be the same. The weighted average income elasticities for all goods consumed must add up to 1.

The implication of Eq. (5-27) is that whenever one commodity is strongly inferior, there must be either (1) an even more strongly normal good or (2) a set of fairly strongly normal goods. Why? To offset the strongly inferior good so that the (weighted) average income elasticity of demand equals 1.

Another way of stating this is that whenever there are strongly normal goods whose income elasticities exceed 1, they must be offset by other goods with income elasticities that are less than 1.

Finally, Eq. (5-27) allows us to predict that the items that take up a large percentage of a consumer's budget generally have income elasticities of demand close to 1. Consider the budget of a low-income family in which 75 percent of the income is spent on food, or $k_{food} = 0.75$. That means that if the income elasticity of the demand of this family for food exceeded the reciprocal of $\frac{3}{4}$ (i.e., was greater than $\frac{4}{3}$, or 1.333), the average income elasticity of demand for all other goods would have to be negative. This is unlikely. Most goods are normal. Thus, we surmise that for this particular family, the income elasticity of demand for food is considerably less than 1.333. To illustrate this point with an exaggeration, consider the possibility that $\mu_{food} = 2.00$. We assume that μ_{food} takes up 75 percent of the budget:

$$1 = k_{food} \cdot \mu_{food} + k_{all\ other\ goods} \cdot \mu_{all\ other\ goods} \tag{5-28}$$

which becomes

$$1 = 0.75 \cdot 2.00 + 0.25 \mu_{all\ other\ goods} \tag{5-29}$$

or $1 = 1.5 + 0.25 \cdot \mu_{all\ other\ goods}$ (5-30)

But for Eq. (5-30) to hold, $\mu_{all\ other\ goods}$ must equal -2! And that is extremely unlikely.

CROSS ELASTICITIES: SUBSTITUTES AND COMPLEMENTS REVISITED

We have already talked about the effect of a change in the price of one good on the quantity demanded of a related good. We defined substitutes and complements in terms of whether a reduction in the price of one good caused a shift leftward or rightward, respectively, in the demand curve of the other.

$$\eta_{xy} = \frac{\Delta q_x/q_x}{\Delta P_y/P_y}$$

Quantity of x demanded increases / Price of y increases $\searrow \nearrow \frac{(+)/q_x}{(+)/P_y} = (+) = \eta_{xy}$

x and y are substitutes

Quantity of x demanded decreases / Price of y decreases $\searrow \nearrow \frac{(-)/q_x}{(-)/P_y} = (+) = \eta_{xy}$

Quantity demanded of x increases / Price of y decreases $\searrow \nearrow \frac{(+)/q_x}{(-)/P_y} = (-) = \eta_{xy}$

x and y are complements

Now we can also use a definition of elasticity to define substitutability and complementarity. Up to this point, we have discussed what happens to the quantity demanded of a good when its *own* price changes; we have been referring to the *own price elasticity of demand*. Now we examine the **cross-price elasticity of demand,** which is defined as

$$\eta_{xy} = \frac{\Delta q_x/q_x}{\Delta P_y/P_y} = \frac{\Delta q_x}{\Delta P_y} \cdot \frac{P_y}{q_x}$$

$$\text{or} \quad \eta_{yx} = \frac{\Delta q_y/q_y}{\Delta P_x/P_x} = \frac{\Delta q_y}{\Delta P_x} \cdot \frac{P_x}{q_y}$$

(5-31)

The subscripts refer to two commodities, x and y. Whenever η_{xy} or η_{yx} is positive, we classify the two commodities as substitutes. When it is negative, we classify them as complements.[5]

We must be careful in our treatment of substitutes and complements. Substitution is primarily a matter of relative price. A common example of substitutes involves margarine and butter because they have similar *physical*

[5]The definition of complementarity or substitutability as implied in Eq. (5-31) is a *gross* definition. We are referring to *gross* substitutes and *gross* complements since there is no way to take account of compensating changes in the level of real income. In other words, we might want to relabel the cross elasticity of demand, as defined in Eq. (5-31), as the *total* cross-price elasticity of demand.

characteristics. However, if butter costs $100 a pound and margarine $1 a pound, we would undoubtedly find out that they empirically were not good substitutes in the market. Even if the price of margarine went up by a large percentage, few consumers could be induced to switch to butter. We wouldn't, therefore, call them substitutes at these relative prices. However, if butter cost $100 a pound and margarine cost $80 a pound, they would turn out to be substitutes.

TABLE 5-6
Selected estimates of price elasticity of demand

Source: For the food category, D. M. Shuffett, The Demand and Price Structure for Selected Vegetables (Washington, D.C.: U.S. Department of Agriculture, 1954; Technical Bulletin no. 1105); for all other categories, H. S. Houthakker and L. D. Taylor, Consumer Demand in the United States: Analyses and Projections (Cambridge, Mass.: Harvard University Press, 1970). Fractions have been rounded.

Category	Estimated η	
	Short-run coefficient	Long-run coefficient
Food		
Potatoes	−0.3	
Peas, fresh	−2.8	
Peas, canned	−1.6	
Tomatoes, fresh	−4.6	
Tomatoes, canned	−2.5	
Nondurable goods		
Shoes	−0.9	
Newspapers and magazines	−0.4	
Tires and related items	−0.8	−1.2
Services		
Auto repair and related services	−1.4	
Radio and television repair	−0.5	−3.8
Travel and entertainment		
Legitimate theater and opera	−0.2	−0.31
Motion pictures	−0.87	−3.7
Foreign travel by United States residents	−0.1	−1.8
Public transportation		
Taxicabs	−0.6	
Local public transportation	−0.6	−1.2
Intercity bus	−0.2	−2.2
Utility services		
Electricity	−0.1	−1.8
Telephone	−0.25	
Miscellaneous		
Jewelry and watches	−0.4	−0.6

Some estimates of price elasticities

In Table 5-6, we are presented with some estimated price elasticities of demand for some food items, nondurable goods, services, travel and entertainment, and public transportation. For a number of these items, there are separate short- and long-run estimates of the price elasticity of demand. All the elasticities are negative. In all cases, the estimated long-run price elasticity of demand was numerically greater than the short-run figure. Therefore, these estimates do not refute our hypothesis that the longer the time for adjustment, the greater the price elasticity of demand.

THE PRICE ELASTICITY OF SUPPLY

We can define the **price elasticity of supply** in the same manner as we defined the price elasticity of demand. We use the Greek letter ε, *epsilon*, to denote the coefficient of the price elasticity of supply. It will be equal to

$$\varepsilon = \frac{\Delta q/q}{\Delta P/P} = \frac{\Delta q}{\Delta P} \cdot \frac{P}{q} \tag{5-32}$$

It is similar to the formula for the coefficient of the price elasticity of demand. However, supply curves are generally upward-sloping: ε will, except in cases of decreasing-cost industries, be positive. We denote supply curves as elastic, unit-elastic, or inelastic, according to whether ε exceeds 1, is equal to 1, or is less than 1. A vertical supply curve has an elasticity ε equal to 0; a horizontal supply curve has an elasticity ε equal to ∞. Thus, the supply curve SS in Figure 5-15 has a price elasticity of supply ε equal to infinity. On the other hand, the vertical supply curve S′S′ has a price elasticity of supply ε equal to 0.

FIGURE 5-15
Extreme price elasticities of supply
Supply curve SS is perfectly horizontal. Its price elasticity of supply, ε, is equal to infinity. Vertical supply curve S′S has ε = 0.

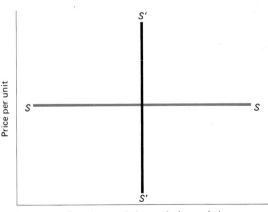

Quantity supplied per unit time period

Slope of the supply curve and price elasticity

As with a linear demand curve, we cannot determine the price elasticity of demand by looking at its slope. Consider supply curves $S''S''$ and $S'''S'''$ in Figure 5-16. They have different slopes, yet both have a price elasticity of supply equal to 1. Look at Eq. (5-32) again. It is equal to the reciprocal of the slope of the supply curve times P/q. In other words, it is equal to P/q divided by the slope of the supply curve. However, for any supply curve that passes through 0, the origin, $\Delta P/\Delta q$, will always equal P/q. Thus, *any linear supply curve passing through the origin has unitary elasticity at each and every price.*

Two linear supply curves with the same slope will have different elasticities, depending on whether they intersect the vertical or the horizontal axis. To see why, consider again the formula for price elasticity of supply:

$$\varepsilon = \frac{\Delta q/q}{\Delta P/P}$$

Now look at supply curve SS in panel (a) of Figure 5-17. Supply curve SS is parallel to supply curve $S'S'$ in panel (b).

SS intersects the vertical axis in panel (a). Consider an increase in quantity supplied from 0 to q. Since we are starting at 0 quantity supplied, $\Delta q/q$ must be equal to 1. In order to obtain q of output, the price P must be fetched. But to go from 0 quantity supplied to q quantity supplied, the change in price is equal only to ΔP, as seen in panel (a) of Figure 5-17. Since ΔP is less than P, the term $\Delta P/P$ is less than 1. Using the price elasticity of supply formula, we know that the numerator, $\Delta q/q$, will equal 1 and the denomi-

FIGURE 5-16
The price elasticity of supply
One cannot tell by the slope of a supply curve whether it is elastic or inelastic. Any supply curve such as $S'''S'''$ that forms a ray from the origin has an elasticity of unity.

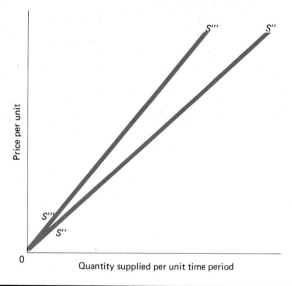

Price per unit

S''' S''

S'''
S''

0

Quantity supplied per unit time period

FIGURE 5-17
Parallel supply curves with different price elasticities
Supply curve SS in panel (a) is parallel to supply curve S'S' in panel (b). Nonetheless, SS in panel (a) will always be elastic, whereas S'S' in panel (b) will always be inelastic.

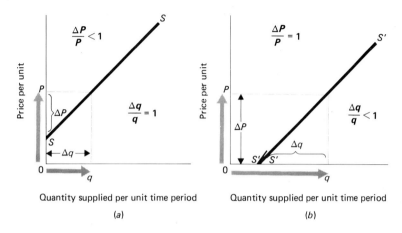

(a)

(b)

nator, $\Delta P/P$, will always be less than 1. Hence, *any supply curve, such as SS, that intersects the vertical axis will have a price elasticity of supply ε that is greater than 1; it will always be price-elastic.*

Now consider supply curve S'S' in panel (b). [It is parallel to SS in panel (a).] It cuts the horizontal axis. Consider a price rise from 0 to P. It is represented by ΔP, which is also equal to P since we started on the vertical axis at the origin 0. Hence, the term ΔP can be chosen to be always equal to 1. But, the change in q, Δq, is shown to be less than the distance from the origin to q. Hence, with a change in price from 0 to P, we get a $\Delta q/q$ that is less than 1. Using our price elasticity of supply formula Eq. (5-32), we realize that the numerator, $\Delta q/q$, will always be less than 1 and the denominator, $\Delta P/P$, will always equal 1. Hence, *all supply curves similar to S'S' which intersect the horizontal axis will have price elasticities of supply ε that will be less than 1; they will be price-inelastic.*

ELASTICITY OF SUPPLY AND LENGTH OF TIME FOR ADJUSTMENT

Earlier in this chapter, we pointed out that the longer the time allowed for adjustment, the more price-elastic is the demand curve. It turns out that the same proposition applies to supply. The longer the time for adjustment, the more price-elastic is the supply curve. Thus, in Figure 5-18 we could hypothesize that the immediate-run (market period) supply curve would be

FIGURE 5-18
Allowing for the time of adjustment
The immediate-run (market period) supply curve S_1S_1 is vertical. Its price elasticity is equal to zero. As more time is allowed for adjustment, it becomes less inelastic (or more elastic).

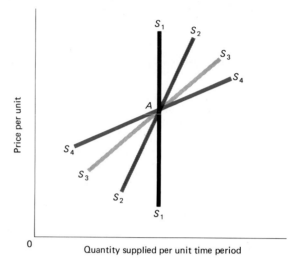

S_1S_1. However, as more time was allowed for adjustment, the supply curve would rotate to S_2S_2, then S_3S_3, then S_4S_4. Otherwise stated, long-run supply curves will be more price-elastic than short-run supply curves, other things being equal (at the point of rotation, A).

The longer the time allowed for adjustment, the more actual and potential firms are able to figure out ways to increase production in an industry. Moreover, the longer the time allowed, the more resources can flow into the industry. As an example, consider the amount of housing services offered for rent or sale in a particular city. Note that we are referring to housing *services* rather than the *stock* of housing available. In the immediate run, it is conceivable that the supply curve of housing services offered for rent or sale is relatively inelastic. However, as more time is allowed for adjustment, two things can happen. First, current owners of the housing stock can find ways to increase the amount of housing services they will offer for rent from the given stock. This is done, for example, by the owner of a large house who decides to have two of his or her children move into one room and rent out the "extra" bedroom. It can also be done by the owner of a large house who decides to move out into an apartment and rent each floor of the house to a separate family. Second, more apartment buildings, condominiums, co-ops, duplexes, mobile homes, and single-family dwellings will be built so that eventually the housing stock will grow and so too, *ceteris paribus*, will the quantity of housing services supplied.

We can also think in terms of how the individual firm responds to a change in the price of its output. Suppose that the firm expects a price increase to be only short-lived. Under those circumstances, additional plant

TABLE 5-7
Estimated price elasticities of supply

Source: M. Nerlove and W. Addison, "Statistical Estimation of Long-Run Elasticities of Supply and Demand," American Journal of Agricultural Economics (formerly Journal of Farm Economics), vol. 40, November 1958, pp. 861–880.

Commodity	Elasticity ε	
	Short-run coefficient	Long-run coefficient
Cabbage	0.36	1.20
Carrots	0.14	1.00
Cucumbers	0.29	2.20
Onions	0.34	1.00
Green peas	0.31	4.40
Tomatoes	0.16	0.90
Watermelons	0.23	0.48
Beets	0.13	1.00
Cauliflower	0.14	1.10
Celery	0.14	0.95
Eggplant	0.16	0.34
Spinach	0.20	4.70

facilities probably would not be constructed. Rather, the company will run its machines longer by paying overtime rates to workers and/or putting on a second or third shift. On the other hand, if the price increase is expected to be permanent, the firm will consider expanding, and indeed will expand, its capacity through purchases of new plant and equipment needed to produce more in response to higher prices offered. As this is done, we would expect per unit cost to fall in the long run as the firm readapts to a larger, now-optimal scale of plant. Thus, we can generate the set of supply curves depicted in Figure 5-18 in this manner.

Real-world estimates of the price elasticity of supply

There are problems in obtaining empirical estimates of supply elasticities. They are similar to the estimation problems for price elasticity of demand. In Table 5-7, we present some estimates of short- and long-run elasticities of supply for fresh vegetables in the United States. In estimating these elasticities, the short run was defined as one "production period." We note that most short-run elasticities are considerably less than their long-run counterparts.

Demand elasticities and fuel economy[6]

The effectiveness of the government's fuel-efficiency program for automobiles illustrates the use of demand elasticities other than price elasticity. A recent study provides an estimate of the improvements in automobile miles per gallon ("fuel efficiency") and the demand for gasoline. There are two offsetting influences at work in this case. With improved fuel efficiency the number of gallons of fuel used for a particular trip decreases. Yet this decrease in fuel used per mile will, *ceteris paribus*, reduce the marginal cost or price of driving an extra mile, thus increasing the quantity of travel and fuel demanded. Using Florida data for a 10-year period, the authors estimate an elasticity of demand for fuel consumption of -0.703, meaning that for every 10 percent savings in gallons of fuel burned per mile of travel, gasoline consumption will fall by 7 percent.

[6]This discussion is based on Roger D. Blair, David L. Kaserman, and Richard C. Tepel, "The Impact of Improved Mileage on Gasoline Consumption," *Economic Inquiry*, vol. 22, no. 2, April 1984, pp. 209–217.

This relation, however, does not tell us whether this legislated policy for fuel economy is more efficient in reducing fuel consumption than would be a simple increase in the price of fuel. In order to know that we would have to know the cost of redesigning and manufacturing the vehicles that are capable of this greater fuel efficiency. We could then compare this cost with the results of achieving the same reduction in fuel consumption through higher fuel prices. The authors of this study do estimate for us a price elasticity of demand for fuel consumption of -0.412 during the period of the study.

This estimate may be too low for present conditions, however, as the database used in the study ends in 1976, before significant increases in petroleum fuel prices. As you will recall, demand elasticity increases along a straight-line demand curve as the relative price of the good demanded increases. It may thus be that we are at a more elastic demand point today than we were in 1976.

Drug addiction and elasticity

Law enforcement agencies around the world are concerned with the problem of drug use and abuse. More specifically, the sale and use of "hard drugs," or physiologically addictive drugs,[7] is usually a felony punishable by imprisonment and/or fines. Clearly, the more re-

[7]With the exceptions of tobacco and caffeine.

sources that are used in enforcing the laws against drug use, the higher the implicit price to the drug user; the total price of illegal drug use is the actual out-of-pocket cost to purchase the drug, plus the anticipated or expected cost associated with getting caught, jailed, fined, harassed, and so on. If drug laws are not enforced at all, this expected cost is

FIGURE 5-19
Hypothetical individual demand curve for heroin
If an individual is willing to pay "any price" for a given quantity of heroin, that individual's demand curve is represented by vertical line dd, at quantity q_1. The price elasticity of demand is equal to zero.

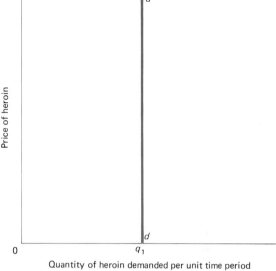

effectively equal to 0. However, the more resources that go into enforcement, the greater the probability of being caught and the greater the total expected cost of using the drug (assuming that enforcement is directed at *users* as well as "dealers").

What is at issue here is the price elasticity of demand for hard drugs. Take the case of heroin. If indeed the individual heroin user's demand curve is dd in Figure 5-19, the quantity demanded will be q_1 "no matter what the price." In other words, no matter how expensive the drug becomes because of increased law enforcement against sellers and users, the same quantity will be demanded. If every individual has a demand curve such as dd *and no budget constraint*, the market demand curve will also be a vertical line. Here the price elasticity of demand is 0; that is, we have a completely inelastic demand curve. Those who contend the users of hard drugs become not only psychologically but physiologically addicted as well are implying that the demand curve is perfectly inelastic, as in Figure 5-19. According to one researcher, "for the heroin user, jail sentences cease to be a deterrent. . . ."[8] Since the quantity of heroin demanded is the same, irrespective of the implicit price charged, researchers in this area often suggest that emphasis must be given to therapeutic programs directed toward altering the addict's life-style (moving his or her demand curve to the left), as opposed to raising the implicit price of the illegal drug.

On a more fundamental level, the entire discussion of the price elasticity of the demand for heroin may often be based on a confusion of averages with margins. The market demand curve for heroin may be relatively inelastic. However, there certainly exist marginal heroin users, such as curious teenagers deciding whether to try the drug once or a few more times, whose demand curves for the drug are relatively elastic. Thus the *market* demand curve will not exhibit a zero price elasticity of demand. After all, there are significant income constraints over any substantial price range.

[8]Raul A. Fernandez, "The Clandestine Distribution of Heroin, Its Discovery and Suppression: A Comment," *Journal of Political Economy*, vol. 77, no. 4, part 1, July/August 1969, p. 487.

The elasticity of the demand for transportation

The concept of demand elasticity reviewed in this chapter has a wide variety of empirical applications. Transportation provides a fertile field for such applications, both because of the historical importance of the industry in economic development—many of the first modern corporations were canal and railroad companies—and because of the many government controls. Price, entry, exits, and operating rules for most interstate transportation modes have long been subject to some form of federal regulation. In addition, many county and municipal governments either own outright or closely regulate local public transportation companies. These considerations, along with the increasing importance of contemporary urban problems such as airport noise and highway congestion, have created the need to understand the nature of competition among alternative ways to transport freight and passengers. Elasticity estimates derived from models of transportation demand are commonly used to guide policy decisions concerning pricing, investment, and other regulatory issues.

BASIC ANALYSIS

The analysis of transportation demand begins with specifying a model of individual choice among various possible modes (auto, bus, or air for passengers; truck, rail, or barge for shippers, for example). The type of transportation chosen is assumed to maximize the chooser's utility or to minimize cost. Economic theory suggests that the model should include as variables the prices of the various transportation alternatives, income, and, perhaps, some attributes of the good being shipped (perishability, shipment size, and so forth). In addition, though, travel (or service) time is an important part of the "price" of transportation. The primary output of any transportation demand model, therefore, consists of estimates of price and service time elasticities of demand.

FAST FREIGHT OR SLOW

Table 5-8 presents some elasticity estimates for the major forms of transportation.[9] As you can see, elasticity estimates in freight transportation vary widely depending on commodity. Lumber and paper products shippers, for example, are not very sensitive to changes in either price or service time. However, shippers of perishable fresh produce are quite responsive to changes in the time required for transporting their product by rail. The magnitudes of the estimated elasticities also indicate the degree of competition for shipping goods. Low values suggest that a transportation firm could raise its rate to shippers without having many of its customers shift to alternative forms of transportation.

UNCLOG THE HIGHWAYS?

The price and service time elasticities for urban passenger transportation modes indicate that reductions in travel time can be as effective as fare reductions in increasing ridership. In addition, however, the generally inelastic nature of the demand for transportation in cities means that policies aimed at reducing highway congestion (e.g., raising tolls, introducing "express" buses to cut travel time) are not likely to be very effective. On the other hand, fare increases can lead to revenue increases for the public transit authority.

[9]Clifford Winston, "Conceptual Developments in the Economics of Transportation: An Interpretive Survey," *Journal of Economic Literature*, vol. 23, March 1985, p. 74.

TABLE 5-8
Transportation price and service time elasticities

A. FREIGHT

	Rail price Elasticity	Rail service time elasticity	Truck price elasticity	Truck service time elasticity
Fresh produce		−2.33		−.69
Leather, rubber, plastic products			−2.97	
Lumber	−.08			
Machinery			−.04	
Mineral products	−.37		−1.81	
Paper products		−.07		−.15
Petroleum products	−1.16		−.58	
Transport equipment	−2.68			

B. URBAN PASSENGER

	Auto	Bus	Rail
Price elasticity	−.47	−.58	−.86
Service time elasticity	−.22	−.60	−.60

C. INTERCITY PASSENGER

	Auto	Bus	Rail	Air
Price elasticity	−45	−.69	−1.20	−.38
Service time elasticity	−.39	−2.11	−1.58	−.43

TAKE THE A TRAIN?

Finally, price and service time elasticities for intercity auto and air transportation are inelastic, but mostly elastic for bus and rail. Interestingly, those taking the bus for long trips are more sensitive to changes in travel time than to changes in price. These companies have probably suffered substantially because of the federally mandated 55 miles per hour speed limit.

Do police deter crime? The case of basketball

Economics can be used to model illegal activities just as we usually employ economic tools to analyze more traditional markets. In the economic model of criminal activity we usually assume that potential criminals weigh the costs and benefits of their actions, so that if the costs of committing crimes are increased, the number of crimes committed will decrease.[10] Two primary factors have been shown to raise the costs of committing crime: (1) being detected, arrested, and convicted, and (2) the level of punishment.

If we were to have a police force so vigilant that they detected almost every illegal act, apprehended the person(s) committing the act, and saw that they were convicted, the expected net benefits from criminal activity would be very low or negative. Even if the punishment was not severe, because the chance of getting away with the illegal act was very low, it would not be very worthwhile. On the other hand, if only a fraction of the suspected criminals are caught, if the punishment were severe, then the expected net benefit would again be reduced. That is, if only one in ten car thieves are apprehended, it may appear that the return to car theft is not too low. But if every apprehended car thief is executed or given life in prison, then the expected value of a car theft is not very high and would be negative for most people.

CRIME ON THE COURT

Two economists applied this economic model of illegal activity to illegal activity in sports—in particular, basketball. They looked at the role of referees as being like that of a police officer and judge.[11] A referee detects illegal activity, identifies the guilty party, and imposes a penalty. What happens when the number of referees is increased? That is, given the same game, the same number of minutes played, the same rules, and the same number of players, what is the consequence of increasing the referees from two to three?

ACC BASKETBALL

Since the authors of the study were located at a school in the Atlantic Coast Conference (ACC), they studied the impact of the increase in the number of referees by 50 percent in the annual ACC tournament. The data they used began in 1954, when the tournament started, through the 1983 tournament. The number of referees was increased in 1979.

Economic theory predicts that if potential criminals know that the chance of being apprehended for their acts has increased (the penalty for illegal acts remaining the same), they will commit fewer acts. This was the case in basketball. The number of fouls called per game dropped by about 17—a 34 percent reduction in the number of offenses detected and called by the officials, despite an increase of 50 percent of the number of officials.

FEWER BAD CALLS

The addition of a third referee apparently not only reduced the incentive of players to commit fouls, because of the increased chance of being detected, but because it allowed each referee to watch a small number of players or monitor behavior in a smaller area; it seems to have increased the quality of the fouls called. That is, the referees made fewer bad calls (false arrests).

Note that the result of this study does not mean that the addition of the third referee was a "good" thing. One cannot conclude, just because a 50 percent increase in the size of a police force may reduce the number of crimes committed and the number of false arrests, that the force should be increased by 50 percent. One must compare the marginal cost of increasing the size of the police force (or the number of referees) with the marginal benefit that results from the value of crimes deterred.

---

[10]Gary S. Becker, "Crime and Punishment: An Economic Approach," *Journal of Political Economy*, March/April 1968, pp. 169–217. Also Isaac Ehrlich, "The Deterrent Effect of Capital Punishment: A Question of Life and Death," *American Economic Review*, June 1975, pp. 397–417.

[11]Robert E. McCormick and Robert D. Tollison, "Crime on the Court," *Journal of Political Economy*, April 1984, pp. 223–235.

SUMMARY

1   The coefficient of price elasticity of demand is

$$\eta = \frac{\Delta q/q}{\Delta P/P} = \frac{\Delta q}{\Delta P} \cdot \frac{P}{q}$$

2   For other than Giffen goods, η is always negative, holding *money* income constant.

3   Price elasticity of demand depends on (a) the existence and closeness of substitutes, (b) the "importance" of the commodity in total expenditures, and (c) the length of time allowed for adjustment to price changes.

4   Long-run demand curves are more elastic than short-run demand curves.

5   If we wish to compute the arc elasticity, we must use a compromise formula; in one of these we estimate price elasticity at the midpoint of the arc.

6   We can derive the point price elasticity of demand by using either the horizontal or the vertical axis formula. In the horizontal axis formula, we draw from the horizontal axis a perpendicular to the point on the demand curve where we wish to measure price elasticity of demand. The ratio of the distance from that line to the intersection of the demand curve on the horizontal axis over the distance from the origin to that line on the horizontal axis is our measure of price elasticity of demand at that point on the demand curve. A similar procedure is used with the vertical axis formula: A line is drawn horizontally from the point on the demand curve to the vertical axis.

7   Price elasticity of demand along the linear demand curve varies from $-\infty$ to 0 as we move from the upper-left extreme of the demand curve down to the lower right, where the demand curve terminates on the horizontal axis.

8   It is important to distinguish between the slope of the demand curve and its price elasticity. Since η is equal to the negative value of the reciprocal of the slope of the demand curve times the fraction P/q, the slope does not uniquely determine price elasticity.

9   When comparing any two straight-line demand curves on the same diagram, the one that intersects the vertical axis closer to the origin is the more elastic at each and every price.

10 Producers' revenues (TR $= P \times Q$) are the mirror image of consumers' expenditures.

11   Marginal revenue becomes zero at the quantity where total revenue reaches its maximum.

12   Marginal revenue is given by the formula $MR = P(1 + 1/\eta)$.

13   A vertical line drawn from the point where the marginal revenue curve intersects the horizontal axis will hit the demand curve where $\eta = -1$.

14   When demand is price-elastic, total revenues change in the opposite direction of a price change. When demand is unitary-price-elastic, total revenues remain constant when there is a price change. When demand is price-inelastic, total revenues change in the same direction as a price change.

15   The classification of goods is based upon their income elasticity of demand (μ): An inferior good has a negative μ; a normal good has a positive μ.

16   The sum of weighted averages of income elasticities of demand for all commodities purchased must equal 1. The weights are the relative shares of total expenditures by the consumer.

17   Given that the weighted income elasticities must add up to 1, if a particular commodity is strongly inferior, there must be at least one even more strongly normal good in the basket of commodities purchased by the consumer.

18   Items that take up a large percentage of a consumer's budget generally have small income elasticities of demand.

19   The cross-price elasticity of demand is defined as $\eta_{xy} = (\Delta q_x/\Delta P_y)\,(P_y/q_x)$. When η_{xy} is positive, the goods are substitutes; when it is negative, they are complements.

20   The price elasticity of supply is defined as

$$\varepsilon = \frac{\Delta q/q}{\Delta P/P}$$

21   Vertical supply curves have a price elasticity of zero. Horizontal supply curves have a price elasticity of infinity.

22   Any linear supply curve passing through the origin has unitary elasticity at each and every point.

23   Any straight-line supply curve that intersects the vertical axis will be price-elastic; any straight-line supply curve that intersects the horizontal axis will be price-inelastic.

24   The longer the time allowed for adjustment the greater the price elasticity of supply.

GLOSSARY

- **point elasticity** Price elasticity of demand measured at a single point on a demand curve; to be constrasted with *arc* elasticity.
- **arc elasticity** Price elasticity of demand measured along a section of a demand curve rather than at a single point; to be contrasted with point elasticity.
- **total revenue** Price per unit times quantity sold per unit time period.
- **marginal revenue** Change in total revenue associated with a one-unit change in the quantity sold.
- **average revenue** Total revenue divided by quantity; the result is price per unit where all units are sold at a uniform price.
- **income elasticity of demand** The responsiveness of the quantity demanded of a good to changes in income; the percentage change in the quantity demanded of a good divided by the percentage change in money income.
- **cross-price elasticity of demand** The relative change in the quantity demanded of good x divided by the relative change in the price of good y; to be contrasted with *price elasticity of demand.*
- **price elasticity of supply** The relative change in the quantity supplied divided by the relative change in the price.

QUESTIONS

(Answers to even-numbered questions are at back of text.)

1 Define price elasticity of demand, income elasticity of demand, and cross elasticity of demand.

2 Looking at the formula $\eta = (\Delta q/\Delta P)\,(P/q)$, how can you tell that when the demand curve is a straight line, the price elasticity of demand *must* be different at every price?

3 Construct on the same graph two straight-line demand curves with the same y intercept, with one flatter than the other. Can you make a general statement about which one is the more elastic curve? If so, what is it?

4 Now construct on the same graph two straight-line demand curves with the same x intercept, with one flatter than the other. Answer the same question which was posed in question 3 above.

5 Draw the Seven-Up Bottling Company's demand curve for 1-liter returnable 7-Up bottles. What is its price elasticity of demand?

6 Can any demand curve possibly be perfectly inelastic ($\eta = 0$) regardless of price? Explain.

7 Like the perfectly (infinitely) elastic and perfectly (zero) inelastic demand curves, the *unitary-elastic* demand curve is somewhat of a curiosity. Give its equation. What is the geometric name for such a curve? Looking at that equation, why is it impossible for the curve ever to "cut" (intercept) either axis? Suppose you were the only owner in the world of a perishable good, the demand for which was unitary-elastic at all prices. How much would you charge per unit, if you wanted to make the most money possible?

8 Explain how you would calculate the point elasticity of a nonlinear demand curve at some price p.

9 What is the difficulty inherent in estimating arc elasticity $(\%\Delta q)/(\%\Delta P)$? How was it suggested that you deal with it?

10 Which of the following cross elasticities of demand would you expect to be positive and which to be negative: (a) tennis balls and tennis racquets, (b) tennis balls and golf balls, (c) dental services and toothpaste, (d) dental services and candy, (e) liquor and ice cubes, (f) liquor and marijuana?

11 For any given relative price, would you think that the demand for canal transportation was more or less elastic in 1840 than in 1880? How about the demand for Pony Express messengers before and after the transcontinental telegraph? The demand for rail transportation before and after the Model T Ford? Before and after the Ford Tri-Motor? The demand for transatlantic cable-laying equipment before and after communications satellites? The demand for slide rules before and after introduction of the pocket-sized electronic calculator? Why?

12 A new mobile-home park makes no charge whatsoever for water used by its inhabitants. Consumption is 100,000 gallons per month. Then the decision is made to charge according to how much each mobile-home owner uses, at a rate of $10 per thousand gallons. Consumption declines to 50,000 gallons per month. Try to measure the demand elasticity. Can you?

13 "A harsh winter in Florida, by wiping out the orange crop, will certainly decrease the revenues of citrus growers." Is this statement true or false, and why?

14 "The demand curves of wealthy persons are consistently less elastic than those of the less affluent." Is this statement true or false?

15 "The demand for sodium chloride (table salt) must be pretty inelastic. Even if the price did change, surely this wouldn't affect the amount people use on hard-boiled eggs, french fries, and the like." Is this statement true or false, and why?

SELECTED REFERENCES

Allen, R.G.D., "The Concept of Arc Elasticity of Demand," *Review of Economic Studies,* vol. 1, June 1934, pp. 226–229.

Baumol, W., *Economic Theory and Operations Analysis* (Englewood Cliffs, N.J.: Prentice-Hall, 1965), pp. 211–214.

Dean, J., "Estimating the Price Elasticity of Demand," in E. Mansfield (ed.), *Managerial Economics and Operations Research,* 3d ed. (New York: Norton, 1975).

Lerner, A.P., "Geometrical Comparisons of Elasticities," *American Economic Review,* vol. 37, March 1947, p. 191.

Norris, Ruby T., *The Theory of Consumer's Demand,* rev. ed. (New Haven: Yale University Press, 1952), chap. 9.

Schultz, Henry, *The Theory and Measurement of Demand* (Chicago: University of Chicago Press, 1938).

Working, E.J., "What Do Statistical 'Demand Curves' Show?" *Quarterly Journal of Economics,* vol. 41, 1927, p. 212–235; reprinted in American Economic Association, *Readings in Price Theory* (Chicago: Irwin, 1952).

APPENDIX TO CHAPTER 5

INDIVIDUAL AND MARKET ELASTICITIES OF DEMAND

We looked at the derivation of individual demand curves and then derived the market demand curve by summing horizontally all individual demand curves. As might be expected, there is a definite relation between the individual price elasticities of demand and the market price elasticity of demand. The market price elasticity of demand is equal to the weighted average of all the individual price elasticities of demand. The weights are equal to each individual buyer's share of the total quantity demanded at any given price. This can be seen in the following exercise. Let

$$X = x_1 + x_2 \qquad (A5\text{-}1)$$

where X is the market quantity demanded and x_1 and x_2 are the individual quantities demanded. Then with a small change, Δ, in x_1 and x_2, Eq. (A5-1) becomes

$$\Delta X = \Delta x_1 + \Delta x_2 \qquad (A5\text{-}2)$$

We now divide both sides of Eq. (A5-2) by the same quantity, ΔP, which is equal to a small change in the market price. When we do so, we preserve the equality because we are dividing both sides of the equation by the same quantity.

$$\frac{\Delta X}{\Delta P} = \frac{\Delta x_1}{\Delta P} + \frac{\Delta x_2}{\Delta P} \qquad (A5\text{-}3)$$

If we multiply both sides of the resulting Eq. (A5-3) by exactly the same quantity, we continue to preserve the equality. The quantity which we will use in this multiplication process is P/X.

$$\frac{\Delta X}{\Delta P} \cdot \frac{P}{X} = \left(\frac{\Delta x_1}{\Delta P} \cdot \frac{P}{X} \right) + \left(\frac{\Delta x_2}{\Delta P} \cdot \frac{P}{X} \right) \qquad (A5\text{-}4)$$

Then multiply each term on the right-hand side of Eq. (A5-4) by x_1/x_1 and x_2/x_2, respectively. We can clearly make these two transformations because $x_1/x_1 = 1$ and $x_2/x_2 = 1$, and multiplying by 1 does not change anything.

$$\frac{\Delta X}{\Delta P} \cdot \frac{P}{X} = \left(\frac{\Delta x_1}{\Delta P} \cdot \frac{P}{X} \cdot \frac{x_1}{x_1} \right) + \left(\frac{\Delta x_2}{\Delta P} \cdot \frac{P}{X} \cdot \frac{x_2}{x_2} \right)$$

$$= \left(\frac{\Delta x_1}{\Delta P} \cdot \frac{P}{x_1} \cdot \frac{x_1}{X} \right) + \left(\frac{\Delta x_2}{\Delta P} \cdot \frac{P}{x_2} \cdot \frac{x_2}{X} \right) \qquad (A5\text{-}5)$$

Rearranging Eq. (A5-5) into some recognizable terms,

$$\frac{\Delta X/X}{\Delta P/P} = \left(\frac{\Delta x_1/x_1}{\Delta P/P} \cdot \frac{x_1}{X} \right) + \left(\frac{\Delta x_2/x_2}{\Delta P/P} \cdot \frac{x_2}{X} \right)$$

$$(A5\text{-}6)$$

In Eq. (A5-6), we recognize three terms representing price elasticity of demand; we can also recognize that the terms x_1/X and x_2/X merely represent the proportion of the total market demand that is accounted for by individuals 1 and 2, respectively. If we let each share be denoted by g_1, and g_2, respectively, we get

$$\eta_{\text{total market}} = g_1 \cdot \eta_{\text{individual 1}} + g_2 \cdot \eta_{\text{individual 2}}$$

$$(A5\text{-}7)$$

The economics of time: planning for the future

*T*ime is a scarce economic resource; it has a positive economic value. Time has positive marginal utility for most people as a source of leisure. It has a market value as one of the factors required to produce goods, either as labor or as a part of the accumulation of human capital. Time also has a role in the consumption of other goods. There is a **time cost** involved in the consumption of goods, and consumers place different values on the consumption of items at different times.

In this chapter, we will extend our basis analysis to include the economics of time, the economics of time preference, the decisions of individuals about how to allocate their time, and decisions about how to use non-human durable factors of production over time.

THE ECONOMICS OF TIME

Clearly, time is required for work effort. There is a time constraint imposed on each individual. We showed that in our analysis of the labor-leisure choice in the Issues and Applications section of Chapter 4. However, consider the fact that the consumption of commodities requires time too. A haircut is not purchased and consumed instantaneously. The purchase of the haircut involves the explicit monetary cost plus the time involved in waiting to be served plus the time consumed sitting in the barber's chair. The consumption of a meal includes the time involved in sitting at the table while the meal is being eaten. A vacation trip entails a time cost. Hence, the cost of a trip is not merely the monetary outlay—the reduction in wealth available for the other consumption activities—but also the value placed on the reduction in time available to engage in other activities.

In this context, rather than separate the notions of consumption and production, we can consider the cost of all facets of the process of satisfying human wants. Thus, the production of a meal will require all the inputs, including groceries, fuel, shopping time, preparation time, and so forth, as well as the time required to eat the meal.

Total cost of consumption

When viewed in this fashion, the total price of consuming any good is the sum of its market price and the opportunity cost of the time required to consume the good, where opportunity cost is the value of that time in its best alternative use.

| Market price (explicit cost) | Opportunity cost (implicit cost) |

Total cost of consumption

Thus, it is possible to say that the total price of consuming a product selling for a fixed monetary price varies with the opportunity cost of the individual consuming the product. Hence, a 15-minute haircut that "costs" $6 is more expensive to an individual whose opportunity cost of time is higher than it is to some other individual. This example leads to an interesting hypothesis.

If we include in the time cost of haircuts the cost of waiting to be served by a barber, an increase in the relative money cost of a haircut will lead to a *decrease* in the total cost of consumption for certain individuals. How can that be? If the price elasticity of demand for haircuts is sufficiently high in numerical value, an increase in the relative money price of haircuts will reduce significantly the quantity demanded at a given barber shop. Some people just won't get haircuts, or won't get them as often. The amount of time one must wait for a barber will therefore fall. Thus, the relatively more highly paid individual whose opportunity cost of time (by definition) is higher may find that the *total* cost of a haircut has fallen, even though he or she must now pay a higher *money* price.

Using this approach, we can explain, at least in part, much of the behavior of certain income groups of individuals who are willing to spend relatively larger amounts of time to consume particular goods. Teenagers, by and large, are more willing than adults to wait in line for tickets to sporting events. This follows from the law of demand. At a lower price, a larger quantity will be demanded. The price to teenagers of purchasing a ticket to an important sporting event plus watching the sporting event will be lower than the cost to an adult who typically has a higher opportunity cost of time. Hence, most teenagers will demand a larger quantity of the product than will most adults.

Similarly, there is a fairly obvious negative correlation or relation between the salaries of married people who work and the number of children they choose to have. If we consider children as a consumption item, the demand for children should be inversely related to the relative price. But the relative price of children includes the time necessary to take care of them. The more a person earns in the marketplace, the higher this opportunity cost; hence, the higher the total cost or price of a child and the fewer children demanded.

Income and the value of time

Finally, using this approach, we can point out what might occur as the value of time rises. Bargaining over the price of clothing, food, and minor personal goods is widespread in less developed countries—and used to be common in this country. Now, we bargain only over the prices of "large ticket" items (automobiles and houses) and, in general, purchase lesser-valued items at advertised or listed prices. The difference probably has to do with the increased value of our time. Similarly, we would predict that, in general, the consumption of time-intensive goods—those which require relatively large amounts of time to consume—will fall, *ceteris paribus*, as wage rates rise. Obviously this is not true for all goods, as we observe highly paid individuals engaging in the time-intensive sport of golf. For the prediction to be correct, the income effect must be outweighed by the substitution effect.

Time and utility

We know that a person's income is, in part, a function of income-leisure trade-offs. It is also true that a consumer's ultimate realized utility is a function of the time costs of the goods that a consumer chooses to consume. A consumer gives up the opportunity to consume goods as income is spent on additional units of a particular good, and the opportunity to consume other goods is also sacrificed as time is spent in the consumption of some particular good. The two do not always correspond. Fishing may have a low money cost but a high time cost. Playing the roulette tables may have a low time cost but a high money cost. The choice facing the utility maximizer is thus not so simple as a balancing between income and leisure. The allocation of time between alternative leisure uses must also be considered.

As helpful as these insights are in analyzing real-world situations, we cannot easily integrate them into our formal theory of choice without cumbersome mathematics (see the appendix to this chapter for such a presentation). We will often continue to assume that the goods available to consumers have no time costs connected to them or that the time costs are the same for all goods but the analysis here shows that we can account for time when we need to do so.

TIME PREFERENCE

When we started our formal analysis, the choice confronting the consumer was between two goods—movies and concerts—or more abstractly, between commodity x and commodity y. The two goods were to be consumed "today." It was a choice of concurrent consumption of either one of the goods or a combination of the two. We carried out that analysis using indifference curves.

Similarly, we can consider consumers making choices now between consuming commodities "today" and consuming them "tomorrow." Clearly, it is possible to forgo spending some of one's income today in order to be able to spend it tomorrow or the next day. Moreover, it is possible for individuals to borrow in order to consume today and to repay tomorrow, thereby reducing tomorrow's consumption. Thus we see that there is a choice between consumption today and consumption tomorrow. This is generally called the **theory of time preference.** How much does the individual prefer current consumption to future consumption? There is a market which deals with time preference. It is the credit market which permits individuals to satisfy their time preferences.

The price of time

In order to obtain consumer equilibrium with respect to the two commodities—present goods and future goods—we have to deal with the budget constraint facing the consumer and the consumer's preferences. In order to derive a budget constraint, we have to introduce a special price. This is the price of time preference and, more specifically, is the **interest rate,** r, which we will define as the rate of exchange between goods today and goods tomorrow. The interest rate arises in the market for credit.

One way to view the credit market is to consider it a market in which individuals are exchanging present and future consumption. In other words, the *suppliers* of credit are willing to trade present consumption (command over current purchasing power) for the expectation of higher future consumption. On the other hand, *demanders* of credit are willing to exchange claims to future consumption for present consumption.

Deriving the interest rate

In Figure 6-1, we show a simple supply and demand model for the credit market. The demand curve shows the wants and resources of borrowers while the supply curve shows the wants and resources of lenders. Whether a given person is a net borrower or a net lender is, of course, in part a function of the prevailing rate of interest, as shown by Figure 6-2. The intersection of the supply curve with the demand curve determines the market rate of interest. In this example, we assume that we live in an unlikely world in which there is no expectation of future inflation. It would be relatively simple to take account of inflation by adding on an inflationary factor to the interest

FIGURE 6-1

Determination of the interest rate

The credit market is essentially a market in which potential debtors are seeking to purchase the rights to current consumption, and potential creditors are seeking to sell these rights in expectation of higher future consumption. The demand curve DD slopes downward. The supply curve SS slopes upward. The intersection yields an equilibrium rate of interest r_e. In this model, we assume no expectation of future inflation.

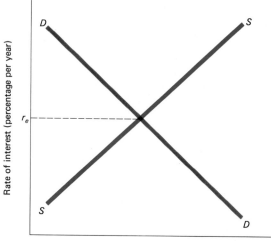

FIGURE 6-2

Individual decision to borrow or lend

The diagram shows the "excess demand" curve for a consumer who is allocating income over 2 or more years by borrowing or lending. If the interest rate is r_0 the consumer will lend $500, reducing consumption this year to increase future consumption. At interest rate r_2 this consumer will borrow $600, increasing current consumption and decreasing future consumption. At interest rate r_1 this consumer will neither borrow nor lend. The consumer's excess demand schedule will shift up or down as expectations about future wealth or income change or as changes in current wealth or income occur.

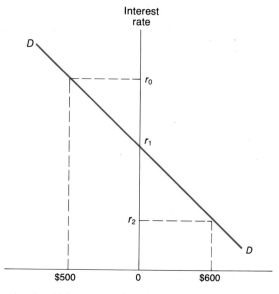

rate r in our model, but we choose not to do so in order to keep the analysis less complicated.

We assume that an individual consumer is a very small part of the entire credit market, and therefore can either borrow or lend as much as he or she wishes at the prevailing market rate of interest. Assume that the prevailing rate of interest is represented by r. Then unity plus the rate of interest, or $(1 + r)$, is the price of current consumption. That is, by consuming $1 today, one forgoes $$(1 + r)$ in the future. Or, looked at another way, one must pay back $$(1 + r)$ in the future in order to borrow and buy $1 of goods now.

This point is sufficiently important to justify another example to make it clear. If the market rate of interest is 10 percent, an individual can save (not consume), say, $100 today and have $110 one year from now. Assuming no inflation, the consumer can purchase $110 worth of consumption a year from now, or 10 percent more, by waiting 1 year rather than consuming the $100 today. Otherwise stated, with a market interest rate of 10 percent, a commodity which costs $110 can be purchased a year from now by setting aside $100 today. Assuming that all income is received at the *start* of each period, we have numerically

$$(1 + 0.10) \ \$100 = \$110 \tag{6-1}$$

Looked at another way, if the consumer's income is $100 in period 1 and $0 in period 2, the consumer can save all $100 in period 1 and have a wealth position of $110 at the beginning of period 2.

Let's reverse the situation. Let's assume that the individual makes no income in period 1 and is certain of making $110 in period 2. A bank may decide to use the certain $110 (to be earned in period 2) as collateral for a $100 loan *now* to this individual, and charge an interest rate of 10 percent.[1] At the beginning of period 2, the principal of $100 plus $10 interest must be paid.

In these two extreme examples, the individual can maximize consumption in the period in which income is not received.

The budget constraint

A general formula can be developed from this analysis to give us the budget constraint that the individual has over the two periods. In period 1, the individual can consume everything earned in period 1 plus the amount that can be borrowed on the basis of income that is expected to be earned in period 2. If we let M_1 equal the income in period 1 and M_2 equal the income in period 2 and call r the interest rate, our formula for the maximum amount of consumption in period 1 will be

$$M_1 + \frac{M_2}{1 + r} = \begin{array}{c} \text{maximum period 1} \\ \text{consumption} \end{array} \tag{6-2}$$

[1] In this analysis we will assume that the rates of borrowing and lending are always equal. There is no "spread" between the two rates.

In the last example, M_1 was zero, M_2 was $110, and the interest rate was 10 percent. Thus, the equation would become

$$0 + \frac{\$110}{1.10} = \$100 \tag{6-3}$$

Now, what about the budget constraint for period 2? The maximum consumable in period 2 is clearly the total amount of money income in period 2 plus the amount of money income available in period 1 (with zero spending) plus the interest earned from saving that, or

$$M_2 + M_1(1 + r) = \frac{\text{maximum period 2}}{\text{consumption}} \tag{6-4}$$

We now have two extreme points from which we may construct the budget constraint. This is done in Figure 6-3. The budget constraint is BB'. Just as the slope of the budget constraint for two commodities purchased concurrently and consumed today was the negative of the ratio of their prices, the same is true in this case. However, the marginal rate of market substitution (MRMS) between one commodity—goods today—and another commodity—goods tomorrow—is $-(1 + r)/1$, since the price of today's goods is 1 and the price of today's goods tomorrow is $(1 + r)$. Thus the slope of BB' is $-(1 + r)$. That is the feasible or market rate at which individuals can substitute present consumption for future consumption, or future consumption for present consumption.

We can better see how we derive the slope of the budget constraint BB' by considering Figure 6-4. We take the point labeled A, which represents

---

FIGURE 6-3
The time of preference budget constraint
If all income is consumed in period 1, total consumption is equal to $M_1 + M_2/(1 + r)$. If, on the other hand, all income is saved in period 1, total income available in period 2 is $M_2 + M_1$ $(1 + r)$, or period 2 income plus income from period 1 plus accrued interest from the saving during period 1. This gives us two points for our budget constraint. The resultant budget line is labeled BB'. Its slope is equal to $-(1 + r)$.

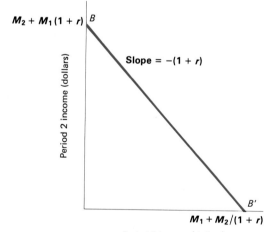

▬▬▬▬

FIGURE 6-4
The slope of the budget constraint
For point $A(M_1, M_2)$, the slope will equal $-M_2B/M_2A$. If we substitute the values for B and A, we obtain a formula for slope which is equal to

$$\text{Slope} = -\frac{M_2 + (1+r)M_1 - M_2}{M_1}$$

which, upon simplification, becomes $-(1+r)$.

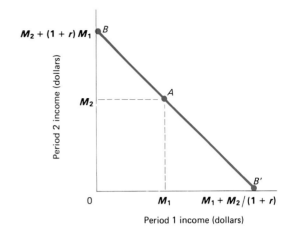

income in period 1 of M_1 and income in period 2 of M_2. The slope at that point will equal the negative of the vertical distance between M_2 and point B divided by the horizontal distance between M_2 and point A, or slope $= -M_2B/M_2A$. Because we know that the exact value of the distance from zero to B is equal to $M_2 + (1+r)M_1$, we can find the value of the distance M_2B. It is equal to $M_2 + (1+r)M_1 - M_2$. Moreover, the horizontal distance between M_2 and point A is merely income in period 1, M_1. Thus, the slope of our time budget constraint can be expressed as

$$\begin{aligned}
\text{Slope} &= -\frac{M_2 + (1+r)M_1 - M_2}{M_1} \\
&= -\frac{(1+r)M_1}{M_1} \\
&= -(1+r)
\end{aligned}$$

The individual time-preference mapping

Now that we have dealt with the budget constraint, let us try to understand the individual's (subjective) marginal valuation of goods today compared with goods tomorrow. In other words, we wish to come up with an indication of the time preference of an individual.

First of all, assume that present consumption is generally preferred to future consumption, *ceteris paribus*. If I am offered a commodity, say a book, with a choice of either having it today or having it next year, assuming there are no storage or insurance costs, I generally will prefer to possess the book today if only for the reason that I have the option of using it over the next year. That option is not available if I have to wait until next year to get the book. Thus, if the book is offered to me today or next year, I generally will be willing to pay a higher price for immediate possession rather than wait a year. This is, of course, the analogue of why individuals generally must be rewarded by a market interest rate in order to induce them to save. Saving is nonconsumption in the current period. If someone else wishes to obtain current command over resources that I presently own, I usually cannot be induced voluntarily to lend that command unless I am rewarded. That reward will be the interest received.

Personal rate of discount

Assuming that present consumption is preferred to future consumption, *ceteris paribus*, we can define an individual's personal valuation of consumption today compared with consumption tomorrow. This is called an individual's **personal rate of discount,** and it is defined as follows:

$$\text{Personal rate of discount} = \left(\begin{array}{c} \text{value an individual} \\ \text{places on this year's} \\ \text{goods in terms of} \\ \text{the forgone goods} \\ \text{of next year} \end{array} \right) - 1 \qquad (6\text{-}5)$$

Another way we can express the individual's personal rate of discount is by considering his or her marginal rate of substitution between consumption in period 1 and consumption in period 2. The rate at which the individual is willing to give up some of this year's consumption C_1 to get more of next year's consumption C_2 is $\text{MRS}_{1:2} = \Delta C_2/\Delta C_1$. Equation (6-5) can now be restated as

$$\text{Personal rate of discount} = \left| \frac{\Delta C_2}{\Delta C_1} \right| - 1 \qquad (6\text{-}6)$$

This definition can be best understood by an example. An individual enjoys drinking 7-Up. The individual is offered a choice: 100 more 7-Ups this year or 110 more 7-Ups next year. Assume that the individual is indifferent to the options. If so, the individual's personal valuation of this year's 7-Ups, in terms of next year's, is 110/100, or 1.1 at that point. He or she values a 7-Up today at 1.1 7-Ups of 1 year hence. Thus, this individual's personal rate of discount is $(1.1 - 1)$ per year, or 10 percent per year. We will represent the individual's personal rate of discount (which is a variable) with the Greek letter *rho* (ρ).

It is the individual's personal rate of discount that determines the shape of the indifference curve between consumption today and consumption next year. We have drawn a typical indifference curve, I, in Figure 6-5. Here the two goods in question are consumption in period 1, C_1, and consumption in period 2, C_2. At any point along indifference curve I, the slope, as measured by the slope of the tangent at that point, represents the marginal (subjective) rate of substitution between future and present consumption, $\text{MRS}_{1:2}$. Remember that $\text{MRS}_{1:2} = \Delta C_2/\Delta C_1$. Using Eq. (6-6), $\rho = |\Delta C_2/\Delta C_1| - 1$. Then, $|\Delta C_2/\Delta C_1| = 1 + \rho$. But because the indifference curve has a negative slope,

FIGURE 6-5
The individual's personal time preference
If the individual values current consumption over future consumption, the indifference curve between consumption today and consumption tomorrow will be convex to the origin. This follows from diminishing marginal rate of valuation between the two commodities: consumption today and consumption tomorrow. The individual's personal discount rate is *rho* (ρ). Therefore, the slope at any point on the indifference curve is equal to the negative of $(1 + \rho)$, or $-(1 + \rho)$.

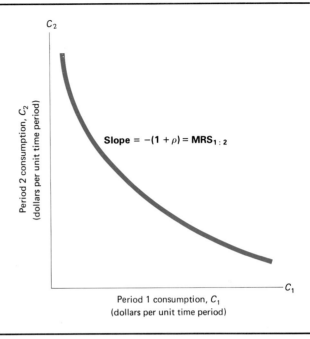

$\Delta C_2 / \Delta C_1 = -(1 + \rho)$. Therefore, the slope of indifference curve I in Figure 6-5 is $-(1 + \rho)$. We have drawn the indifference curve convex to the origin, reflecting diminishing marginal valuation of present consumption in terms of future consumption.

Consumer optimum

We can put together the indifference curve in Figure 6-5 with the budget constraint in Figure 6-3 to find out where the consumer optimum will be. This is done in Figure 6-6. The budget constraint is BB', and the highest indifference curve attainable is indifference curve I. It is tangent to the budget constraint at point E. Thus, the consumer optimum dictates period 1 consumption of C_1 and period 2 consumption of C_2. Note that the horizontal axis depicts period 1 income, consumption, and **saving** (or borrowing, for that matter, because borrowing allows present consumption). In fact, we see that with hypothetical income levels of M_1 in period 1 and M_2 in period 2, there will be saving equal to the distance between M_1 and C_1. In period 2, income is M_2, but consumption is greater because of the saving in the first period and the interest earned. The distance between M_2 and C_2 represents that principal $(M_1 - C_1)$ plus interest.

At the individual point of consumer optimum, E, the rate at which the individual *can* trade future goods for present goods (the marginal rate of market substitution, or MRMS) equals the rate at which he or she is *willing* to trade future goods for present goods (marginal rate of substitution, or

FIGURE 6-6

Optimum consumption between two periods

The horizontal axis measures income, consumption, and saving or borrowing during period 1. The vertical axis measures income, consumption, and saving or borrowing during period 2. A consumption optimum between the two periods will occur when the marginal rate of substitution between consumption today and consumption tomorrow ($MRS_{1:2}$) equals the marginal rate of market substitution (MRMS) between the two. The latter is given by the slope of the budget line and the former by the slope of the indifference curve. In this figure, the optimum occurs at the tangency point E. Assume that income is M_1 in period 1. The optimum consumption rate is C_1; saving will be equal to the difference $M_1 - C_1$. Assume income is M_2 in period 2: consumption will be C_2 and the difference $C_2 - M_2$ will be equal to $M_1 - C_1$ plus the interest accrued.

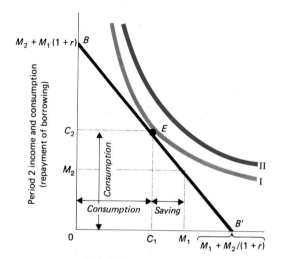

MRS). In other words, at E there is a consumer optimum, the slope of the budget line being equal to the slope of the indifference curve, or

$$-(1 + r) = -(1 + \rho) \tag{6-7}$$

Thus, a consumption optimum requires that $r = \rho$; the market rate of interest must equal the personal rate of discount. We should note that, psychologically, nothing precludes a negative personal rate of discount. That is, some individuals might be willing to pay someone else to force them to save. After all, individuals do purchase savings bonds which impose a penalty (interest is withheld) if they make withdrawals before the scheduled expiration date. At various times, we observe individuals putting away their savings at a 6 percent rate of interest in a savings account, when the rate of inflation is greater than 6 percent. This gives them *less* rather than more purchasing power at the end of their saving period. What we observe then is a demand to consume tomorrow—that is, a demand for savings outlets—and banks provide "safe" storage of wealth that can be consumed in the future. On average, however, individuals usually demand positive rates of interest to give up present consumption.

DISCOUNTING AND PRESENT VALUE

In our analysis of time preference, we employed the notion of a personal rate of discount. We also *implicitly* used it with the present value of the sum of future purchasing power. The two are intimately related. In the example in which the individual was indifferent between 100 bottles of 7-Up this year and 110 bottles next year, the personal rate of discount was calculated to be 10 percent per year. The **present value** (also called "capitalized value" and "discounted value") of 110 bottles of 7-Up 1 year hence, given the personal rate of discount of 10 percent, is 100 bottles.

Think now of the present value of money in terms of a market rate of interest. What is the present value of $110 to be received 1 year from now? That depends on the market rate of interest. If the market rate of interest is 5 percent, we can figure out the present value by answering the question, How much money must I put aside today in a money market mutual fund, for example, at a market rate of interest that will give $110 a year from now? Or

$$(1 + 0.05)P_1 = \$110 \tag{6-8}$$

where P_1 is the sum I must set aside now.

Solving this, we get

$$P_1 = \frac{\$110}{1.05} = \$104.76 \tag{6-9}$$

That is to say, $104.76 will accumulate to $110 at the end of 1 year with a market rate of interest of 5 percent. Thus, the present value of $110 one year from now, using a rate of interest of 5 percent, is $104.76. The formula for present value thus becomes

$$P_1 = \frac{A_1}{1 + r} \tag{6-10}$$

where P_1 = present value for a sum to be paid
   or received 1 year hence
   A_1 = future sum of money paid or
   received 1 year hence
   r = market rate of interest (percent per
   year)

PRESENT VALUES FOR MORE
DISTANT PERIODS

The present value formula for figuring out today's equivalent of dollars to be received at a future date can now be easily seen. How much would have to be put in a savings account today if the account pays a rate of 5 percent per year, compounded annually, to have $110 after 2 years? After 1 year, the sum that would have to be set aside, P_2, would have grown to $P_2(1.05)$. This amount during the *second* year would increase to $[P_2(1.05)]1.05$ or to $P_1(1.05)^2$. To find the P_2 that would grow to $110 over 2 years, set

$$P_2(1.05)^2 = \$110 \qquad\qquad (6\text{-}11)$$

and solve for P_2

$$P_2 = \frac{\$110}{(1.05)^2} \quad \text{or} \quad P_2 = \$99.77 \qquad\qquad (6\text{-}12)$$

Thus the present value of $110 to be paid or received 2 years hence discounted at an interest rate of 5 percent per year compounded annually is equal to $99.77. In other words, $99.77 put into a savings account yielding 5 percent per annum compound interest would accumulate to $110 in 2 years.

TABLE 6-1
Present value table: Present values of a future dollar

Each column shows how much a dollar received at the end of a certain number of years in the future (identified in the extreme left-hand or right-hand column) is worth today. For example, at 5 percent a year, a dollar to be paid or received 20 years in the future is worth only 37.7¢ today. If it is to be paid or received at the end of 50 years, it isn't even worth a dime today. To find out how much $10,000 a certain number of years from now is worth at present, just multiply the figures in the columns by 10,000. For example, $10,000 received at the end of 10 years discounted at a 5 percent rate of interest would have a present value of $6,140.

Year	3%	4%	5%	6%	8%	10%	20%	Year
1	.971	.962	.952	.943	.926	.909	.833	1
2	.943	.925	.907	.890	.857	.826	.694	2
3	.915	.890	.864	.839	.794	.751	.578	3
4	.889	.855	.823	.792	.735	.683	.482	4
5	.863	.823	.784	.747	.681	.620	.402	5
6	.838	.790	.746	.705	.630	.564	.335	6
7	.813	.760	.711	.665	.583	.513	.279	7
8	.789	.731	.677	.627	.540	.466	.233	8
9	.766	.703	.645	.591	.500	.424	.194	9
10	.744	.676	.614	.558	.463	.385	.162	10
11	.722	.650	.585	.526	.429	.350	.134	11
12	.701	.625	.557	.497	.397	.318	.112	12
13	.681	.601	.530	.468	.368	.289	.0935	13
14	.661	.577	.505	.442	.340	.263	.0779	14
15	.642	.555	.481	.417	.315	.239	.0649	15
16	.623	.534	.458	.393	.292	.217	.0541	16
17	.605	.513	.436	.371	.270	.197	.0451	17
18	.587	.494	.416	.350	.250	.179	.0376	18
19	.570	.475	.396	.330	.232	.163	.0313	19
20	.554	.456	.377	.311	.215	.148	.0261	20
25	.478	.375	.295	.232	.146	.0923	.0105	25
30	.412	.308	.231	.174	.0994	.0573	.00421	30
40	.307	.208	.142	.0972	.0460	.0221	.000680	40
50	.228	.141	.087	.0543	.0213	.00852	.000109	50

The discount rate The general formula for discounting becomes

$$P_t = \frac{A_t}{(1 + r)^t} \qquad (6\text{-}13)$$

where t refers to the number of years in the future the money is to be paid or received. Table 6-1 gives the present value of $1 to be received t years hence for various interest rates. The interest rates which were used to derive the present value are sometimes called the rate of discount, or the **discount rate.** We have specified the rate of discount in our examples as the market rate of interest available on savings.[2] We note two important conclusions regarding the interest or discount rate and the present value of a future sum of money: (1) *The farther in the future a sum of money is to be paid or received, the lower is its present value for any given discount rate.* (2) *The higher the interest rate used, the lower is the present value of any given sum of money to be spent or received at a particular future time.*

THE PRESENT VALUE OF AN ANNUITY

We can use Eq. (6-13) to derive the present value of a certain future stream of monies. For example, in the simplest case, we might want to know the present or capitalized value of an **annuity** of $1 per year for 20 years. An annuity is a specific amount of money put aside today to yield a stream of fixed-amount payments at regular intervals throughout a future period. What we want to obtain in our example is that amount of money which must be set aside today at a specified interest rate so that the fixed payments will flow at the intervals and for the period required, just exhausting the original "account" with the last payment. To find this amount, i.e., present value, we have to discount each dollar for each year it is to be received in the future. This would be done using the following formula, where A_1 would be a dollar to be received 1 year hence, A_2 a dollar to be received 2 years hence, and A_{20} a dollar to be received 20 years hence:

$$P_{20} = \frac{A_1}{(1 + r)} + \frac{A_2}{(1 + r)^2} + \frac{A_3}{(1 + r)^3} + \ldots + \frac{A_{20}}{(1 + r)^{20}} \qquad (6\text{-}14)$$

The formula in Eq. (6-14) is usually called a **capital value** formula rather than a present value formula to indicate the computation of the current price

---

[2]Note that we are also implicitly assuming that the interest rate or discount rate is unchanging. If the rate is subject to change we would need a period-by-period calculation.

of the rights to a series of receipts (or obligation of a series of costs) in the future.

When the stream of receipts or costs is to last forever, or to infinity, Eq. (6-13) is simplified to[3]

$$P = \frac{A}{r} \tag{6-15}$$

[3]The proof goes as follows:

Let $S = 1 + R + R^2 + \ldots + R^t$ where R is any number. Multiply by R to obtain

(a) $R \cdot S = R + R^2 + R^3 + \cdots + R^t + R^{t+1}$

Now subtract this equation from the equation we started with:

(b) $S - RS = 1 - R^{t+1}$

which becomes

(c) $S(1 - R) = 1 - R^{t+1}$

or

(d) $S = \dfrac{1}{1 - R} - \dfrac{R^{t+1}}{1 - R}$

If R is less than 1, as t approaches infinity (∞) the numerator in the second term on the right approaches 0 and so does that entire term; and $S = 1/(1 - R)$.

Now let $R = 1/(1 + r)$, where r is less than 1. Assume A_1 to A_t are all equal and $t = \infty$. Then

(e) $P = \dfrac{A}{1 + r} + \dfrac{A}{(1 + r)^2} + \cdots + \dfrac{A}{(1 + r)^\infty}$

If we add and subtract A on the right-hand side, Eq. (e) becomes

(f) $P = -A + A + \dfrac{A}{1 + r} + \dfrac{A}{(1 + r)^2} + \cdots + \dfrac{A}{(1 + r)^\infty}$

Factoring out an A,

(g) $P = -A + A\left[1 + \dfrac{1}{1 + r} + \left(\dfrac{1}{1 + r}\right)^2 + \cdots + \left(\dfrac{1}{1 + r}\right)^\infty\right]$

But the expression in brackets is equal to

(h) $\dfrac{1}{1 - R} = \dfrac{1}{1 - \{[1/(1 + r)]\}}$

so that

(i) $P = -A + A\left\{\dfrac{1}{1 - [1/(1 + r)]}\right\}$

$= -A + \dfrac{A}{r/(1 + r)}$

$= -A + \dfrac{A}{r} + \dfrac{Ar}{r} = -A + \dfrac{A}{r} + A = \dfrac{A}{r}$

TABLE 6-2
Present value of $1 per year for various periods at different discount rates

Here we show the present value of $1 received at the end of each year for a specified number of years. For example, the present value of a dollar received at the end of each year for 10 years at an interest rate of 5 percent would be $7.72. If it were received for 50 years, it would have a present value of $18.30.

Year	3%	4%	5%	6%	8%	10%	20%	Year
1	0.971	0.960	0.952	0.943	0.926	0.909	0.833	1
2	1.91	1.89	1.83	1.83	1.78	1.73	1.53	2
3	2.83	2.78	2.72	2.67	2.58	2.48	2.11	3
4	3.72	3.63	3.55	3.46	3.31	3.16	2.59	4
5	4.58	4.45	4.33	4.21	3.99	3.79	2.99	5
6	5.42	5.24	5.08	4.91	4.62	4.35	3.33	6
7	6.23	6.00	5.79	5.58	5.21	4.86	3.60	7
8	7.02	6.73	6.46	6.20	5.75	5.33	3.84	8
9	7.79	7.44	7.11	6.80	6.25	5.75	4.03	9
10	8.53	8.11	7.72	7.36	6.71	6.14	4.19	10
11	9.25	8.76	8.31	7.88	7.14	6.49	4.33	11
12	9.95	9.39	8.86	8.38	7.54	6.81	4.44	12
13	10.6	9.99	9.39	8.85	7.90	7.10	4.53	13
14	11.3	10.6	9.90	9.29	8.24	7.36	4.61	14
15	11.9	11.1	10.4	9.71	8.56	7.60	4.68	15
16	12.6	11.6	10.8	10.1	8.85	7.82	4.73	16
17	13.2	12.2	11.3	10.4	9.12	8.02	4.77	17
18	13.8	12.7	11.7	10.8	9.37	8.20	4.81	18
19	14.3	13.1	12.1	11.1	9.60	8.36	4.84	19
20	14.9	13.6	12.5	11.4	9.82	8.51	4.87	20
25	17.4	15.6	14.1	12.8	10.7	9.08	4.95	25
30	19.6	17.3	15.4	13.8	11.3	9.43	4.98	30
40	23.1	19.8	17.2	15.0	11.9	9.78	5.00	40
50	25.7	21.5	18.3	15.8	12.2	9.91	5.00	50
∞	33.3	25.0	20.0	16.7	12.5	10.00	5.00	∞

where A in this case represents the sum to be received or spent once per year, in perpetuity. For the formula to be correct, that annual sum must be a fixed one. The formula is a good *approximation* of present value at higher interest rates for periods greater than 20 years. Look at Table 6-2. There we show the present capitalized value of an annuity of $1 that is received at the end of each year. Take a relatively high rate of interest, say 20 percent. The present value becomes indistinguishably close at 40 years to what it is at infinity, $5. Thus Eq. (6-15) is a good approximation, even though the series of $1 payments stops well short of infinity.

The present value of future streams of income or costs turns out to be important for understanding the price that people are willing to pay for goods that last for more than a year.

THE DEMAND FOR DURABLE GOODS

Now that we have the tools of discounting and present value behind us, we can properly analyze the demand for **durable goods,** or goods that last for more than 1 year. We treat the demand for a durable good as a demand not for the good itself, but rather for the net stream of *services* that the good yields. "Net" means after taking account of all costs associated with the use of the durable good. Hence, the demand for an automobile is not treated as the demand for the car per se but rather the demand for the right to use the car day in, day out over a specified period of time. We are dealing with future flow of services to which the consumer will attach some monetary valuation.

For example, take an automobile. Let *A* equal the monetary valuation of the future services (net of operating costs) from the automobile each year. Assume that this valuation is the same over the lifetime of the car; i.e., *A* is a constant annual amount. As usual, the interest rate is represented by r. Thus, the present value of the stream of services from the automobile will equal

$$P_t = \frac{A_1}{1 + r} + \frac{A_2}{(1 + r)^2} + \ldots + \frac{R_t}{(1 + r)^t} \qquad (6\text{-}16)$$

where R_t is the resale value or the scrap value of the automobile when it is no longer desired. The denominator of the last term on the right-hand side of Eq. (6-16) is $1 + r$ taken to the power t, where t is the expected number of years that the individual will keep the automobile.

Clearly, the larger the future flow of services per year, the greater the present value. Moreover, the larger the scrap value, *ceteris paribus*, the larger the present value. If the rate of use and/or return on a durable good or asset changed in each period we would need estimates of each *A* and would use the expanded forms of our calculation formula. And finally, the lower the rate of interest used in discounting, the greater the present value of the durable asset. (Why?)

ASSETS IN GENERAL

Instead of talking solely in terms of durable consumer goods, we can talk in terms of **assets** in general. *Assets* are defined as anything that gives a stream of utility and/or income in the future. Assets include stocks, bonds, automobiles, stereos, a college degree, and so on. The present value of any asset is the discounted future net income stream (or monetary value of the future flow of service) from that asset. Thus we expect the price of an asset to reflect its present value. In fact, we say that the demand price of any asset is the discounted present value of the flow of future services or net income from that asset. Equation (6-16) is thus applicable to explaining the price at which a share of common stock sells at any moment. Equation (6-16) is useful for describing the price of a house at a moment in time. Indeed, that equation can be used to explain the price of any asset.

ISSUES AND APPLICATIONS

Should the project be built?

Businesses and governments are constantly faced with choices about which capital investment projects should be undertaken. We can use present value calculations for deciding on the desirability of a capital investment project.

Every capital investment project will have a present and future stream of costs and benefits. It is not appropriate to look at the stream of costs, add them all up, and compare them with the stream of benefits all added up. The reason it is not appropriate is because a dollar in cost tomorrow is worth less than a dollar in cost today. Also, a dollar in benefits tomorrow has less value than a dollar in benefits today.

What we have to do, then, is calculate the present value of the sum of the stream of future costs and the present value of the sum of the stream of future benefits. Then we look at the difference between the two, as in the following formula:

Present value of net benefits =

$$B_0 - C_0 + \frac{B_1 - C_1}{1 + r} + \frac{B_2 - C_2}{(1 + r)^2} + \cdots$$
$$+ \frac{B_t - C_t}{(1 + r)^t} \quad (6\text{-}17)$$

where B refers to benefits and C refers to costs. The subscript refers to the year in which the benefit is received or the cost incurred (the subscript 0 refers to the current year).

The r chosen for this benefit-cost calculation is crucial. For an individual company, the r is fairly obvious. It is the opportunity cost of capital to that company, or it is the rate of return that the company could earn by taking a dollar and investing it in the next-best alternative project. It could be either the borrowing or the lending rate, depending upon which would be applicable to the next-best alternative. At a minimum, the company could purchase bonds with a specified rate of return over a specified period.

If, when using the appropriate opportunity cost of capital, the present value of net benefits $(B - C)$ does not exceed zero, the project should definitely not be undertaken.

Government agencies have a tougher time figuring out the appropriate r. The capital used in the construction of a government project could have been used not only in some other government project but also in the private sector. Thus, the social opportunity cost of capital might be the appropriate r, and, of course, the social opportunity cost of capital includes the taxes on their profits that private firms pay to the government. If too low a discount rate is used, projects with benefits too far in the future will be undertaken when it is inappropriate. On the other hand, if too high a discount rate is used, not enough projects with future benefits will be undertaken.

To understand in detail how costs and benefits are compared, consider an example

TABLE 6-3
Present value of costs and benefits

End of year (1)	Investment and operating costs C (2)	Revenue B (3)	Net Benefits B − C (4)	Discount factor for r = 5% (5)	Present value of B − C (6)
0	$5,000 ($C_0$)	$0 ($B_0$)	$ − 5,000 = ($B_0 - C_0$)	1.000	− $5,000.00
1	500 (C_1)	3,500 (B_1)	3,000 = ($B_1 - C_1$)	0.952	$2,856.00
2	1,500 (C_2)	4,000 (B_2)	2,500 = ($B_2 - C_2$)	0.907	$2,267.50
3	3,500 (C_3)	3,000 (B_3)	− 500 = ($B_3 - C_3$)	0.864	− $ 432.00
4	1,500 (C_4)	3,000 (B_4)	1,500 = ($B_4 - C_4$)	0.823	$1,234.50
5	2,000 (C_5)	2,000 (B_5)	0 = ($B_5 - C_5$)	0.784	0

Total present value $ 926.00

in which a simple investment cost of $5,000 is incurred at the outset (end of the "zeroth" year). The investment "lives" for 5 more years. We will use a discount rate of 5 percent. Table 6-3 shows all the appropriate calculations. Column (1) shows the year; column (2), the costs; column (3), the benefits or revenues; and column (4), the difference between benefits and costs, or net benefits. Column (5) is the discount factor taken from Table 6-1, and final-ly, column (6) is the present value of net benefits. Notice that the total present value exceeds 0, and hence, this project has a positive discounted net benefits stream. However, if a higher discount rate were used, this would no longer be the case. Go back and redo the calculations, using an interest rate of 10 percent to discount the net benefits stream. Would you then want to undertake this project?

Planned obsolescence, or the "waste makers" revisited

Having developed the tools of present value calculations and their relation to the demand for durable goods, we can analyze the notion of planned obsolescence. This means that the manufacturer of a commodity that is durable allegedly builds into the commodity a reduction in its serviceable life. The easiest example we can take is planned obsolescence by way of style change. An automobile has a planned reduction in resale value after, say, 3 years that is attributable to the introduction of a different style which will render the old-style automobile model "obsolete," if only because it looks different. Another notion of planned obsolescence involves making the product in such a way that it will become use-less sooner than it would have otherwise. Implicit in this notion of planned obsolescence is the dubious notion that the cost to the manufacturer of having the product last longer is minimal, or in the extreme case, zero.

Remember the formula for the present value of an asset, Eq. (6-13)? Let us modify that formula slightly and assume that the resale or scrap value of the durable asset in question is 0 at the end of 3 years. The present value of the asset is therefore

$$PV = \frac{A_1}{(1 + r)} + \frac{A_2}{(1 + r)^2} + \frac{A_3}{(1 + r)^3} \qquad (6\text{-}18)$$

Now consider what happens to the present value when planned obsolescence is effected by producing the asset in such a way that it lasts only 2 years. Now the present value is

$$PV' = \frac{A_1}{(1 + r)} + \frac{A_2}{(1 + r)^2} + \frac{0}{(1 + r)^3} \qquad (6\text{-}19)$$

But clearly $PV > PV'$. To see why, consider this: For a given nominal price of the durable good, the price per constant-quality unit will be higher in the second case than in the first case. If the good costs $100 in both cases, its costs *per year of service* will certainly be higher when the good lasts only 2 years than when it lasts 3 years. If the unit of constant quality is 1 year of service, the price per constant-quality unit will have increased with planned obsolescence. Assuming that the law of demand still holds, the quantity demanded of the durable asset which planned obsolescence makes worthless at the end of 2 years will be less than the quantity demanded of a durable asset that will last 3 years. You can work through the same arithmetic in the case of style changes. Style changes implicitly reduce the monetary value placed on the service flow per year. Thus A_1, A_2, and A_3 will be smaller. At any particular price, when the present value is smaller, the price per constant-quality unit will be larger and the quantity demanded will be less.

At this point, the most we can say about planned obsolescence is that a manufacturer engaging in this process will find the quantity demanded reduced at any given price.

Would publishers and authors be better off if the used-book market were abolished?

A related problem deals with new and used textbooks. Superficially, it would appear that the elimination of the used-book market would benefit the sale of new books by eliminating a substitute. Thus, if the publisher of this book wants to maximize revenues from the sale of this edition, presumably it should not aid in any way the smooth functioning of a used-book market for this text. After all, used price-theory books are substitutes for new ones. When someone purchases a used text from a college bookstore, that person does not purchase a new one. The publisher and the author get paid only when a new book is sold.

PRESENT VALUE FALLS

This analysis is incomplete, however. If you as a student purchase this text new and cannot resell it because a used-book market does not exist, the present value of this book is smaller. In terms of Eq. (6-16), there is no last term that includes R_t' or resale value. Thus, the present value is lower by that amount. At any given nominal price for this textbook, the *price per constant-quality unit* would therefore be higher. Assume that the textbook costs $20. If normally you are able to resell the textbook at the end of the term for 50 percent of its new-book price, you anticipate that the cost for one term's use of the book will be $10; however, if the bookstore absolutely refuses to buy the book back, the cost for one term's use of that same book has doubled to $20. A lower quantity would be demanded.

If you continue this analysis to its ultimate extreme, you would expect individual textbook manufacturers to *aid* in increasing the efficacy of used-book markets so long as their aid was relatively cheap; increasing the efficacy of used-book markets would increase the present value of their textbooks. At the same price, a larger quantity would be demanded, or alternatively, a higher price could be charged for the textbook and the same quantity would be demanded. This is what has actually happened in the market for used IBM typewriters. IBM acts as the intermediary in this market, first buying the used typewriters, then reconditioning them, and finally reselling them. Some textbook publishers also engage in this type of behavior. But there are other publishing houses that instruct their sales staffs to dissuade bookstores from acting as

intermediaries for used versions of the textbooks sold. Presumably these publishers believe that they will have higher profits by reducing the substitutes for new books.

OTHER EFFECTS MUST BE CONSIDERED

It turns out that the preceding analyses are not so simple as outlined there because they focused only on increasing the benefits stream from the ownership of a durable good. However, there is a substitution effect at work. Used versions of durable goods are indeed substitutes for newly produced durable goods. The elimination of part or all of the available supply of substitute used durables leads to a shift outward and to the right in the demand curve for the new durable good.

A case for the elimination of used versions of the durable good can be seen in Figure 6-7. The original demand curve is *DD*. It is drawn by assuming a given availability of substitutes. Assume that the market price per constant-quality unit is P_1. It is the nominal

---

FIGURE 6-7
The case for eliminating the used-durable-good market

The demand curve *DD* is drawn by assuming the existence of a market for the used durable good. The price expressed in present value constant-quality units is, we assume, P_1. Now, the used market is eliminated. This leads to a substitution effect in which the demand curve for the new version of the durable good shifts to the right, outward to *D'D'*, since a substitute has been eliminated. However, the elimination of the used-durable-good market reduces the present value of the good, thus raising its price per present value constant-quality unit from P_1 to P_2. Nonetheless, even at this higher price, the quantity demanded increases from Q_1 to Q_2 because of the shift outward in the demand schedule that resulted from the elimination of the substitute.

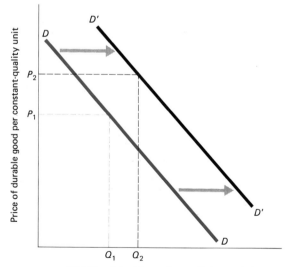

FIGURE 6-8
The case against elimination of the used-durable-good market
This diagram is similar to Figure 6-7; but the shift outward in the demand curve from DD to $D'D'$ was not sufficient to overcome the implicit increase in the price per present value constant-quality unit of the durable good when the used market was eliminated. Thus, the quantity demanded falls from Q_1 to Q_2.

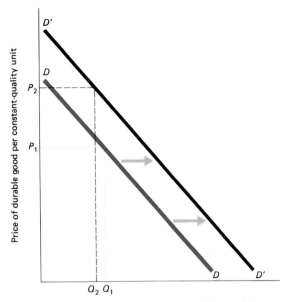

Quantity of durable good per unit time period

price, let us say, for each unit of the durable good. Now consider the elimination of the used-version market of the durable good. The demand curve for the new durable good shifts from DD to $D'D'$. However, the present value of the good has fallen because its resale value is no longer as great as it was when the market for the used version of the durable good existed. In other words, we have cut off a part of the future expected income stream from owning this durable good. We have cut off the possibility of selling the asset after it has been used for a while. If this is the case, at a constant nominal price per nominal unit P_1, the effective price per constant-quality unit must rise. After all, the purchaser of the durable good is purchasing fewer *present value* units with the same amount of dollars. In our example in Figure 6-7, the price rises from P_1 to P_2. However, even at the higher price P_2, the quantity demanded along the new demand curve $D'D'$ increases from Q_1 to Q_2. In this case, the substitution effect outweighed the present value reduction effect.

A case against the elimination of the used version of the durable good can be seen in Figure 6-8. Everything is the same as in Figure 6-7 except that the shift in the demand curve for the new durable good is not as great. At the higher implicit price per constant-quality unit of the durable good, P_2, the quantity demanded, Q_2, is less than the original quantity demanded, Q_1, when the market for the used version of the durable good was in existence.

What you must compare in these situations is the own price elasticity of demand and the cross-price elasticity of demand.[4] This, of course, is an empirical question. From casual

---

[4]Students interested in a more elaborate examination of this problem are referred to Daniel K. Benjamin and Roger C. Kormendi, "The Interrelationship between Markets for New and Used Durable Goods," *The Journal of Law and Economics,* vol. 17, no. 2, October 1974, pp. 381–401. Also see H. Larry Miller, "On Killing Off the Market for Used Textbooks and the Relationship between Markets for New and Secondhand Goods," *Journal of Political Economy,* vol. 82, no. 3, May/June 1974.

observation, however, we can surmise that the IBM Corporation believes that it is better to encourage a used market for its equipment. Specifically, IBM operates an extensive used-IBM-typewriter market, in which you can purchase a reconditioned IBM electric typewriter. Clearly, there is no attempt on the part of IBM to destroy "competition" for new IBM electric typewriters with used IBM electric typewriters.

SUMMARY

1 The total cost of consuming a commodity equals the money cost plus the opportunity cost of the time expended purchasing and/or consuming it. *Ceteris paribus*, as the opportunity cost of time rises, the consumption of time-intensive goods will fall relative to the consumption of less time-intensive goods.

2 As consumer income increases, consumers will spend less time searching for "bargains" or negotiating over the prices of small-ticket items.

3 The theory of time preference assumes that individuals prefer current consumption to future consumption.

4 Whether an individual is willing to borrow or lend an additional dollar will depend on the individual's preferences, current and expected future income, and how much the individual has already borrowed or loaned.

5 The market rate of interest can be derived from the demand for credit (more present consumption) and the supply of credit (more future consumption).

6 In a world of no inflation, the interest rate represents the rate of exchange between goods today and goods in the future. However, if there is an expectation of inflation, the market rate of interest also represents the rate of exchange between dollars today and dollars in the future. A correction then must be made for that expected rate of inflation to arrive at the real interest rate.

7 The slope of the budget line facing the individual in his or her choice between consumption today and consumption tomorrow is equal to $-(1 + r)$, which represents the rate of transformation between consumption today and consumption tomorrow and is determined in the credit market.

8 The individual's time preference is expressed by his or her personal rate of discount and is labeled ρ (rho). The slope of the indifference curve between consumption today and consumption tomorrow is equal to $-(1 + \rho)$.

9 Consumer optimum occurs where the budget constraint is tangent to the indifference curve, or where the rate at which the consumer *can* transform

future consumption into current consumption is equal to the rate at which the consumer *desires* to make this transformation, or when $r = \rho$.

10 All future values must be discounted to obtain their present value, or their value in terms of today's dollars and today's consumption. The general formula for present value is

$$P_t = \frac{A_t}{(1 + r)^t}$$

11 We see that the further in the future a sum or stream of money is to be paid or received, the lower its present value; and the higher the interest rate used, the lower is the present value of any future sum or stream of money.

12 The demand for durable goods is not a demand for the stock per se but rather for the expected stream of useful services from the durable good.

13 The price of durable goods, or any asset for that matter, is equal to the present value of the net future stream of services.

GLOSSARY

- **time cost** The time required for the purchase and/or consumption of a commodity.
- **theory of time preference** Hypothesis relating to the individual's preference for current consumption over future consumption; i.e., the individual prefers current over later consumption, other things being constant.
- **interest rate** The rate of exchange between goods today and goods in the future.
- **personal rate of discount** A measure of the individual's personal time preference or degree of preference for current consumption over future consumption.
- **saving** Nonconsumption of income in the current period.
- **present value** The current value of any sum to be received or paid in the future; sometimes called the discounted value or discounted present value because future sums are discounted back to today.
- **discount rate** The interest rate used to compute present value, or the interest rate used in discounting future sums.
- **annuity** A sequence of future amounts to be paid or received at regular calendar intervals for a specified period of time.
- **capital value** The present value or discounted value of a sequence of future amounts or of an annuity.
- **durable goods** Goods which are expected to yield a stream of services or satisfaction for more than just the current period, e.g., stereos, TVs, washing machines, and automobiles.
- **asset** Anything expected to give a stream of utility in the future; includes durable goods, contracts, stocks, bonds, patents, copyrights, etc.

QUESTIONS

(Answers to even-numbered questions are at back of text.)

1 Food, clothing, and paper towels are examples of so-called nondurable goods. How can a good be nondurable and still be a good? (*Hint:* Is a service durable?)

2 "My wages have increased so much in recent years that I can hardly afford to play golf anymore!" On its face, this is a paradox. Explain what the person really means.

3 Suppose you know someone whose time preference is such that he or she is indifferent between 110 fresh peaches now and 100 a year from now. Does this prove that the interest rate must be negative? Explain.

4 "I can't understand people who will fork over $5 or $10 to see a first-run movie when they could see it for about half that price a few months later, or even watch it on TV 'for free' a few years later." What does time-preference theory say about this?

5 If you have a positive personal rate of discount and the interest rate you face falls, *ceteris paribus*, how would our theory predict that you would respond?

6 Explain why an absolutely certain contractual right to receive a dollar in the future is less valuable than having the dollar right now. Assume, as we have throughout the text, that no inflation or deflation is expected.

7 How is it possible that an absolutely reliable annuity of $1 per year, to be paid or received for 20 years, has a present value of less than $20?

8 A perpetuity is a perpetual annuity. Note that its present value formula ($P = A/r$) is much simpler than those of annuities payable for a finite number of years. If you were able to invest your money at 5 percent per year, without risk, how much would you be willing to pay for an absolutely certain perpetuity of $1 per year? Why? If, after you bought it, the no-risk interest rate fell to 2 percent per year, what would your perpetuity then be worth? Why?

9 Looking at the present value equation, Eq. (6-16), how would you expect an increase in the price of new Honda motorcycles to affect the market price of your used one. Explain.

10 Suppose you buy a United States government bond which entitles you, as the holder, to the following: You will receive $100 per year in interest starting 1 year from today, for the next 10 years. Ten years from today, when the bond matures, you will also receive, in addition to the tenth interest payment, the bond's face value of $1,000. If you are to earn 10 percent per year on your investment, what is the maximum price you will be willing to pay for the bond? What is the most you would be willing to pay if your targeted rate of return were 8 percent per year? Twelve percent per year?

SELECTED REFERENCES

Bailey, Martin, "Saving and the Rate of Interest," *Journal of Political Economy,* vol. 65, 1957, pp. 279–305.

Becker, Gary S., *Economic Theory* (New York: Knopf, 1971), lecture 10, pp. 45–47.

DeHaven, J.C., and J. Hirshleifer, "Feather River Water for Southern California," *Land Economics,* vol. 33, August 1957.
Fisher, Irving, *The Theory of Interest* (New York: Macmillan, 1930), chaps. 4–11.

APPENDIX TO CHAPTER 6

COMPUTING THE TIME ELASTICITY OF DEMAND

We can combine the time constraint with the budget constraint to derive the elasticity of demand with respect to time. First we must consider the usual budget constraint

$$P_x x + P_y y = M \qquad (A6\text{-}1)$$

which is identical to Eq. (3-2) from Chapter 3.

Now we consider the time constraint, which, as you can see, has the same form as the budget constraint, i.e., the income constraint:

$$t_x x + t_y y = T \qquad (A6\text{-}2)$$

where t_x = time cost per unit of good x
  t_y = time cost per unit of good y
  T = total time devoted to the consumption of x and y

Since time can be converted into income, we can combine the two constraints, Eqs. (A6-1) and (A6-2), into one. (In a moment, we'll show what we mean by combining these two constraints.) After all, a consumer can engage in household activities that use time but reduce the need to earn income. For example, time can be used to clean the house rather than hire a housekeeper. Also, the consumer can reduce the time in consumption and use this time for income-earning activities in the job market.

We make the assumption that on the margin, the opportunity cost of an hour used for consumption activities is equal to the hourly wage rate w. In other words, we assume that every hour used in the process of consumption could have been used in an income-earning ac-

tivity in the job market at the going after-tax wage rate w. Thus, the time cost of consumption will be equal to the number of hours used in consumption times the wage rate. We now simply multiply w, the hourly wage rate, by Eq. (A6-2), which gives us

$$w \cdot T = w(t_x x + t_y y) \qquad (A6\text{-}2a)$$

We have here a dollar estimate of the value of the hours used in consumption.

Now we can add Eqs. (A6-1) and (A6-2a) to obtain

$$(P_x x + P_y y) + w)t_x x + (t_y y) = M + wT$$

or

$$(P_x + wt_x)x + (P_y + wt_y)u = M + wT \qquad (A6\text{-}3)$$

The total unit price for good x, for example, is equal to $P_x + wt_x$, since this is the money price plus the monetary value of the time required to consume it. Equation (A6-3) tells us that the effective price of x times the quantity of x plus the effective price of y times the quantity of y cannot exceed money income plus the monetary value of the total number of hours spent in consumption. In other words, we now have a time and money budget constraint.

We can now present the elasticity of demand with respect to the money price of a product and the elasticity of demand with respect to the time price. We define them in the normal way:

$$\eta_{MP} = \frac{\Delta q/q}{\Delta P/P} = \frac{\Delta q}{\Delta P} \cdot \frac{P}{q} \qquad (A6\text{-}4)$$

$$\eta_{\text{time}} = \frac{\Delta q/q}{\Delta wt/wt} = \frac{\Delta q}{\Delta wt} \cdot \frac{wt}{q} \qquad (A6\text{-}5)$$

where η_{MP} is the normal price elasticity of demand and η_{time} is the time price elasticity of demand. We can simplify Eq. (A6-5). If we assume that the wage rate w is constant, $\Delta wt = w\Delta t$; and

$$\eta_{time} = \frac{\Delta q}{w\Delta t} \cdot \frac{wt}{q} \qquad \text{(A6-6)}$$

But the w's cancel out, so that

$$\eta_{time} = \frac{\Delta q}{\Delta t} \cdot \frac{t}{q} \qquad \text{(A6-7)}$$

Very little work has been done in estimating real-world time elasticities of demand. Undoubtedly, however, there will be an increased interest in such work as the time element of consumption becomes more important as a result of higher real incomes and, hence, higher time opportunity costs. We might surmise, for example, that the relatively recent successes of fast-food chains in countries that in the past scorned American hamburger stands is in part due to the rising opportunity cost of time (the real after-tax wage rate) in those countries. This has been particularly evident in France.

Risk and uncertainty in decision making

*I*n the usual analysis of consumer choice we implicitly assume that the consumer is choosing between alternatives which are "certain" or "riskless." A diner who orders and pays for a pepperoni pizza expects to receive what has been ordered, not something else or nothing at all. Some choices that are frequently encountered in the world are not, however, so definite. No one knows with certainty what his or her income or wealth will be within a decade, or even within a year. Fire, flood, illness, or other unexpected disaster may make us substantially poorer. Winning a lottery may make us unexpectedly richer.

This chapter explains how insurance, portfolio diversification, and futures markets are used by consumers and producers in shifting or spreading some of the unwanted risks they face. Why are some people willing to take more risks than others? Why do some people insure against the property loss resulting from an automobile accident but willingly (and happily) gamble in games of chance where the odds are against them?

CHOICES BETWEEN RISKY ALTERNATIVES

To answer these questions economists have invented a vocabulary to talk about preference for or aversion to risk. Imagine, for instance, that someone offers to bet you $10 that the toss of a coin will come up heads. If a "fair" coin is used, your chances of winning or of losing this bet are 50/50. A person interested in the probable gains or losses from making the bet might make the following calculation:

(Probability of losing, 0.5) × (amount that can be lost, $10)

    = (probability-weighted value of losing, $5)

    = (probability of winning, 0.5) × (amount that can be won, $10)

    = (probability-weighted value of winning, $5)

The probability-weighted value of losing or winning the bet, its **expected value**, are the same, since this is a **fair bet**. Hence, this person would be indifferent to the bet unless he or she viewed risk as a good in itself (in which case the bet would be taken) or unless he or she viewed risk as a bad in itself (in which case the bet would be rejected). People who make decisions regarding risky alternatives *solely* in terms of the probability-weighted value (expected value) of winning or losing are said to be **risk neutral**. People who would not accept a fair bet, like the one described above, are said to be **risk averse**. Persons who prefer such a bet to the certainty of keeping their $10 are said to be **risk preferers**.

Risk and income   As you will recall from the section on "Good Goods, Bad Goods, and Indifference Analysis" in Chapter 3, most of those things to which individuals attach utility (either positive or negative) are goods at one rate or level of consumption and bads at a higher rate or level of consumption. This is also true of risk. Most people prefer a low amount of low-loss, low-win risk to no risk at all. That is, most people will gamble, in one form or another in games where their likely losses or winnings are small *relative to their existing income or wealth status.*

However, for most people, risk becomes a bad when the possible losses in a situation become a large share of their income or wealth position. In those situations people prefer a small certain loss, such as an insurance premium, to a much larger possible loss. Just where the turning point between risk-as-a-good and risk-as-a-bad is for each individual is partly a matter of that person's tastes and partly a matter of his or her income or wealth position. Virtually all of us will risk some small proportion of our wealth or income in situations with uncertain outcomes, and most people will become more risk averse in situations involving proportionately greater losses.[1]

In order to analyze these points graphically you might want to try the experiment of using the circular indifference curve graph in Figure 3-20 in Chapter 3, plotting risk as a good/bad on one of the axes. You will note that for low amounts of risk the consumer will pay a positive price; that is, the consumer will be willing to make "unfair" bets. Yet higher amounts of risk will ultimately be taken only if the consumer is paid to do so (that is, at "negative prices").

----

[1]This is true of even those persons who are "morally opposed" to gambling. Such individuals will, nevertheless, double park their cars or drive over 55 mph and thus risk a traffic ticket and a fine.

THE MARKET FOR RISK ASSUMPTION

Security is a scarce good for most people at some level of risk. It has positive value. Individuals are willing to pay to limit risk in their lives, in their income streams, and hence in their consumption streams. Markets have arisen to take care of individual quests for a reduction in risk.

Insurance

One of those markets is the insurance market, in which each individual eliminates his or her *risk* by paying a *certain* periodic premium—that is, incur a *certain* loss—so that when disaster hits any one of them, the pool of funds provided by all of them will take care of the disaster without altering the wealth position of the insured. Take a simple numerical example. There are 100 families. On the average, we assume that one house burns to the ground each year. Each house is worth $50,000. The total annual loss sustained by the group of 100 families is $50,000. The mathematical probability for any one family of a loss in any one year is 1 percent times $50,000, or $500 per year.[2] If all families buy insurance, thus agreeing to pool their risks by paying a "premium" of $505 per year into a common reserve fund, then when the one house burns down per year, the family affected is paid $50,000 out of the reserve fund. The insurance company makes a profit of $500 on these policies, thus making the business of funding and pooling such insurees worthwhile to operate.

The above insurance example is based on the **mutual principle**. When the profit incentive and the costs of administering the program are added, the risk-pooling aspect of insurance remains the same, but the annual premium for insurance will exceed the mathematical expectation of the annual loss.

Market insurance is purchased by firms or individuals to cover those possible losses against which it is difficult or impossible to self-insure. In some cases, however, self-insurance is possible and market insurance is either unavailable or prohibitively expensive.[3] This is often the case for risks connected with an individual's program for investing his or her wealth.

Say that you have a "total worth" of $200,000, of which $100,000 is invested in your home. You can insure your home against loss due to fire, flood, or vandalism by paying for the appropriate market insurance policies. But what can you do about the risk of a general fall in the price of real estate? One answer, which we will consider further below, is never to buy a durable asset, such as a house, on which there may be a capital loss or a capital gain.

---

[2] Given a probability of loss of 1 percent, $500 is called the "expected value of the loss," or the "mathematical expectation of annual loss."

[3] The obvious reason for that is not that markets have failed, but that the party seeking insurance has much better access to information regarding the true risks connected with his or her actions than does a market insurer.

While that alternative may seem attractive in a period when the value of such assets is falling, in a period of rising values it means higher current rental payments with no increase in your wealth.

Portfolio diversification

A way to reduce the risk of holding some of your wealth in the form of real estate is to hold the remainder of your wealth in other forms. This is called **portfolio diversification**. In general, the greater the variety of assets in which you hold your wealth, the lower the risk of your total portfolio of assets. Indefinite diversification of a portfolio is not costless, however. There are usually economies of scale involving each type of asset. That is, transactions costs of purchase and eventual resale are generally higher, per dollar invested, for small purchases than for large purchases of a given asset.

It is sometimes possible to achieve the advantages of risk reduction through portfolio diversification without holding a large number of asset types. Suppose that you determine that asset A tends to increase in real value as the inflation rate increases and decrease in real value as the inflation rate decreases. If you can find another asset, asset B, the real value of which moves inversely with inflation, you can reduce the inflation-related risk of your portfolio by holding both A and B. This is not a perfect answer, however, for there are many such factors which systematically affect the values for various assets.[4] It is thus difficult to construct a portfolio which simultaneously minimizes all these risks.

RISK AND TIME: THE FUTURES MARKET

We have talked about markets dealing in time—the credit market—and we have talked very briefly about a market dealing with risk elimination—the insurance market. There is a market in which both elements, time and uncertainty, are found. This is the **futures market**, in which economic agents agree in the present to the sale or purchase of a particular quantity of a particular commodity for delivery at a particular date in the future at a particular price. Those economic agents who participate in the trading of futures contracts are generally called *speculators*. Before we analyze **speculation** and its effect on the allocation of resources over time and on the degree of risk taking by separate groups of individuals, we will explain briefly the market for futures.

Many of us engage in contracting where a product is to be delivered at a future date. I may order next year's model of a Chevrolet from my local Chevrolet dealer 2 months before the car is scheduled to arrive on the premises. You may order a book from the bookstore that will not be delivered to

---

[4]For instance, the market rate of interest and the level of "general economic activity."

you for 3 weeks. A farmer may sign a contract to deliver a million bushels of grain to a grain elevator operator at a specific month in the future at a price that is agreed upon by both parties today. All such contracts are called forward contracts.

Contracting through time

A **forward contract** is not, strictly speaking, the same as a **futures contract**; the latter applies only to those contracts executed in *formal* commodities exchange markets. There are a number of such markets: the Chicago Board of Trade, the Chicago Mercantile Exchange, the New York Coffee and Sugar Exchange, and others throughout the world. In the United States there are organized open futures markets for frozen orange juice concentrate, oats, soybeans, wheat, corn, cotton, sorghum, sugar, barley, lard, hides, soybean oil, eggs (frozen, powdered, and shelled), frozen chickens, potatoes, silver, rubber, cocoa, pepper, flax seed, copper, wool, pork bellies, platinum, foreign exchange, government-insured mortgages, and T-bills. Futures contracts are made for standard qualities and quantities of a commodity. As an example, in the futures market for frozen orange juice concentrate, a standard contract is for 15,000 pounds of concentrate. It is also necessary for the futures contract to call for delivery at a standard time during the year. Finally, futures contracts can be entered into only through a broker.

The difference between a forward and a futures contract is more profound than the simple explanation above indicates. In a futures market, the dealings are strictly impersonal; buyers and sellers know nothing but the price, the time, a few attributes of the product, and the place of delivery. In other words, in a futures contract it might be stated that 40,000 bushels of Minnesota No. 2 Red wheat will be delivered in Winnipeg between November 3 and November 10, 1986. Clearly there are many economies of transaction here. In other words, the transactions costs are relatively low in a futures market. But it turns out that, comparatively speaking, few futures markets actually exist; there are many more less-organized forward markets. This may be due to the fact that forward markets, in contrast to futures markets, permit more "custom-made" contracting. The buyer and seller engage in a personal rather than impersonal dealing and can specify many more aspects of the transaction than is possible in an organized futures market.

If you *buy* a futures contract today, you agree to *accept delivery* of a specified amount of, say, wheat at a specified date in the future at a specified place. You also agree to pay the price specified in the futures contract. The price that is specified in the futures contract is called the **futures price**. You might look in the newspaper today and find out that the futures price of wheat to be delivered 3 months from now is so many dollars per bushel. You can compare the futures price with today's **spot price**, which is the price of wheat bought "on the spot." It is also called today's *cash* price. Most people who trade in the spot, or cash, market are the actual producers, processors, and distributors of the commodity.

Going long and short

On the other side of the exchange, it is possible to *sell* a futures contract. When you sell one, you agree to *deliver* a specified amount of a commodity on a specified date at a specified price. Those who have agreed to deliver commodities in the future at a stated price are said to have a **short position**, or to be "short" or to have "gone short." They have sold futures contracts. Those who agree to buy a certain quantity at a stated price in the future have a **long position**; they have "gone long." They have bought futures contracts; they have some commodities coming to them.

Note that futures contracts generally are not settled at maturity by actual physical delivery of the commodity to a warehouse. Rather, most futures contracts are either closed out before their maturity date or settled by payment of the difference between the price stipulated in the contract and the spot price of the commodity at the date of maturity. Hence, if the futures price of wheat was $5 when the contract was written, and at the date of maturity the spot price was $5.10, the seller of the futures contract would merely pay the purchaser of the futures contract 10¢ times the number of bushels specified in the contract.[5]

TRANSFERRING RISK: HEDGING AND SPECULATION

A crucial function of the futures market is that it allows individuals to shift risk from those less willing to bear it to those more willing to bear it, for a given fee. The process of using the futures market to eliminate risk is called **hedging**. Those who engage in this activity are called *hedgers*. Consider the operator of a grain elevator (a storage place) who buys corn from farmers at harvest time. The grain elevator operator stores the corn and sells it to processors (millers) over the period between corn harvests. The grain elevator operator wants to specialize in storing corn. He or she does not want to specialize in predicting future spot prices of corn. Knowing that there are fluctuations in the spot, or cash, price of corn, this grain elevator operator may wish to reduce the possibility of loss due to a reduction in the spot price of corn later on. This loss would occur, for example, if the elevator operator bought corn today at $5 a bushel and 2 months from now would get $3 a bushel when it was sold to processors. However, in reducing the possibility of loss, the operator also reduces the possibility of profit.

Using the futures market, it is possible for the grain elevator operator to transfer some of the risk of any reduction in the value of the corn that he or she holds to someone else in exchange for transferring the gains realizable if in fact the spot price of corn rises. What the elevator operator does is sell futures contracts in corn at the same time he or she buys the corn.

---

[5]Note that the volume of futures contracts is not tied to the volume of physical product or even constrained by it.

A numerical example

Let's take a simple example which ignores such things as buying on margin (credit). Assume that the elevator operator has just paid $2 a bushel for 10,000 bushels of corn. The elevator operator plans on selling this corn 6 months from now. During that 6-month period, the operator estimates that inventory costs—insurance, opportunity cost of capital invested, etc.—will be 5¢ per bushel. Thus, for 10,000 bushels, the storage cost will be $500. Assume that market conditions are such that the operator can sell a futures contract for 10,000 bushels of corn to be delivered in 6 months for the sum of $20,500, or $2.05 per bushel. We have assumed that the futures contract has been sold at a price that is just equal to the spot price of corn today ($2) plus the storage costs ($0.05) for 6 months. (Normally, the futures price will be higher than the spot, or cash, price by the cost of insurance, storage, and interest on the money "tied up" for the period of time from today to the delivery date.) Given that assumption, the elevator operator is indifferent to the price of corn remaining the same, going up, or going down over the 6-month waiting period.

The arithmetic is quite simple. Consider these three cases.

Price is unchanged. If the spot price 6 months from now is exactly the same as the current spot price, the value of 10,000 bushels of stored corn will have remained the same. The elevator operator will sell it for exactly the same amount that he or she paid for it. However, the futures contract was sold at a specified price of $2.05 per bushel. (Selling a futures contract is not the same thing as actually selling the physical commodity, corn.) At maturity, the buyer of the futures contract, generally called a "speculator," will settle the account by paying the elevator operator $500; but this just equals the cost of storing the corn for 6 months. The operator neither gains nor loses.

Price goes up. When the spot price of corn goes up by, say, 20¢ per bushel, the elevator operator has an increase in the value of his or her stored corn of 20¢ times 10,000 bushels, or $2,000. But there are costs involved, too. The futures contract specified a price of $2.05 per bushel. The difference, 15¢ per bushel, must be paid to the speculator, or the owner, of the futures contract. The cost, then, is $1,500. Added to that is the other cost of storage, $500. On net, then, a 20¢ rise in the spot price of corn after 6 months yields the elevator operator zero additional profits.

Price goes down. Now you should be able to work through the example when the spot price of corn falls to, say, $1.85 at the end of 6 months. Again, you will find that the elevator operator was not affected by the change in the spot price of corn over the 6-month period.

A recap. Note here that the corn is not really delivered to the speculator, but rather the contract is settled by a payment of the difference between the 6-month futures contract price ($2.05 per bushel of corn) and the actual spot price that prevails 6 months later. Thus, if the spot price in 6 months is only $2, the speculator pays the elevator operator 5¢ per bushel. On the other hand, if the spot price is, say, $2.10 per bushel of corn, the elevator operator pays the speculator 5¢ per bushel. We see, then, that the elevator operator's net revenue from both selling the corn at the spot price in 6 months and settling the futures contract is $2.05 a bushel. Hence, the operator's net revenue is *independent* of the spot price in 6 months.

A selling hedge

What has occurred here? The holder of corn, the elevator operator, has shifted the risk inherent in the ownership of the asset called "corn" to another class of individuals who are typically speculators. The "hedge" that was effected in the transaction mentioned above is called a "selling" hedge. The elevator operator has a "long position" in corn because he or she has actually purchased the corn. To eliminate the risk of the change in the value of that long position, the elevator operator established an equal "short position" by selling futures contracts. The storage operator gets $2.05 per bushel in 6 months from the speculator (the owner of the contract) no matter what the spot price is at that time. If the spot is higher than $2.05 per bushel, the speculator gets to keep the difference; if the price is lower than $2.05 per bushel, the speculator must pay the difference.

A buying hedge

A buying hedge is also possible. A hog farmer may make a forward contract (forward, rather than futures, since there is no organized market in fresh pork) with a meat processor to sell so many pounds of fresh pork at a predetermined price per pound at a future date. However, the hog farmer, until that future date, must feed the pigs. The price established in the forward contract with the same meat processor is based perhaps on the assumption that the cost of grain that goes into fattening the pigs will remain constant. If, however, the price of grain rises, the hog farmer will suffer because the price of the product he or she has agreed to sell at some future date is already agreed upon in the forward contract. As protection, the hog farmer will buy grain in the futures market by buying futures contracts which guarantee delivery of grain at a specified time at a price agreed upon today. That is the price which the hog farmer would put into his or her cost calculations in arriving at the price to charge the meat processor in the forward contract that guarantees delivery of so many pounds of pork. You should be able to work through an example similar to the one just mentioned, in which you can show that after entering the two separate contracts, the hog farmer's wealth position will not change due to a change in either the price of feed or that of fattened hogs.

Speculation

Those who do not enter simultaneously into long and short cash and futures positions in a particular commodity are not hedgers but rather speculators. Speculators are betting that the future spot price of a commodity will be different from the price specified in a futures contract today. In the case of the grain operator, the purchaser of a futures contract from the grain operator at $2.05 per bushel of corn is betting that in 6 months the spot price of corn will not be $2.05 but will be something greater. If it is selling for $2.15 per bushel in 6 months, the speculator who has purchased the futures contract makes a profit of 10¢ per bushel. Speculators also sell futures contracts. When they sell a futures contract, they are betting that the spot price of the commodity on the date of maturity of the contract in the future will be lower than the current futures price (i.e., the price specified on futures contracts sold today). The difference is their profit on each unit of the commodity sold. They are betting that there will be a difference between the actual *future* price and the current *futures* price (and that the difference will exceed all their explicit and implicit transactions costs). The future price is the actual market price at some specified date in the future; the futures price is the anticipated or expected future price that is put into the futures contract.

SPECULATION AND ALLOCATION OF NONPERISHABLE GOODS OVER TIME

The futures market is more than just a market to provide the transfer of risk from hedgers to speculators (or to other hedgers). It is also a market which generates signals that alter the consumption pattern of commodities over time from what it would be in the absence of a futures market.

Consider the two periods, 1 and 2, depicted in Figure 7-1. We assume that it is known with certainty in this example that the corn crop in period 1 will yield a supply of S_1S_1, as illustrated in panel (a). It is also known with certainty that in period 2 there will be a smaller crop, as represented by the supply curve S_2S_2 in panel (b). The demand curve, in the absence of speculation, is D_1D_1 in panel (a) for period 1. It represents the demand curve for corn by period 1 users only. In the absence of speculation, the intersection of D_1D_1 with S_1S_1 would yield a market-clearing price of P_1 at which $0S_1$ would be consumed. In period 2, the demand curve represents the demand by period 2 users only. It is drawn as D_2D_2. It intersects the supply curve of corn S_2S_2 at a price P_2. Notice here that in the absence of speculators, a larger quantity of corn will be consumed in period 1 because of the relatively low price, and a smaller quantity will be consumed in period 2 because of the higher relative price.

SPECULATION AND PRICE VARIATION

Now speculators enter the market. They foresee the possibility of a profit because of a smaller crop being expected for next year. If they can purchase futures contracts for corn somewhere near period 1's spot price, they will make a profit when period 2's spot price exceeds that futures price. The speculators' demand is represented by the horizontal distance between D_1D_1 and $D_1'D_1'$. With a given supply S_1S_1, the price of corn in period 1 will not be P_1 but rather P_1' because this is the intersection of S_1S_1 with $D_1'D_1'$. The

FIGURE 7-1

Speculation smooths out the rate of consumption over time

In the absence of speculation, period 1 supply is S_1S_1 and period 2 supply is S_2S_2. The demand curves for periods 1 and 2 are D_1D_1 and D_2D_2, respectively. The price without speculation, would therefore be P_1 in period 1 and P_2 in period 2. If speculators enter the market, they add to the current demand in period 1. The new demand curve becomes $D_1'D_1'$, and is users' plus speculators' demand. The market-clearing price in period 1 rises to P_1'. The period 1 quantity demanded by users falls to Q_1, and the difference $S_1 - Q_1$ goes into the inventories held by speculators. In period 2, the supply curve shifts out by the amount of these inventories to $S_2'S_2'$. The price in period 2 falls to P_2', which is less than P_2.

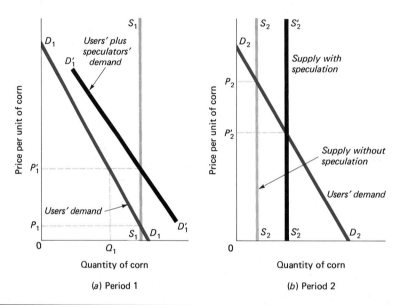

(a) Period 1   (b) Period 2

quantity demanded by current users will now be Q_1, a quantity which is less than the $0S_1$ without speculative demand. The difference $(S_1 - Q_1)$ will be held in storage to deliver to purchasers of future contracts at maturity in period 2. Now go to panel (b), which represents period 2. The supply curve shifts out to the right by the amount of corn that has been stored from period 1 to period 2. The market-clearing price in period 2 ends up being P_2' rather than P_2 because this is where the then-current demand curve of current users, D_2D_2, intersects the supply curve $S_2'S_2'$. In an idealized setting with perfect information, the difference between P_1' in panel (a) and P_2' in panel (b) will be equal to the cost of storage plus a normal risk-corrected profit sufficient to induce speculators to tie up their capital in the futures market during the period of time under study.

Thus, what do speculators do? They induce current owners of inventories of commodities to withhold sale until future periods. Current owners anticipate that the supply of the commodity in the future will be sufficiently low relative to the demand to cause its future spot price to be greater than it is in the present. You should be able to redo panels (a) and (b) under the assumption that speculators anticipate a "bumper" crop of corn in period 2. How would that affect the futures price of corn, and how would that alter the quantity of corn consumed in the present period?

Now you can see why the current price of a nonperishable commodity can rise without any change in the current demand by current users. A premature frost in coffee-growing countries in Latin America may signal to speculators that the future supply of coffee will be lower than anticipated and, hence, that the price of coffee in the future will be higher than had been anticipated. Speculators will bid up the price of futures contracts. As they do this, current owners of inventories of coffee will withhold coffee from the market in order to benefit from higher expected future prices, and this will mean that today's spot price will also rise. The rise in today's price has not been caused by speculation; it has been caused by the premature frost and the expectation that the future crop of coffee will be smaller. Speculators had nothing to do with that premature frost. If their anticipations prove to be incorrect, they will be the ones to suffer a loss of wealth.

SPECULATION AND TOTAL VALUE

The preceding example also serves to show the service that speculators can provide to consumers. The former indirectly even out the latter's consumption of a storable commodity over time. By reducing current supply, speculators are necessarily increasing future supply. Steady consumption, as opposed to feast-famine cycles, is usually preferred by consumers, as we know from our analysis of consumer choice in the previous chapter. Moreover, the total value of the corn in the earlier example has been raised by speculation. Why? Because of the law of demand. Without speculation, the marginal use value of corn in period 1 would have been relatively much less than its marginal use value in period 2. Speculation allows these marginal use values in the two periods to come closer together and thereby raises the *total* use value of corn.

SPECULATION AND RISK TAKING

To be sure, it is possible for hedgers to shift risk onto speculators. However, speculation is not limited to futures markets. Anyone who has any nonindexed assets or liabilities is by definition a speculator. These include an automobile, a house, or major applicances as well as stocks, bonds, or futures contracts. The value of assets can go up or down, depending on shifts in the supply and demand curves of the assets in question. Owners usually have nothing to do with the shifts in supply and demand; unanticipated changes in the rate of inflation, for example, can alter the burden of liabilities. Hence, owners of assets or liabilities are at the mercy of "the market." To the extent that you have a short or long interest in any asset, you are by definition a speculator. You can reduce speculation by renting and leasing assets rather than by owning them because by leasing you don't go short or long. But even then you still cannot eliminate speculation completely. A long-term lease involves speculation because you could be "locked into" a high monthly lease fee during a period in which the value of the asset you are leasing falls in the open market. When this happens, new leases will be written at a lower rate. You will suffer a reduction in your wealth in comparison to what your wealth would have been had you not signed the long-term lease but rather signed a series of consecutive short-term leases.

RISKS IN FACE-TO-FACE TRANSACTIONS

The above discussion of market insurance, self-insurance through portfolio diversification, and insurance through futures market operations generally assumes a context of impersonal market transactions and normally distributed risks. Risks may also arise, however, in face-to-face contractual situations where each party is contemplating future performance of the contract. Parties in this context face two possible sources of risk: first, the risk inherent in the possibly uncertain value of fully performing the contract and, second, the possibility that the other parties to the contract will fail to perform or will perform in a manner different than you expect.

Risk of uncertain value
The risk that full performance of the contract will not be worth what you expected it to be worth can, in most cases,[6] be handled by always being the "payee" of the contract—that is, the party who receives a certain money return rather than an uncertain value in whatever goods or services the money is being exchanged for. Workers for a firm, for example, usually receive a fixed wage per period. The owners of the firm are the "residual claimants" of what the goods or services produced by the workers are worth on the market. The workers have thus shifted the risk of the type of production in which they are engaged to the owners of the firm for which they work. Similarly, the person who assigns goods to a retailer for sale in the retailer's shop is the "residual claimant" of whatever goods remain unsold and whatever revenues (minus sales charges) are derived from the sale of the goods. The retailer assignee receives a certain return for each unit sold but bears no direct loss if the goods turn out not to be a profitable item.[7]

Risk of nonperformance
The risk that a contract will not be performed by the other parties or that it will be performed differently than is anticipated can be dealt with through a meticulous specification of contract terms and remedies for default. Most

---

[6]The one exception to this rule, of course, occurs when there is an unanticipated deflation or inflation which changes the real value of the money received.

[7]The retailer does, of course, bear an implicit loss if there was a higher valued alternative use of his or her sales space.

of the law of contracts is simply the specification of a "standard" set of contract terms for situations which the contracting parties may initially fail to address in their contract. No contract will consider every possible eventuality or every possible interpretation of the terms of the contract since such indefinite specification of the contract is itself costly. The larger the number of contemplated transaction(s) or the more unique the transaction engaged in, the larger the investment to tailor the contract's terms to the specific wishes of the parties.[8]

CONCLUSION

The lesson of this chapter is that the world and all our dealings in it are risky. Reducing that risk by shifting it to others or by taking precautions in the way in which we order our affairs is costly. Just how much risk we are willing to bear rather than pay the price for increased security is largely a function of how much risk we are already bearing and what percentage of our total income or wealth position is at risk. If you reflect on the basic propositions of consumer choice and demand elasticity which you learned in previous chapters, it will become clear that certainty or risk reduction is a scarce good governed by the same general principles of choice as are all other goods.

[8]Microeconomists have spent considerable time considering contract law. For an introduction to the literature concerning these issues, see Richard Posner and Anthony Kronman (eds.), *The Economics of Contract Law* (Boston: Little, Brown & Co., 1979).

ISSUES AND APPLICATIONS

Taking hostages, credible threats, and the enforcement of contracts[9]

In the body of this chapter we discussed different types of risk associated with exchange. One of these types of risk is the risk of nonperformance or misperformance of the terms of a contract. This type of risk usually occurs when the contractual arrangement involves goods or services to be "delivered" at a certain date in the future or over a period of time. Such risks are of particular concern when there are, or are expected to be, no good substitutes available for the good or service contracted for or when monitoring and detection of the nonperformance or incomplete performance of the contract is prohibitively costly during the contract period. A typical example of the first type of situation is that of an express de-

[9]One of the best recent sources on these issues is Oliver E. Williamson's "Credible Commitments: Using Hostages to Support Exchange," *American Economic Review*, vol. 73, September 1983, pp. 519–540.

livery service, dealing in items which "must" reach their destination by a certain specified time. An example of the latter type of situation is the agreement of a leaseholder to take reasonable care of the structure and premises leased.

It was suggested earlier in this chapter that some of these contract risks could be reduced by careful legal drafting of the terms of the contract, so that the elements of performance under the contract were clearly and completely specified. In addition, not all contingencies need to be specifically addressed in every contract, for contract law provides a set of "standard terms" which the courts will read into a contract unless the contract provides otherwise.

The limitation of relying exclusively on careful drafting and the provisions of contract law to reduce the risks of performance is that these precautions can ultimately be enforced only through recourse to the legal system, that is, filing suit and litigating the alleged breach. Use of the legal system is, however, far from free, as anyone familiar with attorneys' fees and court costs is all too well aware.

The alternative to litigating a breach of contract is to arrange the contract so that the other party will have nothing to gain by breach or such that the injured party will "automatically" receive damages. This can be accomplished through the arrangement variously known as "performance bonding," "putting up a security deposit," or, in the good old days, "taking hostages." The idea is simply that the party whose performance is in doubt provides a low-cost way for the other party to collect the equivalent of damages without undertaking the costs of litigating the breach. If both parties' preferences are known with certainty, then a satisfactory result will arise if the bond is limited to damages to the injured party from breach or gain to the breaching party, whichever is less.

It is curious that the law of contracts allows for "liquidated damages" clauses in contracts, which are somewhat analogous to the suggestion above, but that it construes the maximum allowable amount of such damages strictly and is generally hostile to anything which might be interpreted as a "penalty" for breach. Some economists have suggested that this limitation on what may be agreed to between the parties is desirable, for it eliminates strategic behavior by the party receiving the liquidated damages in case of breach and, hence, promotes the performance of the contract. An alternative, if somewhat more cynical, view is that the courts, by refusing to enforce "penalty" terms in contracts, and by strictly construing liquidated damages, are attempting to preserve their own market as the only supplier of remedies for contract breach.

Throwing money down the drain: The case of the new territories

Visitors to the New Territories of Hong Kong marvel at the amount of construction that has been undertaken in the last decade or so. These visitors may even become incredulous when told that the land is leased from the People's Republic of China and must be turned back at about the end of this century. Assume for the moment that, in fact, the land will return to the control of the mainland Chinese at the stroke of midnight, December 31, 1999. Was it irrational for entrepreneurs to build large hotels, apartment buildings, and so on in the New Territories?

Think of the benefit-cost analysis just presented in the previous section. Here, benefits were subtracted from costs in every year into the future for the life of the project. In essence, the net income stream obtained was discounted back to today. Look at Table 6-1 again. Look at some present values of a dollar in future net income 20 years from now. If the appropriate opportunity cost of capital for the entrepreneur investing in a building in the New Territories is, say, 20 percent, the value of a dollar in net profits in 20 years is only $.0261! Thus, it is not so foolish for an entrepreneur to invest in New Territories real estate. Those discounted potential profits in the year 2000 and beyond will not alter significantly the present value of net benefits from engaging in the project. All the entrepreneur need do to carry out the correct profitability calculation is cut off the $(B–C)$'s after the year 1999. If, when using the appropriate rate of discount, the present value of net benefits is still positive, it will be appropriate to invest in the New Territories.[10]

We can speculate about some other aspects of the New Territories. If the lessees were certain that they would not only lose the territory but also would obtain no compensation

---

[10]Apparently, the discounted, or present, value of net benefits for human capital beyond the year 1999 is a significant factor in human migration decisions. Los Angeles is said to be experiencing a "flood" of wealthy people from the New Territories of Hong Kong.

whatsoever for the buildings that they put up on the territory owned by the mainland Chinese, we would predict that they would construct those buildings in such a way that they would have minimal value by the year 2000. In other words, the average durability of assets that were fixed to the land in the New Territories should always be equal to the number of years remaining on the lease. It would not pay to make assets any more durable if there is no anticipation of compensation or scrap value for those assets in the year 2000.

Presumably, however, the Chinese will not want these assets to be completely neglected and, hence, have a relatively small value when they are taken over in the year 2000. If mainland China wants, for example, to maintain the New Territories as a tourist area after the year 2000, it may decide to arrange for appropriate compensation to the current lessees of its land for the durable assets that they are constructing and/or using on it. Our prediction would be that the lessees in the New Territories would treat their durable assets fixed to the land in a less "destructive" manner if the mainland Chinese government set up a system of promised compensations based on, for example, the quality of the buildings that they were going to take over in the year 2000.

████████████████

Uncertainty and the formation of price expectations

Uncertainty is pervasive in economic decision making, and consumers must continually make choices that require them to form some sort of prediction about future prices. How well do they perform this task? That is, are consumers able to make rational decisions by marshalling vast amounts of information in the manner of specialists who trade in financial markets, or are many of their choices short-sighted because they ignore relevant information? Some

evidence about the reaction of consumers to the "energy crisis" of the late 1970s suggest that consumers are able to make rather complex choices in the face of a great deal of uncertainty.[11]

---

[11]George G. Daly and Thomas H. Mayor, "Reason and Rationality During Energy Crises," *Journal of Political Economy,* vol. 91, February 1983, pp. 168–181.

U.S. gasoline prices fluctuated mildly around an essentially flat trend during the middle and late 1950s, then fell slowly throughout the 1960s. Indeed, by 1972, the real price of gasoline was fully 17 percent below its late 1950s level. This tranquility was disturbed by two price shocks during the 1970s, the first resulting from the OPEC (Organization of Petroleum Exporting Countries) oil embargo in 1973, and the second caused by the Iranian revolution of 1979, which interrupted crude oil shipments from that country. During both events, consumers were widely criticized by government policymakers and by the press for ignoring the oil crisis, thus contributing to its severity. These criticisms led to the imposition of automobile fuel efficiency standards and other regulations designed to force consumers to take account of higher energy prices.

ABSORBING THE PRICE SHOCKS

It is, of course, impossible to tell directly whether or not consumers took the oil price shocks seriously. An individual's expectations about future prices cannot be observed. However, Professors Daly and Mayor adopted a simple analytic device for estimating consumer reactions to the unanticipated gasoline price increases. They reasoned that if consumers were informed and expected gasoline prices to be permanently higher as a result of the 1973 embargo and, later, the Iranian shutoff, those changed expectations would have been reflected in changes in the relative prices of automobiles. More specifically, the prices consumers were willing to pay for fuel-efficient autos should have risen relative to the prices they were willing to pay for gas guzzlers.

To test this proposition, the researchers examined the behavior of used car prices during the 12 months following each of the two shocks. They divided a sample of used cars sold during these periods into two fuel-efficiency categories and observed the resulting changes in relative prices. The results showed that consumers did indeed take the two crises seriously, but that only the Iranian revolution led them to expect permanently higher gasoline prices.

GAS UP-GUZZLING DOWN

To illustrate, the price of the 1973 Dodge Monaco, a typical low-mileage automobile of that era, was falling by about $200 every 3 months as a result of normal depreciation. Had that trend continued, Daly and Mayor estimated that given the rate of change in the general price level prevailing prior to the late-1973 OPEC embargo, the price of the car would have been $3,314 in December. In fact, the Monaco sold for $2,630. This price discrepancy was explained almost entirely by the estimated effect of price expectations, suggesting that consumers anticipated (in December 1973) a $673 increase in the present value of future gas costs over the useful life of the model. However, the Monaco's price recovered to $3,200 soon after the lifting of the embargo in the spring of 1974, a level consistent with pre-shock expectations about future gasoline prices. Thus, consumers apparently viewed the 1973–1974 events as temporary.

The results for the period following the Iranian revolution were substantially different, perhaps because the OPEC embargo provided consumers with additional information about the response of gasoline prices to unexpected crude oil supply reductions. Changes in the relative prices of fuel-efficient and fuel-inefficient used cars again indicated that consumers revised their expectations about future gasoline prices upward, and the initial price adjustments gave quite good predictions about the actual behavior of gasoline prices over the following year. Unlike the 1973–1974 experience, though, expectations did not revert to precrisis levels. By March 1980, gasoline prices had risen about 45¢ per gallon above the levels anticipated prior to the revolution, and the change in relative automobile prices suggested that consumers believed that about

74 percent of this increase would be permanent.

RATIONALITY IN THE FACE OF UNCERTAINTY

The study concluded that consumers possess and utilize complex information in a manner consistent with rational decision making even in a market—used automobiles—where the cost of obtaining information is relatively high.

The actual price expectations formed by consumers in response to anticipated oil-price shocks clearly were subject to error. However, they compared favorably with the historical gasoline price series, with contemporaneous forecasts made by industry specialists, government policymakers, and other experts, and with the actual behavior of prices following the unexpected events. The evidence, therefore, suggests that consumers are able to operate rationally in a world of uncertainty.

SUMMARY

1 Risk, like many other elements of our daily lives, can be a good or a bad depending on the amount consumed.

2 Persons willing to take *fair bets*, where the expected value of losses equals the expected value of gains, are *risk neutral*. Persons unwilling to take such fair bets are *risk averse*, and persons willing to take *unfair bets* are *risk preferers*.

3 Most people are risk preferers when the stakes are a small share of their present income and wealth. Most people are risk averse when the stakes represent a large proportion of their income or wealth.

4 Risk averse individuals will insure against the risks to which they are averse, even if the insurance premium is somewhat larger than the expected loss covered by the insurance. Since most individuals are risk averse to relatively large losses, most people will insure against such losses.

5 Individuals and business firms can self-insure against certain sorts of risks by diversification of the assets which they own. This is called *portfolio diversification*.

6 The futures market allows individuals to hedge against future fluctuations in prices. It also provides the mechanism by which speculators, in anticipating consumer wants, smooth out the consumption of nonperishable goods over time.

7 In a futures market, futures contracts are bought and sold by both hedgers and speculators. Hedgers engage in both buying and selling of futures contracts; speculators are defined as those who deliberately take either a short position or a long position in the expectation of profit.

8   Sellers of futures contracts (those agreeing to deliver the goods) are betting that the spot price in the future will be lower than the futures price specified in the contract. Purchasers of such contracts (those agreeing to accept delivery of the goods) are hoping for the opposite.

9   Speculation leads to a smoothing out of consumption over time by forcing up the futures price of the commodity when a lower supply is anticipated and thus causing current owners of the commodity to withhold more from the current spot market. This in turn raises the current spot price and discourages present consumption. The opposite occurs if a relatively larger supply is anticipated in the future.

10   It is virtually impossible to avoid speculation. Any owner of nonindexed assets or liabilities implicitly incurs risk. The real value of any asset can change in an unexpected manner, and so can the relative burden of a liability. Leasing is one way to reduce speculation, but it does not eliminate speculation completely.

11   Many ordinary market transactions involve an assignment of risk between the parties. Such an assignment may be explicit, as in a contingency clause in a contract, or implicit, as in the relationship between employees, who receive a certain wage in exchange for producing a good, and employers, who sell the goods for a risky or uncertain profit.

GLOSSARY

■ **expected value** The probability weighted value of each outcome to a particular game or risky situation.

■ **fair bet** Also called a fair game; a situation in which the probability weighted (expected) values of losses and gains are equal.

■ **risk neutral** An individual who assesses alternative outcomes solely in terms of their expected (probability weighted) values.

■ **risk averse (preferer)** An individual who considers the riskiness inherent in a particular situation or game as a bad (good).

■ **mutual principle** A principle used in insurance whereby individuals pool their funds ("premiums") so as to eliminate the risk faced by any one individual in the group. That risk is thereby converted into a *certain* payment or liability of a specified insurance premium.

■ **portfolio diversification** A collection of assets in which the value of the various assets will move in different directions as certain pervasive exogenous influences change (such as, inflation rates, interest rates, economic growth rates). Diversification of assets in a portfolio tends to lower the riskiness of the entire portfolio, *ceteris paribus*.

■ **futures market** The market in which futures contracts are traded. Such contracts specify the future date of delivery of a certain amount of a commodity and specify the particular price to be paid on that date. This term refers only to organized markets.

- **speculation** The buying and selling of assets and liabilities in the hope of making a profit on their price fluctuations. Both long and short positions are possible. Actually, any ownership of nonindexed assets or obligations to pay (liabilities) involves speculation.
- **forward contract** A contract for the delivery of a specified quantity of a good on a specified date at a specified price and with specified qualities; refers to contracts on goods that are traded in other than organized markets.
- **futures contract** Like a forward contract, except that it refers to standardized contracts traded on organized exchanges.
- **future price** The price that is specified in a futures contract and that must be paid upon maturation of the contract for the specified commodity.
- **spot price** The current or cash price of a commodity. The price for "on the spot" delivery.
- **short position** This is the position of anyone who has agreed to *deliver* a specified quantity of a commodity at a specified time in the future at a stated price.
- **long position** This is the position of anyone who has agreed to *receive* a specified quantity of a commodity at a specified price in the future at a stated price.
- **hedging** The process of using the futures market to reduce risk. In hedging, the individual simultaneously enters into short and long cash and futures positions or simultaneously into long and short cash and futures positions in a commodity.

QUESTIONS

1 What can you say about the risk preferences of visitors to Las Vegas casinos? How do you know that your answer is true? What about the risk preferences of those individuals who always buy used cars?

2 If you had $20,000 to invest and wanted the "safest possible investment," would you: (*a*) buy stock in a "blue chip" corporation? (*b*) buy U.S. government bonds? (*c*) spread your money over several different sorts of assets?

3 Suppose you own a bar near the University of Nevada at Las Vegas. Every time the basketball team wins a home game, business is brisk and you clear $200 for the day. When it loses, business is slow, and on those days you clear only $50. The problem is, you don't like risk; you would prefer a certain income to an uncertain one. Fortunately for you, gambling is legal in Nevada, and there are hordes of people who like to shoulder risk, among other ways, by wagering on athletic events. Assuming you can get even odds, how much should you bet per game and on which team, in order that you will be "hedged" against the team's having a bad (or good) season?

4 Suppose a group of 100 women, all age twenty-five decide to "cut out the middle persons" by forming a mutual pregnancy-insurance league. From statistics they ascertain that for every 100 women of age twenty-five, an average of 15 conceptions occurs per year. Medical expenses in their area average $2,000 per pregnancy. Based upon these figures, what annual "insurance premium" would they assess one another to take care of the expected pregnancies? Can you anticipate any potential problems with their scheme to beat the insurance companies out of some business?

5 In present value terms, what two financial rights do you buy when you purchase a share of common stock? Does the past performance (earnings, etc.) of the firm have any bearing on either of these two rights?

6 Why might a speculator in commodities futures want to have instantaneous reports on changes in weather throughout the world? How much should a speculator spend generating weather information? Should he or she go as far as to have an in-house weather service generating its own weather forecasts?

7 Is it possible for someone to eliminate all financial risk by investing properly? Discuss.

8 Do all people regard risk with the same attitude? Does the size of the risk make a difference?

9 Suppose you run a printing business specializing in "rush jobs." Would you want any special clauses in the contracts you make with your suppliers of ink, paper stock, and other essential inventory?

SELECTED REFERENCES

Hieronymus, Thomas A., *Economics of Futures Trading* (New York: Commodity Research Bureau, Inc., 1971).

Jones, C. E., "Theory of Hedging on the Beef Futures Market," *American Journal of Agricultural Economics*, vol. 50, December 1968, pp. 1760–1766.

Sandor, Richard I., *Speculating in Futures* (Chicago: Board of Trade of the City of Chicago, 1973).

Stevens, Neil A., "The Futures Market for Farm Commodities—What It Can Mean to Farmers," *Federal Reserve Bank of St. Louis Review*, August 1974, pp. 10–15.

Stigler, George, *The Theory of Price*, 3d ed. (New York: Macmillan, 1966), chap. 17.

The firm and production

CHAPTER 8

*U*ntil now we have been concerned essentially with the household sector of the economy. We can call this the "consumption sector" of the economy. But there is another broad sector of the economy that consists of business firms. We want to analyze business behavior to see how firms choose inputs and outputs and determine prices. We will first define production and then discuss the reasons why firms exist. The assumption of the firm as a profit-maximizing entity will be reviewed, as will competing hypotheses about the goals of firms. Then we will analyze production, including many of the aspects of the relation between inputs and outputs.

THE MEANING OF PRODUCTION

We can define **production** in its broadest sense as any use of resources that transforms one commodity into a different commodity. The commodities can be different either in terms of *what* they are, in terms of *when* or *where* they are located, or in terms of what the consumer can do with the commodity. Production therefore includes not only manufacturing but storing, wholesaling, transporting, retailing, repackaging, attempting to alter regulatory agency rulings, using lawyers and accountants to find tax loopholes, and so on.

Production includes both goods and services because the term "commodity" refers to both. Indeed, there is rarely any difference between goods and services from an economic point of view. Both are usually produced using some labor and some capital.

Production is a flow concept. It is an activity that is measured as a *rate of output per unit time*, where output is expressed in constant-quality units. Thus, when we talk of increasing production, we mean increasing the rate of output, with all other dimensions of production held constant. Similarly, the use of resources in a production process is measured in terms of flows. Capital is measured in hours of machine services, not in numbers of machines. Land is measured in acre-years, not in numbers of acres.

WHY DO FIRMS EXIST?

Commodities are produced by firms. Our definition of a **firm** is limited to any **organization** in which there is an employer and one or more employees. More generally, we could define a firm as an organization that buys and hires resources and sells goods and services. The employees are paid a contractually fixed wage per period, no matter what the rate of output of the firm and no matter what the rate of sales or profits. On the other hand, the employer, who is also defined as an **entrepreneur**—the organizer of production and undertaker of business risks—does not receive a contractual wage rate in the capacity of entrepreneur. Rather, the employer receives what revenue is left over, if any, after all contractual payments are made.[1] In accounting, "what is left over" from each year's revenues is called **profit,** or *net income*. Economists call this the *residual* or *net revenues*. We will examine the concept of profit in more detail in later chapters.

Firms do exist. In principle, an individual could, for example, make automobiles, but automobile *firms* in fact produce most automobiles. Many of the production activities that go into the final product called an automobile are carried out within an automobile manufacturing firm. Conversely, we could conceive of an economy in which each step in the process for producing a particular good was done by individual workers who bought partly finished goods from another worker and sold a more finished output to subsequent workers. Typical firms differ from this arrangement by **integrating production** within their organizational framework.

Transaction costs   Much can be understood about the reasons firms exist by recognizing that economic transactions are not costless. Exchange between two individuals has its costs, generally called *transactions costs*. Given the existence of transactions costs, it may be cheaper to organize production in such a way that

---

[1]There are, of course, some real-world firms in which the same person is both an employee and an entrepreneur (workers' cooperatives and some small proprietorships and partnerships).

some market transactions are eliminated and replaced by an entrepreneur who both monitors and directs the production process within an organization.

However, such an organization does have its bad points. Production by a group of individuals who are not the **residual claimants** to any profits—"what's left over"—increases the cost of monitoring, metering, directing, and renegotiating contracts. If 10 Haitian basket weavers operate separately as individual entities, each being an entrepreneur, each will feel the full brunt of "not doing his or her job." Income and profits will fall for each individual who slacks off, in proportion to how much that individual slows down. However, if all 10 are put into one firm in which they work together as a coordinated group, each specializing, say, in one aspect of production, the cost of any one individual member's not doing the job will be spread out among all members. Hence, if a firm is used to organize production, the cost to an individual of slacking off on the job is less than in a situation in which the worker is also the residual claimant to any profits. Moreover, in a firm, it is more difficult to meter the output of each individual in the group because they are all working together. Thus, it is also more difficult to work out a proper incentive system to reward a worker who generates a higher output by way of a greater work effort. The above are factors working *against* organizing firms. Yet, production within firms where workers are not also owners is the norm in today's economy. How do such firms function?

Role of monitors   What we observe in firms is the use of **monitors**. Monitors make sure that workers perform by direct observation and by other attempts to meter the output of workers. The ultimate monitor in a firm is the entrepreneur or employer. That person monitors all other monitors in the firm.

If the entrepreneur or employer doesn't monitor output effectively, his or her net wealth position is reduced. Employees, in choosing to work for a firm, implicitly agree to being monitored by the entrepreneur. It can even be shown that workers in a worker-owned firm would desire some degree of monitoring and penalties for shirking. The larger the firm, the more formal and strict such monitoring would be.

All this leads to the prediction that *firms will exist whenever cooperative group effort results in a larger product than the sum of the products of individual efforts.* The difference, of course, must be at least as great as the costs of organizing, monitoring, metering,[2] and enforcing contracts with em-

---

[2]A detailed discussion of the notion of monitoring and metering and of the existence of firms can be found in A.A. Alchian and H. Demsetz, "Production, Information Costs, and Economic Organization," *American Economic Review*, December 1972, pp. 777–795. See also R.H. Coase, "The Nature of the Firm," *Economica*, new ser., vol. 4, November 1937, pp. 386–408. The latter is also reprinted in G. Stigler and K. Boulding, *Readings in Price Theory* (Homewood, Ill.: Irwin, 1952), pp. 332–335.

ployees less the transactions costs associated with the subcontracting alternative.

THE GOAL OF THE FIRM: PROFIT MAXIMIZATION

Lurking behind the explanation of why firms exist was an implicit assumption about the goal or goals of the firm. It was stated that the buck stopped at the ultimate monitor, the owner-entrepreneur or employer who had a residual claim on whatever was left over after all expenses were paid. This residual claim is called profit. Underlying our assertion that the entrepreneur as monitor will slack off less in his or her duties because of the immediate impact on net worth is an assumption of net worth maximization (in the present value sense). The theory of the firm as we present it in this book is built around this hypothesis.

In demand theory, utility (or satisfaction) maximization by the individual provides the basis for the analysis. In the theory of the firm and production, profit or wealth maximization is at least initially the underlying hypothesis of our predictive theory.

Is this assumption of profit maximization realistic? If we are trying to explain business behavior, we do not have to assume that entrepreneurs consciously try to maximize profits. We hypothesize that their behavior is *consistent with* the maximization of profits.

Our justification for assuming profit maximization by firms is similar to our belief in utility maximization by individuals. In order to obtain labor, capital, and other resources required to produce commodities, firms must first obtain financing from investors. In general, investors are indifferent about the details of how a firm uses the money they provide. They are most interested in the earnings on this money and the risk of obtaining lower returns or losing the money they have invested. Firms that can provide high returns and less risk, therefore, will have an advantage in obtaining the financing needed to continue or expand production. Over time, we would expect a risk-discounted policy of profit maximization to become the dominant mode of behavior for firms that survive. This rationale applies only to "for profit" firms operating within unregulated markets. Nonprofit charitable or education foundations and self-financed sole proprietorships face other constraints on their actions and "maximize" other goals.

THEORIES OF MANAGERIAL DISCRETION

Although we will use the assumption of profit maximization throughout the next several chapters, a brief examination of other possible firm goals that economists have discussed is worth presenting.

FIGURE 8-1
Staff maximization

FIGURE 8-1
Staff maximization
Staff hours per unit time period are measured on the horizontal axis. Total profit is expressed as dollars per unit time period on the vertical axis. Up to S_2 as staff is added, profits increase. After that point, total profits decrease. Thus, the profit-maximizing size of staff is at S_2; however, the managers are assumed to obtain utility from a larger staff size. Thus, they hire staff up to the point where they can reach their highest indifference curve, II, or at point E. Staff hired will be equal to S_1, which is greater than S_2. The corresponding profit A will be less than the maximum profit B.

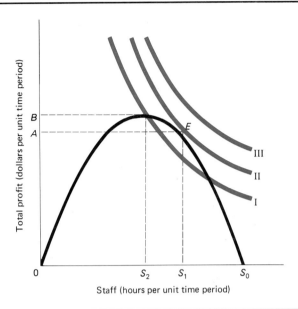

Staff maximization

Whenever there is a separation of the ownership of a business from its control, the possibility arises that the managers will not act in the best interests of the owners.[3] Since monitoring is not a costless activity, owners would not be expected to eliminate completely managerial activities that benefit the managers but harm the owners. Given the *separation of ownership and control*, it is possible that managers may seek to improve their own *real income* by having a larger staff than would be consistent with maximum profit or wealth for the owners. The manager is willing to trade off some of the owner's profit for an increase in his or her staff, particularly when it is unlikely that the managers will "get caught" at not acting 100 percent in the owner's interest. We can represent the trade-off in terms of indifference curves. We show three of these in Figure 8-1.

We see in Figure 8-1 that the horizontal axis measures staff hours per unit time period and the vertical axis measures total profit per unit time period. Assume that the indifference curves for a manager are convex to the origin. There is a profit curve showing the relation between total profit and staff size. *Ceteris paribus*, as more staff members are added, total profit rises to a maximum of B associated with a staff size of S_2 and then falls, reaching zero with a staff size of S_0. To maximize the utility of the manager, the staff size would be set at S_1, for that is where indifference curve II is tangent to the "budget constraint" or trade-off line between profit and staff size (point

[3]See, for example, Adolph A. Berle and Gardiner C. Means, *The Modern Corporation and Private Property* (New York: Macmillan, 1948).

E). If there were no separation of ownership and control, or if monitoring by owners were costless, the size of the staff would be set at S_2 and total profits would be at their maximum of B. In other words, managers would act *as if* they were owners in setting the optimal staff size.

This is a utility-maximizing theory of managerial behavior. It requires the existence of imperfect information among the owners-stockholders. It also requires that the firm have some degree of market power.[4] If the firm were in a completely competitive market, a topic we will discuss in Chapter 10, it would have to maximize profits merely to survive.

Sales maximization[5]

Another type of model that has been offered for the firm is based on sales maximization. Managers may pursue sales maximization if they think that their own compensation and/or professional prestige depends more on sales than on profits. We must insert the constraint here that there be a minimum rate of return on investment that stockholders require. (Note that we are referring now to the percentage *rate* of profit—profit per year/investment— rather than to absolute dollar profits.)

We present the model of sales maximization in Figure 8-2. Profit, ex-pressed as a rate of return on investment, is represented on the vertical axis and unit sales per unit time period on the horizontal axis. The relation between the profit rate and the unit sales rate is given by the curve; the profit rate reaches a maximum at Q_1. However, assume that the point of maximum revenues (price times quantity) occurs at Q_3. Even if management wishes to maximize sales revenues, it will not be able to produce at the quantity Q_3 because there is a constraint upon it. That constraint is the minimum profit rate, which we have drawn in arbitrarily at 10 percent per year. Thus the managers will set sales at Q_2 rather than at the profitability-maximizing rate of Q_1.

We have drawn indifference curves I, II, and III vertically. They are drawn vertically because we assume that management obtains no utility, or satis-faction, at all from profitability; thus, a higher utility curve is merely a vertical line farther to the right. How can managers increase unit sales and hence revenues? Provided that they are operating in the elastic portion of their demand curve, they can lower the price of the product and increase total revenues. Furthermore, they can engage in more advertising to increase sales by shifting the demand curve outward to the right.

Growth maximization

A similar model of the firm involves managers attempting to maximize the *rate of growth* of sales revenues. Presumably this would explain why man-agers are so amenable to mergers with other firms. If they see that their

[4]Oliver E. Williamson, *The Economics of Discretionary Behavior* (Englewood Cliffs, N.J.: Prentice-Hall, 1964).
[5]William J. Baumol, *Business Behavior, Value and Growth,* rev. ed. (New York: Harcourt Brace Jovanovich, 1967).

FIGURE 8-2
Sales maximization

Assume that profitability, expressed as a rate of return on investment, is an increasing function of unit sales up to Q_1; after that profitability diminishes. Assume, also, that there is a minimum annual rate of return of 10% per year that managers must meet. The indifference curves for the managers are I, II, and III. They are vertical, indicating the managers receive no utility from profitability per se. The highest indifference curve that managers can reach is not III, with the rate of unit sales at Q_3, because the rate of unit sales yields a rate of profitability below 10 percent per year. Therefore, the rate of unit sales that managers will strive for is Q_2, which puts them on indifference curve II. Note that this rate exceeds the profitability-maximizing rate of unit sales Q_1.

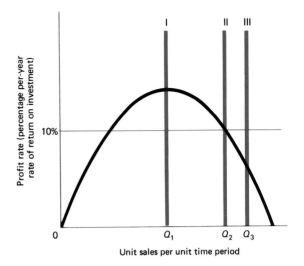

salaries are related to the rate of growth of the firm and to having larger organizations under their control, they will engage in activities to make the firm larger. However, they are still constrained by a minimum profitability requirement. This minimum profitability requirement exists, in principle, because if profitability becomes too low, there exists the possibility that some group of stockholders will attempt to take over the firm and possibly fire some or all of the current managers.

A combination of managerial utility maximization, sales maximization, and growth-rate maximization is inherent in the view of the firm presented in J. K. Galbraith's *New Industrial State* and *Economics and the Public Purpose*. Additionally, Galbraith points to the managerial drive for prestige and technical virtuosity. He further suggests that the managers can carry out their plans because they are able to influence the behavior of consumers, primarily by advertising. Since the corporation is run by managers who wish to have an easy life for themselves, Galbraith emphasizes, large corporations will try to avoid risks and engage in extensive planning to produce stability. This is his so-called planning sector of the economy, and it is run by corporate technocrats: *technically* skilled individuals who, in Galbraith's view, make all the important business planning decisions.

"Satisficing" behavior[6]

According to the "satisficing" theory of firm behavior, the firm sets for itself a minimum standard for performance. It aims at a "satisfactory" rate of profit; presumably, once this rate of profit is obtained, the managers slack off. An

[6]Herbert Simon, "Theories of Decision-Making in Economics and Behavioral Science," *American Economic Review*, June 1959.

implication of the "satisficing" theory of firm behavior is that within the firm there is no consistent attempt to minimize costs for any given level of output, provided that a satisfactory rate of return is being earned. In other words, there is "internal slack."

Criticisms of non-profit-maximizing assumptions

Aside from the question of the role of assumption in economic theory, criticisms have been leveled against the alternative models presented above. One is that there is indeed a market in managers. Every management team of every firm faces the possibility that some other management team may convince the board of directors of the corporation or, more dramatically, the stockholders, that the latter team will increase the profitability of the firm if allowed to take control.

Takeovers may occur by a majority of the stockholders selling their stock to outsiders, as explained below. Alternatively, a majority of shareholders could vote to put a new board of directors in control. The new board could install a new management team that promises to improve profits. Given the existence of a *market for corporate control*, behavior that deviates dramatically from profit maximization presumably will not be allowed to continue indefinitely. (Although clearly, the more impediments there are to controlling corporate management, the more likely is the firm to operate in a non-profit-maximizing dimension.)

Additionally, critics of non-profit-maximizing models of the firm point out that not only existing stockholders but *potential* stockholders must be considered. Remember in Chapter 6 when we said that the price of an asset is the discounted stream of its anticipated future net income? If the asset in question is the common stock of a firm, its value or price in the marketplace will be the present value of the expected stream of future net profits. Thus, to the extent that current management decisions are not maximizing long-run profits, the current market price of the firm's stock will be less than it otherwise would be. Some outsiders may take note of this, making the corporation a sitting duck for a takeover bid. A group of investors would attempt to take over the corporation by buying a large block of its stock at a premium over the current low price, kicking out the current managers, and installing a new set, thereby increasing anticipated future profitability. The market value of the stock would then rise. Those who took over would experience an increase in their net worth—a capital gain—since the stock they owned in the company could be sold for more than they paid for it. Thus, to the extent that there exists a market for corporate takeovers, non-profit-maximizing behavior has some limits set on it.

Accepting for the moment, then, the assumption of profit maximization, we can proceed to examine the determinants of the way in which a firm organizes production. Specifically, we will look at the optimal use of inputs.

PRODUCTION INPUTS

What goes into the production of a commodity? Broadly speaking, the terms *inputs*, *factors of production* (often just called *factors*), or *productive resources* are all synonymous. These terms include managerial talent; entrepreneurial risk taking; raw materials; various types of labor, machinery, and buildings or their service flows; and so on.

Classification of inputs

In order to simplify our analysis, we will group all inputs into either of two categories: *labor* and *capital*. Once the analysis has been done with this simplified division of production inputs, we can refine the classification of inputs to whatever degree is desired, depending upon the exactness of the analysis we want to undertake. Capital may include the skills that a laborer has gained by investing his or her time and other resources. Thus, even services that may superficially seem to involve only the use of labor probably are produced using some "human capital."

A further classification that we will use is the division of inputs into those which are fixed and those which are variable. Complying with tradition, and for ease of exposition, when we want to discuss fixed inputs, we will treat capital as fixed and labor as variable. The distinction between fixed and variable factors of production is clearly arbitrary and is dependent upon the time period for which the firm has to make decisions.

Short versus long run

Commonly, a fixed factor of production is an input that cannot be altered in the short run but can be altered in the long run. But, then, what is the meaning of short run and long run here, and what is meant by "cannot be altered"? Certainly, you would agree that a steam generator already in place must be classified as a fixed factor of production in the short run because it is hard to expand the firm's stock of steam generators in a short period of time. That, however, is an incomplete statement of reality. If it is willing to pay a high price, an electric utility can have a steam generator installed in a relatively short period of time. Furthermore, if there is a large change in relative prices, a firm may junk its existing fixed factors of production in favor of some other set of fixed factors, such as turbine generators for electric utilities.

Again, we will have to make a rather arbitrary distinction between short run and long run as applied to our way of defining fixed and variable factors of production. What we will have to say is that a fixed factor of production is one whose quantity cannot be expanded in a particular situation without *substantially* increasing the cost per unit of the fixed factor; it can, however, be altered in the long run without an increase in cost per unit of the input.

The definition of the long run involves a production situation during which all factors of production are *variable*. Within the context of this reasoning, the long run is a production situation during which all factors can be varied without causing their per unit cost to rise. The long run is thus an investment-decision or investment-planning situation. In the long run, a decision is made whether to invest in, to reinvest in, or to scrap a production process.

It is common, and not usually misleading, to think of the short run and the long run as periods of time, with the short run referring to what is possible in the near future and the long run referring to what is possible over a longer period. In fact, it is more correct in analyzing the production decisions of a firm, to focus our attention on what alternatives are open or not open to the firm when particular decisions are being made. The long run is, thus, a situation where more alternatives are available.

RELATING OUTPUT TO INPUTS

The firm brings together certain types of inputs and combines them in such a way that an output results. The output is what the firm sells. Our theory implies that the way in which the firm uses inputs to produce output is *technologically efficient*.

Technical efficiency

Efficiency concerns relations between inputs and output. Let us first consider the technological aspects of these relations. At any moment in time, the list of all known productive processes in a society is its available technology. We will assume in our economic analysis of production that there is perfect transmission of technological information across firms; thus the available technology is the same for all firms. As time goes on, new ways in which inputs can be used to produce outputs are discovered. As new processes are discovered, old ones remain known, so the list of available technology becomes longer and longer.

Now consider a situation in which a new process has been discovered. Assume this new process uses the same types of inputs and produces the same type of output as an existing process. However, the new process uses less of one or more of the inputs and no more of any other input to produce a given rate of output. Alternatively, it can produce more output with the same amounts of each input. In such a situation, the old process has now become technically inefficient. Clearly, no profit-maximizing or cost-minimizing producer would use more inputs than need be used for a given level of output. It is, therefore, not unreasonable for us to assume that once a process has become technically inefficient, it will never be used.

By definition, then, **technical efficiency** requires *a production process that uses no more inputs than necessary for a particular level of output, given the existing technology.*

Now let us consider a technological change to a new process that uses the same types of inputs to produce the same output as the old process did. However, it uses less of some inputs and more of others to produce any given quantity of output. We cannot automatically call the old process technologically inefficient or efficient. In fact, the old process may continue to be used in some markets, the new process in others. Which is used in each case will depend on the relative prices of the inputs in each market and on the uncertainty of a continued supply (such as natural gas). For example, we have a "new" process for building highways. We use workers and sophisticated machinery. The old process uses relatively more workers with picks and shovels. That process uses more labor and more capital. In a society where there is relatively more labor, the old process may continue to be used in spite of the fact that firms in that society know of the existence of the new process. The choice of processes becomes an *economic* rather than a purely *technical* one. The engineer fades from the picture; the economist enters the scene.

Economic efficiency

Implicit in the notion of **economic efficiency** is the concept of *least-cost* production. In other words, *for any given rate of output, a firm engages in economically efficient production if and only if that firm is utilizing resources in the proportion for which the cost per unit of output (for that given rate of output) is the least.* In other words, a production process is economically efficient for a specified rate of output if there is no other process that can be used to produce that rate of output at a lower (per unit) cost.

In the discussion that follows, we take for granted technological efficiency on the part of the firm. The profit-maximizing firm will never voluntarily select a production process that physically "wastes" inputs. If 10 units of output can be produced with 10 units of labor and 10 units of capital, the firm will never use 10 units of labor and 12 units of capital in the production of 10 units of output. Once we understand the implications of technical efficiency, we will find that the optimal choice of inputs on the part of the firm incorporates the notion of technical efficiency as a part of the concept of economic efficiency.

The production function

We label the relationship between physical output and physical inputs the **production function.** It is defined as the schedule or mathematical equation that gives the *maximum* quantity of output that can be produced from specified sets of inputs, *ceteris paribus.*[7] *Ceteris paribus* in this case refers particularly to possible other techniques available for producing an output from inputs (technology).

In its broadest form, a production function is described by the equation

$$Q = f(K, L) \tag{8-1}$$

[7]A more formal definition is the envelope of the attainable set of technically efficient combinations of inputs.

where Q is the rate of output per unit time period, K is the service flow from the stock of capital per unit time period, and L is the service flow from the firm's laborers per unit time period. All that this equation tells us is that the physical quantity of output is some function of the physical quantities of the inputs: capital and labor. We have not specified the exact relation. Rather, we have left it as an unspecified function. It is important to note, however, that all production functions are statements of mechanical or other physical transformations of inputs into outputs. No production function, in itself, tells us anything about the worth or value of the inputs or the outputs. We will cover that topic when we discuss costs and revenue functions.

Perhaps it is easiest to understand the notion of a production function by working through a hypothetical numerical example. We will deal with only one variable factor of production in this example and work it through in its entirety. Then we will deal with two variable inputs.

Short-run production with one variable factor

We present a short-run production-function relationship in Table 8-1. This short-run production function can be written as

$$Q = f(L, \overline{K}) \tag{8-2}$$

where K is constant as indicated by $\overline{K}$.

Total physical product. Here we are assuming that there is only one variable factor of production, labor. Capital is held constant. As more workers are added, total output increases. The **total physical product** curve that results is presented in Figure 8-3. We have joined the successive points taken from Table 8-1 to form that curve. It reaches a maximum at six workers per year. After that point, total physical product actually declines.

If we examine average physical product and marginal physical product, we will be able to explain why the total product curve is shaped the way it is.

Average physical product. **Average physical product** (APP) is defined as the total product divided by the quantity of the variable input employed.

TABLE 8-1
Total output with one variable and one fixed input

Number of worker-years per year	Number of machine-years per year	Total physical product (pounds of corn per year)
1	2	100
2	2	210
3	2	330
4	2	405
5	2	475
6	2	500
7	2	490

FIGURE 8-3
Short-run total physical product
The production function of Table 8-1 is
transferred to this graph. Total physical product
rises through six workers and then falls.

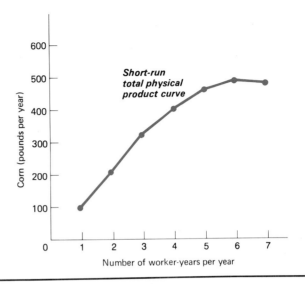

We present average physical product in column (3) of Table 8-2. It is total output per year divided by the number of full-time workers. Column (3) combined with column (1) can be represented graphically, as shown in Figure 8-4. Here we show the average physical product curve, which first rises, then reaches a peak at three workers, and then falls.

Marginal physical product. **Marginal physical product** (MPP) is defined as the change in total output (absolute value) associated with a one-unit increment or decrement in the variable input. In this example, we are considering the effect on output of changes in the amount of labor used along with a constant amount of capital. Therefore, we refer to the marginal physical product of labor, which is presented in Table 8-2. Numerically, the marginal physical product of labor is basically the change in the total output in column (2). Note that we follow the standard convention; all marginal figures in this table, and in all others that follow, will refer to the interval between the indicated amount of whatever is under study and one unit less than the indicated amount. Thus, the marginal physical product for the interval between zero and one worker is 100, and for between one worker and two workers is 110. It also can go in the other direction: From two workers to one worker the marginal physical product of labor is 110, from one to zero workers it is 100.

The data from column (4) are represented graphically in Figure 8-4. The result is the marginal physical product, and it is so labeled. The marginal physical product of labor does not mean the amount of output produced by an additional or last unit of labor. Rather, it refers to the change in total output when the total amount of the labor input used in production is changed

TABLE 8-2
Deriving average and marginal physical product of labor

*All marginal figures refer to an interval between the indicated amount of the variable input and one unit less than that indicated amount. This convention will be used in all tables showing marginal quantities.

Number of workers (1)	Total output (2)	Average physical product of labor [(2) ÷ (1)] (3)	Marginal physical product of labor* $\left(\dfrac{\Delta \text{ total output}}{\Delta \text{ labor input}}\right)$ (4)
0	0	—	—
1	100	100	100
2	210	105	110
3	330	110	120
4	405	101.25	75
5	475	95	70
6	500	83.33	25
7	490	70	−10

FIGURE 8-4
Average and marginal physical product
The average physical product curve is taken from the third column in Table 8-2. It rises up to three workers per year and then falls thereafter. Marginal physical product is taken from the last column in Table 8-2.

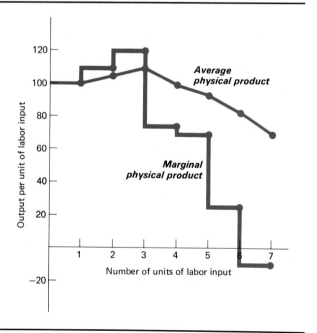

by one unit. It is a comparison, as it were, between total output associated with a particular size of labor input and total output when that size of labor input is increased or decreased by one unit, keeping capital fixed. Thus, marginal physical product of labor never means the amount produced by the *last* unit of labor. This can be seen by examining the exact relation between marginal product and average product.

THE LAW OF DIMINISHING MARGINAL RETURNS

The shape of the total physical product curve in Figure 8-3 and the resulting average and marginal physical product curves in Figure 8-4 were not accidental. The way we have drawn these curves is consistent with the so-called **law of diminishing marginal returns**, or diminishing marginal *physical* product. Actually, in the way we have set up our example, the marginal physical product from adding one more worker per year first rises, going from 100 to 110 to 120, and then falls. At the point at which the marginal physical product of labor falls, we say that diminishing marginal returns have set in. It is relatively easy to understand why the so-called law of diminishing marginal physical product (or returns) would be operative in just about all production functions. After all, we are holding the amount of capital constant and merely adding more workers. Each worker is thus working with a smaller and smaller capital stock. Think of it in terms of the capital stock consisting of hoes for a bunch of workers who are going to weed an acre of cotton. After some point, there will be more workers than hoes, and the hoes will have to be shared. At least at that point, and perhaps even before, diminishing marginal physical returns will probably set in.

Let us formally state the law of diminishing marginal returns:

■ *Holding technology and all inputs except one constant, as the variable input is increased by equal increments, beyond a certain point the rate of increase in product that results will decrease. Otherwise stated, after a certain point, the marginal physical product of the variable input will diminish.*

The law of diminishing returns holds if:

1. Only one variable input is varied and all others are held strictly constant.
2. The "state of the arts" is fixed; i.e., technology does not change.
3. The coefficients of production are variable; i.e., we are not dealing with a fixed-proportions function in which one unit of labor has to be used with, say, two units of capital.

For example, we rule out a road-building production process which requires that only one laborer with one pick be used. We assume that it is possible to substitute more sophisticated machinery in order to use fewer workers, or vice versa.

The law of diminishing returns is an empirical assertion about reality. It is not a theorem derived from a set of assumptions or an axiomatic system. It is not a logical proposition and hence is not susceptible to mathematical proof or refutation. It is merely a statement concerning physical relationships that has been observed to hold in the real world. One of the reasons that we accept this "law" is that we would otherwise find it difficult to explain why firms *stopped* hiring additional labor (or any other input) at some point.

TOTAL, AVERAGE, AND MARGINAL PHYSICAL PRODUCT

One way of looking at marginal physical product is to see that it represents the average physical product corrected for any change in the average physical product due to a change in the variable factor of production. In other words, marginal physical product is average physical product plus the change in average product times the number of workers. Or

$$MPP_L = APP_L + (\Delta APP_L)L \qquad \text{(8-3)}$$

where the subscript L refers to labor.[8]

[8]To prove this, start with average physical product of labor Q/L, where Q = output; then

(a) $Q = L\left(\dfrac{Q}{L}\right)$

For simplicity, let $Q/L = X$.

(a') $Q = L \cdot X$

(b) $Q + \Delta Q = (L + \Delta L)(X + \Delta X)$

$\qquad\qquad = LX + L\Delta X + \Delta LX + \Delta L\Delta X$

(c) $\Delta Q = L\Delta X + \Delta LX + \Delta L\Delta X$

(d) $\dfrac{\Delta Q}{\Delta L} = L\dfrac{\Delta X}{\Delta L} + X + \Delta X$

As $\Delta L \rightarrow 0$, ΔX also approaches 0, since $X = Q/L$, then (d) becomes

(e) $\dfrac{\Delta Q}{\Delta L} = L\dfrac{\Delta X}{\Delta L} + X$

(f) $\dfrac{\Delta Q}{\Delta L} = L\dfrac{\Delta(Q/L)}{\Delta L} + \dfrac{Q}{L}$

(g) $MPP_L = APP_L + L\dfrac{\Delta APP_L}{\Delta L}$

which is Eq. (8-3) when ΔL is assumed equal to one unit.

The term ΔAPP_L is negative in cases where a one-worker change reduces the average productivity of all workers. In the example we have been dealing with, this occurs when the seventh worker is added or laid off. The workers get in each other's way so much that total physical product actually falls when the seventh worker is put on the labor force and rises with the seventh worker's removal. We can use Eq. (8-3) to determine the marginal physical product when seven laborers are working. The average physical product of seven workers is 70. The change in average physical product when we go from six to seven workers is $-13\frac{1}{3}$ ($70 - 83.33 = -13.33$). We multiply $-13\frac{1}{3}$ by 6, and we get -80; $70 + (-80) = -10$, which is exactly equal to the marginal physical product of labor when seven workers are working.

We can also use Eq. (8-3) to figure out the relation between average and marginal physical product on a graph. (Note that all these relations apply only when it is possible to produce different levels of output with different proportions of capital and labor inputs. It would be impossible for us to draw the curves that we have drawn if capital and labor had to be used in fixed proportions. Thus we say that the above relations apply only to variable-proportion production functions.)

The geometry of the relationships

We will see this when we work out their geometry. Look at Figure 8-5. Here we have shown a smoothly drawn total physical product curve. In order to figure out average physical product, pick any amount of the variable input, for example, L_1. The amount of output produced is Q_1. The definition of

---

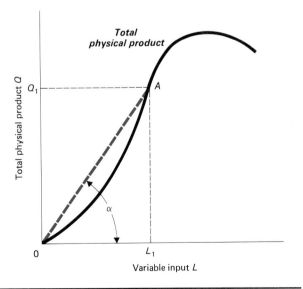

FIGURE 8-5
Deriving average physical product from total physical product
We draw in a smooth total physical product curve here. Pick a point, such as A, where L_1 of workers are hired. Their total physical product is measured on the vertical axis as Q_1. Average physical product is, therefore, Q_1/L_1; but this is equal to the numerical value of the slope of the line connecting point A with the origin, or with the tangent of angle α.

average physical product tells us that it is measured by the vertical distance $0Q_1$ (which is also equal to L_1A) divided by the horizontal distance $0L_1$. Thus, average physical product of $0L_1$ units of the variable inputs equals $L_1A/0L_1$. But $L_1A/0L_1$ is identically equal to the slope of the line, or dashed ray, connecting point A with the origin. Otherwise stated, APP is the slope of the straight line that connects point A with the origin and is equal to the tangent of angle α.

We now have a geometric way to figure out what happens to average physical product as we increase the use of the variable input. It is shown in Figure 8-6. Consider first quantity A of the variable input, then B, then C, all the way through H. We see that the slope of the straight lines from the origin to the input-output combination quantities in question gets steeper and steeper, reaches its maximum at E, and then gets less steep. Thus, average physical product increases up to the amount of E units of the variable input

---

FIGURE 8-6
Changing APP
We show increases in the quantity of the variable input L, from zero to q_A to q_B all the way through q_H. The points corresponding to these quantities of inputs are shown as A through H on the total physical product curve. When we connect lines (rays) from the origin, 0, to points A through H, we see that the lines (rays) have an increasing slope up to E and then have a decreasing slope. Thus, APP of the variable input increases up to E and decreases thereafter.

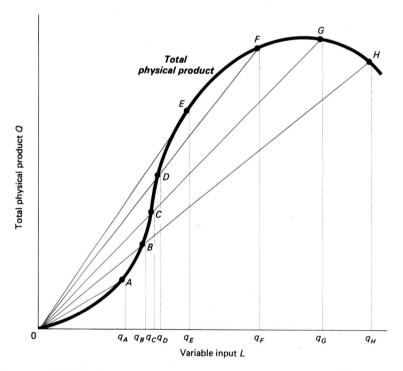

and thereafter decreases. Quantity E would correspond to three workers in Table 8-2.

The relation between total, average, and marginal physical product curves. Marginal physical product is defined as the change in total physical product due to a one-unit change in the variable input. When we are dealing with infinitesimally small changes in the variable input, marginal physical product can be defined as the slope of the total physical product curve at the point in question. It is important to make the distinction between average physical product and marginal physical product. Average physical product is determined by the slope of the line (a ray) from the origin to the point in question on the total physical product curve.

Marginal physical product is determined by the slope of the tangent line drawn at the point in question on the total physical product curve. This is shown in Figure 8-7, where eight amounts, q_A through q_H of the variable

---

FIGURE 8-7
Deriving MPP from the total physical product curve
Marginal physical product is defined as the change in total physical product associated with a one-unit change in the variable input. Thus, it is equal to the slope of a tangent drawn to any point on the total physical product curve. We see, then, that marginal physical product increases as it moves from point A to points B and C, then decreases after the inflection point D through points E and F, finally becomes zero at point G, and is negative thereafter.

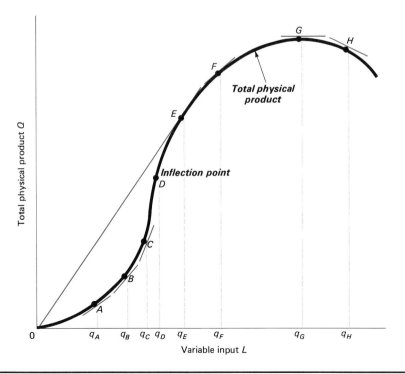

input, are pinpointed on the total physical product curve. A tangent is drawn at each of these points. The slope of the tangent first rises and then falls and eventually becomes negative after point G. Notice two things about the slope of these tangent lines. At some point D, corresponding to quantity input q_D, the slope of the tangent line stops getting steeper and starts getting less steep. This is the *inflection point* on the total physical product curve. Note also that the tangent line at point E, corresponding to quantity input q_E, intersects the origin. Thus, at point E, average physical product and marginal physical product are equal.

To summarize the relations between average product and marginal product that we have derived from our total product of labor graphs, we can note that marginal physical product will exceed average physical product only

FIGURE 8-8
***The relationship between total, average, and
marginal physical product***
In the top panel, we draw a smooth total physical product curve. Its inflection point is at point A, where marginal physical product changes from increasing to decreasing, i.e., reaches its maximum at variable input level $q_{A'}$ in the lower panel. At point B in the top panel on the total physical product curve, marginal physical product is equal to average physical product; i.e., the two curves intersect. This is seen in the bottom panel at quantity of variable input $q_{B'}$. Thereafter, average physical product declines. At point C, total physical product has reached its maximum; marginal physical product is zero, and thereafter it is negative. In the top panel, we have shown stages I, II, and III. Stage II is called the *economic region of production.*

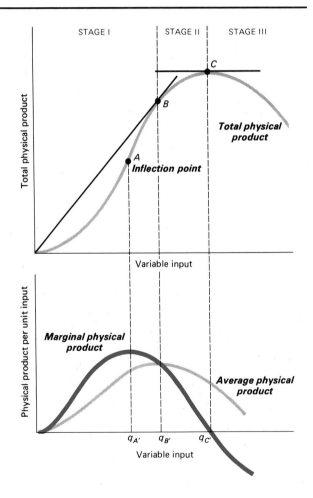

when average physical product is rising. Marginal physical product will be less than average physical product only when average physical product is falling. Thus we know that whenever the average physical product curve is rising, the marginal physical product curve must be somewhere above it; when the average physical product curve is falling, the marginal physical product curve must be somewhere below it. This is as we have drawn it in Figures 8-4 and 8-8. We also know from Figure 8-7 that the only time marginal physical product equals average physical product is when average physical product is "constant," or horizontal. This occurs at the maximum point on the average physical product curve. These same rules apply to any average and corresponding marginal relation. Consider your class average and your score on the next test or a baseball player's batting average and his hitting during a single game.

Putting it all together

In Figure 8-8, we have put all the above geometric information together. We show a total physical product curve in the top half of the diagram. From information in this total physical product curve, we can derive various points on the average and marginal physical product curves and learn the exact relations between them. These are shown in the bottom half of the diagram. First of all, point A is the inflection point on the total physical product curve. At the inflection point, marginal physical product reaches its maximum. This is shown in the marginal physical product curve in the bottom part of the diagram. At point B, we know two things: Average physical product is at its maximum, and average physical product equals marginal physical product. Thus, in the bottom half of the diagram, we see that the average physical product curve has reached its maximum at input quantity $q_{B'}$ and that the average physical product curve intersects the marginal physical product curve there. Finally, at point C, we know that marginal physical product is equal to 0. Thus we show the marginal physical product curve intersecting the vertical axis in the bottom half of Figure 8-8, and becoming negative for levels of variable input greater than input quantity $q_{C'}$.

THE THREE STAGES OF PRODUCTION

The top part of Figure 8-8 has also been partitioned into three regions: stage I, stage II, and stage III. These are the so-called *three stages of production.* In the first stage of production, the average physical product of the variable input is increasing. In stage II, its average physical product is decreasing, as is its marginal physical product, but the marginal physical product is still positive. In stage III, the average physical product continues to decrease and so, too, does the total physical product because the marginal physical product is negative in this stage.

No producer will want to produce in either stage I or stage III. Clearly, it is disadvantageous to be in stage III because a higher total physical product can be obtained by reducing the amount of the variable input. Marginal physical product of the variable input is negative beyond $q_{C'}$.[9]

THE LONG-RUN CASE OF TWO VARIABLE INPUTS

Perhaps a more interesting production decision involves not the choice of *how much* of one variable input to use but rather *what combination* of *two variable inputs* to use.

In long-run decision making, we assume that the capital and labor available to the firm are both variable and that both capital and labor are available to the firm in very small increments. Certain combinations of capital and labor will produce certain levels of output. We can use a geometric device in our theory of production that is similar to the one we used in the theory of consumer demand. Remember the indifference curve that gave the various combinations of two commodities that yielded a constant level of satisfaction? If we now consider that we are talking about a constant level of output, we can imagine a similar geometric device showing the various combinations of labor and capital that yield a constant level of output.

Production isoquants

The technical term for this geometric device is a **production, or output, isoquant**. It is defined as a curve in an **input space** that shows all the possible combinations of two inputs (capital and labor, in our example) that are physically capable of producing a given rate of output.

We show a hypothetical isoquant in Figure 8-9. The horizontal axis measures physical amounts of labor, expressed in service flow per unit time period; physical amounts of capital, expressed in service flow per unit time period, are depicted on the vertical axis. The isoquant is drawn for a particular production rate Q_1. Thus any combination of capital and labor given by a point along the isoquant will yield exactly Q_1 of output. As we move along Q_1, we simultaneously vary the input amounts *and* the proportions in which capital and labor are used.

Fixed-proportion production functions

Up until now we have implicitly or explicitly been dealing with variable-proportion production functions; such production functions allow for varying proportions of capital and labor to be used. It is possible, however, that two inputs, such as tires and wheels, must be used in fixed proportions in order to produce a particular output (automobiles).

We demonstrate what the isoquants would look like in the case of a

---

[9]Additionally, it can be shown that this argument is symmetrical. Using less of the variable input than at $q_{A'}$ results in the marginal physical productivity of the *fixed* input being negative. Thus, too many roadworkers trying to work with too few shovels may lower output, as may too few workers trying to work with too many shovels. The reason that the latter does not seem to be such a serious problem is that the cost of disposing of or storing excess shovels is very near zero. This holds, at a minimum, whenever the production function is homogeneous of degree one.

FIGURE 8-9
An output isoquant
When we are dealing with a variable-proportion production function, we can vary labor and capital inputs so as to produce a constant level of output. This is shown by a constant output curve called an *isoquant* and here labeled Q_1.

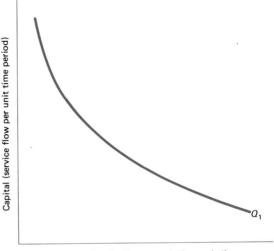

Labor (service flow per unit time period)

fixed-proportion production function. The ratio of capital to labor is fixed physically in the particular example illustrated in Figure 8-10. The ratio is given by the slope of the ray $0N$. The isoquants are necessarily right angles. For output Q_1, it is necessary to use labor and capital in the proportion L_1/K_1. In other words, given the amount of labor L_1, it does not matter if more capital than K_1 is used. In fact, more than K_1 would be technically (and

FIGURE 8-10
Fixed-proportion production function
The ratio of capital to labor is physically fixed in this particular production function. That ratio is given by the slope of the ray $0N$. For output Q_1, it is necessary to use L_1 of labor and K_1 of capital. It does not matter if more capital is used, holding the quantity of labor constant; that will not increase output. It does not matter if more labor is used, holding the quantity of capital constant; it will not increase output. In other words, the MPP of either input is zero.

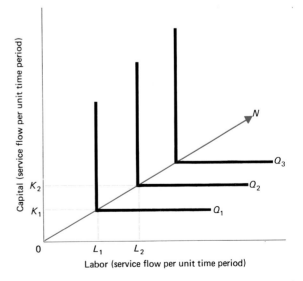

economically) inefficient. The maximum output available is Q_1 using L_1 of labor. Conversely, given the amount of capital K_1, it does not matter if more labor than L_1 is used; output cannot be expanded beyond Q_1. More than L_1 would be technically inefficient. Go on to the next output level, Q_2. Here the amount of labor necessary is L_2 and the amount of capital is K_2. The *proportion* L_2/K_2 is equal to the *proportion* L_1/K_1. In other words, $L_2/K_2 = L_1/K_1$. That is the nature of the fixed-proportion production functions. Suffice it to say here that the real world does not exhibit a great number of fixed-proportion production functions. When the isoquants are perpendicular, as in Figure 8-10, we say that the inputs are either joint or perfectly complementary; i.e., they must be used in fixed proportions. For such cases, it is useful to speak of the demand for bundles of the two inputs in their fixed proportion.

Distinguishing between movements along and among isoquants

Look at Figure 8-11. Each isoquant represents the combinations of capital and labor that may be used to produce given outputs Q_1, Q_2, and Q_3, where $Q_1 < Q_2 < Q_3$. Now, what happens when we move from A to B along the isoquant corresponding to output level Q_1? We merely change the combination of labor and capital—both the proportion *and* the absolute amounts—but we do not change the output level. We see the change in the proportion

FIGURE 8-11
Distinguishing between a movement along a single isoquant and a movement among isoquants
As we move along isoquant Q_1, with the quantity of output held constant at Q_1, we change the *proportions* of the two inputs. In other words, the movement from A to B involves an increase in the capital/labor ratio. However, a movement along any ray, such as $0N$, entails a movement among isoquants where *output* is changing while the factor proportion remains fixed such as at points E, E', and E''. The capital/labor ratio is the same, but output has increased.

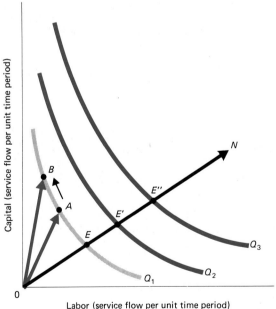

Capital (service flow per unit time period)

Labor (service flow per unit time period)

of labor to capital by the change in the angle of the ray (straight line) from the origin to points A and B. At point B, more capital is used and less labor; i.e., the ratio of capital to labor is greater, and clearly the slope of the ray 0B is greater than the slope of the ray 0A, for at A less capital and more labor are used.

Movements out along a particular ray, such as 0N, guarantee that the proportion of capital to labor will remain constant, but the output level associated with each will rise because more of both capital and labor is being used. Thus, for movements along any ray (which is a straight line from the origin), we will find the level of output changing continuously but the input ratio (K/L or L/K) remaining constant. The input ratio at E, E', and E'' is constant in Figure 8-11.

SUBSTITUTION AMONG INPUTS

We have assumed that substitution among inputs is feasible. It turns out that the shape of an isoquant indicates the amount of substitution that is *technically* feasible. We can better understand the slope of an isoquant by relating it to the marginal physical product of the input.

The slope of an isoquant

When we move along an isoquant, we increase the usage of one input and decrease the usage of the other input, all the while keeping output constant. The degree to which the usage of one input is increased while the other is decreased is given by the slope of the isoquant. The slope of the isoquant is clearly the change in capital divided by the change in labor as output is held constant, or

$$\text{Slope of isoquant} = \frac{\Delta K}{\Delta L} \qquad Q = \overline{Q} \qquad \text{(8-4)}$$

i.e., output is held constant.

The slope of the isoquants that we have drawn in Figures 8-9 and 8-11 is negative. The direction of a change in capital will always be opposite to that of a change in labor.

We can relate the slope of a convex isoquant, which is always changing, to the marginal physical product of labor and of capital. Remember that MPP_L is defined as the change in output resulting from a one-unit change in the amount of labor used, *keeping the capital input fixed*. The marginal physical product of capital MPP_K is the change in output resulting from a one-unit change in the amount of capital used, *holding the labor input constant*.

Let us begin the analysis on the isoquant relating to a level of output Q_1 in Figure 8-12 at point A. We increase the amount of labor used by ΔL, which lands us at point B. The movement from A to B is the result of a positive

▰▰▰▰

FIGURE 8-12

The slope of an isoquant
The slope of an isoquant is given by the ratio of the change in capital to the change in labor. A change in labor from point A to point B will change output by $\Delta L \cdot \mathrm{MPP}_L$. In order to keep output constant, we must now reduce it by reducing capital. Capital must be reduced by the amount ΔK, and output will then fall by $\Delta K \cdot \mathrm{MPP}_K$. These two quantities must be equal to keep output constant; hence, $-\Delta K/\Delta L$, negative of the slope of the output isoquant, must be equal to $\mathrm{MPP}_L/\mathrm{MPP}_K$.

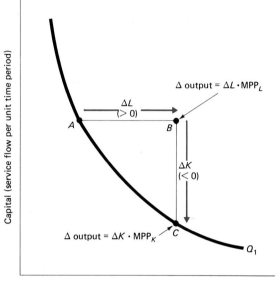

$(+)$ ΔL change in the amount of labor. The movement from B to C is caused by a negative $(-)$ ΔK change in the use of capital. Now, along the Q_1 isoquant, output is held constant at Q_1. Thus for any movement along the isoquant, $\Delta L \cdot \mathrm{MPP}_L + \Delta K \cdot \mathrm{MPP}_K = 0$. In words, if one input, say labor, is increased, total output will increase by that change in labor times labor's marginal physical product. But along an isoquant, output does not change, by definition. Therefore, there must be a corresponding reduction in the other input, capital. That reduction must reduce output back down to where it was before. Another way of stating this is that along any isoquant

$$\Delta L \cdot \mathrm{MPP}_L = -\Delta K \cdot \mathrm{MPP}_K \qquad (8\text{-}4a)$$

If you think back to the discussion in Chapter 3 of the marginal rate of substitution, you will recall that when we defined marginal rate of substitution along a given indifference curve, the changes were very small. The same thing is true here; to have accurate measures we can consider the slope of the isoquant only at a single point, such as point A in Figure 8-13. The change illustrated in Figure 8-12 was simply to show the concept involved. To be accurate, we measure the slope at a single point where a very small change in inputs labor and capital is occurring. To rearrange Eq. (8-4a):

$$\frac{\mathrm{MPP}_L}{\mathrm{MPP}_K} = -\frac{\Delta K}{\Delta L} \qquad (8\text{-}4b)$$

FIGURE 8-13
The slope of an isoquant
The slope of an isoquant is given by the ratio of a very small change in capital to the change in labor. The slope at point A is equal to the slope of the line tangent to the isoquant at point A. At that constant level of output, the changes in the inputs, $\Delta K/\Delta L$, equal the slope of the isoquant, and equal $\text{MPP}_L/\text{MPP}_K$.

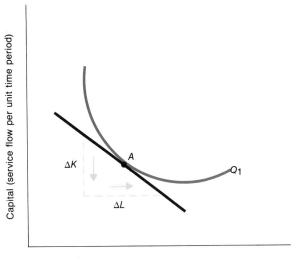

We now see that the numerical value (ignoring its sign) of the slope at any point on the isoquant is going to be equal to $\text{MPP}_L/\text{MPP}_K$. The name for this ratio is the marginal rate of technical substitution.

MARGINAL RATE OF TECHNICAL SUBSTITUTION

The ratio $\text{MPP}_L/\text{MPP}_K$ is the numerical value of the slope of the isoquant and is called the **marginal rate of technical substitution** of labor for capital, or MRTS. Formally, then,

$$-\frac{\Delta K}{\Delta L} = \text{MRTS}_{K:L} = \frac{\text{MPP}_L}{\text{MPP}_K} \qquad \text{(8-5)}$$

Verbally, the MRTS is defined as the change in labor required in order to keep output constant when there is a one-unit change in the usage of capital.

With convex isoquants, the marginal rate of technical substitution diminishes as L increases (and K decreases). In other words, the consequence of moving down a convex-to-the-origin isoquant is a diminishing MRTS. The analysis here is analogous to what we did in the theory of consumer demand. There we talked about convex indifference curves and diminishing marginal rates of substitution in consumption. Now we are talking about convex isoquants and diminishing marginal rates of technical substitution in production.

Presumably, we could talk about a law of diminishing MRTS in which we would state that as labor was substituted for capital along an isoquant, the marginal rate of technical substitution declines. The only time this is true, however, is where isoquants are convex and have negative slopes.

Uneconomic regions of production

Consider the lowest isoquant Q_1 in Figure 8-14. Look at point D. Here Q_1 of output can be produced with L_1 of labor and K_1 of capital. What if more labor—that is, a quantity in excess of L_1—is used? In order to use more than L_1 of labor, more than K_1 of capital would have to be used to maintain Q_1 of output. That is going to be uneconomic for any producer. After all, both capital and labor have a positive price. Thus, why would any entrepreneur want to hire more labor to produce the same quantity of output if doing so required the hiring of more capital services as well? Clearly, it would never pay to use more than L_1 of labor to produce Q_1 of output. This would be technically inefficient.

A symmetrical analysis can be done for point A. It would never pay to use more capital services to produce Q_1 than the amount indicated at point A; doing so would require the use of more labor services just to keep output from falling below Q_1. Points A, B, C, D, E, and F all have this same property. They are points beyond which the isoquant turns back on itself. It is never economic to use the factors of production indicated by the section of the isoquants past points A, B, C, D, E, and F. If we connect these lines with the lines $0R$ or $0R'$, we have sectioned off the economic area of production.

FIGURE 8-14
Ridge lines
Points A, B, and C constitute the upper ridge line. Combinations of labor and capital above the upper ridge line are uneconomic because they require an increase in the use of both inputs with no corresponding increase in output. Points B, E, and F are connected to form the lower ridge. Combinations of labor and capital to the right of the lower ridge line also require more of both labor and capital with no corresponding increase in output and, hence, such combinations are also uneconomic. Everywhere along ridge line $0R$, the marginal physical product of capital is zero. Above the ridge line $0R$, marginal physical product of capital is negative. Everywhere along the ridge line $0R'$, the marginal physical product of labor is equal to zero. Everywhere below $0R'$, the marginal physical product of labor is negative.

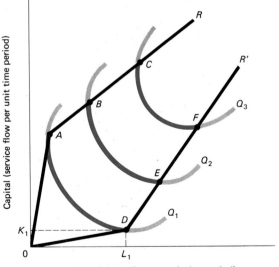

Capital (service flow per unit time period)

Labor (service flow per unit time period)

FIGURE 8-15
Diminishing MRTS

As labor is increased at a constant rate, L_1 to L_2 to L_3, etc., as a substitute for capital, K_1 to K_2 to K_3, etc., the marginal rate of technical substitution declines. Visually we see that each added unit of labor replaces less capital as we become more labor intensive, output held constant at Q_1. Comparing points A and B we can see that in the uneconomic region of production, the additional use of a factor of production, an increase from L_A to L_B, causes a decrease in output.

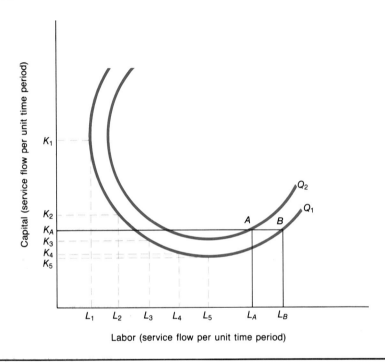

Labor (service flow per unit time period)

The lines $0R$ and $0R'$ are called the **ridge lines**. On one side of a ridge line, the input ratios are economic; on the other side, they are not. The area enclosed by the two ridge lines is stage II, similar to stage II in the top half of Figure 8-8.[10]

Now that we understand that the numerical value of the slope of the isoquant is given by the numerical value of the ratio of the marginal physical product of labor to the marginal physical product of capital, we can understand even better why the area outside the ridge lines in Figure 8-14 is uneconomic. (Actually, that area corresponds to stages I and III in Figure 8-8.)

When production declines

Look again at Figure 8-14. Notice that the isoquants turn back on themselves at points A, B, C, D, E, and F. At point A, for example, as we move upward along the isoquant, we now have an increasing marginal rate of technical

---

[10]This symmetry holds for *linear homogeneous* production functions.

substitution, but the only way we can have an increasing marginal rate of technical substitution is for one of the marginal physical products to be negative. This is exactly what occurs outside the ridge lines. In the case of moving along the first isoquant past point A in Figure 8-14, the marginal physical product of capital becomes negative. This is true anywhere above the ridge line $0R$. At any point below the ridge line $0R'$, the marginal physical product of labor becomes negative. Along $0R'$, $MPP_L = 0$; and along $0R$, $MPP_K = 0$. Below $0R'$ is stage III for labor; above capital $0R$ is stage III for capital. (See the end of Chapter 3, "Good Goods, Bad Goods, and Indifference Analysis," for an analogous graphical presentation.)

The fact that the marginal rate of technical substitution declines is illustrated in Figure 8-15. There we add equal increments to the labor being used in a constant level of production, Q_1. The labor replaces capital, but at a declining rate. Whether or not a firm will actually do this depends, of course, on the relative prices of the two inputs. Furthermore, if we go beyond the ridge lines identified in Figure 8-14, out into the uneconomic region of production, as are points A and B in Figure 8-15, we can see that added units of inputs will actually decrease output. If we hold capital constant at K_A, but increase labor from L_A to L_B, we see that output falls from A to B, since Q_2 is a higher isoquant than Q_1. In such a case, apparently so many workers have been placed into a production situation with a limited amount of capital that they are simply impeding each others' work, cutting output.

OPTIMAL INPUT COMBINATION

In order to find out the optimal (least-cost) input combination for a firm working to produce a given level of output, we must add some *cost data*. This is what we had to do with consumer theory when we wanted to find the consumption optimum. We added price and income data. There we drew a budget line; now we draw what is called an **isocost curve**.

Isocost curve

We assume that input prices are taken as given as far as any one producer is concerned and are determined by the forces of supply and demand in the input market. The producer is a small part of that market and can buy as much or as little as he or she wants at the market price.

We will call the unit price of labor services w and the unit price of capital services r, where r is *not* an interest rate. Sometimes r is called the implicit rental value per unit of capital. If, for example, a firm is able to rent a dump truck for $500 a week, the weekly price for the services of the dump truck, r, is equal to $500. If the firm owns the dump truck for which it paid $130,000, the unit price of services from the dump truck does not change to $130,000. Rather, it implicitly would stay the same: $500 per week, if that continues to be the going weekly price at which dump trucks can be rented. Remember that the only true or choice-relevant costs for economists are alternative costs. *Sunk costs are by definition unrecoverable and are thus irrelevant for decision making.* Here, the total cost for any volume of labor and capital will equal

$$TC = wL + rK \qquad \text{(8-6)}$$

where TC equals total cost.

A line along which total costs are constant is called an *isocost curve* or *isocost line*. It is similar to the budget line along which total consumer expenditures are constant. Look at Figure 8-16. We can find the extreme point on the horizontal axis for a particular constant amount of total costs, TC, by dividing total costs by the wage rate. This gives us the maximum quantity of labor, t', that could be purchased with total costs equal to TC. With the other extreme point on the vertical axis, we do the same thing for capital. We divide total cost, TC, by the implicit rental price per unit of capital, or TC/r, and get a maximum quantity of capital, t. The resultant isocost line is tt'.

The slope of the isocost curve. The slope of the isocost curve tt' in Figure 8-14 will be equal to $-0t/0t'$. But $t = TC/r$ and $t' = TC/w$, so that

$$\text{Slope of } tt' = \frac{TC/r}{TC/w} = -\frac{TC}{r} \cdot \frac{w}{TC} \qquad \text{(8-7)}$$

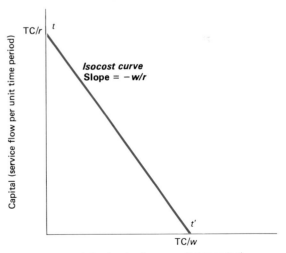

FIGURE 8-16
An isocost curve
If we divide total cost by the wage rate, we obtain the maximum quantity of labor that can be hired, t'. If we divide total cost by the price per unit of capital, we obtain the maximum amount of capital that can be purchased, t. When we connect these two points, we obtain the firm's isocost curve. It represents the combinations of capital and labor that can be purchased with a particular outlay TC. Its slope is equal to $-w/r$.

Isocost curve
Slope = $-w/r$

TC/r

Capital (service flow per unit time period)

TC/w

Labor (service flow per unit time period)

FIGURE 8-17
Optimal combination of inputs
The firm's optimal combination of inputs for a given outlay TC is obtained when an isoquant is tangent to the isocost curve, here at point E. The optimum combination of capital and labor would be K_e and L_e, respectively.

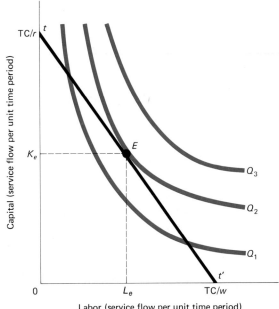

The TCs cancel out,[11] leaving

$$\text{Slope of isocost curve} = -\frac{w}{r} \tag{8-8}$$

Changing total costs. If input prices remain constant, an increase in total cost will shift the isocost curve tt' in Figure 8-16 to the right without changing its slope. With input prices fixed, an infinite number of isocost curves can be drawn in the input space in Figure 8-16.

---

[11]An alternative way of deriving the slope of the isocost curve is to consider the equation for total cost:

(a) $TC = rK + wL$

Now, subtracting wL from both sides of Eq. (a), we obtain

(b) $TC - wL = rK$

If we divide both sides of Eq. (b) by r, we obtain

$K = TC/r - (w/r)L$

But this is the equation of a straight line whose intercept is the first term on the right-hand side of Eq. (c) and whose slope is the coefficient of L, or $-w/r$.

**Attaining
production
optimum**

It is now possible to combine isocost curves with isoquants to find the input combination that would maximize output obtained from a given "budgeted" cost. In other words, the entrepreneur takes as given input prices w and r. For a given total cost TC, there is one and only one combination of labor and capital that will maximize total product. (Note that maximizing output for a given TC is *not* equivalent to maximizing profits.)

Output is maximized for a given TC only when the highest isoquant possible is attained. In Figure 8-17, the highest attainable isoquant is the one which is just tangent to the isocost line tt'. That isoquant corresponds to an output level of Q_2, which is clearly greater than Q_1. The tangency occurs at point E. The optimal quantity of labor used will be L_e, and the optimal quantity of capital used will be K_e. (For simplicity, we have drawn in only the portion of each isoquant that is contained within the ridge lines.)

At the point where the isoquant is tangent to the isocost line tt', their slopes are, by definition, equal: At point E, the negative of the slope of the isoquant is equal both to the marginal rate of technical substitution and to the marginal physical product of labor divided by the marginal physical product of capital. The negative of the slope of the isocost curve is equal to the ratio of the wage rate per unit of labor and the implicit rental rate per unit of capital. Thus, optimal use of capital and labor for a given total cost requires that[12]

$$\text{MRTS} = \frac{\text{MPP}_L}{\text{MPP}_K} = \frac{w}{r} \tag{8-9}$$

---

[12]The proof is as follows: If capital is decreased by ΔK, the resulting change in Q will be $-\text{MPP}_K\Delta K$. Capital costs will change by $-r\Delta K$. But we want TC to remain a constant, and so we must somehow increase labor costs by an equal amount, or

(a) $+w\Delta L = -r\Delta K$

We can divide (a) by w to get

(b) $\Delta L = -\frac{r}{w}\Delta K$

Now we ask what the change in output will be if labor is changed by ΔL. We can find out by multiplying ΔL by its marginal physical product MPP_L; thus our answer is (b) multiplied by MPP_L or

(c) $\text{MPP}_L\Delta L = -\frac{r}{w}\text{MPP}_L\Delta K$

The net change in output is

$$\Delta Q = \text{MPP}_K\Delta K + \text{MPP}_L\Delta L$$

(continued)

In other words, *the optimal combination of labor and capital occurs when the ratio of the prices of labor and capital is equal to the marginal rate of technical substitution of labor for capital.* From Eq. (8-9), we also know that the optimal combination occurs when the price ratio of labor to capital equals the ratio of the marginal physical product of labor to the marginal physical product of capital.

At this point, we could show why a diminishing MRTS is important. If isoquants were not convex to the origin but rather concave to the origin, we would end up with a corner rather than an interior solution. In Figure 8-17, the optimal combination would be at either the vertical intercept of tt' or the horizontal intercept. In other words, concave-to-the-origin isoquants (increasing MRTS) imply specialization in input usage. Since we do not observe such specialization in the real world, we use convex- rather than concave-to-the-origin isoquants. This analysis is similar to the one presented in Chapter 3 where we talked about convex- versus concave-to-the-origin indifference curves in the theory of consumer demand.

From Eq. (b) we know what ΔL is equal to, and we substitute it in the expression above to get

$$\Delta Q = MPP_K \Delta K + MPP_L \left(-\frac{r}{w} \Delta K \right)$$

Simplifying terms, we get

(d) $\quad \Delta Q = \Delta K \left(MPP_K - \frac{r}{w} MPP_L \right)$

But along an isoquant, $\Delta Q = 0$ so that (d) becomes

(e) $\quad 0 = \Delta K \left(MPP_K - \frac{r}{w} MPP_L \right)$

Dividing (e) by ΔK we get

(f) $\quad 0 = MPP_K - \frac{r}{w} MPP_L$

or $\quad -MPP_K = -\frac{r}{w} MPP_L$

$$\frac{MPP_K}{MPP_L} = \frac{r}{w}$$

which we must invert to arrive at

(g) $\quad \dfrac{MPP_L}{MPP_K} = \dfrac{w}{r}$

Q.E.D.

The least-cost solution

We can arrange Eq. (8-9) as follows:

$$\frac{\text{MPP}_L}{w} = \frac{\text{MPP}_K}{r} \tag{8-9a}$$

Equation (8-9a) simply tells the firm that the least-cost combination of labor and capital is such that the same output should be obtained per last dollar spent on each of the resources. If not, purchases of labor and capital can be rearranged so that Eq. (8-9a) will hold.

WARNING: PRODUCTION THEORY NOT CONSUMER DEMAND THEORY

Superficially, it would appear that the theory of production as presented above is identical to the theory of consumer demand. Isoquants *look like* indifference curves, and isocost curves *look like* budget lines. However, the similarity ends there. The theory of consumer behavior does indeed explain the nature of the consumer's optimum. However, the optimum presented in Figure 8-17 and in Eq. (8-9) is incomplete. It does not represent a final optimum. It tells us how the producer will combine inputs to maximize output *for a given total cost.* Alternatively, Eq. (8-9a) tells us how a producer would combine inputs to minimize costs *of producing a given output.* But we have yet to show which output rate is the profit-maximizing one. We will answer that question in Chapter 10.

Two other points need to be mentioned in distinguishing between the formal characteristics of consumption and production theory. First of all, although the concept of utility or satisfaction can probably not be measured cardinally, there is no difficulty in obtaining cardinal measures of output. Thus, while we can say only that the consumer is more or less satisfied, we can make the more definite statement that a firm produced twice as much or one-half as much in one period compared to another. Second, while we could easily imagine a consumer being in equilibrium while consuming none of one good (a corner solution), production using no labor, for example, is less feasible. Thus we generally will not consider corner solutions in our discussion of production.

ISSUES AND APPLICATIONS

What do real-world production functions look like?

Many researchers have investigated the nature of real-world production functions. A variety of techniques have been developed to estimate these functions. Researchers have analyzed data from a long period of time to show the various inputs used in each period in the past and the amount of output that resulted in each period. For example, one could obtain information on the amount of labor and capital used in the primary aluminum industry during each year from, say, 1950 to 1978. The researcher would then have 29 observations, and from these observations an estimate of the relation between inputs and the resulting output could be obtained.

An alternative technique involves analyzing statistically data either from a large number of firms or from different sectors of the industry at a particular time. Information on the amount of capital and labor used by firms in the tire manufacturing industry could be obtained for a particular year, say, 1977. The number of observations would be equal to the number of firms from which data were obtained. From such data, an estimate of the relation between inputs and the resulting output could be obtained.

Statisticians dealing with the data used to estimate production functions run into many problems. It is often difficult to measure the capital input since at any point in time the stock of capital is composed of equipment that is not of the same type or of the same age and productivity. Even the measurement of the labor input is difficult because the labor in any one firm is of varying quality. A complete list of the problems in the measurement of production functions could fill an entire book.

The exact mathematical form of the production function must also be chosen. If you'll go back to Eq. (8-1), you will see that we did not specify the form, but rather left it implicit. Researchers in this area have often simply assumed that a production function was of the "Cobb-Douglas"[13] nature. This broad class of production functions has the following appearance:

$$Q = AL^{\alpha}K^{\beta} \qquad \text{(8-10)}$$

where Q = output

L = the quantity of labor services

K = the quantity of capital services

A, α, and β are parameters that vary from firm to firm and from industry to industry.

This type of production function is multiplicative. An additive type of production function would look like the following:

$$Q = A + \alpha L + \beta K \qquad \text{(8-11)}$$

To give you an idea of some of the estimates of the coefficients of labor and capital, α and β, we present in Table 8-3 a variety of estimates for different industries in different countries.

The coefficient of labor α from the Cobb-Douglas production function [Eq. (8-10)] is the percentage increase in output that would result from a 1 percent increase in labor, the quantity of capital being held constant. Similarly, β is the percentage increase in output that would result from a 1 percent increase in capital, the quantity of labor being held con-

---

[13]Named after two earlier researchers who used such functions extensively.

TABLE 8-3
Estimates of α and β for selected industries

Source: A. Dobell, L. Taylor, L. Waverman, T. Liu, and M. Copland, "Communications in Canada," Bell Journal of Economics and Management Science, 1972; A. A. Walters, "Production and Cost Functions," Econometrica, January, 1963; J. Moroney, "Cobb-Douglas Production Functions and Returns to Scale in U.S. Manufacturing," Western Economic Journal, 1967.

Industry	Country	Year	α	β
Metals and machinery	United States	1909	.71	.26
Cotton	India	1951	.92	.12
Coal	United Kingdom	1950	.79	.29
Jute	India	1951	.84	.14
Food	United States	1909	.72	.35
Sugar	India	1951	.59	.33
Coal	India	1951	.71	.44
Telephone	Canada	1972	.70	.41
Paper	India	1951	.64	.45
Chemicals	India	1951	.80	.37
Gas	France	1945	.83	.10
Electricity	India	1951	.20	.67

stant. In other words, α and β are elasticities; they are the elasticity of output with respect to each input. So we see, for example, that the estimate for α in the cotton industry in India in 1951 is 0.92. We would predict, there-fore, that a 1 percent increase in the labor input would result in a 0.92 percent increase in the output of cotton. Similarly, given a β of 0.12, a 1 percent increase in the capital input would increase output by 0.12 percent.

SUMMARY

1 Production includes all uses of resources that transform a commodity into a different commodity. It is a flow concept and is measured as a rate of output per unit time period.

2 Firms exist whenever cooperative (or team) effort results in a product larger than the sum of the products of individual effort.

3 The assumption of profit maximization is the one we use in this text; however, there are alternative theories of managerial behavior, such as staff maximization, sales maximization, growth maximization, and "satisficing."

4 To the extent that a market for corporate control exists, there is a limit to the non-profit-maximizing behavior of managers.

5 While there are many inputs used in the production of a good, for simplicity we usually group inputs into labor and capital. We assume all inputs to be variable in the long run, while in the short run only some inputs can be changed at a "reasonable cost."

6 Production functions state a relationship between inputs and outputs; while we presume these relationships to be technically efficient, we are searching to determine economic efficiency.

7   Whenever average physical product is rising, marginal physical product will be above it; whenever average physical product is falling, marginal physical product will be below it. Marginal physical product equals average physical product at the latter's maximum.

8   The law of diminishing marginal returns does not follow from a set of assumptions; it is an assertion about reality.

9   There are three stages of production. In stage I, the average physical product APP of the variable factor is rising since the marginal physical product MPP is above it. In stage II, both average and marginal physical product are falling, but MPP is positive. In stage III, both APP and MPP are decreasing, but MPP has become negative. No producer would willingly produce in stage I or stage III.

10 When dealing with two variable inputs, we find the optimal combination of the two inputs at the point where an isoquant is tangent to the isocost curve. At this point, the marginal rate of technical substitution is equal to the ratio of the price of labor to the price of capital.

11 It is important to distinguish between movements along and among isoquants. The former refers to changes along an isoquant where both the ratio and the absolute amount of the inputs change, with one input increasing and the other decreasing. The latter refers to a northeastward movement along a line from the origin from one isoquant to the next. The ratio of capital labor is constant, but output increases.

12 The uneconomic regions of production in a capital-labor input space are bounded by so-called ridge lines. Above the upper ridge line, the marginal physical product of capital is negative; below the bottom ridge line, the marginal physical product of labor is negative.

13 In that area where isoquants are convex to the origin, the firm is experiencing a diminishing marginal rate of technical substitution of labor for capital.

14 The production optimum is not strictly analogous to the consumption optimum. All it tells us is how the producer will combine inputs to maximize output for a given total cost or, alternatively, how the producer will combine inputs to minimize costs of a given output. We have not yet dealt with the determination of the profit-maximizing rate of output.

GLOSSARY

■   **production** Any use of resources that converts one commodity into a different commodity; production, therefore, includes storing, wholesaling, transporting, repackaging, and manufacturing.

- **firm** An organization in which there is an employer and one or more employees.
- **organization** A group of individuals engaged jointly in production
- **entrepreneur** The organizer of production and undertaker of risk in a business. The entrepreneur's income is the residual, if any, after all expenses are subtracted from revenues.
- **profit** The residual after all expenses are paid in a business; the difference between total revenues and total costs, including the opportunity cost of all resources used.
- **integrating production** To reduce costs firms may move various steps in the production process, whether physical inputs like steel or contractual inputs like accounting work, into the firm itself rather than purchase the inputs from the outside.
- **residual claimants** Individuals who have a right to that which is left over after all contractual expenses of a business are paid. They claim the residual, if any.
- **monitors** Individuals within firms who observe others within the firm to insure that they perform their assigned tasks.
- **technical efficiency** The technical relation between output and inputs; measured in terms of physical units of output compared with physical units of inputs.
- **economic efficiency** A production process is economically efficient for any given rate of output if there is no other process that can be used to produce that rate of output at a lower cost.
- **production function** The mathematical expression of the technical relation between output and one or more inputs.
- **total physical product** The physical output that results from production.
- **average physical product** Total physical product divided by the number of units of the variable input used.
- **marginal physical product** The change in total physical product due to a one-unit change in a single variable factor of production, all other factors of production held constant.
- **law of diminishing marginal returns** With a given technology and all inputs but one fixed, as equal increments of that one variable input are added, beyond a certain point the *rate* of increase in output will decrease.
- **production or output isoquant** The locus of points showing all the combinations of capital and labor that will yield a constant amount of output.
- **input space** In our two-dimensional production situation, a quadrant representing combinations of capital and labor; similar to a commodity space.
- **marginal rate of technical substitution** The rate at which labor can be substituted for capital, holding output constant; or the ratio of the marginal physical product of labor to the marginal physical product of capital, i.e., $MRTS = MPP_L/MPP_K$.
- **ridge lines** The lines connecting the points on isoquants where those isoquants turn back on themselves. To the left of the upward ridge line and to the right of the rightward ridge line lie the uneconomic areas of production. Along the ridge line either MPP_L or MPP_K is zero.
- **isocost curve** Also called an *isocost line;* the business firm's "budget constraint" that gives the different combinations of capital and labor that can be purchased with a fixed outlay and with the nominal (and therefore relative) prices of capital and labor fixed. The line along which total costs are constant in an input space.

QUESTIONS

(Answers to even-numbered questions are at back of text.)

1 Using this chapter's definition of production, examine each of the following two statements to determine whether any production took place:

   a Five minutes after buying a used car for $500, and without so much as washing it, the dealer turns around and sells it to someone else for $600.

   b A ton of pitted apricots, with a market value of $300, is exposed to the sun's rays for a week and then sold (only half a ton now that much of the water has evaporated) for $400.

2 Can you think of a good or service that is produced solely with labor and without the use of any capital equipment whatsoever?

3 If production is a flow concept measured with reference to a period of time, how would you describe the "output" of a speculator who merely buys, say, an ounce of gold, holds it a year, and then resells it?

4 Is it possible to be in the freight delivery business without owning any trucks, and if so, who in his or her right mind would do so? How? Why?

5 "The way to have the best of both worlds (low transactions costs and low costs of supervision) is to have all your employees working on piecework and pay them according to just how much they produce." If this statement were accurate, we would expect to see few, if any, workers paid according to their time input. Yet the vast majority of employees are paid by the hour, week, or month. The evidence is in conflict with the assertion. What do you think has been overlooked here?

6 By definition, an entrepreneur must be willing to take risks. Aside from such a willingness to shoulder risks, what other quality would you expect a good entrepreneur to possess?

7 "Since 'proxy fights' (the attempted takeover of a corporation by a united block of stockholders) rarely occur, they obviously cannot be a very important factor in keeping inefficient managements in line." Is this statement true or false? Why?

8 Why is it difficult to give a concrete definition of when a firm's short run "ends" and its long run "begins"?

9 What is meant by technical efficiency, and how does it differ from economic efficiency?

10 Suppose you are an industrial engineer charged with keeping your firm's production costs at a minimum. (You are *not* asked to make decisions as to the rate of output of the firm; such decisions are made for you by the marketing division on the basis of orders obtained by salespeople in the field.) In order to do your job well, what information do you need to know besides that given by the production function? Why? (*Hint:* Look at Figure 8-17.)

11 Why, if average physical product is falling, must marginal physical product be less than average physical product? Also, explain why total physical product can be declining only if marginal physical product is negative.

12 Why would a firm in full competition never operate in either stage I or stage III of its production function?

13 What information is shown by a single production isoquant? What is signified by a move to the northwest along an isoquant, and what might induce a firm to make such a move?

14 Look at Figure 8-17. Suppose a firm is producing output Q_2 at point E and using K_e of capital and L_e of labor; r and w are the respective input prices, and total cost is TC. If the firm is to expand output to Q_3, clearly more resources must be employed (assuming no change in the underlying production function). Focusing now on the isocost curve, what are the three variables that, with a sufficient change in any one of them, would enable the firm to expand output to Q_3?

15 "Our union represents all the city's garbage collection engineers. The city-owned trash company is a monopoly requiring all residents to pay for trash collection even if they don't generate any trash. Consequently, even a 50 percent increase in our hourly wages will have no adverse effect on how many hours of our labor will be hired per week." Is the statement true or false? Why?

16 What would the economic and uneconomic regions of production look like for a fixed-proportion isoquant map?

SELECTED REFERENCES

Cassels, John M., "On the Law of Variable Proportions," in American Economic Association, *Readings in The Theory of Income Distribution* (Philadelphia: Blakiston, 1946), pp. 103–118.

Douglas, Paul, "Are There Laws of Production?" *American Economic Review,* March 1948.

Hicks, J.R., *Value and Capital,* 2d ed. (Oxford: Clarendon Press, 1946), chaps. 6 and 7.

Knight, Frank H., *Risk, Uncertainty and Profit* (Boston: Houghton Mifflin, 1921), pp. 94–104.

Machlup, Fritz, "Theories of the Firm: Marginalist, Behavioral Managerial," *American Economic Review,* March 1967.

Reder, Melvin W., "A Reconsideration of the Marginal Productivity Theory," *Journal of Political Economy,* vol. 55, October 1947, pp. 450–458.

Scitovsky, Tibor, "A Note on Profit Maximization and Its Implications," *Review of Economic Studies,* vol. 2, no. 1, 1943, pp. 56–60.

The costs of production

osts are incurred when a firm produces a commodity. The costs of production include wages for workers, interest costs, rent for land, and expenses for raw material. For purposes of analysis, we must go beyond the ordinary notion of the meaning of costs, and we must place costs into a number of subclassifications.

OPPORTUNITY COST

Cost has a special meaning in economics, but it is the same meaning whether we are referring to the theory of the firm or to consumer decision making. Cost in economics means one and only one thing: **opportunity cost**. Opportunity cost is defined as the value of a resource in its next-best or alternative use. Note: In this definition, *opportunity cost does not depend on who is using the resource.* Strictly speaking, for opportunity costs to be known with accuracy, the economic decision makers must have "perfect knowledge" (a concept we will consider in Chapter 10). Even without perfect knowledge, however, the owner of a productive resource will always have an incentive to seek higher values (more profitable uses) for his or her resources, whether they be within a particular firm or elsewhere. For example, the opportunity cost of a piece of machinery to a firm is not just its best alternative use *within* the firm but the value of its highest alternative use *anywhere*. Thus, if we define capital as a machine in place, we can define the cost of the use of the machine to its owner as equal to the price that could be fetched if the services of the machine were sold to the highest bidder. The highest bidder could pay for the services of that machine in several ways, the most obvious being leasing or renting it. Indeed, the owner of a machine has the option not only of leasing the machine but also of selling it and earning interest on the money previously "tied up" in the machine.

What is the opportunity cost of having that machine? It is the value that could be obtained from the machine in its highest alternative use. That may be the value obtained by renting the machine, or it may be the value in selling it to someone else and putting the proceeds in certificates of deposit yielding 14 percent per annum.

Another way to look at cost is that it is a currently available alternative *that is sacrificed*. With a machine in place, the alternative that is sacrificed is leasing the machine or selling it and investing the proceeds. Strictly speaking, when there is no currently available alternative that is being sacrificed, there is no cost involved in using the resource. For example, if a machine in place is so highly specialized to a particular production process that no one else will lease it or buy it even at a zero price, no alternative is sacrificed. The opportunity cost of the machine is effectively zero.

PRIVATE COSTS: DECISION RELEVANT COSTS

For the firm, the cost of any action is the opportunity cost, or the most valued opportunity forgone. We would expect a firm's decisions to be based only on costs that are incurred by the firm even though such decisions may entail additional costs which the firm does not take into account. The costs incurred by the firm or the individual decision maker as a result of their own decisions are called **private costs**.

Social costs are real costs

These are the costs that affect the decisions of the firm's owners. However, the production activities of the firm (or the consumption activities of consumers) can impose economic benefits or costs upon others that are beyond the control of those other people. A firm producing paper pulp incurs the cost of raw materials, the cost of labor, and the cost of capital. These are the private costs of producing pulp. However, in the process of production, such by-products as foul odors and liquid and solid wastes, called effluents, are emitted. Foul odors visit economic damages or costs upon those in the vicinity of the paper mill. Effluents visit damages on those who use the waters into which the effluents flow. These added costs of production, beyond the private costs recognized by firms, are often known as *externalities*. That is, they are costs external to a firm's decision-making process. If we add together the private costs of production of paper pulp and the economic damage (externality) imposed upon others, we come up with what are called **social costs**.[1]

We will deal with this distinction between private and social costs in Chapter 19 when we examine the concept of market failure or externalities. Suffice it to say here that *the costs of any activity include the social opportunity costs and not just the private costs.*

SHORT AND LONG RUNS

We introduced the concept of the short and the long run in the last chapter when we made the arbitrary distinction between fixed and variable factors of production. We defined the short run as a period during which *at least one* input could not be increased without appreciably increasing its cost per unit. We defined the long run as the period during which all factors of production became variable. Short run and long run do not refer to specific clock or calendar time but rather to the time required for individuals to adapt to new conditions.

Our definition of short run is obviously loose; at a sufficiently high cost, decision makers can adjust rapidly to a change in economic conditions. (The length of the short run also depends on the industry and the production techniques used.) In a world with zero transactions costs and complete nonspecialization of production inputs, there would be no distinction between long and short run. However, in our world there are costs of renegotiating long-run contracts, for example, and there are resources that are specialized in the production of particular goods and have negligible value in producing other goods. Hence, it is meaningful to make the distinction between long- and short-run cost curves.

We could talk in terms of short runs of varying lengths, intermediate runs, and then the long run. However, at this point in your study of microeconomics, it will suffice to stick with the standard division of short and long run, and therefore we will consider only short-run costs and long-run costs. In this discussion we must constantly keep in mind that the alternative uses of a particular resource will be different and fewer in the short run compared with what they are in the long run. In other words, the opportunity cost of a given resource changes when a longer time is allowed for adjustment.

---

[1]The terms private and social costs were first employed by A. C. Pigou, *The Economics of Welfare*, 4th ed. (London: Macmillan, 1932), part II, chap. 9. Pigou and some later economists failed to distinguish carefully between those social costs which are reflected in private costs and those which are truly external to a firm. In order for a social cost to be external to a firm it must be one over which the firm has no control or no incentive to exercise control.

SHORT-RUN TOTAL COST CURVES

The concept of total costs used in this section includes all costs associated with the production of a commodity. We have divided total cost (TC) into two components: total fixed costs (TFC) and total variable costs (TVC).

Total fixed cost

Total fixed costs (TFC) are often defined as those costs which are "sunk," i.e., cannot be reduced no matter what the rate of output. In other words, fixed costs are those costs which are invariant to the rate of production.[2]

We should be careful here because *fixed, or sunk, costs are not costs at all in the sense that we described them above.* That is, sunk costs are not opportunity costs because they do not represent any currently available alternative that must be sacrificed. Nonetheless, we follow convention in

[2]A sunk investment is one that cannot be transferred to some other *profitable* use. Its true opportunity cost equals 0 (e.g., a stamping machine which makes only grilles for Ford's Edsel!).

TABLE 9-1
Deriving total, marginal, and average cost

Rate of output per unit time period (units) (1)	Total fixed cost (TFC) ($) (2)	Total variable cost (TVC) ($) (3)	Total cost (TC) ($) (4)	Marginal cost ($/unit) $\Delta TC (= \Delta TVC)$ / Δ output (5)	Average total cost (ATC) ($/unit) [(4) ÷ (1)] (6)	Average variable cost (AVC) ($/unit) [(3) ÷ (1)] (7)	Average fixed cost (AFC) ($/unit) [(2) ÷ (1)] (8)
0	10.00	0	10.00	—	—	—	—
1	10.00	4.00	14.00	4.00	14.00	4.00	10.00
2	10.00	7.50	17.50	3.50	8.75	3.75	5.00
3	10.00	10.75	20.75	3.25	6.92	3.58	3.33
4	10.00	13.80	23.80	3.05	5.95	3.45	2.50
5	10.00	16.70	26.70	2.90	5.34	3.34	2.00
6	10.00	19.50	29.50	2.80	4.92	3.25	1.67
7	10.00	22.25	32.25	2.75	4.61	3.18	1.43
8	10.00	25.10	35.10	2.85	4.39	3.14	1.25
9	10.00	28.30	38.30	3.20	4.26	3.14	1.11
10	10.00	32.30	42.30	4.00	4.23	3.23	1.00
11	10.00	38.30	48.30	6.00	4.39	3.48	0.91
12	10.00	47.30	57.30	9.00	4.78	3.94	0.83
13	10.00	60.30	70.30	13.00	5.41	4.64	0.77
14	10.00	78.30	88.30	18.00	6.31	5.59	0.71
15	10.00	102.30	112.30	24.00	7.49	6.82	0.67

this chapter and consider that total fixed costs are the costs of all fixed inputs of production.

Total variable cost

In their most simplified form, **total variable costs (TVC)** are those costs incurred by the use of variable inputs in the production process. In other words, variable costs, by definition, are a function of the rate of output. Variable costs would then include the wage bill, the raw materials bill, and so on.

We present a hypothetical set of total cost schedules in Table 9-1. The resultant cost curves are presented in Figure 9-1.

Total cost

Total cost is defined as the sum of total variable cost and total fixed cost. We show total cost in column (4) of Table 9-1. The data points in this column are presented graphically as the TC curve in Figure 9-1. The only difference between the total cost curve and the total variable cost curve in that figure is that the TC curve is $10 higher than the TVC curve at each rate of output. That is, the vertical distance between the TC and the TVC curves in Figure 9-1 is always $10. Notice that the TFC curve is merely a horizontal line at $10.

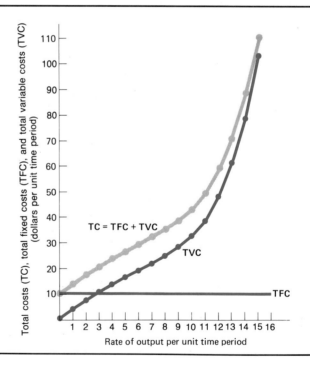

FIGURE 9-1
Total cost curves
From columns (1) and (2) in Table 9-1, we obtain total fixed costs which are invariant to the rate of output at $10. Total variable costs are taken from columns (1) and (3) in Table 9-1. Total costs are total variable costs plus the total fixed costs ($10 in this case).

SHORT-RUN AVERAGE COST CURVES

The three short-run total cost curves presented in Figure 9-1 can be converted to average cost curves. In the following sections, we will look at average fixed costs, average variable costs, average total costs, and marginal costs.

Average fixed cost

An average is the total divided by the number of units over which the total is spread; thus, **average fixed cost (AFC)** equals total fixed cost divided by the number of units of output, or AFC = TFC/Q. We find average fixed cost for a hypothetical cost situation in column (8) of Table 9-1. This column is represented graphically as the continuously downward-sloping AFC curve in Figure 9-2. The AFC curve (a rectangular hyperbola) never meets the horizontal or vertical axes (but it approaches each axis asymptotically).[3]

Average variable cost

Average variable cost (AVC) is merely defined as total variable cost divided by output, or AVC = TVC/Q. We find AVC in our example in column (7) of Table 9-1. When we transfer these data to Figure 9-2, they become the AVC curve, which is first downward-sloping and then upward-sloping.

The relation between AVC and APP

We can show a relation between the average variable cost curve and the average physical product curve. Again, we will assume that there is only one variable factor of production. Total variable costs then equal the price per unit of the variable factor of production times the number of units used. In our example, in which labor is the only variable factor of production, TVC = $w \cdot L$. But AVC is defined as

$$\text{AVC} = \frac{\text{TVC}}{Q} \tag{9-1}$$

If we substitute wL for TVC in Eq. (9-1), we get

$$\text{AVC} = \frac{wL}{Q} = w\left(\frac{L}{Q}\right) \tag{9-2}$$

We can see, however, that the term in parentheses is the reciprocal of the average physical product of labor [$\text{APP}_L = (Q/L)\ \overline{K}$]:

$$\text{AVC} = w\frac{1}{\text{APP}} \tag{9-3}$$

We assumed in Chapter 8 that average physical product first rises and then falls. Thus average variable costs must first fall and then rise.

---

[3]The AFC curve is a "rectangular hyperbola" with the algebraic form: $y = \text{constant}/x$, or $xy = \text{constant}$. Thus output times AFC equals TFC.

Combinations of variable resources. When there are several variable resources that can be used, each one must be considered in relation to the others. Let us consider a situation where there are just two variable resources: labor and capital. We suppose that the cost curves in Figure 9-2 are based on different ratios of amounts used, and different costs per unit, of each of these two variable resources. We now also assume that there is a given market price for each resource. From these assumptions it turns out that there is only one way in which the resources can be combined in order to minimize costs for a given level of output.

Cost minimization at a given output level. From Chapter 8 we know that a firm can minimize the costs of producing a given level of output by distributing expenditures among various inputs so that the marginal physical product of the last dollar spent on any input is equal to the marginal physical product of the last dollar spent on any of the other inputs used. Notice that, since we are concerned with opportunity costs, we do not talk about the

FIGURE 9-2
A family of cost curves
These curves are taken from columns (1) and (5) through (8) in Table 9-1. Note that the AFC curve is a rectangular hyperbola. Furthermore, the MC curve intersects both the ATC and the AVC curves at their respective minimum points.

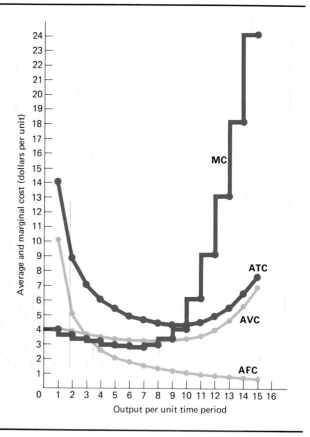

price of capital but about the implicit rental value which is the implicit opportunity cost of this factor of production. The formula for cost minimization, given output, is therefore

$$\frac{\text{MPP}_{labor}}{\text{Wage rate/unit of labor}} = \frac{\text{MPP}_{capital}}{\text{(implicit rental) price/unit of capital}} \tag{9-4}$$

The formula for MPP, the marginal physical product, was given in Chapter 8. We obtained the formula by finding out where the optimal combination of inputs would be for a given total cost. This least-cost combination of inputs occurred when the isocost curve was tangent to an isoquant.

Average total cost

Average total cost (ATC) is defined as total cost divided by output, or ATC = TC/Q. We show average total cost in column (6) of Table 9-1. This column is represented by the ATC curve in Figure 9-2. The vertical distance between the ATC curve and the AVC curve is, of course, AFC. Average total cost has the same property as average variable cost. It first falls and then rises. This is a consequence of the shape of the production function that we implicitly assumed in Chapter 8 and which is conventionally assumed in these discussions.

Marginal cost

Marginal cost (MC) is defined as the change in total cost when there is a one-unit change in the rate of production. Otherwise stated, marginal cost is equal to the change in total cost per unit change in output, i.e.,

$$MC = \frac{\Delta TC}{\Delta Q} \tag{9-5}$$

where $\Delta Q = 1$. We present marginal cost for our example in column (5) of Table 9-1. Columns (1) and (5) are transferred to Figure 9-2, and the resulting curve is labeled MC. Since we are working in discrete-unit changes, the curve is a stepladder rather than a smooth line.

The relation between MC and MPP

There is a relation between marginal cost and marginal physical product, just as there is a relation between average variable cost and average physical product and a relation between total variable cost and total physical product. Consider an example in which we have only one variable input, and that input is labor. In this situation, any change in total costs is a change in total variable costs due to a change in labor input

$$\Delta TC = \Delta TVC = w\Delta L \tag{9-6}$$

where w is the given wage rate and L is the quantity of labor per unit time period. If we substitute $w\Delta L$ from Eq. (9-6) for ΔTC in Eq. (9-5), we come up with

$$MC = \frac{w\Delta L}{\Delta Q} = w\left(\frac{1}{\Delta Q/\Delta L}\right) \tag{9-6a}$$

But $\Delta Q/\Delta L$ is the marginal physical product of labor. Therefore

$$MC = w\left(\frac{1}{MPP_L}\right) \tag{9-7}$$

For any given wage rate w, a diminishing marginal physical product will result in an increasing marginal cost. In other words, whenever we have diminishing marginal physical product (see Figure 8-8) or diminishing marginal returns, we will have an increasing marginal cost.

THE GEOMETRY OF SHORT-RUN COST CURVES

We can go through the geometry of the relation between the various short-run cost curves just as we did when we showed the relation between the various physical product curves in Chapter 8.

Total cost and average total cost

Average total cost is total cost divided by the rate of output. In Figure 9-3, panel (a), we have shown a total cost curve. Pick any output level along the horizontal axis, say, Q_1; total costs equal the vertical distance from Q_1 to A. The rate of output is the horizontal distance 0 to Q_1. Therefore, average total cost ATC = $Q_1A/0Q_1$, but this is merely the slope of a straight line drawn from the origin 0 to point A on the total cost curve. Therefore, we know that *average variable cost is the slope of a straight line drawn from the origin to the corresponding point on the total cost curve for any given level of output.* As a result, we also know that at output Q_2 average total cost reaches a minimum, for here the slope of the ray is as small as it is going to get (for this particular total cost curve); after output Q_2 the slope of that ray will increase again. The ATC curve generated in panel (b) below panel (a) therefore reaches its minimum point at output Q_2.

It is now relatively easy to derive geometrically the average variable cost curve. To remove fixed cost from total cost graphically, all we need do is shift the total cost curve down to where it starts at the origin in panel (a) of Figure 9-3. The same graphical procedure that was used for average total cost would then be used. The slope of the rays to various points on the newly constructed total variable cost curve would give average variable cost.

The relation between total cost and marginal cost

Marginal cost is defined as the change in total cost due to a one-unit change in output. If we think in terms of very small changes in output, *marginal cost at a particular output rate is defined as the slope of a tangent drawn to the particular point on the total cost curve corresponding to that output rate.* Remember that the slope of a curve is equal to $\Delta y/\Delta x$, where y is the

FIGURE 9-3
The relationship between TC and ATC
For any output rate such as Q_1 or Q_2, we can obtain the ATC curve by measuring the slope of the ray drawn to the respective point on the TC curve. This is exactly the way we derived the average physical product curve from the total physical product curve in the last chapter. At output rate Q_2 we know that average total costs reached their minimum because before that point B, the slope of any ray drawn to the TC curve was decreasing and after B the slope was increasing. The resultant ATC curve is shown in panel (b).

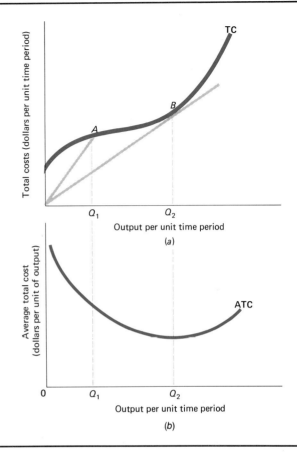

variable measured on the vertical axis and x is the variable measured on the horizontal axis. If total cost is on the vertical axis and the rate of output is on the horizontal axis, the slope of a total cost curve at any point will give the change in total cost due to a change in the rate of output, which is marginal cost. We find the slope of a nonlinear curve at a particular point by drawing a tangent to the curve at that point and finding the slope of that tangent; hence, marginal cost is measured at any point along the total curve by finding the slope of the tangent to that point.

We draw tangents to various points on the total cost curve in panel (a) of Figure 9-4. Points A, B, C, and D correspond to rates of output of Q_1, Q_2, Q_3, and Q_4. Notice that the slope of the tangent at A is greater than the slope of the tangent at B. The way we have drawn the total cost curve, the slope of the tangent corresponding to output Q_2 is the smallest (MC is the lowest) that it will be. Notice the special nature of the output rate Q_3. The tangent at point C on the total cost curve also is the ray from the origin. Thus, at output rate Q_3, we know that marginal cost and average total cost will be

FIGURE 9-4
Relationship between TC and MC
Just as we derived marginal physical product
from total physical product by measuring the
angle of the tangents at five points on the total
physical product curve, we can derive the
marginal cost curve in panel (b) from the
respective slopes of tangents drawn to the total
cost curve at various output rates such as Q_1,
Q_2, Q_3, and Q_4. Marginal costs reach their
minimum point in panel (a) at the inflection
point B on the TC curve, or at output rate Q_2.
Note that at output rate Q_3, the tangent to the
TC curve at point C is also the ray to the origin;
thus, MC and ATC would be equal at this
output rate. Beyond output Q_4, MC > ATC.

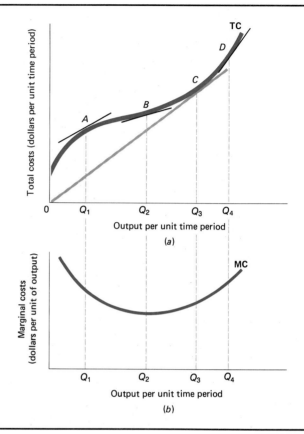

equal. The resulting marginal cost curve is shown in panel (b) of Figure
9-4.

**The relation
between
marginal cost
curves and
average cost
curves**

It should be clear from Figures 9-3 and 9-4 that there is a distinct relation
between marginal cost and average cost curves.[4] We noted that when the
ray to the origin was tangent to the total cost curve, average costs were at
their minimum. But when this ray is tangent to the total cost curve, its slope
also indicates marginal cost. Hence, just from the geometry, we know that
*marginal costs and average costs are equal at the point where average cost
is minimum.* Examine Figure 9-2 again. Note that the marginal cost curve

---

[4]We learned this relation in Chapter 8. Recall that whenever a marginal curve lies above
the corresponding average curve, the average will rise. When the marginal curve is below the
average curve, the latter will fall. When the marginal curve is equal to the average curve, the
average curve will be horizontal (a constant).

MC intersects both the AVC curve and the ATC curve at their minimum points.

We can see that MC must equal AC when AC is at its minimum by writing down the formula for marginal cost:

$$\text{MC} = \text{AC} + \frac{\Delta \text{AC} \cdot Q}{\Delta Q} = \text{AC} + \Delta \text{AC} \cdot Q \tag{9-8}$$

where $\Delta Q = 1$.

Marginal cost is defined as the change in total cost brought about when there is a one-unit change in the rate of production. Taking the case where $\Delta Q = 1$, we can explain Eq. (9-8) in exactly the way we explained Eq. (8-3) (when we related marginal physical product to average physical product). In fact, the relations between marginals and averages are the same no matter what we are talking about.

Now, when will marginal costs equal average costs? When the average costs are neither rising nor falling as small changes in output occur. Where does this occur on a continuous average cost curve? It occurs only where the slope of the tangent drawn to a point on the curve is 0. This occurs at the minimum point of the average cost curve. An infinitesimal change in output involves no change in average costs. Marginal cost equals average cost at the average cost curve's minimum point.[5] This holds for either average total cost or average variable cost.[6]

Furthermore, we can deduce from either the geometry of the relationship between marginal and average costs or Eq. (9-8) that *when average costs are falling, marginal costs must be below average costs, and when average costs are rising, marginal costs must be above average costs.* This can be seen by rearranging Eq. (9-8) into

$$\text{AC} = \text{MC} - \frac{\Delta \text{AC} \cdot Q}{\Delta Q} = \text{MC} - \Delta \text{AC} \cdot Q \tag{9-9}$$

where $\Delta Q = 1$.

When average costs are falling, ΔAC is negative. Thus, $- [(\Delta \text{AC} \cdot Q)/\Delta Q]$ is positive, and for the equality to hold, marginal costs must be less than average costs. When average costs are rising, ΔAC is positive; thus the term $- [\text{AC} \cdot Q)/\Delta Q]$ is negative. For the equality to hold in Eq. (9-9), marginal costs must be greater than average costs.

---

[5]Note in Eq. (9-8): $\text{MC} = \text{AC} + [(\Delta \text{AC} \cdot Q)/\Delta Q]$ becomes $\text{MC} - \text{AC} = (\Delta \text{AC} \cdot Q)/\Delta Q$. When $\text{MC} = \text{AC}$, then $(\Delta \text{AC}/\Delta Q) \cdot Q = 0$. Dividing by Q, we obtain $\Delta \text{AC}/\Delta Q$. Ergo, AC is at its minimum point where its slope $= 0$.

[6]The proof has been given for the relation between marginal physical product and average physical product in footnote 8 in Chapter 8. Also note that AC can be either ATC or AVC, since $\text{ATC} - \text{AVC} = \text{AFC}$; but AFC is invariant to changes in output. Therefore $\Delta \text{ATC}/\Delta Q = \Delta \text{AVC}/\Delta Q$.

LONG-RUN COST CURVES

The long run, as you will remember, is defined as a situation in which full adjustment can be made to any and all changes in the economic environment. Thus, in the long run, all factors of production are variable. Long-run curves are sometimes called planning curves, and the long run is sometimes called the **planning horizon.**

We start our analysis of long-run cost curves by considering a single firm which operates with a single plant. The firm has, let us say, three alternative plant sizes from which to choose on its planning horizon. Each plant size generates its own short-run cost curves. Now that we are talking about the difference between long-run and short-run cost curves, we will label all short-run curves with an S; short-run average (total) costs will be labeled SAC; all long-run curves will have an L before them.

As we noted earlier in this chapter, we derive marginal and average cost curves from total cost curves. So first we derive the long-run total cost curve; we do this from the isoquant-isocost analysis presented in Chapter 8.

The expansion path

A profit-maximizing entrepreneur combines capital and labor so that the ratio of their marginal physical products is equal to the ratio of their prices. Otherwise stated, capital and labor are combined such that the marginal physical product per last dollar spent on each is equal, or $MPP_L/P_L = MPP_k/P_k$. This occurs at the tangency point between an isocost curve and an isoquant. What happens to the capital/labor ratio when output expands? We indicate this in Figure 9-5. We pick three successively higher rates of output, Q_1, Q_2, and Q_3. Then we ask what will be the cost-minimizing ratio of capital to labor and hence the minimum total costs necessary to produce at these three different rates of output. This is done by drawing in isocost lines that are tangent to the isoquant curves. The resulting isocost lines are labeled by their respective total costs, TC_1, TC_2, and TC_3. The extreme points on the vertical and horizontal axes are obtained by dividing each successive total cost by the implicit rental rate of capital and the wage rate of labor, respectively. The tangency points E, E', and E'' are then connected by a line called the **expansion path.** This is the line along which output will expand when the input factor price ratio remains constant. It is the expansion path which depicts how input factor proportions change when output changes while relative input prices remain constant. Note that for normal inputs there can never be a vertical or horizontal section in an expansion path because this would indicate that output could be increased without increasing the use of one of the inputs.

When we ask, for each level of total cost, what the maximum output will be, we get exactly the same diagram as in Figure 9-5; but now the expansion path is given the name of **isocline.** An isocline is defined as the locus of points along which the marginal rate of technical subsitution (MRTS)

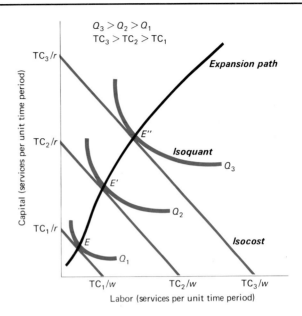

FIGURE 9-5
The expansion path
To find the expansion path, we increase output from Q_1 to Q_2 to Q_3. We then draw in the minimum isocost curves (all of slope $-w/r$), i.e., the ones that are tangent to the isoquants corresponding to those three rates of output. When we connect the tangency points E, E', and E'', we obtain the expansion path.

is constant. Remember that the slope of the isoquant is equal to the negative of the marginal rate of technical substitution. Otherwise stated, the isocline is the locus of points along which the ratio of the marginal physical product of capital to the marginal physical product of labor is constant.

Long-run total cost

It is easy to derive the long-run total cost curve from the expansion path. We merely ask the following question: For each rate of output, given the relative price of L and K, what is the minimum total cost given by the expansion path? We see from Figure 9-5 that for the rate of output Q_1, total cost would be TC_1. This gives us one point on the long-run total cost schedule presented in Figure 9-6; it gives us point A. The combination of rate of output Q_2 and total cost TC_2 gives us point B, and finally, the rate of output Q_3 and level of total cost TC_3 gives us point C. In the input space of Figure 9-5, there are an infinite number of combinations of rates of output and levels of total cost. This infinite number of combinations gives us an infinite number of points which become our LTC curve in Figure 9-6.

It would now be relatively simple to obtain the long-run marginal cost curve and the long-run average cost curve. The long-run marginal cost curve would be obtained by getting the slopes of the tangents to different points along LTC; the long-run average cost curve would be obtained by getting the slopes of the rays to different points along the LTC curve. There is no difference between the LTC curve, the LAC curve, and the LMC curve derived

FIGURE 9-6
Deriving the long-run total cost curve
The LTC curve can be derived from the
expansion path. The total outlays for each rate
of output can be read from Figure 9-5.

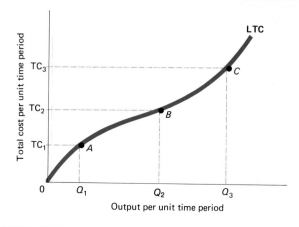

in this manner and those derived in the previous sections. We will consider
the LAC and LMC curves in detail, but first let us examine the relation
between LTC and STC.

The relation between STC and LTC

The long run is all the short-run possibilities combined. This is true whether
we look at total, average, or marginal costs. In Figure 9-7 we return to our
example of three short-run production possibilities and show they are related
to the long run. Figure 9-7 is the same as Figure 9-5 except that we show
that three particular points on the expansion path, E, E', and E'', represent
the least-cost combination of capital and labor associated with a given output
level. For point E, capital is fixed at level K, labor is variable. Only the least-
cost point of that short-run period is included in the many possibilities
available in the long run.

Our example shows three different least-cost combinations possible in
the short run, given fixed levels of capital K, K', and K''. The notion that
there is only one least-cost production point in each short-run period (during
which capital is fixed) carries over to Figure 9-8, where we see the relation
between the many short-run total cost curves that exist and the long-run
total cost curve. *The LTC is made up of all the minimum average cost points
from the STCs.* Hence, there is only one point in common, a tangency,
between each STC and the LTC. That is, point E in Figure 9-8 corresponds
to the minimum point on the SAC that is derived from the STC (the equivalent of point B at output level Q_2 in Figure 9-3). E, E', and E'' in Figure
9-8 correspond to the lowest total costs at which Q, Q', and Q'' can be
produced. The reason why total costs are minimized at E, E', and E'' can be
observed by examining Figure 9-7 once again.

FIGURE 9-7
Short-run and long-run points on the
expansion path
The expansion path illustrates the least-cost
production points available in the long run. In
the short run, capital is assumed to be fixed in
each time period, at K, K', or K'' for example.
Only one point in the short run is identical to
one point in the long run, because in the long
run all points on the expansion path are
possible as any level of capital may be
employed.

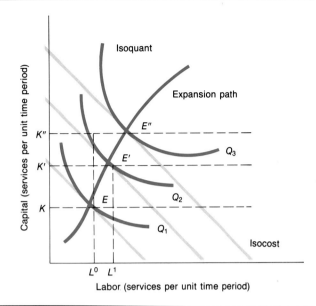

FIGURE 9-8
The relationship between STC and LTC
The long-run total cost curve represents an "envelope" of the cost-minimizing points on all the short-run total cost
curves. Each STC has only one point in common with the LTC. This point (minimum SAC) is the same as the point
the STC and LTC had in common on the expansion path, E, E', or E'' in this example.

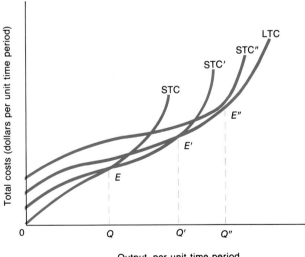

Output level Q_2 can be produced using any of the input combinations along the isoquant labeled Q_2. Given the factor-price ratio that determines the slope of the relevant isocost lines, the lowest-cost combination of factors along Q_2 is $K'L'$. We know that this is true because point E' forms a tangency between isoquant Q_2 and the "lowest" isocost line that shares a point with Q_2. However, note that *if* the level of capital usage is fixed in a particular short run at K'', Q_2 can still be produced using input combination $K''L^0$. This combination, pictured in Figure 9-7, lies on a higher isocost curve than E'. This input combination corresponds to a higher level of total costs. In fact, every K and L combination along isoquant Q_2 other than E' corresponds to higher total costs for producing Q_2. Each combination that is "nonoptimal" in the long run would, however, be optimal (least-cost) in some possible short run, where either K or L were fixed and the firm was required to operate within that constraint.

Seeing the relation between the short-run and the long-run total cost curves helps illustrate the point that while in this analysis we will derive a single least-cost production point for the long run, we must remember that in the short run it may not be possible or desirable to be at the long-run solution. Hence, we always have an incentive to search for the least-cost solution—given the circumstances of the moment. We will explore this further by examining the average cost and marginal cost curves.

The optimal plant size. Look at Figure 9-9. Here we show three short-run average cost curves for three successively larger plant sizes. Which is the optimal plant size to build? That depends on the anticipated permanent rate of output per unit time period, which in turn hinges on the firm's expected demand. Assume for a moment that the anticipated permanent rate of output is Q_1. If Q_1 is produced with plant size 1 (corresponding to SAC_1),

FIGURE 9-9
The optimal plant size
If the anticipated permanent rate of output per unit time period is Q_1, the optimal plant to build would be the one corresponding to SAC_1 because average costs are lowest. However, if the permanent rate of output increases to Q_2, it will be most profitable to have a plant size corresponding to SAC_2. Unit costs fall to C_3.

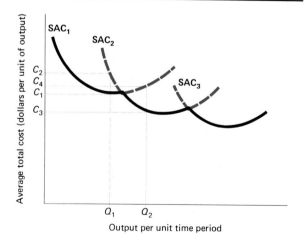

then it will cost C_1. However, if plant size 2 is used to produce Q_1, then average cost will rise to C_2. Thus, if the anticipated permanent rate of output is Q_1, plant size 1 (SAC_1) is preferable (lower cost) to plant size 2 (SAC_2).

Note, however, that if the anticipated permanent rate of output per unit time period goes from Q_1 to Q_2, and plant 1 had been decided upon, average costs would be C_4. However, if plant 2 had been decided upon, average cost for output rate Q_2 would be C_3, which is clearly less than C_4. There is, therefore, no such thing as the lowest-cost plant size for all levels of output. Different rates of output are produced more "efficiently" by using different levels of capital (smaller or larger plants).

In choosing the appropriate plant size for a single-plant firm during the planning horizon, the firm will pick that plant size whose short-run average cost curve generates an average cost which is lowest for the expected "permanent" rate of output.

Long-run average cost curve

If we make the further assumption that the entrepreneur is faced with an infinite number of choices of plant sizes in the long run, we can conceive of an infinite number of SAC curves similar to the three in Figure 9-9. We are not able, of course, to draw an infinite number; we have drawn quite a few, however, in Figure 9-10. If we then draw the "envelope" to all these

---

FIGURE 9-10
Deriving the long-run average cost curve
If we draw all the possible short-run average cost curves that correspond to different plant sizes, and then draw the envelope to these various curves, $SAC_1, \ldots, SAC_8$, we obtain the long-run average cost curve, or the planning curve.

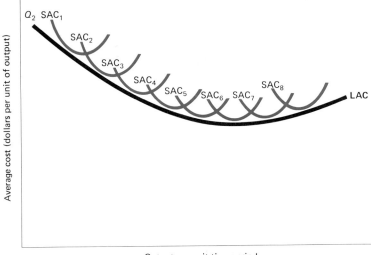

Output per unit time period

various short-run average cost curves, the result is the **long-run average cost curve (LAC)**. This long-run average cost curve is sometimes called the **planning curve**, for it represents the various average costs attainable at the planning stage of the firm's decision making. The LAC curve is the locus of points that represent the least cost of producing each given rate of output. Note that the LAC curve is *not* tangent to the minimum point of each individual SAC curve. *Only that SAC curve which is tangent to the LAC curve at the minimum of the LAC curve has its own minimum point at that point.* There, and only there, is the minimum long-run average cost equal to the minimum short-run average cost. In drawing the LAC and associated SAC curves, a simple rule is helpful. To the left of the minimum of LAC, each SAC has its tangency with LAC to the left of its minimum. To the right of the minimum of LAC, each SAC has its minimum to the left of its tangency with LAC.[7]

Long-run marginal cost

We can draw a **long-run marginal cost curve (LMC)** using methods similar to those used to draw the short-run marginal cost curve. LMC is defined as the locus of points showing the minimum amount by which total cost is increased, when the rate of output is expanded. We show a long-run marginal cost curve LMC in Figure 9-11. It is marginal to the long-run planning curve LAC. As with all marginal curves, it intersects its average curve at the minimum point of that average curve. To reemphasize the discussion in the last paragraph, we have drawn in two short-run average cost curves, SAC_1 and SAC_2, in Figure 9-11. SAC_1 is tangent to LAC at point B where output rate Q_1 is produced. The curve marginal to SAC_1 is labeled SMC_1. SMC_1 intersects SAC_1 at the latter's minimum point, which is point C. Point A represents the point where SMC_1 is equal to LMC. At point A the rate of output, Q_1, is such that SAC_1 is tangent to LAC. This follows from the definition of the long-run average cost curve as the locus of points representing the minimum unit cost (in the long run) of producing any given rate of output.

Thus, *short-run marginal costs and long-run marginal costs will be equal only at that output level where short-run average costs and long-run average costs are equal.*

Hence, this is why we know that the intersection of any short-run marginal cost curve with the long-run marginal cost curve will be at a rate of output which corresponds to the point of tangency of the respective short-

---

[7]In preparing a classic article on the short- and long-run cost curves, an economist named Jacob Viner had given instructions to a draftsperson which were literally impossible to execute. Viner had told the draftsperson to construct the LAC curve so that it was tangent to the minimum point on every single SAC curve. Apparently, it was only after a considerable amount of argument from the draftsperson, who was not an economist, that Viner finally realized that it is impossible to have all SAC curves tangent to the LAC curve at the formers' minimum points. See Jacob Viner, "Cost Curves and Supply Curves," *Zeitschrift für Nationalökonomie*, vol. 3, 1931, pp. 23–46. Also reprinted in George J. Stigler and Kenneth E. Boulding (eds.), *Readings in Price Theory*, American Economic Association (Homewood, Ill.: Irwin, 1952), pp. 198–232.

FIGURE 9-11

Long-run marginal costs

The long-run marginal cost curve intersects the minimum point of the long-run average cost curve. Since at the minimum point of LAC the short-run average cost curve is also tangent to LAC at its minimum point, we know that at point E, $LMC = LAC = SAC_2 = SMC_2$. Every short-run marginal cost curve (such as SMC_1) intersects its respective short-run average cost curve at the latter's minimum point (such as point C). LMC will always intersect a short-run marginal cost curve (such as SMC_1 at point A) at the rate of output where SAC_1 is tangent to LAC (point B).

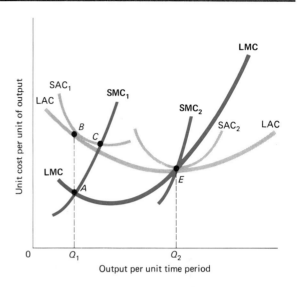

run average cost curve with the long-run average cost curve. Or as shown in Figure 9-11, $SMC_1 = LMC$ at Q_1, where $SAC_1 = LAC$.

Summarizing the relation between the short-run and long-run curves

Since this notion can be hard to understand, let us consider it in more detail. We will do so from the perspective of total cost, but first, remember that the rate of change of total cost is equal to marginal cost.

At point B in Figure 9-11, where output rate $= Q_1$, short-run and long-run average costs are equal because at that point SAC_1 is tangent to LAC. When short-run and long-run *average* costs are equal, short-run and long-run *total* costs are also equal.

Now consider a similar output rate between 0 and Q_1. Short-run average costs as measured on SAC_1 will be greater than long-run average costs as measured on LAC. Hence, short-run total costs will be greater than long-run total costs.[8] In order for long-run total costs to catch up with short-run total costs at point B (output rate Q_1, where $SAC_1 = LAC$), long-run total costs must be rising at a more rapid rate than short-run total costs. But the rate of change, or rise, in STC is SMC, while the rate of change in LTC is LMC. Thus, below output rates of Q_1, short-run marginal costs must be less than long-run marginal costs.

Next, consider output rates greater than Q_1. Short-run average costs, as exhibited on SAC_1, are not only greater than long-run average costs, but as

[8]If AC = TC/Q and we are evaluating SAC_1 and LAC at the same Q, then, if $SAC_1 > LAC$, $STC_1 > LTC$.

we move outward to the right, they are becoming increasingly greater than long-run average costs. Hence, the rate of increase of short-run total costs (i.e., short-run marginal costs) must be greater than the rate of increase of long-run total costs (i.e., long-run marginal costs). Thus, after output Q_1, SMC_1 must be greater than LMC.

Therefore, only when short-run average costs and long-run average costs (and hence, short-run and long-run total costs) are equal can short-run and long-run marginal costs be equal. The intersection or equality of SMC_1 and LMC occurs at point A in Figure 9-11, and it is directly below point B where LAC is tangent (equal) to SAC_1.

LMC will intersect LAC at the latter's minimum point. This point will also necessarily be at the minimum point on the short-run average cost curve which is tangent to the long-run average cost curve at the SAC minimum point. This particular SAC is labeled SAC_2 in Figure 9-11. Thus, at point E, where output is Q_2, short-run marginal costs $SMC_2 = SAC_2 = LMC = LAC$. Why? Because each marginal curve always intersects the minimum point of its average curve, and the output level where $SAC_2 = LAC$ is also the output level where $SMC_2 = LMC$. Thus, when the minimums on SAC_2 and LAC coincide, this point is also the point of intersection between SMC_2 and LMC.

CAPACITY

You often read about the fact that manufacturing capacity is being used only 70 percent, or 60 percent, or 80 percent. You often hear the phrase "at full capacity." The notion of full capacity for a firm is an elusive one. It cannot refer to some physical notion of using plant and equipment to its ultimate limit. At a high enough cost just a little bit more output can always be obtained from a plant, even one already running 24 hours a day; but the marginal cost of obtaining that additional "bit" may be astronomical. Thus the notion of capacity in some way must relate to unit cost.

Indeed, it is possible, but not very meaningful, as we will see, to define capacity in terms of minimum average cost. In fact, one suggested definition of capacity is the output at which short-run average cost is at a minimum. If this definition were used in Figure 9-12 for plant size 1, which yields short-run average cost curve SAC_1 (intercepted at its minimum point by SMC_1), capacity would be Q_1. But something seems wrong here. The long-run average cost curve is defined as the minimum unit cost of producing at every feasible rate of output. Average costs for output rate Q_1 in Figure 9-12 are represented by the vertical distance from point A, the minimum point on SAC_1, to the horizontal axis. However, if the firm expected to produce this rate of output indefinitely, it would not build so large a plant; it would build a smaller plant whose short-run average cost curve would be tangent to the LAC curve at point B. Average costs per unit would drop from AQ_1 to BQ_1.

FIGURE 9-12
Defining capacity
Capacity is often defined as the rate of output at which short-run average costs are at a minimum. One such output rate is Q_1, but, at that output rate, the difference between short-run average costs and long-run average costs is the vertical distance between A and B. The firm would not, in the long run, keep that plant size if the expected permanent rate of output were Q_1. If capacity is defined as the rate of output at which there is no incentive to alter the size of the plant, output rate Q_2 is the measure of capacity because, at that output rate, short-run average costs are equal to long-run average costs.

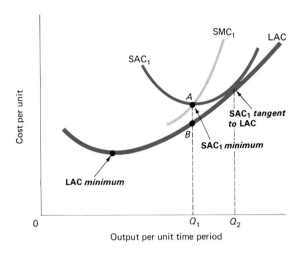

This gives a hint of what the appropriate definition for capacity for a given size of plant might be. **Capacity** will be defined as the rate of output at which there is no incentive to alter the size of the plant, if that rate of output is expected to be permanent. Thus, for plant size 1, as represented by SAC_1, the capacity would have to be at output rate Q_2 because here long-run average costs and short-run average costs are equal.

Thus our notion of capacity, even though short-run in nature, relates to long-run considerations. There are, of course, many other ways of defining capacity. The important thing is that it be defined and that the definition be relevant to the alternatives being considered.

RETURNS TO SCALE

We would now like to be able to answer the question of how output responds in the long run to changes in the scale of the firm. This topic is generally referred to as **returns to scale**. In discussing this topic we are mainly interested in what the payoff is, if any, from increasing the scale of the firm (or plant) in the long run.

There are three possibilities for returns to scale: Output may increase by a larger proportion than each of the inputs is increased; output may increase by the same proportion; output may increase by a smaller proportion than each of the inputs. Accordingly, we talk about **increasing**, **constant**, and **decreasing returns to scale**. In talking about returns to scale it is very important to remember that we are talking about altering all inputs by the same proportion. This is unlike the case of marginal returns, where all the change occurs in one input, with all other inputs held constant. Thus, when we say a doubling of scale, we mean doubling all labor inputs and all capital inputs (and keeping input prices constant).

The isoquant approach

Increasing, constant, and decreasing returns to scale can be shown by using the isoquant approach.

Look at Figure 9-13. Here we have three panels. Panel (a) represents increasing returns to scale; panel (b), constant returns to scale; and panel (c), decreasing returns to scale. We start off with a given rate of output of 1 in each of the three panels. We also start out with a given capital/labor ratio, K_1/L_1, which is the same in each of the three panels. Now we ask the question: How much do we have to increase capital and labor, while keeping their ratios constant, in order to increase the rate of output from 1 to 2? Isoquant 2 represents exactly twice the output of isoquant 1.

We see in panel (a) that when there are increasing returns, the increase

---

FIGURE 9-13

Increasing, constant, and decreasing returns to scale

We wish to increase output by proportional changes in both capital and labor. Along any ray from the origin, the capital/labor ratio remains the same. In other words, K_1/L_1 will be equal along all the rays shown in panels (a), (b), and (c). In panel (a) we see increasing returns to scale. An increase in the output from 1 to 2 requires a less-than-proportional increase in capital and labor. In panel (b), we see constant returns to scale. An increase in output from 1 to 2 requires a proportional increase in both inputs. Finally, in panel (c), we show decreasing returns to scale. An increase in output from 1 to 2 requires a more-than-proportional increase in both inputs.

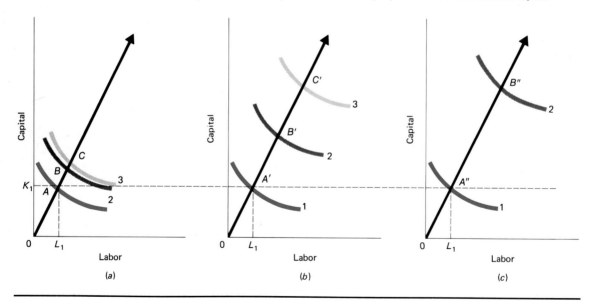

in capital and labor inputs is less than in proportion to the increase in output. That is, since the output level at any point along isoquant 2 is twice that of any point along isoquant 1, and the amount of capital and labor used at *B* is less than twice the amount of capital and labor used at *A*, the firm is getting more than doubled output for a doubling in its use of factors of production.[9] We can see this by looking at the respective distances along the ray from the origin. Remember that along any (straight-line) ray from the origin in an input space, the capital/labor ratio remains the same. Since we are dealing with proportional changes in all inputs, we can look only at what happens along any given ray. The rays drawn in panels (*a*), (*b*), and (*c*) all have equal slopes. In panel (*a*), the length of the ray between zero and where it intersects the isoquant associated with the rate of output of 1 is more than the length of the portion of the ray between the isoquant labeled 1 and the isoquant labeled 2. Otherwise stated, a doubling of output is achieved by less than a doubling of inputs. The same experiment is even more persuasive when we increase output from a rate of 2 to a rate of 3, where isoquant 3 represents exactly three times the output of isoquant 1. (Thus the numbers 1, 2, and 3 are cardinal as opposed to ordinal.)

In panel (*b*), we show constant returns to scale. Here the distance measured along the ray is the same between output rates of 0–1, 1–2, and 2–3. A doubling of inputs results in an exact doubling of output.

Finally, in panel (*c*), we show decreasing returns to scale. The distance between the isoquants gets larger for equal increments in output. Hence it requires more-than-proportionate increases in inputs to increase output. Otherwise stated, a doubling of output requires more than a doubling of inputs.

The long-run average cost approach

If we assume constant input prices no matter what the scale of the firm, we can translate the results of panels (*a*), (*b*), and (*c*) in Figure 9-13 into the shape of long-run average cost curves. We see this in Figure 9-14 panels (*a*), (*b*), and (*c*). In panel (*a*), the long-run average cost curve falls over the relevant range of outputs; in panel (*b*), it is horizontal; and in panel (*c*), it rises. The reason for this result is that, when input prices are constant, a doubling in the firm's usage of inputs will exactly double *total* cost. Yet, average cost is total cost divided by the amount of output which can be produced from the inputs purchased by the firm.[10]

[9]In general, if λ and γ are symbols for any two different positive numbers, and we state the generalized production function as $\lambda Q = f(\gamma K, \gamma L)$, we have increasing returns to scale if $\lambda > \gamma$, decreasing returns to scale if $\lambda < \gamma$, and constant returns to scale if $\lambda = \gamma$.

[10]Using our previous symbols, $LAC = \gamma LTC/\lambda Q$, if $\lambda > \gamma$ then we have a negatively sloped LAC and increasing returns to scale; if $\lambda < \gamma$ we have a positively sloped LAC and decreasing returns to scale; if $\lambda = \gamma$ we have a horizontal (constant) LAC and constant returns to scale.

FIGURE 9-14

Increasing, constant, and decreasing returns to scale with cost curves

The implication of Figure 9-13 is that long-run average costs will fall when there are increasing returns to scale [panel (a)], will be constant when there are constant returns to scale [panel (b)], and will rise when there are decreasing returns to scale [panel (c)].

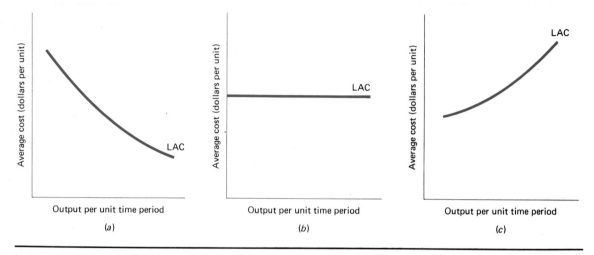

THE DISTINCTION BETWEEN RETURNS TO SCALE AND ECONOMIES OF SCALE

Increasing, constant, and decreasing returns to scale are related to the *technological* relation between a proportionate change in all inputs and the resultant change in output. In other words, returns to scale refer only to the *technological* phenomena that occur *within* a firm. The ability to combine inputs in a more efficient manner as the output rate increases would be an example of a technological phenomenon within a firm.

When we consider the possibility of things changing *externally* to the firm, we are considering the possibility of changes in things such as the prices of factors. These are determined outside the firm. If all the firms in a competitive industry are expanding production and, therefore, demanding more factors of production at each and every price, this may cause the prices of those factors to increase. When we allow for such external changes, we are considering what have been called (external) **economies** and **diseconomies of scale**.

As an industry expands, new input-production methods may be adopted by suppliers. In other words, the expansion of one industry that requires inputs from another industry may create the incentive for the other industry to develop improved technology. The resulting reduced price of inputs into the expanding industry will reduce costs for *all firms* in that industry. These are examples of economies of scale.

The opposite scenario is also possible. Diseconomies of scale may occur when input prices rise as an industry expands production. The rise in input prices may be due to inelastic supply conditions in the input-producing industry.

Thus, economies of scale and increasing returns to scale are related but are not exactly the same. Increasing returns to scale are the *technological* or production basis for economies of scale. Economies of scale are represented by a declining average *cost* of larger-scale production. Economies of scale can arise solely on the basis of technologically increasing returns to scale, or they can come about solely from price effects on inputs. Hence, it is possible for there to be increasing returns to scale but no economies of scale if the firm must buy its inputs at prices that rise when the industry (or firm) expands production. It is important, however, to distinguish between changes in factor prices which result from the expansion or contraction of an industry and those which result from causes outside the industry. The former are reflected in the *shape* of the firm's LAC curve; the latter are reflected in the position (upward or downward shift) of the firm's long-run and short-run cost curves.

Increasing returns to scale

Here we list several reasons why a firm might be expected to experience increasing returns to scale.

Specialization. As a firm's scale of operation increases, the opportunities for specialization in the use of resource inputs also increase. This is sometimes called increased division of tasks or operations, or an increased "division of labor" among tasks. Gains from increasing the division of labor, or increased specialization, are well known; see, for example, Adam Smith's famous pin-factory case.[11] When we consider managerial staffs, we also find that larger enterprises may be able to put together more highly specialized staffs. Larger enterprises may have the ability to tap better managerial technology.

Dimensional factor. Large-scale firms often require proportionately less input per unit of output simply because certain inputs do not have to be physically doubled in order to double the output. Consider the cost of oil storage. The cost of storage is basically related to the cost of steel that goes into building the storage container; however, the amount of steel required to build the shell of the container goes up less than in proportion to the volume of oil that the container can hold.

Transportation factor. The transportation cost per unit will fall as the market area increases. The market size increases by πr^2, which is the formula for the area of a circle where r is the radius. However, transportation distance

---

[11]Adam Smith, *The Wealth of Nations* (1776), book I, chap. 1, pp. 4–5.

from the center of the circle is equal to r, the radius. For example, transportation distance only doubles when market area quadruples.

Improved productive equipment. The larger the scale of the enterprise, the more it is able to take advantage of larger-volume or specially "tailored" types of machinery. Small-scale operations may not lend themselves to machines that require a large volume of output to be used profitably, and such operations will seldom find it profitable to have a machine built or modified to the details of their particular production situations.

Decreasing returns to scale

One of the basic reasons we can eventually expect to observe decreasing returns to scale at the firm level is that there are limits to the efficient functioning of management. Moreover, as more workers are hired, a more-than-proportionate increase in managers may be needed, and this can cause increased cost per unit. For example, it may be possible to hire from 0 to 10 workers and give them each a shovel to dig ditches; however, as soon as 10 workers are hired, it may also be appropriate to hire an overseer to coordinate their ditch-digging efforts. Thus, perhaps constant returns to scale will obtain until 10 workers and 10 shovels are employed; then decreasing returns to scale set in. As the layers of supervision grow, the cost of information and communication grows more than in proportion. So average monitoring costs and shirking per unit of output will usually be greater in a large-scale firm than in a small-scale firm.

Physical constraints. Some inputs are subject to physical constraints. For example, a firm can double the number of machines while it doubles the use of all other inputs and not necessarily double the machines' contribution to output. Consider the possibility of the machines generating "excessive" noise and heat, thus requiring a larger space, that is, larger than double the working space, in order to keep the machines physically efficient. There are numerous other examples of such physical problems which can cause decreasing returns to scale.

TECHNOLOGICAL CHANGE

Throughout the last two chapters, we have taken the production function of the firm as given. In other words, we have been concerned with the optimal choice of inputs (under stationary conditions) with no changes in technology. We have taken the "state of the arts" as given. In other words, technology has been considered fixed. However, technology is not always fixed. Technological change consists of discovering new methods of producing old products, of developing new products, and of introducing new techniques of marketing, organization, and management.

In this section we are assuming that factor prices remain constant. Remember that although an improvement in technology will always lower the firm's costs, *ceteris paribus*, every decrease in costs is *not* due to an improvement in technology. The level of costs is a function of the prices a firm must pay for factors of production as well as the physical amounts of these factors required to produce a unit of output. Technological change is motivated by the desire to produce the same quantity at a lower average cost. We can examine technological change by using the isoquant technique that we have used so much already. We will examine three types of technological change: neutral, labor-saving, and capital-saving.

Neutral technological change

Neutral technological change occurs when the increase in MPP_L is equal to the increase in MPP_K at a given capital/labor ratio. Remember that the marginal rate of technical substitution of labor for capital is equal to

$$MRTS_{K:L} = \frac{MPP_L}{MPP_K} \tag{9-10}$$

Therefore, technical change is neutral if $MRTS_{K:L}$ remains unchanged at the originally given capital/labor ratio. Panel (a) in Figure 9-15 depicts a

---

FIGURE 9-15
Technological change
In panel (a), we show neutral technological change. Output equal to 1 can be attained using less capital and less labor. This is shown by movement from isoquant Q to isoquant Q', both of which have an output rate equal to 1. At point E on isoquant Q, we have drawn a tangent, the slope of which gives the $MRTS_{K:L}$. We have also drawn a tangent at point E' on isoquant Q'. That tangent is parallel to the previous tangent, indicating that the technological progress at the given capital/labor ratio did not change the $MRTS_{K:L}$. In panel (b) we show labor-saving technological change. There is a movement similar to the one in panel (a) from isoquant $Q = 1$ to isoquant $Q' = 1$; however, with constant factor prices, the firm would not stay at point E' because at that point $\Delta L/\Delta K = MPP_L/MPP_K$ is no longer equal to the ratio of the price of capital to the price of labor. The firm would have to use more capital and less labor. More importantly, as can be seen by the difference in the slope of the tangents at E and E', the $MRTS_{K:L}$ has changed. It has diminished, indicating that technical change is labor-saving. In panel (c) we see that the $MRTS_{K:L}$ has increased, indicating that there has been capital-saving technological change.

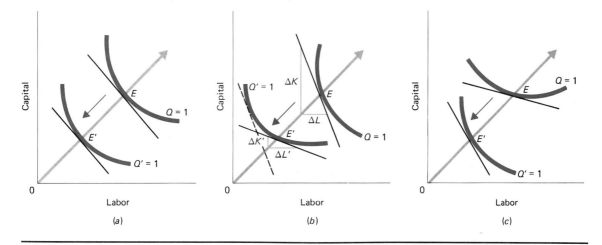

(a) (b) (c)

situation of *neutral* technological change. We start off on the isoquant labeled $Q = 1$. The rate of output per unit time period is 1. As a result of technological change to obtain the same output, we now have to use less of both labor and capital. We move from the isoquant labeled $Q = 1$ to the lower isoquant labeled $Q' = 1$. We are shifting the entire set of isoquants—on the new set we can obtain the same level of output for fewer inputs because of the technological changes. That is, the old isoquant Q may now be equivalent to, say, $2Q'$—which means that we could obtain twice as much output as before given the new technology.

The tangency along a particular ray drawn from the origin [which has the same slope as the rays drawn from the origin in panels (b) and (c)] is given at points E and E'. The slope of the tangents along that ray are equal. That means that the MRTS is constant before and after technological change. That means that the marginal physical product of labor and the marginal physical product of capital have not changed (since MRTS = $\text{MPP}_L/\text{MPP}_K$). In this sense, the technological change is neutral. It is referred to as "neutral" because it does not induce the firm to change the capital/labor ratio because, in turn, the ratio of their marginal physical products has not changed—or, otherwise stated, because the marginal rate of technical substitution has not changed.

Labor-saving technological change

Panel (b) in Figure 9-15 represents **labor-saving technological change**. The original position is given by the isoquant labeled $Q = 1$, where output is at the rate of 1 per unit time period. Now technological change takes place. The isoquant shifts downward so that an output of 1 per unit time period can be obtained with less labor and less capital. However, there is a difference between what has happened in this situation and what happened in the previous situation [panel (a)]. In panel (b), look at the respective slopes of the tangents drawn at point E and point E'. The slope is much steeper at point E than it is at point E'. This means that for any given ratio of capital to labor, such as the one represented along the ray drawn from the origin in panel (b), the marginal rate of technical substitution has diminished, or otherwise stated, the ratio of the marginal physical product of labor to the marginal physical product of capital has diminished. In fact, in this situation it is clear that the marginal physical product of labor has fallen relative to the marginal physical product of capital. Thus, given the relative prices of labor and capital, w/r, less labor will be used per unit of output than before. In this sense, technological change is labor-saving. Otherwise stated, technological change is labor-saving if the MPP_L increases by less than the MPP_K at a given capital/labor ratio. This encourages the firm to use relatively less labor (and relatively more capital).

Clearly, if, for example, E is an optimum position, then E' is *not* an optimum position for the firm if factor prices are constant. For given constant factor prices, the optimum position will require that less labor be used and more capital be used. Why? Because of the law of diminishing marginal physical returns. At point E', the marginal product of capital has increased relative to the marginal product of labor. At firm optimum, however, we know that the ratio of the two marginal physical products must be equal to the ratio of their respective prices. But the price of capital and labor is given. The only way to decrease the marginal physical product of capital is to increase the amount of capital used relative to labor. Conversely, the only way to increase the marginal physical product of labor is to decrease the amount of labor used relative to capital. Hence, this is why the technological change depicted in panel (b) is called labor-saving. (It could also be called capital-using.)

Capital-saving technological change

We could go through a similar analysis to describe the **capital-saving technological change** which is depicted in panel (c) of Figure 9-15. The marginal physical product of labor increases relative to capital in such a situation. Hence, less capital need be used per unit of output with a given quantity of labor. The only way to get to the firm optimum will be to increase the amount of labor used and decrease the amount of capital, thereby affecting their relative marginal physical products. This is why it is called capital-saving. (It could also be called a labor-using technological change.) Otherwise stated, technological change is capital-saving if the MPP_L increases by more than the MPP_K at a given capital/labor ratio. This encourages the firm to use relatively less capital (and relatively more labor).

ISSUES AND APPLICATIONS

Social versus private costs: The case of two roads

The apparent originator of the terms "social costs" and "private costs," British economist A. C. Pigou, presented what has become a classic case illustrating what can happen when there is a divergence between social and private costs. This case was written up in Pigou's first edition of *The Economics of Welfare*, published in 1918. Pigou contended that in situations where social costs exceeded private costs, individuals freely left to their own initiative would end up overinvesting and overconsuming, from "society's" point of view, in such activities. He demonstrated his point by comparing two roads.

Road 1 was a well-paved but narrow road

that, when uncrowded, could get motorists to their destination faster than the alternative road. The alternative road was unpaved, and hence, relatively slow speeds had to be observed on it. It had the virtue, however, of being very broad and was capable of handling (in Pigou's hypothetical example) any volume of traffic without congestion.

When making a choice between road 1 and road 2, motorists would choose road 1 as long as it did not become crowded, for they could get to their destinations more cheaply in terms of time. However, after road 1 became crowded, the decision was not so easy. After some point, the increased congestion on road 1 would slow traffic down so much that it would be as cheap in terms of time to use road 2.

We can illustrate the situation in Figure 9-16. Panel (a) represents the situation on road 1 and panel (b) the situation on road 2.

Panel (b) is easier to understand. By assumption, in Pigou's example, no matter how many cars use road 2, the time cost of travel remains the same. If we measure time on the vertical axis and cars per unit time period on the horizontal axis, the average cost curve expressed in terms of time will be a horizontal line at T_2. On road 2, average costs are constant, and therefore marginal time cost must

equal average time cost and also be constant, i.e., $0T_2 = AC_2 = MC_2$.

In panel (a), the time-cost situation is depicted for road 1. Until the quantity of cars per unit time period Q_1 is reached, the time cost remains at T_1. Thus, from T_1 to point A, average costs equals marginal cost, or $AC_1 = MC_1$. After Q_1, when cars enter road 1, congestion arises and the time cost increases. Average cost rises after point A; marginal cost, therefore, is above average cost. Remember, we are expressing cost in terms of travel time.

Until what volume of traffic would motorists continue to enter road 1? According to Pi-

FIGURE 9-16
Private versus social costs: the case of two roads
In panel (b), we show road 2, which can accommodate any volume of cars at a constant time cost of $0T_2$; therefore, $AC_2 = MC_2$. In panel (a), we show a constant time cost for road 1 at $0T_1$ up to volume $0Q_1$. Thereafter, average cost rises, and marginal cost MC_1 is above it. If no one owns the better road, 1, cars will enter the road until the time costs are equated or until volume $0Q_3$, when the time cost will equal the vertical distance from Q_3 to point E, which is also equal to $0T_2$ in panel (b). However, at that volume, the social cost of the last driver entering the road is equal to the vertical distance Q_3 to F, since that driver imposes a cost on all other drivers by slowing them down. If someone owns the road, a toll can be charged. It will equal the monetary value of the reduction in time saved by using road 1 instead of road 2. The maximum toll that can be charged, therefore, is BA. The optimum toll is equal to DC. In this case, social costs equal private costs to the individual driver because that driver will pay marginal costs rather than average costs.

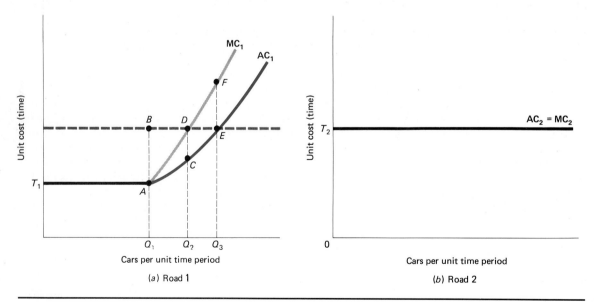

(a) Road 1

(b) Road 2

gou, motorists would continue entering road 1 until the total travel time was equal to what it would be on road 2. This occurs at quantity Q_3 of cars per unit time period. Here, total travel time is equalized between the two roads and is equal to T_2. Motorists would not enter road 1 at a rate in excess of Q_3 because it would be cheaper in time cost to switch to road 2.

DIVERGENCE OF SOCIAL AND PRIVATE COSTS

The private time cost of using road 1 is equal to the vertical distance between point E and Q_3, which is equal to $0T_2$. In other words, the private cost to the individual motorist is equal to the average cost or average total travel time spent on road 1. The marginal social cost, however, is greater. It is equal to the vertical distance between point F and Q_3. Why? Because all Q_3 motorists using road 1 are not only incurring a private total time cost of EQ_3, but each is also slowing down every other motorist on road 1. The amount that any given user slows down every other motorist is given by the distance between F and E. The delay per motorist might be trivial, but the total is large. For example, consider 100 motorists who each take 60 minutes to travel the road. When the 101st driver enters, he or she causes congestion, slowing down all 100 other drivers. They each require 61 minutes to drive the road. He or she, therefore, adds 1 minute times 100 drivers, or 100 minutes of driving time for that road. The social marginal cost of his or her entering the road in time units is 61 minutes plus 100 minutes, or 161 minutes. In other words, the social marginal cost of the last motorist's entrance onto road 1 is given by the marginal cost curve MC_1. Social cost is defined as all costs associated with an activity. These social costs must include not only the total private time cost incurred by the last motorist on road 1 but also the total additional time costs incurred by all other motorists. If you will remember Eq. (9-8), this can be stated as

$$MC_1 = AC_1 + \Delta AC_1 \cdot Q \qquad (9\text{-}11)$$

where Q equals the cars per unit time period on road 1.

According to Pigou's original analysis, road 1 is used too much and road 2 is used too little. The individual undertaking the decision to enter road 1 is not forced to take into account the greater travel time cost that he or she imposes on all other drivers on road 1. In such a free entry onto a highway situation, he or she does not have to consider social costs, only private costs.

THE EFFECTS OF CHARGING A TOLL

In a rebuttal to Pigou's analysis, Professor F. H. Knight[12] pointed out that Pigou's prediction would hold true only if both roads were free to all comers. Knight then went on to demonstrate that if road 1 charged the proper toll, there would be the optimal number of cars per unit time on road 1 and there would be no overuse of the resource (that road).

Suppose that there were private property rights in road 1 or that the state operated in a profit-maximizing manner. Then suppose that the owner of road 1 would like to make some income from that road. Let's assume for the moment that there are no costs of collecting tolls or of physical maintenance of the road. Clearly, the owner of road 1 could not charge a toll in excess of the monetary value of the time cost between A and B. This distance represents the time saving by using road 1 rather than road 2 when road 1 is uncongested. No motorist would be willing to pay a toll that was higher in monetary terms than the value placed on the time saving between road 1 and road 2. Thus we have the *maximum* toll that could be charged; it is equal to the monetary value of the time saving and is represented by the distance between A and B. If this toll were charged, quantity Q_1 of cars per unit time

[12]F. H. Knight, "Some Fallacies in the Interpretation of Social Costs," *Quarterly Journal of Economics*, vol. 38, 1924, pp. 582–606.

period would use road 1. If the minimum toll, i.e., no toll at all, were charged, we would be back in the first situation discussed by Pigou. The quantity Q_3 of cars per unit time would use road 1.

We now have two extreme points between which the owner of the road must set the toll in order to maximize revenues collected. Let's start from the maximum toll and keep decreasing it until we find the optimal toll. We must realize that as the toll is decreased from (in monetary terms) AB, more motorists will enter road 1. Thus, the owner of the road will have a larger volume of traffic. However, this is obtained only by reducing the toll to all who come on the road. Note that the toll is equal to the difference between average costs on road 2 and average costs on road 1, or $AC_2 - AC_1$. The maximum toll AB is equal to $T_2 - T_1$.

The owner of the road will want to continue lowering the toll as long as the amount collected on the marginal motorist, $AC_2 - AC_1$, exceeds the reduction in revenue collected from the other motorists. This reduction in revenue from other motorists is equal to $\Delta AC_1 \cdot Q$.

Rearranging this we obtain the optimum toll when

$$AC_1 + \Delta AC_1 \cdot Q = AC_2$$

Notice that the left-hand side of this expression is exactly equal to our definition of MC_1 given in Eq. (9-11). In other words, the optimal toll is charged so as to make the marginal cost on road 1 equal to the average cost (which is equal to the MC of road 2 by assumption) on road 2. This occurs in panel (a) of Figure 9-16 when the toll is equal to CD and the quantity of cars per unit time period on the road is Q_2. The owner of road 1 would make all those who used road 1 take account of the full social cost of their actions; and the social cost is represented by the marginal cost curve in panel (a). In other words, motorists on road 1 would be forced to pay for the additional time cost that they impose on other motorists.

Knight's qualification of Pigou's argument is based on road 1 being privately owned and operated for profit. The charging of a price in the form of a toll forces the individual motorists to recognize the full social cost of their actions.

One plant or two? Coordinating Multiplant production

We usually show a single marginal cost curve for a firm since we assume a single production process. Of course some firms have more than one production facility and, since the costs of operating the facilities may be different, the firm managers must decide when to use only one plant or expand production to two plants. Suppose a firm has plant New and plant Old. Plant New has a lower minimum marginal cost at a higher level of output than plant Old. Assuming that demand for the products produced by these plants is lower than they are capable of producing, there is some cost minimizing mix of production between the two

plants; or, it is possible, that the cost-minimizing solution is to produce everything at only one plant.

Figure 9-17 shows such a situation. We see the marginal cost curve for the new plant and for the old plant. At output level Q the firm will be indifferent between producing Q all at plant New or producing Q_1 at plant New and $Q-Q_1$ at plant Old. Note that while MC_{New} is a traditional marginal cost curve, MC_{Old} begins at Q and is read backward in terms of quantity, so that it produces from Q going left along the axis to point Q_1. The reason the firm is indifferent between having plant New pro-

FIGURE 9-17
The two-plant firm
Initially the firm produces quantity Q per time period. It faces MC_{New} for its newer production plant and MC_{Old} for its older production plant. It can not operate plant Old and have all production (level Q) produced by plant New, or it can have plant New produce output level Q_1 and have plant Old produce output level $Q - Q_1$. In that case, since area A equals area B, the cost savings and cost increase of plant Old are just offset, so that the total cost is the same as if all production were by plant New. When output per time period rises to Q', the firm still faces MC_{New}, but at a higher point on the curve, so that production from plant Old now becomes more attractive (remember that MC_{Old} begins at point Q or Q_1). Cost savings, area B', are greater than the region of higher costs, area A', so that it will be most efficient to use both plants.

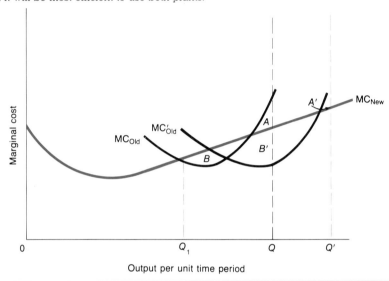

duce everything or having the plants split production is that the lower costs incurred by plant Old, area B (where MC_{Old} is below MC_{New}), is just offset by area A, where plant Old has higher per unit costs of production than plant New.

EFFECT OF AN INCREASE IN QUANTITY

Now suppose that the firm suddenly sees an increase in the demand for its product, so that it can increase output to level Q'. That moves the firm further along MC_{New}. Since we measure MC_{Old} from point Q', we shift from the original MC_{Old} to MC'_{Old} (the curves are identical).

At the new, higher level of quantity produced, MC_{Old} still has a range of production where its costs are greater than those of plant New, area A'. But this time the area of cost saving from plant Old, area B', are larger than A', so that the cost-minimizing strategy for the firm will be a mix of production from plant New and plant Old.

DISCONTINUOUS MARGINAL COST

This set of curves has shown us that up to production level Q, the firm will cost-minimize by only using plant New. Once the quantity produced during the relevant time period rises beyond Q, the firm will use some mix of plant

FIGURE 9-18
Discontinuous marginal cost curve
The decision-relevant marginal cost curve for the firm takes into account plant New and plant Old. After the firm passes point Q level of output per unit time it is cheaper for the firm to begin production in plant Old rather than only use plant New. This enables the firm to operate at a lower point on MC_{New}, since it cuts production at plant New, and takes advantage of the range of production in plant Old that is less costly per unit than in plant New.

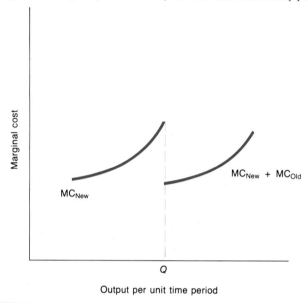

Output per unit time period

New and plant Old, so that, for the firm as a whole, there is a discontinuous marginal cost curve, as shown in Figure 9-18.[13]

This does not change the analysis of mar-

[13]This analysis draws on the article by Edward L. Sattler and Robert C. Scott, "Price and Output Adjustments in the Two-Plant Firm," *Southern Economic Journal*, April 1982, pp. 1042–1048.

ginal cost curves and their implications, but this particular firm will face some interesting pricing problems for its output when it crosses the discontinuous point on its marginal cost curve as demand expands or contracts. You might think about this problem during the next few chapters where we study price determination.

Economies of scale: Large firms and large plants

Stories are told about large private firms being so complex that they are just like a large government bureaucracy. The inference is drawn that big firms (and perhaps big production plants) must suffer from inefficiencies not suffered by smaller organizations. That may in fact be true, but there is empirical evidence that whatever added costs are imposed by

TABLE 9-2
Evidence of economies of scale

This table summarizes studies that show that labor productivity is higher in large firms compared to smaller firms across a wide range of industries. It also indicates that due to the higher productivity, the larger firms compensate their employees better than average.

*These values are a comparison of the average of the four largest firms in an industry to all other firms in an industry, across 443 industries. All figures are mean (average) values.

Large firm values compared to other firms		
Variable	1972	1977
Labor productivity		
Shipments per employee	39%	45.4%
Value added per employee	37	41.7
Materials per employee	43	50.8
Value added per production worker manhour	41	45.6 .
Profit margin per employee	57	60.6
Labor compensation		
Payroll per employee	15.4	15.8
Production worker wages per manhour	17.2	18.3

large-scale organizations that may be avoided by smaller organizations are offset by other factors that produce economies of scale.

One economist who has studied economies of scale has produced estimates of the benefits of being a large firm in an industry.[14] In Table 9-2 some of the results of his work are produced. These estimates were based on Census Bureau data for approximately 443 industries in the U.S.

The first part of the table concerns labor productivity. It compares the average labor productivity, using the different measures shown, for the four largest firms in a given industry to all other firms in the industry. Hence, we see that in 1977 the largest firms,

on average, shipped 45.4 percent more goods (in dollar value) per employee than did the smaller firms. By all measures of production, the four largest firms (which usually have large production plants), had higher measures of labor productivity than smaller firms. This higher level of productivity, reflecting economies of scale enjoyed by the larger firms, also produced a 60 percent higher profit margin per employee.

As can be seen from the second part of the table, the benefits of higher productivity are shared by the workers. Workers at the larger firms averaged over 15 percent higher pay than their counterparts at smaller firms.

Further empirical work has indicated that the advantages enjoyed by the larger firms were greater the larger the largest plant size. Hence, economies of scale do exist in the technology of production and are reflected in labor productivity.

[14]Edward M. Miller, "Extent of Economies of Scale: An Update," *Southern Economic Journal*, October 1984, pp. 582–587.

SUMMARY

1   The cost of any action is the cost of the most valued currently available alternative that is sacrificed.

2   Firms and consumers generally take account of private costs rather than all social costs; the latter includes all costs of any activity, both private and "external."

3   All productive resources that are identical have the same opportunity cost.

4   Fixed costs are usually defined as the cost that is invariant to the rate of output; however, a true fixed, or sunk, cost, which is the cost of assets that cannot be transferred to some other profitable use, actually has an opportunity cost equal to zero.

5   If a machine is highly specialized and, therefore, has no alternative use and also no scrap value, its cost of acquisition is equal to its price; the resale value by definition is equal to zero.

6   Average fixed costs can be represented by a rectangular hyperbola; the axes are the asymptotes.

7   The marginal cost curve intersects both the average variable cost curve and the average total cost curve at their minimum points.

8   Whenever AVC and/or ATC are falling, marginal cost is below them; whenver they are rising, marginal cost is above them.

9   Cost minimization for a given output level requires that the ratio of marginal physical product of an input to its price be equal for all inputs.

10   Average variable cost is equal to the input price divided by the average physical product of the input.

11   Marginal cost is equal to the input price divided by the marginal physical product of the input.

12   In the long run, the firm is able to alter all inputs. It therefore faces a planning horizon.

13   The appropriate plant size for a single-plant firm during the planning horizon is the one that minimizes the short-run average cost at the expected permanent rate of output.

14   If we connect the points of tangency between successively higher isoquants and parallel isocost curves, we obtain the expansion path; it shows us how factor proportions change (if they do) when output increases, while input prices remain constant.

15   The long-run average cost curve is obtained by drawing the envelope of all the short-run average cost curves. Only at the minimum point on the LAC curve is the LAC curve tangent to the minimum point of a short-run average cost curve. The long-run marginal cost curve will always intersect each short-run marginal cost curve at the output rate at which the respective short-run average cost curve is tangent to the long-run average cost curve.

16   Capacity in the short run is the output at which the firm has no incentive to alter the size of plant when the rate of output is expected to be

permanent. Thus, capacity must be at a point on a short-run average cost curve where it is tangent to the long-run average cost curve; only at that tangency point will the firm keep that size of plant if that output is considered permanent.

17 Returns to scale relate to the change in output due to a proportionate change in all inputs. Returns to scale are a technological phenomenon *within* the firm.

18 Economies of scale can result from returns to scale but can also be caused by such changes outside the firm's control as a change in the input price due to a change in the *industry's* rate of output.

19 Increasing returns to scale may be due to (a) specialization, (b) dimensional factors, (c) transportation factors, and (d) improved productive equipment.

20 Decreasing returns to scale may be due to the managerial limits within a firm.

21 Technological change is a change in the production function. If the same output can be obtained with less of at least one input, and if such a change induces the firm to keep constant, increase, or decrease its capital/labor ratio, the technological change is said to be neutral, labor-saving, or capital-saving, respectively.

GLOSSARY

- **opportunity cost** The forgone value of resources in their next-best alternative use; a currently available alternative that is sacrificed.
- **private costs** All costs explicitly or implicitly incurred by individuals or firms.
- **social costs** Private costs plus costs imposed on other members of society who are not parties to the transaction (third parties).
- **total fixed cost (TFC)** Cost that is "sunk"; cost that is invariant to the rate of output.
- **total variable cost (TVC)** The cost that is related to the rate of output; i.e., it varies as output changes.
- **average fixed cost (AFC)** Total fixed cost divided by output.
- **average variable cost (AVC)** Total variable cost divided by output.
- **average total cost (ATC)** Total of all fixed and variable costs divided by output.
- **marginal cost (MC)** The change in total cost (or in variable cost) due to a one-unit change in the rate of output.
- **planning horizon** Another name for long-run cost curves; all inputs are variable during the planning horizon.
- **expansion path** The line along which output will expand while relative factor prices remain constant; shows how factor proportions change when output changes and relative input prices are constant.

- **isocline** The locus of points along which the marginal rate of technical substitution is constant; shows how output changes as successively higher total outlays are incurred while holding relative price of inputs constant.
- **long-run average cost curve (LAC)** The locus of points representing the minimum unit cost of producing any given rate of output, given current technology and resource prices.
- **planning curve** Another name for the long-run average cost curve.
- **long-run marginal cost curve (LMC)** The locus of points showing the minimum amount by which total cost is increased as the rate of output is expanded by one unit.
- **capacity** That permanent rate of output at which there is no incentive for the firm to alter plant size in the long run.
- **returns to scale** The relation between changes in output and proportionate changes in all factors of production.
- **increasing returns to scale** Output increases more than in proportion to the change in inputs.
- **constant returns to scale** Output increases by the same proportion that all inputs increase.
- **decreasing returns to scale** Output increases less than in proportion to the increase in inputs.
- **economies of scale** Output increases more than in proportion to the change in inputs; may result from both increasing returns to scale or such external-to-the-firm changes as falling factor prices.
- **diseconomies of scale** Output rises less than in proportion to a change in inputs; may result from either decreasing returns to scale or such external changes as an increase in the price of inputs.
- **neutral technological change** A technological change is neutral when the $MRTS_{K:L}$ remains unchanged. Otherwise stated, technological change is neutral when the MPP_L increases by the same amount that the MPP_K increases at a given capital/labor ratio.
- **labor-saving technological change** A change in the production function such that the $MRTS_{K:L}$ diminishes. Otherwise stated, technological change is labor-saving when the MPP_L increases by less than the MPP_K at a given capital/labor ratio, thus encouraging the firm to use relatively less labor (and relatively more capital).
- **capital-saving technological change** A change in the production function such that the $MRTS_{K:L}$ increases at the originally given capital/labor ratio. Otherwise stated, technological change is capital-saving when the MPP_L increases by more than the MPP_K at a given capital/labor ratio, thus encouraging the firm to use relatively less capital (and relatively more labor).

QUESTIONS

(Answers to even-numbered questions are at back of text.)

1 How would you go about determining the opportunity cost of going to college from September until June? Who bears this cost?

2 "We seldom use that old machine, but it doesn't cost us anything to keep it because it's been completely depreciated on the company books." Criticize this statement.

3 "We demand that Riskyroad Market be investigated by the state consumer ombudsperson. It is widely known that their meats are centrally butchered and that the better cuts are trucked out to the affluent suburban stores while only the fat- and bone-laden meat (chuck steak, ham hocks, chicken wings, and the like) is stocked in the inner-city stores. This discrimination must be brought to a halt." What does the opportunity cost of preparing food at home have to do with the above situation?

4 The concept of social costs was introduced in this chapter. Its counterpart is social benefits. Suppose an X-rated film at a drive-in movie is visible from an adjacent highway. Is this an example of an external cost or an external benefit?

5 Suppose that Congress changed the tax laws so that stock dividends became a tax-deductible "expense" for corporations. What impact would such a move have on the relative attractiveness of *debt* financing (issuing new bonds or borrowing from a bank to raise capital) and *equity* financing (issuing new shares of stock to raise capital)? Why?

6 "I know that the 'short run' for my gas station won't end for at least 10 more years, since that's how long my lease runs." Assuming that this person does not have the right to sublet, do you agree or disagree? Why?

7 Is a fixed cost ever a function of output in the short run? Why or why not? What is the formula for average fixed cost? What is a curve of that sort called?

8 Suppose you were producing a rate of output Q, employing a combination of inputs such that the marginal physical product of capital was 8 times that of labor. If the implicit rental price per unit of capital were 10 times as much as the wage rate per unit of labor, are you minimizing your costs for that output? Why or why not? What change in inputs will lower your cost of producing output Q? Explain.

9 Define marginal cost. Does your definition refer to a change in total cost or in variable cost? Does it matter? Why or why not?

10 Define long-run average total cost. In light of the fact that businesses are operated day to day in the short run, of what use is the concept of long-run average total cost to an entrepreneur?

11 "Despite all the developments in power gardening equipment which have occurred in recent years, the typical home gardening service consists of a single gardener, sometimes two, and a pickup truck full of equipment. One of these days, one of them is going to get smart and increase the scale of operations to six or eight workers and operate with a very large truck full of highly specialized equipment. The result will be lower costs, and the smaller traditional operators who are unable to purchase the larger-scale equipment will be driven out of business." Criticize this statement.

12 Consider a three-plant firm. At present output Q, each plant is producing one-third ($Q/3$) of the total. You are hired as the company's new industrial engineer. The first thing you do is ascertain the marginal cost of each plant at the present output rate of $Q/3$. Your figures show plant 1's marginal cost to be \$10 and that of plants 2 and 3 to be \$8. Assuming that you wish to continue output at the same level Q, how should you rearrange production shares so as to decrease costs? Does it make any difference to your decision if all sales occur at the location of plant 1 and the outputs of plants 2 and 3 must be shipped to 1 in order to be sold?

13 Why is it that a significant expansion of an entire industry, particularly a fairly rapid one, will often shift the marginal cost curve of each individual firm leftward?

14 What is the relationship between the "commerce clause" ("Congress [rather than the individual states] shall have power . . . to regulate commerce with foreign nations, and among the several states. . . .") of the United States Constitution and the LAC concept?

15 Why do you think that the federal government allows taxpayers using their own personal cars in their work (other than just to and from) to deduct as an expense an amount (about 22¢ per mile at this writing) which is approximately equal to the ATC of the vast majority of car owners? Why doesn't Congress limit the deduction to one's marginal cost?

SELECTED REFERENCES

Chamberlin, Edward H., "Proportionality, Divisibility, and Economies of Scale," *Quarterly Journal of Economics*, vol. 62, February 1948, pp. 229–262.

Clark, J.M., *The Economics of Overhead Costs* (Chicago: University of Chicago Press, 1923), chaps. 4–6.

Coase, R.H., "The Problem of Social Cost," *Journal of Law and Economics*, vol. 3, October 1960, pp. 1–44.

Liebhafsky, H.H., *The Nature of Price Theory*, rev. ed. (Homewood, Ill.: Dorsey-Irwin, 1968), chap. 7.

Mansfield, Edwin, *The Economics of Technological Change* (New York: Norton, 1968).

Moore, Frederick T., "Economies of Scale: Some Statistical Evidence," *Quarterly Journal of Economics*, May 1959.

Stigler, George J., "The Economies of Scale," *Journal of Law and Economics*, vol. 1, October 1958, pp. 54–71.

The competitive firm: Pricing and output

We presented the theory of demand and the theory of the firm in the first nine chapters. We have not yet, however, devoted much space to finding out how much will actually be produced and sold and at what prices. In order to do so, we must specify the market organization or structure in which the firm operates. In this chapter, we will analyze a perfectly competitive market. In later chapters, we will analyze market organizations which deviate from the model of **perfect competition**.

THE MEANING OF COMPETITION

At the outset, let's make a distinction between a fairly relaxed notion of competition and a model of perfect competition. The more relaxed view of the competitive process focuses on the concept of rivalry among economic transactors.

Rivalry

In a world of scarce resources, there will be **rivalry** among sellers and among buyers. Rivalrous behavior among sellers takes on many forms: advertising, improvement in the quality of the product, sales promotion, development of new products, modification of old products, and so on. Rivalry among buyers also takes on many forms: finding better deals, figuring out ways to take advantage of quantity discounts, offering a higer price to obtain a product which is in fixed supply, and so on.

Competition and survivorship

In the preceding two chapters, we examined the total, average, and marginal cost and product curves; however, exact knowledge of these curves and of the demand curve is not necessary for rivalry to exist. In a world of scarce resources, consumers will opt for the lower-priced product, other things held constant. That the firm has exact information on its cost and on demand is immaterial. For the firm that chooses the best combination of output qualities, quantities, and price will ultimately survive, forcing other firms to imitate if they also wish to survive. This is sometimes called the **survivorship principle**. It helps us understand the nature of real-world rivalry.

However, the more commonsense notion of rivalry outlined here is absent in the typical analysis of a perfectly competitive firm.

Perfect competition

In essence, a market characterized by perfect competition is one in which no individual buyer or seller can influence the price by his or her purchases or sales alone. There are four conditions under which a perfectly competitive market arises *in theory*, and the presence of all four is required. We list them here.

Homogeneity of product. In perfect competition, we are dealing with a homogeneous product. There are a large number of sellers, each selling an identical product. The important thing about homogeneity is that buyers are able to choose from a large number of sellers who are offering for sale a product that all buyers believe to be exactly the same.

Unconstrained resource mobility.[1] Firms must be able to enter or leave any industry; resources must be able to move without friction among alternative uses; and goods and services must be salable wherever the price is highest.

Large numbers of buyers and sellers.[2] In order that each economic agent have no influence upon price, there must be a large number of them and they must act independently. In addition, the largest buyer or the largest seller must provide only a small fraction of the total quantities bought and sold. Strictly speaking, perfect competition does not require large numbers of sellers if there is free entry into the industry and all actual or potential firms face constant costs (linear homogeneous production functions).

Perfect information. All buyers and sellers must have perfect information about their demand curves and their cost curves and about market supply and demand. Thus, there is perfect information about the prices at which commodities can be bought and sold. This guarantees that the price per constant-quality unit, corrected for transportation charges, will be uniform.

---

[1]Although the model of perfect competition is central to most modern economic reasoning, the older politial economy of Adam Smith, David Ricardo, and John Mill did not use this concept. Instead, those economists were concerned with a notion of competition built upon resource mobility unconstrained by legal barriers.

[2]Under certain reasonable conditions in a general equilibrium model, it is correct to state that in a perfectly competitive market, no producer has any effect on market price. See E. Fama and A. Laffer, "The Number of Firms in Competition," *American Economic Review*, vol. 62, 1972, pp. 670–674.

Perfect competition and rivalry

The definition of perfect competition might have added the additional attribute of a complete *lack* of rivalry in the market. For once we assume perfect information, and insignificance of each market participant, there is really no market rivalry and therefore no market process to analyze. Indeed, in a perfectly competitive market, all the signs of rivalry will be absent and there will be no motivation to advertise, no need for market research, and certainly no differentiation because the product is homogeneous. On the buyers' side, no buyer ever need search for a more favorable deal, no buyer will ever regret having made a purchase, and certainly no buyer will ever bother to look at brand names. In short, no activity on the part of individuals can be classified as rivalry in a perfectly competitive market.

Realism of theoretical models

The point to be made here is not that the perfectly competitive model has no value. Indeed, we will find that it allows us to understand the consequences of a number of common restrictions on economic behavior. Rather, we must realize that in dealing with a perfectly competitive model, we will have to relax, to some extent, the assumptions in order to apply it to real-world phenomena.

Assertions that the perfectly competitive model should be abandoned because its assumptions make it inapplicable to the real world are incorrect. The model is useful as a first approximation to understanding how markets operate and for predicting the results of proposed microeconomic policies. As long as its limitations, as well as its strengths, are recognized, the model of perfect competition is a valuable tool of economic analysis.

INDUSTRY ALTERNATIVES IN THE IMMEDIATE RUN

In the last few chapters, we have introduced the concept of the short run and the long run. Indeed, in what follows, we will reintroduce those concepts and talk about equilibrium in the short run and the long run. For the moment, let us consider a situation that we will call the **immediate run, or market period**. This is a situation in which there is *no time allowed for adjustment* on the part of suppliers of a product. We then ask what the price will be in an industry in such a situation. We define an **industry** as any group of firms that produces a homogeneous product.

Industry equilibrium price

We see in Figure 10-1 the situation described above. The supply curve is vertical (perfectly inelastic), indicating that there is no possibility for a change in the quantity supplied by firms in the industry from Q_0. The industry supply curve is *SS*. What will the equilibrium price be? First remember that we derive the market demand curve by horizontally summing all the individual demand curves. Thus if the market demand curve is *DD*, the intersection with the industry supply curve *SS* is at *E*. The market-clearing price

FIGURE 10-1
Rationing a fixed supply in the immediate period
In the immediate run (market period), the supply curve is vertical. The equilibrium quantity Q_0 is uniquely determined by supply. The market-clearing, or equilibrium, price is determined by the intersection of market demand curve DD with SS (at price P_e). If demand increases to $D'D'$, the market-clearing price will increase to P'_e, but the equilibrium quantity will remain at Q_0.

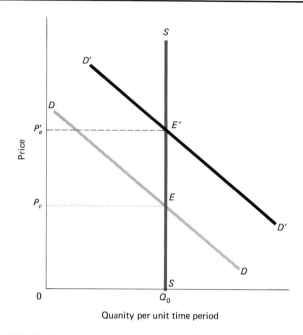

will be P_e. If, however, the market demand curve is $D'D'$, the intersection with SS is at E' and the industry equilibrium price will be P'_e.

SS might represent the amount of fresh fish available after all the fishing boats come in early some morning. If the demand curve for fish that day is DD, the market-clearing price will be P_e. However, if the demand curve for fish that day is $D'D'$, the market-clearing price will be higher at P'_e.

Price rations the fixed supply

Clearly, the price in the situation shown in Figure 10-1 serves only as a rationing function. Supply in that figure *bears no relation to any costs of production*. The price in the immediate run that obtains in the industry is such that the quantity demanded equals the quantity supplied. The price rations the fixed supply of goods among actual and potential demanders. Do not get the impression that in other situations price does not also serve as a rationing device. Rather, this immediate-run situation demonstrates to an extreme degree the manner in which price rations scarce resources.

Note that using price as a rationing system, or as a way in which resources are allocated, is discriminatory. Those who are discriminated against are those who are unwilling or unable to pay the going price. Those who are being discriminated in favor of are those who are willing or able to pay the price for a desired quantity. Thus, we can categorically state that the price system is discriminatory in the way in which it rations scarce resources. However, all systems which allocate scarce resources discriminate according to some criterion (or set of criteria). The existence of scarcity implies that some demands will be satisfied and others will remain unsatisfied. Given scarcity, any allocation system, whether via market prices, a centralized allocation system, or a system based on "need," will, of necessity, employ discriminatory criteria. Social policies concerned with discriminatory allocation criteria attempt to regulate which criteria are used and which are to be discouraged. Elimination of all such allocation criteria is impossible.

THE DEMAND CURVE FACING THE PERFECTLY COMPETITIVE FIRM

A firm in a perfectly competitive industry does not influence the price of the commodity sold; it must take price *as given*. The firm is such a small part of the market that by itself it is insignificant. How is this given price determined? By the interaction of *market* demand and *market* supply, not by demand as perceived by nor supply provided by the individual competitive firm. Later in the chapter, we will derive the market supply curve; the market demand curve has already been derived in Chapter 4.

If the individual firm in a perfectly competitive market must take the price as given, the demand curve facing that firm will look like *dd* in Figure 10-2, which is a line parallel to the horizontal axis at the vertical

FIGURE 10-2
The relationship between market demand and the demand curve facing a perfect competitor
In (a) we see the determination of market equilibrium price P_e by the intersection of market demand and market supply. The individual perfectly competitive firm will perceive the equilibrium price P_e as its demand curve. The firm will act as if it can sell any quantity at that price and that it will sell nothing if it charges more than that price. Its demand curve is horizontal, as we see in B, so the price elasticity of demand is $-\infty$.

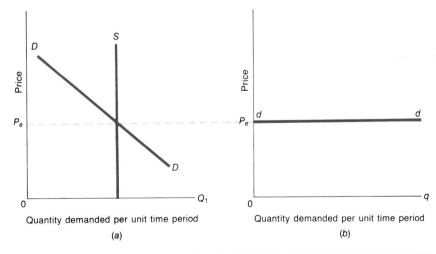

distance $0P_e$, where P_e is the "going" (equilibrium) price determined by the intersection of the market demand curve and the market supply curve. It has a price elasticity $\eta = -\infty$; i.e., it is perfectly elastic. The reason that the demand curve dd facing the individual competitive firm is perfectly or infinitely elastic is that this firm will lose all of its sales if it attempts to charge more than the market price for its product. In other words, a perfect competitior will sell zero units at a price that is even slightly above price P_e. However, the perfect competitor would never set a price below P_e because he or she can, by assumption, sell any and all output at that price. Therefore, charging a price below P_e would not be profit-maximizing.

The demand curve depicted in Figure 10-1 represents total or market demand facing the entire industry composed of numerous perfect competitors. The demand curve labeled with lowercase d's in Figure 10-2 represents the demand curve facing only one perfect competitor in that industry. The position of the dd curve faced by a competitive firm is determined by the intersection of market supply and demand.

Price elasticity of demand

Remember that the mathematical expression for the price elasticity of demand is the relative change in quantity demanded divided by the relative change in price. However, by definition, the individual seller in a perfectly competitive industry cannot influence the price. Price must be taken as given. Thus, we see that the demand curve dd in Figure 10-2 exhibits a price elasticity of demand of $-\infty$. An infinitesimally small increase in the price leads to a very large reduction in the quantity demanded; the latter goes to zero. Alternatively, an infinitesimally small percentage decrease in the price leads to an infinitely large percentage increase in the quantity demanded. Hence, the price elasticity of demand is $-\infty$. Another way of seeing this is by remembering the formula for price elasticity of demand $\eta = (\Delta q/\Delta P) \cdot (P/q)$. As the demand curve dd facing the individual firm gets flatter and flatter, its slope $\Delta P/\Delta q$ gets closer and closer to zero. Thus the reciprocal of the slope, $\Delta q/\Delta P$, gets bigger and bigger. In the limit, η becomes $[(-\infty)(P/q)] = -\infty$, and that's what it is for dd in Figure 10-2.

Marginal revenue for the perfect competitor

Remember that we defined marginal revenue as the change in total revenue due to a one-unit change in sales. We also came up with an alternative definition of marginal revenue which related it to the price elasticity of demand. From Chapter 5, we repeat this formula:

$$\text{MR} = P\left(1 + \frac{1}{\eta}\right) \tag{10-1}$$

However, we have just indicated that price elasticity of demand for the firm in a perfectly competitive industry is $-\infty$. Thus, Eq. (10-1) becomes

$$\text{MR} = P\left(1 + \frac{1}{-\infty}\right) = P(1 + 0) = P \tag{10-2}$$

Hence, for the perfectly competitive firm, marginal revenue is equal to price. This should come as no surprise. Since every unit the competitive firm sells is sold at the same price, then the addition to total revenues for the next (or incremental) unit sold (or MR) is always equal to this price. Thus, if $P = \$5$ per unit, then $MR = \$5$ per unit. One of the differences between a perfectly competitive firm and other firms is that the perfect competitor need not lower the price at which he or she sells in order to expand sales.

PROFIT MAXIMIZATION FOR THE FIRM IN THE SHORT RUN

We continue to assume that the firm's goal is profit maximization. Profits are defined here as the difference between total revenue, TR, and total cost, TC.

The concepts of profits

Profit is perhaps one of the most misunderstood economic concepts. Non-economists tend to include as part of profit some dollars which really go toward costs. To get a picture of this misconception, let's assume that you have accumulated savings of $100,000 and that you can purchase a variety of assets which will each yield a 12 percent annual return. Now let's assume that instead of purchasing one of those assets, such as a certificate of deposit or shares in a money market fund, you use your savings to start your own business. At the end of the year, after paying all costs, including a wage for yourself, your records show that there is a $12,000 "profit." Is that really a profit? It is in an accounting sense, but it is not an economic profit, because you could have earned that $12,000 elsewhere. Economic profit in this particular case would be exactly zero. You would have to earn revenues greater than all costs plus the opportunity cost of capital—the $12,000—to have made an economic profit.

Those investors who invest in a firm, whether they be proprietors or stockholders, must anticipate a rate of return that is at least as great as that which they could have earned elsewhere in investments of equal risk.

The divergence of accounting and economic profits

In our analysis, the average total cost curve includes the full opportunity costs of capital. Indeed, the average total cost curve includes the opportunity cost of *all* factors of production used in the production process. We define **economic profits** as those profits over and above what is required to keep capital in the firm. When economic profits are zero, **accounting profits** may still be positive. Consider an example. A baseball bat manufacturer sells bats at price P_1. The owners of the firm have invested their own capital in the business; they have borrowed no money from anyone. Moreover, assume that they explicitly pay the full opportunity cost of all factors of production, including any labor that they personally contribute to the business. In other words, they pay themselves salaries which show up as costs on the books, and those salaries are equal to what they could have earned in the next-best alternative occupation. At the end of the year, the owners find that after they subtract all explicit costs from total revenues they have earned $100,000. Their investment, we will say, was $1 million; thus, the rate of return on that investment during the first year was 10 percent per year. This turns out to be, we will assume, equal to the rate of return that, on average, all other baseball-bat manufacturers make in that industry.

This $100,000 per year income, or 10 percent rate of return, is actually a competitive or *normal* rate of return on invested capital in that industry. If the owners were making only $50,000 per year, or 5 percent, on their $1 million investment, they would have been able to make higher profits by leaving the industry and investing their $1 million elsewhere. Thus, we say that the 10 percent rate of return was the opportunity cost of capital. The accountants showed it as a profit; we call it a cost. We also include that cost in the average total cost curve that we draw.

Another case in which accounting profits exceed economic profits is that of the owner-run business in which the owner is an employee who does not explicitly pay himself or herself a market wage rate. In the typical "Mom and Pop" grocery store, the proprietors may not pay themselves any explicit wages at all. They may, however, work a combined total of 140 hours a week. Had they rented out their labor services, they would have received wages. In order to obtain economic profits, the hourly wage rate that they could have earned in their next-best alternative job times the number of hours they actually worked in the grocery store must be added to total costs. If there is still an excess of total revenues over total costs, the couple has earned an economic profit. We sometimes find owner-run enterprises in which economic profit is negative. The owners are willing to pay a premium for self-employment; that is, one of the goods consumed by the owners of such a business is self-employment, and this good, like all other scarce goods, has a positive purchase price.

The profit-maximizing rate of output

Since profits are defined as TR − TC, the profit-maximizing firm in a perfectly competitive industry (or any industry, for that matter) will produce the output at which the positive difference between TR and TC is maximized.

We have taken the cost data used in Chapter 9 and presented some of them in Table 10-1. We have also added some revenue information. The price per unit is given in column (2) and is assumed to be $9 per unit, regardless of the number of units produced and sold. Column (3) represents total revenues and is equal to price per unit times rate of output (all of which is sold). Total profits, then, are given in column (5) and are the difference between total revenues and total costs. We see that total profits are maximized at a rate of output of 11 as well as 12. The reason there are two rates of output which maximize profit is that we are working with discrete units. If

TABLE 10-1
Revenues, costs, and profits

Rate of output (units/ time period) (1)	Price ($/unit) (2)	Total revenues ($/unit time period) [(2) × (1)] (3)	Total costs ($/unit time period) (4)	Total profits ($/unit time period) [(3) − (4)] (5)	Marginal costs ($/unit) (6)	Marginal revenue ($/unit) (7)
0	9.00	0	10.00	−10.00	—	—
1	9.00	9.00	14.00	− 5.00	4.00	9.00
2	9.00	18.00	17.50	0.50	3.50	9.00
3	9.00	27.00	20.75	6.25	3.25	9.00
4	9.00	36.00	23.80	12.20	3.05	9.00
5	9.00	45.00	26.70	18.30	2.90	9.00
6	9.00	54.00	29.50	24.50	2.80	9.00
7	9.00	63.00	32.25	30.75	2.75	9.00
8	9.00	72.00	35.10	36.90	2.85	9.00
9	9.00	81.00	38.30	42.70	3.20	9.00
10	9.00	90.00	42.30	47.70	4.00	9.00
11	9.00	99.00	48.30	50.70	6.00	9.00
12	9.00	108.00	57.30	50.70	9.00	9.00
13	9.00	117.00	70.30	46.70	13.00	9.00
14	9.00	126.00	88.30	37.70	18.00	9.00
15	9.00	135.00	112.30	22.70	24.00	9.00

FIGURE 10-3
Profit maximization for the perfect competitor: TR − TC approach
Profit maximization dictates that the rate of output be set such that the positive difference between TR and TC is maximized. This occurs at an output rate of either 11 or 12. We know that the firm is a perfect competitor because the total revenue curve is a ray from the origin. Any quantity can be sold at $9 per unit. Note also that the tangent to the total cost cuve (which has the same slope as the total revenue curve) gives the profit-maximizing rate of output. That tangent is labeled *AA*. It is parallel to TR.

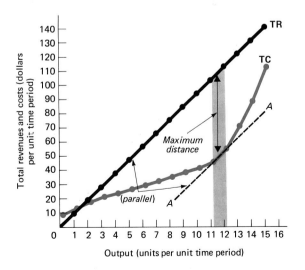

output was infinitely divisible, so that our profit and revenue measures were continuous, there would be only one profit-maximizing rate of output. To simplify matters we can arbitrarily say that the firm will always choose the larger of the two profit-maximizing rates of output.

Column (3) and column (4) from Table 10-1 are represented graphically in Figure 10-3. The total revenue curve TR is a straight line from the origin and has a slope of +9 (since the firm can sell all that it wants at a constant price of $9). The total cost curve is taken from column (4) of Table 10-1. The profit-maximizing rate of output is that rate which maximizes the vertical distance between the TR curve and the TC curve (if TR > TC). This is shown to be an output rate of 11 as well as 12 units per unit time period.

SHORT-RUN FIRM PROFIT-MAXIMIZING: THE MARGINAL APPROACH

We can do exactly the same thing we did in the previous section by looking at marginal quantities rather than total quantities.

In Figure 10-4, we have drawn in the marginal revenue curve horizontally at $9 per unit. This marginal revenue curve is the same as the demand curve *dd* facing each individual firm in a perfectly competitive market. It is given in column (7) of Table 10-1. The marginal cost curve is obtained by plotting the data from column (6) of Table 10-1.

Now we ask the question: What is the rate of output per unit time period that will maximize profits? The answer is that rate of output at which marginal revenue equals marginal cost.[3] This rate is indicated in Figure 10-4 by the shaded area below the marginal revenue curve between the output rates of 11 and 12 units per unit time period. If the rate of output were in excess of 12 units, marginal cost would exceed marginal revenue for the additional units and total profits would be less than at 11.5 units. If the output rate were less than 11 units per unit time period, marginal revenue would exceed marginal cost and total profits could be increased by expanding production to 11.5 units. Again, the profit-maximizing rate of output is 11 as well as 12 units (Figure 10-4) per unit time period because we are dealing in discrete units.

The short-run break-even price

Rather than continuing to deal in discrete units, we will generalize our diagrammatic analysis and deal with smooth curves that still retain the essence of cost and revenue conditions facing the firm. We will no longer use the specific data contained in Table 10-1.

Look now at Figure 10-5. Here we have shown a marginal cost curve,

---

[3]We must further specify that the marginal cost curve cut the marginal revenue curve from below. If the marginal cost curve cuts the marginal revenue curve from above and MR = MC, we have *loss* maximization.

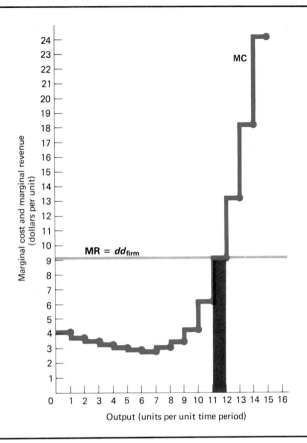

FIGURE 10-4
Profit maximization: MR − MC approach
Profits are maximized at an output rate at which marginal revenue equals marginal cost. For the perfectly competitive firm, marginal revenue is the same as its demand curve *dd*. It is a horizontal line, here at $9 per unit. The marginal cost curve is taken from column (6) of Table 10-1. The profit-maximizing rate of output is either 11 or 12 units per unit time period.

an average total cost curve, and an average variable cost curve. At any price above P_1, the firm will find that each unit it sells fetches a price that exceeds average total cost and hence generates positive economic profits. However, at price P_1, the price line is just tangent to the minimum point on the average total cost curve; the firm will find that there is no difference between price per unit and average total cost. This is, of course, the output at which the marginal cost curve intersects the average total cost curve at the latter's minimum. We call point E the short-run break-even point, and we call price P_1, the **short-run break-even price**.

The short-run shutdown price

Will the firm automatically shut down if the price at which it can sell its output falls below P_1? The answer is no, not necessarily. It is true that at a price below P_1, average *total* costs are not being covered. However, at prices below P_1 but above average variable cost the firm has more than covered the costs of staying in operation, and shutting down does not become necessary. If the firm chose to shut down, it would lose all of its revenues but end only

FIGURE 10-5
The firm's short-run break-even and shutdown points
Any price line represents a marginal revenue curve for the perfect competitor, and the profit-maximizing rate of output is always the output at which the price line intersects the marginal cost curve. The short-run break-even point is at E. The short-run break-even price is P_1, the price that just covers average total costs. The short-run shutdown point is at E'; the short-run shutdown price is P_2 and is equal to the minimum average variable cost. It does not pay the firm to continue production if it cannot at least cover variable costs.

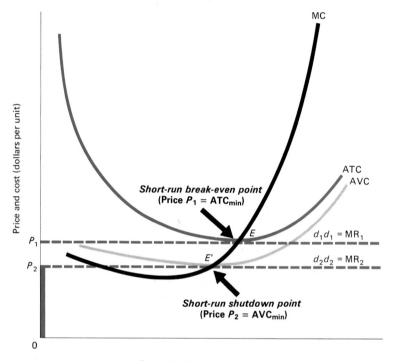

Output (units per unit time period)

its variable costs. It would still have to cover its fixed or unavoidable costs. Since a firm for which ATC > MR > AVC is more than covering its variable costs of operation, such a firm can minimize the losses it experiences, due to the existence of fixed costs, by continuing to operate.

The firm will never want to produce at a price below average *variable* cost. For by doing so, it would be actually lowering the net worth position of the owners. In other words, they would be suffering short-run losses greater than fixed costs. For example, if average variable cost is $2 but the given market price of the commodity is $1.50, the firm will lose out-of-pocket (immediately) 50¢ for every unit it produces. It is better to shut down since variable costs are not even covered and operation, thus, merely adds to losses.

In Figure 10-5, we can see this more explicitly. Price P_2, which is obtained by finding the intersection of the marginal cost curve with the (minimum point on the) average variable cost curve, is a price below which this firm will not continue production in the short run. This intersection is labeled E'. It is marked the short-run shutdown point. The price P_2 is the **short-run shutdown price**. Another way of looking at this is to consider any price between P_1 and P_2. Such a price yields a rate of return on invested capital of only, say, 4 percent per year when the rate of return on capital elsewhere in the economy is, say, 8 percent per year. In other words, the rate of profitability in this firm is one-half what it could be elsewhere. However, due to the fact that the investor must meet certain fixed contractual obligations, or due to the fact that there has been an investment in specialized machinery with little or no resale value, the investor is better off accepting a below-market return on the sunk investment rather than "writing off" the entire amount invested.

As long as the market price exceeds the shutdown price, the investor gets something back on the original investment, even though he or she may not be earning very much on it. If, however, the market price falls *permanently* below the shutdown price, the investor loses forever everything that was invested.

Even if the market price falls below the shutdown price P_2, the firm may shut down only temporarily. The shutdown point is defined only at a moment in time. The firm might want to wait out a downturn in the market by easing current production and then start up again if and when the market price moves up. If we take this consideration into account, average variable costs ought to include the opportunity costs of closing down and starting up again.

TOTAL COSTS AND PROFITS

Perhaps the fact that we labeled E in Figure 10-5 the break-even point may have disturbed you. At E and price P_1, price is just equal to average total costs. If this is the case, why would a firm continue to produce if it were making no profit whatsoever? To answer this question we again make the distinction between accounting profit and economic profit. At price P_1 the firm has zero economic profit but positive accounting profit. Normal profit for the firms in this industry is one of the elements incorporated into the firms' cost curves.

The ATC curve and economic profits

While it is true in the short run that minimum short-run ATC can be below or above the price line, we should be aware that in the long run the ATC curve can move up or down. Assume for a moment that at some outputs short-run ATC is below the price line. That means that the firm receives positive economic profits. What would happen now if the owner of this firm sold the firm to someone else? With competition in the market for assets, the selling price of the firm would be a price that would just yield the new owner a *normal* rate of return. This is a rate of return that would just equal the opportunity cost of the owner's invested capital. Otherwise stated, the future stream of positive economic profits associated with this firm would be capitalized and included in the sale price of the firm, so long as the assets responsible for these higher than normal profits are transferable with the firm (see Chapter 6). Now, what would the average total cost curve for the *new* owner look like? It would rise to take account of the price that was paid for the firm. In fact, it would rise so that it became tangent to the price line, and the new owner would be making zero economic profits and "normal" accounting profits.

Since the original owners of the firm always have the option to sell it, whether they actually do so or not, their decision not to sell would mean that they have higher alternative costs than before. Thus, regardless of who owns the firm, economic costs will rise to eliminate any economic profits in the long run.

The ATC curve and economic losses

In the opposite situation, if a firm were suffering economic losses and potential buyers anticipated that these losses would persist into the future, the sale price of the firm would be reduced from what it was previously by the present discounted value of the economic losses. Thus, the average total cost curve for owners would be lower than before. It would move down until it was just tangent to the price line, and the owner would make a normal rate of return in the long run, nothing more and nothing less. (Note that if the price fell below P_2 in Figure 10-5 and was expected to stay there, the firm would be worth only the scrap value of its physical assets.) Moreover, if the industry rate of return is not sufficiently high compared with that of other industries, no new plants will be built in the industry. Investment decisions are made on the basis of comparisons among alternative possibilities.

THE FIRM'S SHORT-RUN SUPPLY CURVE

We saw in the preceding several sections that the firm would never produce at a price below average variable cost. The firm will, however, produce at prices above the average variable cost curve. Remember that the price line coincides with the marginal revenue line, which in turn coincides with the individual firm's demand curve. We can in principle draw an infinite number of price lines above the intersection of the marginal cost curve with the average variable cost curve, and we can then find the resultant quantities that will be supplied at each of these prices. (Those quantities are found at each of the points of intersection between successively higher price, or MR, lines and the marginal cost curve.) Therefore, the firm's short-run supply curve, which by definition shows the quantity the firm will supply at each

FIGURE 10-6
The individual firm's supply curve
Here we show the marginal cost curve MC and three different individual demand curves. The first one is *dd*. If the demand curve is *dd*, the equilibrium, or profit-maximizing, point for the firm will be at the intersection of *dd* and MC, or at *E*. It will produce q_1. If the firm's demand curve shifts up to *d'd'*, the new intersection will be at *E'* and output will be q_2. If the demand curve falls to *d"d"*, the new intersection is at *E"*. The firm will produce only q_0. The supply curve, then, for the individual firm is that portion of its marginal cost curve above the shutdown point, or point *A*. That is at the point of the intersection of the average variable cost curve and the marginal cost curve. Thus, the supply curve is only the heavily shaded portion of the MC curve.

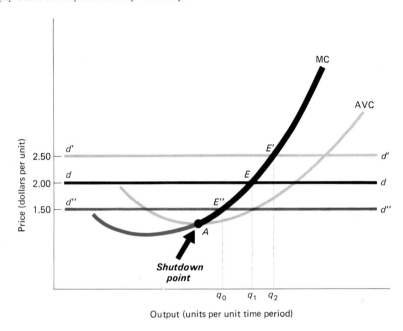

price, is coincident with its marginal cost curve above the average variable cost curve. We have drawn the firm's supply curve as the heavy solid portion of the marginal cost curve in Figure 10-6.

THE SHORT-RUN INDUSTRY SUPPLY CURVE

The short-run industry supply curve can be found by horizontally summing all the individual firms' short-run supply curves. In order to "horizontally sum" these short-run firm supply curves, we add together the quantities supplied by each firm at each price. We do this for a simple example of two firms in Figure 10-7, panels (*a*) and (*b*). The marginal cost curves for the

▬▬▬▬▬▬

FIGURE 10-7

Deriving the industry supply curve

We assume there are only two firms in this industry. Marginal cost curves above average minimum variable cost
are presented in panels (a) and (b) for firms a and b. We horizontally sum the two quantities supplied, q_1^a and q_1^b
at price P_1. This gives us point F. We do the same thing for the quantities at price P_2. This gives us point G. When
we connect those two points, we have the industry supply curve SS which is the horizontal summation of the
firms' marginal cost curves above their respective average minimum costs.

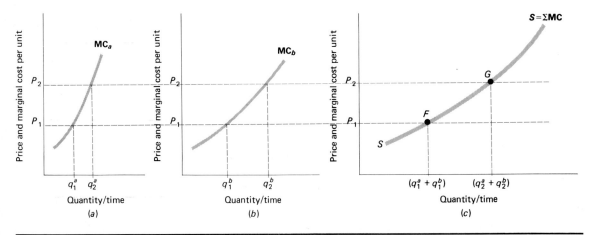

two separate firms are presented as MC_a in panel (a) and MC_b in panel (b).
Those two marginal cost curves are drawn only for prices above the minimum
average variable cost for each respective firm. Hence, we are not including
any of the section of the marginal cost curves below minimum average variable cost. In panel (a) for firm A at price P_1, the quantity supplied would
be q_1^a. At price P_2, the quantity supplied would be q_2^a. In panel (b), we see
the two different quantities corresponding to the two prices that would be
supplied by firm B. Now we horizontally add for price P_1 the quantity q_1^a
and q_1^b. This gives us one point, F, for our short-run **industry supply curve**,
SS. We obtain the other point, G, by doing the same horizontal adding of
quantities at P_2. When we connect points F and G, we obtain short-run
industry supply curve SS, which is also marked as Σ (the summation sign)
MC, or horizontal summation of the marginal cost curves (above the respective minimum average variable cost of each firm).

We note also that this short-run industry supply curve is the horizontal
summation of each individual firm's marginal cost curve only so long as
input prices remain constant. It is possible that the simultaneous increase
in the output of *all* firms in an industry may cause input prices to rise. In
such cases, the industry supply curve will be more steeply sloped (and less
price-elastic) than if input prices remain constant.

FIRM PROFITS AND LOSSES

For the perfectly competitive firm, the price of the commodity is given. The economic profits or losses that the firm incurs depend in the short run on the position of its average total cost curve in relation to the price of the commodity.

In panels (a) and (b) in Figure 10-8, we depict the situation facing two firms in a competitive industry. Both firms face a horizontal demand curve at price P_e. In panel (a), the profit-maximizing rate of output is found at the intersection of the marginal cost curve with the demand (or marginal revenue) curve. In panel (a), this is at point e; the equilibrium rate of output for firm 1 is q_1. The average total cost curve is ATC_1. At the rate of output of q_1, firm 1 makes a profit per unit equal to the vertical distance between point e and point A. When we multiply the per unit profit by the quantity, we get the shaded-in rectangle labeled "profits," which represents pure economic profits: revenues over and above all opportunity costs, including capital. In

FIGURE 10-8

Economic profits and losses

In panel (a) we show a situation where the marginal cost curve MC intersects the marginal revenue curve $(=dd)$ at point e. At the profit-maximizing rate of output q_1, average total costs are A. Economic profits are represented by the shaded area. In panel (b) we show economic losses; the differences between price P_e and average total cost is the vertical distance between A' and e'. When we multiply that by quantity sold, we obtain the shaded rectangle labeled "losses."

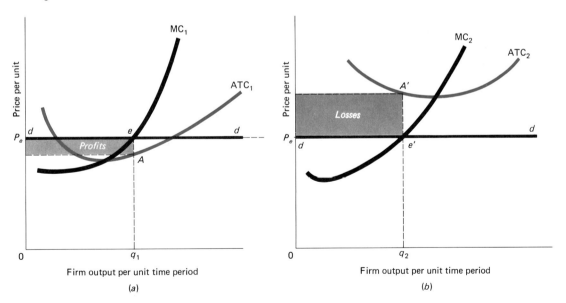

panel (b), we show a situation where pure economic losses are being incurred. The important difference between firm 2 in panel (b) and firm 1 in panel (a) is that firm 2 has a higher average total cost curve. Its losses per unit are given by the vertical distance between A' and e'. Total losses are represented by the shaded-in rectangle.

LONG-RUN EQUILIBRIUM FOR THE FIRM: THE SELECTION OF AN OPTIMAL SCALE OF OPERATION

In the long run the firm can change the scale of its plant. We should assume that in the long run the firm would adjust plant size in such a way that it had no further incentive to change. Since we are assuming profit maximization, in the long run the firm should be producing in such a way that profit is maximized. In the short run it will do this by setting short-run marginal cost equal to price. This same principle will also govern in the long run. Long-run marginal cost will also equal price, and as we shall see, long-run marginal cost will also equal short-run marginal cost at the profit-maximizing rate of output and equilibrium scale of plant.

Consider the firm depicted in Figure 10-9. Assume that the anticipated long-run equilibrium price of the commodity in question is P_1. Assume that the firm is starting out with a plant whose scale leads to the short-run cost curves given by SAC_1 and SMC_1. The firm will produce quantity q_1 because this is the output at which the short-run marginal cost curve for plant size 1 intersects the price line (which is the firm's demand curve and marginal revenue curve). Given costs represented by SAC_1, the firm will make a per unit profit equal to the vertical distance between P_1 and C_1 and a total profit equal to P_1C_1FE.

This is not, however, a long-run profit-maximizing position for the firm. It can expand the scale of plant and increase its profit. First of all we note that at output rate q_1, the firm was not "on" its long-run average cost curve. That is, with a plant size given by SAC_1, minimum costs of producing a unit of output at q_1 are $0C_1$ not $0C_3$. However, at output rate q_2, the firm is on its long-run average cost curve if it produces with a plant size given by SAC_2. Note that SAC_2 is just tangent to the long-run average cost curve at point A and point A is directly below the point where $SMC_2 = LMC = P_1$. Profit per unit will increase from the vertical distance P_1 to C_1 to the vertical distance between P_1 and C_2, and total profit will increase from P_1C_1FE to P_1C_2AB. The important thing to realize about the long-run profit-maximizing rate of output is that the firm's short-run marginal cost = long-run marginal cost = the price of the product:

$$SMC = LMC = P \qquad\qquad\qquad \textbf{(10-3)}$$

(and at the same long-run q, SAC = LAC).

FIGURE 10-9
Long-run equilibrium for a competitive firm
If the long-run equilibrium price is P_1, the optimal plant is not given by the cost curves SAC_1 and SMC_1, for, at the profit-maximizing rate of output with that plant, q_1, the firm is not operating on the long-run average cost curve LAC. The firm would want to expand its plant until its cost curves were given by SAC_2 and SMC_2. The profit-maximizing rate of output is q_2; the firm is operating on LAC. Profits per unit have increased from the vertical distance between P_1 and C_1 to the vertical distance between P_1 and C_2.

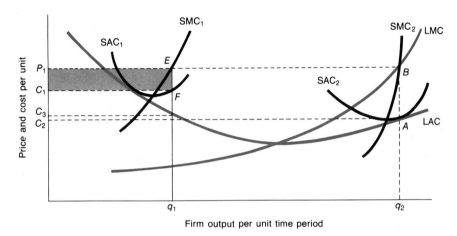

Profits: inducement to entry

However, even though this may be the long-run desired profit-maximizing position of the firm with respect to plant size—or, otherwise stated, the firm's optimal plant size—the competitive firm does not operate in a vacuum. It cannot regulate its market conditions or the behavior of other economic decision makers. The area of P_1C_2AB represents total economic profits earned by a firm in this industry in each time period. Such economic profits will induce other firms to enter the industry. Entry into the industry will cause the industry supply curve to shift outward, as seen in panel (a) of Figure 10-10. But the shifting outward of the supply curve from SS to S'S', due to entry into the industry, reduces the equilibrium price from P_e to P_e'. The industry rate of output per unit time period will increase from Q_e to Q_e'. The reduction in the price will clearly have an effect on the optimal plant size in the long run for the perfectly competitive firm. At this lower price, the optimal plant size will no longer be represented by plant size 2 in Figure 10-9. It will be a smaller plant. There will be a movement down the long-run average cost curve LAC.

When does this process stop? It stops when the perfectly competitive firm is making zero economic profits in the long run. This is represented by panel (b) in Figure 10-10. The long-run equilibrium of a perfectly competitive firm occurs when the price, or dd curve, is equal to the minimum long-run average cost, which necessarily corresponds to the minimum short-run av-

FIGURE 10-10
Long-run competitive equilibrum

If economic profits such as those depicted in Figure 10-9 are being made, there will be entry into the industry. The supply curve will shift rightward in panel (a) from SS to S'S'. The industry output will increase from Q_e to Q'_e; the market-clearing price will fall from P_e to P'_e. The firm eventually will find itself in the situation depicted in panel (b) where, at the profit-maximizing rate of output q_e, LAC = LMC = P'_e = SMC = SAC. No economic profits or losses are being made.

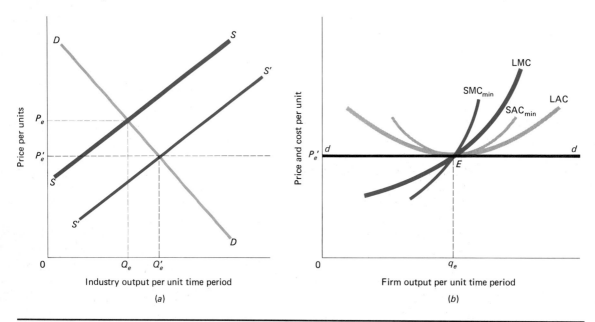

(a)   (b)

erage cost, and, necessarily, to both the short-run marginal cost and long-run marginal cost. This point at output q_e is marked E in panel (b), where SMC = SAC = LAC = LMC = P'_e. The long-run equilibrium rate of output for the perfectly competitive firm is rate q_e.

Note again that zero economic profits mean *positive* accounting profits. Zero economic profits mean that all factors of production, including equity capital, are paid their opportunity cost.

ECONOMIC RENTS

Even though the long-run equilibrium position of the competitive firm is one of zero economic profits, there may be, in full equilibrium of the competitive firms and industry, returns above this level. We call these returns **economic rents**.

Consider an individual with extraordinary entrepreneurial talents. That person may be able to generate positive economic profits, even in a perfectly competitive industry. These economic profits will, however, necessarily be paid out by the firm to the entrepreneur in the form of a higher wage for his or her services. This unusually productive entrepreneur, or any unusually productive factor, can extract the full value of any higher-than-normal profits generated for a firm, because of competition for such services. Thus, although one firm may have more productive factors than other firms, it must pay these factors higher wages equal to their superior productivity or lose them to other firms. Ultimately, then, each firm in an industry ends up with the same costs and profit rates as all others, although some will have high costs in one category and others higher costs in other categories.[4]

PERFECT COMPETITION AND OPTIMUM RESOURCE ALLOCATION

The perfectly competitive solution is one in which price equals marginal cost. Remember that marginal cost represents the cost of changing production by one unit. Suppose a marginal cost curve shows that an increase in production from 10,000 bushels of wheat to 10,001 bushels of wheat will cost $3. That $3 represents the opportunity cost of producing one more bushel of wheat. The marginal cost curve, therefore, is a graphic representation of the opportunity cost of production or the true scarcity of the product.

The perfectly competitive firm will produce at a quantity such that price equals marginal cost. The perfectly competitive firm sells its product at a price that just equals the incremental cost to society—that is, the opportunity cost—for that is what the marginal cost curve represents. A competitive situation where $P = MC$, therefore, is a situation in which the marginal (opportunity) cost is just equal to the marginal value of the good to "society," reflected in the price that people will pay for that rate of output. Hence, if price were raised higher than marginal cost, there would be "too little" produced. If price were below marginal cost, "too much" would be produced. The perfectly competitive market mechanism causes suppliers to produce whatever output consumers desire. The allocation of resources is therefore at an optimum. (A fuller discussion is presented in Chapter 18).

AN ASIDE: ECONOMIES OF SCOPE

In this text we generally follow the convention of considering only single-product firms. However, many firms produce more than one product, and the proportion of such firms is growing rather than declining.

Given what we already know about the advantages of specialization,

---

[4]Recall, however, that if an owner/manager of a firm does not pay himself or herself a full market wage, the accounting profit of the firm can exceed its economic profits.

why would firms divide resources and efforts between two or more production processes? In other words, what can be the origin of **economies of scope**—the savings in costs to firms engaged in multiproduct production? The explanation may be found in the technical characteristics of the firm's production process.

The notion of economies of scope rests upon the existence of some input that is owned by a firm as a necessary ingredient in the production of one of its outputs, but which can also be used, without "crowding" (affecting the cost of production of the "first" output), in the production of some other output(s). When any input has this characteristic it is said to be *shareable* or *quasi-public*, and the costs of providing the outputs produced with this input are said to be "subadditive."

For example, consider a firm that, due to zoning regulations, must construct a building that is larger than originally planned to house its operations. If this firm is prohibited from renting the "excess" space, or prefers not to share its facilities with outsiders, it may decide to use the space for a new production process. Laws and regulations, or simply the institutional or physical infeasibility of dividing up units of an input between different firms, can be the source of the saving in costs resulting from a combination of production processes within one firm.

Other examples of economies of scope from the real world include electric power generation during peak and off-peak periods, indivisible equipment (machines or assembly lines), heat sources that are only partially used in the primary production process, and multiuse human capital. You should also note that the long-recognized category of *joint products*, like leather and beef from the input "cattle," is properly a subset of "shareable inputs."

ISSUES AND APPLICATIONS

The soil bank program

In Chapter 2 we presented an analysis of price supports in agriculture. As with all situations in which the government attempts to set a minimum price (price support) which exceeds the market-clearing price, the result is an excess quantity supplied at that minimum price. This excess quantity supplied has often been given the name "surplus" in agriculture. In order to eliminate surpluses, the government has at times engaged in "conservation" or soil bank programs in which a certain amount of arable land had to be left unused in order for the owners of the land to participate in the price-support program. The results of the soil bank program can be seen in Figure 10-11.

We start off in equilibrium with DD and SS intersecting at point E, an equilibrium price of P_e, and an equilibrium quantity of Q_e. A price support is put into effect at the price P_{min}. The government knows that at that price there would be surpluses, and so it restricts the amount of land available. However, when it restricts the amount of land available, it changes the shape of the supply curve. Even-

FIGURE 10-11
Soil bank program
If price controls are set at P_{min}, there will be a "surplus" at that price equal to the difference between Q_S, the amount of output farmers will provide at that price level, and Q'_e, the amount consumers will buy at that price. To eliminate the surplus, the government restricts the amount of land that may be devoted to producing the crop that receives the price support. That is reflected at point A—the number of acres that farmers may plant. As they increase other inputs the supply curve rotates to now become SAS'. If the soil bank program is effective, the surplus is eliminated and there is an equilibrium at E', due to the constraint on supply.

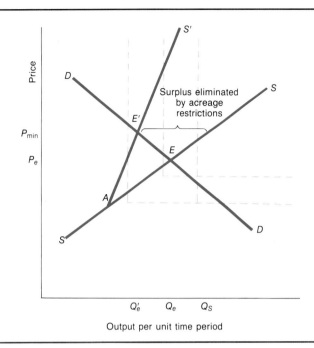

tually, the supply curve rotates to SAS'. Point A is the point on the supply curve that reflects the amount of product that would be produced from the existing land treated in the same manner as before—but eliminating some land from production. That is, the soil bank program may take 25 percent of all farmers' land out of production. If they did not change their treatment of that land they would produce at point A. However, that land is unrestricted and is now farmed more intensively. The farmer cultivates the noncontrolled land more diligently—applying more fertilizer, labor, seed, pest control, etc. This then causes the cost per unit of production to rise along segment AS' of the supply curve. If the soil bank program meets its objectives, there is no surplus.

This example shows how constraining the market in one manner (the introduction of price supports) can produce a problem (the surplus) that leads to another constraint (the soil bank program).

The effect of a per unit tax on relative prices

Consider a commodity that is sold in various qualities. Take the example of cigarettes. A package of cigarettes can contain cigarettes using higher-quality tobacco or lower-quality tobacco. What happens to the *relative* price of higher-quality tobacco cigarettes when a per unit (specific) tax of, say 10¢ is put on each package of cigarettes? It falls. This can be seen in the following numerical example.

In Table 10-2, we see that prior to the 10¢ tax on a pack of cigarettes, the relative price of higher quality to lower quality is 2:1. That

TABLE 10-2
Effect of a specific tax on the relative price of differing qualities of cigarettes

	Higher quality	Lower quality	Relative prices
Price before tax	40¢	20¢	2:1
Price after tax	50¢	30¢	5:3

is, lower-quality cigarettes cost 50 percent of what higher-quality cigarettes cost. After the per unit tax of 10¢, however, the relative price of higher-quality to lower-quality cigarettes changes from 5 to 3. After the tax, lower-quality cigarettes cost 60 percent of the price of higher-quality cigarettes. Their relative price has gone up. A smaller quantity will be demanded after the tax than before, relative to higher-quality cigarettes.[5] Indeed, this ac-

[5]This discussion ignores income effects and certain other problems. See John P. Gould and Joel Segall, "The Substitution Effects of Transportation Costs," *Journal of Political Economy*, January/February 1968, pp. 130–137. Additionally, in order for the price of cigarettes to go up by exactly 10¢, we are assuming perfect competition and free entry.

tually happened in the United States, and as the theory would predict, lower-quality cigarettes gradually disappeared from the market. Had an equal *percentage* tax been put on all brands of cigarettes, the situation would have been different. An equal percentage tax per pack of cigarettes, based on the selling price of each pack, would not have affected the relative prices of the various qualities of cigarettes. That is to say, high-quality- and low-quality-tobacco products would have maintained their relative prices even after the equal percentage tax was put on. The consumer may, of course, change the proportion of income devoted to the purchase of this good in any case—whether the good is inferior or superior and the proportionate tax alters real income.

Can price controls work?

We can use the analysis of the competitive industry to predict the effects of price controls. When the maximum price that is imposed by law is below the market-clearing price (or the price that would prevail in the absence of any centralized coercion), the results can be predicted.

PRICE CONTROLS IN THEIR SIMPLEST FORM

Let us take a simple case in which a maximum price is put on the product of an industry that sells its product directly to the consumer. We

represent this situation in Figure 10-12. The market-clearing price is P_e, and the equilibrium quantity supplied and demanded at that price is Q_e. The government sets the maximum price at P_{max}. At that price, however, the quantity demanded increases to Q_D but the quantity supplied falls to Q_S. The difference is an excess quantity demanded (or "shortage") at price P_{max}. If the only amount available remained at Q_S, consumers would be willing to pay P'_e. If indeed it is legally impossible for consumers to pay a higher price, the excess quantity demanded will manifest itself in queues. More realistically, ways

▬▬▬

FIGURE 10-12
Price controls: no black markets
If an effective price control is put on at price P_{max}, the quantity demanded Q_D will exceed the quantity supplied Q_s. For that quantity supplied, the differences will be called a shortage. That quantity Q_s could be sold at price P'_e.

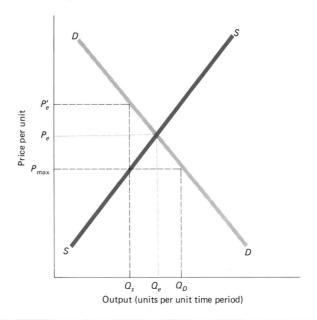

around price controls—black markets and decreases in quality—will be devised.

TAKING ACCOUNT OF BLACK MARKETS

The analysis given for Figure 10-12 is incomplete because it does not take account of the possibility of black markets arising. We define a **black market** as a market in which the product in question is sold at a price above the legal maximum.

SANCTIONS IMPOSED ON SUPPLIERS ONLY

In this situation, we assume that there are no sanctions imposed whatsoever on demanders, and moreover, the demanders find no distastefulness in using a black market. Hence, we are assuming no legal or psychic costs involved in black market transactions on the demander's side. On the supplier's side, however, we will assume added risk and added cost because of the possibility of sanctions,

which may include public chastisement, fines, and jail terms.

In Figure 10-13, we draw in the unrestricted supply and demand curves SS and DD. The market-clearing price without restrictions would be P_e, and the equilibrium quantity would be Q_e. A price maximum is imposed at P_{max}. At such a price, without a black market, the quantity demanded is given by Q_D and the quantity supplied is given by Q_S. Now, producers enter the black market. The supply curve becomes SCS_B. It pivots at the intersection of the maximum price with the original supply curve. It pivots counterclockwise because suppliers willing to offer the product in the black market at a price in excess of the legal maximum incur additional costs equal to the risks of penalty. Thus, the only way that they will offer more of the product is by being compensated for this additional expected cost.

In this situation, the black-market supply curve, SCS_B, intersects the original demand curve DD at price P_B. Consumers will purchase the quantity $Q_S Q_B$ in the black market at price P_B.

FIGURE 10-13
Price controls: black-market sanctions on suppliers only

It is assumed that demanders run no risk when engaging in black-market dealings and also incur no moral costs. The supply curve SS now becomes SCS_B. It pivots at the intersection of P_{max} with the original supply curve. This is because firms engaging in illegal black-market dealings incur higher costs and must be compensated. The intersection of the black-market supply curve with the demand curve DD is at P_B. The black-market quantity supplied and demanded will be Q_sQ_B at that price.

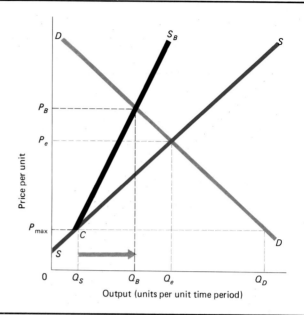

In this particular case, the black-market price exceeds the original unregulated market-clearing price but is lower than that price which would prevail at output Q_S were there no black-market production.

MODIFYING OUR ASSUMPTIONS

Let us consider the same set of assumptions as we did in the analysis presented in Figure 10-13, but note how the assumptions one makes can change some of the details of the analysis, although not the basic result.

The shape of the supply curve in Figure 10-13, SCS_B, was drawn under the assumption that it becomes increasingly costly to supply more and more units of the good to the market—that is, that the possibility of punishment by the price enforcers rises continuously. That is why the new curve diverged from the original supply curve and the distance between the two curves grows as supply increased.

One can assume a different enforcement policy of the price controls. Perhaps every supplier incurs a fixed cost for operating in the black market, but it does not matter how much the individual sells in the black market. Maybe every seller has to pay a $10 bribe every month to the price controllers to look the other way. In this case the supply curve looks like $SCC'S_B'$ in Figure 10-14. That is, the cost of supplying the good jumps up the distance CC' (to reflect the suppliers' cost of paying the bribe), so the new supply curve is higher than the original supply curve but parallel to it.

The result of the analysis is the same—less is supplied to the public than if the market were unconstrained, and the price paid by many consumers is higher than it would have been in the uncontrolled market. This is the equivalent of a "lump-sum tax" on the good in question, rather than the equivalent of a progressive tax as in the case in the previous figure.

FIGURE 10-14
Price controls: black-market sanctions on suppliers only, another possibility
As in the last figure, it is assumed that the demand curve is unchanged by the price control. The supply curve SS in this case becomes SCC'S'$_B$. It is a discontinuous supply curve, jumping from point C up to C' once level Q$_s$ has been supplied. This increase means that the cost of doing business at all points has been increased the same amount for all suppliers.

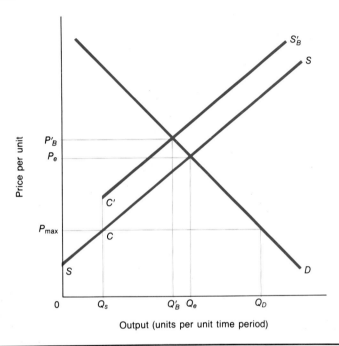

Output (units per unit time period)

SUMMARY

1   Scarcity implies rivalry and competition.

2   The definition of perfect competition implies a complete absence of rivalry because the product is homogeneous and there is perfect information. Thus, in order to analyze real-world issues, we must relax one or more of the assumptions in the model of perfect competition.

3   Claims that the assumption of the model of pure competition are unrealistic are not important. The test of a model's usefulness is its ability to predict compared to alternative models.

4   Price acts as a rationing criterion, and this is discriminatory; however, all systems of rationing are, by necessity, discriminatory by virtue of the criteria established for distribution of commodities.

5 The demand curve facing a perfectly competitive firm is horizontal. Its elasticity is $-\infty$.

6 Marginal revenue for a perfect competitor is equal to price.

7 The profit-maximizing rate of output for the perfect competitor is the output at which marginal revenue equals marginal cost. Since marginal revenue equals price in a perfectly competitive industry, the firm produces the output at which marginal cost equals price.

8 In the short run, the firm makes no economic profits at a price which just covers average *total* costs. In the short run, the firm will shut down below the price which just covers minimum average *variable* costs.

9 The industry supply curve is the horizontal summation of each firm's marginal cost curve above its respective average variable cost curve.

10 It is important to distinguish between accounting and economic profits; the latter refers to those profits which are left over after the opportunity cost of all inputs is subtracted from total revenues.

11 In the long run, the short-run break-even point is actually the going-out-of-business point; if price falls below that point, the opportunity cost of capital will not be covered; the firm will not stay in the industry (at least not with that set of facilities).

12 In a price system, resources flow to industries that are making higher-than-average, risk-adjusted rates of return (economic profits) and resources flow out of industries or are not reinvested in industries that are making economic losses.

13 In the long run, the competitive firm produces an output q_e at which $LMC = LAC = SMC = SAC_{min} = P_e$.

GLOSSARY

- **perfect competition** A model of industrial or market organization that requires (1) homogeneity of product, (2) unfettered resource mobility, (3) large numbers of buyers and sellers, and (4) product divisibility.
- **rivalry** The commonsense notion of competition in which economic agents attempt to improve their net worth by advertising, marketing, developing new products, and so on.
- **survivorship principle** In a world of scarce resources, firms which make the "right" decisions survive, and others must imitate them.
- **immediate run or market period** That period of time in which the stock (supply) is fixed and cannot be increased.
- **industry** A group of firms that produces a homogeneous product.
- **economic profits** The pure profit left over when all costs, including the full opportunity cost of all inputs, are subtracted from total revenues.

■ **accounting profits** The profits shown on the firm's books which may not have taken full account of *all* explicit and implicit costs of production, including the opportunity cost of capital; to be contrasted with the broader notion of economic profits.

■ **short-run break-even price** That price which just covers short-run average total costs.

■ **short-run shutdown price** A price equal to minimum short-run AVC; the price below which the firm will shut down production in the short run.

■ **industry supply curve** The locus of points showing the minimum prices at which given quantities will be forthcoming; also called the market supply curve.

■ **economic rents** Any payment in excess of that just necessary to maintain a resource in its current activity at its current quantity.

■ **economies of scope** Cost savings that occur because of the ability to combine two or more product lines within a single firm more cheaply than if produced separately.

■ **black market** A market in which goods are sold at prices which exceed the legally stipulated maximum.

QUESTIONS

(Answers to even-numbered questions are at back of text.)

1 In our model of a perfectly competitive market, does an individual firm compete with others and, if so, how?

2 In a perfectly competitive market, what is the difference between the demand facing the industry and the demand facing an individual firm?

3 Explain how goods are rationed in the immediate run (market period) in a perfectly competitive market.

4 List five criteria, other than price, which might be used to ration a scarce good.

5 Look at Figure 10-3. Geometrically speaking, how would MC and MR be portrayed? What then would be the geometric solution, using Figure 10-3, for profit maximization?

6 Why might a firm continue to produce in the short run, even though the going price was less than its average to total cost?

7 Why would the perfect competition model predict that if price is above ATC and is expected to remain there, new firms will enter the industry?

8 You have a friend who earns $10,000 per year working for a collection agency. She quits her job, takes $100,000 out of the savings and loan where it was earning 8 percent per year, and buys a car wash. She shows you her tax return after a year of operations, and it shows that the car wash had a pretax "profit" of $16,000. "What do you think about that?" she remarks. What is your answer?

9 What is one possible danger in deriving an industry's short-run supply curve by summing the MC curves (above AVC) of the individual firms?

10 "When a good's price is 'clearing the market' (at equilibrium), everybody is happy, but disequilibrium prices are bound to make somebody mad." Criticize this statement.

11 "If there's anything I can't stand, it's a bar or restaurant that sets its prices *too low*." Complete this person's statement.

12 Construct a supply-and-demand diagram for a "free" good (one which is not scarce).

13 In long-run equilibrium, what is the relation between the various per unit cost and revenue variables? Why must these equalities hold?

14 Suppose you know someone who is very good at making economic profits in perfectly competitive industries in which everyone else is barely covering all the costs. How would you explain (or explain away) this phenomenon?

15 Do you see any inconsistency between a federal "farm program" and a federal "wage-price control program"? If so, what is it?

SELECTED REFERENCES

Knight, Frank H., *Risk, Uncertainty and Profit* (New York: Harper & Row, 1921; reprint edition, 1965), chaps. 1, 5, and 6.

Machlup, Fritz, *Economics of Sellers' Competition* (Baltimore: Johns Hopkins, 1952), pp. 79–85, 116–125.

Marshall, Alfred, *Principles of Economics,* 8th ed. (London: Macmillan, 1920), book 5, chaps. 4–5.

Panzar, John C., and Robert D. Willig, "Economies of Scope," *American Economic Review,* vol. 71, May 1981, pp. 268–272.

Samuelson, Paul A., "Dynamic Process Analysis," in H.S. Ellis (ed.), *A Survey of Contemporary Economics* (Philadelphia: Blakiston, 1948), chap. 10.

———, "Dynamics, Statics, and the Stationary States," *Review of Economics and Statistics,* vol. 25, February 1943, pp. 58–68.

Smith, Vernon, "An Experimental Study of Competitive Market Behavior," *Journal of Political Economy,* vol. 70, April 1962, pp. 111–137.

Stigler, George, "Perfect Competition, Historically Contemplated," *Journal of Political Economy,* vol. 65, February 1957, pp. 1–17.

Wicksteed, P.H., *The Common Sense of Political Economy* (London: Routledge, 1934), vol. 2, book 3.

Competitive markets and the role of entrepreneurship

*T*he previous chapter considered the competitive firm and its adjustment to equilibrium in the short run and in the long run. The significant feature of a competitive firm, distinguishing it from a monopolist or a less-than-perfect competitor, is that the competitive firm is a price taker. It can do nothing about the market revenue conditions (demand equals market price) that it faces, but it can sell all it wants at the prevailing market price.

THE COMPETITIVE INDUSTRY

Our definition of a perfectly competitive firm would seem to give us some hint about what a **competitive industry** is like. By definition, an industry composed entirely of competitive firms would, itself, have to be competitive. That observation is less revealing than it might appear to be. For what is given for the individual firm within a competitive industry (the market price) must necessarily be variable for the industry as a whole. The industry, after all, is the market, or, at least, the supply side of the market. Therefore, we usually define a competitive industry in terms of conditions that mean the lack of control over price that is characteristic of the competitive firm. That characteristic is: the freedom of any firm to enter into or exit from the industry, simply by purchasing or selling the required means of producing the output of the industry—the capital, land, and labor used to produce that output—given prevailing technological knowledge.

Profits as a signal

The main thing that induces firms to want to enter into an industry is that the firms already in the industry are making economic profits (which, you will remember, are an excess of revenues above both direct and alternative costs). The thing that causes a firm to want to leave its present industry is, of course, that it is experiencing an economic loss; that is, there are better opportunities in some other industry. Any time that firms in one industry are making economic profits, firms in other industries with similar production techniques must, by definition, be experiencing economic losses. That is merely to say that firms in the less profitable industries have higher-profit alternatives.

Not every industry presents an immediate source of opportunity for every firm. In a brief period of time it is difficult for a firm that produces bubble gum to switch to the production of microcomputers, even if there are very large profits to be made. Over the long run, however, we would expect to see such a change, whether or not the bubble gum producers want to change over to another product.

Investors supply firms in the more profitable industry with more investment funds, which they take from firms in less profitable industries. Similarly, resources needed in the production of more profitable goods, such as labor, will be bid away from lower-valued opportunities. Investors and other suppliers of needed resources respond to market **signals** about their highest-valued opportunities. Market adjustment to changes in demand will occur regardless of the wishes of the managers of firms in less profitable markets. They can either attempt to adjust their product line to respond to the new demands or be replaced by managers who are more responsive to new conditions.

Adjustment process

Now let's look at the graphs that illustrate the adjustment of a competitive industry to changes in market demand. Assume that minicassette players, which are a source of entertainment for joggers, suddenly become more popular. This results in an increased demand for the complementary good of magnetic recording tape because market demand has increased. This is seen in Figure 11-1 by a shift from DD to $D'D'$. With the increase in demand, market price increases. Each firm already in the recording-tape market will immediately move along its marginal cost curve, as shown by the movement from q_1 to q_2 for a firm in the industry, or the movement from Q_1 to Q_2 for the industry as a whole.

Note, however, that along with this short-run industry adjustment that something else has happened in the recording-tape industry. Market price has increased from P_1 to P_2 and each firm in the industry is making economic profits equal to the shaded area in Figure 11-1(b). As would-be competitors observe the economic profits being earned by firms in the industry, some

FIGURE 11-1
Impact of an increase in demand on the firm and on the industry
A sudden increase in demand for magnetic tapes is reflected by the shift from DD to $D'D'$ in (a), which increases the market price of tapes and the quantity sold in this time period. The "ordinary" firm in the industry is able to increase its output from q_1 to q_2 in (b). This is done as the firm moves along its marginal cost curve from a to b, allowing the firm to earn economic profits. Similarly, the industry as a whole is earning economic profits, sending a signal to would-be members of the industry.

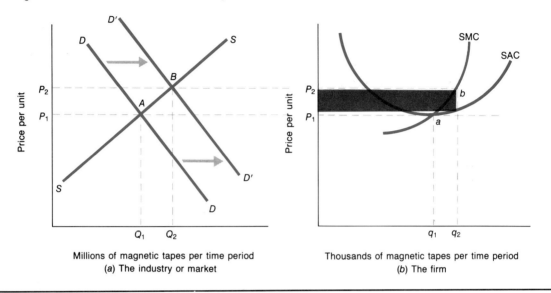

Millions of magnetic tapes per time period
(a) The industry or market

Thousands of magnetic tapes per time period
(b) The firm

will decide to take the plunge and go into competition. How many new firms will enter before the industry will be back in equilibrium? To answer this we need to know what happens in the market or industry when firms enter.

We observed that the increase in demand for magnetic tapes moved the industry along its supply curve [up SS in Figure 11-1(a)]. A change in the number of firms in the industry will, however, lead to a shift in the supply curve. The shift will be to the right as the number of firms increases. As the industry supply curve shifts to the right, market price will begin to fall, as we see in Figure 11-2.

Firms will continue to enter the industry as long as there are economic profits to be made. Economic profits exist so long as the market or industry price is above the minimum point on a firm's long-run average cost curve. We define industry equilibrium as the situation in which firms in the industry are making zero economic profits and there is no incentive for any firm to enter or leave the industry, so that the number of firms in the industry is constant.

FIGURE 11-2
Long-run adjustment of supply in a constant-cost industry
Initially there was a sudden increase in demand for magnetic tapes. The equilibrium shifted from point A to point B. In the long run more firms entered the industry until all economic profits were eliminated. Supply increases from SS to $S'S'$, and the new equilibrium in the market is at point C, where Q_3 is sold at P_1, the same price as before since costs are constant.

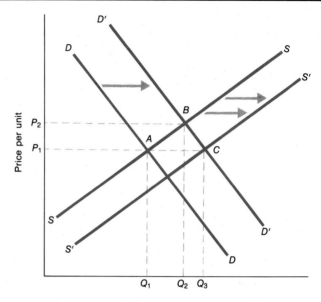

Millions of magnetic tapes per time period

Constant-cost industry

In the simplest case, as we see in Figure 11-2, the magnetic-tape industry will arrive back at full equilibrium when supply has shifted far enough to the right that market price returns to P_1, the price before the demand increase. We call this the "constant-cost case" and we call the industry that adjusts to a change in market demand in this way a **constant-cost industry**.

However, in many industries, firms experience an increase in their costs when industry output expands—in the long run—and a related decline in their costs when industry output contracts. In Figure 11-3 the fall in demand from DD to $D'D'$ causes economic losses to be incurred by firms in the industry and for some firms to exit from the industry. As industry output falls and firms exit, the LAC of each firm that remains falls.

Increasing-cost industry

As you study Figure 11-3, notice several points about the adjustment to a new long-run equilibrium. When demand falls for the industry, existing firms have no choice but to sell at the new market price, P_2, so that they incur economic losses, as illustrated by the shaded box in panel (b). These losses cause firms in the industry to start departing for other alternatives. When they do so, resources they employed are released. In the example here, unlike the example if Figure 11-1, those resources decline in demand so that their market price falls. Hence, in this industry, if there is a contraction, prices decline in the long run; if there is an expansion, prices rise in the long run. This is an **increasing-cost industry**.

FIGURE 11-3

Long-run adjustment in an increasing-cost industry following a decline in demand
Demand suddenly falls from DD to $D'D'$, leading to new price level P_2, at which Q_2 is sold. The firm in (b) moves from point a to b and suffers economic losses shown by the shaded area. After some firms exit the industry, the lower demand for resources used in producing the product causes costs to fall, from LAC_1 to LAC_2 for the firm. The lower costs and smaller number of firms in the industry cause supply to fall from SS to $S'S'$, so new industry equilibrium occurs at point C in (a) and the firm is at equilibrium at point c in (b).

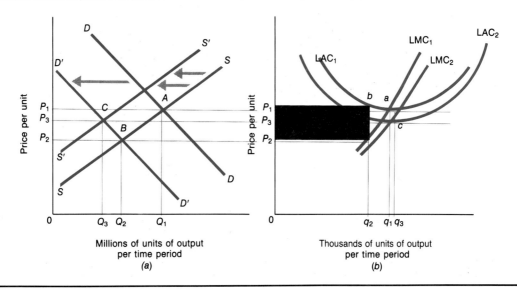

Millions of units of output per time period
(a)

Thousands of units of output per time period
(b)

Because resource prices decline, firms that remained in the industry see their long-run average cost curve decline—from LAC_1 to LAC_2 in this case.[1] Hence, as the industry adjusts to the new, lower demand, the equilibrium price at point C (P_3), is lower than old equilibrium price at point A. It is higher than the short-run price of P_2 because that price was merely a signal for some producers to exit from the market. It was not a price that could persist in the long run since the firms that remain must earn a normal profit.

Long-run industry supply

Note that in the example here and the one in Figure 11-2 we can construct at least a part of the *long-run industry supply* curve. In Figure 11-3 points A and C are on that curve. In Figure 11-2 points A and C are on that curve. In that case it is horizontal at least over the range for which we have observations. The long-run industry supply curve is, like the long-run firm supply curve, derived from the short-run curves.

[1]Note that in this example, in (b), we use the long-run curves. This is for simplicity only, to show the long-run adjustment the firm makes. In fact, we know that in the short run the firm is on a short-run set of curves, but the results of our analysis would not change.

Search for equilibrium

The long-run industry supply curve is derived from the short-run industry supply curves where they intersect demand curves—when the firms in the industry, as a whole, are earning a normal profit (zero economic profits). Short-run "equilibrium" points, like point B in Figure 11-3, are not on the long-run supply curve because at such points the industry is not at equilibrium as we define it. Economic losses are being incurred, so firms are adjusting to the new market situation. They will keep adjusting—firms leaving the industry or working to lower costs—until a new market equilibrium is attained.

The reason that some industries are constant-cost and others are increasing-cost (you can envision what a decreasing-cost industry supply curve would look like, but would you expect it to exist without any technological changes?) lies in the conditions under which firms in these industries purchase inputs or factors of production. If an industry can expand without pushing up the price of the factors it uses in production, then it will be a constant-cost industry. If, however, when an industry expands and demands more factors of production, it forces up the price of those factors, the cost of producing an average unit of output will also rise. This is an increasing-cost industry.

We should not think of any industry as being increasing- or constant-cost in nature forever. Many industries are increasing-cost only until the factor markets that serve them can adjust to the changes in demand for their outputs.

COMPETING CONCEPTIONS OF MICROECONOMIC ANALYSIS

Many of the microeconomic concepts we have studied have been familiar to economists for over a century. Since the 1930s, however, there has been increasing emphasis in microeconomics on the "pure logic" of choice; that is, on what can be said in general about the decisions made by consumers and businesses without reference to the characteristics, histories, or detailed circumstances of individuals and firms. Most of the chapters in this text are concerned with this generalized theory of consumer and firm choice, because that is what predominates in microeconomic thinking at this time. There are, however, at least two other major lines of inquiry in microeconomics.

"Market theory" and microeconomics

One of these approaches is illustrated by the discussion of market adjustment in this chapter and by parts of Chapters 17 to 19. This type of microeconomic analysis is focused on the role played by markets in an economic system and assumes as given the choice calculus of the various economic actors in these markets. An early statement of market function is found in Adam Smith's masterwork, *An Inquiry into the Nature and Causes of the Wealth of Nations,* first published in 1776. More recent and modern treatments have been offered by numerous economists, but seldom in college textbooks.

According to this microeconomic **market theory**, the organization of an economy via competitive and decentralized decision making performs two important tasks. First, competitive markets present knowledge, which consumers and producers must have in order to account for increases and decreases in the scarcity of goods (or productive resources), in the simplified and easy-to-understand form of changing relative prices. Second, markets motivate consumers and producers to respond "appropriately" to this information by rewarding those who do so with higher incomes, profits, or utility.

Note the difference in focus and emphasis in these remarks versus our previous discussion of microeconomic topics. In most of the microeconomics you have learned in this course, the central question is how a decision maker will respond to some particular change in his or her economic environment— an environment over which the economic actor has little or no control. The most important elements of this environment are summarized in the given relative prices of available courses of action. In market theory, the concern is, rather, on why or under what circumstances relative prices change and what adjustments between and within markets might be expected in response to these changes.

The Austrian school

Market process analysis is given another slant by the *Austrian school* of economists, which includes authors such as Nobel laureate F. A. Hayek.[2] Such writers start from the premise that individuals make most of their decisions in a state of partial ignorance. That is, individuals plan their future actions with incomplete or incorrect views about what the economic world will look like in the future. Markets *coordinate* the divergent plans and expectations of the large number of people who participate in the economy by providing a continuous source of feedback about the changing plans and actions of other individuals in the economy and other relevant changes in the economic environment. While some individuals may be frustrated in their plans, they will learn how to adjust their behavior by observing the changes that occur in relative prices, so they can be better off than they would have been otherwise.

An illustration of this principle can be provided by tracing through the economic effects of an especially severe freeze that destroys most of the Florida orange crop. Such an event results in a large increase in the price of oranges in Florida, which signals consumers to cut back on consumption.

---

[2]Hayek's works illustrating his "market analysis" of the functioning of a capitalist economy are listed at the end of the chapter, as are some works of another leading Austrian school economist, Israel Kirzner. A masterful summary of the themes in market and entrepreneurial theory is presented in the book by Thomas Sowell, cited there.

The large increase in world price is noticed by orange growers in California and Latin America, who are interested in marketing their output for the highest profit. Under the new conditions, these growers can secure a higher price and profit by diverting some of their crop to the market normally served by Florida. The supply of oranges to this market increases as more oranges are shipped in from other markets. The price of oranges in that market then falls below its immediate postfreeze level. Simultaneously, of course, the supply of oranges declines in Latin America and California, so the price rises above what it would have been otherwise. The unexpected event of a severe Florida freeze thus signals a redistribution of oranges between locales and, in the course of doing so, has signaled all consumers and producers that oranges are more scarce than they were before.

The "entrepreneurial" interpretation of market function

Market theory reformulates the concept of a static equilibrium of a market in terms of the mechanisms or incentives that cause economic actors (producers and consumers) to act in ways that create a new equilibrium once the old equilibrium has been upset by an exogenous disturbance. That is, standard microeconomic analysis studies equilibriums. As we have seen in most of this text, we begin with a market or a firm in equilibrium, then we introduce a *shock* to the equilibrium, such as a sudden decline in demand, and then observe the new equilibrium that results. These equilibrium positions can be compared to understand the consequences of change. Market theory recognizes the equilibriums but focuses more attention on the *mechanism of change* itself. Both the conventional static equilibrium analysis of markets and the dynamics of market theory analysis assume that consumers and producers are passive reactors to the environment of prices and given alternatives that surrounds them.

The theory of *entrepreneurial behavior* or **entrepreneurial economics** shifts the focus of microeconomics from the impersonal feedback mechanisms of the market to the creative attributes of profit and utility seekers. While we have thus come full circle in our focus—from the calculus of individual choice, to the feedback mechanisms of a market, to the creative choices of producers and consumers in a changing and imperfectly known world—the choice makers of entrepreneurial theory are quite different from the "mechanical" reactors of traditional neoclassical microeconomic theory.

Dynamic role of consumers and producers

The consumer portrayed in entrepreneurial theory is engaged in continuous market search. Consumers seek not just a lower price for the goods they purchase, but also new uses for known goods and new goods for known uses. The choice set of goods available to a consumer is as much a function of that consumer's "investment" in knowledge about what is available, and his or her perceptions about the possible uses of the choices available, as it is a function of the physical availability of these items in the market and their prices.

Similarly, producers no longer are conceived of as applying a given technology and resources to the satisfaction of a set of given demands. Entrepreneurs seek out new and less expensive substitutes for the inputs they have been using, they reform the organization as well as the physical technology of their production processes, and they actively seek customers by reducing the cost of information concerning the uses of their product by advertising. The world of entrepreneurial economics is thus a dynamic world in which the function of markets is to reward those who find ways, through either creative consumption or creative production, to extract more utility from previously unknown or undervalued goods or productive resources. In entrepreneurial economics, there is not as much concern about physical changes as there is an emphasis on peoples' knowledge about and perceptions of what alternatives exist, and a recognition that these alternatives are subject to continual change.[3]

ASSESSING THE ALTERNATIVES TO NEOCLASSICAL MICROECONOMICS

In Chapter 1 we considered the trade-off between the complexity or "realism" of a theory and the simplicity and scope of its analytical structure. Simpler theories tend to explain more (have a broader scope) and are easier to work with, but they may assume away some aspects of a particular situation that are critical to an accurate analysis of that situation. On the other hand, a theory can become so complex that it is little more than an historical account of one unique event or of a series of events and is thus without power to predict future events stemming from a slightly different set of circumstances.

The attempts discussed above to make microeconomics more realistic by creating a more dynamic view of the world serve to illustrate the trade-off between simplicity and predictability on one side and complexity and inapplicability on the other.

Dominance of neoclassical microeconomics

While traditional neoclassical microeconomists have been eager to apply their models to every aspect of the world, market theory and entrepreneurial analysis still remain in about the same position that they were a half-century ago. The reasons for this seem clear. It is easy for the market theorist to conclude that the outcome of a market process must be the best of all possible worlds, since no one individual can know more about the world than what is summarized in the prices generated by the vast information network of

---

[3]The literature interpreting economics in terms of the inventive, risk-bearing, and opportunity-seeking activities of entrepreneurs has a long history. Among the major economists in history who can be tied to this strain are Jean Baptiste Say, Jeremy Bentham, Alfred Marshall, Frank Knight, and Joseph Schumpeter. More recently, works by F. A. Hayek, Israel Kirzner, and G. L. S. Shackle have contributed to this theory.

the market. The principle exceptions to this rule—as we will see soon in the theory of monopoly and externalities—have been well developed.

It is even easier for the entrepreneurial theorist to believe that all, or almost all, restrictions on the actions of individuals potentially inhibit the use by people of their own special insights and knowledge in the pursuit of gain that benefits us all. Once the world comes to rest upon invention and discovery, one can conceive of enormous costs arising from even the most trifling inhibition to free creativity.

Importance of ability to predict

Although there may be much truth in the insights of market and entrepreneurial theory, it is easy to see why they have been, in general, not popular among economists. Even though many economists sympathize with the basic notions in these theories, it appears to many that these theories do not allow us to do much. These theories stress the unknowable aspects of the multitude of markets in the world. While it is true that we cannot, by definition, know the unknown aspects of the future, we typically try to estimate the costs and benefits from alternative courses of action on the basis of what we do know.

The *ceteris paribus* methodology of any social study, such as neoclassical microeconomics, presumes that certain things will not change. While that may, in fact, be false over a sufficiently long period of time, we are often interested in what will happen next month, rather than what will happen in the next decade. Any change in social policy will probably have unforeseen effects, but so will leaving social policies as they presently stand. The observation that the market works tells us little about the expected consequences of making automobile drivers strictly liable for damages inflicted on pedestrians rather than holding them to a negligence standard. Similarly, it says little about the possible differences in the effects of using tariffs rather than an income tax to raise a certain fixed sum of government revenues. Presumably, economists can say something about these issues, although neither market theory nor the theory of the entrepreneur can do so without stepping outside their basic premises.

The lesson to be learned from this digression into competing theories of microeconomic analysis is not that one theory is right and one is wrong, but that different perspectives are sometimes helpful in answering different questions. The basic operation of a market is undoubtedly captured better by market theory and by the general equilibrium tools of neoclassical microeconomics, which we will study in Chapter 17, than it is by the supply and demand curves that we examined in Chapter 2. Similarly, what happens to consumer choice and the successful producer's method of production over long periods of time is nicely portrayed in the discussions of entrepreneurial theory. Neither of these perspectives are, however, as useful as applied neoclassical microeconomics in evaluating the month-by-month and year-by-year choices between alternative public policies that occur continuously in all societies. While the static tools of conventional microeconomics are not perfect representations of the complex world, they can be good guides in helping us to understand what has happened and what is likely to happen, so they can help guide us in making better choices in many situations.

▅▅▅▅▅▅▅▅▅

ISSUES AND APPLICATIONS

What is the meaning of competition in the stock market?

The market for stocks approximates as closely as possible the perfectly competitive situation, at least for shares of stock listed and traded on the major stock exchanges. Information concerning prices and quantities and transactions is readily available at very small per unit costs. All you need do is telephone or visit a brokerage firm to learn, within seconds, the latest price and quantity sold of any stock on a major exchange. We are dealing with homogeneous products within each particular company category. Moreover, there is mobility of resources: People buy and sell all the time. And finally, in most cases the individual buyer or seller represents an insignificant part of the total market. Therefore, the individual buyer or seller of shares of stock must take prices as given. (However, when there is institutional trading, which involves the purchase or sale of large blocks of shares by institutions such as pension and mutual funds and insurance companies, these traders are not an insignificant part of the total market and hence do have some influence over price. This influence, however, will be diminished when the institutional large quantity of block trading is done through a computerized system which will break up the block into many small transactions.)

The price for an individual share of stock in a company traded on a major exchange is determined by the supply of and demand for that stock. (The total number of outstanding shares of that stock is fixed at any moment in time.)

INFORMATION COSTLY TO OBTAIN

Here we are more interested in how far we can push the competitive model to understand pricing of shares of stock on major stock exchanges. First, we know that a share of stock is an asset. Its price reflects the discounted present value of the expected future stream of net income. What determines the expectations of future net income for a particular stock? To a large extent, knowledge of the current and expected future profits of the company in question. Here is where the notion of competition continues in our analysis. There is certainly no such thing as free information, even about prices and quantities of stock sold. This is *a fortiori* correct when we talk about information concerning the future profitability of a company, an industry, or all industries within the nation. Information about companies is costly to obtain.

Nonetheless, there is rivalry among those who buy and sell shares of stock. This rivalry causes many of them to expend resources to obtain information about the future profitability of companies or industries. They engage in research or analysis. But since there is rivalry among literally millions of individuals, all wishing to get rich, we know that lots of resources are spent to obtain this valuable information. In fact, resources for each individual researcher are expended up to the point where marginal cost equals expected marginal revenue. When we add all the results of these researchers together, we come up with a tremendous amount of information on individual companies.

THE VALUE OF PUBLIC INFORMATION

Now, this is the question: Given that we are dealing with a very competitive market (even though it may not be *perfectly* competitive), can we say anything about the value of research information? Yes, we can. The value of research information that is *publicly* known is zero, for such information has already been "used" by the time it reaches the public. In other words, be it bullish (good) or bearish (bad), all public information is discounted very quickly by a change in the stock's prices. Those who first find out about the increased present or future profitability of a company will bid up the price of the shares of stock in that company, and those who first find out that the company is going to be less profitable in the future will, by their selling, cause the price of the stock to fall. Actually, what is involved is many individuals doing this simultaneously. That is why we say that the current price of a stock reflects all presently available information, properly discounted, concerning the future profitability of the firm. This is also known as the **efficient-market hypothesis**. In a highly efficient market, such as the stock market, rates of return on investment will tend toward equality on the margin (when these rates of return are corrected for risk).

THE DYNAMIC COMPETITIVE PROCESS

This is no different from the dynamic process outlined in this chapter when we showed what would happen in an industry making positive economic profits or negative economic profits (losses). In any highly competitive, efficient market, capital flows to wherever rates of return corrected for risk are highest. When we say "corrected for risk," we mean that even with perfect competition, the rate of return necessary to induce capital into a more risky venture will be higher than the rate of return necessary to induce capital into a less risky venture. As capital moves around to where rates of return are anticipated to be highest (corrected for risk), this shuffling around tends to drive down expected high rates of return (corrected for risk). If one area of potential investment has an extremely high risk-corrected expected rate of return, the capital that will flow in will constitute an additional supply. With a given demand for capital, the additional supply (shifting the supply curve outward to the right) will drive down that high anticipated risk-corrected rate of return to capital. The reverse will occur when there is a relatively low risk-corrected expected rate of return to capital somewhere in the economy.

In a highly competitive investment market, it therefore usually does little good to obtain public information, that is, information which is known to more than a relatively small number of individuals who can make timely use of that information to make capital gains or avoid capital losses. Public information includes not only research service results, presented free of charge by stockbrokerage firms, but also schemes on how to get rich quick that are printed in magazines, newspapers, and books, and investment services offered by the numerous investment firms in this country and elsewhere.

The conclusion to be reached is perhaps best summed up in the words of Paul Samuelson:

■ *Even the best investors seem to find it hard to do better than the comprehensive common-stock averages, or better on the average than random selection among stocks of comparable variability.*[4]

[4]P. A. Samuelson, "Proof That Properly Discounted Present Values of Assets Vibrate Randomly," *The Bell Journal of Economics and Management Science*, vol. 4, no. 2, Autumn 1973, pp. 369–374.

We must point out one caveat in this discussion. If, as an investor, you are better at *interpreting* public information than the market in general, you can make higher-than-normal rates of return using this public information. In other words, if you are the sole possessor of a truly superior *theory* that allows you to use public information to predict the future course of a stock market, as long as you are able to keep your theory secret from everyone else, you can "make a killing" in the market (if your trade is small relative to the total volume).

Another way that you can do better than the market is to have access to *inside information* and the ability to trade on such information. Inside information is information about a firm's earnings or future plans which is not known outside of the firm. For many years there has been an attempt to prohibit insiders from taking "unfair advantage" of their special knowledge in buying or selling the stock of their company. The economic assessments of the usefulness of these prohibitions has been mixed. But from our discussion regarding the scarcity of investment information we can deduce that someone will gain from learning insider facts before they become more generally known. This person may be a company insider, a stock broker, or someone else with a valuable information source depending upon the rules of the game, but it will almost never be the "average investor," who devotes few resources to keeping informed about details of each company's operations.

Contestable markets

Students, professors, and policymakers have long complained that the model of perfect competition is too abstract to be helpful in analyzing real-world phenomena. Despite the weaknesses inherent in that complaint (see Chapter 1), it now appears that the assumptions of perfect competition are more restrictive than they need to be to obtain a model of firms that are efficient and sell their output at the lowest possible price.

The new model of efficient firm behavior is called the *theory of contestable markets*.[5] This model results in most of the same outcomes as the theory of perfect competition.[6]

Specifically, the firm, absent mistakes, will produce the output where price equals marginal cost in the short and long runs. All other characteristics of efficient operation of the firm will be attained in the long run, and the firm will receive a price that exactly results in zero economic profits in the long run.

Unlike perfect competition, however, the theory of contestable markets requires only two firms in an industry for these conditions to emerge. There is no gradation of industry structures from very competitive to somewhat competitive to not very competitive in the theory of contestable markets as there often is in a classification of industries based on perfect competition. Similarly, there is no indeterminacy of firm behavior in an oligopolistic

[5]See the reference at the end of the chapter. For some implications of the theory, see Elizabeth Bailey and William Baumol, "Deregulation and the Theory of Contestable Markets," *Yale Journal of Regulation*, vol. 1, 1984, pp. 111–137.

[6]One efficient outcome not secured by a theory of contestable markets is dynamic efficiency. Given the conditions for perfect contestability, no firm, even the most efficient, is fully protected against entrants into the industry in the long run. A contestable market may be subject to temporary oversupply.

market that is perfectly contestable, because the behavior of the industry depends upon the constraints facing potential entrants, not upon the game strategies played among firms already in the industry.

FREE AND COSTLESS ENTRY AND EXIT

In order for a market to be perfectly contestable, it is necessary that firms be able to enter and leave the market freely. Free entry and exit implies an absence of nonprice constraints and an absence of sunk costs associated with a potential competitor's decision to enter a contestable market. Such an absence of sunk costs results if the firm need buy no specific durable inputs in order to enter, if it uses up all such inputs it does purchase, or if all of its specific durable inputs are saleable upon exit without any losses beyond those normally incurred from depreciation or user costs.

The mathematical model of perfect contestability is complex, but the underlying logic is straightforward. So long as conditions for free entry prevail, any excess profits, or any inefficiencies on the part of incumbent firms, will serve as an inducement for potential entrants to enter. By entry new firms can temporarily profit at no risk to themselves from the less-than-competitive situation in the industry. Once competitive conditions are again restored, they will leave the industry just as quickly.

───────────

Consequences of different ownership forms: Restaurants and liquor stores

Market economies are presumed to be "driven" by entrepreneurs who seek profitable opportunities and try to manage business organizations so as to maximize profits. Various studies have been done to examine the consequences of different forms of ownership if enterprises to test the implications of economic theory concerning the incentives created by private ownership. Here we look at two examples: franchise restaurants run by owners or by hired managers and liquor stores that are privately owned or publicly owned.

FRANCHISE RESTAURANTS

Restaurant chains are common today where almost all inputs—physical location and plant, menu, prices, employee training, food, etc.— are determined by the parent company. In many cases an individual pays a franchise fee to the parent company for the right to run the restaurant. The income of these individ-uals is dependent upon the profitability of the restaurant. One chain studied had restaurants that were owner-operated and others that were managed by a company employee when an acceptable franchise buyer had not been found, or when the franchisee had sold the restaurant back to the parent company.[7] These company managers were experienced and were salaried; in other words they did not have to rely solely on profits.

On average, when a company manager followed an owner-operator, sales dropped 7.3 percent. When owner-operators followed company managers, sales rose an average of 19.1 percent. Even more impressive was the impact on profits. The profit margins for company managers averaged 1.8 percent compared to 9.5 percent for owner-operators. The

[7]John P. Shelton, "Allocative Efficiency vs. 'X-Efficiency': Comment," *American Economic Review*, December 1967, pp. 1252–1258.

average weekly profit during company manager supervision was $56.81, while it was $271.83 under owner-operators.

LIQUOR STORES

Unlike the restaurant study that considered privately owned enterprises, the study of liquor stores compared the consequences of public ownership of liquor retail outlets to private ownership of liquor retail stores.[8] Fifteen states that are geographically scattered around the U.S. have complete state control over liquor—a state agency buys liquor and sells it through state owned and operated stores. The other 35 states have private liquor retail stores.

Under government ownership there is no way to estimate the profits of liquor stores, so other measures were looked at to compare the consequences of public versus private organization. There were major differences in employment. In 1977, the average salary per clerk was $8191.62 in the public ownership states. That is 41 percent higher than the average

[8]Asghar Zardkoohi and Alain Sheer, "Public versus Private Liquor Retailing," *Southern Economic Journal*, April 1984, pp. 1058–1076.

salary of $5,803.77 in private ownership states. One factor that apparently contributed to the higher pay in the public ownership states was the dominance of unions in those states, whereas no liquor store workers were unionized in the private ownership states. As one would expect, among the private ownership states, the higher the wage rate, the fewer the workers employed relative to sales. In contrast, among the public ownership states, higher wages made no difference to the number of workers hired relative to sales. Possibly to offset the higher wage costs in the public ownership state, the stores there hired fewer workers relative to sales than did the private ownership states.

Finally, the study determined that private ownership produces more stores. Holding income, liquor prices, and population density constant, the number of stores per capita is higher in the private ownership states than in the public ownership states. What was the difference in average liquor prices in the private ownership states compared to the public ownership states? Prices were higher in the private ownership states. The authors attributed this to the consequences of taxes imposed on liquor in the private ownership states and the revenue maximization objective of the state liquor organizations.

SUMMARY

1 A competitive *industry* is one in which there is "free" entry and exit of firms.

2 "Free" entry and exit means there are no *legal* restraints on entry or exit, as there are in regulated or licensed industries. Firms enter or exit solely on the basis of their estimates of actual or likely profit or loss.

3 An economic profit is a signal to firms already in the industry that there are no higher returns to be made in other alternative lines of production. An economic profit is also a signal to firms in other alternative ("commensurate") lines of production to exit their present industries and enter the industry where the economic profits are available.

4   An economic loss is a signal to firms in the industry, and in alternative lines of production, that there are higher profits to be made in some other industry.

5   Constant-cost industries are those in which the long-run equilibrium price is always the same regardless of the level of market demand and long-run equilibrium industry output. A constant-cost industry is an insignificant source of demand for the inputs used by the industry. So an increase or decrease in the output of the constant-cost industry will not alter the prices of these inputs.

6   Increasing-cost industries are those in which the long-run equilibrium price is higher, the larger is the level of market demand and long-run equilibrium industry output. An increasing-cost industry is a significant part of the total demand for inputs used by the industry; so, an increase or decrease in the output of an increasing-cost industry will increase or decrease the prices of these inputs.

7   The microeconomic analysis presented in this book is only one of several views of microeconomic analysis which is now or has been used by economists.

8   Classical economists, like Adam Smith, emphasized the adjustment of markets to changes in relative demands and costs, as described in this chapter.

9   The economists of the "Austrian school" emphasize the role of markets in economizing on and distributing knowledge needed to make "correct" allocations of goods and factors of production between competing uses.

10   "Austrians" and other economists have also explored the role of markets in encouraging and directing innovation and invention, whether in new forms of consumption, the organization of production, or distribution of products produced.

11   None of these emphases, however, contradict the theory which you will learn from this text. They are merely extensions and applications of this theory to issues and problems beyond the scope of our discussion.

GLOSSARY

- **competitive industry** An industry in which firms are free to enter or exit in response to economic profits or economic losses.
- **signal** A compact way of indicating to an economic decision maker information needed to make a decision. A "true signal" not only conveys information but also provides the incentive to "act appropriately" to the signal given. Economic profits and economic losses are such signals.

- **constant-cost industry** An industry in which the long-run equilibrium price of output is unaffected by the level of market demand.
- **increasing-cost industry** An industry in which the long-run equilibrium price of output rises or falls with the level of market demand.
- **market theory** The view of economic analysis which emphasizes market adjustment to changes in relative demands and relative costs.
- **"entrepreneurial" economics** The view of economic analysis which emphasizes the role of markets in economizing on, distributing, and discovering knowledge about resources supplies, uses of goods and factors, and technical processes. The view that the ultimate "scarcity" is a scarcity of knowledge about how things are and how they can be changed.
- **efficient-market hypothesis** In a highly competitive market that is working efficiently, the value of any asset completely reflects the discounted present value of all information about the future income stream derivable from the asset.

QUESTIONS

(Answers to even-numbered questions are at back of text.)

1 What would happen to the production and price of ice cream if the medical profession became convinced that butter fat caused cancer? Is the dairy industry a constant-cost or increasing-cost industry?

2 If there were no National Guard, Coast Guard, or other emergency services to respond to floods, what would happen to the allocation of rowboats and small crafts if there were a sudden flood in Houston, Texas, which stranded many families on rooftops?

3 In the sixteenth century in Europe, forests were becoming increasingly depleted and the price of wood was rapidly rising. Wood was the main source of fuel for heating and lighting homes. What happened next? (*Hint:* The answer is *not* that the noble families of many European nations attempted to lay claim to forest lands, although that did happen during this period.)

4 Tomatoes were once thought to be poisonous and no one would think of eating one. Why isn't this still the case today?

5 Chile was the world's largest producer of nitrates in the nineteenth and early twentieth centuries. Nitrates are an essential input into the production of gunpowder. With the coming of World War I Chile decided to "conserve nitrates for future generations" by restricting the quantities which could be exported to other countries, and, hence, the quantities which would be extracted from Chilean deposits. What happened next?

6 Famine is increasingly less of a problem in India and parts of southeast Asia. Why?

7 Some "Austrian" economists remain extremely skeptical about the economists' ability to predict exact numerical values for future production, future prices, etc. If, for the sake of argument, one accepts this skepticism as justified, what roles are left for economists?

8 "Austrians" often argue that centralized planning of an economic system is not merely undesirable; it is also impossible. How would you interpret and justify this statement, given the above description of an Austrian's belief about what is important in an economy?

SELECTED REFERENCES

Baumol, William J., "Contestable Markets: An Uprising in the Theory of Industry Structure," *American Economic Review*, vol. 72, March 1982, pp. 1–15.

Becker, Gary S., and George J. Stigler, "De Gustibus Non Est Disputandum," *American Economic Review*, vol. 67, March 1977, pp. 76–90.

Herbert, Robert F., and Albert Link, *The Entrepreneur: Mainstream Views and Radical Critiques* (New York: Praeger, 1982).

Hayek, Friedrich, *Individualism and Economic Order* (Chicago: University of Chicago Press, 1948).

Kirzner, Israel, *Competition and Entrepreneurship* (Chicago: University of Chicago Press, 1973).

Sowell, Thomas, *Knowledge and Decision* (New York: Basic Books, 1981).

Monopoly pricing and output

We have just studied perfect competition. We will now analyze its opposite, pure monopoly. Just as the conditions for perfect competition are rarely met in the real world, the conditions for pure monopoly also are rarely met. Nonetheless, we find the pure monopoly model useful for analyzing and predicting price and output changes in less competitive industries.

In this chapter, we will analyze pure monopoly, where there is only one firm in an industry. Indeed, we will define the **monopolist** as a single seller, or supplier, of a well-defined commodity for which there are no "good" substitutes. We will take as given the possibility of a monopoly arising and the methods by which individuals attempt to establish and maintain monopoly power. After we develop our analytical tools for studying the implications of pure monopoly, in the next chapter we will consider how monopolies can arise in practice and study some of the consequences.

THE DEMAND CURVE FACING A MONOPOLY

The monopoly is the only firm in the industry; the demand curve facing the monopoly is in the industry demand curve, or market demand curve. The entire market buys from only one supplier. Assuming that the law of demand holds, the industry demand curve will be downward-sloping with an elasticity between $-\infty$ and 0. We draw such a curve shown as DD, in Figure 12-1, panel (a).

FIGURE 12-1
Elasticity and total revenues
In panel (a) we show a linear demand curve along which the price elasticity of demand decreases numerically as we increase quantity. At the midpoint of the demand curve, price elasticity of demand is equal to -1 and marginal revenue is equal to 0. In panel (b) we can see that total revenues start at 0, reach a peak at output rate Q_1, and then fall to 0 when price reaches 0 at output Q_2. Total revenues are maximized at the output rate at which $\eta = -1$. (The horizontal axis measures output for both (a) and (b).)

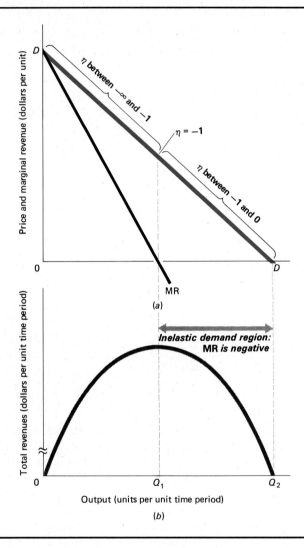

Price elasticity of demand

It is often asserted that a monopolist faces an inelastic demand curve. However, this does not follow from the definition of monopoly. The demand curve shown in Figure 12-1 (a) is linear and hence has a price elasticity of demand which goes from $-\infty$ to 0 as we move rightward along the curve. (Why?)

If you recall the discussion of elasticity in Chapter 5, you will remember that we cannot talk about the elasticity of a demand curve because the elasticity changes as you move along a downward-sloping demand curve. For the monopolist, we will see, profits are maximized when elasticity of demand is equal to or greater than one. Of course, as we learned before, the elasticity of demand is affected by the closeness of substitutes—that is, the closeness of the competition faced by the monopolist.

Monopoly marginal revenue

You will remember that marginal revenue is defined as the change in total revenue due to a one-unit change in volume sold. We also saw in Chapter 5 that marginal revenue was related to price and elasticity of demand. The relationship was mathematically shown to be

$$MR = P\left(1 + \frac{1}{\eta}\right) \tag{12-1}$$

In the case of a perfect competitor, $\eta = -\infty$ by definition; therefore, marginal revenue equals price because Eq. (12-1) becomes $MR = P(1 + 1/-\infty) = P(1 - 0) = P$. The monopolist, however, does not face a horizontal demand schedule with η always equal to $-\infty$. The monopolist would never willingly operate where marginal revenue is less than 0, even if there were zero costs of production, for it could always reduce output and thereby increase revenues, and consequently profits. MR becomes 0 in Eq. (12-1) when $\eta = -1$ [then $MR = P(1 + 1/-1) = P(1 - 1) = 0$]. When η is between -1 and 0, MR is negative. That means that the monopolist will never operate on that portion of the demand curve where demand is inelastic. This can be better seen by looking at the relation between marginal revenue, total revenue, and elasticity of demand. We developed the technique for drawing the marginal revenue curve back in Chapter 5.

Marginal revenue, total revenue, and elasticity of demand

We have drawn panel (b) in Figure 12-1 to show the relation between total revenue, marginal revenue, and price elasticity of demand. Total revenue is clearly 0 when unit sales are 0; thus, in panel (b), the total revenue curve starts at the origin. Total revenues are also 0 when the price is 0, so total revenues are equal to 0 at the rate of output Q_2, at which demand curve DD intersects the horizontal axis in panel (a) of Figure 12-1. In between the output of 0 and that output Q_2, total revenue first rises and then falls. It reaches a peak at the rate of output Q_1 where marginal revenue is equal to 0, i.e., where elasticity of demand must be -1. It is clear from panel (a) that the monopolist would never operate at a rate of output larger than Q_1, because marginal revenue is negative. This is equivalent to saying that the monopolist will never operate in the inelastic region of the (straight-line) demand curve DD.

It should be noted here that this entire discussion of monopoly assumes that the monopolist charges the same price for all units of its product. This is the case of a **nondiscriminating monopoly**. Later in this chapter, we consider the possibility of a **discriminating monopoly**, where different units of the same product are sold at different prices.

Price adjustments in the short run and the long run

The perfect competitor has no effect on the price of its product; the marginal revenue of the perfect competitor is equal to price, which is taken as given. For planning purposes, the short-run and the long-run prices and marginal revenue are the same for the perfect competitor. This follows from the assumption that the current market price is the long-run equilibrium price.

Such is not the case with monopolists who cannot ignore the fact that the price they set today may influence tomorrow's sales. Specifically, a reduction in price this year may lead to an increase in sales next year. That would occur whenever buyers have delayed responses to price changes. Indeed, the responsiveness of consumers to changes in prices is greater the longer the price change has been in effect. That is to say, long-run price elasticities of demand are greater (numerically) than short-run price elasticities of demand. The perfectly competitive firm does not worry about this distinction because, by definition, its demand curve always has $\eta = -\infty$.

Since the long-run price elasticity of demand is greater than the short-run price elasticity of demand, a monopolist must be careful in interpreting any short-run responsiveness in quantity demanded to a change in price that the monopolist has just posted. For example, the monopolist may raise the price and not see much effect for a few weeks, or longer. Nonetheless, the monopolist can anticipate that the reduction in quantity demanded will be measurably greater a year later. Remember that, unlike the firm that is a perfect competitor and must take price as a given, the monopolist is the firm and the industry—it is a *price maker*.

The monopolist's costs

The fact that a firm is a pure monopoly in the product market implies nothing about its position in the *input market*. To simplify our analysis, we will assume that our pure monopolist has to buy all its input in purely competitive input markets. Thus, the cost curves for a monopolist can be derived in the same manner as the cost curves for a perfectly competitive firm. (In Chapter 15, we examine the case of monopoly in the *buying* of inputs.)

SHORT-RUN EQUILIBRIUM

We assume that profit maximization is the goal of the pure monopolist, just as we assumed that it was the goal of the perfect competitor. With the perfect competitor, however, we had to decide only on the profit-maximizing rate of output, because price was given. For the pure monopolist we must seek a profit-maximizing *price-output combination*. We can determine this in either of two ways: the total revenue–total cost approach or the marginal revenue–marginal cost approach. Both approaches will be demonstrated. We present some hypothetical cost data that for the sake of simplicity are the same as the cost data we used for the perfect competitor in Chapter 10.

Total revenue–total cost approach

Column (3) of Table 12-1 shows total revenues of our hypothetical monopolist, and column (4) shows total costs. We graphically represent these two columns in Figure 12-2. The only difference between Figure 12-2 and the similar figure (Figure 10-3) we drew for a perfect competitor is that the total revenue line is no longer a linear ray from the origin. Rather, it is a nonlinear curve. For any given demand curve, in order to sell more, the monopolist must lower the price; and after a certain point (where elasticity of demand equals -1), a further lowering of price causes total revenues to fall. [Refer to Figure 12-1, panel (b).]

Profit maximization involves maximizing the difference between total revenues and total costs. This occurs at a rate of output of 10. We must be careful to be maximizing the *positive* difference between total revenues and total costs; otherwise, we could end up maximizing losses rather than profits. Thus, we are interested only in that range of outputs (if it exists) of Figure 12-2 where the total revenue exceeds total cost. Consequently, in this case we won't consider output rates below 3 or above 13.

Marginal revenue–marginal cost approach

Profit maximization occurs where marginal revenue equals marginal cost. This is as true for a monopolist as it is for a perfect competitor. If the firm goes past the output at which marginal revenue equals marginal cost, total profits will be less because, for each additional unit sold, costs would in-

TABLE 12-1
Monopoly costs, revenues, and profits

Rate of output (units/time) (1)	Price per unit (average revenue) (2)	Total revenues [(2) × (1)] ($/time) (3)	Total costs ($/time) (4)	Total profit [(3) − (4)] ($/unit) (5)	Marginal cost ($/unit) (6)	Marginal revenue ($/unit) (7)
0	8.00	0	10.00	− 10.00	—	—
1	7.80	7.80	14.00	− 6.20	4.00	7.80
2	7.60	15.20	17.50	− 2.30	3.50	7.40
3	7.40	22.20	20.75	− 1.45	3.25	7.00
4	7.20	28.80	23.80	5.00	3.05	6.60
5	7.00	35.00	26.70	8.30	2.90	6.20
6	6.80	40.80	29.50	11.30	2.80	5.80
7	6.60	46.20	32.25	13.95	2.75	5.40
8	6.40	51.20	35.10	16.10	2.85	5.00
9	6.20	55.80	38.30	17.50	3.20	4.60
10	6.00	60.00	42.30	17.70	4.00	4.20
11	5.80	63.80	48.30	15.50	6.00	3.80
12	5.60	67.20	57.30	9.90	9.00	3.40
13	5.40	70.20	70.30	− 0.10	13.00	3.00
14	5.20	72.80	88.30	− 15.50	18.00	2.60
15	5.00	75.00	112.30	− 37.30	24.00	2.20

FIGURE 12-2
Profit maximization: TR–TC approach
The monopolist maximizes profits where the positive difference between TR and TC is greatest. This is at an output rate of approximately 10. Notice the difference between the TR curve here and the one shown in Chapter 10 for a perfect competitor. This one is curved to reflect a downward-sloping linear demand curve.

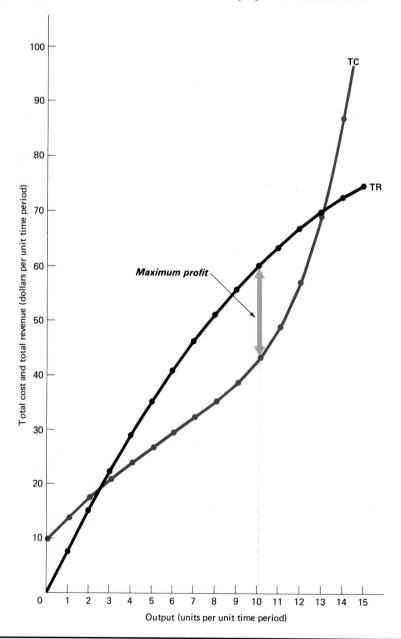

■■■■■

FIGURE 12-3
Profit maximization: MR–MC approach
Profit maximization occurs where marginal revenue equals marginal cost. This is at an output rate of approximately 10. (Also, the MC curve must cut the MR curve from below.)

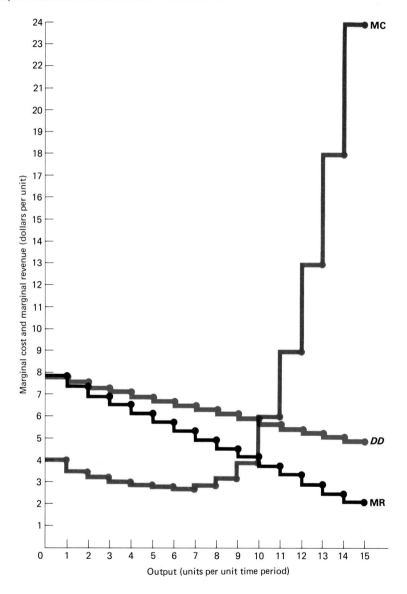

crease more than revenues. If the firm does not produce up to the output at which marginal revenue equals marginal cost, total profits will be less than they could be, because an additional unit sold would increase revenues by more than it would increase costs.

We graphically represent the marginal cost and marginal revenue curves from columns (6) and (7) of Table 12-1 on the graph in Figure 12-3. Marginal revenue equals marginal cost at an output rate of about 10. This is the profit-maximizing rate of output for a pure monopolist; the optimal output rate is the same as in Figure 12-2.[1]

Searching for a price to charge

The monopolist must set the price. It is said to be a **price searcher**. What price will be set? The profit-maximizing price, of course, but this is related to the profit-maximizing rate of output. Indeed, these two variables are determined simultaneously. At a profit-maximizing rate of output of 10 in Figure 12-3, the firm can charge a maximum price of $6 and still sell all the goods produced. The maximum price that can be charged for this putput is "read" off the demand curve, *DD*, which indicates the price at which the profit-maximizing quantity can be sold.

The procedure for finding the profit-maximizing short-run price-quantity combination for the monopolist is first to determine the profit-maximizing rate of output, either by the total revenue–total cost method or by the marginal revenue–marginal cost method, and then to determine, by use of the demand schedule *DD*, the maximum price that can be charged in order to sell that output.

A MONOPOLIST'S SUPPLY CURVE

We were able to derive the single firm's supply curve in a perfectly competitive industry from the firm's marginal cost curve. We were able to derive an industry supply curve by the horizontal summation of all individual firms' marginal cost curves above average variable cost. It would seem, then, that the monopolist's supply curve would also be its marginal cost curve.

Even though it would seem so, it turns out *not* to be so. *The monopolist has no supply curve.* A supply curve is defined as the locus of points showing the minimum price at which a given quantity will be forthcoming. There is *no* unique relation between price and the quantity supplied by a monopolist. This can be seen by looking at Figure 12-4.

We draw one marginal cost curve MC. The first demand curve is D_1D_1. It has a marginal revenue curve MR_1. The intersection of marginal revenue and marginal cost curves is at a rate of output per unit time period of Q_1. The monopolist facing this demand curve D_1D_1 will charge a price of P_1.

[1]Note that the MC curve must cut the MR curve from *below*.

FIGURE 12-4
No supply curve for a monopolist
Since a supply curve is defined as the locus of points showing the minimum prices at which given quantities will be forthcoming, a monopolist does not have a supply curve. We show two different demand curves, D_1D_1 and D_2D_2, that yield exactly the same profit-maximizing price but two different quantities supplied by the monopolist. Hence, there is no unique relationship between price and quantity supplied by a monopoly.

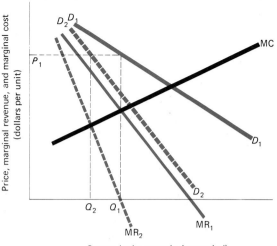

Now consider another demand situation with the same marginal cost curve. Demand has now shifted to D_2D_2. The marginal revenue curve that results from that is MR_2. It intersects the marginal cost curve at a profit-maximizing rate of output per unit time period of Q_2. But as you can see, this rate of output will be sold at the same price P_1 as before. Thus we find that price P_1 is associated with two different rates of output: Q_1 and Q_2.[2] Any particular price can result in a wide variety of optimum rates of monopoly output, depending on the price elasticity of demand and the position of the demand curve. Thus, for a monopolist there is no unique relation between price and quantity forthcoming; i.e., there is no supply curve.

MONOPOLY SHORT-RUN PROFIT

We have talked about the monopolist maximizing profit, but we have yet to indicate how much profit the monopolist makes. We can do this by putting a short-run average total cost curve (SATC) into Figure 12-3. We do this in Figure 12-5. When we add the average total cost curve, we find that the profit that a monopolist makes is equal to the shaded area (which is P − SATC high and Q long). In Figure 12-5, the monopolist earns a pure profit in the short run. Perfect competitors may also earn a pure profit in the short run. Thus, in the short run, one important difference between monopoly and

---

[2]We can also have a case in which two different prices, from two different demand curves, correspond to the same quantity. Can you draw this?

FIGURE 12-5
Monopoly profit
We find monopoly profit here by subtracting total costs from total revenues at an output rate of 10, which is approximately where MR = MC. Monopoly profit is given by the shaded area. This diagram is similar to Figure 12-3, except that we have added the short-run average total cost curve SATC.

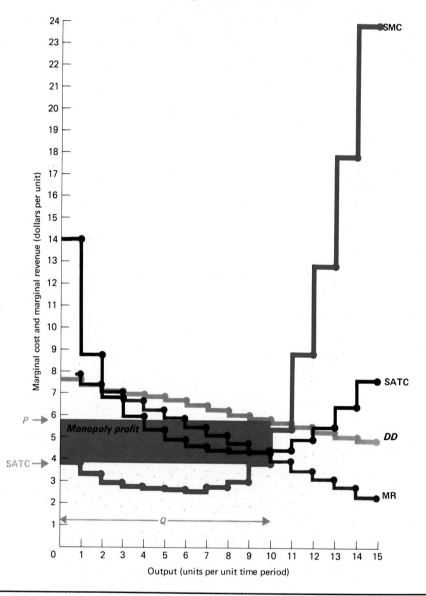

perfect competition is in the slope of the demand curve. Both types of firms may earn pure economic profits; of course, either may also incur a loss.

Monopoly doesn't necessarily mean profits

The term "monopoly" conjures up the notion of a greedy firm ripping off the public and making exorbitant "monopoly" profits. However, the mere existence of a monopoly does not guarantee economic profits. Look at Figure 12-6. Here we show the demand curve facing the monopolist as *DD* and the resultant marginal revenue curve as MR. It does not matter at what rate of output this particular monopolist operates; total costs cannot be covered. Look at the position of the average total cost curve. It lies everywhere above *DD* (the average revenue curve). Thus, there is no price-output combination that will allow the monopolist to earn monopoly profits. This monopolist will always suffer economic losses and, hence, will move to another line of business in the long run. The diagram in Figure 12-6 depicts the situation for numerous monopolies that exist; they are called "patented inventions." The owner of a patented invention has a (temporary) pure legal monopoly, but the demand and cost curves may be such that it is not profitable to produce. Every year there are inventors' conventions where one can see many inventions that have never been put into production, having been deemed "uneconomic" by potential users.

FIGURE 12-6
Monopolies aren't always profitable
This diagram depicts the situation confronting some monopolists. The average total cost curve ATC is everywhere above the average revenue or demand curve *DD*.

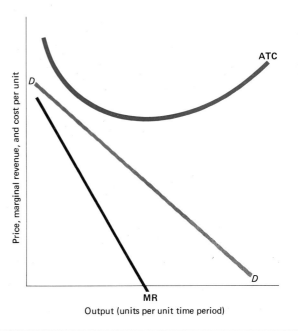

MULTIPLANT SHORT-RUN EQUILIBRIUM

Consider for a moment how a monopoly firm should operate two plants to maximize profits in the short run. We examined this problem in Chapter 9. The plants should be operated at an output rate such that marginal cost in plant 1 is equal to marginal cost in plant 2, both being equal to price. For the monopolist, the rule would be

$$MC_1 = MC_2 = MC = MR$$

With two plants that have different marginal cost curves, the monopolist's marginal cost curve for operating both plants can be derived by running both plants in different combinations of rates such that *total* cost is minimized at each output rate. This can be seen by looking at the example shown in Table 12-2. The first column is the rate of output, the second column is the marginal cost in plant 1, and the third column is the marginal cost in plant 2. Now we derive the sixth column, which is the marginal cost for the monopoly firm (both plants taken together). At a rate of output of 1 per unit time period, it is clear that the firm would operate plant 1 at that rate and not operate plant 2 at all. The marginal cost for the firm, therefore, at that rate of output is $3.

Now, what about a rate of output of 2 per unit time period? If both units are produced in plant 1, marginal cost is $5. However, if 1 unit is produced in plant 1 and 1 unit in plant 2, marginal cost is $4. Thus, marginal cost for the firm at a rate of output of 2 is $4.

For a rate of output of 3 per unit time period, if all 3 are produced in plant 1, marginal cost is $6. However, if 1 is produced in plant 2 and 2 in plant 1, the *marginal* cost will equal $5. Finally, at a rate of output of 4, the firm can minimize total cost by producing 3 units per unit time period in plant 1 at a marginal cost of $6 and 1 unit per unit time period in plant 2 at a cost of $4; the firm's marginal cost at a rate of output of 4 is $6 per unit.

TABLE 12-2
Multiplant monopoly

Output	MC_1 ($/unit)	MC_2 ($/unit)	Output Plant 1 (q/t)	Plant 2 (q/t)	MC ($/unit)
1	3	4	1	0	3
2	5	7	1	1	5
3	6	9	2	1	6
4	8	10	3	1	8
5	.	.	.	.	.
6	.	.	.	.	.
7	.	.	.	.	.

Adding up the marginal costs

We have transferred the information from Table 12-2 graphically onto Figure 12-7. MC_1 is the marginal cost curve for plant 1. MC_2 is the marginal cost curve for plant 2. Their *horizontal* summation is labeled ΣMC. In other words, we have added the horizontal distance between the vertical axis and any point on MC_1 to the horizontal distance between the vertical axis and MC_2 to derive the points that we connect for ΣMC. We then draw in a hypothetical demand curve with its resultant marginal revenue curve MR. Profits are maximized where marginal revenue equals (summed) marginal cost or where the MR curve intersects ΣMC. This is a rate of output of 3 units per unit time period for which the monopolist can charge a price P_m per unit (which is approximately equal to $10.40).

The monopolist will operate each plant so that marginal cost in each plant is equal to the marginal revenue from selling the combined outputs.

FIGURE 12-7

Profit maximization for the multiplant monopolist

The multiplant monopolist with two plants faces marginal cost curves MC_1 and MC_2. The horizontal summation of these two cost curves gives ΣMC. The profit-maximizing rate of output is at the intersection of ΣMC with MR. Now the firm produces such that $MC_1 = MC_2 = MC$. Plant 1 will operate at an output rate of approximately 1.2.

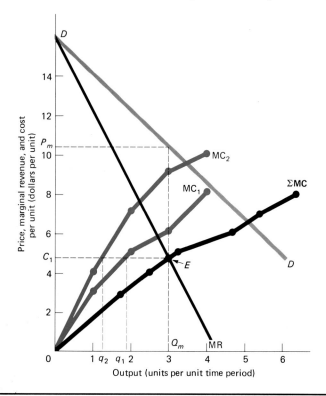

Marginal revenue and marginal cost at the profit-maximizing rate of output is given by C_1 on the vertical axis in Figure 12-7 and is approximately equal to $4.80. In order to produce 3 units per unit time period, the monopolist will produce approximately 1.2 units in plant 2, which is q_2 on the horizontal axis, and 1.8 units in plant 1, which is q_1 on the horizontal axis. Notice that there is a slight difference between the marginal cost per unit for a rate of output of 3 in Table 12-2 and C_1 in Figure 12-7. In Table 12-2, we see in the last column that the marginal cost per unit per 3 units of output per unit time period is equal to $5. That is because this table does not allow for continuous production rates, in which fractions of a unit can be produced. In other words, production is depicted in discrete units. In Figure 12-7, however, we will allow for the possibility that fractions of a unit can be produced. Thus, the marginal cost at the rate of output of 3 is slightly less than $5, as is given in Table 12-2.

ON THE EXISTENCE OF LONG-RUN MONOPOLY PROFITS

Can monopoly profits persist in the long run? Some economists will answer no to this question, not because the monopoly loses its monopoly power but because any monopoly's (economic) profits will be capitalized and thus will be included in the average total cost curve. We referred to this when we talked about the suspicious nature of the ATC curve in Chapter 10. In other words, if a monopoly is really making monopoly profits and you were to purchase the monopoly firm, you would have to pay a price that reflected the (discounted) present value of those monopoly profits. The average total cost curve that you would face would therefore be higher than the average total cost curve that the original owner of the monopoly faced.[3]

Consider a case in which one firm has obtained the right to be the only food vendor on your campus. The firm has a monopoly in selling food on campus. If we assume that the company is making monopoly profits every year it is in operation and is expected to continue to do so, how much would you have to pay to buy that firm?

Importance of source of monopoly power

That would depend upon how the monopoly has been obtained and maintained. If the firm has been granted this exclusive privilege, by contract, forever, then the monopoly is based on a transferable and capitalizable asset. So you would have to pay a price for the firm that reflected the expectation that it would make monopoly profits into the future (forever, in this case). Hence, only the original owner of the firm would benefit directly from the monopoly position that was bestowed upon the firm by the school.

Another possibility is that the school sells an exclusive (monopoly) contract every so often by open bidding. In this case, the winner of the bid has

---

[3]The analysis of economic losses is symmetrical; they are "capitalized" into the market value of the monopoly. The ATC curve would shift down.

a monopoly for the duration of the contract, but is willing to pay a price for the monopoly that reflects the expected future monopoly profits. In this case, the school collects the monopoly profits, and the firm has paid a price for the contract that should allow it to earn a normal rate of return. Again, the new owner of the firm will expect to earn only a competitive rate of return on investment, because the price paid reflected the expectation of future monopoly profits.

Still another possibility is that the monopoly is based on some nontransferable asset. Suppose, for example, the previous owner of the firm was given a monopoly on food service because his sister was the president of the school. In this case, the monopoly profits are what we call *rents* (which we will discuss in Chapter 16). Unless you expect to have such monopoly power transferred to you as new owner, you will again pay a price that will allow you to earn a competitive rate of return.

Regardless of whether the monopoly right is being sold, the *implicit* price for the resource exists. The total costs of operation to the monopolist include the opportunity cost of the sale value of the firm, whether or not the monopoly firm is actually sold. This will be discussed in more detail in the next chapter.

MEASURING MONOPOLY MARKET POWER

It is quite one thing to say that a monopoly exists; it is quite another to measure the *degree* to which it exists. There are several methods that can be used. We will look at the two most popular.

Industry concentration

Sometimes the measure of monopoly power is given by the amount of industry concentration. Industry concentration can be measured in a number of ways. The most popular is the percentage of total sales or production accounted for by, say, the top four or top eight firms. Thus, a four-firm **concentration ratio,** as it is called, of 80 percent—the top four firms together make 80 percent of the total revenues in the industry—implies more monopoly power than a four-firm concentration ratio of 50 percent, in which the top four together make only 50 percent of total industry revenues. An example of an industry with 25 firms is given below.

	Sales	
Firm 1	$150,000,000	
Firm 2	100,000,000	
Firm 3	80,000,000	= $400,000,000
Firm 4	70,000,000	
Firms 5–25 (together)	50,000,000	
Total	$450,000,000	

$$\text{Four-firm concentration ratio} = \frac{\$400,000,000}{\$450,000,000} = 88.9\%$$

TABLE 12-3
Concentration ratios (percent)

*Withheld by Commerce Department to avoid disclosing figures for individual companies.

Source: U.S. Department of Commerce

	Share of value of shipments accounted for by the:			
	Largest four companies		Largest eight companies	
	1967	1972	1967	1972
Motor vehicles	92	93	98	99
Primary copper	77	72	98	*
Aircraft	69	66	89	86
Synthetic rubber	61	62	82	81
Blast furnaces and steel mills	48	45	66	65
Industrial trucks and tractors	48	50	62	66
Construction machinery	41	43	53	54
Petroleum	33	31	57	56
Paper mills	26	24	43	40
Meatpacking	26	22	38	37
Newspapers	16	17	25	28
Fluid milk	22	18	30	26

Concentration ratios for the top 8, 20, and 50 firms in major industries are also computed and reported by the Bureau of the Census. In Table 12-3, we see concentration ratios that have been computed for various industries for the largest four and largest eight firms.

Although at first glance the concentration ratio seems to be a useful measure of monopoly power, it has a serious shortcoming: Monopoly power is a function not only of a firm's market share but of potential supply from either existing firms or firms that *could* enter the industry. As Paul Samuelson pointed out,[4] a one-firm industry concentration ratio would be 100 percent— i.e., one firm produces or sells the entire industry's output—and yet the monopoly power of that one firm would be zero if the potential supply elasticity were great enough. In other words, a price-output combination which yields economic profits in this situation will cause the existing monopoly to be deluged by new entrants into the industry. This point is also made in the theory of contestable markets that we considered at the end of the last chapter.

The Lerner Index

Professor Abba Lerner provided us another measure of monopoly power that avoids the necessity of inferring the degree of monopoly power from sales data. This index is as follows:

[4]Paul A. Samuelson, *Foundations of Economic Analysis* (New York: Atheneum, 1965), p. 79.

$$\text{Lerner Index of monopoly power} = \frac{P - \text{MC}}{P} \qquad (12\text{-}2)$$

where P = the price of the product and MC = marginal cost of production of the product. In essence, this index looks at the performance of a monopolist. This index measures the degree to which price deviates from marginal cost. For example, if MC = \$5 and monopoly price = \$10, the Lerner Index is

$$\frac{\$10 - \$5}{\$10} = 0.5, \text{ or } 50 \text{ percent}$$

The Lerner Index of monopoly power requires the ability to measure marginal cost. This is no easy task. We should remember, for instance, that long-run marginal cost will usually be different from short-run marginal cost. Moreover, price must refer to a constant-quality unit. Thus, when one attempts to compute the Lerner Index of monopoly power in order to compare firms across industries, you must try to quantify the qualitative aspects of products.

COMPARING PURE MONOPOLY WITH PERFECT COMPETITION

We will compare perfect competition and pure monopoly from just two perspectives: costs and output rates. Strictly speaking, in order to compare monopoly with competition, we must first obtain the long-run optimum plant size of the pure monopolist. We know that in the long run, if the monopolist can find no plant size that at least results in a competitive rate of return, the monopolist will go out of business. If, on the other hand, the monopolist is making a profit in the short run with one plant size, that monopolist must determine whether an even greater profit can be obtained with a larger or a smaller plant size. As with the long-run equilibrium of a competitive firm, the monopolist will adjust plant size so that it is operating on the long-run average cost curve. The long-run profit-maximizing rate of output will be such that the long-run marginal cost equals marginal revenue, as we see in Figure 12-8(b).

Comparing costs   Conceptually, in the long run, a perfectly competitive firm operates with an optimal plant size such that short-run average cost = long-run average cost = marginal revenue = price (= average revenue) = long-run marginal cost = short-run marginal cost. This is seen in Figure 12-8(a). However, compare this situation with the long-run equilibrium for the single-plant monopolist depicted in panel (b) of Figure 12-8. The profit-maximizing rate of output is Q_m. It is the output at which long-run marginal cost = marginal revenue = short-run marginal cost. But at that rate of output, neither short-

FIGURE 12-8
Comparing monopoly and competitive per unit costs and revenues
In panel (a) we show long-run equilibrium for a perfectly competitive firm. Its rate of output q_e is such that
SMC = SAC = LAC = LMC = MR = P. Moreover, average total cost is at a minimum. In panel (b) we show the
situation for a monopolist. At the profit-maximizing rate of output Q_m, the monopolist is not operating at the
minimum point A on its short-run average cost curve SAC or at the minimum point B on its LAC curve.

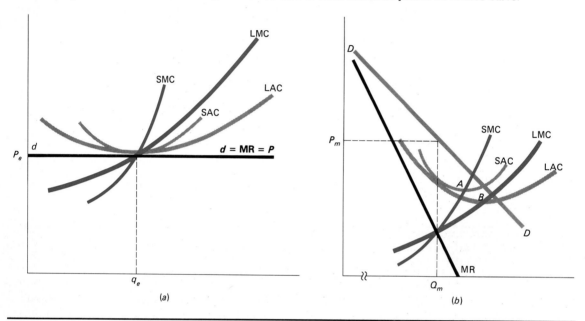

(a)　　　　　　　　　　　　　　　　(b)

run average cost nor LAC is at a minimum. The minimum SAC occurs at
point A, where SMC intersects SAC. The scale of the plant will not be such
that short-run and/or long-run average costs are a minimum at the rate of
output chosen to maximize profits. Thus in comparing monopoly with competition, some observers infer from a comparison of panels (a) and (b) that
monopoly is inefficient because average costs are not at a minimum.

We must be quick to point out, however, that although it may be possible
and even probable that the monopolist will not produce at the minimum of
the long-range average cost curve, no economist can present such a proposition with certainty. In fact, we could redraw panel (b) of Figure 12-8,
giving the demand curve a slope one-half as great as it had been given. The
monopolist's profit-maximizing rate of output would then end up closer to
where LAC is at a minimum. We see this in Figure 12-9, where, by chance,
the monopolist's profit-maximizing equilibrium looks like the profit-maximizing equilibrium for a firm in a perfectly competitive industry, except that
the monopolist is a price-maker instead of a price-taker, so that there are
monopoly profits.

The only way we can analyze the supposed inefficiency of a monopoly

FIGURE 12-9
Monopoly equilibrium that looks like competitive equilibrium
In this case, the slope of the demand curve facing the monopolist, and hence the slope of the MR curve, happens to produce an equilibrium for the monopolist firm-industry at the least-cost point on the LAC. This means that the monopoly output level (Q_m) appears to be the same as the output that would occur if the competitive price (P_e) existed, since that price is the demand and MR curve for the competitive firm. Obviously, the monopolist earns monopoly profits, but are the costs the same as if the monopolist was in a competitive industry?

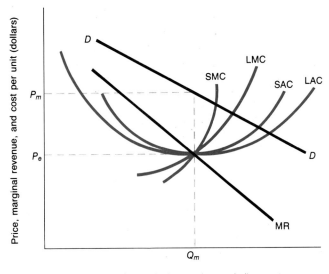

Output (units per time period)

is to set up the cost curves for a set of perfect competitors and then suddenly (somehow) make those costs into the costs of a monopolist. That we could effect this switch in market structure is an heroic assumption. That is, in Figure 12-9, the cost curves facing the monopolist appear to be the same as those facing a firm in a competitive industry; only the demand curve *looks* different for the monopoly firm compared to that facing the competitive firm. As we will see later, however, there are reasons to presume that the cost curves are in fact not identical. But let us put that assumption aside for the moment and compare the long-run price and output combinations in the two extreme market situations.

Comparing price and output

In Figure 12-10, we have drawn an industry demand schedule *DD*. Assume now that the industry is perfectly competitive and that each competitor has a horizontal marginal cost curve depicted by the horizontal line MC. Thus the horizontal summation of each firm's marginal cost curve is going to be the horizontal line at price P_c. The intersection, then, of the industry supply curve, which is MC, will be at *E*; the market-clearing price will be P_c; and an equilibrium quantity will be Q_c. Now we assume that overnight the in-

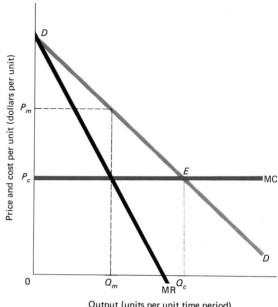

FIGURE 12-10
Comparing price and output for monopoly and competition
Assume constant marginal cost for the industry. Given an industry demand curve *DD*, and assuming that the industry supply curve is MC, the competitive industry output would be Q_c; the industry price would be P_c. Now consider the possibility that all firms become a single-monopoly firm overnight and that there are no changes in costs. The profit-maximizing rate of output will now fall to Q_m; the price will go up to P_m. The conclusion is that monopolization of a perfectly competitive industry restricts production and increases price, *ceteris paribus*.

dustry is fully monopolized—say, by government fiat—and owned by one person, and further that all cost curves remain exactly the same. The monopolist sets the rate of output where marginal cost = marginal revenue. (Perfect competitors do also, but for them MR = P.) The monopolist, then, sets the rate of output at Q_m. The monopolist can sell this rate of output at a price of P_m. Thus, under the assumption that the cost curves remain the same when the industry goes from competition to monopoly, we can state that the monopolist restricts production and raises price.

A monopoly with strong cost advantages

If there are strong cost advantages for the monopoly firm, it is conceivable that a monopoly could be selling more output at a lower price than a group of numerous competitors selling the same product. Consider this possibility in Figure 12-11. Here we have shown the market demand curve as *DD*. The market supply curve under competition is, for numerous firms, ΣMC. It is the horizontal summation of all individual firms' marginal cost curves above the minimum point of their average variable cost curves. Equilibrium occurs at price P_c and quantity Q_c. Now assume that the firms are monopolized; that is, all the firms are organized together into one firm, a monopoly firm. If there are really substantial cost advantages, the new marginal cost curve may be below the old industry supply curve at every point. This marginal cost curve for a monopolist is labeled MC. The monopolist will set the rate of output where marginal revenue = marginal cost. This rate of output will

FIGURE 12-11
Monopoly with strong cost advantage

Assume that the horizontally summed marginal cost curve ΣMC for a competitive situation is as drawn. Now the firm is monopolized, and it experiences tremendous cost advantages such that the marginal cost curve for the monopolist "shifts" downward as drawn. Profit-maximizing rate of output goes from Q_c out to Q_m, and price falls from P_c to P_m.

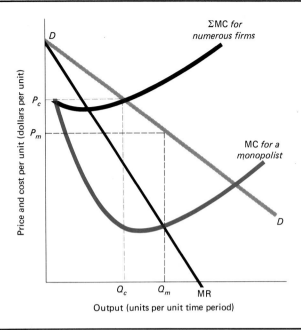

be Q_m. The monopolist will be able to sell that rate of output at a price of P_m. In this case, monopolization leads to an increase in the rate of output, which can be sold only at a lower price. We will see why this may arise when we study economies of scale in the next chapter.

PRICE DISCRIMINATION

In a perfectly competitive market, each buyer is charged the same price for every unit of the particular commodity (corrected, of course, for quality differences and differential transportation charges). Since the product is homogeneous and since we also assume full knowledge on the part of the buyers, a difference in price per constant-quality unit cannot exist. Any seller of the product who tried to charge a price higher than the going market price would find that no one would purchase from him or her. In this chapter, we have assumed up until now that the monopolist charged all consumers the same price for all units. A monopolist, however, may be able to charge different people different prices and/or different unit prices for successive units purchased by a given buyer. Either one or a combination of these is called **price discrimination**. The reason a firm wishes to engage in price discrimination is that, where feasible, such a practice will lead to increased revenues and profits from the same level of output and unit sales. It must be made clear at the outset that charging different prices to different people and/or for different units as a result of differences in the cost of service does *not* amount to price discrimination. This is **price differentiation**: differences in prices that reflect differences in marginal cost.

It is also true that a uniform price does not necessarily indicate an absence of price discrimination. If production costs vary by customer and all are charged the same price, this is also a case of price discrimination.

Necessary conditions for price discrimination

There are three necessary conditions for the existence of price discrimination:

1 The firm must have some market power (i.e., it is not a price taker).
2 The firm must be able to separate markets, both in terms of identifying persons or units of output with their part of the market and in terms of preventing resale between markets.
3 The buyers in the different markets must have different price elasticities of demand.

It is necessary that these two or more identifiable classes of buyers can be separated at a reasonable cost. Additionally, the monopolist must be able to prevent, at least partially, reselling by those buyers who paid a low price to those buyers who would be charged a higher price. For example, charging students a lower price than nonstudents for a movie can be done relatively easily. The cost of checking out student IDs apparently is not significant. Also, it is fairly easy to make sure that students do not resell their tickets to nonstudents—for example, if the use of the tickets requires a student ID card. As another example, price discrimination for medical services is easy. Resale of a coronary bypass operation is impossible.

Segmenting the markets

We know that for profit to be at a maximum, marginal revenue must equal marginal cost. For the monopolist who is able to discriminate between two classes of buyers, I and II, for profit to be at a maximum, $MR_I = MR_{II} = MC$. It is as if the goods sold to class I and class II were two *different* goods having exactly the same marginal cost of production. In other words, to maximize total profits, the monopolist wants to set marginal revenue equal to marginal cost in all markets in which it is selling. If marginal revenue in market I exceeded marginal cost, profits could be increased by expanding sales (lowering price) in market I. The same holds for market II. On the other hand, if marginal revenue in market I were less than marginal cost, profit could be increased by reducing sales (raising price) in market I. Again, the same holds for market II.

We show this in Figure 12-12. Class I buyers are represented in panel (*b*), class II buyers in panel (*a*). Note that in panel (*a*), the quantity sold to class II buyers gets larger as we move from the origin, 0, to the left. We assume for simplicity's sake that the marginal cost for servicing both classes of consumers is both equal and constant. Marginal cost equals marginal

FIGURE 12-12
Price discrimination in two separate markets with constant marginal cost

Assume that the monopolist has been able to separate two classes of demanders, I and II. The profit-maximizing rate of output for each class will be given by the respective intersection of MR_I and MR_{II} with the common marginal cost MC. The output rate for class I demanders will be Q_I; the price charged will be P_I. For class II demanders the price will be lower, P_{II}. The demand curve for class II consumers is more elastic at any given P because it cuts the vertical axis closer to the origin.

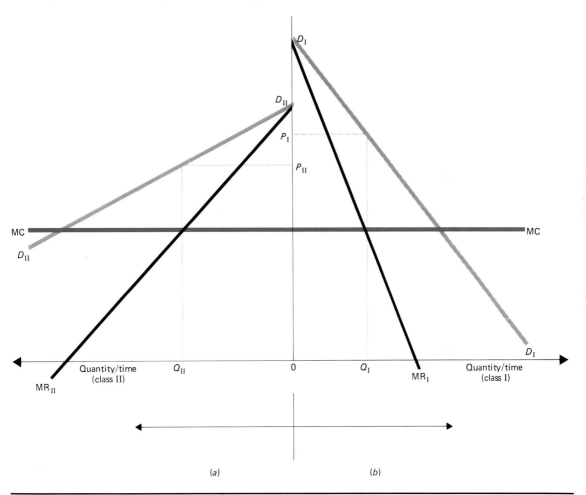

for class I at quantity Q_I. The price at which this quantity can be sold is P_I. On the other hand, for buyers in class II, who have a more elastic demand curve (at any given P) than class I buyers, the intersection of marginal cost with MR_{II} is at quantity Q_{II}. The price at which this quantity is sold is P_{II}, which is lower than P_I. In other words, the price-discriminating monopolist will sell that same product to the class of buyers with a relatively less elastic demand curve at a higher price than that charged to the other class of buyers with a relatively higher elasticity of demand.

This can be seen by using the formula in Eq. (12-1) and equating the two marginal revenues:

$$MR_I = P_I\left(1 + \frac{1}{\eta_I}\right)$$

$$MR_{II} = P_{II}\left(1 + \frac{1}{\eta_{II}}\right)$$

(12-3)

At Q_I for class I buyers and Q_{II} for class II buyers, these two marginal revenues are equal. Since $MR_I = MR_{II} = MC$, we get

$$P_I\left(1 + \frac{1}{\eta_I}\right) = P_{II}\left(1 + \frac{1}{\eta_{II}}\right)$$

(12-4)

We know, however, that class I buyers have a market demand schedule that is more inelastic than that of class II buyers. In order for the two sides of Eq. (12-4) to be equal, P_I must be greater than P_{II}.

The general case   We can take the more general case with an upward-sloping marginal cost curve to show the profit-maximizing prices that a price-discriminating monopolist will charge to two identifiably different classes of demanders. In Figure 12-13, we have shown a demand curve for class I as $D_I D_I$. Its marginal revenue curve is labeled MR_I. Class II demanders have a demand curve represented by $D_{II}D_{II}$ and a marginal revenue curve MR_{II}. In this case, the relative elasticity of demand is numerically greater for class II demanders than for class I demanders. (This is so even though $D_{II}D_{II}$ at first glance looks more inelastic than $D_I D_I$ because it is steeper; however, remember from Chapter 5 that we cannot determine the elasticity of demand by the *slope* of the demand curve. Using the vertical axis formula for elasticity, we found in Chapter 5 that whichever demand curve intersects the vertical axis closer to the origin will be the relatively more elastic one.)

We now derive the summed marginal revenue curve labeled $MR_I + MR_{II}$ in Figure 12-13. Here we are horizontally summing the two separate marginal revenue curves. The horizontally summed marginal revenue curve intersects the common marginal cost curve at point E; thus, the profit-maximizing quantity to be produced and sold is Q_m. We now have a marginal cost labeled C_1 on the vertical axis. To satisfy the profit-maximization criterion, which requires that marginal revenue be equal to marginal cost, a monopolist will allocate quantity Q_I to class I and quantity Q_{II} to class II; $Q_I + Q_{II} = Q_m$. These quantities are given by the respective intersections of specific marginal cost C_1 with marginal revenue in each separate market. The prices that will be charged are P_I and P_{II}, or the prices at which the profit-maximizing quantities can be sold in each individual market. As in the previous example, in the market with the more numerically elastic demand curve, the price will be lower than in the market with the less elastic demand curve, i.e., $P_{II} < P_I$.

FIGURE 12-13
Price discrimination: the general case
We horizontally sum the marginal revenue curves to derive $MR_I + MR_{II}$. The summed marginal revenue curve intersects the common marginal cost curve at point E. The total output rate will be Q_m. It will be distributed between the two classes so that the first receives Q_I and the second receives Q_{II}. We find the prices that the monopolist can charge for those rates of output on their respective demand curves: Class I buyers will pay a higher price P_I than the P_{II} charged class II buyers.

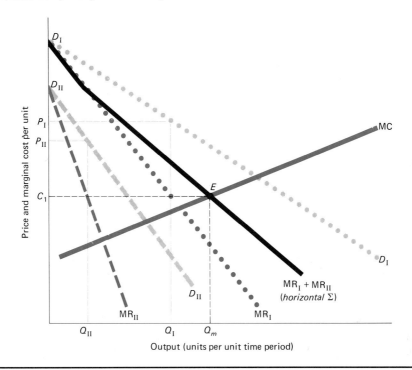

The different types of price discrimination

Economists define three types of price discrimination. (There are more if one wishes to stretch the point.) They are labeled first, second, and third degree. We summarize these in Table 12-4. What we have just talked about, and seen in Figure 12-13, is third-degree price discrimination.

Third-degree price discrimination. **Third-degree price discrimination** occurs when a monopolist charges different prices in different markets for the same product. That is exactly what we have shown above. There were two different markets for the product. A higher price was charged in the market with the less elastic demand. Charging students a lower price than nonstudents for movies, magazines, and professional journals is a common example of third-degree price discrimination. Charging senior citizens a lower price than other buyers for movies and spectator events is another common example. So-called dumping—selling domestically produced products abroad at lower prices than are charged domestically—is yet another example of price discrimination.

TABLE 12-4
Forms of price discrimination

Type of price discrimination	Attributes	Examples
Third-degree	Different classes of buyers charged different prices for same product.	Student and senior-citizen discounts at entertainment events and on public transportation.
Second-degree	Declining rate schedules; lower price per unit as larger quantities purchased.	Electricity pricing; quantity discounts at supermarkets.
First-degree (perfect)	Each buyer charged exactly that price which leaves him or her indifferent between buying and not buying.	Wholesale diamond sales; haggling over prices of souvenirs in "tourist traps."

Second-degree price discrimination. **Second-degree price discrimination** is found when there are many buyers within each market and there are differences among buyers in the number of units of the good they purchase. A declining rate schedule embodying "quantity discounts" is an example of this type of discrimination. Some electric utilities charge lower prices for each additional "block" of electricity used. Those customers who use a specified large amount of electricity can buy the next block at a lower price. Second-degree price discrimination induces greater consumption by offering quantity discounts that are made in a stepladder fashion. Look at Figure 12-17 in the Issues and Applications section at the end of this chapter for an example of block pricing or step pricing.

Another name for second-degree price discrimination is **multipart pricing**. Multipart pricing involves charging successively lower prices for the marginal unit of a commodity as more of the commodity is purchased. Multipart pricing occurs, for example, in supermarkets when you are allowed to buy one can for 50¢ and two cans for 99¢. In other words, the first can is 50¢ and the marginal price of the second can is 49¢. A uniform price of 49.5¢ is charged to all those who buy two cans, and so on.[5]

There is a difference between multipart pricing, which is second-degree price discrimination, and first-degree, or perfect, price discrimination. Mul-

---

[5]Some economists contend that multipart pricing in supermarkets is not a form of price discrimination but rather a classic case of price *differentiation*. They point out that supermarkets are highly competitive and that multipart pricing is merely a method by which they economize on transactions costs; e.g., it takes less cashier time per unit sold when larger quantities are purchased. This saving in cashier time is, in essence, "passed on" to the consumer who buys in larger quantities. (A way to reconcile these two hypotheses is to point out that the competitors must use multipart pricing merely to survive.)

tipart pricing is an *imperfect* way to extract as much money as possible from each consumer. It is a way of dealing with broad, discrete intervals of quantity purchased and charging appropriate revenue-maximizing prices for each additional unit purchased without ever selling any unit below MC.

First-degree price discrimination. In **first-degree, or perfect, price discrimination** the monopolist is able to charge each buyer the maximum amount that the person would be willing to pay rather than do without the specified quantity of the commodity being offered. Consider, for example, a situation in which you are a diamond purchaser. You go into a small room in which a sack of diamonds is exhibited to you. You are faced with the choice of "take it or leave it." If the seller of the diamonds can figure out exactly the shape of your demand curve, you can be charged a price which leaves you indifferent to buying or not buying the sack of diamonds. You will then be the "victim" of perfect price discrimination. This is illustrated in Figure 12-14, where we see that the monopolist has been able to move down its demand curve so that every buyer pays the highest price, unit by unit, he or she is willing to pay for the good in question. The seller then earns the highest revenues possible, as shown by the shaded area under the demand

---

FIGURE 12-14
First-degree (perfect) price discrimination
The seller knows the highest price that each buyer is willing to pay for each unit of the good, or is able to determine that information by a pricing strategy that forces each buyer to reveal their demand for each unit. This allows the monopolist to capture the full value that buyers have for the good—the shaded area QQ_mAD.

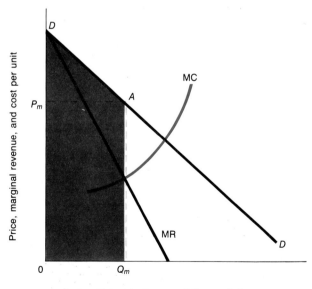

Output (units per unit time period)

curve, starting from the most highly valued customer's purchase down to the last units sold at P_m. This is unusual in practice because of the many special conditions required for it to work.

WHEN PRICE DISCRIMINATION IS REQUIRED FOR "EXISTENCE" OF AN INDUSTRY

Sometimes price discrimination is necessary if an industry is to continue to exist (or to begin in the first place). Consider the situation depicted in Figure 12-15. We have drawn the demand curves for two different classes of buyers of the product in question. Those curves are labeled D_1D_1 and D_2D_2. We know that demand curve D_2D_2 is relatively more price-elastic than D_1D_1 because it cuts the vertical axis closer to the origin. We now horizontally sum these two demand curves in order to derive the total, or market, demand curve that would face a monopolist in this industry. This demand curve is the heavily shaded line labeled D_1D_T. This market demand curve coincides with the demand curve D_1D_1 until the price at which D_2D_2 begins.

We have drawn in a long-run average cost curve, LAC, which is *everywhere* above the market demand curve D_1D_T. Thus, if a single price had to be charged in this market, there would be no single price that would allow the monopolist to cover long-run average costs. The industry would not exist.

Now consider the possibility of third-degree price discrimination. The profit-maximizing prices for the two different classes of demanders are given as P_1 and P_2. They are derived in the same manner employed in Figure 12-13. We have, for the sake of simplicity, drawn in neither the separate marginal revenue curves nor horizontally summed marginal revenue and

FIGURE 12-15
Price discrimination necessary for industry's existence
If the long-run average cost curve is everywhere above the market demand curve D_1D_T, the firm cannot exist without price discrimination. If, however, the monopolist is allowed to charge P_1 to those with less elastic demand and P_2 to those with more elastic demand, the weighted average price P_3 would just equal long-run average cost at point A. The industry can and will exist.

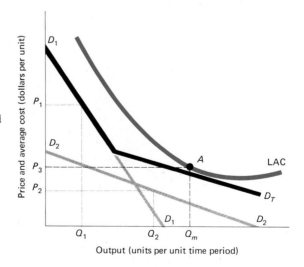

marginal cost curves. The profit-maximizing quantity that would be sold to class 1 demanders is given as Q_1, and to class 2 demanders it is Q_2. The total quantity that the price-discriminating monopolist would provide is given as Q_m ($= Q_1 + Q_2$). It is sold at a (weighted) average price of P_3, which, in this particular example, is just equal to long-run average costs at rate of output Q_m, or point A. The weighted average price is

$$P_3 = \frac{Q_1 P_1 + Q_2 P_2}{Q_m}$$

In this instance, unless price discrimination is both feasible and permitted, the industry will not exist; i.e., the product will not be offered for sale.

A FINAL NOTE: BUSINESS PRICING BEHAVIOR

It is not unrealistic to assume that most businesses face downward-sloping demand curves. Although they are not pure monopolists, they are certainly not perfect competitors. A common method of business pricing is called **markup pricing**. It involves tacking a markup of, say, 20 percent or 40 percent onto the unit cost of production. Is such behavior consistent with anything we have said in this chapter? It turns out that it is.

Remember that profit maximization requires in every instance that marginal cost equal marginal revenue. Using the formula for marginal revenue given in Eq. (12-1), if MC = MR and MR = $P(1 + 1/\eta)$, to maximize profits, it is necessary that

$$\text{MC} = P\left(1 + \frac{1}{\eta}\right) \tag{12-5}$$

Dividing both sides of Eq. (12-5) by $(1 + 1/\eta)$, we find that price equals

$$P = \text{MC}\left(\frac{1}{1 + 1/\eta}\right) \tag{12-6}$$

which becomes

$$P = \text{MC}\left(\frac{1}{\eta/\eta + 1/\eta}\right) = \text{MC}\,\frac{1}{[(\eta + 1)/\eta]} \tag{12-7}$$

which becomes

$$P = \text{MC}\left(\frac{\eta}{\eta + 1}\right) \tag{12-8}$$

Now consider the case in which there are constant returns to scale over a very wide range of output. With constant returns to scale, long-run average cost equals long-run marginal cost. We also know that LAC is the same as long-run variable cost (in the long run all costs are variable). Thus Eq. (12-8) becomes

$$P = \text{AVC} \left(\frac{\eta}{\eta + 1} \right) \tag{12-9}$$

Assume, as an example, that $\eta = -4$. Using Eq. (12-9), we obtain

$$\text{Price} = \text{AVC} \left(\frac{-4}{-3} \right) = \text{AVC}(1.33) \tag{12-10}$$

Hence, if $\eta = -4$, price should be set equal to average cost plus a one-third markup. In other words, markup pricing, based on average costs, may be an attempt by a business to guess at the coefficient of price elasticity of demand.

Note that even if a monopolist could use markup pricing, it would not follow that all business people who use such markup pricing are, therefore, monopolists.

ISSUES AND APPLICATIONS

Price controls for a monopoly

It turns out that a price control put on a monopolist can result in not only a lower price but a larger quantity supplied. This can be seen in Figure 12-16. In panel (a) the monopolist's demand curve is DD, and the resultant marginal revenue curve is labeled MR.

The marginal cost curve (MC) intersects the marginal revenue curve at a rate of output Q_m, which can be sold at a price of P_m. Now assume that the government sets a maximum price of P_{max}, as shown in panel (b). How much will the monopolist produce at this price? We want to find out where marginal revenue = marginal cost. There is a new marginal revenue curve which is different from the old one. It is the heavily shaded line from P_{max} to point A on the demand curve, for at quantities from zero to Q'_m they can all be sold at a price of P_{max}, which is the legal maximum price. After point A (quantity Q'_m), however, the monopolist faces the remainder of the downward-sloping demand curve; then the

original (pre-price control) marginal revenue curve becomes relevant. We have shown a new marginal revenue curve, then, which is $P_{max}ABMR$; it is discontinuous at quantity Q'_m. The heavily shaded portion on the original (pre-price control) marginal revenue curve coincides with the new marginal revenue curve. If MC intersects the perpendicular dashed line between point A and point B, for marginal revenue to "equal" marginal cost, the quantity to be sold would be Q'_m at price P_{max}. We find that an appropriately established price control on the monopolist can, in principle, lead to a higher quantity sold with no "shortages."

An excess quantity demanded ("shortage") would result if the legal maximum price were set below the intersection of the marginal cost curve and the marginal demand curve, that is, below point E. (Can you show why on Figure 12-16?) Moreover, the diagram that we have worked with does not show what

FIGURE 12-16

Price controls on a monopolist

In panel (a) we show the unrestricted monopoly profit-maximizing price as P_m and output as Q_m. If the maximum price is set at P_{max}, panel (b) indicates that the monopolist can sell all it wants at that price up to quantity Q'_m. Thus, the heavily shaded horizontal line now becomes marginal revenue up to quantity Q'_m. It then has a discontinuous portion from A down to B and is coincident with the old marginal revenue curve thereafter. Profit maximization requires that MC = MR. This occurs at quantity Q'_m in the discontinuous portion of the new marginal revenue curve. The monopolist's output will have increased (from Q_m to Q'_m) as a result of the price control.

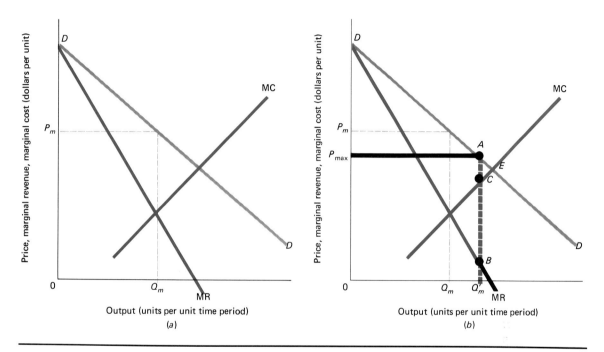

Output (units per unit time period)

(a)

Output (units per unit time period)

(b)

the rate of return to investment is for the monopolist. If the price control were set at a price ($P <$ ATC) that resulted in economic losses, the monopolist would go out of business in the long run.

PRICE CONTROLS AND THE "REAL WORLD"

There are problems with the "two-dimensional" price-quantity analysis just given. In the real world, the output of the monopolist is typically a combination of several commodities. As an example, consider the commodity

"telephone services." There are numerous qualities of telephone services. A price control on the monopolist who provides telephone services will result in one or more of the *quality* dimensions being compromised. For example, the telephone company, in the face of price controls, can reduce the availability of service personnel, the quality of voice transmission, the speed with which new phones are installed, and so forth. The regulatory agency can easily exert control over price but cannot easily, if at all, exert control over the many other dimensions of the commodity. The monopolist has, in effect, monopoly power despite price controls.

Do public utilities price-discriminate?

It is often asserted that public utilities engage in price discrimination. We can, indeed, analyze some of their pricing policies in terms of second-degree price discrimination. Public utilities do use multipart pricing, or what they call declining-block pricing.

Consider Figure 12-17. Here we are looking at the hypothetical demand curve of an individual customer of the electric utility. We now consider the total revenues that are available to the electric utility from this one customer. If the electric utility wanted to sell the quantity q_1, it could do so by charging the uniform price of P_1 [the demand curve in panel

(a) and panel (b) is the same]. The utility would receive a total revenue equal to the area $0P_1Aq_1$.

However, if the utility engages in multipart pricing, or second-degree price discrimination, it may use the price schedule seen in panel (a). It charges P_2 for the first q_2 of kilowatts consumed per month, then charges P_1 for kilowatts consumed between q_2 and q_1. It would then earn the same revenues as it earned before—for selling the same number of kilowatts—but would now add more revenues because of the block pricing. It would add the area P_1P_2CB to its total from before.

If the utility moves to an even more com-

FIGURE 12-17
Declining block pricing
Public utilities often use declining block pricing in which separate "blocks" of electricity can be purchased at declining prices. If the utility charges a uniform price of P_1, its revenues will be $0P_1Aq_1$. If the utility charges a price of P_2 for the first q_2 kilowatts used, in panel (a), and then P_1 for the next "block" of electricity used up to q_1, its total revenues will equal what it earned before, $0P_1Aq_1$, plus the new revenues from the block pricing, P_1BCP_2, for total revenues of $0P_2CBAq_1$. If the utility goes to a more elaborate, four-part pricing scheme, in panel (b), from the same customers it can extract more revenues for the same quantity sold: $0P_4GFEDCBAq_1$.

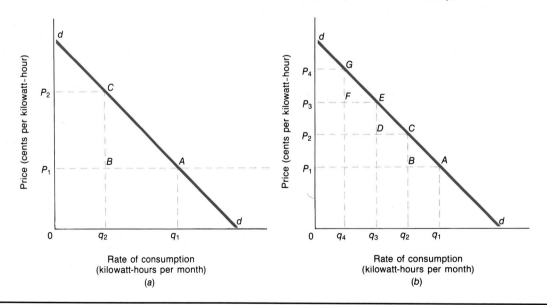

plicated pricing scheme, with more steps in the pricing schedule, it could obtain a result like we see in panel (b). Here the same consumer pays even more to the utility for consuming the same amount as before. The first quantity of electricity consumed, level q_4, costs the most—P_4. The next quantity of electricity

consumed during the month, from q_4 to q_3, costs the consumer P_3; and so on down to quantity q_1. The utility extracts more revenues than before, capturing the dollars under the steps in the diagram—$0P_4GFEDCBAq_1$ in total.

Third-degree price discrimination: 25¢ off on your next box of cereal

BRINGING IN NEW CUSTOMERS

We have all seen coupons in magazines, newspapers, and other places that can be used to purchase some product for less than its current retail price. These coupons usually give a specific amount, such as 25¢, that is to be cut from the price of a specific product, such as Ryan's Half-Grain Cereal, and states "one per customer." This is an example of third-degree price discrimination. Contrary to the negative implication of the words "price discrimination," this is something that clearly improves the welfare of society—both the producers and the customers are made better off.[6]

BRINGING IN NEW CUSTOMERS

The primary purpose of such coupons is to get new customers to purchase the product in question. If the producer could somehow make sure that existing customers, who were already buying the product, did not get the coupons, the market would have been "sealed"—the new customers and the old customers separated—and the price discrimination would be perfect. Even without the ability to seal the market, the primary effect is still the same—new customers are induced to purchase a

product that they previously did not buy because its price was higher than they valued the product.

We can see this in Figure 12-18. For simplicity we assume the marginal cost of the product to be constant. The producer faces an existing demand curve, D_0, for its product, which is composed of all of the "old" customers. Behaving as a monopolist, price is set where $MC = MR_0$, so that quantity Q_m is sold at price P_m. Now coupons are issued to induce new customers to buy the product who would not do so previously, so there is a new demand curve that begins at P_m, located at point a along D_0. We label this D_n, the demand curve of the new customers. If the coupon discount has been set properly by the producer, it is where $MC = MR_n$, so that the retail price for the new customers is P_n. The difference between P_m and P_n is the coupon discount.

EVERYONE BENEFITS

Obviously we are observing profit-maximizing pricing by the use of price discrimination. The producer has benefited because total profits have increased from the old level of $MCeaP_m$ to $MCdcbaP_m$. Consumers have benefited because all of the new customers are obtaining a product that they now value more highly than its market price. When this occurs we can say that there has been improvement in

[6]This analysis is drawn from Sumner J. La Croix, "Marketing, Price Discrimination, and Welfare," *Southern Economic Journal*, January 1983, pp. 847–852.

FIGURE 12-18
Third-degree price discrimination: a sealed market
Facing demand D_0, the producer maximized profits by equating MR_0 and MC, so that price is P_m, at which Q_m is sold. Profits are equal to the box, $MCeaP_m$. Coupons are sent to induce new customers to buy their product. Their demand curve is D_n. For this group of customers, profits are maximized by equating MR_n and MC. The coupon reduces the price they pay from P_m to P_n, so they purchase quantity Q_n. Additional profits equal to the box $edcb$ are collected, raising total profits to $MCdcbaP_m$.

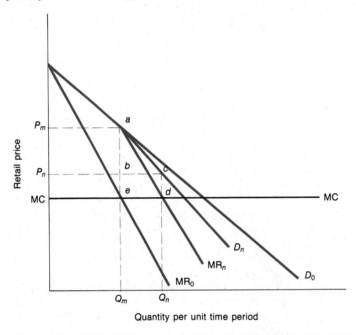

Quantity per unit time period

general welfare—everyone is better off, no one has been hurt.

We know that it is difficult to seal markets, so that some old customers obtain the coupons and pay price P_n rather than price P_m. This has, of course, made them better off. The producer suffers from the loss of profits from the customers who would have paid P_m, but, as long as the added profits from the new customers outweigh the reduction in profits from the old customers, the producer is still better off by allowing the coupons to be used.

SUMMARY

1 A pure monopolist is the only firm in the industry and faces the industry demand curve, which is, by necessity, downward-sloping. The demand curve facing a monopolist will be more elastic the more numerous, better, and lower-priced are the substitutes. However, there is a trade-off between closeness of substitutes and number; a large number of imperfect

substitutes will lead to a relatively elastic demand curve in the same manner as will a few good substitutes.

2 Since price elasticity of demand for the monopolist's product is numerically greater than 0 and less than $-\infty$, marginal revenue is less than price.

3 The monopolist will never willingly operate on the inelastic portion of the demand curve.

4 Monopoly marginal revenue is greater in the long run than in the short run because is takes time for buyers to respond to price changes.

5 The profit-maximizing price-output combination is found by discovering that rate of output at which MR = MC and then determining the maximum price at which that quantity can be sold, the latter being obtained from the demand curve.

6 A monopolist does not have a supply curve (defined as the locus of points showing the minimum prices at which given quantities will be offered for sale). Any particular monopoly price can result in a wide variety of rates of output; and the output produced will depend on the shape and position of the demand curve.

7 Economic profit occurs when average total cost is less than price. Monopoly should not, however, be equated with profits; many monopolists go out of business or never go into business because average total costs are everywhere above their demand curve.

8 A monopolist will operate several plants so that
MR $= \Sigma$MC $=$ MC$_1$ $=$ MC$_2$ $= \ldots$.

9 Anyone wishing to purchase a monopoly can expect to pay the fully discounted present value of future economic profits. Thus, the expected rate of return to the new buyer will be the normal rate of return corrected for risk, rather than the monopoly rate of return.

10 There are a number of measures of monopoly power, such as the concentration ratio and the Lerner Index. All of them have deficiencies. The concentration ratio, for example, does not take potential suppliers into account.

11 In general, we can predict that a monopoly will produce a lower rate of output and sell at a higher price than will a competitive industry, *ceteris paribus*. Moreover, the monopolist will generally not operate at a rate of output at which long-run average costs are at a minimum.

12 A monopolist can usually make a higher profit by engaging in price discrimination; this, however, requires that consumer classes be identifiable and separable and that those who purchase the product at a

lower price be effectively prevented from reselling it to those who would have to purchase it at a higher price.

13 The discriminating monopolist who engages in third-degree price discrimination will charge those with more elastic demands a price lower than the price it charges to those with less elastic demands.

14 Quantity discounts are a common type of multipart pricing in which the price of the last unit purchased is less than the price of previous units; however, in many cases, this may be a form of price differentiation because transactions costs per unit typically fall as larger quantities are purchased.

15 Price discrimination is necessary for an industry to come into existence or to continue to exist when the long-run average cost curve is everywhere above the industry demand curve.

GLOSSARY

- **monopolist** Single seller or supplier of a well-defined commodity for which there are no close substitutes.
- **nondiscriminating monopoly** A monopolist that charges a uniform price for all units sold.
- **discriminating monopoly** A monopolist that charges different prices for different units of an identical product.
- **price searcher** A firm that does not take as given the price at which it can sell its product; rather, it searches out the profit-maximizing price-output combination; to be contrasted with a price taker in a competitive industry.
- **concentration ratio** The percentage of total sales in an industry accounted for by a specified number of firms, such as the top four or the top eight.
- **Lerner Index of monopoly power** A measure of supposed monopoly power given by the ratio $(P - MC)/P$, where P = price and MC = marginal cost.
- **price discrimination** Charging different classes of buyers a different price for different units of an identical product; or alternatively, charging the same price for products that have different marginal costs.
- **price differentiation** Price differences which reflect differences in marginal cost.
- **third-degree price discrimination** Different classes of demanders are distinguished by their relative price elasticities of demand; those with relatively less elastic demands are charged a higher price than those with relatively more elastic demands.
- **second-degree price discrimination** Discrimination on the basis of quantity purchased. A declining rate schedule embodying quantity discounts is an example.
- **multipart pricing** A type of second-degree price discrimination in which the customer is charged a successively lower price for each marginal unit as more is purchased.

- **first-degree, or perfect, price discrimination** Price discrimination in which every bit of consumer surplus is extracted by charging from each consumer the highest price they would be willing to pay for each unit of the good purchased.
- **markup pricing** A type of business practice in which a gross profit margin of some specified amount (20 or 40 percent, for example) is added on to the unit cost of production to determine the price.

QUESTIONS

(Answers to even-numbered questions are at back of text.)

1 "Since a monopolist is the only supplier of a well-defined product, there is no limit to the price it may charge." Is this statement true or false? Explain.
2 Explain why a monopolist will never set a price (and produce the corresponding output) at which the demand is price-inelastic.
3 If you were the monopoly owner of a perishable good, the demand for which was linear, would it be in your best interest to let some of the good "perish" rather than sell it all? Assume that you charge a single unit price for the good (i.e., there is no price discrimination). Also, how would you decide how much to charge?
4 Summarize the relation between price elasticity of demand and marginal revenue.
5 Why should a monopolist's long-run marginal revenue (and elasticity) be greater than its short-run marginal revenue (and elasticity)?
6 Explain how a non-price-discriminating monopolist determines the profit-maximizing output, the price to charge per unit, and what the resultant economic profits, if any, will be.
7 Will a non-price-discriminating monopolist whose total revenue (TR) is less than total cost (TC) go out of business? Explain.
8 Explain how monopoly profits or losses are capitalized into the market value of a firm.
9 Why is it impossible to construct a monopolist's supply curve?
10 Why in the world would a monopolist making economic profits want to "rock the boat" by making long-run changes in its scale of operations? Why tinker with a good thing?
11 "The ultimate monopoly product would be one whose cross elasticity of demand, with respect to any and all other products, was zero." Comment.
12 Contrast the long-run equilibrium of a non-price-discriminating monopolist with that of a perfectly competitive firm. Assume constant returns to scale.
13 What type (degree) of price discrimination might a doctor practice with respect to vasectomies, and what might limit his or her power to do so? What problem might a shoe repair shop owner have in discriminating that the above doctor wouldn't have?
14 In what way is first-degree price discrimination merely a special case of second-degree (multipart) price discrimination?
15 "The reason movie theaters charge youngsters and oldsters less than the rest of us is because theater owners want to help these two low-income groups." Comment.

16 The airlines have a long history of price discrimination in fares, whether or not the airlines were regulated. Often they charge the least for tickets purchased substantially in advance of travel and charge less for travel on certain days of the week. Construct a graph that shows the different fare arrangements and see if this implies that the "full fare" passengers are subsidizing the "discount fare" passengers.

SELECTED REFERENCES

Dewey, D., *Monopoly in Economics and Law* (Chicago: Rand McNally, 1959).

Harrod, R.F., "Doctrines of Imperfect Competition," *Quarterly Journal of Economics,* vol. 48, May 1934, pp. 442–470.

Hicks, J.R., "Annual Survey of Economic Theory: The Theory of Monopoly," *Econometrica,* vol. 3, January 1935, pp. 1–20; also in George J. Stigler and Kenneth E. Boulding (eds.), *Readings in Price Theory,* American Economic Association (Chicago: Irwin, 1952).

Machlup, Fritz, *The Political Economy of Monopoly* (Baltimore: Johns Hopkins, 1952).

Mansfield, Edwin, *Monopoly Power and Economic Performance,* 3d ed. (New York: Norton, 1974).

Marshall, Alfred, *Principles of Economics,* 8th ed. (London: Macmillan, 1920), book 5, chap. 14.

Robinson, E.A.G., *Monopoly* (London: James Nisbet & Company, Ltd., 1941).

Robinson, Joan, *The Economics of Imperfect Competition* (London: Macmillan, 1933), chaps. 2, 3, 15, and 16.

The creation, regulation, and destruction of monopolies

*T*he popular conception of what constitutes a monopoly and the economic definition of what constitutes a monopoly often differ. In the last chapter we defined a monopolist as the single seller of a commodity for which there are no close substitutes. We will examine some of the implications of that definition here as we consider how monopolies arise, the forces that would tend to perpetuate or reduce monopoly power, and the ways in which certain types of monopolies are regulated.

One popular concept that we will dismiss is the notion that high profits necessarily imply monopoly power. As the chapter on competitive pricing and output noted, a change in demand may produce high profits for firms in very competitive industries—in the short run. Those profits signal firms in the industry to expand output and signal other firms to enter the industry, soon driving profits back to the competitive level. Also remember the importance of the notion of "no close subsitutes" for the product or service produced by the monopolist. Only the Apple Computer Company may sell the MacIntosh computer. But does that make Apple Computer a monopolist? Apparently not, since many people find other computers to be close substitutes for the MacIntosh. What then, is required to produce a monopoly as we define it in economic theory? We start by discussing the ways in which barriers to entry allow firms to receive monopoly profits in the long run.

BARRIERS TO ENTRY

For monopoly power to continue to exist in the long run, there has to be some way in which the market is closed to entry. Either legal means or certain aspects of the industry's technical or cost structure may prevent entry. Below we will discuss several of the **barriers to entry** that have allowed firms to reap monopoly profits in the long run.

Ownership of resources without close substitutes

Preventing a newcomer from entering an industry is often difficult. Indeed, there are some economists who contend that no monopoly acting without government support has been able to prevent entry into its industry unless that monopoly had control of some natural resource essential to the production of that industry's output. For instance, suppose one firm owns the entire supply of a raw material that is essential in the production of a particular commodity. This exclusive ownership of a vital resource serves as a barrier to entry until an alternative source of the raw material is found or an alternative technology not requiring the raw material in question is developed. A good example of this is the Aluminum Company of America (Alcoa), a firm that, prior to World War II, controlled the world's bauxite, the essential raw material in the production of aluminum. (We'll look more closely at the Alcoa experience in this chapter's Issues and Applications section.)

Such exclusive ownership must be distinguished from cases in which a unique resource happens to earn large payments (called rents). For example, Michael Jackson has earned many millions of dollars from his entertainment ability. These earnings, from recordings and concerts, are not monopoly profits in an economic sense. That would be the case if Mr. Jackson had been able to control the production of all records and cassettes, so that his current or would-be competitors could not offer their competing talents to the public. Similarly, the founder of Apple Computers was made very wealthy by his entrepreneurial talents, but he did not have the advantage of any barrier to entry against competitors.

Economies of scale

Sometimes it is not feasible for more than one firm to exist in an industry in the sense that costs are too high for more than one firm to make a normal rate of return. This would occur when the industry demand curve's relation to the firm's long-run average cost curve is such that two (or more) firms sharing the market could not each cover average total costs individually. Only when one firm engages in the production of the product can there be economies of scale and can average total costs be covered.

Consider the situation depicted in Figure 13-1. Here the industry demand curve is DD, and the long-run average total cost curve is LAC. Notice that long-run average total costs are falling over a wide range of outputs. Indeed,

FIGURE 13-1
Economies of scale and monopoly
Assume that the industry demand curve is *DD*. A single monopolist has a long-run average total cost curve LAC. It produces where long-run marginal cost LMC intersects marginal revenue MR, or at point *E*, which is at quantity Q_m. It can sell this quantity at price P_m. It makes a profit per unit of the vertical distance between points *A* and *B*. Now, if two (equivalent) firms enter the industry and each shares the market equally, each firm's demand curve would be equal to d_1, which is equal to $\frac{1}{2}DD$. d_1 coincides with the original marginal revenue curve facing the monopolist. However, with two firms in the industry, each would suffer economic losses because the average total cost curve LAC is everywhere above the proportionate demand curve facing each of the two firms in that industry. Only one firm can survive.

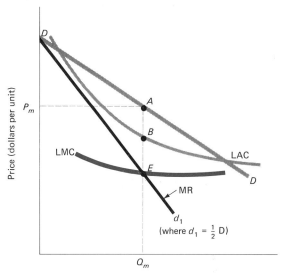

over the entire range of outputs for which the long-run average total cost curve lies below the industry demand curve, average total costs are falling. One firm can successfully operate in this industry at a rate of output of Q_m and make a profit per unit equal to the vertical distance between points *A* and *B*. The profit-maximizing output rate Q_m is determined by the intersection of the monopolist's long-run marginal cost curve LMC and its marginal revenue curve MR. That intersection occurs at point *E*.

Now consider what would happen if the industry were split evenly between two firms, firm 1 and firm 2. Each firm's demand curve would look like the demand curve d_1.[1] (Demand curve d_1 is identical to the single monopolist's marginal revenue curve MR.) Notice that each duopolist's demand (average revenue) curve is everywhere below the long-run average total cost curve. Thus it would not be profitable for a second firm to enter this industry and share the sales. As you can see, we have a situation in which economies of scale are so great in relation to demand that the long-run average total cost curve falls over such a large range that only one firm can successfuly exist in this market. This is called a **natural monopoly**, which we will discuss later in this chapter.

[1]They each have identical price elasticities of demand at any given price because they intersect the vertical axis at the same point.

Licenses, franchises, and certificates of convenience

In may industries it is illegal to enter without a governmentally provided license or "certificate of convenience and public necessity." As a specific example, you could not form an electric utility to compete with the electric utility operating in your area. You would first have to obtain a certificate of convenience and public necessity from the appropriate authority, which is usually the state's public utility commission. However, public utility commissions rarely, if ever, issue a certificate to a group of investors who want to compete directly in the same geographic area with an existing electric utility; hence, entry into the industry in a particular geographic area is prohibited, and long-run monopoly profits could conceivably be earned by the electric utility already serving the area.

In order to enter interstate (and also many intrastate) markets for pipelines, television and radio signals, the production of natural gas, and so on, it is necessary to obtain the equivalent of a certificate of convenience and public necessity.[2] Since these franchises or licenses are not given very often, long-run monopoly profits might be earned by those firms already in the industry. The logic behind issuing few certificates of convenience has to do with supposed economies of scale in the industries in which they are required. If those industries do indeed experience large economies of scale, allowing a large number of firms to compete would, it is reasoned, prevent consumers from benefiting from one firm being able to sell a large output with significantly reduced average costs.

Patents

Closely related to the franchise required for entry is a patent. A patent is issued to protect an inventor from having the invention copied for a period of 17 years. Suppose that I discover a new, inexpensive fertilizer compound that makes all flowers, fruit trees, and plants grow three times larger than they do with any other fertilizer. If I am successful (or my attorneys are) in obtaining a patent on this discovery, I can prevent other individuals from copying it. Note, however, that I must expend resources to prevent them from imitating me even if I do have a legally watertight patent. A patent provides the right to sue others who violate the right to exclusive production or assignment. It is not a criminal law or regulatory rule that is enforced by public prosecution. Many resources are devoted by patent owners to enforcing their exclusive rights. Indeed, I can have a patent on a particular commodity or production process and end up having no economic profits at all, because the costs of policing are so high that I don't bother to protect my patent or, if I do, I end up spending so much on policing costs that I eat up all of my economic profits.

It is contended that patents are necessary for defining and enforcing

---

[2]A poll of professional economists taken several years ago indicated that about 80 percent agreed that regulation of certain industries by regulatory agencies like the Interstate Commerce Commission reduces economic efficiency, because of restrictions on entry into the industry. J. R. Kearl et al., "A Confusion of Economists?" *American Economic Review*, vol. 69, May 1979, pp. 28–37.

property rights in new ideas. However, there is little theoretical justification for a patent's extending to 17 years. Why not 10, 20, or 50 years, or infinity? Economists do not have any generally accepted answers. There is a trade-off involved when the patent is made longer. The longer an individual can anticipate having a property right or monopoly in a specific invention, the more resources will presumably go into inventing patentable items. However, the longer a patent exists, the longer the monopoly exists and presumably the longer the price will remain at a monopoly level rather than a competitive one. To find the socially optimal length of a patent, we must weigh the benefits of inducing more research and creative efforts going into patentable products against the higher price tags that those products will carry during the length of the patent. Some economists even believe that the optimal length of patent rights is 0 years. (Other economists advocate that bounties be paid by the government to inventors instead of awarding them patent rights.)

CREATION AND MAINTENANCE OF MONOPOLY PROFITS

We have just listed a number of ways in which a monopoly profit can be created. When a legal barrier to entry can be erected, then, a monopoly profit is possible. It is not unreasonable to predict that resources will be spent on efforts to create and maintain monopoly profits. Resources will be allocated, for example, for seeking legislation to set up barriers to entry into an industry. Those already in the industry will spend the resources to create and maintain such barriers. We can say, then, that there is a market for the creation of monopoly profits or for the creation of barriers to entry into an industry.

Although we speak in this section of a market which is defined in the political sense (because *legal* barriers are constructed by the political process), we could consider the much broader market for barriers to entry. This would include, among other things, the ways of obtaining an essential resource and cornering the market in it. In any event, there is competition among net worth-maximizing entrepreneurs to set up legal barriers to entry so that they, rather than someone else, will obtain the resulting monopoly profits. Thus, we know at the outset that even if an individual firm obtains a legal barrier which will generate monopoly profits, those profits will not be so great as they might appear. This is because resources had to have been expended in order to erect the legal barrier and additional resources probably will be required to maintain the barrier. Thus, if we disregard these costs when we attempt to calculate monopoly profits, we will end up with an overly high estimate of such profits.

Additionally, once a legal barrier is firmly established, there will be competition to obtain the ownership of that legal barrier. In other words, "outsiders" will see the benefits of operating beneath the umbrella of that legal barrier, and they too will seek its protection. Consider the competition among entrepreneurs to obtain licenses for radio and television broadcasting. This competition takes many forms. It may take the form of demonstrating to the Federal Communications Commission that the proposed candidate for a license will operate "in the public interest." Or it may take the form of a potential licensee using resources in a legal or illegal manner to influence the authorities ruling on the proposed license.

Customers are the losers in the case of successful monopolization. Therefore, they also have an incentive to spend resources; they wish to *stop* the barrier from being set up. Nonetheless, we predict that consumers will spend relatively few resources for the purpose of preventing monopolization. After all, organization costs are relatively much higher for customers—typically a diffuse group—than for suppliers, who are relatively few in number. This topic will be developed in more detail in Chapter 18.

DISSIPATION OF MONOPOLY PROFITS

Given that there is competition for the creation of monopoly profits and competition for the rights to those monopoly profits once they are created, some economists contend that this competition effectively dissipates any monopoly profits that arise through artificial barriers to entry. Take, as an example, the offering of a new television station license in a particular city. According to a competitive model or a rivalry model of analysis, potential licensees will expend resources up to the point where the expected rate of return from obtaining the monopoly license will be no greater than the rate of return from entry into any other business. Thus, the model would predict that monopoly profits, once created, will be competed away and that this competition will entail an expenditure of resources that is socially wasteful.

Look at Figure 13-2. Assume that the figure represents a single firm that has monopoly power because of politically granted control of a market. The firm earns monopoly profits defined by the area P_cP_mAB. If the firm knows it can earn such profits by gaining monopoly control of its market, or knows it can keep earning such profits only if it is allowed to keep its current monopoly control, the firm will be willing to spend a sum equal to as much as the monopoly profits it earns in order to earn the profits, in which case it would earn a normal rate of return. It may have to dissipate its profits in paying for lobbying efforts, political contributions, lawyers' efforts to maintain the power, and the like. This form of competition for favored political status is unlike the competitor in between firms for customers. The latter lowers costs and produces better or cheaper goods. The former raises costs and produces the right to raise prices, neither of which benefits consumers. We will study some further implications of the inefficiencies generated by monopolies later in the text when we consider welfare economics.

FIGURE 13-2

Increasing profits via perfect cartelization
We assume that all firms are of equal size and are faced with identical costs. The proportional demand curve facing each firm is given as dd. The associated marginal revenue curve is mr. For the individual firm in this industry, if it is competitive, profit maximization will be at an output where price P_c will be equal to its marginal cost mc. Each firm will produce q_c. If there are 100 firms in the industry, total industry output will be $100 \times q_c$. Now assume that output is allocated by a single agency directing the entire industry. If there is no cheating, each firm will be assigned output q_m and will sell its output at price P_m. Monopoly profits will be made.

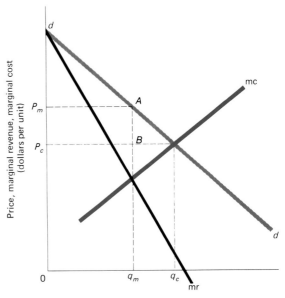

Individual firm's output (units per unit time period)

CARTELS AND COLLUSION

We have yet to talk about how monopoly profits can be created by the formation of a **cartel** or, more specifically, by *collusion* among an industry's members. In this section we will discuss the desire on the part of individual firms to collude and also the reasons why collusive agreements often tend to break down.

When a collusive agreement is legal and open, it is generally called a cartel. However, you must realize that economists often talk in terms of cartels even for illegal collusive agreements among firms that are in the same industry. A cartel can be thought of as a group of firms in the same industry that have banded together in order to increase the net worth position of their owners. This can be done by price fixing and restriction of output, as was once accomplished rather successfully by the Organization of Petroleum Exporting Countries (OPEC). It may also be accomplished by getting legislation passed to prevent entry into an industry.

Increase in profits through cartelization

We can analyze the effects of cartelizing an industry on the rate of profit to each individual firm. In the simplest of all cases, each firm in the industry has identical average and marginal cost curves.

To start the analysis, consider a competitive situation. Assume that there are 100 firms in the industry. Assume further that we are in a situation of perfect competition. Thus, the price at which each individual firm sells its output is equal to its perceived marginal revenue. Each firm's output is the output at which $P = MC$. This price, P_c, is set by the interaction of the industry supply curve, which is the horizontal summation of 100 identical MC curves, and the industry demand curve. The individual firm, of course, does not observe the industry demand curve; rather, it responds to its horizontal demand curve at price P_c. In any event, it will produce an output, q_c, which is one one-hundredth of total industry output Q_c.

Assignment of cartel shares

Now let us see what happens when the industry is cartelized. A cartel is formed with a central agency assigning production quotas. It assigns a production quota of one one-hundredth of the industry's total output to each individual firm. Assuming now that all firms *obey* these quotas, they will all produce the same output. Thus, we know that if each firm increases output by 1 unit, the industry will increase output by 100 units. It is no longer true that the individual firm can sell all it wants at the market-clearing price. Price now depends on the rate of output of the firm, because all the firms are acting in unison. We can now draw a demand curve ($= DD/100$) that faces the individual firm, which is labeled dd in Figure 13-2. The reader should note that dd is based on two assumptions: (1) equal shares for each firm, and (2) no cheating, i.e., costless monitoring and enforcement of the cartel agreement by the central agency. Since this demand curve is downward-sloping, we draw a marginal revenue curve mr ($= MR/100$) that is below dd.

The profit-maximizing rate of output for each firm is given by q_m, and the profit-maximizing price for the firm and the industry is P_m. For the cartel, total industry output is 100 times q_m. The cartelized industry output is less than it was when the firms were in perfect competition; however, each individual firm in the cartel is now making economic profits. In the competitive situation, price was equal to marginal cost; in the cartel situation, price exceeds marginal cost and there is clearly a higher rate of profit for each firm. Thus, we can see the incentives for cartelization of an industry. Cartelization does not have to be thought of as being desired for "evil" purposes but rather as a natural phenomenon consistent with our profit-maximizing assumptions. But these assumptions should hold throughout the analysis, and therefore, you should be skeptical about the long-run stability of the situation depicted in Figure 13-2. There will be forces preventing the successful formation of a cartel, such as squabbles over the appropriate allocation of output reductions and resulting higher profits among firms. Even if a cartel is initiated, there will be difficulty in its successful continuation.

**The incentive
to cheat**

The incentive to cheat in a cartel arrangement is great. The incentive not to join an existing cartel is also great. We can see this in Figure 13-3. In panel (b), the industry demand curve is DD. The curve marginal to that is MR. We assume a large number of equally efficient individual firms that are operated by a cartel manager. The summation of their individual marginal cost curves above their average variable cost curves is labeled ΣMC in panel (b). The profit-maximizing rate of output for the cartel is $Q_{industry}$, and the profit-maximizing price is P_{cartel}.

The relevant curves concerning the individual firm are given in panel (a). Note that the horizontal axes in panels (a) and (b) use vastly different scales. In panel (b), we are representing the industry output; in panel (a), we are representing the output of an individual firm. We assume now that

---

FIGURE 13-3
The incentive to cheat on the cartel agreement
The industry demand curve is DD in panel (b). Its marginal curve is MR. The summation of the individual firm's marginal cost curves is labeled ΣMC. A perfect cartel would set industry output at $Q_{industry}$. The cartel price would then be P_{cartel}. Assume that the individual firm's allotted output shown in panel (a) is q_{cartel}. It sells that output at price P_{cartel}. Its average total costs are C_1; therefore, its profit is the horizontally lined area. However, if the individual firm believes that no one else will cheat, it will take P_{cartel} as given and therefore equal to marginal revenue. It will move out to point E, where mc = P_{cartel} = mr. It will produce at output rate q_1. If indeed no other firm does cheat on the cartel, this firm's profit will increase to the entire horizontally shaded and vertically shaded area, since its cost at output rate q_1 per unit will be C_2, but the price will remain the same as before.

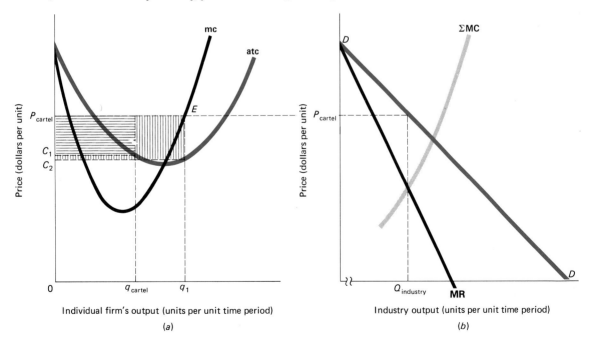

the cartel manager has assigned an equal share of total industry output to each of the firms and that it is represented by q_{cartel} in panel (a). At that rate of output, the individual firm's average total cost is C_1. The total profit that each firm in the cartel makes is therefore the difference between total revenues and total costs, or $(P_{cartel} \cdot q_{cartel}) - (C_1 \cdot q_{cartel})$.

If a disobedient firm attempts to cheat in the cartel, it might assume that the output rate of all other firms will remain constant. It can take, therefore, as a first approximation the cartel price as its demand curve and also as its marginal revenue curve. It will, therefore, profit-maximize by expanding output until marginal revenue equals marginal cost, or out to point E. At output rate q_1, it will make total revenues of $(P_{cartel} \cdot q_1)$. Its cost will be $(C_2 \cdot q_1)$ because at the new output rate q_1, the average total cost is equal to the vertical distance $0C_2$. Therefore, its profits will equal the sum of all the horizontally and vertically lined areas. The increased profit by either not joining the cartel or by being a disobedient firm once in the cartel is equal to the vertically lined area.[3]

Different firm efficiencies

When we initially discussed the possibility of cartelization, we assumed that all firms were equally efficient. The quota for each firm would clearly be an equal share of the industry's output. If firms have different cost curves, however, there is a problem in determining the appropriate quota for each firm, and then decisions must be made in terms of allocating profits among cartel members. While we can state how the industry should be divided among the member firms to maximize the profitability of the cartel, each firm has an incentive to gain at the expense of the other members. Hence, firms will lie about their costs and will be represented at cartel decision-making meetings by people with different bargaining skills—all of which will result in a different allocation to members of the cartel than would exist if we could engineer the result.

To maximize profits for the cartel as a whole, outputs should be assigned as they are under a multiplant monopoly. Such a firm would operate where marginal revenue equals marginal cost of plant 1 = marginal cost of plant 2. The cartel should operate where industry marginal revenue = marginal cost of firm 1 = marginal cost of firm 2 = $\cdots$ = marginal cost of firm n, where there are n firms. This means that profit maximization for the industry cartel as a whole can occur only if quotas are inversely proportional to marginal costs. That is, those firms which are relatively less efficient will be given a quota to produce relatively less of total industry output; the more efficient firms will be given larger quotas. We identify the former by the fact

---

[3]Strictly speaking, the "cheater" would have to lower price a slight amount to get the extra sales. Thus, we are really overstating the potential increased profits from cheating. Also, depending on the profit-maximizing rate of output, new costs C_2 could be greater than C_1. In other words, because of the way we have drawn the hypothetical curves, the costs of the "cheaters" are lower.

that they have higher marginal cost curves; the latter have relatively lower marginal cost curves.

Cartels and policing costs

Throughout our discussion of the instability of cartels, the notion of policing or enforcement costs has been implicitly included. For any cartel to work, there has to be a manner in which the cartel arrangement is successfully policed. We could actually consider the whole cartel-collusion problem in terms of crime and punishment. Any firm that violates a collusive agreement commits a "crime" against the cartel members. The cartel members, on the other hand, will try to detect and deter such crimes by punishing the "criminals." An "ideal," or "perfect," cartel results when monitoring the actions of members of the cartel and enforcing the rules of the cartel are costless. Unfortunately, for cartels, monitoring is not costless and, even more important, enforcement of cartel rules can be very expensive. In such cases, the members of the cartel must decide how much cheating on the cartel they can tolerate, and they must guess what the consequences of trying to punish cheaters will be. It could lead to cheaters quitting the cartel and, hence, becoming full-time competitors against the cartel. If punishments—and thus the cartel—become ineffective, the competitive solution results.

The costs of policing any given collusive agreement will be lower the smaller the number of firms and customers in the industry. It is not surprising, then, that the degree of industry concentration often is used as a measure of the degree of monopoly power. However, the relation clearly is not exact, and much must be inferred from industry data in order to come up with a notion of monopoly power using industry concentration ratios. As we pointed out in Chapter 12, such a measure tells us nothing about the likelihood of potential producers entering.

Electrical equipment conspiracy

Understanding the nature of enforcement costs for collusive agreements helps us understand the now-infamous electrical equipment conspiracy of the 1960s. A number of electrical firms in the United States got together regularly to determine prices and market shares for electrical equipment. This cartel had its greatest successes with electrical equipment that was sold to publicly owned electric utilities. The reason was not hard to find. Public utilities purchase electrical equipment through "competitive" sealed bids. In such a situation, potential suppliers of a particular piece of equipment submit sealed bids to the public utility. At a specified hour on a specified date, all the sealed bids are opened. Generally, the lowest bid is awarded the contract. The reason sealed bids are beneficial to any cartel is that all the sealed bids are opened and made available for public inspection at the same time. Late bids are disallowed. Thus, if a collusive agreement were reached beforehand and a particular firm in the cartel had been chosen to get the job, that firm would put in the "lowest" bid. All the other firms in the cartel would deliberately submit higher bids. If any one of them attempted to cheat, it would be known immediately because when the sealed bid was opened, the cheater would have placed the lowest bid, not in accord with the agreement of the conspiracy, and would be made known to the noncheating conspirators.

We might point out that the electrical equipment cartel broke up. The individual firms engaged in implicit price "shading" by discounting tied-in equipment in other than sealed-bid-type negotiations. In other words, the cartel member firm would sell a particular piece of equipment that was covered by the cartel agreement at the stipulated cartel price; however, if another piece of equipment had to be used and it was not covered by the cartel agreement, the cheating firm would offer a discount on it. It might sell a switch at the cartel price and give (at zero price) a transformer to the buyer in order to take away business from some other cartel member. Such "kick-back" or tie-in sales arrangements are often used by cartel members as a form of disguised discounts or price reductions to customers.

MERGERS TO ENHANCE MONOPOLY POWER

All the analysis above has been in terms of collusion or cartelization in an industry. There is an alternative way to obtain monopoly power. This is by **merger**, which is the joining of two or more firms under a single ownership or control. There are two types of mergers that concern us. One involves **horizontal integration**; the other, **vertical integration**.

Even though we are discussing mergers in terms of increasing monopoly power, we must note that not all mergers are effected with the goal of enhancing monopoly power. Furthermore, even if a merger is desired to enhance monopoly power, the end result may nonetheless do nothing to increase the merging firm's monopoly power.[4]

Horizontal integration

Horizontal integration involves mergers among firms selling a similar commodity. If two shoe-manufacturing firms merge, that is horizontal integration. If a group of firms, all producing steel, merge into one, that also is horizontal integration. Almost all the cartel analysis we just presented also applies to horizontal integration. But none of the enforcement costs are incurred when there is a single owner. Therefore, it might be stated that whatever monopoly power and monopoly profits can be obtained by way of collusion, they can be obtained better by merger as long as this latter process is not "too" costly. Mergers which result in "unreasonable" restraint of trade are, however, usually prevented or prosecuted by the Justice Department and/or the Federal Trade Commission under existing antitrust statutes, as are collusive agreements when detected.

[4]For a further discussion of benign versus "beneficial" mergers, see B. Klein et al., *Journal of Law and Economics*, 1978.

Vertical integration

Vertical integration occurs when one firm merges either with a firm from which it purchases an input or with a firm to which it sells its output. Vertical integration occurs, for example, when a coal-using electric utility purchases a coal-mining firm or when a shoe manufacturer purchases retail shoe outlets.

It turns out that there are few instances in which our analysis can explain vertical integration in terms of increasing monopoly power. Consider the simplest case, in which the purchaser of an input is a monopolist in selling the output but purchases its inputs in a competitve market.

Buying a competitive supplier. The price that the monopolist pays for its input, we have assumed, is a competitive price. This means that the monopolist is but one of many firms purchasing the output of the supplier; the supplier's output is the monopolistic firm's input. That input is then used in the monopolist's product. The question is, How much will the monopolist benefit by this "backward" integration? Assume that it purchases the company that supplies the input. What is the appropriate **internal transfer price** that should be built into the cost of producing the final product and, hence, into the marginal cost curve for the monopolist? The internal transfer price of an input is the price that is carried on the company's books when it computes its costs of production. From these costs, a marginal cost curve can be derived. If anything other than the full opportunity cost of the input is built into the monopolist's marginal cost curve, a non-profit-maximizing price and rate of output will result. In other words, it makes no difference to the monopolist whether the input supplier is independent or part of the firm. The price of the input will remain the same, whether it be implicit or explicit.

Consider the case in which an automobile manufacturer purchases mufflers from an outside supplier for $20 apiece. In that situation, the automobile firm considers the $20 a cost. Assume that the automobile manufacturer then purchases outright a supplier of mufflers. It will continue to "charge itself" $20 per muffler, even though the muffler firm was making, say, $5 "profit" on each muffler. It would be a mistake to consider for cost calculations that the price of the muffler was only $15 just because the automobile manufacturer now owned that supplier.

This is exactly the same reasoning behind the incorrectness of the notion that funds generated internally within the firm are less expensive than funds that must be borrowed or raised by selling additional shares in the company. Funds that are obtained by corporate saving (retained earnings plus depreciation allowances) have an opportunity cost of whatever they could earn if they were loaned to someone else.[5] If the firm does not charge itself this opportunity cost (at least implicitly) in making its investment decisions, it

---

[5]Some economists do point out, however, that funds generated within a firm assure that firm a source of supply with first priority and without the transactions costs associated with searching for the best outside source of financing.

will not be maximizing the net worth of the shareholders. That is to say, the firm might make more income for its shareholders if it sold some of its output at a higher price after it took account of the true, higher opportunity cost of its inputs.

On foreclosing the market. Antitrust law discourages some vertical integration. Somehow it is assumed that such mergers "foreclose one part of the market for rivals." The purchase of retail tire outlets by a tire manufacturer is supposed to prevent rival tire manufacturers from being able to sell tires to these retail outlets. But if we think about it, the ability of rivals to sell tires is impaired only if the *retail* chain of stores had monopolistic powers in the retail market when the tire manufacturer purchased it. And if this were true, we would know that the monopolistic chain of retail outlets would be sold to the tire manufacturer at a price that capitalized the future stream of monopoly profits; the tire manufacturer would not capture any of those profits.

The point to be made is that monopoly power at one particular place in the production and distribution chain in no way confers monopoly power to any other point in that chain. If you own the only supply of a critical raw material in the production of record albums, all you need do is set the monopoly profit-maximizing price on the critical input that you own. You can hope to make a competitive rate of return only on the additional investment needed to purchase record-manufacturing companies and/or retail record outlets. They will not yield you any additional profits. (However, integration will occur, just as the organization of the firm did in the first place, whenever the benefits outweigh the cost of a larger collective unit or to forestall monopolization by some other firm or firms.)

Integration to avoid exploitation. Sometimes a firm relies to a great extent on another firm either for an input needed in the production process or for the purchase of the output of the firm. In such cases, when there is no close substitute, there is the potential for **opportunistic behavior**. Since the possibility of opportunistic behavior is common, we have learned to account for its existence by the use of contracts that make clear various parties' rights, responsibilities, and legal recourses. Opportunistic behavior is the unexpected exploitation of another party that results in the other party incurring higher costs and possibly in the exploiting party's earning higher profits.

Consider a situation in which Boeing has been awarded a contract to build 500 sophisticated jets for the military. Boeing then asks your company to design and produce a particular piece of equipment needed for these jets. These pieces of equipment would have no value in any other use, nor could anyone else cheaply or quickly produce them. Once the equipment had been designed and production of it and of the jets by Boeing had begun, what is to prevent either party from trying to exploit the other? On the one hand, you could tell Boeing that the price had just gone up 50 percent or you would cease production. Boeing would know it could not obtain the equipment from anyone else in time to finish the jets. On the other hand, Boeing could tell you that you were going to have to cut your price 50 percent or they were going to look elsewhere for a supplier. You would then be stuck with equipment and special knowledge of no value to anyone else. Contracts are supposed to be written and enforced to prevent parties from engaging in such opportunistic behavior. Nevertheless, contracts do not always offer the perfect solution or give complete security; therefore, the two firms involved may merge into one firm so that neither party will have an incentive to try to exploit the other one later.

Vertical integration to enhance monopoly power

The preceding discussion should not be taken to indicate that there is no situation in which vertical integration will not increase monopoly profits. There are, in fact, a number of situations that might result in a higher profit through vertical integration. We give some of them below.

The squeeze play. In some instances, it is alleged that a "powerful" firm will be able to squeeze out independent and nonintegrated firms. Assume, for example, that the *integrated* firm has a monopoly on an output at an early stage in the production of a final product. The integrated firm can raise the price it charges for the input to the nonintegrated firm; then the integrated firm can lower the price of the final product that it produces. The unintegrated and independent firm has to buy the unfinished input at the "monopoly" price but is forced to be competitive in selling its final product. Independents can be forced out of business by this "squeeze." As logical as this may seem, it is not a costless ploy on the part of a vertically integrated firm. The vertically integrated firm must forgo monopoly profits during the period in which the price of the final product is kept lower than it would be otherwise. This is sometimes known as "cutthroat" competition. Its rationality in terms of net worth maximization of the owners is certainly not without questions. It can be shown that it is less costly to buy rivals outright (but that may be illegal).[6]

Price discrimination. Vertical integration can sometimes allow a monopolist to practice more price discrimination than would be possible without such integration. The manufacturer of an intermediate product may perceive that the final product is being sold to classes of individuals who have different price elasticities of demand. Perhaps the manufacturer of the intermediate product can more easily exploit these differences if that manufacturer is also the manufacturer of the final product. An example might be aluminum. Assume that exactly the same aluminum ingots are sold to all types of end-use manufacturers. Since the aluminum producer is unable to prevent resale, that producer cannot discriminate in the price of aluminum

[6]See Lester Telser, "Abusive Trade Practices: An Economic Analysis." *Law and Contemporary Problems*, vol. 30, no. 3, Summer 1965, pp. 465–477; and John S. McGee, "Predatory Price Cutting: The Standard Oil (N.J.) Case," *Journal of Law and Economics*, vol. 1, October 1958, pp. 137–169.

ingots for the different final products, such as pots, pans, and car grilles, *unless* that aluminum producer is also the producer of those final products. Otherwise stated, if I am a buyer of an intermediate product that I use in the manufacture of my product, I may be able to buy out the producer of that intermediate product and discriminate perfectly in favor of myself. I would charge myself the true marginal value of that intermediate product; I would charge others monopoly prices on a discriminating basis. In other words, I would engage in third-degree price discrimination as the sole owner of the input supply.

Preventing entry. Vertical integration may be used as a way in which entry into the industry can be prevented. The manufacturer of aluminum products may prevent entry into that industry if that manufacturer buys up the entire supply of all the ingredients that go into making aluminum.

THE NATURAL MONOPOLY

We have already mentioned that one barrier to entry may be (industry) economies of scale. If economies of scale are so great that the long-run average total cost curve is *downward-sloping* over the relevant range, only one firm can survive. That firm will be the one that expands output the most and, hence, enjoys the greatest decrease in average total cost. It is able to "undersell" rivals and eventually drive them out of business. A natural monopoly situation is depicted in Figure 13-4.

There we see that the LAC curve is downward-sloping over a relevant range of outputs. Now assume that the market demand curve is DD. The monopolist's profit-maximizing rate of output is where MR = LMC, or at output rate Q_m. The profit-maximizing monopolist would then charge price P_m. Clearly, a competitive solution to the price-output decision could not prevail in this industry. For it to be a competitive solution, price must equal marginal cost; but if price were equal to marginal cost P_1, the firm in this industry (i.e., the natural monopolist) would suffer a loss on every unit sold because the LAC curve is above the DD curve at the rate of output Q_c. The loss on each unit sold would be the vertical difference between C_1 and P_1 in Figure 13-4. Some theorists, in their desire to have price equal to marginal cost, have suggested that a subsidy be given equal to the distance between C_1 and P_1 per unit of output sold in this natural monopoly situation. It may be true that, with the subsidy, each consumer pays a retail price for the product equal to (long-run) marginal cost. However, taken together, consumers of the product do not pay a total price equal to the true social opportunity cost of the total quantity of this commodity consumed. After all, part of the total opportunity cost is the cost absorbed by taxpayers who pay the subsidy. And these taxpayers are not typically the consumers of the subsidized products.

FIGURE 13-4
The natural monopoly situation
The long-run average cost curve LAC is downward-sloping over the entire relevant range of outputs. In a competitive solution, price is equal to long-run marginal cost. If this natural monopolist were forced to sell at price P_1 and to produce output rate Q_c, it would incur a loss per unit equal to the difference between C_1 and P_1. Unrestrained, the monopolist would produce where marginal revenue equals marginal cost, or at output rate Q_m. It would charge a price equal to P_m.

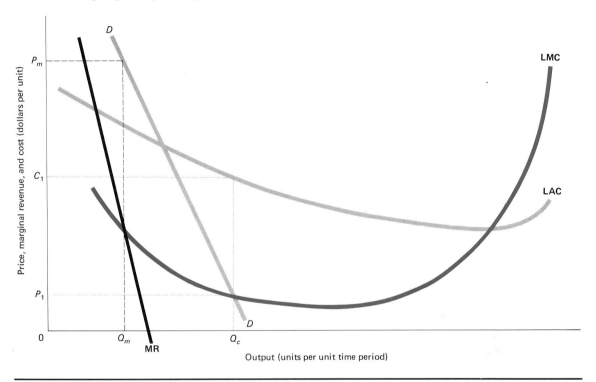

There are two alternatives which can be used in this natural monopoly situation.

Multipart pricing   Conceivably, the natural monopolist that would otherwise suffer a loss if the uniform price of P_1 were charged could engage in multipart pricing. Those demanders of the product with relatively inelastic demand curves would pay prices higher than P_1. The revenues in excess of the marginal cost of providing the units of output to these demanders with relatively inelastic demand curves could be used to cover some or all of the fixed costs.

Selling the rights to produce   In the absence of any regulation, the natural monopoly will set output at a rate at which marginal revenue equals marginal cost. In Figure 13-5, this is rate Q_m. The price that would be charged would be P_m, and the cost per unit

FIGURE 13-5

Selling the exclusive right to produce
This is a natural monopoly. If no regulation restricts its activities, the monopolist will set output at Q_m and price at P_m. If the government sells the right to produce on the basis of price per constant-quality unit, competition for the franchise will result in price equal to P_1, which will equal long-run average costs C_1. The output rate will be Q_b. Price will remain, however, above MC.

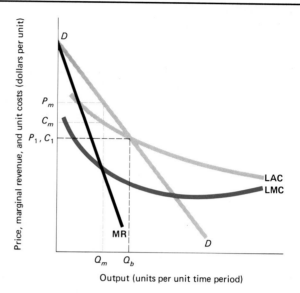

would be C_m. Therefore, the monopoly profits will be the vertical distance between P_m and C_m times the quantity produced Q_m.

Consider the possibility of the government auctioning off the right to produce (on the basis of the price per constant-quality unit to be charged the public). The company offering to sell a constant-quality unit of output at the *lowest* price is awarded the right to produce and sell at that price. If the bidding is competitive, the end result will be a unit price charged that just equals long-run average cost (which includes a normal competitive rate of return on "investment"). Thus we can see that the auctioning off of the right to produce will result in a price equal to P_1 (which is also equal to long-run average costs of C_1) and a quantity produced of Q_b. There would be no monopoly profits, only a normal rate of return. This is an alternative way of regulating natural monopolies if and when it is decided that they need regulation.

THE REGULATION OF MONOPOLIES

The regulation of monopolies in the United States takes basically two forms: antitrust legislation and regulatory activities of such agencies as the Federal Power Commission, the Federal Communications Commission, state regulatory commissions, and so on. Presumably, antitrust legislation attacks the problem of monopoly at its root and therefore obviates the need for any other type of regulation. Monopolies are broken up or not allowed to form so that competitive pricing prevails. In what follows, we will discuss regulatory activities and omit any discussion of antitrust legislation.

Cost-of-service regulation

One type of regulation involves a regulatory commission attempting to ascertain what the cost of service is for the provision of some commodity, for example, electricity. Cost-of-service regulation requires detailed knowledge of the costs of production and distribution of the commodity to be regulated. Moreover, cost-of-service regulation requires that, in many instances, **common costs** be allocated to specific products. For example, the U.S. Postal Service has a truck that it uses to haul first-, second-, and third-class mail to various addresses. The cost of the truck constitutes a common cost for first-, second-, and third-class mail delivery. In what way can such a common cost be meaningfully allocated? It turns out that there is no way other than an arbitrary one that can be used. (By definition, common costs are indeed common to all products.) Thus, cost-of-service regulation faces the problem of arbitrarily allocating common costs.[7]

Moreover, cost-of-service regulation has to grapple with the problem of distinguishing between historical costs and opportunity costs. This is particularly relevant in the inflationary setting of the last two decades. The historical cost of a steam generator may be very much lower than its opportunity cost because of inflation. Price based on historical cost will not then cover current opportunity costs.

Additionally, prices based on all costs rolled in together ignore the long-run marginal cost, which may be many times greater than current average cost. This, again, is particularly true in an inflationary setting. An electric utility that must expand in order to satisfy the demand at the current regulated price may have to incur costs that are many times greater than what it had to pay in the past for capital equipment. This is due in part to inflation and also in part to increased pollution-abatement equipment that must be purchased along with the "productive" capital equipment. In some instances, it has been shown that the long-run marginal cost of electricity is 5 to 10 times the price that is charged for it. If electricity consumers are not charged a price which reflects true long-run marginal costs of providing additional generation of that type of energy, the quantity demanded by consumers will be greater than it would be otherwise, and the utility's willingness to invest in added capacity or to maintain existing generating capacity will be diminished. Thus, not allowing electric utilities to "pass on" increased costs of expanding output leads to consumers *not* being faced with the true social opportunity cost of the electricity they use. This causes an economically inefficient use of resources and potential problems with excess quantities of electricity demanded at regulated prices (e.g., brownouts, rolling outages, etc.).

[7]See Marshall, *Principles of Economics*, 8th ed., book V, chap. VI, and mathematical appendix (New York: The Macmillan Company, 1949).

Rate-of-return regulation

Rate-of-return regulation involves a public utility commission, or some other commission, establishing a price that allows a "fair" rate of return on investors' equity in the regulated industry. Presumably, rate-of-return regulation prevents the monopoly, whether it be an electric utility or telephone company, from reaping monopoly profits. In the simplest model of the regulatory process, the company in question produces one output and uses two inputs—labor and capital—each of which is available to it in unlimited quantities at market-determined prices. The decisions of the firm are affected by regulation in only one way. No more than some fixed percentage of the value of its capital is allowed to be earned in any year. This fixed percentage is the fair rate of return computed on its so-called **rate base**, which is its capital stock. In the simplest of regulatory models, the management of the regulated firm is allowed to pursue its objective of maximizing profits exactly as it would in the absence of regulation, except for the establishment of prices. And for the model to make any sense, the fair rate of return and, therefore, the product price allowed by the regulatory agency is less than the rate of return that would be earned without constraints. In equation form, the regulated firm maximizes total profits subject to a regulatory constraint, or it maximizes

$$\text{Profit} = Pq - wL - rK \tag{13-1}$$

where P = output price

q = output

L = labor

w = wage rate

K = capital stock

r = unit cost of capital (implicit rental rate per unit)

subject to
$$\frac{Pq - wL}{K} \leq z \tag{13-2}$$

where

$z = r + v$ = rate of return allowed by regulation $\tag{13-3}$
(above the unit cost of capital with $v \geq 0$)

The regulated firm is allowed to have a rate of return at least equal to the implicit rental value of the capital stock. The rate of return may be greater than r and depends on what v is. The regulators decide on v and hence on z. Presumably, z is less than the profit-maximizing rate of return since the regulators do not want to allow monopoly profits.

We know that with constraints, the way in which the profit-maximizing firm will act will be different from an unconstrained situation. Employing the simplified assumptions of the model above, it can be shown that the firm will overinvest in capital. This is called the **Averch-Johnson effect** because it was first noted by these two economists in a 1962 article.[8] The overinvestment occurs because when the permitted percentage rate of return on investment is fixed at z and is less than the profit-maximizing rate, the regulated companies will have an incentive to "overinvest." The object of the game is to maximize total profits. If the rate of profit that can be earned on an investment is fixed, why not increase capital investment to get higher absolute profits? The ratio of capital to labor in regulated industries is going to be higher than it would be without regulation. This is called an expansion of the rate base, and it is inefficient.[9]

Problems with regulation

Regulation, even in principle, is not an easy job. In reality, it has proven to be extremely complicated. Next, we will examine only a few of the problems associated with regulaton.

Quality of service. For regulation to have any effect, the price per constant-quality unit must be regulated. If only the nominal price per nominal-quality unit is regulated, a change in the quality of the commodity in question will alter the *real* price. So long as regulators are unable to regulate the quality of the commodity sold, the difficulty of effective regulation becomes relatively greater.

Consider regulating the price of a constant-quality unit of telephone service. Look at the many facets of the quality of telephone service. Getting a dial tone, hearing the voice at the other end clearly, getting the operator to answer quickly, having out-of-order telephones repaired rapidly, and putting through a long-distance call quickly are just a few of those facets. Regulation of the telephone company usually deals with the prices charged for telephone service. Regulators are concerned with the quality of service, but they can regulate only some of the dimensions of quality. If the telephone company wants to raise the price per constant-quality unit and the regulatory agency refuses a nominal price increase, the telephone company can cut down on the quality of the service and thereby implicitly raise the price per constant-quality unit.

Pricing policies and "excess" profits. Regulatory commissions are presumably in the business of preventing higher than "fair" rates of return. It is not surprising, therefore, that regulatory agencies are reluctant to allow long-run marginal cost pricing or peak-load pricing.

Long-run marginal cost pricing often results in temporarily higher than "fair" profits if long-run marginal costs exceed average costs by a great amount.

[8]H. Averch and L. L. Johnson, "Behavior of the Firm under Regulatory Constraint," *American Economic Review*, vol. 52, December 1962, pp. 1053–1069.

[9]When the model becomes more complicated, however, it is not clear that the A-J effect works the way it is supposed to work. See, for example, William J. Baumol and Alvin K. Klevorich, "Input Choices and the Rate of Return Regulation: An Overview of the Discussion," *The Bell Journal of Economics and Management Science*, vol. 1, no. 2, Autumn 1970, pp. 162–190.

LMC does exceed SAC for electricity in many areas of the country because of the increased costs of building plants and adding pollution-control equipment and the cost of financing capital expenditures. Prices, which are based on average costs, therefore, are much lower than prices based on long-run marginal costs. A regulatory agency presumably does not like the idea of allowing a firm to charge for long-run marginal costs, even if that is the most efficient pricing solution, because "excess" profits may temporarily result.

Peak-load pricing involves the same problem. The demand for electricity has peaks during different times of the day and different times of the year, and storage is "too" costly. Regulatory agencies have been reluctant to require, or allow when requested, electric utilities to charge higher rates for peak-load times than for non-peak-load times. Even though peak-load pricing leads to an allocation of scarce resources in a way that requires those who purchase the scarce resources to pay the full social opportunity cost, we have only recently seen peak-load pricing in regulated industries.

The Environmental Defense Fund (EDF) developed the arguments and the records that led the Wisconsin Public Service Commission in 1974 to order the Madison Gas & Electric Company to inaugurate a system of peak-load pricing. Higher rates were set for summer months when air conditioning pushes the system's capacity to its limits. In addition to calling for a winter-summer price differential, the company was directed to differentiate between daytime and nighttime rates for large industrial users. It was determined that the cost of metering was too high to institute a time-of-day pricing system for all users.

In 1975 an experiment was started in Vermont by Central Vermont Public Service Corporation. From 8 A.M. to 11 A.M. and from 5 P.M. to 9 P.M., the families in the experiment were charged a higher rate for electricity; the rest of the day, they were charged a lower rate. Some families started running the dishwasher and cooking dinner before 5 P.M. Others did their laundry before 8 A.M. in order to save on electrical bills. That experiment led to a permanent system of peak-load pricing.

Who regulates the regulators? Another problem with the regulation of monopolies—one that has been alluded to previously—is the political nature of the regulatory process. Regardless of the form of regulation, there is no reason to expect that a more efficient result would be produced by regulation than from a competitive market. In the area of public utilities, different methods of regulation are used in various states and localities, all of which produce some undesirable results.[10]

Several studies indicate that after regulation was imposed on electric utilities in states that had previously allowed competing companies to exist,

---

[10]For an overview of some of the studies of public utility regulation, see L. DeAlessi, "The Economics of Property Rights: A Review of the Evidence," *Research in Law and Economics,* vol. 2, 1980, pp. 1–47.

the result was higher prices, lower output, and an increase in owners' wealth—exactly what the regulation was supposed to prevent.

Regulators obviously do not operate in a vacuum; they respond to the interests that determine their fate. If regulators are elected to office, as are some state utility commissioners, then they may try to enhance their appeal to the voters by setting a price for electricity that is too low to enable the electric company to attract more capital to expand or improve facilities for the long run. On the other hand, if the commissioners are appointed by the state legislature or by the governor, they will have to act in ways that will appeal more directly to those interests. If the utilities contribute heavily to the campaigns of elected officials, then they may pressure the utility regulators to treat the utilities the way they would like to be treated—to include more costs in their rate base and be allowed to earn nice, high rates of return.

There is no simple solution to this issue. No model of regulation has been able to produce a result that is identical to the efficient results that would emerge if a competitive market existed.

Barriers to entry and effective cartels: Aluminum and diamonds

A case in which a monopoly was maintained because a firm owned an essential raw material is found in the history of the Aluminum Company of America (Alcoa). It was the sole manufacturer of aluminum ingots in the United States from the late nineteenth century until World War II. The monopoly position of the firm was at first maintained by the many patents it had obtained for the different phases of the aluminum ingot production process. For example, the first person who discovered a process by which oxygen could be eliminated from bauxite assigned the patent to Alcoa. This patent, however, expired on April 2, 1906. Another process was invented to permit the smelting to be carried on without the use of external heat. This patent was assigned to Alcoa in 1903 but expired on February 2, 1909. Essentially, Alcoa had either a monopoly on the manufacture of virgin aluminum ingots or

a monopoly on the cheapest production process, and this eliminated all competition. After that date, one of the major ways in which Alcoa kept its monopoly position was by cornering sources of bauxite, the raw material. It did this by signing long-term contracts with the companies owning rights to this essential raw material; the contracts specified that those companies could not sell the essential ore to any other company. As early as 1895, Alcoa obtained electrical energy from three power companies and signed with each of them contracts prohibiting these companies from selling or leasing power to anyone else for the manufacture of aluminum. Unfortunately for Alcoa, in 1912 the courts invalidated these agreements.

In order to maintain its monopoly position in the industry after 1912, Alcoa expanded its productive capacity as fast as necessary to meet the increase in demand at the going price for aluminum. Indeed, it lowered prices in many markets in order to increase the quantity demanded for aluminum. In its defense against an antitrust suit, Alcoa contended that its dominance in the "virgin" ingot market in the United States did not give it a monopoly in that market. It was subject to the competition of imported virgin ingot and to the competition of secondary ingot, which is scrap aluminum. It is true that since aluminum does not deteriorate very quickly, the supply of secondary aluminum over time will become sufficiently large to provide competition for virgin aluminum. This is exactly the same problem facing the owners of the supply of "new" diamonds.

In terms of an actual cartel, which Alcoa was not (it was a single-firm monopoly), the owners of diamond mines in South Africa have been successful for many years. They have operated a cartel which has been able to keep the world price of diamonds higher than a competitive price. This has been done by regulating the export of diamonds. This, in turn, has been possible because the owners of diamond mines in South Africa control over three-fourths of the world's diamond production. The first ingredient in this successful monopoly was the control of an essential resource. Second, the diamond mine owners used a single firm as their sole export agent. That firm is DeBeers. Most of the world's diamonds come out of the mines that use DeBeers as their sole export agent. Thus, it is possible to set a monopoly price on diamonds and not leave any individual mine owner able to cheat by offering diamonds at a lower price unless that diamond owner somehow goes around the DeBeers export agency. And finally, no close substitute for diamonds has yet been developed.

Interestingly, the Soviet Union understands the value of the DeBeers cartel. It markets its diamonds through DeBeers. When there was a major diamond find in Australia recently, DeBeers offered to take the Australians into the cartel and, according to news reports, threatened to flood the market with diamonds similar to those being produced in Australia if the new producers did not join the cartel.

The creation of monopoly profits: The case of taxicabs

One way to obtain monopoly profits is to foreclose entry into the market by legal means. If a law can be passed that requires that a license be obtained in order to do business in a particular industry, those in the industry prior to the licensing restriction (and assuming a **grandfather clause**[11] in the law, which is nearly *always* the case) will obtain monopoly profits. A clear-cut case can be seen if we examine the market for taxi services throughout the United States. In many, if not most, cities, in order to operate a taxi, a license must be obtained. In New York City, this license is called a medallion. Before 1937 in New York, the taxicab industry had free entry. The price of taxi medallions was near zero since they were given to anyone who wanted to operate a taxi. Little by little, the city began to restrict its issuance of new medallions. And little by little, anyone wishing to buy a medallion from the then-current owner had to pay a higher and higher price to purchase it. As the market price went up, those who obtained the medallions at lower

---

[11]Under such a clause, everyone in the industry is "grandfathered in" automatically when licensing is required. That is, existing firms obtain a license by virtue of already being in the industry.

than the market price were treated to increases in their net worth. By the end of the 1970s, the market price of a medallion had reached $50,000.

What does that price represent? It represents the fully discounted present value of the expected stream of monopoly profits that can be obtained by having a legal taxicab in New York City.

Medallion owners who purchased or received them in the late 1930s and early 1940s obtained "monopoly" profits. However, owners today recieve no more than a competitive rate of return on their labor and capital. Why? Because they have typically paid the market price for their medallions, and this cost has been added to their other costs. An elimination of the restrictions on entry into the New York taxicab market would immediately subject all the present owners of medallions to a large loss. The emergence of "gypsy" cabs (whose owners do not have medallions) in New York City has already partially eroded the market value of medallions. Gypsies are cabs

which have no *legal* right to pick up passengers for hire. Nonetheless, New York authorities have, for the most part, allowed these illegal cabs to operate in the city in recent years.

We can understand this situation by looking at Figure 13-6. Here we show that the City of New York has issued a fixed number of medallions equal to Q_1. The supply curve of medallions is thus completely price-inelastic at Q_1, and is represented by SS. As the city has grown and real income has increased, the demand curve for taxi services and, hence, the demand for medallions has increased from DD to $D'D'$. The price of medallions has risen from P_1 to P_2. If free entry into the taxicab industry were allowed, the supply curve of medallions would shift to the right so as to always intersect any demand curve at a price of zero. (This is a point not lost on current medallion owners!) In other words, the authorities would issue medallions to anyone who wanted them at a zero price. No matter how many medallions were demanded at a zero price, the au-

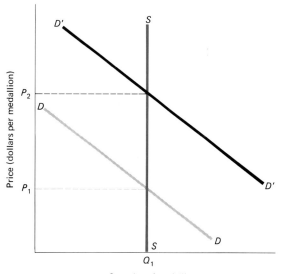

FIGURE 13-6
The rise in value of medallions
If the City of New York sets the number of medallions at Q_1, the supply curve is vertical, SS. If the demand curve a number of years ago was DD, the going price was P_1. As population and real incomes rise, however, the demand curve shifts outward to the right to $D'D'$. The price or value of a medallion rises to P_2 because the quantity supplied is fixed.

thorities would provide them, thus authorizing all comers to operate a taxi in New York City.

MEDALLIONS AND HOURS ON THE STREET

It is conceivable that the limited supply of medallions leads to longer hours per cab on the street and more intense searching for customers. The reason is quite straightforward: With a system that restricts entry by limiting the number of cabs, there is a restriction only on the *number of cabs* rather than on the *amount of cab services*. The amount of cab services is a function, among other things, of the amount of time that the cabs are utilized. In other words, a monopoly restriction on one aspect of the business does not prevent competition in all other aspects. Hence, we can

predict with some certainty that given the possibility of competition in other aspects of providing cab services, there will be more than just medallion restrictions. In addition, we would expect to see fares being set (and they usually are) and the hours of operation per cab and per cabbie also being regulated.

The monopoly profit per medallion will still be positive, but any other monopoly profits on the other inputs into cab services will be less. Why? Because the additional restrictions—fares and hours of use—will raise the cost of service and, hence, lower the quantity demanded. Thus, the demand for other factors in the production of cab services must fall.

Typically, regulated industries follow the example we just gave. Not only is entry restricted, but once entry is restricted a whole set of other restrictions on prices, output qualities, ways of producing the output, and so on are eventually added.

Another case of foreclosing the market: Tobacco

More than four decades ago, owners of tobacco-producing land got Congress to pass legislation which allotted to the then-current half million growers of tobacco the right to grow tobacco on lands that were *then* in use. Since that time, there has been no new land put into tobacco production, and this is for a very good reason. Any tobacco that is grown on unlicensed land is taxed at 75 percent of its value. This tax is prohibitive. No potential tobacco farmers could hope to make any money if they had to pay this tax, because they would be in competition with the tobacco growers who do not have to pay it.

Who are the beneficiaries of restricting the supply of tobacco? Certainly not anyone who today purchases land that is licensed for tobacco growing. The price of licensed land was

long ago bid up to levels that yielded new owners only a competitive rate of return. The ones who benefited from the monopoly position granted by Congress were the owners who had the land at the time the legislation was passed. To be more accurate, it was the original owners who had the land at the time it was generally known that the legislation was going to be passed. They reaped monopoly profits to the tune of $1,500 to $3,000 an acre because they could sell their land for more than they could prior to the acreage allotments.[12]

---

[12]See F. H. Maier, J. L. Hedrick, and W. L. Gibson, Jr., *The Sale of Flue-Cured Tobacco Allotments*, Agriculture Experiment Station, Virginia Polytechnic Institute Technical Bulletin No. 148, April 1960.

▬▬▬▬▬▬

Mergers and monopolies: Federal antitrust law

The first federal antitrust statute, designed to deal with monopoly power and its undesirable consequences, was passed in 1890. It was followed by two other statutes in the early 1900s with the result that we now have a substantial body of antitrust law. While private antitrust actions are not uncommon, most major cases are filed by the federal antitrust authorities—either the Department of Justice or the Federal Trade Commission.

To guide the staff of the Department of Justice, in 1982 the senior administrators issued "Merger Guidelines" (which were essentially agreed upon with the Federal Trade Commission). The Guidelines focus on many of the issues economists discuss in monopoly theory; the closeness of substitutes is understood to be a key to a firm (or two firms proposing to merge) having monopoly power in a product or geographical market. Regardless of firm size (e.g., the multibillion dollar Texaco-Getty merger), if the new firm faces substantial competition in the geographical markets in which it operates and substantial competition in the products it produces, mergers are not likely to be challenged.

HERFINDAHL-HIRSCHMAN INDEX

When a proposed merger is studied, it will be determined whether or not it is a horizontal merger—that is, whether the merging firms are in the same product and geographical markets. If they are, then the Herfindahl-Hirschman Index (HHI) will be used as a guideline to decide whether or not the merger should be challenged.

The HHI is calculated by summing the squares of the individual market shares of all the firms included in the market under discussion (defining the market is a major task). Unlike the traditional four-firm concentration ratio, the HHI accounts for both the distribution of the market shares of the top firms and the composition of the market outside those firms. For example, if the relevant market consists of five firms with market shares of 40 percent, 30 percent, 20 percent, 9 percent, and 1 percent, the HHI is 2982 ($40^2 + 30^2 + 20^2 + 9^2 + 1^2 = 2982$). The highest possible HHI is 10,000, when one firm has 100 percent of the market; the lowest HHI is near zero, in the case of a perfectly competitive market.

The HHI is calculated for the industry in question as if the merger had occurred. That is, if the merging firms had market shares of 10 percent and 5 percent, together they would have a share of 15 percent, so that figure would be used in calculating the HHI. The general standard then is as follows: If the postmerger HHI is under 1000, the market is considered unconcentrated and the merger is unlikely to be challenged. If the postmerger HHI is between 1000 and 1800, the merger is likely to be challenged only if the merger causes the HHI to increase by more than 100 points. If the postmerger HHI is above 1800, the merger will not be challenged if it produces an increase in the HHI less than 50; it may be challenged if it produces an increase between 50 and 100; and it will most likely be challenged if the increase is over 100 points.

The standard sounds mechanical, but in practice it is not. In each case the peculiarities of the market are considered, the likelihood of increased or decreased competition in the market in the future, the possibility that one of the merging firms would go out of business without the merger, and a guess as to the ease of entry into the market in question. The use of such criteria, which are based on economic theory and empirical studies, is a major reason why some mergers involving relatively small firms will be challenged by the antitrust authorities and why other mergers involving giant firms will be uncontested.

The profitability of regulated firms

As we have seen in this chapter, government regulation provides regulated firms the opportunity for earning higher than normal profits. There are numerous examples, past and present, of such regulatory benefits, including federal control of commercial airline fare structures and landing rights under the now-defunct Civil Aeronautics Board; similar regulations affecting interstate rail, truck, and water transportation under the Interstate Commerce Commission; state licensing of architects, physicians, morticians, and other professionals; and local governmental regulation of taxicabs, garbage collections, and other services. The list could go on and on, but let us pause to raise an important question: Do firms get to keep the profits created by regulation? The answer is no. That is because regulation typically limits rivalry on only one or two dimensions (e.g., price or entry), and firms operating under government control may have an incentive to compete in ways not restricted by the regulatory authority. Such competition may increase the regulated firms' costs, dissipating a portion of the economic profits from regulation. Some or all of the potential profits may not materialize.

THE CASE OF TELEVISION STATIONS

Regulation of television broadcasting by the Federal Communications Commission (FCC) provides a good illustration. Through its authority to issue operating licenses, the FCC limits the number of television stations serving local markets. Such entry restrictions serve to raise the profitability of the industry as a whole, but the nature of broadcasting admits a number of possible activities beyond the control of the FCC which might allow an individual station to enhance its share of the total profits. For example, stations may adjust the quality and type of programs offered to viewers, the number of broadcast hours per day, the number and length of commercial interruptions per program, and so forth. Although the industry has attempted to limit rivalry on these and other dimensions by adopting a voluntary code of ethics under the auspices of the National Association of Broadcasters, one activity that is difficult to restrain is a station's expenditures on programs. Almost all stations bid for a substantial amount of their local entertainment programming in the syndication market, and many produce their own news programs. Acting alone, a station may be able to raise its share of the total television audience by increasing its programming expenses. Of course, if any such action is duplicated by competitors, it becomes ineffective—audience shares remain stable, operating costs rise, and a portion of the profits associated with regulation is dissipated.

EMPIRICAL RESULTS

To test whether or not profit dissipation is prevalent in television broadcasting, one economist analyzed a sample of 394 licensed stations that filed earnings reports with the FCC in 1977.[13] His basic methodology was to determine whether factors yielding potential economic profits in the industry were also associated with levels of programming expenditures, despite the fact that such expenses contribute little to revenues for the industry as a whole.

The variables employed in the analysis and listed in Table 13-1 have been used by a number of researchers in explaining televi-

---

[13]The following discussion is based upon Gary M. Fournier, "Nonprice Competition and the Dissipation of Rents from Television Regulation," *Southern Economic Journal*, January 1985, pp. 754–765.

TABLE 13-1
Variables used in regressions

Variable	Definition
UHF	Equals one if the station is UHF, and zero otherwise
AV	Equals one if the market contains no UHF stations, and zero otherwise
NET	Equals one if the station is a network affiliate, and zero otherwise
INDV	Equals one if there are independent VHF stations present in the market, and zero otherwise
H/N	The number of households per station
CRZ	The share of the total audience accounted for by the two largest stations in the market
INCOME	Per capita income of households in the station's market area
AGED 65	Percentage of the population in the market area aged 65 or older

---

sion station profitability. As can be seen from the descriptions given in the table, the variables basically describe the salient characteristics of each local television market, including such things as the number of and types of stations, network affiliations, and audience demographics. The distinction between very-high frequency (VHF) and ultrahigh frequency (UHF) stations is important because VHF broadcasters have a significant cost advantage due to the nature of television transmission technology.

The study estimated two separate regression equations employing these variables, one to explain television station profits (measured as 1977 pretax earnings), the other to explain all explicit programming expenses, such as payments for exclusive program rights, film and tape rental, music license fees, payroll for programming department employees (including on-air personalities), and related program expenses. The results are reported in Table 13-2. As the estimated coefficients show, station profitability is enhanced (variables with positive coefficients) by network affiliation, with this effect being magnified in bigger markets (those having an above-average number of households per station), and in high-income markets. In contrast, an increase in audience age and the use of UHF broadcast

technology tends to reduce station profits. Moreover, VHF-stations' profits fall if there are no UHF rivals in its market area. (The result is explained by the fact that in the absence of UHF competitors, the VHF cost advantage disappears.)

The main results of this study are drawn from a comparison of the coefficient estimates in the two equations, however. Overall, this comparison reveals that while rivalry in programming does not fully dissipate profits in the industry, its effects are substantial. The estimated coefficients in the program expenses equation are roughly one-third to two-thirds of the corresponding magnitudes in the profit equation, suggesting that approximately these proportions of station profits are dissipated by self-defeating programming cost increases. For example, about $1.21/1.62 = 74.7$ percent of the profitability attributable to market size, H/N, is engrossed by additional expenditures on programs. Similarly, the coefficients on INDV suggest that rivalry to increase audience share intensifies when an independent VHF station enters the market.

It is apparent, then, that firms do not get to keep all of the profits associated with regulation. If competition is restrained on one dimension, rivalry between firms may simply shift to other dimensions. It is important to

TABLE 13-2
Regression results

*Not statistically significant.

Explanatory variable	Coefficient in profit equation	Coefficient in program expenses equation
UHF (H/N)	−0.88	−0.33
AV (H/N)	−0.21	−0.18
NET (H/N)	0.29	0.09
INDV (H/N)	0.00*	0.23
H/N	1.62	1.21
CRZ	−415.64*	−128.21
INCOME	0.12	0.16
AGED 65	−37.69	−6.90

point out, however, that the type of competition described here provides little or no benefits for consumers. Rivalry between television stations that bids up the prices of syndicated programs mostly benefits program suppliers at the expense of station owners. From a policy perspective, it may be argued that consumer welfare would be enhanced by relaxing the restraints on entry into television broadcasting.

SUMMARY

1 Barriers to entry include the following: ownership of "essential" resources that have no close substitutes, large capital requirements, government franchises and licenses, patents, and economies of scale.

2 Resources will be spent to obtain monopoly positions. These resources may be spent in the political arena. Further expenditures of resources will be required to keep the monopoly privilege.

3 Monopoly profits will be reduced by competition for them. However, some firms may still be capable of obtaining long-run monopoly profits from their specialized resources.

4 One form of monopolization is cartelization.

5 If firms can be assigned output quotas so that the marginal cost for each firm is equal to industry marginal revenue, profits can be maximized for the cartelized industry. However, it is difficult to prevent cheating, and if firms are of unequal efficiencies, the less efficient will be unhappy with their smaller allocations.

6 The cheating firm in a cartel or a collusive arrangement believes that the established cartel price will be its "going" price, even if it expands

output. When it does expand output, it can increase profits, provided that other firms do not also cheat. Since each cartel member sees the same possibility, every cartel that is not policed by government is inherently unstable.

7 The smaller the number of firms and customers in the industry, the lower the cost of policing any collusive agreement.

8 Sealed bidding allows illegal colluders to monitor the price and output of member firms.

9 Mergers may involve either horizontal integration or vertical integration. Antitrust laws apply to both.

10 Backward vertical integration does not necessarily mean increased profitability, because the opportunity costs of all inputs are the same whether or not the input supplier is owned by the firm purchasing the input.

11 Forward vertical integration does not necessarily foreclose the market. Moreover, even if one firm merged with the monopoly seller of its products, the purchase price of that retail outlet would include the discounted value of all future monopoly profits. The purchasing firm would therefore make only a normal rate of return on that investment.

12 Arguments in favor of vertical integration to enhance monopoly power include (a) being able to squeeze out independent, nonintegrated firms, (b) price discrimination, (c) prevention of entry by controlling a critical resource, and (d) forestalling monopolization by others.

13 When economies of scale are so great that the long-run average total cost curve is downward-sloping over a large range of outputs in relation to the industry demand, a natural monopoly exists. The monopolist will be the firm which is able to exploit the economies of scale first and thereby undercut its competitors.

14 If a natural monopolist is forced to charge a price equal to marginal cost, the monopolist will suffer a loss if it is producing in the downward-sloping portion of its LAC.

15 A natural monopolist cannot, therefore, merely be "instructed" to charge a price equal to marginal cost, for to obtain this price, the monopoly would have to be covered for its losses in the form of a subsidy. It could also be allowed to engage in multipart pricing, or price discrimination. Finally, the government could sell the rights to produce to the highest bidder. In this case, the price charged would be equal to the LAC of the firm, including the opportunity cost of the capital paid out to acquire the franchise.

16 Regulation has two forms. Both cost-of-service and rate-of-return regulations require intimate knowledge of regulated firms' costs curves.

17 In both types of regulation, it is impossible to meaningfully allocate common costs. Moreover, it is virtually impossible to regulate the price per constant-quality unit because it is impossible to regulate all the aspects of quality.

18 When the rate of return on the capital stock is regulated, the regulated firms have an incentive to expand the capital stock or rate base as long as the rate of return permitted exceeds the marginal cost of capital. Accordingly, the ratio of capital to labor in regulated industries will be higher than it would be without regulation.

19 Efficient use of resources would require that higher prices be charged during peak periods. However, regulatory commissions generally have not favored this type of pricing by public utilities because these utilities would earn higher than a "fair" rate of return in the short run and embarrass the commission regulating them. Also, a simpler rate structure is easier to administer.

GLOSSARY

- **barriers to entry** Such impediments to entry into an industry as legal franchises are large capital requirements; allow for monopolization.
- **natural monopoly** A monopoly that comes into existence when the minimum average cost of production occurs at a rate of output that is sufficient for one firm to supply the entire market at a price covering all costs.
- **cartel** An organization of firms in an industry that coordinates output and pricing decisions.
- **merger** The joining of two or more firms together under a single ownership.
- **horizontal integration** Merger activity which involves firms selling the same commodity, e.g., two tennis-racket manufacturers merging into one firm.
- **vertical integration** Merger activity which involves one firm buying either a seller of one of its inputs or a purchaser of its outputs, e.g., an electric utility buying out its supplier of fuel.
- **internal transfer price** The cost figure used within one firm for the output of one part of the firm "bought" by another part of the firm, e.g., the price that the nuts and bolts division of General Motors Corporation charges the Cadillac division for nuts and bolts (also called a "shadow" price).
- **opportunistic behavior** Situations in which parties doing business with one another have the ability to extract a higher than previously agreed upon price for a continuation of the same goods or service.
- **common costs** Costs which are common to the production of more than one output. For example, one building may be used for the production of many products. Its cost is common to all those products.

- **rate base** The net worth or capital stock base upon which a "fair" rate of return can be earned by a regulated utility; it may include the purchase price of buildings and equipment, for example.
- **Averch-Johnson effect** A fixed rate of return on investment will lead to a higher capital-to-labor ratio than in an unregulated situation. Sometimes called an inefficient expansion of the rate base.
- **peak-load pricing** A pricing system in which consumers are charged a higher price during peak demand periods than during off-peak periods. A toll bridge, for example, could charge a higher price during rush hours than it charges during all other hours.
- **grandfather clause** A legal device which allows individuals or firms already engaged in an industry or occupation to avoid being subjected to the requirements of the new law. A law requiring the examination and licensing of water-sprinkler installers might have a grandfather clause which automatically gave a license to all those who were in the industry when the law was passed.

QUESTIONS

(Answers to even-numbered questions are at back of text).

1 Of the barriers to entry discussed in the text, which are government-created and which arise in the absence of government action?

2 "The elimination of all tariffs would dissipate more monopoly power than any other single governmental action." What do tariffs have to do with monopoly power?

3 Suppose you own the only natural mineral-springs spa in your state. Why would we *not* expect to see the state government regulating the price you charge?

4 "Whenever a government entity creates a new monopoly right, there will be competition for its award." Having created the right, how might the government determine who gets it? What criteria might it use?

5 Would you expect to find more or less corruption of government officials in a regulatory agency which auctioned off "certificates of convenience" or in one which rationed them according to nonpecuniary criteria? Why?

6 "All we milk producers need do is persuade the government to set a legal minimum on the price of milk, say 20 percent above the open-market price, and we'll all be set for life." What's wrong with this argument?

7 "Philosophically, I am vehemently opposed to government interference in the marketplace; however, as the owner of a liquor store, I can tell you that deregulation would be very bad for the citizenry. You wouldn't want a liquor store on every corner, would you?" Why would you predict that a liquor store owner would defend regulation of his or her industry?

8 Distinguish between a cartel and other collusive agreements restraining competition.

9 Why might the existing firms in a cartelized industry prefer to be regulated by the government?

10 Is the ABA (American Bar Association) a cartel? What factors would you look for in attempting to make an informed judgment?

11 Why is the incentive so great for an individual firm to cheat on a cartel agreement?

12 Explain what a "natural monopoly" is. Why is the right of free entry insufficient here to prevent sustained economic profits?

13 "If a governmental regulatory agency ordered a public utility to price all of its output at marginal cost, the firm would lose money unless subsidy payments were made by the government." Is this statement true, false, or uncertain? Why?

14 Suppose your monopoly is regulated by the government. You are allowed to price your product at an average cost which includes a 10 percent per year rate of return on the fair market value of your investment. Does it matter to you whether "investment" is defined as your firm's net worth or by the value of its assets? Why or why not?

15 Rate-of-return regulation requires that a firm's investment (rate base) be established. What would be wrong with adding up the market value of all the firm's outstanding common stock and using that figure? Isn't that the best indicator of the fair market value of the firm?

SELECTED REFERENCES

Bain, J.S., *Barriers to New Competition* (Cambridge, Mass.: Harvard University Press, 1956).

Kahn, Alfred E., *The Economics of Regulation*, vols. 1 and 2 (New York: Wiley, 1970).

Klein, Ben, Robert Crawford, and Armen Alchian, "Vertical Integration, Appropriable Rents, and the Competitive Contracting Process," *Journal of Law and Economics*, vol. 22, October 1978, pp. 297–326.

McGee, John S., "Predatory Price Cutting: The Standard Oil (N.J.) Case," *The Journal of Law and Economics*, vol. 1, October 1958, pp. 137–169.

Phillips, Almarin (ed.), *Promoting Competition in Regulated Markets* (Washington, D.C.: The Brookings Institution, 1975).

Posner, Richard A., "Taxation by Regulation," *The Bell Journal of Economics and Management Science*, vol. 2, no. 1, Spring 1971, pp. 22–50.

Solomon, Ezra, "Alternative Rate of Return Concepts and Their Implications for Utility Regulation," *The Bell Journal of Economics and Management Science*, vol. 1, no. 1, Spring 1970, pp. 65–81.

Stigler, George J., "The Theory of Economic Regulation," *The Bell Journal of Economics and Management Science*, vol. 2, no. 1, Spring 1971, pp. 3–21.

Monopolistic competition and oligopoly

*T*he models of perfect competition and pure monopoly represent two forms of market structure. In the perfectly competitive model, we assume that there are numerous firms which produce a homogeneous product and that no one firm has any influence over price—all firms are price takers. In the pure monopoly model, we assume that the firm is a single seller of a good—the firm is a price searcher or maker. There are, however, market situations which seem to fall in between these two extremes. After all, many firms have some control over price—i.e., do not face a perfectly elastic demand curve—but are not really pure monopolists.

In this chapter, we will study market structures in which it is explicitly recognized that firms take account of and react to other firms' pricing and output decisions. Each of the few sellers is aware that the other sellers of the same product may take retaliatory actions to offset or hinder aggressive pricing and output behavior. When there are only two firms in an industry, we call it a **duopoly**. When there are more than two firms but not enough to make the industry perfectly competitive, we call such an industry an **oligopoly**. The main thing is that there is rivalry among the few firms in the industry. Before considering these models, we will first consider another model that was posed to bridge the gap between pure competition and monopoly.

The search for a model that had the qualities of both perfect competition and pure monopoly led, in this case, to the theory of **monopolistic competition**, developed by Harvard's Edward Chamberlin and Cambridge's Joan Robinson. Chamberlin's book was *The Theory of Monopolistic Competition* and Robinson's, *The Economics of Imperfect Competition*. Both appeared in

1933. The theory that we outline in this chapter is derived mainly from Chamberlin's work.

CHARACTERISTICS OF MONOPOLISTICALLY COMPETITIVE INDUSTRIES

In his work, Chamberlin presented some of the key characteristics of monopolistically competitive industries. We outline them below.

Product differentiation

Perhaps the most important feature of the monopolistically competitive market is *product differentiation*. The products, though similar, are not identical. Remember that in a perfectly competitive market we talked about homogeneous products, and in a monopoly we also referred to a homogeneous product that the firm sold. Now we are in a situation in which each individual manufacturer of a product has monopoly over a product which is slightly differentiated from other similar products. There are numerous examples of such product differentiation: cigarettes, toothpaste, soap, jeans, and so on. Indeed, it appears that product differentiation characterizes most, if not all, American markets. We are able to buy more than one type of television set, more than one type of suit, and more than one type of automobile. There are usually a number of similar but differentiated products to choose from in each product classification.

Actually, monopolistic competition is only one instance of this differentiation, which is sometimes called **variation of production**. Each firm has to decide on what it thinks might be an optimal product assortment; each firm has to decide on the appropriate level of quality for each product. But when viewed in this light, product variation can be found in market structures other than monopolistic competition.

Some economists like to distinguish between product differentiation that is "real" and product differentiation that is "artificial." Real product differentiation involves variations in physical characteristics, such as an actual chemical difference between two brands of detergent. Artificial product differentiation would involve different packaging materials, brand names, and advertising outlays. (There are cases in which product differentiation takes the form of an imaginary quality differential; e.g., a Calvin Klein label on what appears to be otherwise an $18 pair of jeans.)

The types of product differentiation we just mentioned, of course, represent only the tip of the iceberg. Firms can differentiate their products on the basis of location and service provided with the product sold.

The point to be made here is that in a monopolistically competitive market, each individual producer has some market power (i.e., ability to raise price above MC) in the production and sale of a differentiated product, but there are many close substitutes for that product.

Sales promotion: advertising

Monopolistic competition differs from perfect competition in that the latter requires no sales promotion. No individual firm in a perfectly competitive market will advertise. After all, if the firm can sell all that it wants at the going market price and cannot affect price, it has no incentive to incur advertising costs because the gains from advertising would be distributed across *all* firms in the industry, not solely to the single firm that would pay for the advertising. But such is not the case for the monopolistic competitor. Since the monopolistic competitor has at least some monopoly power, advertising may result in increased profits. How much advertising should be undertaken? As much as is profitable. It should be carried to the point where the additional revenue associated with a rightward shift of the *DD* curve from an additional dollar of advertising just equals one dollar of marginal cost.

Often it is stated that the goal of the advertiser is to make the demand curve more inelastic for his or her product. However, this is an incorrect assessment of the goal of advertising.

Consider Figure 14-1. We have drawn two demand curves, *DD* and *D'D'*. Using the vertical axis formula for price elasticity of demand, it is clear that *D'D'* is more elastic than *DD*. Does that necessarily mean that a firm would like to have advertising cause the demand curve to rotate around point *A* from *D'D'* to the more inelastic *DD*? That depends on the profit-maximizing rate of output. At rates of output in excess of Q_1, the demand curve *D'D'* is more profitable because any given quantity greater than Q_1 can be sold for a higher price.

The goal of advertising is to shift the demand curve to the right. A monopolistic competitor who advertises will always prefer a demand curve more to the right to a demand curve more to the left, whether the former is more or less elastic.

In the strictest model of monopolistic competition, advertising by one monopolistic competitor does not induce retaliatory action—more advertising—by others. That is to say, advertising is not undertaken as a reaction to encroachments of other firms on the particular market in question.[1] Nonetheless, we generally observe advertising by all the firms in a monopolistically competitive industry. Sometimes this advertising is called competitive or defensive in the sense that it has no effect on *increasing* sales; rather, it is necessary to *keep* sales at what they are and to prevent other firms from taking business away. **Competitive advertising** is sometimes contrasted with

---

[1]This at first blush is a strange assumption since, with stable market demand, shifting one's own demand curve outward means shifting someone else's inward. However, if there are a large number of firms, a perceptible shift in one firm's demand curve will be matched by imperceptible shifts in the demand curves of all other firms. Actually, in the purest model of monopolistic competition, there are a large number of firms; this model conforms to the competitive one in terms of the nonreaction by other firms. It is only when we move toward a situation where there are *not* a large number of monopolistically competitive firms that the assumption appears "strange."

FIGURE 14-1
Advertising and the price elasticity of demand
It is often asserted that advertising is undertaken in an attempt to make demand more inelastic. However, consider demand curves *DD* and *D'D'*. The latter is more elastic than the former; however, *D'D'* would be preferable at output rates in excess of Q_1 because it is to the right of *DD*, even though *DD* is relatively less elastic.

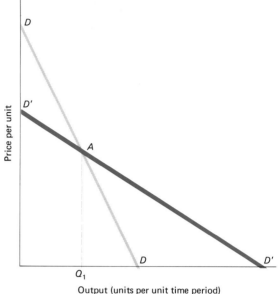

informative advertising, which actually imparts information that can be used by the consumer in deciding which product to buy. The distinction between competitive and informative advertising is a murky one; operationally meaningful modus operandi have not been well developed to make that distinction.

Product groups   We have defined an industry as a collection of firms producing a homogeneous commodity. However, it is difficult to use this definition of an industry when we talk in terms of differentiated products. Each firm has a distinct product and thus is itself an industry, and we could describe each industry in terms of the differentiated product and the firm that produces it. Chamberlin sought to solve this problem by lumping together firms producing very closely related products. These are called **product groups**. Some product groups that come to mind are jeans, breakfast cereals, toilet paper, and hand soap.

DEMAND FOR THE MONOPOLISTICALLY COMPETITIVE FIRM

The monopolistically competitive firm perceives that it has some small amount of monopoly power. Hence, it does not consider that its demand curve is perfectly horizontal at the going market price for the product.

We can best analyze the individual firm in a monopolistically competitive industry (product group) in terms of each firm facing a **proportional demand curve**. This is, in fact, what Chamberlin used as his definition of the demand curve facing the individual monopolistic competitor. "Such a curve will, in fact, be a fractional part of the demand curve for the general class of product, and will be of the same elasticity."[2] If there are 50 sellers, the demand curve for the individual seller will show at each price one-fiftieth of the total quantity demanded at that price. We are implicitly assuming, then, that all firms are of equal size. We will make the further assumption that all firms have identical costs.

Look at Figure 14-2. Here we show the *proportional* demand curve $d_p d_p$. It represents the amount of demand faced by a typical firm when all firms are charging the same price. In other words, the proportional demand curve is constructed by taking one-fiftieth of total market quantity demanded at each price when we assume that there are 50 equal-sized firms. In general, when there are n equal-sized firms, the proportional demand curve is constructed by taking $1/n$ of the total market quantity demanded at each price.

Price determination

Let us start out at a price of P_1. We assume that each firm is charging P_1. Each would therefore sell q_1 units of output per unit time period. However, the individual firm, according to Chamberlin's assumption, will act as if all other firms kept their price at P_1. Thus we assume with Chamberlin that the individual firm *perceives* a firm demand curve of $d_f d_f$ at price P_1. Notice that this firm demand curve $d_f d_f$ has more elasticity to it at price P_1. It has more elasticity to it at every price than the proportional demand curve $d_p d_p$ because the individual firm in this model does not think that other firms will react to changes in its price. Therefore, if the individual firm lowers its price in order to capture a larger share of the market, it perceives that it will be able to take business away from other firms because they will keep the higher price on their products. If this were a perfectly competitive case (and indeed we can analyze perfect competition in this way also), $d_f d_f$ would be perfectly horizontal at price P_1. This is not an instance of a perfectly competitive case, and therefore $d_f d_f$ has a marginal revenue curve, mr_f, that is everywhere below it. To repeat, the individual monopolistic competitor perceives its demand curve to be $d_f d_f$, the one that obtains if it changes its price while all other firms leave their price unchanged.

Under the above assumptions, P_1 is not a price that the individual monopolistically competitive firm will charge. It will increase output until marginal revenue equals marginal cost, which occurs at output q_2. It perceives that it can sell this quantity at price P_2.

However, q_2 is unattainable at price P_2. Figure 14-2 is drawn for a typical firm. All firms acting together in an attempt to increase output *cannot* move

[2]Edward H. Chamberlin, *Theory of Monopolistic Competition*, 5th ed. (Cambridge, Mass.: Harvard University Press, 1948), p. 90.

FIGURE 14-2
Monopolistic competition: the firm and the industry
The proportional demand curve $d_p d_p$ is drawn by assuming that all firms charge the same price and that all firms are of equal size. At a price of P_1, the firm will be able to sell q_1. It perceives a firm demand curve of $d_f d_f$, which is drawn by assuming that all other firms will keep their prices at P_1. At price P_1, however, marginal revenue does not equal marginal cost. This occurs at output rate q_2. The individual firm believes that it can sell this quantity at price P_2. Such an output rate is not attainable at that price, however, because all firms acting together will individually face $d_p d_p$.

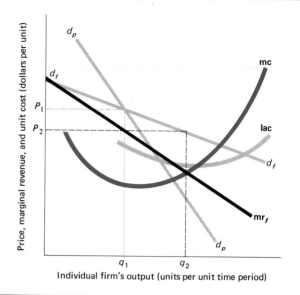

along an imagined individual demand curve $d_f d_f$. Rather, they must move along their respective proportional demand curves $d_p d_p$. Price P_2 and quantity q_2 is not an equilibrium combination because the relevant curve is $d_p d_p$. The firm optimum occurs on each firm's own imagined firm demand curve, $d_f d_f$, where marginal revenue equals marginal cost; for industry equilibrium, the firm must also find itself on the proportional demand curve $d_p d_p$.

EQUILIBRIUM IN MONOPOLISTIC COMPETITION

Short-run equilibrium is defined as a situation in which the going market price is such that no firm has an incentive to change its own price or output. This can occur only where marginal revenue equals marginal cost. Furthermore, the price must be such that the quantity demanded corresponding to the point where marginal revenue equals marginal cost ($mr_f = mc$) also corresponds to the quantity where the proportional demand curve $d_p d_p$ intersects the firm demand curve $d_f d_f$. Only at this point is the firm not frustrated in its attempts to set a price at which the intersection occurs. Look at Figure 14-3. Here we show such a situation. At price P_e, the firm demand curve $d_f d_f$ intersects the proportional demand curve $d_p d_p$. The firm is operating

FIGURE 14-3
Short-run equilibrium under monopolistic competition
Eventually an output rate q_e will be found where $mr_f = mc$ and where the firm's perceived demand curve $d_f d_f$ intersects its proportional demand curve $d_p d_p$. It will sell its output at price P_e; its average total costs are C_1; and its profits are the shaded area.

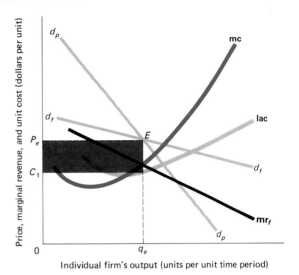

both on its own perceived demand curve and simultaneously on the proportional demand curve. Moreover, this is a profit-maximizing rate of output because it occurs at the point where the marginal cost curve intersects the firm's perceived marginal revenue curve mr_f.

Notice that in this short-run example of equilibrium, positive economic profits are being made by each individual firm. This can be seen by the position of the long-run average cost curve lac. It intersects the quantity line, $q_e E$, below the price line, $P_e E$. Economic profits are shown in Figure 14-3 by the shaded rectangle, $(P_e \cdot q_e) - (C_1 \cdot q_e)$.

Equilibrium in the long run

Figure 14-3 could represent the long-run equilibrium for the individual firm in a monopolistically competitive industry only if entry into the industry were *blocked*. We say this because if entry is not blocked, the existence of positive economic profits will attract new firms into that industry, competing these positive economic profits away.

The long-run equilibrium will be defined in exactly the same way as the short-run equilibrium, but *economic profits will be zero*. They will be competed away by entry of new firms into the industry where they exist, just as they are competed away in the perfectly competitive industry in the short run. In other words, the long-run average cost curve must be tangent to the firm's demand curve at the short-run equilibrium price.

This can be seen in Figure 14-4. The profit-maximizing quantity produced per unit time period is perceived by the individual firm as q_e, for this

FIGURE 14-4

Long-run equilibrium of the firm, monopolistic competition

Positive economic profits will cause entry into the industry. The proportional demand curve $d_p d_p$ will eventually shift leftward until, at the equilibrium price, each individual monopolistic competitor will be earning zero economic profits. At point E, price P_e is just equal to long-run average costs. At this equilibrium there is "excess" capacity, because in perfect competition lac = mc at point M. Hence, the monopolistic competition equilibrium generates a higher price and lower output, as measured by the difference between E and M.

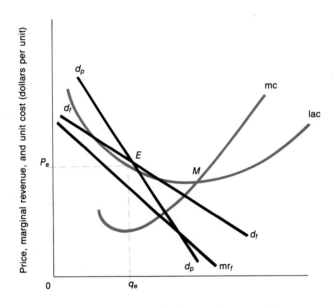

Individual firm' output (units per unit time period)

is where marginal revenue equals marginal cost. The price that can be obtained for that quantity is P_e, and that is the price at which the perceived firm demand curve intersects the proportional demand curve. The long-run average cost curve is also tangent to the perceived firm demand curve $d_f d_f$ at the rate of output q_e and price P_e, or at point E. Thus at price P_e, no economic profits are being received by any individual firm in the monopolistically competitive industry. This occurs because positive economic profits, as represented in Figure 14-3, create a situation in which other firms want to enter the industry to reap those positive economic profits. With a stable market demand curve, the proportional demand curve $d_p d_p$ would shift toward the origin, as n increases by entry of new firms, until economic profits are driven to zero. That is what competition is all about (as new firms enter, the number of substitutes increases, causing the demand curve to become more elastic).

THE LAC TANGENCY POINT
AND "EXCESS" CAPACITY

Remember back in Chapter 10 when we showed the long-run equilibrium for a perfectly competitive industry, in which each firm produced at the minimum on its long-run average cost curve and its short-run average cost curve? This was because the horizontal demand curve facing any individual firm shifted until the price line or individual demand curve just touched or was tangent to the lowest point of the long-run average cost curve. Then entry or exit would cease in the perfectly competitive industry. The same kind of analysis applies to monopolistic competition. However, since the demand curve perceived by the firm is downward-sloping because of the monopoly given it by product differentiation, the tangency point must be to the left of the minimum point on the long-run average cost curve. This can be seen in Figure 14-4. The minimum point M is where the long-run marginal cost curve intersects lac. This is to the right of rate of output q_e.

Why "excess" capacity?

Two reasons why excess capacity, or a rate of output that is not "ideal," exist in the monopolistically competitive firm have been posited traditionally. One is attributable to an inefficient utilization of society's resources; it occurs whenever $P > MC$. The other is attributed to the fact that the monopolistically competitive firm does not produce enough and does not employ enough of society's resources to attain minimum average costs.

Paying for differentness

Note that as long as there is any slope whatsoever (greater than 0) to the individual demand curve $d_f d_f$, there is no way that the individual firm can operate at the *minimum* point on a long-run average cost curve or a short-run average cost curve and still cover those costs. Chamberlin contended that the difference between the actual long-run average cost of production for a monopolistically competitive firm in an open market and the minimum long-run average cost represented the "cost" of producing "differentness." In other words, Chamberlin did not label this difference in unit cost a measure of excess capacity; that was an idea of economists who took up the model after him.

Indeed, Chamberlin argued that it is rational for consumers to have a taste for differentiation; consumers willingly accept the resultant increased production cost in return for choice and variety of output. We know that the so-called excess capacity situation is a result of heterogeneity in the product; if there were no heterogeneity and all other assumptions in the model were retained, the firm would operate at the minimum point on its long-run average cost curve and on its short-run cost curve. Output would be ideal.

"Excess" capacity and waiting costs

Research since Chamberlin's time has disclosed another reason for $P > \text{MC}$ within the framework of competitive markets. Just as some consumers are willing to wait in line to get a lower price for some products, some suppliers may adopt a marketing and production strategy that reduces consumer waiting time. Even if the goods in question are homogeneous and mass-produced, there is a cost to producers for holding enough inventories so as to meet demand fluctuations. In the case of specially tailored products, a reduction in consumer waiting time can be accomplished only through a firm's investment in "excess" capacity, held ready to produce the marginal order.

In either of these cases the firm would appear superficially to be operating above the minimum or short-run and long-run average cost curves with excess capacity, while charging a price above marginal cost. That perception does not, however, account for the cost saving to consumers caused by a reduction in waiting time required to obtain the products they want.

In one sense Chamberlin was exactly correct. The kind of market we have described is one in which the output of different firms is differentiated by the waiting time required to purchase its output, and in the money price paid. In all cases, however, the social cost of the product to the consumer is minimized and the total price paid (money plus waiting costs) is equal to the consumer's marginal cost of the purchase.

OLIGOPOLY AND DUOPOLY

In a duopoly or oligopoly, rivals may spend much of their time trying to second-guess each other. Their rivalry may include such forms of nonprice competition as advertising and product modification rather than price competition. The number of possible ways in which oligopolists can act and react is large. Because of the many forms rivalry can take, we do not have a single theory of oligopoly behavior. We start with a very simple model of oligopoly and then present some classical solutions to duopoly situations. Discussions of price rigidity, price leadership, and nonprice competition follow.

THE SIMPLEST OLIGOPOLY MODEL

Assumptions

To begin this discussion of oligopoly on its most general level, we make five assumptions.

■ *The industry has only a small number of firms. The position and shape of the LAC curve relative to the industry demand curve is such that the industry can support only a small number of efficient plants and firms.*

■ *The firm (and plant) LAC is upward-sloping over the relevant range of outputs. The total cost curve of each firm is continuous and normal in the sense that marginal costs will always be positive and above LAC.*

■ *Single-plant firms are the only possibility. Single-plant firms are the only possibility because of large diseconomies at the firm level, the possibility of antitrust action, etc. In other words, the cost of combining plants under common ownership and control is prohibitive.*

■ *Free entry. There are no barriers to entering or leaving the industry.*

■ *Homogeneous product. The firms produce similar products.*

The oligopolist's demand curve

Now we are faced with the difficult task of drawing the demand curve for an oligopolist. We cannot use the industry demand curve because the oligopolist is not a monopolist. We cannot use a horizontal demand curve at the market-clearing price because the oligopolist is, by definition, not a perfect competitor. We can say nothing about the demand curve of an oligopolist until we make an assumption about the interaction among oligopolists. We have to know something about the *reaction function* that we are looking at. Does each oligopolist believe that others will not react to changes in its price and/or output? If the typical oligopolist believes that they will react, we must specify the manner in which the oligopolist *expects* them to react. In a perfectly competitive model, each firm ignores the reactions of other firms because each firm can sell all that it wants at the going market price. In the pure monopoly model, the monopolist does not have to worry about the reaction of rivals, since by definition there *are* none.

Being able to ignore what other firms are doing in an industry—whether it be perfectly competitive or purely monopolistic—is therefore the key distinction to be made between those two forms of market structure and the one under study, oligopoly. We are referring here to interdependence. This interdependence lies at the heart of every oligopoly model, and as you might imagine, every time a new assumption about interaction among oligopolists (or a reaction function) is made, a new oligopoly model is born. For this simplest of oligopoly models, we will assume the following:

■ *Each firm expects that any change in price will be matched by all other firms in the industry.*

We can see in Figure 14-5 the result of this assumption. The industry demand curve is DD. If the industry has only two firms each of equal size, each firm will believe that its demand curve is equal to the one labeled $\frac{1}{2}D\frac{1}{2}D$. This follows from our assumption that whatever price it chooses will be matched by its rivals.

If we assume three equal-sized firms in the industry, each individual demand curve, as perceived by the individual oligopolist, will be $\frac{1}{3}D\frac{1}{3}D$.

FIGURE 14-5
Establishing the equilibrium number of firms
If each firm expects that any change in price will be matched by all other firms in the industry, and if there are two equal-sized firms in the industry, each will face a demand curve that is $\frac{1}{2}D\frac{1}{2}D$. If there are three equal-sized firms in the industry, each will face a demand curve that is $\frac{1}{3}D\frac{1}{3}D$. If the long-run average cost curve for the industry is LAC, only three firms can be supported in this industry. If a fourth firm enters, each will face a demand curve equal to $\frac{1}{4}D\frac{1}{4}D$. The LAC curve is everywhere above that proportionate demand curve; all firms make losses.

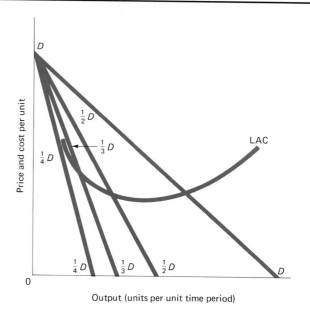

The equilibrium number of firms

We have assumed unrestricted entry and exit. Further, we assume that all firms have cost curves exactly alike. We can determine the number of firms that will be in the industry by comparing the long-run average cost curve with the firms' demand curves. This is shown in Figure 14-6. If there were one firm in the industry, other firms would be attracted because the long-run cost curve lies below the industry demand curve *DD* for a large range of outputs. If there were two firms in the industry, there would still be an incentive to enter. Finally, if three firms were in the industry, a fourth firm would not desire to enter because the LAC curve is everywhere above the proportional demand curve $\frac{1}{4}D\frac{1}{4}D$. If four firms were in the industry, by our assumptions, none could cover long-run average costs. They would all suffer economic losses.

Long-run economic profits

It is possible in this simple model that in the long run, economic profits will be obtained. This can be seen by transferring the proportional demand curve for an individual oligopolist when there are three firms to Figure 14-6. The demand curve facing each of the three individual firms is $\frac{1}{3}D\frac{1}{3}D$. The long-run average cost curve is given as LAC, and the long-run marginal cost curve is LMC. The profit-maximizing rate of output for each individual oligopolist is at the intersection of marginal revenue and long-run marginal cost, or at a rate of output q_1. The price that the product will sell for is identically equal

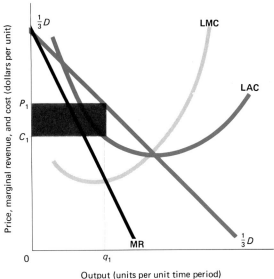

FIGURE 14-6
Long-run economic profits
We have assumed that three equal-sized firms will exist in this industry. Each faces a proportionate demand curve $\frac{1}{3}D\frac{1}{3}D$. The marginal revenue curve facing each firm is MR, the output for each firm is q_1, and the price is P_1. Costs are equal to C_1 and, thus, each firm's profit is the shaded area.

for each firm at P_1. Unit cost, given LAC, is C_1. Economic profits per unit time period are equal to the shaded area in Figure 14-3.

Given the assumptions in this model, this is the long-run equilibrium situation.

INTERDEPENDENCE AND UNCERTAINTY

Now we change our assumptions. Firms now recognize their interdependence, but they are still not completely certain how interdependent they are. In other words, pricing and output decisions are made on the basis of inaccurate or incomplete information about rivals' reactions. Again, it is difficult to proceed with model building unless we make specific assumptions about how firms *think* other firms will react. What we will do is consider several so-called classic solutions to a situation in which there are only two firms, that is, a situation of duopoly.

THE COURNOT DUOPOLY SITUATION

Well over a century ago, Antoine Augustin Cournot, a Frenchman, published a theory of duopoly.[3] Unfortunately for Cournot, this theory did not become

---

[3]Antoine Augustin Cournot, *Recherches sur les principes mathématiques de la théorie des richesse* (Paris, 1838). English translation by N. T. Bacon, *Researches into the Mathematical Principles of the Theory of Wealth* (N. V., Macmillan & Co., 1897, reprinted 1927).

widely known or discussed until the 1930s. Although the model is intrinsically interesting and used as a basis of departure for further analysis, it does embody some rather restrictive assumptions.

Assumptions

The assumptions for this duopoly model are similar to those of the simplified three-firm model presented above. The producers produce identical products at identical costs. We assume that costs are constant and that the two producers know exactly what the market demand curve is. They have perfect information about every point on *DD* in Figure 14-5. Furthermore, both producers behave in exactly the same way. We are further assuming that buyers have perfect information. Therefore, each duopolist will always sell the product at exactly the same price.

Now we come to the behavioral rule that Cournot specified:

■ *Each duopolist, in selecting its own rate of output, assumes that the other duopolist's output will remain constant.*

Of course, this assumption involves self-delusion on the part of each firm. Each duopolist assumes that it can act without provoking an output reaction from the other. This is, in essence, a no-learning-by-doing model. Nonetheless, Cournot was able to show that, given his assumptions, the duopolist will approach an equilibrium rate of output and price.

The Cournot approach toward equilibrium

In order to understand how the model works, we start with an industry demand function for the commodity. To keep the flavor of Cournot's original publication, we will use mineral water as the commodity. We assume for simplicity that marginal cost is equal to zero.

Look at Figure 14-7. The industry demand curve is *DD*, and the marginal revenue curve is MR. The two firms are I and II. Firm I starts the ball rolling, while firm II is temporarily inactive. Hence, *DD* is the demand curve facing firm I. It sets the rate of output where marginal revenue equals marginal cost. In this case, this is the output at which the marginal revenue curve intersects the horizontal axis. It sets a rate of output of Q_1^I. The superscript refers to the firm and the subscript refers to the period, or "round." Thus Q_1^I indicates the output produced by duopolist I in the first round, or first period. It does 1933. The theory that we outline in this chapter is derived mainly from Chamberlin's work.

Now firm II enters the market. It takes as given firm I's output rate of Q_1^I. Firm II believes that its demand durve is *DD* minus the rate of output Q_1^I. Its demand curve is *D'D'*, which is derived by subtracting firm I's rate of output, Q_1^I from *DD*. Firm II will maximize profit by setting its rate of output at the point where its new marginal revenue curve MR' intersects the horizontal axis, which is its marginal cost curve. Firm II will produce at rate Q_1^{II}. Now firm I has the next move since Q_1^I is no longer optimal. It assumes that firm II will keep its rate of output at Q_1^{II}. Firm I perceives its new demand curve as the market demand curve minus the rate of output of firm II. This newly perceived (by firm I) demand curve is *D''D''* in Figure

FIGURE 14-7

The Cournot duopoly model

Marginal cost is equal to zero and, therefore, coincides with the horizontal axis. We start with demand curve DD. Duopolist I maximizes profit by setting its output rate at Q_1^I because this is where MR = MC. Firm II now believes that its demand curve is D'D', which is derived by subtracting the rate of output Q_1^I from demand curve DD. Duopolist II therefore maximizes profit by setting output at Q_1^{II}. Now firm I has the next move. It assumes that firm II will keep its rate of output at Q_1^{II}. It therefore perceives demand curve D''D'', which is drawn by subtracting output rate Q_1^{II} from demand curve DD. Duopolist I now sets its profit-maximizing rate of output at the new intersection of MR'' with MC, or at rate Q_2^I. This process continues. A determinate equilibrium will be reached where price is P_e, total output is Q_e, and each firm's profit-maximizing rate of output is $\frac{1}{2}Q_e$. If there were only one firm, the profit-maximizing output would be at Q_1^I sold at price P_m.

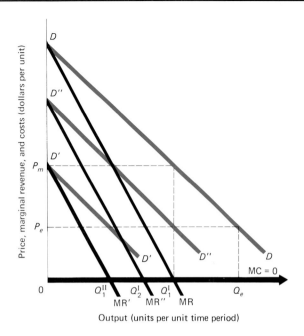

14-7. The curve marginal to this demand curve is labeled MR''. Firm I will change its rate of output so that marginal revenue MR'' = marginal cost = 0. This is where MR'' intersects the horizontal axis, or at a rate of output Q_2^I.

Each firm takes the other firm's output as given and then maximizes its profits by choosing the appropriate profit-maximizing rate of output. This process, however, will not go on indefinitely. Ultimately, the rate of output for each firm will tend toward an equilibrium amount equal to $\frac{1}{2}Q_e$ in Figure 14-7 in the case of two firms. The price at which each firm sells its output is P_e. Notice that this differs from the perfectly competitive solution, which would require that price be equal to marginal cost, which in this case would be zero. Thus, in the Cournot duopoly model, price exceeds marginal cost and the rate of output is less than it would be under perfect competition. However, in the Cournot model, the rate of output is greater than it would be in a pure monopoly. In a pure monopoly, the rate of output would be set at Q_1^I since there MR = MC.[4] The monopoly price would be P_m in Figure 14-7.

---

[4]It can be shown that the Cournot solution applies for more than two sellers. Mathematically, if we assume a linear demand curve given by $P = a - bQ$, the equilibrium rate of output for each firm is equal to $a/[2b + b(n - 1)]$ or $a/b(n + 1)$, where a/b is the quantity intercept of the demand curve and n is the number of firms in the industry. In our simple duopoly model, $n = 2$; in a monopoly solution, $n = 1$; and in a perfectly competitive solution, n approaches ∞. See Roy J. Ruffin, "Cournot Oligopoly and Competitive Behavior," *The Review of Economic Studies*, vol. 38, 1971, pp. 493–502.

THE EDGEWORTH DUOPOLY SOLUTION

There were and still are many criticisms of Cournot's model. One of the basic criticisms was that each firm assumed that the other firm's output was held constant. A French mathematician, Joseph Bertrand, suggested that a solution should be based on the assumption that the *price* charged by the other firm is constant. An English economist named Edgeworth (1845–1926) took up this suggestion and developed a new duopoly solution.

Assumptions

In Edgeworth's model, there are two changes from Cournot's assumptions. The first is that the two suppliers of mineral water have a limited productive capacity. The quantity demanded at zero price exceeds what one single producer can supply. The second change is that in the very short run, two different prices for mineral water may be quoted in the market.

Most importantly, the assumption made by Edgeworth was that each duopolist selects the price that will maximize profit, and this price is selected on the assumption that the other duoplist will continue to charge the same price even after the first has set a different price.

Moving toward equilibrium in the Edgeworth model

Edgeworth assumes that in the long run, the duopolists will charge the same price for the product and will divide the market equally. Thus, we can use Figure 14-8. The rate of output for duopolist I is shown on the right-hand side, and the rate of output for duopolist II is shown on the left-hand side. The common vertical axis measures the price per unit. The demand curve for duopolist I is d_1d_1, and the demand curve facing dupolist II is $d_{II}d_{II}$. *Both these demand curves are constructed on the assumption that in the long run both sellers charge the same price.* Each proportional demand curve equals one-half the market demand.

The maximum productive capacities for duopolists I and II are q_{max}^I and q_{max}^{II}, respectively. As in the Cournot model, the sellers persistently attempt to maximize profit and are incapable of learning. This, again, is a no-learning-by-doing model.

We start with duopolist I (who is temporarily a monopolist) setting a profit-maximizing price P_1. This is profit-maximizing because the corresponding rate of output q_1^I occurs where the marginal revenue curve intersects the horizontal axis, which is also the marginal cost curve in this example. For simplicity we have not drawn in the marginal revenue curve. (To check up on the artist, see whether q_1^I lies equidistant between point 0 and the point where the demand curve hits the horizontal axis.)

But duoplist II sees price P_1 charged by duopolist I and believes that by setting its price just below P_1, it can take customers away from duopolist I, which will continue to charge P_1.

However, when this is done, duopolist I sees that customers can be taken away from duopolist II if an even lower price is charged. This price war

FIGURE 14-8
The Edgeworth duopoly model

The proportionate demand curves are marked as $d_I d_I$ and $d_{II} d_{II}$. The assumed maximum rate of output for each firm is q_{max}^I and q_{max}^{II}, respectively. Duopolist I sets a profit-maximizing price of P_I. (Remember that the horizontal axis in these models is equal to marginal cost because MC $= 0$.) However, duopolist II will set price below P_I and attempt to take customers away from duopolist I. This process will continue until price P_n is reached. At this price, each firm will start increasing price toward the profit-maximizing P_I. There is no unique equilibrium output or equilibrium price. (Without an effective output constraint, price would fall to zero: the competitive solution.)

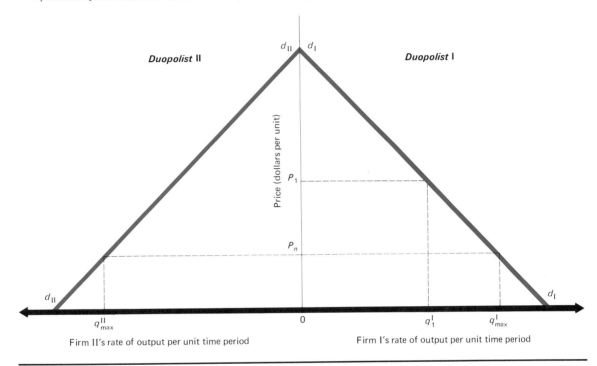

continues until price P_n is reached. At this price neither firm can increase its output because its output is equal to its production capacity. At price P_n, both duopolist I and duopolist II are each producing at the respective maximum, q_{max}^I and q_{max}^{II}. Now what will happen? Clearly, if P_1 is a profit-maximizing price, one duopolist will see that by raising the price above P_n, he or she can increase total profits. The other duopolist will follow suit and raise price. Thus, the Edgeworth model does not yield a solution at all. It merely gives the limits on the price and rate of output that will be seen in the duopoly market. The maximum price to be charged will be P_1, and the minimum price will be P_n. There is *no unique equilibrium price*; there is *no unique equilibrium output*. But there is a *range* of possible prices and outputs.

Before going on to other oligopoly models, we note here that the Cournot and Edgeworth models are not presented because of their relevance or re-alism. Rather, we show them to demonstrate the difficulties inherent in theorizing about oligopoly. There are difficult problems in obtaining the demand curve facing the firm when there is mutual interdependence between the oligopolists. That is at the crux of all problems with oligopoly theory.

THE CHAMBERLIN DUOPOLY MODEL

Edward Chamberlin, of monopolistic competition fame, came up with per-haps a more useful model than those of Cournot and Edgeworth. Chamberlin assumes that after the initial round, firm I recognizes that firm II will react to firm I's actions. After this recognition takes place in firm I, it also takes place within firm II. In other words, the two firms each recognize that the best thing they can do is *share the monopoly profits*. Chamberlin's solution is presented in Figure 14-9. The profit-maximizing rate of output for the two firms taken together is the output at which marginal revenue intersects the horizontal axis at the point where marginal cost equals zero. This is at output rate Q_e. The profit-maximizing price for the shared monopoly would be P_e. Thus, each firm would produce exactly one-half Q_e and sell at a price P_e. This is a stable duopoly solution, in contrast to the Edgeworth solution, which is unstable.

FIGURE 14-9
The Chamberlin model
Chamberlin's model of duopoly assumes that the two firms jointly recognize that they want to share full monopoly profits; thus, total output is equal to Q_e and is sold at price P_e. Each firm produces one-half of that output. The demand curve is the summation of two proportionate demand curves.

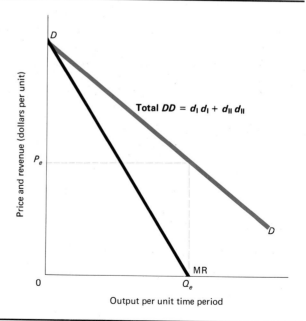

Implicit in the Chamberlin model is a system of stable prices charged by all firms without explicit collusion. No written or even verbal agreement is in evidence. This is a form of noncollusive behavior that leads to the same results that a perfectly operated cartel would have.

The problem with such a model is that it implies joint profit splitting with zero enforcement costs. If such a model could be used to describe a situation with two firms, why could it not be used to describe a situation with three firms, four firms, or five firms? In other words, at what point does the number of firms become so large that the incentive to cut price is great enough that the implicit cartel breaks down? This model does not tell us the answer.

IMPLICIT COLLUSION: THE STIGLER OLIGOPOLY MODEL

All the so-called classic models of oligopoly include reaction functions. The results, or predictions, of such models have been shown to be rather inconclusive, the price-quantity solution varying from the monopoly to the competitive depending upon the conditions assumed. In fact, there are very few testable implications that one can derive from such models. George Stigler, in his model of oligopoly, eliminated reaction functions.[5] He accepts the hypothesis that oligopolists would like to collude to maximize joint profits. However, collusion is costly to undertake and even more costly to police. It goes without saying that if all the firms in an industry acted together, they could set output and price to maximize total profits in the industry. Monopoly profits therefore would exist. Oligopoly, however, occurs in a world that is imperfect because transactions costs are not zero.

In the Stigler approach to oligopoly, the agreed-upon goal of the oligopolists is to collude; however, each recognizes that none can be restrained from cheating on any collusive agreement. Some optimum amount of resources will be used to detect trickery and cheating, but it is certainly not sufficient to allow the oligopolists to collude as if they were one. There will be some equilibrium quantity of deviation from any collusive solution that would represent a monopoly maximum for the oligopolists. Stigler treats oligopoly as an implicit or explicit cartel that is formed with full knowledge that the policing scheme used will be imperfectly, although tolerably, effective.

Testable implications

The testable implications of the Stigler collusive oligopolist model are as follows:

1   The fewer firms involved, the more effective the cartel. A smaller number of firms means lower costs of policing a cartel arrangement.

[5]George Stigler, "A Theory of Oligopoly," *Journal of Political Economy*, vol. 72, February 1964, pp. 44–46.

2   Secret price cuts will be offered relatively more often to large than to small buyers. This is because the payoff from getting more business from the large buyer for any given price reduction is greater than that from a small buyer.

3   The more homogeneous the product, the easier it is to enforce a collusive pricing agreement. When the product is heterogeneous, price cuts can take the form of quality improvements and are difficult to eliminate.

4   The more unstable the industry demand and/or cost conditions, the less likely it is that collusion will be successful. It is more difficult to enforce an agreement in an industry that has to adapt to constantly changing circumstances of demand and supply.

SWEEZY'S KINKED DEMAND CURVE

The Chamberlin model implied stable prices without overt collusion. Another model, presented by economist Paul Sweezy, also implies price rigidity without collusion. Indeed, it is a more sophisticated model of price rigidity with interdependence.[6]

Assumptions

In the Sweezy model, the assumption is made that the market consists of rivals who will quickly match price reductions, but only incompletely, and follow price increases, but very hesitantly. This assumption allows us to postulate a demand curve facing an individual oligopolist.

The nature of the kinked demand curve

In Figure 14-10, we draw the **kinked demand curve** which is implicit in the Sweezy model. We start off at a given price of P_0 and assume that the quantity demanded at that price for this individual oligopolist is q_0. This oligopolist assumes that if it lowers its price, rivals will react by matching that reduction to avoid losing their respective shares of the market. Thus, there will not be a great increase in the quantity demanded for the oligopolist who lowers price. Over the portion of the demand curve below the kink price of P_0, the demand curve is much less elastic. This is shown by the demand curve to the right of point E in Figure 14-10. On the other hand, if the oligopolist increases price, no rivals will follow suit. (If they do follow, they will follow incompletely.) Thus, the quantity demanded at the higher price for this oligopolist will fall off dramatically. The demand schedule to the left of point E will be relatively elastic. This is the flatter part of the curve to the left of point E. Consequently, the demand curve facing the oligopolist is dd, which has a kink at E.

[6]Paul Sweezy, "Demand under Conditions of Oligopoly," *Journal of Political Economy*, vol. 47, August 1939, pp. 568–573. This model was advanced almost simultaneously by R. C. Hall and C. J. Hitch, "Price Theory and Business Behavior," *Oxford Economic Papers*, vol. 2, May 1939.

FIGURE 14-10
The kinked demand curve

Start with the price of P_0. The firm assumes that if it raises its price, no firm (or at least not all firms) will follow. Its demand is relatively elastic; however, if it lowers price, other oligopolists will follow. Its demand is much less elastic; thus, there is a kink at E. The kinked demand curve is dd; the marginal revenue curve is discontinuous at the output rate q_0 and is labeled MR.

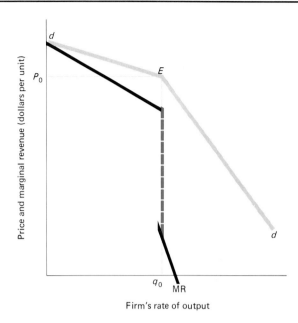

The marginal revenue curve

To draw a marginal revenue curve for the kinked demand curve in Figure 14-10, we first draw a marginal revenue curve out from the vertical axis for the elastic portion of the demand curve (from the upper d to point E on the demand cruve dd). At quantity q_0, however, the demand curve abruptly changes slope and becomes steeper. The marginal revenue curve therefore is discontinuous at the kink, or at quantity q_0. We see, therefore, that that discontinuous part is represented by the dashed line at quantity q_0 in Figure 14-10. The length of the discontinuity is proportional to the difference between the slopes of the upper and lower segments of the demand curve at the kink. [You can draw one in on any other kinked demand curve. Just remember that the MR curve always bisects any horizontal line (parallel to the horizontal axis) drawn from the vertical axis to the demand curve.]

Reactions to fluctuations in marginal cost

Over the discontinuous portion of the marginal revenue curve, the oligopolist does not react to relatively small changes in marginal cost. Look, for example, at Figure 14-11. Assume that marginal cost is represented by mc. The profit-maximizing rate of output is q_0, which can be sold at a price of P_0. Now assume that the marginal cost curve rises to mc'. What will happen to the profit-maximizing rate of output? Nothing. Both quantity and output will remain the same for this oligopolist. What will happen when marginal cost falls to mc"? Nothing. This oligopolist will continue to produce at a rate of output q_0 and charge a price of P_0. Thus, whenever the marginal cost curve

FIGURE 14-11
Changes in cost may not alter the profit-maximizing price and output
The marginal revenue curve has a discontinuous portion between points A and B. So long as the marginal cost curve intersects the line segment AB, shifts in the marginal revenue curve within this range will lead to no change in the profit-maximizing price output combination, P_0, q_0.

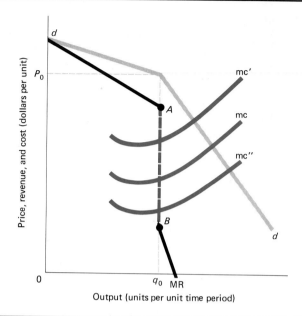

intersects line segment AB in Figure 14-11, fluctuations of marginal cost within this range will not affect output or price because the profit-maximizing condition MR = MC will continue to hold.

Reactions to changes in demand

It also is possible to show situations in which a shift in demand will not affect the price charged by the oligopolist. It will, however, change the quantity produced (unless the kink remains at P_0, q_0).

Consider panel (a) in Figure 14-12. The profit-maximizing rate of output for this oligopolist is q_0. The profit-maximizing price is P_0. The marginal cost curve intersects the marginal revenue curve in its discontinuous part.

Now there is a change in demand from dd in panel (a) to $d'd'$ in panel (b) of Figure 14-12. However, the kink stays at the same price P_0. We are assuming, therefore, that the shift in the demand curve dd to $d'd'$ is an exact outward shift, with the slopes of the two different parts of the curve remaining the same. The cost curve does not change either. The marginal cost curve, mc, in panel (b) is the same as the marginal cost curve in panel (a). Clearly, the marginal cost curve intersects the new marginal revenue curve at a higher rate of output, and the profit-maximizing rate of output therefore increases from q_0 to q_1. So long as the increase in demand is such that the marginal cost curve continues to "intersect" the discontinuous portion of the marginal revenue curve, the price will remain at P_0 even though output has changed. This example could be altered so that there would be a decrease in demand, and the results would be the same as long as the decrease in

FIGURE 14-12
Changes in demand may not change profit-maximizing price
In panel (a) we show demand curve dd with a kink at output rate q_0. The price that is charged is P_0. In panel (b) we show a shift or increase in demand to $d'd'$. However, if the kink remains at price P_0, that price will be maintained in the market, but output will increase for the oligopolist to q_1.

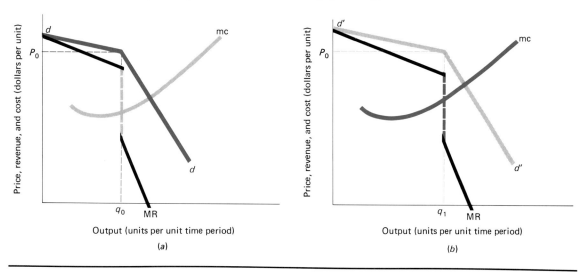

demand was sufficiently small to allow the marginal cost curve to continue "intersecting" the marginal revenue curve in its discontinuous portion. The price would remain the same with a decrease in demand, but the quantity provided by each oligopolist would fall.

Criticisms of the Sweezy model

After Sweezy's article first appeared, it was regarded by many economists as a definitive new general theory of oligopoly. Subsequent research and theoretical questioning have, however, cast some doubt on its general usefulness.

Theoretical problems. The theoretical problems are many. Not the least of them concerns how the initial price P_0 was determined. We start off the model with P_0 given. But if we do not know how P_0 was reached, we do not have a general theory of oligopoly pricing and output decision making.

While it may be true that the kinked demand curve is accurate when interim knowledge about rivals' reactions is low, it is difficult to imagine that it is a long-run stable situation. Some economists contend that the kinked demand curve applies to a new industry in its early stages or to an industry in which new and previously unknown rivals enter the market.

One problem that we still have with the kinked demand curve model is that it represents another no-learning-by-doing model; it is as if the participants—the oligopolistic decision makers—never seem to learn from experience what the reactions of their rivals would be in the future. Therefore, the kink mentality appears to be a barrier to changes in price. Such a barrier seems to be wholly of the oligopolist's own making; that is, it is his or her own cerebral fabrication. We can presume that there must be quite a number of ways in which such a mental barrier could be circumvented. After all, one behavioral definition of a business enterprise is that it is an institution composed of a collection of devices for circumventing barriers to higher profits. In other words, couldn't profit-maximizing oligopolistic decision makers figure out ways to make higher profits that in effect will eliminate the kink?

Empirical evidence. The empirical evidence is not strong enough to support the existence of a kink. A study by George Stigler showed that in seven oligopolistic industries, price rises by one firm were met by price rises by other firms. Thus there seemed to be no asymmetry in the reaction of rivals to changes in price inherent in the kinked demand curve.[7] One empirical study does not disprove a theory, but it does cast doubt on the completeness of the Sweezy solution to the oligopoly pricing and output problem.

IMPLICIT COLLUSION

Various models of implicit collusion have been presented to try to explain oligopolistic industries. One model that has had a relatively long life is the model of price leadership. In this model, and others that have been proposed, there is no formal or explicit cartel arrangement.

Price leadership by the dominant firm

It is sometimes alleged that pricing in oligopolistic industries is controlled by the dominant firm, i.e., the largest firm in the industry. The basic assumption in this model is that the dominant firm sets the price and allows other firms to sell all they can at that price. The dominant firm then sells the rest. Given this assumption, a determinant solution for price and quantity can be derived.

The first thing we must do is derive the demand schedule for the dominant firm. This is done in Figure 14-13. First we draw the market demand schedule DD. Then we draw the supply schedule of all the smaller firms taken together. This is shown as Σmc_{small}. It is the horizontal summation of all the marginal cost curves of the smaller firms above their respective minimum average variable cost curves. To find the demand curve of the dominant firm, we need to find (1) a point at which all the smaller firms supply the entire market demand and the dominant firm supplies zero demand, and (2)

[7]George J. Stigler, "The Kinky Oligopoly Demand Curve and Rigid Prices," *Journal of Political Economy,* vol. 55, no. 5, October 1947, pp. 432–449.

FIGURE 14-13
Price leadership by the dominant firm
The market demand curve is DD. Assume that at price P_1 all the small firms taken together will provide the entire output that is, the horizontal distance from P_1 to point E. At price P_2, the small firms will provide a quantity P_2A. The dominant firm would therefore provide the rest. Thus, we derive point B on the dominant firm's demand curve by subtracting the horizontal distance from P_2 to point A from the demand curve DD. In other words, $BC = P_2A$. At price P_3, the small firms will provide none of the output, for marginal cost exceeds that price. The dominant firm's demand curve becomes coincident with the industry demand curve. The dominant firm's demand curve is the heavy line P_1BFD. When we draw in the marginal revenue curve up to the discontinuous point, F, on the dominant firm's demand curve, we find the profit-maximizing rate of output for the dominant firm at $q_{dominant}$ or at point G, where $mr_{dominant} = mc_{dominant}$. The profit-maximizing price is found on demand curve P_1BFD; it is P_2.

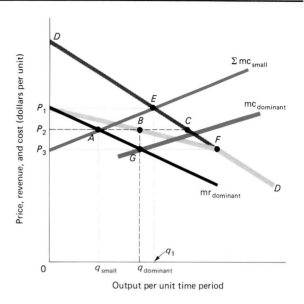

a point where the dominant firm supplies the entire market and the small firms supply zero. In what follows, we add a third point in between.

Look at price P_1. At this price the small firms would supply the entire output for the industry. For at price P_1, the small firms would want to supply the total quantity that the market would purchase at that price, or the quantity from the vertical axis to point E on the demand curve DD. Remember that by assumption, the dominant firm sets the price and *allows* other firms to sell all they can at that price. If the dominant firm set the price P_1 and followed this assumption, it would allow the small firms to supply everything, or $0q_1$; the dominant firm would supply nothing at price P_1. P_1 is therefore the vertical intercept of the dominant firm's demand curve.

Now pick a price P_2 less than P_1. The smaller firms will provide output P_2A: the horizontal distance from the vertical axis to point A on the summed marginal cost curve. At price P_2, total quantity demanded is equal to P_2C, or the horizontal distance from the vertical axis to point C on the demand curve. We measure back from point C an amount equal to P_2A to find out how much is left over for the dominant firm. This gets us to point B. Thus, the dominant firm will supply output equal to the horizontal distance from P_2 to point B. (Note that $BC = P_2A$.)

Now we go to price P_3. At this price the small firms will provide nothing. Their costs are too high. The dominant firm will provide the entire market, or the horizontal distance from the vertical axis to point F on the market demand schedule. The dominant firm's demand curve is the thick, kinked demand curve that runs from the vertical axis at price P_1 through B to point F and then along the *industry* demand curve.

Given this demand curve, the dominant firm acts as a monopolist. We must now draw in a marginal revenue curve that is marginal to P_1FD. It is labeled $mr_{dominant}$. (For simplicity, on the diagram we have not drawn in the marginal revenue curve past the "kink" price P_3, that is, beyond point F on DD.)

The marginal cost curve for the dominant firm is labeled $mc_{dominant}$. It intersects the dominant firm's marginal revenue curve $mr_{dominant}$ at point G. The dominant firm's profit-maximizing rate of output is therefore given as $q_{dominant}$. The profit-maximizing price set by the dominant firm will be P_2. The smaller firms, in the aggregate, will produce q_{small}.[8] At price P_2, total market demand is satisfied by the combined outputs $q_{dominant}$ and q_{small}. A price-quantity solution is obtained. It is stable because of our assumption that the small firms behave passively as price takers. In other words, small firms are eliminated from consideration as rivals in the usual sense of the term.

Problems with price-leadership models

There are a number of problems with price-leadership models that we could discuss. We mention just one here.

Information about future demands for a commodity, future alternative sources of supply, future production costs, and future changes in technology is not free. Information is a scarce resource and requires the expenditure of other resources to obtain it. The information necessary for a firm to make a decision as to where to set output and price in order to maximize profits is costly. Thus, we might predict that in some instances some firms would prefer to allow other firms to generate that information. Firms would like, if they could, to be free riders on the information obtained by other firms that would help each firm set its profit-maximizing prices.

What better way to be a free rider than to allow the dominant, "richest" firm in the industry to do all the market research to determine what the profit-maximizing price is? It is possible that price leadership by a dominant firm has nothing to do with collusion or shared markets but rather with the fact that smaller firms are allowing the larger firm to spend all the resources necessary to obtain the information for setting a profit-maximizing price. Price leadership by a dominant firm can be couched within the theory of information and the problem of the free rider.

---

[8]In order to simplify the diagram, $mc_{dominant}$ was drawn to intersect $mr_{dominant}$ at the quantity $q_{dominant}$ so that a new price line would not have to be drawn in.

NONPRICE COMPETITION

According to some observers, oligopolistic markets do not exhibit very active forms of price competition. Price wars do erupt occasionally, but this is seen to be an implicit indication that communication channels among firms in oligopolistic markets are temporarily disrupted. With the exception of the Edgeworth model, the usual prediction for an oligopolistic market is stable prices. Therefore, competition for an increased market share must take on some other form. The alternative form is what is generally called **nonprice competition**. Nonprice competition cannot be subdivided neatly into two or more categories because it can take on a large number of forms. Nonprice competition is an attempt by one oligopolistic firm to attract customers by some means other than a price differential.

Some economists argue that the lack of price competition in oligopolistic industries results from the fact that no single firm has a cost advantage that would make it beneficial for it to cut prices. Moreover, if we are dealing with a large firm in an oligopolistic industry, that firm may be worried about antitrust problems. Thus, firms in such situations may opt for nonprice competition where they feel a greater freedom to act without being followed immediately by competing firms. Product differentiation takes on many forms, but we will consider only advertising and quality differentials.

Advertising

As we pointed out previously, the primary purpose of advertising is to shift the demand curve to the right. This allows the seller to sell more at each and every price. Advertising may also have the effect of differentiating the product and making the product's availability better known. To go into a complete theory of advertising here would require us to get into the theory of information dissemination; we will not do this. Whatever can be said about advertising, its effects on the firm are certainly not completely predictable. Whether advertising in oligopolistic industries is beneficial to society as a whole is a question we cannot answer. It does exist, and hence, by assumption, it is perceived to be beneficial by each of the firms engaging in it.

Quality variations

Quality differentiation results in a division of one market into a number of submarkets. We talked earlier about product differentiation by quality differentials when we discussed monopolistic competition. A prime example of product differentiation is the automobile industry. There are specific, physically definable differences between different automobile models within one single firm. A General Motors Citation and a General Motors Seville are certainly not the same auto. If we were to examine automobiles, we would see that competition among firms creates a continuous expansion and redefinition of the different models that are sold by any one company. There is competition to create new quality classes and thereby gain a competitive edge. Being the first in the market in a new-quality class has often meant higher profits. Witness the phenomenal success of the original Mustang. But also witness the dismal failure of Ford's Edsel a few years before the introduction of the successful Mustang.

WHERE ARE WE IN THE THEORY OF OLIGOPOLY?

If you found this chapter to be analytically somewhat less conclusive than the chapters on competition and monopoly, you are not alone. Most economists consider the theory of oligopoly and monopolistic competition to be the most perplexing of the models of industrial structure. It is particularly perplexing because oligopoly is so widespread and is especially common in manufacturing industries. We need only mention primary aluminum, primary copper, and automobiles to come up with clear cases of oligopoly. A very high concentration of total output is in the hands of the largest three or four firms, and there is a small number of firms within each industry.

Of course, the problem with oligopoly theory is that it is characterized by a recognized interdependence among sellers. We then must deal with what economists call conjectural variations in the firms' expectations about how other firms' outputs and/or prices will change as a result of its own changes in output and/or price. Depending on the specific assumptions we make, we come up with different models and different solutions. Unfortunately, economic theory does not suggest which assumptions to use. In any event, each of these theories must ultimately stand or fall on its predictive powers.

ISSUES AND APPLICATIONS

Greasing the maitre d's palm

In most cities and towns, there is at least one relatively well-known restaurant where, on weekends, a 1- to 2-hour wait is not uncommon. Seemingly, the only certain method of obtaining immediate seating is to go on a weekday and arrive, say, at 5 o'clock. Most people do not, however, want to eat dinner at 5 P.M. Furthermore, dining out on the town is often limited to 7 or 8 P.M. on a Friday or a Saturday night by custom or desire. The inevitable occurs: The famous restaurant that everyone knows has good food at reasonable prices is packed on weekends.

"GREASING" AND FAST SERVICE

It is not unusual on such Friday or Saturday evenings to observe someone come in, talk to the maitre d', and be seated almost immediately. The maitre d's palm, of course, has been "greased." He or she has received a very handsome tip, perhaps a $10, $20, or even $50 bill folded neatly and quickly slipped to the maitre d' without anyone seeing the transfer. An economic explanation for what has occurred involves both price discrimination and price differentiation.

PRICE DISCRIMINATION

In a large, thriving establishment such as one just mentioned, it would be impossible for waiters personally to determine each party's price elasticity of demand and to charge accordingly. In fact, if tried, such a procedure probably would outrage the clientele and cause a loss of business. Alternatively, if waiters tried to price-discriminate and were successful, they might find some individuals with relatively more elastic demands ordering more food than they could eat at the relatively lower price and surreptitiously selling it to individuals with a relatively more inelastic demand who would have been charged a higher price. Clearly, no restauranteur would allow this to happen.

However, there is a way to charge people with more inelastic demands a higher price. That is what "greasing" the palm of the maitre d' is all about. Presumably, those people who have more highly inelastic demand will be willing to pay more for their meals. One way they can be "charged" more is to confront them with a very long wait. In order to avoid the wait, they must pay the maitre d' a tip of $10, $20, or $50.

WHO ENGAGES IN TIPPING?

We can determine which individuals would, in general, be engaged in tipping the maitre d' in order to be seated more quickly. They will be individuals who have a high opportunity cost of time. A party of four lawyers entertaining an out-of-town client may have a collective opportunity cost of $500 an hour.

If they can save 1 hour by tipping the maitre d' $50, they certainly will be better off. On the other hand, individuals who place a low value on their time will not tip the maitre d'.

WHY DON'T ALL RESTAURANTS PRACTICE SUCH PRICE DISCRIMINATION?

An important question is, Why isn't this price-discriminating technique used at virtually every restaurant? The answer lies in the requirements for price discrimination to work. One of the most important requirements is that there be at least two classes of buyers with significantly differing price elasticities of demand. At restaurants where tipping the maitre d' is common practice, there is a whole range of individuals with different price elasticities of demand who eat there. Such restaurants are not either the cheapest or the most expensive. The clientele usually ranges from middle-class to wealthy. Thus, we can presume that the opportunity cost of time for the different individuals who eat in such establishments varies greatly.

Now consider luxury restaurants such as the The Four Seasons and 21 Club in New York City. Basically, they use a reservation-only system. It would be difficult, if not impossible, to show up unannounced on a Saturday night at The Four Seasons without reservations *and* be seated. Now, why wouldn't the system of tipping the maitre d' work here? It usually won't work because virtually all the people who go to such high-priced establishments will almost by necessity have high opportunity cost of time. In essence, they will have relatively similar price elasticities of demand for the product.

At the other end of the spectrum, in restaurants where relatively cheaper fare is offered, no reservations are ever accepted and there is no maitre d'. No profitable way in which tipping would work is in evidence. At such relatively low-priced food establishments, virtually every customer has a relatively lower opportunity cost of time and also a relatively higher price elasticity of demand. Therefore, the payoff to the restaurant for attempting to price-discriminate in such establishments would be very low.

A FURTHER EXAMPLE: LAS VEGAS DINNER SHOWS

A similar analysis can be applied to the way patrons are treated at Las Vegas dinner shows. All tickets usually are sold at a flat price. Clearly, though, some tables are preferred to others because they provide a better view of the stage. For a sufficient tip or "grease," the headwaiter will seat an individual with a dinner-show ticket at one of the better tables. Since tourists and out-of-town guests cannot be sure what the "going" price for a good seat is, they will end up paying different prices (tips) to obtain the better seats. The existence

of a wide range of prices for the different types of seats is tantamount to a system of price discrimination.

PRICE DIFFERENTIATION, TOO

Price differentiation is occurring, however, in both the restaurant case and the case of the Las Vegas dinner show. A different product is being offered to the person who is seated immediately at a busy restaurant than is offered to the person who waits. A different product is given to a person who gets a preferred table at a Las Vegas dinner show than is given to one who does not. To the extent that rapid seating and preferred tables are rationed to the highest bidders, we are witnessing price differentiation. It is only when an *array* of prices for *equivalent* products exists that we can truly talk about price discrimination.

Pricing in an allegedly oligopolistic industry: The case of automobiles

The automobile industry has been used as an example of an oligopoly for many years. What we would like to show in this application is that even though GM, for example, may appear to have a significant amount of monopoly or oligopoly power, that power is attenuated by the supply elasticity of the other automobile firms.

DERIVING THE RELATION BETWEEN ONE FIRM'S DEMAND AND ALL OTHER FIRMS' SUPPLY

Let General Motors produce q_i. Then

$$Q_s = q_i + q_0 \qquad (14\text{-}1)$$

where Q_s = industry supply
$\quad\quad\;\; q_0$ = supply of all other firms

Both supply and demand are a function of price, and in equilibrium

$$Q_D(P) = Q_S(P) = q_i + q_0 \qquad (14\text{-}2)$$

where Q_D = market demand for autos. Then:

$$q_d = Q_D - q_0 \qquad (14\text{-}3)$$

where q_d = demand for GM's cars.
The complete notation is then

$$\left.\begin{array}{l} Q_s = \text{industry supply} \\ q_i = \text{GM supply} \\ q_0 = \text{all other supply} \end{array}\right\} \text{supply}$$

$$\left.\begin{array}{l} Q_D = \text{industry demand} \\ q_d = \text{GM demand} \end{array}\right\} \text{demand}$$

In other words, what's left over from industry demand is the demand for GM cars.

Change each of the variables in Eq. (14-3) by a little bit, Δ, and

$$\Delta q_d = \Delta Q_D - \Delta q_0 \qquad \text{(14-4)}$$

Divide Eq. (14-4) by $q_d \Delta P$ to get

$$\frac{\Delta q_d}{q_d \Delta P} = \frac{\Delta Q_D}{q_d \Delta P} - \frac{\Delta q_0}{q_d \Delta P} \qquad \text{(14-5)}$$

Now multiply Eq. (14-5) by P to get

$$\frac{\Delta q_d}{q_d} \cdot \frac{P}{\Delta P} = \\ \left(\frac{\Delta Q_D}{q_d} \cdot \frac{P}{\Delta P} \right) - \left(\frac{\Delta q_0}{q_d} \cdot \frac{P}{\Delta P} \right) \qquad \text{(14-6)}$$

We rearrange Eq. (14-6). Multiply the first right-hand term by Q_D/Q_D and the second by q_0/q_0

$$\frac{\Delta q_d}{\Delta P} \cdot \frac{P}{q_d} = \\ \left(\frac{Q_D}{q_d} \right) \frac{\Delta Q_D}{Q_D} \cdot \frac{P}{\Delta P} - \left(\frac{q_0}{q_d} \right) \frac{\Delta q_0}{q_0} \cdot \frac{P}{\Delta P} \qquad \text{(14-7)}$$

But this equals

$$\eta_d = \left(\frac{Q_D}{q_d} \right) \eta_D - \left(\frac{q_0}{q_d} \right) \varepsilon_0 \qquad \text{(14-8)}$$

where ε_0 is the supply elasticity of the other auto manufacturers, η_D is price elasticity of demand for the industry, and η_d is the price elasticity of demand for GM.

From Eq. (14-8), we see that the price elasticity of demand for General Motors products η_d is a function of the market price elasticity of demand η_D and price elasticity of supply of other firms, as well as the (inverse of the) relative share of industry output accounted for by the firm under study, Q_D/q_d. What is clear from Eq. (14-8) is the importance of ε_0. Since η is always negative, when we subtract ε_0, we always increase absolutely the price elasticity of demand facing the individual firm. In the short run, a demand curve for General Motors products might be inelastic. However, in the long run, if ε_0 is sufficiently large, that is no longer true. This analysis explains why

a firm such as General Motors will sell in a market in which the demand is relatively inelastic and set a price lower than expected.

SOME HYPOTHETICAL NUMBERS

Various estimates have been made of the price elasticity of demand for new automobiles in the entire industry. A good average of those estimates is $\eta_D = -2$.

Remember that when the firm maximizes profits

$$\text{MR} = P \left(1 + \frac{1}{\eta_D} \right) = \text{MC} \qquad \text{(14-9)}$$

Thus, if we rearrange Eq. (14-9), we get

$$\frac{P - \text{MC}}{P} = -\frac{1}{\eta_D} \qquad \text{(14-10)}$$

Now, if we make the assumption that marginal cost is approximately equal to average cost (not an unreasonable assumption for firms selling millions of cars annually), Eq. (14-10) becomes

$$\frac{P - \text{AC}}{P} = -\frac{1}{\eta_D} \qquad \text{(14-11)}$$

Then, if the industry price elasticity of demand is approximately equal to -2.0, we would expect that

$$\frac{P - \text{AC}}{P} = -\frac{1}{-2.00} = \frac{1}{2.0} \qquad \text{(14-12)}$$

This would indicate that 50¢ of each dollar would be a profit margin. However, if we look at the data relating to General Motors and other automobile companies, we do not find anything near a 50 percent profit margin on sales. What we find are figures much closer to 6 to 10 percent of sales. A profit of 10 percent on sales is consistent with a price elasticity of demand facing an individual firm of about -10 when we use Eq. (14-11).

We can approximate, then, the price elasticity of supply facing, for example, General Motors, by using this information. Let us substitute for $\eta_d = -10$ and for $\eta_D = -2$ in Eq. (14-8). The share of industry output accounted for by General Motors is about 50 percent so that $Q_D/q_d = 2$, and $q_0/q_d = 1$. Thus, Eq. (14-8) becomes

$$-10 = (2)(-2) - (1)\varepsilon_0 \qquad \textbf{(14-13)}$$

The price elasticity of supply of other firms, ε_0, is approximately equal to 6. A 1 percent increase in the price that General Motors charges for its cars will elicit a 6 percent increase in the quantity supplied from other companies. Thus, the monopoly or oligopoly power that General Motors has is limited by the supply of the other firms in the industry.

Advertising, search goods, experience goods, and competitive pricing

Advertising is subject to frequent criticism. It is often derided as tasteless, offensive, or stupid. As you have learned by now, economics does not have much to say about such taste-oriented claims. However, there has been a history of arguments in economics about the usefulness of advertising. Claims have been made that advertising does not provide useful information for consumers, but rather subliminally seduces consumers to want things they otherwise would not. In this sense, it is viewed as a waste of resources and, some have claimed, it is essentially anticompetitive because larger, established firms can spend more on advertising than smaller, newer firms, so the former's market position will be protected by noninformative advertising. This view is less popular now than it was a decade or two ago because of some new theories about the role advertising plays and because of some empirical evidence about the benefits to consumers from advertising.

A NEW LOOK AT ADVERTISING: TWO TYPES OF GOODS

Even if price information about goods is easy to obtain, which is not always the case, consumers have a difficult time determining product quality. Mass-media advertising is viewed as providing consumers with useful information about the quality of products.[9] Goods can be viewed as being in two basic categories: search goods and experience goods.

Search goods

Search goods are products whose quality can be checked out before purchase. A suit, a dress, and a steam generator are examples. Most of the advertising about these products is of the kind that contains direct information about the quality and characteristics of the product. This information is generally accurate because it would be nonprofitable over time to give misleading information. While we see some advertisements that contain some detailed information, others convey a simple message, such as the name of a famous designer who has put his or her name on the product in question. Such simple identification alone is a signal about quality because consumers have learned to expect certain names to be associated with a certain level of quality. If the famous person were to place his or her name on a shoddy product, just as if a manufacturer were to run a deceitful (expensive) advertising

---

[9]Philip Nelson, "Advertising as Information," *Journal of Political Economy*, July/August 1974, pp. 729–754.

campaign about a shoddy product, consumers would learn not to trust that name, so its value would drop substantially.

Experience goods

Experience goods are products that are often consumed before the consumer can determine their quality or desirability. Examples would be soft drinks, soaps, and deodorants. Advertising about these products cannot give much information about quality—its main concern must be to let consumers know the product exists and convince them to try it. Advertising about experience goods does, however, inherently contain information about quality. Producers of relatively high-priced, low-quality products would not get repeat purchases from consumers who were fooled into buying the product one time. In other words, companies advertise products they believe will be winners. It would be financially foolish for a company to spend substantial sums to advertise an inferior product. Indeed, to continue to advertise an inferior product that consumers believed was not a good value would reinforce their memory about the lack of trust for the company as a whole.

COMPETITIVE PRICING AND ADVERTISING

A number of studies have examined the impact of advertising on price competition. Many states used to prohibit price and/or nonprice advertisements for retail eyeglasses. By comparing prices in states that had such restrictions to prices in states that did not have the restrictions, one economist found that in the states with the restrictions retail eyeglass prices were 20 to 100 percent higher.[10] The annual costs to consumers from the higher prices

was in the hundreds of millions of dollars per year. This study and others have not found that the restrictions on advertising produced any public health or safety benefits. Indeed, as one might expect when consumers face higher prices, purchases of eyeglasses were 17 to 35 percent lower in the states with the advertising restrictions.

Another study found that even if advertising increased the prices that manufacturers charged for their products, the advertising seemed to produce lower retail prices.[11] The sales of the toy industry in 1971 and 1972 were examined. The 100 toys with the largest Christmas sales have a 25 percent markup, while poorer sellers (which were not as heavily advertised) had an average markup of 42 percent. Data from Canada showed the same thing. Toys that were advertised on television in Canada had 20 percent markups on average, while nontelevised toys had 46 percent markups.

Finally, another study looked at the consequences of the ban on posting gasoline prices by gas stations in New York City in 1970, by comparing that gasoline market to the market in Los Angeles, where there were no restrictions on price posting.[12] Holding other factors constant, the posting of gasoline prices in Los Angeles was estimated to reduce the price of regular gas by 0.7¢ per gallon compared to the price in New York. Since the average retail price was 36¢ per gallon, this meant that the price was about 2 percent lower due to posting. For premium gasoline, the savings due to posting was 1.5¢ per gallon, or almost 4 percent on an average retail price of 40¢ per gallon. The study estimated that if gasoline price posting was as competitive all across the U.S. as it was in Los Angeles, the annual savings to consumers would have been about $325 million in 1970, or about $1 billion in today's dollars.

[10]Lee Benham, "The Effect of Advertising on the Price of Eyeglasses," *Journal of Law and Economics*, October 1972, pp. 337–351.

[11]Robert L. Steiner, "Does Advertising Lower Consumer Prices?" *Journal of Marketing*, October 1973, pp. 19–26.

[12]Alex Maurizi and Thom Kelly, *Prices and Consumer Information*, American Enterprise Institute, 1978.

SUMMARY

1   Monopolistic competition is characterized by product differentiation and sales promotion.

2   Some investigators have attempted to differentiate between "real" and "artificial" product differentiation. The task, however, is not an easy one.

3   The goal of advertising is not to make the demand curve more inelastic but rather to shift it to the right.

4   Some investigators have attempted to differentiate between competitive advertising and informative advertising. However, the distinction has not been made operationally meaningful.

5   In long-run equilibrium, no firm in a monopolistically competitive industry will make economic profits.

6   In long-run equilibrium, each monopolistic competitor will be operating on the downward-sloping portion of its long-run average cost curve and will not operate at the minimum point on that curve as firms in a perfectly competitive industry do.

7   It has been argued that monopolistic competition leads to "excess" capacity. Chamberlin contended that that was the "price" consumers had to pay for variety in the goods they bought. Excess capacity is no different from having any asset that is not always utilized, such as bathrooms and automobiles. Price may also be greater than marginal cost because producers bear the expense of holding inventories to meet demand fluctuations; this helps to reduce waiting costs that consumers would bear otherwise.

8   In addition to competition, monopoly, and monopolistic competition, we study the market structures of duopoly and oligopoly, in which each firm realizes that other firms will react to any changes in its price and/or output.

9   In the simplest oligopoly model, each firm assumes that any change in price will be matched by all other firms in the industry.

10 In the Cournot duopoly model, the two producers are identical and each selects its rate of output under the assumption that the other will continue to produce whatever it is presently producing. Although this is a no-learning-by-doing model, a determinate equilibrium can be reached.

11 In Edgeworth's model, each firm has a limited productive capacity and different prices for the product can temporarily prevail. Price is selected on the assumption that the other duopolist will continue to charge the same price currently charged. There is no determinate solution.

12 In the Chamberlin model of duopoly, each firm produces exactly one-half total industry output and each sells at the joint profit-maximizing price (the price a monopolist would charge if it owned both firms).

13 In the Stigler model, the agreed-upon goal of the oligopolists is to collude, but each recognizes that none can be restrained completely from cheating. Oligopoly is an implicit cartel that is formed with full knowledge that the policing scheme used will be imperfectly, although tolerably, effective.

14 The implications of the Stigler model are: (a) The fewer the firms, the more effective the cartel. (b) Secret price cuts will be offered relatively more often to large as opposed to small buyers. (c) The more homogeneous the product, the easier it is to enforce a collusive price agreement. (d) The more unstable the industry demand and/or cost conditions, the less likely the collusion will be successful.

15 In a kinked demand curve oligopoly model, the individual oligopolist assumes that if price is lowered, rivals will match the reduction, but if price is raised, rivals will not match the increase.

16 Marginal revenue for a kinked demand curve has a discontinuous portion at the kink price (quantity).

17 It is possible that changes in cost and/or demand conditions will leave unchanged the price that the oligopolist will charge.

18 The kinked demand curve has been subject to criticism. No indication is given as to how the initial price was arrived at, and the empirical evidence used to support the existence of a kink is weak at best.

19 Implicit collusion models include (a) price leadership by the dominant firm, and (b) price leadership by the low-cost firm.

GLOSSARY

- **duolopy** A market structure in which there are only two sellers.
- **oligopoly** A market structure in which there are several sellers and each takes account of the others' reactions.
- **monopolistic competition** A model of industrial organization in which there are numerous firms producing slightly differentiated products and each firm has some market power. However, there is enough competition among firms so that economic profits are eliminated in the long run by entry.
- **variation of production** The array of product assortments and levels of quality that each firm produces.
- **competitive advertising** Advertising which is used only to keep a firm's market share intact rather than to inform the consumer about real qualities of the product; sometimes called defensive advertising, to be contrasted with informative advertising.

- **informative advertising** Advertising which gives information about the product; to be constrasted with competitive advertising.
- **product groups** Groups of products that a supposedly well-defined set of firms are making, e.g., designer jeans, breakfast cereals, and hand soap.
- **proportional demand curve** A proportional demand curve is drawn under the assumption that all firms charge the same price and that each firm faces 1/nth of total demand when there are n firms.
- **kinked demand curve** A demand curve that has a kink, or abrupt change in slope, at some price; related to a theory developed by Paul Sweezy.
- **nonprice competition** Competition by means of quality changes, design changes, reliability, service, and so on; to be contrasted with price competition.

QUESTIONS

(Answers to even-numbered questions are at back of text.)

1 Compare the assumptions underlying the perfectly competitive market with those of the monopolistically competitive market. How are they similar and how do they differ?

2 Assuming that all firms are faced with identical cost curves, compare the long-run equilibrium result (the relationship between the various per unit cost and revenue variables) of a perfectly competitive industry with that of a monopolistically competitive industry.

3 What are some of the ways in which gas stations differentiate their products?

4 Which of the product variations in question 3 are "real" differences and which are merely "artificial"?

5 Service stations at or near freeway entrances and exits typically charge a few cents a gallon more than other stations. How do they get away with it?

6 In what sense does the "marginal revenue" resulting from advertising differ from the marginal revenue concept we have been dealing with up to this point?

7 Suppose your monopolistically competitive firm "Fine-Tune" is presently selling 100 tune-ups per week at a price of $50 each. As the owner-operator, you initiate an ad campaign on a local FM radio station, promising to "mellow-out any machine for four bits" ($50 in this context). As a result, you find yourself fine-tuning 140 cars per week instead of 100. What is the "marginal revenue" of the ad campaign? What additional information do you need to determine whether your profits have risen?

8 Assuming that the advertising in question 7 in fact increased your profits, should you advertise even more? If so, at what point should you cease increasing your weekly outlay on advertising?

9 Distinguish between the motives underlying advertising by your Dairyowners' Association and advertising by one of the individual dairies.

10 Are most toothpaste advertisements competitive or informative? How about the advertising of vacation spots? Typewriters? Mercedes Benz automobiles?

11 How is a proportional demand curve derived? Can you think of any objection(s) to this technique?

12 What is the implication of Chamberlin's assumption that each firm will act as though others will not react?

13 Describe the short-run equilibrium situation in a monoplistically competitive industry.

14 Explain how, in the long run, any economic profits will be competed away in a monopolistically competitive industry.

15 If people do not prefer differentiated products to standardized products, why would a business expend resources seeking to destandardize its particular product? Is a "Chiquita Banana" really just a banana? If so, according to whom?

16 Look at Figure 14-5. It appears that two firms could supply the industry demand more efficiently, from a cost standpoint, than could three. Why, then, does this model predict that three firms will emerge?

17 Figure 14-6 portrays long-run economic profits. How can that be the case if entry is unrestricted?

18 In Cournot's duopoly model: (*a*) What are his assumptions? (*b*) What is the long-run result predicted by the model?

19 How does Edgeworth's duopoly model differ from that of Cournot (*a*) in its assumptions and (*b*) in its solution?

20 Criticize the Cournot and Edgeworth models.

21 On what assumptions does Chamberlin's duopoly model rely? What result is obtained?

22 Explain why Paul Sweezy's kinked demand curve is kinked.

23 Under the kinked demand theory of Sweezy, why do shifts in the marginal cost curve often cause no change whatsoever in price or output?

24 If the dominant firm sets the price, what sort of behavior is assumed on the part of the rest of the oligopolists?

25 If the low-cost firm is the price leader, how can it run the other firms out of business? Why might it prefer *not* to do so?

26 Why do you think that advertising and minor changes in product design are so prevalent in many oligopolistic industries?

27 Suppose that oligopoly pricing and output policies were deemed to be a social evil and declared illegal. Can you imagine any problems that a government attorney, armed with the theories in this chapter, would have in prosecuting a case in which collusion had been alleged?

SELECTED REFERENCES

Chamberlin, Edward H., *The Theory of Monopolistic Competition*, 8th ed. (Cambridge, Mass.: Harvard, 1962), chaps. 4 and 5.

Dewey, Donald, *The Theory of Imperfect Competition* (New York: Columbia, 1969).

Fellner, William, *Competition among the Few: Oligopoly and Similar Market Structures* (New York: Knopf, 1949).

Machlup, Fritz, *The Economics of Sellers' Competition* (Baltimore: Johns Hopkins, 1952), chaps. 4–7 and 10–16.

Modigliani, Franco, "New Developments on the Oligopoly Front," *Journal of Political Economy,* vol. 66, June 1958, pp. 215–232.

Nutter, G.W., "Duopoly, Oligopoly, and Emerging Competition," *Southern Economic Journal,* vol. 30, April 1964, pp. 342–352.

Samuelson, Paul, "The Monopolistic Competition Revolution," in Robert Quenne (ed.), *Monopolistic Competition Theory* (New York: Wiley, 1967).

Scherer, Frederic M., *Industrial Market Structure and Economic Performance* (Chicago: Rand McNally, 1971), chap. XIV.

"The Theory of Monopolistic Competition after Thirty Years," *American Economic Review, Papers and Proceedings,* vol. 54, no. 3, May 1964, pp. 28–57; papers by Joe S. Bain, Robert L. Bishop, and William J. Baumol; discussants; Jesse W. Markham and Peter O. Steiner.

Van Cise, Gerrold G., *The Federal Anti-Trust Laws,* 3d ed., rev. (Washington, D.C.: American Enterprise Institute for Public Policy Research, 1975).

APPENDIX TO CHAPTER 14

THE THEORY OF GAMES AND ECONOMIC ANALYSIS

As was mentioned in the introduction to this chapter, an oligopolistic situation is one in which each firm recognizes that the price and output of other firms has a bearing upon its own optimal price and output decisions. Thus each firm tries to estimate the behavior of other firms in working out its own strategy for achieving maximum profits. Situations in which decision makers consciously interact in attempting to achieve their goals can be described by the language and mathematics of game theory. Game theory is fundamentally a way of describing the various possible outcomes in any situation involving two or more interacting individuals when these individuals are aware of the interactive nature of their situation and plan accordingly. The plans made by these individuals are known as "game stategies."

TYPES OF INTERACTIONS BETWEEN INDIVIDUALS

Interactions between individuals are of two general types, competitive and cooperative. The ordinary interaction between firms serving the same market is competitive. Each firm is attempting to attract customers away from other firms. The standard cartel arrangement is, however, cooperative. The firms in the cartel are acting in a coordinated fashion to achieve a common goal (reduced industry output, a higher price for the product they produce, and higher profits). Most real-world game like situations have both competitive and cooperative aspects, however, a fact that we can illustrate by considering the three major types of games.

Gamelike situations are generally classified as being of one of three basic types: negative-sum, zero-sum, or positive-sum games. A *negative-sum game* is one in which the players all lose or are worse off after the game is played out than they were before it started. The game of "spite 'n' malice" is usually one such game. A zero-sum game is one in which one player's losses (if any) are exactly offset by other players' gains. An ordinary bet or wager between friends is such a game if we measure gains and losses solely in terms of money. *Positive-sum games* are those in which both players are better off after the game than they were before the game. A voluntary exchange between individuals who are informed about the characteristics of the goods being exchanged is such a game if we measure gains in terms of utility.

Although it might seem that positive-sum games are cooperative while zero-sum games are competitive, that is not strictly true. Even in the positive-sum context, there can still be competition over the division of the gains so long as each player ends up better off than he or she was before the game began. It is also important to note that few real-world situations correspond exactly to one of the above types of games. Often a real-world situation will involve several different games running simultaneously, or it will have the potential to change from one type of game to the other. That possibility can be illustrated by the often discussed "prisoner's dilemma."

PRISONER'S DILEMMA

A particular type of gamelike situation which has attracted considerable attention among economists is the "prisoner's dilemma."[13] A prisoner's dilemma exists whenever there are gains to be realized by cooperation between a group of individuals, yet there are even greater gains possible for each individual if that party can "cheat" on the cooperative arrangement while all other parties continue to abide by it.

The most obvious example of such a situation in economics is a cartel agreement between otherwise independent firms. In this case, each firm benefits, in the form of higher profits, so long as the agreement is adhered to by all other firms. Yet, each firm knows that it would obtain even higher profits if it could cut price and expand output while other firms continued to restrict their output and charge a higher price.

Another example of a prisoner's dilemma in economics is found in any contractual arrangement under which performance cannot be costlessly monitored. Such an arrangement is said to involve "shirking" or "agency cost." The logic of this situation is that each employee or agent will know that some amount of shirking (acting in ways which contributes to the personal welfare of the employee at the expense of the firm) will go undetected. To engage in shirking is thus "costless" to the employee. Similarly, a decision to refrain from shirking would generate no benefits for the employee, since the employer wouldn't be able to distinguish his or her exemplary behavior from the performance of other employees. When all agents or employees realize this situation, and shirk in response to it, however, the profits of the firm for which they are working decline, as will their wages.

A final situation involving a prisoner's dilemma is voting on the provision of, and apportionment of the costs of, public goods, a topic which we will examine in Chapter 19.

---

[13]The prisoner's dilemma is named for the original parable which was used to describe this kind of situation. Imagine a setting in which two partners in crime are apprehended by police and placed in different examination rooms. Each suspect is told that if he confesses, and his partner doesn't, the prosecutor will ask the court for leniency in his case (i.e., 2 years in prison) but will ask for the maximum sentence in his partner's case (i.e., 15 years in prison). If they both confess, they both get the regular sentence (i.e., 10 years in prison), and if neither confesses, they will both go free, as the evidence is insufficient to convict without a confession by one of the two suspects. Each suspect then knows that if he confesses he may get a reduced sentence or he may not, depending upon whether his partner also confesses. He also knows, however, that if he doesn't confess he will either go free or serve a longer sentence than he would if he did confess, depending, again, upon what his partner does. If both suspects are risk-averse and neither is certain of what his partner will do, both will confess. Neither would confess, of course, if they could work out a binding agreement between themselves.

FIGURE A14-1
Prisoner's dilemma
The optimal strategy for the two arrested prisoners, who are kept apart, is to be silent so there is no evidence for a conviction. If one prisoner confesses and the other does not, the one who confesses has punishment reduced as the other takes most of the blame. If both confess—the most likely outcome—both lose as the blame is shared.

	Person II's strategy choice	
	Don't confess (keep the pact)	Confess (cheat)
Don't confess (keep the pact)	I's gain = + 400 utils II's gain = + 400 utils	I's loss = − 200 utils II's gain = + 200 utils
Confess (cheat)	I's gain = + 200 utils II's loss = − 200 utils	I's loss = − 100 utils II's loss = − 100 utils

Person I's strategy choice

A NOTE ON "PAYOFF MATRICES"

It is conventional to represent the alternative outcomes possible in a simple game situation in a diagram called a "payoff matrix." This diagram shows the gain or loss to each player for each combination of strategies adopted by that player and by other players. Figure A14-1 illustrates a prisoner's dilemma situation for two players choosing between two possible strategies. This matrix has been constructed so that the game between the players is zero-sum so long as they do not both confess. If it was possible to work out a binding agreement between the players, however, that agreement would be zero-sum, as illustrated by the comparison of the "both confess" versus the "neither confess" outcome.

Input demand

*W*e have now examined the economic bases for decisions made by producers and consumers. From these analyses we have derived a deeper understanding of what determines or lies behind the market demand and supply curves for a commodity.

Looking back at the flow diagram in Figure 1-1, you will see that we have considered only some of the markets that make up the economy. We know something about how consumers determine their expenditures and how producers determine their optimal output levels and input combinations. Yet we have not considered how consumers earn the income that they spend or what determines the value of the labor and other resources supplied to producers. Our discussion of these topics does not need to be as long as our consideration of commodity markets, for many of the principles of analysis that you have learned apply readily to the new context of markets for factors of production or productive resources (labor, land, and capital).

DEMANDERS ARE SUPPLIERS AND SUPPLIERS ARE DEMANDERS

One point about factor markets is sometimes confusing. There is a reversal of the roles played by business firms and households in these markets as compared with the roles played by these same firms and households in commodity markets. Business firms produce or supply goods to commodity markets, and households purchase or demand these goods. In exchange for commodities supplied, businesses receive revenue in the form of money, while households give up or exchange money in demanding "real" (non-money) goods and services. In factor markets the opposite is true. Businesses demand factors of production, for which they give up money in the form of wages, rents, and profits, and households sell or supply these real factors in exchange for money income.

You might say that a business's demand for factors of production is "derived from" that business's ability to sell the commodities it produces by using these factors in production. Similarly, a household's supply of factors is derived from its desire for income, which it will use to purchase commodities. This chapter is devoted largely to a detailed consideration of what those statements mean in competitive and noncompetitive factor markets.

OPTIMAL INPUT EMPLOYMENT

We first dealt with the firm's optimal input combination when we studied the theory of the firm in Chapter 8. What we did there and in Chapter 9 was look at two variable inputs, capital and labor. We assumed that each could be purchased at a constant unit price. We further assumed that their quantities could be infinitesimally varied. This permitted us to draw, on a graph representing capital-labor input combinations, a smooth isoquant curve convex to the origin. It was convex because of a diminishing marginal rate of technical substitution of capital for labor.

Starting out with a given dollar outlay, we asked the following question: What is the optimal or cost-minimizing combination of capital and labor? It was found to be where an isoquant curve is tangent to the given isocost or total outlay line. Given that the slope of the isocost line is equal to $-w/r$ and the slope at any point of the isoquant is MPP_L/MPP_K, we know that the optimal input combination of capital and labor is such that

$$\frac{w}{r} = \frac{MPP_L}{MPP_K} \quad \text{or} \quad \frac{MPP_K}{r} = \frac{MPP_L}{w} \tag{15-1}$$

where r = the implicit rental rate per unit of service flow from capital (capital-user charge) and w = the wage rate for a constant-quality unit of labor. We can generalize Eq. (15-1) to more than two inputs. When there are n inputs,

$$\frac{MPP_x}{P_x} = \frac{MPP_y}{P_y} = \cdots = \frac{MPP_n}{P_n} \tag{15-2}$$

In other words, input cost minimization or output maximization requires a combination of inputs such that the marginal physical product of each input divided by its price is the same for all inputs.

Marginal cost, marginal revenue, and price

Look at the reciprocal of any one of the terms in Eq. (15-2), e.g., P_x/MPP_x. The numerator is the price of a unit of the input.

Thus, an increase of one unit in one of the inputs such as x adds P_x to total cost, but it also adds to the total physical product by the amount MPP_x. The ratio P_x/MPP_x is therefore the change in the firm's total cost per unit change in physical output. But this is the same as our definition of marginal cost. We know, then, that marginal cost equals P_i/MPP_i for each ith input, when output is expanded by increasing that particular input. Equation (15-2) can thus be rewritten as

$$\frac{\text{MPP}_x}{P_x} = \frac{\text{MPP}_y}{P_y} = \cdots = \frac{\text{MPP}_n}{P_n} = \frac{1}{\text{MC}} \qquad \textbf{(15-3)}$$

Equilibrium in competition

Now consider the profit-maximizing firm selling its product in a perfectly competitive market. In equilibrium, it will produce the output at which marginal revenue equals marginal cost and marginal revenue is equal to the price of the output for a competitive firm.

Thus we know that Eq. (15-3) can be written as

$$\frac{\text{MPP}_x}{P_x} = \frac{\text{MPP}_y}{P_y} = \cdots = \frac{\text{MPP}_n}{P_n} = \frac{1}{\text{MC}} = \frac{1}{\text{MR}} = \frac{1}{P} \qquad \textbf{(15-4)}$$

or

$$\frac{P_x}{\text{MPP}_x} = \frac{P_y}{\text{MPP}_y} = \cdots = \frac{P_n}{\text{MPP}_n} = \text{MC} = \text{MR} = P$$

where P (without a subscript) is the price per unit of the product.

If the firm is to maximize profits, this equation must hold for all inputs. We can rearrange the terms of this equation to obtain the firm's profit-maximizing decision rule; it tells the firm how much of each input to employ. Let's do it for one input, x.

We have from Eq. (15-4) that

$$\frac{\text{MPP}_x}{P_x} = \frac{1}{\text{MR}}$$

When we multiply this through by $(\text{MR} \cdot P_x)$, we obtain

$$\text{MPP}_x \cdot \text{MR} = P_x$$

For the perfect competitor, MR = P, and so this becomes

$$\text{MPP}_x \cdot P = P_x$$

Thus for all inputs we have

$$\text{MPP}_x \cdot \text{MR} = P_x \quad \text{or} \quad \text{MPP}_x \cdot P = P_x$$

$$\text{MPP}_y \cdot \text{MR} = P_y \quad \text{or} \quad \text{MPP}_y \cdot P = P_y \qquad \text{(15-5)}$$

$$\text{MPP}_n \cdot \text{MR} = P_n \quad \text{or} \quad \text{MPP}_n \cdot P = P_n$$

Thus firms selling and hiring in perfectly competitive markets will employ each input up to the quantity where the price per unit of input equals the marginal physical product of that input times the price per unit of the output— that is, to the point where the *value* of the output produced from using an additional unit of the input is equal to the price paid for a unit of the input. This forms the basis for the firm's demand for an input. For example, consider a nursery that sells its planting services in a perfectly competitive market. Assume that it can purchase unskilled labor to dig holes at $4 an hour in a perfectly competitive labor market. It will hire workers up to the point where the marginal physical product of its hole-digging labor force times the price it receives for that output from the customers is equal to $4.

THE DEMAND FOR ONE VARIABLE INPUT

With this refresher and additional background, we will now start our discussion of *factor demand*. We consider the case of a single variable input in the same short-run production situation that we first examined in Chapter 8. We assume that all inputs except labor are fixed. Labor can be used in any discrete quantity. It is subject to the law of diminishing marginal physical returns.

We show below the same table that we used in Chapter 8, relabeled as Table 15-1. We have added two columns, which we will explain in a moment.

Marginal physical product is the increase in total physical product associated with a one-unit increase in the variable input. Remember that the marginal physical product of an input is *not* the *added* amount of output produced by an *additional* unit of the input. It is the increase in output that results when the amount of the variable input used *in combination with all other inputs* is increased by one unit. This added output results from the use of a *larger total amount of the variable factor together with fixed amounts of other factors.*[1]

The amount that an additional worker produces is his or her *average product*, or simply Q/L. After all, when an additional worker is hired, that worker produces some output, but more important, he or she alters the average amount of output that all other workers produce because they all work together. For a one-unit increase in labor ($\Delta L = 1$), this change is[2]

$$\text{MPP}_L = \text{APP}_L + \Delta\text{APP}_L \cdot L$$

[1] In defining marginal product we are talking about alternative production plans, not about sequential changes in an operating production plan. The resulting output in each of these plans arises from the cooperative or combined use of all factors in the production process.

[2] See Chapter 8 for the derivation of this equation.

TABLE 15-1
Derivation of value of marginal product

*All marginal figures refer to an interval between the indicated amount of whatever is in the denominator and one unit less that indicated amount. This convention is used in all tables showing marginal quantities.

Number of workers L (1)	Total output q (2)	Average physical product of labor $[(2) \div (1)]$ APP_L (3)	Marginal physical product of labor* $\left(\dfrac{\Delta \text{ total output}}{\Delta \text{ labor input}}\right)$ MPP_L (4)	Price of product P (5)	Value of marginal product $[(4) \times (5)]$ VMP_L (6)
1	100	100	100	$9	$900
2	210	105	110	9	990
3	330	110	120	9	1080
4	405	$101\frac{1}{4}$	75	9	675
5	475	95	70	9	630
6	500	$84\frac{1}{3}$	25	9	225
7	490	70	-10	9	-90

Value of marginal product

If we multiply the marginal physical product times the price of the product, we come up with what is called the **value of marginal product (VMP)**. In this case it is the value of the marginal product of labor, or VMP_L. This is presented in column (6) of Table 15-1, where we see that $VMP_L = MPP_L \cdot P$. We show the derivation of the value of marginal physical product curve in the two panels of Figure 15-1. Since we know that the firm will be operating only in stage II (somewhere between the two ridge lines in an isocost-isoquant diagram), we know that the firm will be operating only in the region of diminishing marginal returns. Hence, in panel (*a*) in Figure 15-1, we show only the downward-sloping portion of the marginal physical product curve. All we have to do to obtain the VMP curve in panel (*b*) in Figure 15-1 is find marginal physical product for a given rate of use of the input labor and then multiply it by the price of the output (*P*).

The short-run demand curve for labor, or the optimal employment of labor

We have already seen that a profit-maximizing firm will hire an input to the point where the price per unit of an input equals the marginal physical product of the input times the price of the output. This was seen in Eq. (15-5). For example, if the price per unit of input is $10 and the price per unit of output is $5, workers will be hired up to the point where the marginal physical product is two units of output per worker, such that

$$\text{MPP} \times P_{\text{output}} = P_{\text{input}}$$

$$2 \text{ units of output} \times \$5 = \$10$$

FIGURE 15-1
Deriving the VMP curve from the MPP curve
In panel (a), we show the MPP curve of column 4 of Table 15-1. We multiply that curve by the price of the product, $9, and obtain the value of marginal product curve, VMP, in panel (b). It is taken from column (6) in Table 15-1. Note the difference between the vertical axes in panel (a) and (b).

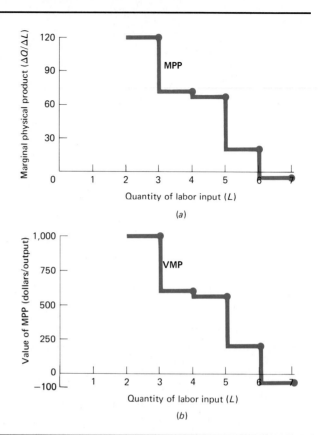

We already have a name for the unit price of output times marginal physical product: value of marginal product (VMP). Thus, it turns out that the value of marginal product curve for labor is the firm's short-run demand curve for labor in a perfectly competitive market, *the quantity of all other inputs held constant.* For the perfectly competitive individual firm, the price of output remains constant no matter how much is sold. The price of the input, we will assume in this chapter, also remains constant; its suppply is perfectly elastic to the individual firm. Thus we can see that the profit-maximizing quantity of labor will be obtained where the wage line (the "going" wage rate for the skill in question) intersects the firm's value of marginal product curve. This is presented in Figure 15-2. If the going wage rate per constant-quality unit of labor is w_0, the optimum quantity of labor demanded will be L_0. The line horizontal at w_0 represents the supply curve of labor to each firm when labor is purchased in a perfectly competitive labor market.

FIGURE 15-2
The profit-maximizing employment of labor
We assume that labor can be obtained at wage
rate w_0. The optimal quantity of labor
demanded by the firm will be L_0, or where the
wage line intersects the VMP_L curve.

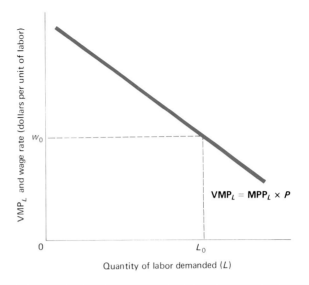

THE INPUT DEMAND CURVE WITH MORE
THAN ONE VARIABLE INPUT

Our analysis becomes more complicated if we vary more than one factor of
production. In order to keep the problem manageable, however, we will
confine our example to a situation in which there are only two variable
factors of production. We will consider labor and capital. In a situation where
there is more than one variable factor of production, the VMP curve no longer
represents the demand curve for the input under study.

A verbal
explanation

When the price of labor falls, the quantity of labor demanded will increase, as represented by a lower wage line which will intersect the VMP
curve at a larger quantity of labor. However, as the quantity of labor used
increases, the marginal physical product of the given fixed capital stock,
MPP_K, will increase because each unit of capital is now being used with
more laborers. If a die-stamping machine is operated by two workers instead of one, the marginal physical product of the die-stamp machine will
be greater because the workers can take turns, thereby eliminating "down-
time" and mistakes due to fatigue and boredom. In other words, each unit
of the fixed amount of capital has more _complementary_ input units with
which to work. We assume **complementarity** between capital and labor
throughout.

A graphical explanation

Look at Figure 15-3. We start off with a wage rate of w_1. The firm can hire all the labor it wants at w_1. This horizontal wage line intersects the value of marginal product curve (VMP$_1$) at A. The quantity of labor demanded is L_1. Now the wage rate falls to w_2. We move down the value of marginal product curve (VMP$_1$) to point B. The new quantity of labor demanded is L_2.

However, with this amount of labor used, the marginal physical product of capital will rise. Each unit of capital now has more units of labor working with it. Since we have assumed that capital and labor have complementary factors of production, MPP$_K$ will rise as more labor is used. By assumption, the price of a unit of capital services has not changed, but its marginal physical product has gone up. The profit-maximizing firm hires each unit of input up to the point at which its value of marginal product equals its price. Since MPP$_K$ has increased, the firm is no longer using the profit-maximizing quantity of capital. The firm must therefore use more units of capital in order to lower MPP$_K$. (Remember that we are in the region of diminishing marginal physical returns.)

However, when the firm increases the amount of capital that it uses, it shifts the VMP curve for labor to the right, since each unit of labor will now be working with more units of capital (and we are assuming complementarity between capital and labor). The increased use of capital therefore shifts the VMP curve from VMP$_1$ to VMP$_2$. The new wage rate, w_2, now intersects the new VMP curve (VMP$_2$) at point C. The new quantity of labor demanded increases from L_2 to L_3. If we connect points A and C, we obtain the demand curve for labor when there are two variable factors of production. This demand curve for labor is labeled $d_L d_L$.

FIGURE 15-3
The demand curve for labor with two variable inputs
We start out with wage rate w_1. The optimal employment of labor is L_1, given at point A on VMP$_1$. The wage rate falls to w_2. Optimal employment apparently increases to L_2, where the new horizontal wage line, w_2, intersects VMP$_1$. However, the marginal physical product of capital will now rise because we are assuming complementarity of the inputs. This will shift the value of marginal product curve of labor to the right from VMP$_1$ to VMP$_2$. The new intersection of the horizontal wage line (supply curve of labor) is at point C. The optimal employment will increase to L_3. If we connect points such as A and C, we have the demand curve for labor, which is labeled $d_L d_L$.

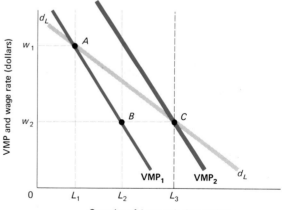

**The slope
of the input
demand curve**

Can we be guaranteed that when there is more than one variable factor of production the demand curve will always be downward-sloping? After all, we did come up with the possibility of an upward-sloping demand curve for a product whenever the income effect for an inferior good was so strong that it overrode the pure substitution effect. (This was the Giffen good case in Chapter 4.) It has been demonstrated by C. E. Ferguson that the factor demand curve must always be negatively sloped because, on balance, all the effects of an input price change must cause the quantity demanded to vary inversely with the price.[3]

**The elasticity
of factor
substitution**

When the price of labor fell, in the preceding example, the quantity of labor demanded increased. With a given output level, there would have been a substitution effect and labor would have been substituted for capital. The responsiveness of the firm to a change in the relative prices of inputs can be measured by what is called the **elasticity of factor substitution**. This measures the relative responsiveness of the capital/labor ratio to a change in relative factor prices. The elasticity of substitution equals

$$\sigma = - \left[\frac{\Delta(K/L)}{K/L} \Big/ \frac{\Delta(r/w)}{r/w} \right] \tag{15-6}$$

where σ (sigma) is the Greek letter used for elasticity of substitution.[4] When $\sigma = -1$, a 1 percent decrease in the price of capital relative to the price of labor results in a 1 percent increase in the capital/labor proportion.

Numerous studies have been undertaken to estimate the elasticity of substitution of capital for labor. Quite a few have concluded that it is numerically close to -1; however, it varies from industry to industry and from short run to long run. Empirically, the firm can and does respond to changing relative input prices. The notion of fixed proportion production functions does not hold up in the real world.

THE INDUSTRY DEMAND CURVE

An industry's demand curve for any input is obtained by looking at all the individual firms' input demand curves. However, we cannot simply add together each firm's demand curve. The reason we cannot do so is that as

---

[3]C. E. Ferguson, "Production, Prices, and the Theory of Jointly Derived Input Demand Functions," *Economica*, new ser., vol. 33, 1966.

[4]The elasticity of substitution is equal to the responsiveness of the capital/labor ratio to changes in the marginal rate of technical substitution of capital for labor. However, we substitute for the marginal rate of technical substitution the ratio of the two marginal products. We continue using the profit-maximizing rule given in Eq. (15-1) to get the ratio of the factor prices instead of the ratio of the marginal products.

the price of labor falls and more of it is hired, output increases.[5] As the output of the entire industry increases, the price of the product must fall in order for the additional output to be sold. This results in a shift in VMP. Thus, we must take account of this reduction in the price of the output in deriving the market demand curve for an input.

We do this in panels (a) and (b) of Figure 15-4. We start off with the assumption that each firm is identical and that its demand curve for labor is $d_L d_L$, as shown in panel (a). The going wage rate per constant-quality unit of labor is w_1. This is the supply price of labor, the price per unit that the firm must pay. It intersects the firm's demand curve for labor at point A in panel (a). The quantity of labor demanded by the firm will be q_1. We multiply q_1 times the number of firms and find that the quantity of labor demanded by the industry is Q_1, as shown in panel (b). The wage rate w_1 and the quantity demanded in the industry Q_1 give us one point on our industry demand curve, and that point is labeled A'.

Effect of a decline in a factor price

Now assume that there is a reduction in the wage rate of workers to w_2. Each individual firm moves along its demand for labor curve. Thus, there is a movement from point A to point B on $d_L d_L$ in panel (a) of Figure 15-4. Each firm would like to hire q_2 workers. However, if *each* firm were to hire q_2 workers, they would end up producing more. When they produce more, the only way they can all sell this increased input is by reducing the price of the output.[6] But a reduction in the output's price will shift the value of marginal product curve. The firm's demand curve for labor will shift inward; each firm will see its own demand curve for labor shifting inward from $d_L d_L$ to $d_L' d_L'$. Rather than demanding quantity q_2, each firm will demand quantity q_3, where the firm's supply curve for labor (the horizontal line drawn from w_2) intersects the demand curve for labor at point B'. If we multiply quantity q_3 by the number of firms, we obtain the quantity Q_3 in panel (b). We now have another point for our industry demand curve for labor. It is at the intersection of the wage line with the new quantity demanded, or point B''. When we connect all such points, we get the industry demand curve $D_L D_L$ in panel (b).

We can see that the industry demand curve for an input is steeper than the curve we would get if we simply summed horizontally all the firms' demand curves. Consider the possibility that you work for a consulting firm that has been paid to predict what the increase in industry employment will be after a fall in the price of labor employed in that industry. If you make a prediction based on the present price of the product in that industy, you may be led astray. You would be looking at the summation of a set of individual demand curves such as $d_L d_L$ in panel (a) of Figure 15-4. You would

[5]There are exceptions when there are several variable inputs.

[6]We ignore here problems that arise when *several* variable factors are used, for then we would have to account for changes in the prices of other inputs. See M. Friedman, *Price Theory: A Provisional Text* (Chicago: Aldine, 1962), pp. 180–183.

FIGURE 15-4
Deriving the industry demand curve for labor
Assume a wage rate of w_1. The individual firm demand curve is $d_L d_L$ from Figure 15-3. This gives a point on the industry demand curve $D_L D_L$, which is point A' in panel (b). The quantity demanded is Q_1 for the industry, and q_1 for the firm. Now the wage rate falls to w_2. The firm increases quantity demanded to q_2; however, point B cannot be maintained for long. As all firms increase output, the price of the product must fall. The VMP curve shifts to the left to $d_L' d_L'$; the quantity of labor demanded falls from q_2 to q_3 in panel (a). Point B' gives us a new point in panel (b), point B''. Industry quantity demanded increases to Q_3. If we connect points A' and B'', we obtain the industry demand curve $D_L D_L$ for the input over wage rate range w_1 to w_2.

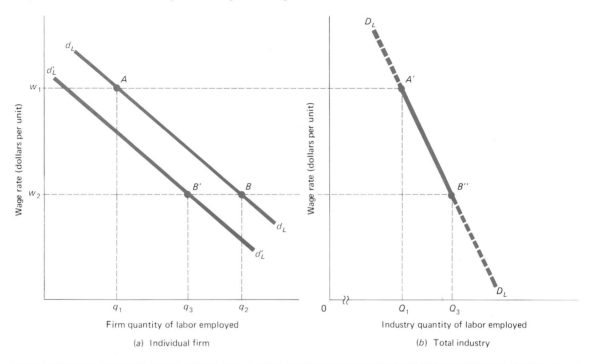

(a) Individual firm

(b) Total industry

be predicting that each firm would increase its quantity of labor demanded from q_1 to q_2, but you would be ignoring the fact that each firm will not be able to sell all that additional output unless the price of output falls, thus moving each firm's demand curve for labor inward to $d_L' d_L'$. Hence you should instead discount the firm's intentions and make allowances for the fall in the product price that will result when all firms expand their production.

INPUT DEMAND BY A MONOPOLIST

Recall that when the firm *purchases* its inputs in a perfectly competitive market it can obtain all it wishes at the going price. Thus, in the case of labor, a horizontal wage line represents the supply curve of labor to the firm.

For the moment we will retain the assumption of a perfectly competitive market in which the firm buys inputs. However, we alter the assumption that the firm *sells* its product in a perfectly competitive market. We consider the case of a monopolistic seller. A monopolist, you will remember, faces a downward-sloping demand curve which is the industry demand curve. The monopolist cannot sell all it wants at a single going price. It is necessary to lower the price in order to sell more. We will consider only the case of a non-price-discriminating monopolist. The price at which the monopolist sells each unit of the product is the same.

In order to find the demand of a monopolist for an input, we must find out the value to the monopolist of increasing employment by one unit of a particular input in question.

Earlier, we found the marginal physical product for a variable input and then multiplied it by the price of the output to obtain the value of marginal product for that input. VMP ($=$ MPP $\times$ price of output product) gave us the demand curve for the labor input of an individual firm, purchasing its labor in a perfectly competitive market and selling its output in a perfectly competitive product market.

Marginal revenue product

We are now interested in finding out the demand curve for labor when the firm sells its output in a noncompetitive market. In other words, what should we look at to find a monopolist's demand for labor curve? It would be inappropriate to do as we did for a competitive firm; that is, we cannot merely multiply MPP times a market-determined price of the output. Why? Because the monopolist, in order to sell an additional unit of output, must reduce the price on all units sold. (Again, here we are considering the case of a non-price-discriminating monopolist.) If the monopolist wants to find out the change in total revenues that results from an increase in the use of a variable input, say, labor, the monopolist must look at the change in physical output due to the additional unit of labor and the revenue resulting from the sale of each additional unit of output, that is, *marginal revenue*.

Thus, to find the increase in total revenues due to a one-unit increase in labor, the monopolist will look at marginal physical product multiplied by the marginal revenue that results from the sale of that increased output.

When we find MPP $\times$ MR, we obtain the increase in total revenues due to a one-unit increase in the variable input. This quantity is called **marginal revenue product (MRP)**. MRP ($\equiv$ MPP $\times$ MR) is similar to VMP except that it takes into account the necessity of lowering price in order for a monopolist to sell a larger quantity of output.

We show an example of the derivation of marginal revenue product in Table 15-2. Note that the law of diminishing marginal physical returns is working. We see this in column (3), where we see listed the marginal physical product of labor; it is continuously declining. To find marginal revenue product in column (6), we obtain total revenues in column (5) for the various output rates obtainable by first two, then three, then four, up to six workers

TABLE 15-2
Derivation of marginal revenue product
*All marginal figures refer to an interval between the indicated amount of whatever is in the denominator and one unit less than the indicated amount.

Number of workers (1)	Total output (2)	$MPP_L =$ Δ total output/ Δ labor input* (3)	Price of output (4)	Total revenues (5)	$MRP_L =$ Δ total revenue/ Δ labor input (6)
2	210	—	$9.00	$1,890.00	—
3	330	120	8.00	2,640.00	$750.00
4	405	75	7.50	3,037.50	397.50
5	475	70	7.00	3,325.00	287.50
6	500	25	6.80	3,400.00	75.00
7	490	−10	6.50	3,185.00	−215.00

FIGURE 15-5
Deriving the MRP curve
Panel (a) is the familiar marginal physical product curve taken from column 3 of Table 15-2. Panel (b) shows the marginal revenue product curve which represents the change in total revenues due to a one-unit change in labor input.

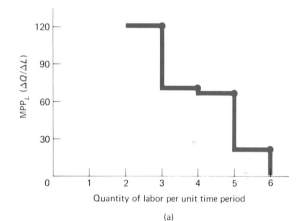

(a)

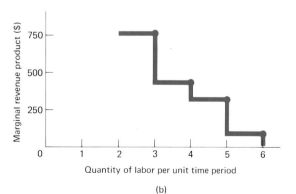

(b)

per unit time period. MRP is then obtained by looking at the difference between total revenues each time we add one more worker.

In Figure 15-5, we plot the marginal physical product of labor MPP_L in panel (a) for two to seven workers. In panel (b), the resultant marginal revenue product curve is plotted (ignoring its negative portion). It is downward-sloping just as the VMP curve was in Figures 15-1 and 15-2.

MONOPOLY DEMAND FOR A SINGLE VARIABLE INPUT

We have been assuming that there is only one variable input, labor. Assume again that the monopolist purchases labor in a perfectly competitive input market. Therefore, the going wage rate per constant-quality unit of labor is given to the monopolist by a line horizontal at that wage rate which represents the perfectly elastic supply curve of labor to the monopolist.

Both competitive and monopoly firms that are maximizing profits will choose their inputs and outputs such that in every case marginal revenue equals marginal cost. That is a general optimization rule for any firm (or for any individual). Every optimization situation therefore requires that an appropriate measure for marginal revenue and marginal cost be obtained. When we looked at output decisions, marginal revenue was the change in total receipts generated by a change in the *production and sale* of one unit of the product. Marginal cost was the change in total cost generated by a *one-unit change in production*. Previously we were dealing with demand for input factors under perfect competition. There, again, we were looking at marginal revenue and the marginal cost of using a particular input. Considering labor alone, the marginal cost of using one more unit of labor was identically equal to the going wage rate since, by definition, the firm could purchase all units of labor at a constant wage. Marginal revenue resulting from hiring one more unit of labor turned out to be equal to VMP, or MPP × price of final output.

Profit-maximizing solution

We now wish to look at the profit-maximizing quantity of input demanded by a firm selling in a monopoly market. To do this, we will rework the formulas we used earlier. We will use those equations to reflect the fact that the monopolist cannot sell additional output at a constant price. Rather, the monopolist faces a downward-sloping demand curve. Therefore, in order to sell the additional output due to an increase in the use of the variable input, the monopolist must lower the price on all units of the product sold. Go back to Eq. (15-4). We now substitute marginal revenue for price and use

$$\frac{P_i}{MPP_i} = MC = MR \qquad \text{[for all } i \text{ (inputs)]} \tag{15-7}$$

which means that generally

$$MPP_i \cdot MR = P_i \qquad \text{(15-8)}$$

or more specifically for labor,

$$MRP_{labor} = P_{labor} \qquad \text{(15-9)}$$

Profit maximization dictates that the monopolist hire labor up to the point where the *marginal revenue product of labor equals the price of labor* (the wage rate). We can determine the profit-maximizing employment level for a monopolist by looking at the price of labor and the monopolist's marginal revenue product of labor curve. This is presented in Figure 15-6. Remember that we are still assuming that the firm can purchase its inputs in a perfectly competitive market. Thus, it faces a horizontal supply curve of the labor input at the going price of labor, or wage rate w_e. That wage rate equals the MRP at the intersection of the wage line with the MRP curve in Figure 15-6. The profit-maximizing monopolist facing the wage rate for the variable input labor at w_e will therefore purchase Q_e units of labor per unit time period.

Essentially, then, we have shown that the monopolist's demand curve for a *single* variable input, holding all others constant, is its marginal revenue product curve. The monopolist faces a labor supply curve, if it buys the labor input in a perfectly competitive market, that is a horizontal line at the going market wage rate per unit of labor.

FIGURE 15-6
Monopoly employment determination
If the going wage rate is w_e, the point at the intersection of that supply curve of labor with the marginal revenue product curve gives the optimal employment Q_e of the input.

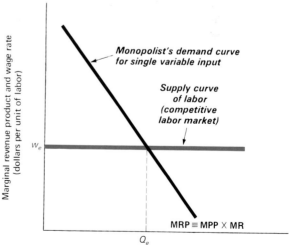

THE MONOPOLIST'S DEMAND CURVE WHEN SEVERAL INPUTS ARE VARIABLE

What happens if the monopolist can vary other inputs besides labor? We are back to the situation which we described earlier when we had to consider that a change in the quantity of one variable input used also changes the marginal physical product of the other variable inputs used. Exactly the same analysis applies to a monopolist as applies to a perfectly competitive producer. The only difference is that for the monopolist we show a marginal revenue product curve shifting instead of the VMP, which is the equivalent construct for the competitor. (See Figure 15-3.)

This can be seen in Figure 15-7. We start off with a wage rate of w_1. The firm can hire all the labor it wants at w_1. This horizontal wage line intersects the marginal revenue product curve (MRP$_1$) at A. The quantity of labor demanded is Q_1. Now the wage rate falls to w_2. We move down the marginal revenue product curve (MRP$_1$) to point B. The new quantity of labor demanded is Q_2.

However, with this amount of labor used, the marginal physical product of capital will rise. Each unit of capital now has more units of labor working with it. Assuming that capital and labor are complementary factors of production, MPP$_K$ will rise as more labor is used. By assumption, the price of a unit of capital services has not changed, but its marginal physical product has risen. The profit-maximizing firm hires each input up to the point where that input's marginal revenue product equals its price. Since MPP$_K$ has in-

FIGURE 15-7
The monopolist's demand curve when there are several variable factors
We start out with wage rate w_1. The optimal employment of labor is Q_1 at point A on MRP$_1$. The wage rate falls to w_2. Optimal employment apparently increases to Q_2, where the w_2 line intersects MRP$_1$. However, the marginal physical product of capital will now rise because we are assuming complementarity of inputs. Since the firm will now employ more capital, this will shift the marginal revenue product curve of labor to the right to MRP$_2$. The new intersection of the wage line (supply curve of labor) is at point C. The optimal employment will increase to Q_3. If we connect points such as A and C, we have the demand curve for labor $d_L d_L$.

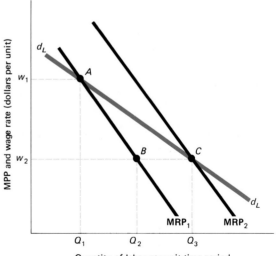

creased, the firm is no longer using the profit-maximizing quantity of capital. In order to satisfy the optimum condition [Eq. (15-8)], the firm must now use more units of capital in order to lower MPP_K. (Remember that we are in the region of diminishing marginal physical returns.) However, when the firm increases the amount of capital that it uses, it will shift the MRP_1 curve for labor to the right, since each unit of labor will now be working with more units of capital and we are assuming complementarity between capital and labor. The MRP_1 curve shifts to MRP_2. The new wage rate w_2 intersects the new MRP_2 curve at point C. The new quantity of labor demanded is Q_3. We connect points A and C to obtain the demand curve for labor when there is more than one variable factor of production. It is labeled $d_L d_L$.

SUPPLY OF A COMPETITIVE INPUT

Up to this point in the chapter we have studied the demand for inputs for competitive firms and firms with monopoly power. We will now turn to the supply of resources (inputs) that are demanded by producing firms. Back in Chapter 4 we discussed one important variable input, labor. We used indifference curve analysis to show how individual labor suppliers react to a change in the wage rate. In Figure 15-8 we see the supply curve of labor that we derived in Chapter 4 (and ignore its backward-bending portion). This curve will allow us to study pricing and employment of the input labor.

FIGURE 15-8
The supply curve of labor
We assume an upward-sloping supply curve of labor $S_L S_L$.

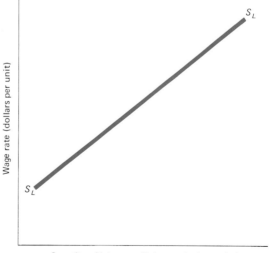

FIGURE 15-9
The three supply curves of labor
Here we see that the individual firm in an industry faces a perfectly horizontal supply curve at the going wage rate. Under the assumption of a perfectly competitive labor market, the industry faces an upward-sloping supply curve. So, too, does the entire economy ("all industries").

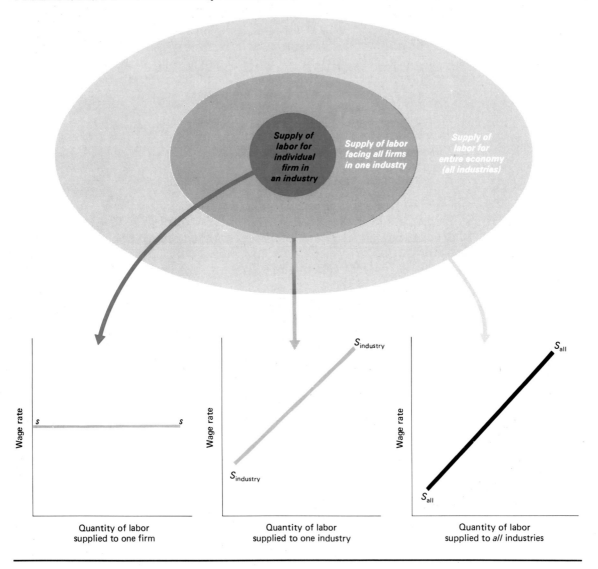

Labor supply to the firm, one industry, and all industries

Perhaps it is important here to distinguish between the supply curve of labor facing (1) the individual firm, (2) one industry, and (3) all industries. In Figure 15-9 we show that the individual firm faces a horizontal supply curve of labor at the going wage rate. We assume that each firm purchasing the labor is an insignificant part of the market demand for that input. Then we see that the supply curve facing one industry is upward-sloping. So too is the supply curve of labor facing all industries.

THE DETERMINATION OF INPUT PRICE AND EMPLOYMENT

All we need do now is put together the market supply curve and the market demand curve to find the market-clearing price of a factor of production and the associated equilibrium quantity. This is shown in Figure 15-10 for labor. It could be drawn similarly for any other factor of production.

Note that in Figure 15-10 both the demand curve and the supply curve for labor are drawn for constant-quality units. Furthermore, the wage rate is an all-inclusive wage rate and includes the value of all fringe benefits. It is the implicit or alternative cost per unit of constant-quality employment that the employer incurs and that the employee receives.

FIGURE 15-10
Equilibrium in the labor market
We combine an industry demand curve $D_L D_L$ and an industry supply curve of labor $S_L S_L$. The equilibrium wage rate will be w_e. The equilibrium quantity of labor will be L_e.

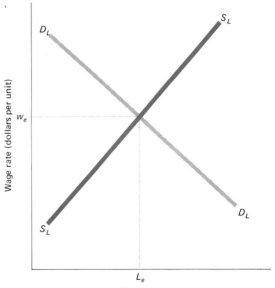

THE DETERMINANTS OF FACTOR
DEMAND ELASTICITY

We have not yet looked at what determines the price elasticity of a demand curve such as D_LD_L presented in Figure 15-10. There are basically five determinants of an input's price elasticity of demand: (1) the technological feasibility of substituting one input for another, (2) price elasticity of demand of final output, (3) supply elasticity of other inputs, (4) percentage of total cost of all inputs accounted for by the cost of the particular input under study, and (5) length of time allowed for adjustment. We will treat these in that order here.

Technological feasibility of substitution

The price elasticity of demand for an input will clearly depend on the technical feasibility of substituting one input for another. In some cases this technological feasibility is very limited; in others it is substantial. We measured technological feasibility by the elasticity of technical substitution σ presented in Eq. (15-6). The coefficient is calculated with output held constant. In other words, it reflects a movement along an isoquant. The more sharply convex the isoquant is, the lower σ will be. The extreme is, of course, an isoquant that demonstrates fixed proportions. It is composed of a horizontal and a vertical line, drawn from the point representing the required K/L ratio. (For a graphic illustration, refer to Figure 8-10.) For a fixed proportion isoquant σ is equal to 0. In such a case, the price elasticity of demand for capital or for labor, all other things taken into account, would also be 0.[7] The other extreme involves a $\sigma = -\infty$. This is represented by linear (straight-line) isoquants, representing perfectly substitutable inputs.

Price elasticity of demand of final output

Since the demand for any input is a **derived demand**, one derived from the demand for output, we would expect the price elasticity of demand of an input to be a direct function of the demand for final output. The more elastic the demand for the output, the more elastic will be the demand for each input, *ceteris paribus*. Think of this in terms of, say, a 10 percent increase in the relative price of an input. This will ultimately result in some increase in the relative price of the final product. The more elastic the demand for the final product, the greater will be the reduction in the quantity demanded, and hence the greater will be the reduction in the demand for the input required to produce this now-smaller output. Consider as an example the price elasticity of demand for the labor input used in the production of electricity. If the price elasticity of demand of the final output—electrical

---

[7]In other words, changes in the relative prices of the inputs will not alter the optimal combination of capital and labor.

energy—is close to 0, an increase in the price of the labor input (a higher wage rate) can be passed on to the consumer of electricity without the quantity of electricity demanded falling appreciably. Therefore, the reduction in the profit-maximizing rate of output will be very small, and hence, *ceteris paribus*, there will be little reduction in the quantity of labor demanded by electric utilities.

Supply elasticity of other inputs

The greater the price elasticity of supply of other inputs, the greater the price elasticity of demand for the input under study. In other words, if firms in an industry can easily turn to a substitute input and obtain more of it by paying a very small increase in price, the reduction in the quantity demanded of the input in question will be relatively great for any given increase in its price. Assume that aluminum and plastic are close substitutes for use in automobile grilles. If the supply elasticity of aluminum is very high—i.e., increasing quantities can be purchased without affecting the unit price of aluminum—then whenever the price of plastic goes up, automobile manufacturers can easily switch to aluminum. This switch will be accomplished without a significant increase in the unit price of the input for making grilles, since the supply elasticity of aluminum is, in this example, very high. Thus, the price elasticity of the demand by automobile manufacturers for the input plastic will, *ceteris paribus*, also be high.

Factor payments as a percentage of total costs

In many circumstances, the following proposition is true: The smaller the percentage of total costs represented by the cost of the variable input under study, the less the price elasticity of demand will be for that input. If the percentage of the total cost of some product paid to the input in question is only 1 percent, a 100 percent increase in the price of that input will result in only a one percentage point increase in total cost. It turns out that this proposition is usually correct, but it is not always true.[8]

Short versus long run

The price elasticity of demand for any input, just like the price elasticity of demand for any final product, will be greater the longer the time allowed for adjustment. The reasoning here is identical with the reasoning employed in looking at the demand for final output. The longer the time allowed for adjustment, the more adjustments can be made. For example, if the price of a certain type of machinery happens to increase, it may not be possible for plants to reduce appreciably the quantity of that machinery that they use in the short run; but in the long run, when they replace the machinery, they can substitute a different kind of machine or employ more labor and less machinery.

[8]See Martin Bronfenbrenner, "Note on the Elasticity of Derived Demand," *Oxford Economic Papers*, October 1961.

SUPPLY IN AN IMPERFECTLY COMPETITIVE INPUT MARKET

Up to this point we have assumed that the labor market is characterized by a great number of buyers and sellers, each of whom is unable to affect the equilibrium wage rate. We now turn to an imperfectly competitive input market. Specifically, we now assume that the firm buying labor is sufficiently large relative to the market that a change in its demand for labor affects the market demand for labor and the wage rate for labor. This occurs whenever a firm faces a *less than perfectly elastic supply curve* for the input in question. We now return to the assumption that the purchaser of the input is a producer selling its output in a perfectly competitive market. Thus, we are looking at imperfect competition in the input market and perfect competition in the output market.

In its most extreme case, the situation of a large buyer or demander is one of **monopsony**, which means a single buyer. Several buyers might be called **oligopsony**, but this term is not often used. We will consider a monopsonist in the following section. Here we will be talking about a monopoly in the purchase of an input. (In Chapter 12, we talked about monopoly in the *sale* of an *output*.)

Average and marginal factor cost curves

The monopsonist faces an upward-sloping supply curve of the input in question because, as the only buyer, it faces the entire market supply curve for the input. The monopsonist must pay a higher price for the last unit of the input, but in the case in which no price discrimination in purchasing is possible, the monopsonist must also pay a higher price on all previous units purchased.

The supply curve of an input can be called the **average factor cost curve (AFC)**, just as the demand curve for an output is often called the average revenue curve. We derived a curve marginal to the average revenue curve to represent the marginal revenue obtained by a monopolist from an extra unit of sales. Now we look at a curve marginal to the average factor cost curve; we will call it the **marginal factor cost curve (MFC)**. It will give the increase in factor cost that results from a one-unit increase in the purchase of the input under study.[9]

Numerical example. Consider the numerical example in Table 15-3. Here we show the quantity of labor purchased, the wage rate per hour, the total cost of the quantity of hours of labor purchased per hour, and the marginal factor cost per hour for the additional labor bought.

We can represent the data in the columns of Table 15-3 graphically, as shown in Figure 15-11. We show the supply curve as SS, which is taken

---

[9]Marginal factor cost has been called a number of things: marginal expense of input, marginal expenditure for input, marginal resource (input) cost, and probably a dozen other names. They all refer to the same thing.

TABLE 15-3
Derivation of marginal factor cost

Quantity of labor used by management (1)	Wage rate ($ per hour) (2)	Total wage bill [(1) × (2)] (3)	Marginal factor cost MFC = Δ wage bill/Δ labor = Δ (3)/Δ (1) (4)
0	—	—	—
1	$1.00	$ 1.00	$1.00
2	2.00	4.00	3.00
3	2.40	7.20	3.20
4	2.80	11.20	4.00
5	3.60	18.00	6.80
6	4.20	25.20	7.20

FIGURE 15-11
Derivation of a marginal factor cost curve
The supply curve is a graphical representation of columns (1) and (2) of Table 15-3. The marginal factor cost curve MFC is a graphical representation of columns (1) and (4); it is the increase in the total wage bill resulting from a one-unit increase in labor input.

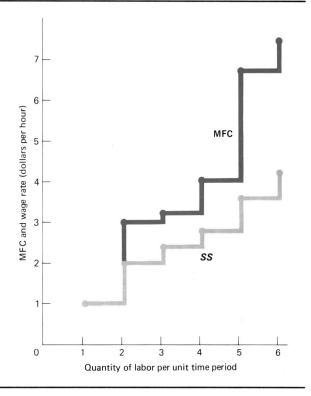

from columns (1) and (2). The marginal factor cost curve MFC is taken from columns (1) and (4). The marginal factor cost curve must be above the supply curve whenever the supply curve is upward-sloping. If the supply curve is upward-sloping, the firm must pay a higher wage rate in order to attract a larger supply of labor. This higher wage rate must be paid to all workers; thus, the increase in total costs due to an increase in the labor input will exceed the wage rate. Remember that in a perfectly competitive input market, the wage rate facing each firm is fixed or horizontal and is its supply curve for labor; the marginal factor cost curve is identical with the supply curve at this fixed wage.

PRICING AND EMPLOYMENT OF A SINGLE VARIABLE INPUT UNDER MONOPSONY

We assume that the pure monopsonist, like anyone else, maximizes profit. We now have to alter Eq. (15-7) because the price of the variable input is no longer constant. Instead of the price of input, we use marginal factor cost of input; Eq. (15-7) becomes

$$\frac{\text{MFC}_i}{\text{MPP}_i} = \text{MC} = \text{MR} = P \qquad \text{[for all } i \text{ (inputs)]} \tag{15-10}$$

Equation (15-10) represents the profit-maximizing combinations of inputs for a firm which is a *perfect competitor in the output market* and a *pure monopsonist in the input market*. Rearranging Eq. (15-10), we get

$$\text{MPP}_i \cdot P = \text{MFC}_i \tag{15-11}$$

or

$$\text{VMP}_i = \text{MFC}_i \tag{15-12}$$

The firm that is a competitor in its output or product market and a monopsonist in the input market will hire a resource up to the point at which the value of marginal product equals the marginal factor cost. We can see the pricing and employment of such an input by the profit-maximizing monopsonist in Figure 15-12.

If labor is the only variable factor of production, we are looking at a VMP curve for labor. The profit-maximizing monopsonist will hire labor up to the point where MFC = VMP. This occurs at the intersection of the MFC curve with the VMP curve, or at point A. That gives the profit-maximizing rate of employment of labor, Q_L. Now, how much does the monopsonist have to pay per unit for that amount of labor? That is given by the supply curve, SS. Point B on curve SS corresponds to the desired quantity of labor, Q_L. The wage rate that must be paid is w_1. We have, then, the wage and employment optimum for a monopsonist input user selling its output in a purely competitive market when there is only one variable factor of production which is purchased in an imperfectly competitive market.

FIGURE 15-12
Price and employment of a single variable input purchased by a pure monopsonist that is a competitor in the product market.
When we consider only a single variable input, the pure monopsonist will hire the input up to the point where MFC = VMP. This is point A. In order to obtain that quantity of labor Q_L, the pure monopsonist will have to pay only the wage rate w_1, which is read off the supply curve SS, where it intersects the quantity line at point B.

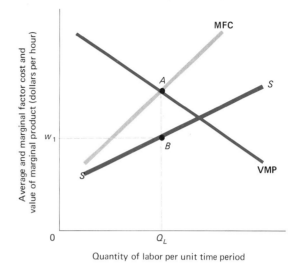

Quantity of labor per unit time period

The first time Figure 15-12 is examined, readers may feel that A should be the wage rate. After all, that is where we observe the intersection of the marginal factor cost curve with the VMP curve (which is the demand curve for labor). But that intersection at A gives us information only about the quantity of labor that should be hired by the pure monopsonist. Once that optimal quantity is determined, the pure monopsonist does not have to pay that high a wage rate (A) to attract the quantity Q_L of labor per unit time period. The monopsonist has to pay only the wage rate w_1, which is read off the supply curve for labor, SS. Remember, it is the supply curve of labor that indicates the quantity of labor forthcoming at each and every wage rate.

WHEN THE MONOPSONIST IS ALSO A MONOPOLIST

We can alter the analysis above to take into account the monopsonist input buyer who is also a monopolist in the output market. Instead of looking at the price of the product, we focus on its marginal revenue. Instead of using the value of marginal product curve, we want to use the marginal revenue product curve. The analysis above will be redone utilizing the MRP curve rather than the VMP curve. Thus, instead of VMP as in Figure 15-12, we show MRP as in Figure 15-13. The profit-maximizing quantity of employment is obtained where the marginal factor cost curve intersects the marginal revenue product curve. This is at point A in Figure 15-13. The optimum quantity of input is therefore Q_1. Since the monopsonist faces supply curve SS, the monopsonist need pay a uniform wage rate of only w_2 in order to

FIGURE 15-13
Pricing and employment of an input hired by the monopsonist-monopolist.
If the monopolist is also a monopsonist, it will hire the input up to the point where MFC = MRP at point A. This gives the optimal employment of Q_1. The minimal wage rate that will have to be paid is w_2, the wage at which Q_1 of labor will be supplied.

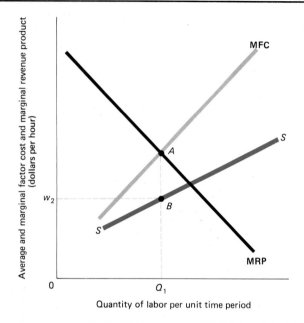

obtain quantity Q_1 of labor. That is, the wage rate necessary to obtain Q_1 is given at the intersection of the vertical line drawn from Q_1 through SS, or at point B.

Notice that because marginal revenue is always less than output price, the quantity of labor demanded, Q_1, will be smaller in Figure 15-13 than it was in Figure 15-12. Moreover, since we are at a point on the supply curve that is closer to the origin, the wage rate w_2 in Figure 15-13 will also be below the wage rate w_1, in Figure 15-12.

TABLE 15-4
A summary of monopsony and monopoly situations. Optimal output and input employment: the case of labor

Input market structure	Output market structure	
	Perfect competition	Monopoly
Perfect competition	(a) MC = MR = P w = MFC_L = MRP_L = VMP_L	(b) MC = MR($<P$) w = MFC_L = MRP_L($<VMP_L$)
Monopsony	(c) MC = MR = P $w < MFC_L$ = MRP_L = VMP_L	(d) MC = MR($<P$) $w < MFC_L$ = MRP_L($<VMP_L$)

FIGURE 15-14

Summary of pricing and employment under various market conditions

The panels in this diagram correspond to the sections marked (a), (b), (c), and (d) in Table 15-4. In panel (a) the firm operates in perfect competition in both input and output markets. It purchases labor up to the point where the going wage rate w_e is equal to VMP. It hires quantity Q_c of labor. In panel (b) the firm purchases the variable input labor in a perfectly competitive market but has a monopoly in the output market. It purchases labor up to the point where the wage rate w_e is equal to MRP. It hires a smaller quantity of labor Q_m than in panel (a). In panels (c) and (d) the firm is a monopsonist in the input market. In panel (c) it is a perfect competitor in the output market. It hires labor up to the point where MFC = VMP. It will hire quantity Q_1 and pay a wage rate w_c. In panel (d) the monopsonist is also a monopolist. It hires labor up to the point where MFC = MRP, which is quantity Q_2. It pays wage rate w_m.

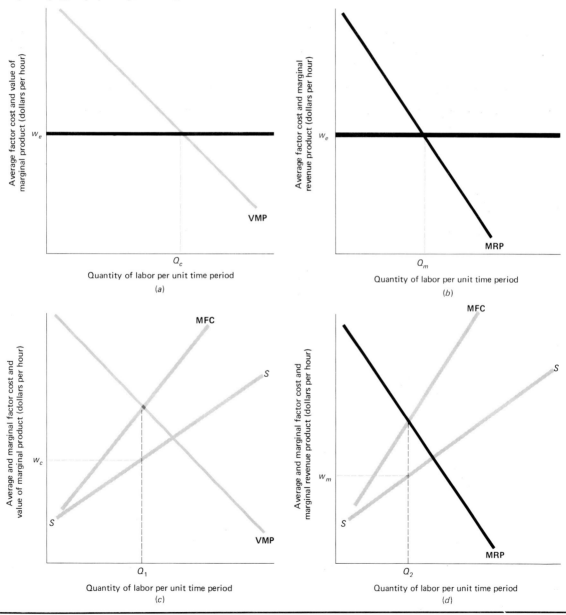

A SUMMARY OF MONOPSONY AND MONOPOLY SITUATIONS

We have studied input factor pricing and employment with pure competition in the input and the output markets and with monopoly in the input and the output markets. In Table 15-4, we present a summary of the various conditions under which output will be produced and a variable input, labor in this case, will be demanded. Table 15-4 is presented graphically in panels (a) through (d) in Figure 15-14.

The notion of exploitation

Exploitation is defined as paying a resource less than the value of its marginal product. Otherwise stated, labor exploitation is the difference between the wage rate and the value of marginal product of labor.

We consider the amount of exploitation that exists in a situation where a firm is both a monopolist and a monopsonist. This is depicted in Figure 15-15. The profit-maximizing monopolist/monopsonist will determine the quantity of labor demanded at the intersection of MFC and MRP, which is labeled E in Figure 15-15. It will pay a wage rate w_m for the quantity Q_m of labor. **Monopolistic exploitation** occurs because the monopolist looks at its MRP curve rather than its VMP curve, which would be relevant for a perfect competitor. **Monopsonistic exploitation** occurs because the monopsonist looks at the MFC curve rather than the input supply curve, as does the buyer of labor in a perfectly competitive market.

FIGURE 15-15
Exploitation

Exploitation is defined as paying an input less than the value of its marginal product. In the situation depicted here, we have both monopoly and monopsony. The monopolist finds the profit-maximizing rate of labor use at the intersection of MFC and MRP, or point E. The profit-maximizing quantity of labor demanded will be Q_m, which will be paid a wage rate w_m. Monopoly exploitation equals $(VMP_L - MRP_L)$. Monopsony exploitation equals $(MRP_L - w_m)$. Total exploitation equals $(VMP_L - w_m)$.

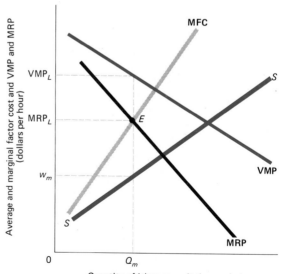

An analysis of the minimum wage laws

If you look at Figure 15-16, you can see that in an unrestricted labor market there will be an equilibrium wage rate at which equal quantities of labor are demanded and supplied. What if a legal minimum wage rate were set above the equilibrium wage rate? Who benefits and who loses from the imposition of a minimum rate above w_e?

We analyze the effects of a minimum wage in Figure 15-16. We start off in equilibrium with the equilibrium wage rate of w_e and the equilibrium quantity of labor demanded and supplied equal to Q_e. A minimum wage w_m, which is higher than w_e, is imposed. At w_m the quantity demanded for labor is reduced to Q_D and some workers now become unemployed. Note that the reduction in employment

from Q_e to Q_D, or the distance from B to A, is less than the excess quantity of labor supplied at wage rate w_m. This excess quantity supplied is the distance between C and A, or the distance between Q_s and D_D. The reason the reduction time employment is smaller than the excess supply of labor at the minimum wage is that the latter also includes a second component which consists of additional hours supplied at the new higher minimum wage. Some of this labor will be unemployed and some will be employed elsewhere in the non-covered sectors of the economy at an even lower wage. After all, when workers leave the covered sector, they increase the supply of labor in the uncovered sectors. With any given demand for labor in each of the uncovered

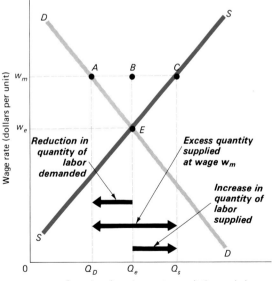

FIGURE 15-16
The effect of a minimum wage rate
The market-clearing wage rate is w_e. The market-clearing quantity of employment is Q_e and is determined by the intersection of supply and demand at point E. A minimum wage equal to w_m is established. The quantity of labor demanded is reduced to Q_D; the reduction of employment from Q_e to Q_D is equal to the distance between A and B. That distance is smaller than the excess quantity of labor supplied, AC, at wage rate w_m. The distance between B and C is the increase in the quantity of labor supplied at the higher minimum wage rate.

sectors—that is, industries not covered by federal minimum wage laws—an increase in the supply of labor to those sectors must cause the equilibrium wage rate there to fall.

In the long run, some of the reduction in labor demanded will result from a reduction in the number of firms, and some from changes in the number of workers employed by each firm. The former cases occur when the firms affected by minimum wage legislation compete in the product market with other firms that somehow are unaffected or manage to evade the law. Assume, for example, that other firms pay wages higher than w_m for superior-quality labor. The minimum wage raises wages in the lower-wage market without causing any improvement in the quality of its labor. Thus, if the low-wage-paying firms had been successfully competing with the high-wage-paying firms before the minimum wage law, they would now be at a competitive disadvantage and might have to move out of the local labor market or go out of business altogether.

ENFORCEMENT OF THE LAW

The effects of a minimum wage law depend crucially upon whether it is enforced. If the law is not enforced, it may have no effect whatsoever. The analysis of minimum wages is identical with the analysis of other price controls. Although it is easier to see the effects of minimum wage legislation because the law will spell out specifically which kinds of labor are covered and what exemptions are allowed, it still does not always follow that the minimum wage is effective.

There are ways to get around minimum wage laws. In every instance where low-paid workers are receiving benefits in kind, such as below-cost lunches and free tickets to professional football games, there can be a reduction of such benefits. For example, if a minimum wage forces *money* wages to go up, the employer can raise the price of lunches or charge for the football tickets to make up the difference between the new minimum wage and the former lower money wage rate paid.

Furthermore, firms may require kickbacks from employees, establish company stores, or require workers to live in company-owned housing. The price for company-store products or company-owned housing may exceed the marginal cost to the firm. This is a way of paying a lower wage. Thus, if a minimum wage is established, the actual wage can still be kept below the legal minimum by use of such devices. Another method of avoiding the minimum wage laws is to hire relatives. In many cases, relatives of employers, particularly close relatives, are not covered under minimum wage laws and/or are not monitored closely by the Department of Labor. This particular way to avoid minimum wage laws may be a clue to understanding how small neighborhood grocery stores and restaurants can compete successfully with larger, presumably more efficient competing enterprises in their area. Dry-cleaning establishments owned by retired couples apparently are competing very effectively with dry-cleaning chains, presumably because of the former's ability to avoid minimum wage legislation, since the "workers" in the firm—the retired couple—are proprietors who don't have to "pay" themselves any particular wage rate.

We also must be careful to distinguish between the short run and the long run. It is a general proposition that short-run curves tend to be less elastic than long-run curves. Hence, we would expect that the minimum wage will have a much smaller effect in the short run than in the long run. What we would like to know (in order to assess its full impact on employment) is what happens in the long run.

THE HOMOGENEITY ASSUMPTION

All the analysis so far has hinged on the common assumption that labor is homogeneous and that the minimum wage law applies to all labor. We know that this is not an accurate description of reality. There are many kinds of labor, and minimum wage laws typically make explicit statements about which groups are to be affected and by how much. Therefore, we should not look at total employment but at employment of those groups affected.

This type of analysis, by the way, is consistent with the law's motivation. It is aimed at improving the living standards of lower-paid, lower-skilled workers. However, minimum wage laws appear to hurt exactly those groups they are intended to help. Minimum wage laws narrow the range of employment opportunities available to those at the lower end of the wage spectrum. This seems to be especially true for urban black teenagers. What happens is that there is substitution which works against the groups that are being "protected." Employers raise their skill standards[10] and become more capital-intensive wherever possible. Moreover, minimum wages may prevent some employers from offering ap-

prenticeships and on-the-job training to low-skilled workers at relatively low money wages.

MONOPSONY: A JUSTIFICATION FOR THE MINIMUM WAGE LAW?

One justification for a minimum wage rate has been the alleged existence of employer monopsony power. Look at Figure 15-17. Here we show the monopsony pricing and employment of labor. The profit-maximizing monopsonist that sells its output in a perfectly competitive market will set the rate of employment at the intersection of MFC and VMP, or at point A. The quantity of the input employed is Q_1. The wage rate that must be paid to get that quantity of labor is w_1, which is determined by the intersection of the line drawn from A to Q_1 with the supply curve, intersecting at point B.

Some economists have argued that a minimum wage can reduce this monopsonistic exploitation. If the minimum wage is set at w_m, the supply curve facing the monopsonist be-

---

[10]Workers may even overuse society's training resources by obtaining education, etc., in order to qualify for higher-paying jobs.

FIGURE 15-17
The minimum wage and monopsony
Assume that the monopsonist faces labor supply curve SS (=AFC) and marginal factor cost curve MFC. Now, MFC = VMP at the quantity of labor demanded Q_1 and the wage rate paid will be w_1. Assume a minimum wage is established at w_m. The monopsonist can hire up to Q_m of labor at that wage rate. Thus with the minimum wage, its supply curve of labor is the horizontal line at w_m to point E on the old supply schedule. (Then the old supply curve becomes relevant.) The horizontal line which is heavily shaded is also equal to marginal factor cost. After the quantity of labor Q_m is hired, however, the monopsonist must pay a higher wage and marginal factor cost than coincides with the original marginal factor cost curve. The profit-maximizing monopsonist faced with this minimum wage will hire where marginal factor cost equals value of marginal product. This is at point E. This monopsonist will increase employment to Q_m and pay a higher wage rate w_m.

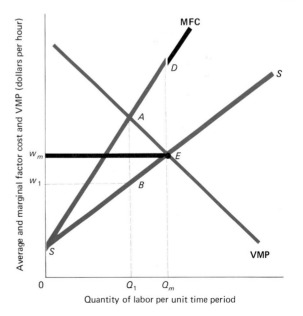

comes a horizontal line at the minimum wage rate, w_m, out to the old supply schedule, or point E. Then the supply curve becomes coincident with the old SS. In other words, there is a kink in it at quantity of labor Q_m.

The new marginal factor cost curve facing the monopsonist becomes a horizontal line between the vertical axis and point E. There is a discontinuous part at Q_m between E and D. Beyond Q_m the marginal factor cost curve coincides with the old marginal factor cost curve. The profit-maximizing monopsonist will employ the input where marginal factor cost equals value of marginal product. This occurs at point E, at the start of the discontinuous part of the MFC curve, if the minimum wage is w_m. The profit-maximizing rate of employ-ment will be Q_m, and this will be at wage rate w_m, which is the same as the wage rate in a perfectly competitive labor market.[11]

According to some critics of the minimum wage law, monopsony is the sole intellectual argument for minimum wages, and it is only in the discussion of minimum wages that the monopsony argument even comes up. Moreover, there is no empirical evidence that is widely accepted as support of this contention.

[11]This model is strictly correct only for the nondiscriminating monopsonist. The minimum wage would have no effect if it were set below w_1, and it would have its maximum employment effect if it were set at the intersection of SS and VMP, or at E.

The demand for baseball players: A bilateral monopoly situation

Collusive agreements among potential monopolists are often difficult to enforce. However, for many years the professional sports leagues in the United States had the sanction of Congress and the Supreme Court to monopolize professional sports. One result of monopolization shows up in the factor markets, most notably in the salaries paid to players. In the past decade, as the effects of the reserve clause in baseball and some other impediments to competition for labor inputs have been eroded, a great increase in player salaries has been witnessed. In the case of baseball, this increase was predicted by the use of the economic analysis we have developed in this chapter.

Specifically, in Table 15-5 we see the empirical evidence presented by economist George Scully to measure the difference between marginal revenue product and the wage rate (estimated salary). He tried to take player quality into account by netting out the expenses relating to player development. He came up with a "net" MRP for players of three different qualities: mediocre, average, and star. Because team owners often expend $500,000 developing every player signed and because team owners cannot predict accurately which players will develop into stars, sometimes net MRP (ex post facto) is negative. If the baseball players' market is purely competitive, the annual salary should roughly equal net MRP. In a monopsony situation, however, annual salary, on average, would be less than net MRP. The latter is exactly what Table 15-5 shows.

SALARY DETERMINATION: MONOPOLY AND BILATERAL MONOPOLY

We first assume that the players are unorganized and do not bargain collectively. The team owners, however, have formed a monopsony and agree that no team will attempt to bid away any other team's players. They

TABLE 15-5
*Monopsony exploitation in
professional baseball*

Source: G. W. Scully, "Pay and
Performance in Major League Baseball,"
American Economic Review, vol. LXIV,
no. 6, December 1974, p. 928.

Pitching ability (ratio of strikeouts to walks)	Pitchers' net MRP ($/playing season)	Estimated salary ($/playing season)
1.50	−20,800	9,000
2.30	169,200	36,900
3.09	405,300	66,800

Slugging average (total bases per 1,000 at-bats)	Hitters' net MRP ($/playing season)	Estimated salary ($/playing season)
255	−39,100	9,700
350	137,800	32,700
427	296,500	42,200
525	383,700	68,000

further agree not to raise wages. This is the simplest model that can be applied to the baseball situation.

The marginal revenue product curve of the baseball team owners, taken as a group, is represented by MRP in Figure 15-18. The marginal factor cost curve facing the team owners, taken as a whole, is MFC. The intersection of MRP and MFC is at A. The quantity demanded of baseball players is Q_m. The wage rate presented to baseball players is w_m. The amount of monopsonistic exploitation is the distance between A and C. The amount of monopolistic exploitation is the distance between A and B. Total exploitation is the vertical distance between B and C.

Now, what happens when the baseball players band together and form a monopoly in the sale of their services? This is the situation called **bilateral monopoly;** in this case, it's the factor market in which there is a single buyer and a single seller. We show it in Figure 15-19. The marginal revenue product curve of the baseball team owners, taken as a whole, is represented by MRP. We draw a curve that is *marginal* to MRP and label it MR. MR is, in effect, a marginal revenue curve (for the monopoly seller of baseball players' services), when we consider that MRP is the demand

curve for baseball players' services by monopoly team owners. Thus, MR is no different from any other marginal revenue curve in a monopoly situation. The union of baseball players has a supply curve of SS. The curve marginal to that SS curve is called marginal factor cost curve, or MFC. The baseball team owners would like to set a wage rate of w_m, because this is where the team owners could obtain the profit-maximizing number of players, and it is determined by the intersection at point A of the marginal factor cost curve (MFC) and the marginal revenue product curve (MRP). However, the union, acting as the sole bargaining agent for all the employees, would, if it were maximizing the equivalent of monopoly profits, want to set a wage rate of w_u. We determine the maximizing wage rate w_u by considering that the union is acting as a monopolist. Every monopolist will set output where MR = MC. What is marginal revenue in this case? It is the curve labeled MR, which is marginal to the demand curve for baseball players (MRP) by monopoly team owners. What is marginal cost? It is given by the supply curve of baseball players, or SS. MR and SS intersect at point B. That amount of baseball players' services can be sold to the team owners at a price of w_u given by the team owners'

FIGURE 15-18
Monopsony and the demand for baseball
players
The baseball teams taken as a whole have an
effective monopoly in the product market.
Accordingly, they look to their MRP. They are
also a monopsonist in the factor market. They
hire workers to the point where MFC = MRP,
which is at point A. They hire Q_m baseball
players and pay a wage rate of w_m. The
amount of monopolistic exploitation is the
vertical distance between B and A; the amount
of monopsonistic exploitation is the vertical
distance between A and C.

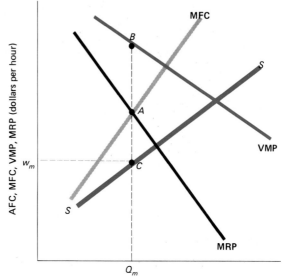

FIGURE 15-19
The players' union versus the team owners:
bilateral monopoly in the factor market
Baseball team owners would like to hire a
quantity of players where MFC = MRP; this
occurs at point A. They would, therefore, want
to set wage rate w_m. However, if the baseball
players form a union, they want to sell the
quantity of their labor where MR = MC(SS).
Marginal revenue is given by the curve that is
marginal to the MRP curve. This curve is
labeled MR. The intersection, then, of marginal
revenue and marginal cost, of SS, is at point B.
Because the supply curve SS represents the
summation of the individual marginal cost
curves of the individual players, the players'
union would like to set a wage rate of w_u. Joint
wealth maximization would dictate that the
team owners and team players' union get
together to offer quantity Q^*.

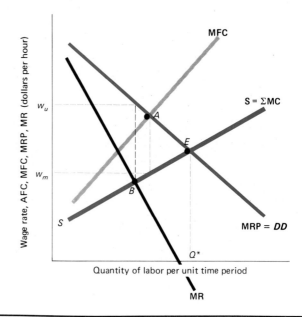

demand curve MRP. All we can say is that, in a situation of bilateral monopoly, the agreed-upon wage rate is indeterminate, but it will be in between w_m and w_u. (The quantity of the players employed will also be indeterminate.) If we were to assume that the union is pro-prietary—*privately* owned for the purpose of making a profit—we would state that the union would attempt to attain w_u because that is the wage rate which maximizes the difference be-tween total wages that are paid to employed baseball players and the minimum amount of wages required to bring this quantity of labor into the baseball playing market.

JOINT WEALTH MAXIMIZATION

Actually, there is a determinate level of em-ployment at which both the players and the team owners maximize their joint wealth. If we assume that transactions costs are zero, the two groups would agree to employ the number of players at which the supply curve intersects the marginal revenue product at point E. At this point the two groups are not attempting to exploit one another; rather, they are conspiring to jointly exploit the specta-tors. There is a problem at point E, however. The problem is how wealth should be split between the group of players and the group of team owners.

This analysis indicates that the reason the baseball team owners complain about play-ers' salaries being "too high" is because there is a transfer of wealth from owners to players. From the standpoint of baseball observers, there would seem to be no reason to think it more "fair" that the owners get the funds in question rather than the players. Look back at the MRP estimates in Table 15-5. Those numbers were based on data from the late 1960s. If we assume that wages have kept pace with consumer prices, the player salaries would be about three times the MRP estimate today. Indeed we see most "star" players earning over a million dollars, so Scully's es-timates appear to have been reasonably ac-curate. In fact, he estimated that during the late 1960s Hank Aaron was worth about $600,000 per year and Sandy Koufax was worth about $725,000 per year, which would translate to about $2 million per year today—a number consistent with the earnings of our current "superstars."

Can paraprofessionals replace professionals?

In Chapter 13 we discussed how monopoly power can be created by regulation or licens-ing requirements. The problem of how regu-lators should and do behave also arises in the context of markets for professional services. In this country and in many others, physi-cians, lawyers, dentists, veterinarians, brick-layers, and many other professional groups are self-regulated. That means licenses to practice the profession are issued under the control of a board typically composed of es-tablished members of the profession. This board, usually organized at the state or local level, often also approves education pro-grams for the training of new professionals. Practicing the profession without a license is prohibited by law, and in many cases an ap-plicant must have graduated from an ap-proved educational program as a step to ob-tain a license. There are good arguments for and against this type of system.

Proponents of the system point to the need to protect consumers of the services provided from unscrupulous or incompetent practitioners. Arguments against professional regulation point out that such groups will restrict the supply of new entrants into the profession on bases irrelevant to competence or integrity, thus elevating the wages of those currently practicing in the profession.

An interesting development in the major professions in recent years is the dramatic increase in "paraprofessionals." A paraprofessional is a practitioner with less comprehensive or extensive training than a full-fledged member of the profession. The paraprofessional is licensed to carry out limited, but frequently encountered tasks. Paraprofessionals are usually required to practice under the direction and supervision of a licensed professional, rather than deal directly with the public as a "solo" practitioner.

If a paraprofessional is a good substitute for the professional in certain frequently provided types of services, then the prohibition against paraprofessionals engaging in solo practice is one way in which professionals could restrict the extent to which paraprofessionals undercut their position in the market. However, if paraprofessionals have skills that can substitute for those skills required of a licensed professional, we would expect to see licensed professionals hire (lower-priced) paraprofessionals in lieu of (higher-priced) newly licensed professionals to do work within the professional firm.

THE ELASTICITY OF FACTOR SUBSTITUTION

Paralegals have increased substantially in numbers in recent years. One study looked to see if paralegals were being hired by senior law firm attorneys in lieu of licensed junior attorneys.[12] The study estimated the elasticity of substitution between paralegals, licensed junior attorneys, and legal secretaries (and other existing skilled law firm workers). It found a very low elasticity of substitution between paralegals and lawyers (.15), but a high elasticity of substitution between paralegals and legal secretaries (.92). Similarly, the study found the demand price elasticity of junior lawyers to be low ($-.14$), and that of paraprofessionals to be more elastic ($-.58$).

Paralegals provide competition for legal secretaries, but do not seem to be a direct market substitute for lawyers. Senior attorneys apparently have discovered that paralegals are not good substitutes for trained and licensed lawyers doing in-house legal work. Thus, it is not surprising that lawyers in general have not opposed the increase in the number of new paralegals in the last decade, but have consistently favored supervision over the services they provide.

[12]Robert M. Feinberg, "Paralegals and Substitution among Labor Inputs in the Law Firm," *The Journal of Industrial Economics*, vol. 33, September 1984, pp. 99–104.

SUMMARY

1   The firm's profit-maximizing combination of inputs will be such that

$$\frac{MPP_x}{P_x} = \frac{MPP_y}{P_y} = \cdots = \frac{MPP_n}{P_n} = \frac{1}{MC} = \frac{1}{MR} = \frac{1}{P}$$

or, inverting,

$$\frac{P_x}{MPP_x} = \frac{P_y}{MPP_y} = \cdots = \frac{P_n}{MPP_n} = MC = MR = P$$

for the competitive firm buying inputs in a competitive market.

2　The profit-maximizing competitive firm's decision rule for input utilization is to use each input up to the point where the price per unit equals the value of its marginal product.

3　The value of marginal product curve is derived by multiplying marginal physical product times the price of the product.

4　The optimum quantity of labor hired by the competitive firm will be determined from where the wage line, or supply curve of labor, intersects the VMP curve.

5　When capital and labor are complements, the demand curve for either will be less steeply sloping than the corresponding value of marginal product curve.

6　It can be proved that the factor demand curve will always be negatively sloped.

7　The total demand curve for an input is not the horizontal summation of the individual firms' demand curves because as every firm increases output, the output price must fall in order for the increased output to be sold. The market demand curve for an input is more inelastic than the individual firm's demand for that input.

8　The pure monopolist's demand curve for a single variable factor of production, all other factors held constant, is its marginal revenue product curve (if it purchases the input in a perfectly competitive market).

9　Marginal revenue product equals marginal physical product times marginal revenue.

10　For the monopolist purchasing inputs in a perfectly competitive market, the profit-maximizing combinations of inputs will be such that $P_i/MPP_i = MC = MR$ [for all i (inputs)], or marignal revenue product for each input will equal its unit price.

11　When there are several variable inputs, the monopolist's demand curve for an input is more elastic than the input's given marginal revenue product curve.

12　The equilibrium price and rate of utilization of an input are determined by the intersection of the industry supply curve and the industry demand curve for the input.

13　Factor demand elasticity depends on (a) technological feasibility of substitution, (b) price elasticity of demand of final output, (c) supply elasticity of other inputs, (d) percentage of **total** costs accounted for by that factor, and (e) the length of time allowed for adjustment.

14   The equilibrium input price and rate of employment for the monopolist is at the intersection of its marginal revenue product curve and the supply curve of the input.

15   The marginal factor cost curve is everywhere above an upward-sloping supply curve.

16   The monopsonist that sells its product competitively will hire inputs to the point where the value of marginal product of each input is equal to the marginal factor cost. If a monopsonist is also a monopolist, it will hire an input to the point where the marginal factor cost equals marginal revenue product. The factor price will then be obtained from the supply curve for that equilibrium labor quantity.

17   Exploitation can come about because of monopoly and/or monopsony. It occurs whenever an input is paid less than its VMP.

18   The price-discriminating monopsonist would pay different wages to different workers. It would hire an input to the point where the supply curve intersects the value of marginal product curve, paying only the last unit a wage equal to its VMP.

19   The monopsonist has no demand curve for an input, just as the monopolist has no supply curve for its output.

GLOSSARY

- **value of marginal product (VMP)** Marginal physical product of an input times the price per unit of output, or MPP·P. The market value of the marginal physical product of a factor of production.
- **complementarity** As applied to production inputs, we say that two factors are complementary if increased use of one raises the marginal physical product of the other.
- **elasticity of factor substitution** A measure of the relative responsiveness of the capital/labor ratio to a relative change in the ratio of factor prices:

$$\sigma = -\left[\frac{\Delta(K/L)}{K/L}\bigg/\frac{\Delta(r/w)}{r/w}\right]$$

- **marginal revenue product (MRP)** The change in total revenue that results from a unit change in a particular variable input ($\equiv$ MPP · MR).
- **derived demand** Demand for an input that is derived from the demand for final output produced from the input. The demand for production inputs is a derived demand.
- **monopsony** A single buyer.
- **oligopsony** A few or several buyers.
- **average factor cost curve (AFC)** Another name for the input supply curve; at any point on the supply curve, the price given is equal to the average (per unit) factor cost.

- **marginal factor cost curves (MFC)** A curve showing the increase in total factor cost due to a one-unit increase in use of that factor.
- **exploitation** Paying a resource unit less than its VMP in its *current* use.
- **monopolistic exploitation** Paying a resource its marginal revenue product instead of its value of marginal product ($\equiv$ VMP $-$ MRP).
- **monopsonistic exploitation** Exploitation due to monopsony power. It leads to a unit factor price that is less than its MRP ($\equiv$ MRP $-$ w).
- **bilateral monopoly** A situation in which a monopolist sells to a monopsonist.

QUESTIONS

(Answers to even-numbered questions are at back of text.)

1 Most of the discussion in this chapter deals with examples in which labor is the variable input in the short run. Can you imagine a firm whose short-run fixed costs are labor and whose variable costs are capital?

2 "Capital and labor compete with one another. This point was not lost on the workers of Flanders who sabotaged the machines of the early industrial era with their wooden shoes (*sabots*, thus the origin of the word 'sabotage'); they knew well what the situation was." Comment critically.

3 What factors determine the amount of labor a perfectly competitive firm will hire in the short run if labor is the sole variable input?

4 Does a perfectly competitive firm have to worry about the impact of its own demand for labor on the going wage rate?

5 If the capital input of a firm is not fixed, and it generally is not, why can't a firm simply "ride" its VMP curve up and down as the relative price of labor changes?

6 Explain the "substitution effect" of a fall in the relative price of labor.

7 Explain the "output effect" of a fall in the price of labor.

8 Explain the "profit-maximizing effect" of a fall in the price of labor.

9 Give the formula for the elasticity of substitution of capital for labor, and explain what it measures.

10 The price elasticity of demand for the final output product directly affects the elasticity of demand for the input factor. Why?

11 A chicken sexer is someone who is skilled at distinguishing male and female chicks. Often earning upward of $100 per day, a good chicken sexer can sex several thousand chicks in a single shift with a high degree of accuracy. Which determinant of factor demand elasticity do you think would bear most heavily on the demand for sexers' services? Why?

12 Does the reserve labor hypothesis apply to a barbershop owner's demand for labor? Why or why not?

13 Why is it inaccurate to sum horizontally the labor demand curves of individual firms to arrive at the total industry demand for labor?

14 "I can see why the market supply curve of labor would be upward-sloping in a free society where people aren't required to work. The supply of land, however, must be straight up and down (perfectly inelastic with respect to its price). After all, there's only so much land." Comment critically.

15 When there is only one variable input, how does a monopoly seller's demand for that input differ from that of a perfectly competitive seller?

16 Would the Wham-O Manufacturing Company's demand for Frisbee production workers be a good example of a monopoly seller hiring in a perfectly competitive labor market? How would you decide?

17 Why is it that if an input is hired only by monopolists, the horizontal summation of the individual firms' input demand curves establishes the market demand curve, while in a perfectly competitive market this technique would overstate the demand for the factor?

18 "Just because sellers may be monopolists in the product market doesn't mean they are able to exploit nonunionized labor in a competitive labor market." Is this statement true or false, and why?

19 Under what circumstances can a firm selling in a perfectly competitive product market exploit workers?

20 Give examples of perfectly competitive sellers having monopsony power in the input market.

21 "Nonunion company towns epitomize the evils of economic power. If the worker doesn't like the wages offered, what can he or she do? In fact, the worker will surely be sacked if there are complaints or attempts to organize a union." Comment critically.

22 "People with highly specialized skills who are employable only by a handful of firms are often exploited. What few employers there are may agree, tacitly or otherwise, to keep those persons' wage rates down." Comment.

23 Can you give some examples of firms that are monopolists in their product market and also monopsonists in the input market?

24 Why will a monopsony hirer of labor, who is able to price (wage)-discriminate "perfectly," hire the same amount of labor as a price (wage)-taking hirer of labor, *ceteris paribus*?

25 With a perfectly wage-discriminating monopsonist, is there any exploitation?

26 Can economic theory explain the traditional reluctance of many individuals to discuss their earnings?

SELECTED REFERENCES

Cartter, Allan M., *Theory of Wages and Employment* (Homewood, Ill.: Irwin, 1959), pp. 11–133.

Hicks, John R., *Value and Capital,* 2d ed. (Oxford: Clarendon, 1946), pp. 78–111.

Russell, R.R., "On the Demand Curve for a Factor of Production," *American Economic Review,* vol. 4, September 1964, pp. 726–733.

Scitovsky, Tibor, *Welfare and Competition,* rev. ed. (Homewood, Ill.: Irwin, 1971), chap. 7.

Fellner, William, *Modern Economic Analysis* (New York: McGraw-Hill, 1960), chap. 19.

Rees, Albert, *The Economics of Work and Pay* (New York: Harper & Row, 1973), pp. 75–80.

Robinson, Joan, *The Economics of Imperfect Competition* (London: Macmillan, 1933), pp. 218–228 and 281–304.

Wages, rents, and income differences

*T*he difference between the annual income of a dishwasher in a restaurant and that of the president of General Motors is immense. The difference between average wages in one industry and another can be significant. Individuals who seemingly have the same qualifications and do the same job often appear to earn different money incomes. In short, there are differences in both wage rates and money incomes. In this chapter we examine theories of wage determination and reasons why income differences arise.

In examining why there are income differences, you must keep in mind that income goes to the owners of resources. The price fetched by a resource is determined by the interaction of the demand and supply for that resource. Hence, the owner of a labor resource is paid an income because he or she possesses intelligence, attractiveness, ability to reason, business acumen, muscle power, and all the other things that constitute a labor resource. Similarly, the owner of a parcel of land receives the income generated by that land.

MARGINAL PRODUCTIVITY THEORY

The theory of pricing and employment of inputs in Chapter 15 has generally been called the **marginal productivity theory** of the demand for factors of production.

The marginal productivity theory has often been termed a theory of wages. However, marginal productivity concerns itself only with the *demand side* of the market for labor. We pointed out, for example, that a competitive firm buying labor in a perfectly competitive market will employ workers up to the point where the wage rate equals VMP. In essence, then, the VMP curve is the individual firm's demand curve for labor. Although marginal productivity is important when discussing employment and pricing of the labor input, we rarely speak of a demand theory of prices for other commodities. Rather, we talk in terms of demand and supply interacting to determine the relative price of the product in question. The same is true for labor. The demand side of the picture cannot be looked at in isolation.

Wage rates and employment are jointly determined by the interaction of supply and demand. To speak of the marginal productivity theory of wages is to speak of a demand theory of prices; and no one speaks of a demand theory of prices because price is determined by *both* demand and supply.

On being paid one's VMP

In the case of a firm selling its output in a perfectly competitive market and hiring inputs in a perfectly competitive market, marginal productivity theory indicates that workers are hired to the point where the *wage rate equals the value of their marginal product.* But if workers are paid just what they are worth, or the value of their marginal product, how do entrepreneurs cover the costs of the other factors as well as obtain any profits? To find the answer, we look at the MPP component of VMP. The marginal *physical* product of labor is *not* the amount of output produced by an additional unit of labor. Rather, MPP is the increase in total output when one more unit of labor is used in a productive process. In other words, we cannot technically assign the quantity called marginal physical product to the *last* worker hired.

Consider Figure 16-1. Assume that the going market wage rate is w_1. The perfect competitor hiring workers in a perfectly competitive market will hire Q_1 of labor. Each worker will be paid w_1. However, the amount of revenue obtained by the employer is the price of the product times the *average* physical product of each worker, or $P \cdot$ APP. This is given in Figure 16-1 by the curve labeled "Value of APP." With Q_1 workers, the vertical distance between Q_1 and B (or between the origin and R_1) represents the average revenue received per worker from selling the product of all the workers using other factors of production. On the vertical axis this is labeled R_1. We see that for each worker the employer pays a wage rate of w_1 but obtains a revenue of R_1. Consequently, the area of the rectangle $w_1 R_1 BA$ represents the amount of revenues available to pay the other factors of production.

If the workers are paid their VMP, by definition, they are each being paid an amount equal to the decrease in total revenues the firm would experience if one worker quit. The workers are not paid the value of what they produce in combination with other factors. Therefore, they are not paid R_1, for if that were so, there would be nothing left over to remunerate any other factors.

FIGURE 16-1
The distinction between the value of marginal product and the value of average product
When the quantity of labor employed per unit time period is Q_1, the worker is paid a wage rate w_1, or the value of marginal product (equal to the price of the output times marginal physical product). The wage rate is equivalent to the reduction in total revenues that the firm would suffer if one worker quit, other inputs remaining constant. However, the "contribution" of any worker (in conjunction with the nonlabor inputs) is equivalent to that worker's average physical product times the price of the output; APP $\cdot$ P = R_1. Thus, the firm pays a wage rate equal to the value of marginal product. Its total wage bill is therefore equal to the rectangle $0w_1AQ_1$. That leaves it with a rectangle, w_1R_1BA, available to pay the other factors of production, in particular, capital. That shaded rectangle, therefore, is the return to nonlabor factors.

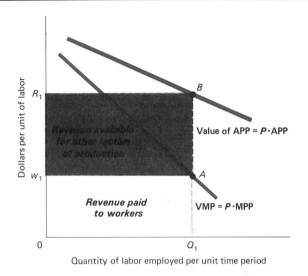

Value of APP = $P \cdot$ APP

Revenue available for other factors of production

Revenue paid to workers

VMP = $P \cdot$ MPP

Dollars per unit of labor

R_1

w_1

B

A

0 Q_1

Quantity of labor employed per unit time period

THE PROCESS OF WAGE EQUALIZATION

Where all industries are identical, we would expect that wage rates of a given quality of labor would be the same in all industries. This is the process that we depict in Figure 16-2.

Assume that there are only two industries and that all resources are fully employed. We start out in equilibrium with a wage rate w_e, which is the same in industry I and in industry II. It is determined by the intersection of the respective demand and supply curves in those two industries: D_ID_I and S_IS_I in industry I and $D_{II}D_{II}$ and $S_{II}S_{II}$ in industry II. D_ID_I depends on wages in industry II; $D_{II}D_{II}$ depends on wages in industry I. (Why?)

Assume now that there is a shift in tastes and that the demand for the product produced in industry I increases. The demand for the output of industry II therefore decreases. The demand curve for labor is derived from the demand for the final product. The demand curve for labor in industry I, represented in panel (a), shifts out to $D_I'D_I'$. On the other hand, the demand curve for labor in industry II shifts inward to $D_{II}'D_{II}'$ in response to the declining demand for that product. The new short-run equilibrium wage rates are w_e' in industry I and w_e'' in industry II. The new intersections of supply and demand for labor are labeled E' in both panels (a) and (b).

Competition for labor

Given our assumptions, this is not a long-run equilibrium. The differential wage rate will attract workers from industry II into industry I. This will cause the supply curve of labor in industry I to shift outward to $S_I'S_I'$. Similarly, it

FIGURE 16-2
Wage adjustment

Assume the economy consists of two industries. The demand and supply curves of labor are given for industries I in panel (a) and for industry II in panel (b). The initial equilibrium wage rate is w_e in both industries I and II. It is determined by the intersection of supply and demand in each industry [found at point E in panels (a) and (b).] An increase in demand for industry I's output shifts the demand curve for workers rightward in that industry to $D'_I D'_I$. Initially the wage rate rises in industry I to w'_e (found at the intersection of the new demand curve with the old supply curve at point E'). The wage rate in industry II falls to w'_e because the demand curve for its output and therefore labor has shifted leftward to $D'_{II} D'_{II}$. Assuming homogeneity of the labor force and perfect mobility, the supply curve of labor will now shift so that the wage rate in industry I depicted in panel (a) will fall back down to w_e; the wage rate in industry II depicted in panel (b) will rise back up to w_e as the supply of labor falls in this industry. The new long-run equilibrium intersections are labeled E'' in both diagrams.

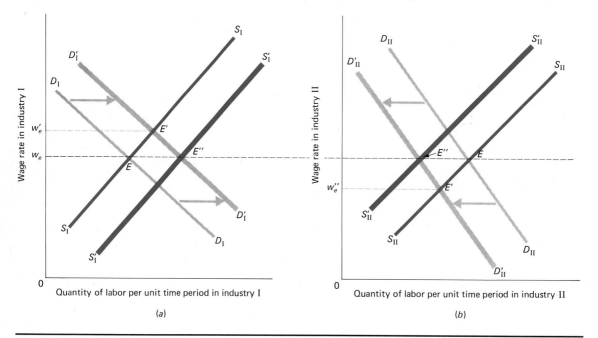

(a)   (b)

will decrease the supply curve of labor in industry II to $S'_{II} S'_{II}$. This process will continue until wages are equalized (assuming that labor is homogeneous between industries and perfectly mobile). The new intersections of the demand and supply curves will be at E'' in both panels (a) and (b), and the long-run equilibrium wage rate will again be w_e in both industries. The only difference is that $E - E''$ of labor has shifted from industry II to industry I. The long-run industry labor supply curves are seen to be horizontal lines at wage rate w_e.

This analysis assumes *mobility* of workers among industries and *knowledge* of the wage differentials. It also assumes that the industries are equally desirable from the point of view of the marginal workers and that all workers are of the same "quality" and have the same training. We will now see what happens when each of these assumptions is relaxed.

Equalizing wage differences

When we realize that different workers attain different levels of satisfaction (or dissatisfaction) from the same type of work, we open our analysis to the possibility of wage differences which reflect varying tastes for different jobs. This is sometimes called the *theory of equalizing wage differences*. Individuals are willing to make a trade-off between less desirable occupations and increased income. The supply and demand in different industries, therefore, determines relative wages and the relative numbers of employees in different occupations. This is also considered a part of the theory of job choice or labor supply.

Look at Figure 16-3. We assume that there are only two occupations. We plot the relative wage rate w_I/w_{II} in the two occupations on the vertical axis. The horizontal axis measures *relative* employment in the two occupations. It is labeled E_I/E_{II}.

The derived demand curve for labor is, as always, downward-sloping. As the relative wage rate in occupation I goes down, a larger quantity of that skill is demanded and a smaller quantity is demanded of the other skill, and vice versa.

The supply curve is upward-sloping. As the relative wage rate in occupation I increases, the number of individuals induced to leave occupation II to enter occupation I will increase. We assume in this analysis that all

---

FIGURE 16-3
Equalizing wage differences
The relative wage ratio is shown on the vertical axis; the relative employment ratio is plotted on the horizontal axis. The supply curve SS is upward-sloping, indicating that workers have different preferences for the two jobs in question. If they didn't, the supply curve SS would be a horizontal line. The steeper the supply curve, the more individuals dislike occupation I relative to occupation II. The equalizing wage difference will be $w_I w_{II} = 1.4$, for example. The relative employment ratio, $E_I E_{II}$, will be, say, 0.8.

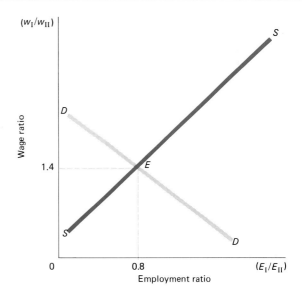

individuals can do *either* job equally well. The reason the supply curve slopes upward is that individuals have different preferences for the two jobs in question. If individuals were indifferent between these two jobs, the supply curve SS in Figure 16-3 would be a horizontal line. The steeper the supply curve, the more there are differences in worker preferences. In this situation, equilibrium occurs at the intersection of DD and SS, or point E. This gives a relative wage ratio of 1.4, for example, and a relative employment ratio of 0.8. That means that in equilibrium, the wage rate in occupation I will be 40 percent higher than in occupation II.

The theory tells us that higher relative wages must be offered to get individuals to enter less desirable occupations. We do, however, observe individuals making relatively low wages in what we might consider "less desirable" jobs. We have to take into account not only the tastes of the workers but also the *supply* of workers relative to the quantities that employers desire. Washing dishes in a restaurant may be undesirable, but there may be a sufficient number of individuals who do not have the skills for other occupations and are willing to wash dishes. This abundant supply of applicants for the job of dishwasher will keep the wage rate down.

Wage differences and geographical preferences

We can continue the analysis above by considering the geographical preferences of individuals. Real wage rates sometimes differ dramatically between less desirable and more desirable geographic locations. For example, secretarial wages in real terms in Honolulu may be quite a bit lower than in Chicago. Part of the difference can be explained by the differences in potential supplies of those persons seeking to work as secretaries in Hawaii and in Chicago.[1] The relatively larger potential supply of secretaries available in Hawaii is the result of its preferred climate. (One might say that the difference in real wages is the price that has to be paid for sunshine.) What we see is that the differences in real pecuniary incomes compensate for differences in the *nonpecuniary* aspects of employment. Figure 16-3 can be used for all such problems by redefining the term "job" to include all its nonpecuniary aspects.

QUALITATIVE DIFFERENCES IN FACTORS OF PRODUCTION

Until now we have assumed that the factors of production under consideration were homogeneous. Once we eliminate this assumption, we can account for some of the differences in wages we observe among individuals within the same occupation and among individuals working for the same

---

[1]We must, of course, normalize for population size. Also, geographical mobility is based on present value of wage differences over the life of a worker relative to the cost of migrating. See Lary Sjaastad, "The Cost and Returns of Human Migration," *Journal of Political Economy*, vol. LXX, no. 2, part 2, October 1962, pp. 80–93.

firm. One worker may not be the duplicate of another because their skill levels are different. Remember that the profit-maximizing firm will hire an input up to the point where the price per unit of the input equals its marginal physical product times output price if we are talking about a perfect competitor, or MPP times marginal revenue if we are talking about a monopolist. If we have two groups of workers doing the same job but with unequal productivities, we will find that the profit-maximizing firm selling in a competitive market will hire each type of worker up to the point where

$$\text{MPP}_I \cdot P = w_I \tag{16-1}$$

$$\text{MPP}_{II} \cdot P = w_{II} \tag{16-2}$$

The two distinct marginal physical products are represented by the subscripts I and II, and the corresponding unequal wage rates are represented by the same subscripts. The differential in wages between the more skilled and the less skilled will equal the differential in their respective marginal physical products. We can see this by multiplying Eq.(16-1) by $1/(P \cdot w_I)$ and then multiplying Eq.(16-2) by $1/(P \cdot w_{II})$. Then it is seen that these adjustments in Eqs.(16-1) and (16-2) are both equal to $1/P$. We can set them equal to each other, which yields

$$\frac{\text{MPP}_I}{w_I} = \frac{\text{MPP}_{II}}{w_{II}} \tag{16-3}$$

$$\frac{w_I}{w_{II}} = \frac{\text{MPP}_I}{\text{MPP}_{II}}$$

Long and short run

Occupational wage differentials can be expected to be greater in the short run than in the long run. The short-run supply curve of labor for a particular kind of skill is going to be relatively inelastic compared with the equivalent long-run curve. In the immediate run it would be vertical, the number of people in the occupation being independent of the wage rate. However, given adequate time for training and/or the establishment of new training facilities, the number of qualified individuals in an occupation can and will increase if wage differentials are sufficient to justify the costs of training and/or retraining. These considerations determine just how long the long run is in a particular labor market. Thus in the long run, the supply curve of labor for an occupation will be elastic, unless of course there are significant barriers to entry (e.g., professional licensing).

Uncertainty

The greater the amount of uncertainty about the stability of demand in an occupation, the greater will have to be the average wage rate for such an occupation compared with all other occupations that are similar but have less uncertainty. Such uncertainty about demand leads to uncertainty about the dispersion of income over a lifetime in a given occupation. We expect, then, that two occupations with equal *average* incomes but unequal disper-

TABLE 16-1
Compensating wage differentials for differential risk of loss of life, selected occupations, 1967

Source: Richard Thaler and Sherwin Rosen, "The Value of Saving a Life: Evidence from the Labor Market," in N. Terleckyj (ed.), Household Production and Consumption (New York: National Bureau of Economic Research, 1975).

Occupation	Incremental annual deaths per 100,000 workers	Estimated addition to annual salary (in dollars)
Boilermakers	230	405
Fire fighters	44	77
Mine operatives	176	310
Police and detectives	78	137
Teamsters	114	201

sions will have different wage rates attached to them. The one with more dispersion of income will have a higher wage rate. This, of course, assumes that marginal individuals are averse to risk taking, i.e., that they prefer certainty.

Compensating wage differentials

One important determinant in some jobs is the degree of risk involved. Two economists have estimated the wage differences that can be attributed to the risk of loss of life. In Table 16-1 we show the results presented by Richard Thaler and Sherwin Rosen. Jobs with a higher risk of loss of life have higher annual wages, other things held constant. Thaler and Rosen estimated that, in 1967, individuals placed an implicit value of around $175,000 on their own lives (over $500,000 in today's dollars). Their conclusion, to be sure, is controversial. Many economists believe this figure to be too low, and most would agree that it would increase as average real income in the society increases. That is, safety is a normal and, perhaps, a superior good.

Another economist, R. E. B. Lucas, has attempted to assess compensating differentials for so-called unpleasant work. His evidence, presented in brief in Table 16-2, does seem to show that individuals obtain higher wages for repetitive jobs or jobs that are done in noisy, cold, or hot environments.

TABLE 16-2
Compensating wage differentials: "unpleasant" working conditions

Source: R. E. B. Lucas, "Hedonic Wage Equations and Psychic Wages in the Returns to Schooling," American Economic Review, vol. 67, no. 4, September 1977, table 1, p. 554.

	Percent addition to wage provided by job attribute			
	Black females	Black males	White females	White males
Jobs in a poor work environment	19.5	−7.7	3.3	6.8
Repetitive jobs	25.6	7.7	22.3	10.3

RENTS, "SUPERIOR" FACTORS, AND THE EQUALIZATION OF COSTS

Many factors of production are more or less productive as a result of the investment which has been made in their development. To a certain extent, one worker is "better" than another worker in the same trade or profession because the first worker has had better training, is more experienced, or has invested more time and energy in mastering the skills and knowledge that are important in the field. We refer to improvements in the productivity or skills of a worker due to this kind of investment as a difference in *human capital formation.*

Not all differences in productivity between different units of a factor are *exclusively* attributable to differences in the amount of human capital, however. Longer legs will, *ceteris paribus*, make one a faster runner. Certain configurations of the vocal cords, the tongue, and the mouth are better adapted to forming certain sounds and, hence, can make one a better singer. The existence of "natural" differences in the productivity of factors is even more marked in the case of nonhuman factors. Some mines contain veins of ore which are richer or more pure. Certain forest lands contain more trees of harvestable age and more hardwoods. David Ricardo and Henri von Thunen, famous nineteenth-century economists, pointed out that certain parcels of land are worth more simply because of their location. That is, certain parcels are nearer to a center of economic activity and thus have a higher "site value" than more distant parcels.

Economic rents

How do these observations fit into our theories of factor pricing and of the costs of firms? A factor that is *naturally* more productive than other factors of the same type will receive a "bonus" payment over and above its normal wage. Under conditions of competition for the factor, this bonus payment will be exactly equal to the *added* value produced by using this factor, as compared to the value produced by the use of the least productive unit of a factor of the same type. This bonus is called a rental payment or **Ricardian (economic) rent** for the *superior natural productivity* of the factor. As we can see in Figure 16-4, a rental return is attached to some aspect of the factor that is neither created by investment nor can be destroyed by mere neglect. This rent is purely *demand determined*. That is, it will be higher or lower as the demand for the service being produced rises or falls. The amount supplied *due to the rental aspect of the factor* would be the same at a zero rate of return as it is at a very high rate of return.

Let us briefly consider how rental payments are determined. Suppose that Accountant A is the least skillful accountant employed. Accountant A creates a value per period of $800. If we can assume that this is the marginal accountant working the marginal period of time then the equilibrium competitive wage for accountants should be $800 per period. Can any other

FIGURE 16-4
Pure economic (Ricardian) rent
If indeed the supply curve of a factor of production were completely price-inelastic in the long run, it would be depicted by SS. At the quantity in existence, Q_1, any and all revenues are pure rent. If demand is DD, the price will be P_1; if demand is $D'D'$, price will rise to P_2. Economic rent would be $P_1 \cdot Q_1$ and $P_2 \cdot Q_1$, respectively.

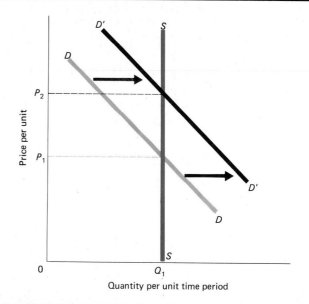

accountant make more than $800 if there is free competition on both sides of the accounting market? Yes; in fact, by our assumption that Accountant A is the least skillful worker in his market, all other accountants will make more than $800. In some cases, the more skillful accountants will simply be reaping profits on their investment in human capital. In a few such cases, however, there will be individuals who are innately suited to accounting by disposition and talent. These individuals will be making a rent on their natural traits.

This rental return will be higher than the market wage of $800 by whatever "surplus" amount they produce for their employer. If they are currently receiving less than this, it will pay some other employer to make them an offer at a higher rate. That process will be repeated, presuming perfect competition and costless information, until the entire surplus is paid to the worker as an "above market" bonus. This same story could, of course, be repeated for the mining example mentioned above. The richer any mine is, compared to the marginal mine still in operation, the greater will be its market value. The only difference between the case of the accountant and the case of the mine is that the surplus amounts yielded by the mine until it is exhausted can be "capitalized" into a higher sales price for the mine. The same is not true of the accountant, who cannot be bound to a nonvoidable lifetime service contract.

Effect of rents on costs

What does all of this mean for the costs of various firms, some of which own or hire more "superior" factors and some of which own or hire less superior factors? It means, surprisingly, that all firms in the same industry will have identical costs, if they purchase all their inputs in competitive input markets. The rationale for this conclusion is straightforward. If any firm hires a superior factor of production it must pay that factor the competitive market wage plus a rental bonus exactly equal to the factor's superior value productivity. Although superior factors will produce more, they do so at a cost which wipes out any differential gain from their employment. A similar logic applies to firms which own but have not "purchased" superior factors (e.g., a mining firm that discovered and staked out a particularly rich "strike"). The value of the factor or asset on the market exactly reflects its normal rate of return over its expected lifetime plus a capitalized rental payment for its superior productivity. The firm, by deciding to keep and use this factor rather than sell it, bears an implicit cost of its retention equal to its market price. Thus firms which own such superior productivity factors again experience offsetting costs, but in an implicit rather than explicit form.

Our discussion so far has been connected with traits of a factor which are neither created nor destroyed and which, therefore, cannot be increased or decreased over time. This is the case with a *pure economic rent*. Pure economic rents are long-run phenomena. We now turn to a related short-run phenomenon known as quasi-rent.

Quasi-rents

Any fixed factor earns an economic rent in the short run. This is because of the perfectly inelastic supply of such factors in the short run. We call the return to factors that are fixed only in the short-run **quasi-rent**. Thus we can also define quasi-rent as the difference between total revenues and total variable costs. Quasi-rents are those revenues, if any, available for fixed factors and/or economic profits. The reason we call this a quasi-rent rather than an economic rent is that the fixed factors are fixed only in the short run and not in the long run. The quasi-rent must be at least equal to the interest plus depreciation on a durable asset for that durable asset to be maintained. In other words, quasi-rents are payments to durable factors of production which do not influence the *current* quantity supplied of those factors of production but do influence the *future* quantity supplied.

In a competitive capital market, we know that rates of return (corrected for risk) tend toward equality on the margin. Thus if the investment in a particular capital asset yields a long-run net rate of return that is below the yield on other investments, in the future there will be less investment in the relatively less profitable asset. The short-run gross return to a specialized capital good is indeed a quasi-rent, but if that gross return does not equal the long-run net return to all capital goods, the capital good in question will be allowed to depreciate and will eventually disappear.

We can illustrate quasi-rents by using the traditional cost curves of the firm. In Figure 16-5, we examine a firm in a perfectly competitive market receiving zero economic profits. The short-run average total cost curve is just tangent to the price line *dd*, which is the demand curve faced by a perfect competitor. The tangency occurs at the minimum average total cost and is where marginal cost intersects average total costs. The profit-maxi-

FIGURE 16-5
Measuring quasi-rents
If output for the firm is q_1, the difference between average variable costs and price will be the quasi-rent per unit of output, since the firm will continue to produce in the short run as long as price exceeds minimum average variable costs. Its quasi-rents are equal to the rectangle C_1P_cEA.

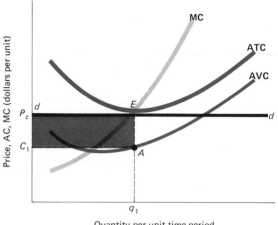

mizing rate of output is q_1, but the firm's economic profits are zero. However, the return to the fixed factors of production is the rectangle C_1P_cEA and is equal to $AFC \cdot q_1$ = total fixed costs. This rectangle is also the quasi-rent, for it is payment to fixed factors of production which, by definition, have no alternative cost in the short run. Such factors represent a sunk cost. If the firm obtained a price for its product that yielded just enough to cover average *variable* cost, the firm in the short run would remain in operation. However, the rate of return to investment in that firm would be *negative*. In the long run, the firm would go out of business. Hence, any revenues over and above average variable cost are considered quasi-rents because those revenues do not affect the current quantity of the fixed resources supplied.

When quasi-rents are not enough

In some cases, quasi-rents fail to be sufficient to induce reinvestment in the capital asset in question. How can this arise? Simply because of mistaken expectations on the part of those who made the original investment. The investors failed to predict accurately the future course of the demand for and/or supply of the services of the durable capital good when it was first purchased and installed. This might occur, for example, if an investment were made in a machine that became inefficient as the result of the subsequent innovation of a superior machine. Alternatively, the demand for the final output that the specialized machine helped produce may have declined because of a change in tastes or because of a fall in the price of substitute goods.

Prediction errors can rarely be eliminated. Moreover, they are more serious the more specialized the investment. A highly specialized machine that can be used only to make one specific product is much more at the mercy of the shifts in the supply of and the demand for the services of the machine that can be transferred only imperfectly to some alternative use. We say, then, that the demand for a machine is more stable the less specialized the machine. And we might predict that we would find relatively more specialized machines in those industries with relatively more stable demand for their products.

THE DISTRIBUTION OF INCOME

Much of the explanation of the distribution of money income can be found in the determinants of wage differentials. However, there are other considerations that need to be examined. They are, in a sense, refinements on what we have just discussed. Before we go into them, let us take a look at the actual distribution of income in the United States.

The bottom row of Table 16-3 shows why it is difficult to draw many conclusions from a study of income in current income dollars over time. The effects of inflation (and of economic growth to a much lesser extent) have made current income dollar numbers nearly meaningless over time. Contrast the current-dollar income figures with the constant-dollar income figures and note especially what happened from 1970 to 1982.

Income class

We learn more by examining the distribution of constant-dollar income by income class. As we see in Table 16-3, since 1960 there has been a gradual upward movement in income classes, although the 1982 figures may represent a slip in the other direction. Table 16-4 tells a similar story with a different measure—that of percentage income shares by quintiles. That is, what share of income went to the poorest fifth of the population and what share went to the wealthiest fifth. In the 35 years covered by this table we see that the top fifth of the population has "lost" some of its income share to less wealthy families.

TABLE 16-3
Percent distribution of families by constant-dollars income level and median incomes in constant and current dollars

Source: U.S. Bureau of the Census, Current Population Reports, various issues; totals may not equal 100 because of rounding.

Income class	1982	1975	1970	1960
Under $10,000	16.6	14.5	14.0	22.5
$10,000–$19,999	24.5	24.0	27.3	37.8
$20,000–$34,999	31.7	39.0	37.3	⎱39.7⎰
Over $35,000	26.9	22.4	21.4	
Median income (constant 1982 dollars)	$23,433	$24,604	$24,528	$18,317
Median income (current dollars)	$23,433	$13,719	$ 9,867	$ 5,620

TABLE 16-4
Percentage share of income for families before direct taxes

Source: U.S. Bureau of the Census, Current Population Reports, various issues; totals may not equal 100 because of rounding.

Income group	1982	1973	1960	1947
Lowest fifth	5.9	5.5	4.8	5.1
Second fifth	13.0	11.9	12.2	11.8
Third fifth	18.1	17.5	17.8	16.7
Fourth fifth	24.0	24.0	24.0	23.2
Highest fifth	39.0	41.1	41.3	43.3

All income classes increase their real incomes if the increases in economic growth are evenly distributed across all income groups. Increases in real income may not alter the *relative* shares of income earned by families. For example, in Table 16-3 we see that the percentage of families earning less than $10,000 per year in constant dollars has dropped since 1960. Similarly, the percentage of all families earning less than $20,000 per year (constant dollars) has dropped from about 60 percent of the population in 1960 to about 40 percent of the population in 1982. Looking at Table 16-4 we see that the change in income *distribution* has not been as dramatic.

Accordingly, the conclusion has been drawn that there have been only slight changes in the distribution of money income. And, indeed, considering that the definition of money income used by the U.S. Bureau of the Census includes only wage and salary income, income from self-employment, interest and dividends, and such government cash-transfer payments as social security, welfare, and unemployment compensation, we have to agree that the distribution of money income has not changed. Money income, though, is not total income for individuals who receive in-kind transfers from the government in the form of food stamps, public housing, and so on.

The distribution of *total* income

If we include in-kind transfers in estimating the distribution of *total* income, we find a very different picture of what has happened to the poor in the United States since World War II. In 1973 there were 23 million people officially regarded as poor. However, those 23 million people received $18.8 billion of such restricted and in-kind transfers as food stamps, health care, and public housing. The lowest-fifth income group in 1960 was estimated to have 4.8 of total money income. In terms of total income, it had 5 percent. For 1973 it was estimated, as given in Table 16-4, that this lowest fifth obtained only 5.5 percent of total money income. However, when in-kind transfers are added to the money-income figures for 1973, the estimated share of the first quintile reaches about 12 percent.[2] Indeed, when these noncash

[2]Edgar K. Browning, "How Much More Equality Can We Afford?" *The Public Interest*, Spring 1976, pp. 90–110.

forms of income are included, the relative positions of the poorest fifth of families improved by *over 100 percent* between 1960 and 1973.

Causes of income differences

We now list some of the causes of differences in incomes. A detailed discussion of these causes is beyond the scope of an intermediate price theory text.

Age. Most workers follow a lifetime real-income pattern that is typified in Figure 16-6. This figure is called an **age-earnings profile**. It shows how earnings rise with age, reach a peak somewhere between ages forty-five and fifty-five, and then fall. Note that this curve is drawn for a fixed level of nationwide labor productivity. Any change in national productivity would shift the curve.

Its shape is explained by a number of factors. First of all, younger workers typically have less training and experience. Their marginal physical products are lower on the average than those of older and more experienced workers. Second, the number of weekly hours worked by the average worker goes up until around age forty-five or fifty-five and then declines. This explains to some extent the downward slope of the age-earnings profile to the right of the peak. Furthermore, the age-earnings profile levels off and slopes down because of the eventual adverse effects of age on marginal productivity. And finally, the curve usually drops abruptly at retirement. However, if we included the earnings from capital ownership, social security benefits, and other annuities, income would not drop at retirement.

Inherited characteristics. Many characteristics of entertainment stars are to a large extent inherited or innate. If one is born with a beautiful voice, one has an edge over someone who can't carry a tune. If a person is born with an IQ of 160, all other things being equal, that person should have a higher income-earning potential than someone with half that IQ. There is currently a debate raging over the extent to which income-earning characteristics are actually innate or inherited and the extent to which they are determined by environment and society.

FIGURE 16-6
The age-earnings profile
Real annual earnings (abstracting from changes in the national labor productivity) typically rise until they reach a peak somewhere between ages forty-five and fifty-five and then fall.

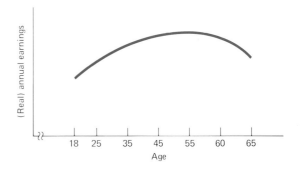

Risk taking. Those who work at more hazardous jobs will earn more, on the average, than those who do not. The relatively high salaries of those who walk steel beams on skyscrapers can be explained in large part by the increased risk of injury or death. *Ceteris paribus*, we expect that the earnings of those with safer jobs will average below those with less-safe jobs.

Uncertainty and variance of income. As we pointed out before, if individuals on the margin are risk-averse, they require a larger expected income from a job which generates income with a higher variance than in other occupations. Thus, we would predict that individuals in jobs of the former type will have higher incomes, on average, than those with jobs of the latter type.

Training. Given a set of individuals with exactly the same innate characteristics, those with more training will earn higher incomes. The training may be formal, obtained either by higher education or mail-order home study courses, or informal knowledge and training acquired on the job. Indeed, the role of on-the-job training is very important in explaining the variation of earnings with age. The reason training leads to higher income is that workers who are better trained have higher marginal physical products than the less skilled. We will discuss this topic in more detail below when we discuss investment in human capital.

Inherited wealth. Those who inherit wealth can earn incomes which are higher than those with similar abilities and training who do not inherit wealth, because wealth will yield them an income. The degree to which inherited wealth affects the distribution of money income in the United States is surprisingly small. It is more important in less-developed countries where a smaller percentage of national income accrues to labor.

Market imperfections. Monopoly, monopsony, union policies, government-mandated minimum wages, licensing requirements, certification, and the like all lead to differences in money incomes among classes of workers. Those who benefit from these market imperfections receive higher money incomes at the expense of others.

Discrimination. In the labor market, discrimination by race, religion, or sex can explain certain income differences. Studies that attempt to correct for the differences in marginal physical productivities of different classes of workers grouped by race or sex generally show an unexplained "residual" that may be the result of discrimination. In other words, even after taking into account the quantity and quality of schooling and other training, age, number of years in the labor force, and so on, when wage rates of men and women are compared, an unexplained differential still remains; likewise, when wage rates of whites and blacks are compared, a differential persists. This differential is attributed by some to discrimination. What is at issue, of course, is how much of that differential results from discrimination on the basis of sex and/or race or from unmeasured differences in productivity-related characteristics. The extent of discrimination cannot be measured by the difference between the median earnings of two such groups, if it is not adjusted for differences in marginal productivity.

INVESTMENT IN HUMAN CAPITAL

Much of the explanation for differences in labor incomes can be explained by the individual worker's (and his or her employer's) **investment in human capital**. This is a term that has taken on a very broad meaning. In general, it is any activity on the part of a worker or potential worker that raises that worker's present or future marginal productivity. Thus, activities which come under the heading "investment in human capital" include the following:

1   On-the-job training
2   Formal education
3   Informal education
4   Health maintenance and improvement activities
5   Migration

There are other activities which could not be classified with the above. The activity that has received the most attention from economists is formal education.

The private rate of return to formal schooling

Look at Figure 16-7. Here we show two age-earnings profiles. One is for a high school graduate and the other is for a college graduate. Note that the latter's profile is below the former's for a number of years and then eventually rises above it. It turns out that to assess properly the investment in formal schooling, we must discount the higher future earnings that the college graduate typically makes. We also have to subtract the out-of-pocket costs and the forgone earnings incurred while remaining in school rather than going to work. Note that we do not subtract food and lodging as a cost of going to college because this cost would be incurred anyway and therefore

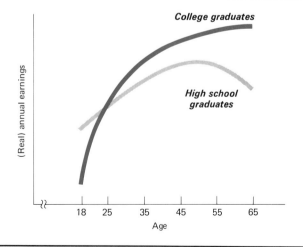

FIGURE 16-7
Comparing age-earning profiles of high school and college graduates
A college graduate's age-earnings profile is below a high school graduate's between the ages of eighteen and about twenty-five. Thereafter, however, the college graduate has a higher age-earnings profile that is a reflection of increased productivity.

does not constitute a cost by our definition. As you might expect, it turns out that the largest cost of formal education is the forgone earnings.

When all three of these calculations are completed, we find that the annual rate of return on a college education is somewhere between 9 and 15 percent. This rate of return is roughly equivalent to what could be earned in the *nonhuman* capital markets. These figures may be biased, however; they don't attempt to assess the nonpecuniary benefits of going to college, and the data are only for those who *complete* college. Those who drop out may have been forced to do so, since some of the rate of return from going to college is no doubt a reflection of differential abilities.

ISSUES AND APPLICATIONS

What do unions maximize?

Unions can be looked upon as setters of minimum wage rates. Through collective bargaining, unions establish minimum wage rates below which no individual worker may offer his or her services. We can analyze the effects of a union in the face of a monopsony employer to show the possible effects of a union minimum wage that exceeds the wage paid by a monopsonist. In such situations, it could be shown that a union setting a wage rate above that which would prevail in the monopsony labor market could actually increase employment and increase wage rates at the same time. However, we are again faced with the necessity of showing that monopsony is a significant factor in American labor markets (although we have shown that it is important in professional sports).

WHEN THERE IS NO MONOPSONY

In a labor market where there is labor unionization but no monopsony, any wage rate set higher than a competitive market-clearing wage rate will reduce total employment in that market. This can be seen in Figure 16-8. We have a competitive market for labor. The market demand curve is *DD,* and the market supply curve is *SS.* The market-clearing wage rate

will be w_e; the equilibrium quantity demanded and supplied of labor will be Q_e. If the union establishes a minimum wage rate by collective bargaining that exceeds w_e, there will be an excess quantity of labor supplied. For example, if the minimum wage established by collective bargaining is w_u, the quantity supplied would be Q_S; the quantity demanded would be Q_D. The difference is the excess quantity supplied, or "surplus." We see that one of the major tasks of a union which establishes a wage rate above the market-clearing price is to ration available jobs among the excessive number of workers who wish to work at the unionized wage rate. We see that there is a trade-off here which must be faced by any union's leadership. Higher real wages inevitably mean a reduction in total employment, as more persons seek to fill a smaller number of positions, e.g., the United Mine Workers during the past few decades.

TYPES OF UNION BEHAVIOR: WHAT DO THEY MAXIMIZE?

Our analysis of union objectives considers three possibilities. We view a union here as a monopoly seller of a particular service.

FIGURE 16-8
Unions must ration jobs
If there is no monopsony, and if the union succeeds in obtaining a wage rate w_u, the quantity of labor demanded will be Q_D, and the quantity of labor supplied Q_S. The union must ration a limited number of would-be workers.

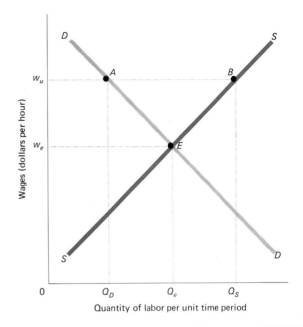

Employing all members in the union. Assume that the union has Q_1 workers. If it faces a demand curve such as *DD* in Figure 16-9, the only way it can "sell" all those workers is to accept a wage rate of w_1. This is a naive theory because unions could use some form of second-degree price discrimination to increase the average wage rate without reducing employment below Q_1.

Maximizing total wages. If the union is interested in maximizing the gross income of its members, it will not want a membership of Q_1 workers but will want to have Q_2 workers employed in Figure 16-9 and have them paid wage rate of w_2. The marginal revenue curve intersects the horizontal axis at the quantity at which total revenues are maximized. Total revenues in this case represent the aggregate income of the union membership, $w_2 \cdot Q_2$.

Note that in this situation, if the union started out with Q_1 members, there would be $Q_1 - Q_2$ members who would be out of union work at the wage rate w_2.

Maximizing the wage rate for a given number of workers. Assume that the union wants to maximize the wage rate for a portion of the union's members, perhaps those with the most seniority. If it wanted to keep employed, say, Q_3 workers, it would seek to obtain a wage rate w_3. This would require deciding which workers would be unemployed and which workers would work and for how long each week they would be employed.

A pure monopoly approach. We can analyze unions as pure monopolies. If business monopolies behave as if they maximized profits, why don't we analyze unions in a similar manner? In other words, why don't we assume that they behave as if they maximize the equivalent of monopoly profits or members' wealth? We could then say that unions would behave to maximize the difference between the total wage bill and the wage bill which is necessary to bid workers away from alternative employment. The problem with such an analysis is that it assumes that the union is proprietary, that is, that it is privately owned and the owners obtain all noncontractual income, or profits. Once we abandon this assumption, it is difficult to continue our anal-

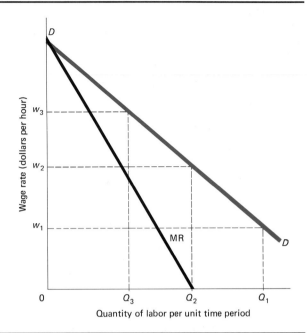

FIGURE 16-9
What do unions maximize?
Assume that the union wants to employ all of its Q_1 members. It will attempt to get a wage rate w_1. If the union wants to maximize total wage receipts, it will seek wage rate w_2, where the elasticity of demand is equal to -1. If the union wants to maximize the wage rate for a given number of workers, say Q_3, it will negotiate for wage rates w_3.

ogy with business monopolies, which are, by the way, analyzed by assuming private property rights in the ownership of the monopoly.

A PROPERTY RIGHTS APPROACH TO THE ECONOMICS OF UNIONS

Recently there have been a number of developments in the analysis of trade unions. One in particular that we will treat here examines the property rights structure within unions. This approach has been successfully used by Donald L. Martin.[3] Martin first points out that the theory of the profit-maximizing firm is based at a minimum on an implicit assumption of private property rights in resources and in the wealth increments arising from resource use. Models of union behavior cannot ignore the

ownership characteristics of trade union organizations. These characteristics define the alternative opportunities of unions.

Legal structure of unions. Labor organizations are legally and structurally constituted to behave as collusive or monopolistic actors in the labor market. Legal, enforceable, and *exclusive* bargaining rights and the legal right to withhold production provide unions with the tools to generate monopoly profits for their members. Of particular importance is the fact that unions are exempted from antitrust laws. We cannot conclude, however, that unions will *behave* as if they were seeking to maximize the profits of union labor leaders simply because unions are *capable* of generating those profits. Here is where the institutional arrangements become relevant.

Capturability of results of current actions on present value of future wealth. Current actions of utility-maximizing individuals normally generate future consequences. However, unless individuals can capitalize these

[3]Donald L. Martin, *An Economic Theory of the Trade Union: A New Approach* (Berkeley: University of California Press, 1980).

future consequences into current transfer prices, they will not be as sensitive to all opportunities that would truly maximize their wealth. We note that with very few exceptions, private property in union membership is nonexistent. Unlike shareholders of a corporation, union members may not sell their membership rights to would-be unionists. Such sales are not legally enforceable and are almost universally prohibited in union constitutions; hence, the present value of future economic profits *cannot* be capitalized in the current value of membership to incumbents. Members must wait and hope that they will survive to claim such profits if and when they materialize.

Economic analysis suggests that the interests of utility-maximizing members, when confronted with the nonproprietary constraint, will generate union behavior inconsistent with the hypothesis that the organization is attempting to maximize its wealth. Whenever wealth-increasing opportunities cannot be captured in the immediate value of membership rights, union collective bargaining goals will be biased toward *current* as opposed to future interests, despite the obvious negative consequences for the organization and its members *in the long run*.

Younger members and vacancies. We predict, then, that since current members cannot completely capture future wealth increases, they will attempt to bargain for more, i.e., higher wages now, despite the adverse future employment consequences for incumbents or potential additions to the firm's work force. We come up with another implication of the nonproprietary nature of unions. We expect them to practice nonprice rationing for vacant membership slots. That is, in the nonproprietary unions, the capitalized value of membership entry fees and dues payments will be lower than the present value of expected monopoly profits to would-be members. Entry into unions will be rationed, instead, on the basis

of race, sex, nationality, and religion, as well as other personal characteristics.

Strikes. The nonproprietary nature of most trade unions has an effect on the nature and characteristics of strike activity. Strikes impose immediate costs on strikers in the form of lost wages. They also impose future costs on union members, because in the future higher assessments will have to be made to build up a depleted strike fund. After all, when strikes occur, workers are often given money out of such a strike fund; the burden of rebuilding those depleted funds is only vaguely perceived in the present in nonproprietary unions, since they are unable to capitalize the value of membership rights. This suggests an explanation for strikes and strike lengths that often appear irrational to outside observers because the present value of the increments in wages is equal to or less than the present value of the total cost of the strike. But such strikes may be perfectly rational to the member of the nonproprietary union if a larger fraction of benefits may be captured earlier, while most strike costs are spread out over a longer period of time and are incurred by future members.

Union leadership. The absence of private property in union membership rights lowers the returns to members from participating in efforts to police and change union management. As a result, the nonproprietary character of most unions provides greater opportunities for leaders, if they choose, to increase their own utility at the expense of rank and file members. This may take the form of (1) "sweetheart" contracts with employers, (2) collective bargaining packages that enrich union treasuries directly rather than increase the current wages and benefits of rank and file members, (3) diversion of union resources to prolong tenure and leadership, (4) the pursuit of local, regional, or national political interests at union expense, and (5) blatant corruption.

Opportunity in the labor market: Women and divorce

Economics has been accused by some non-economists of being an imperialistic discipline because economists apply economic theory to areas that other sciences thought were their private domains. In the past decade there has been a substantial amount of literature on the economics of marriage, divorce, and other nontraditional subjects. One interesting development is the relationship between labor force participation and divorce. At the same time that participation by women in the labor force has been increasing, there has been an increase in the divorce rate. While there are many factors at work here, careful economic analysis can help to explain what is happening.

HOW YOU GOING TO KEEP 'EM DOWN ON THE FARM?

Detailed analysis about marriage and divorce has led to predictions about which characteristics of the partners in a marriage will tend to enhance its stability and which will increase the likelihood of divorce.[4] Here we examine some of the questions involved by comparing the divorce rates and labor force participation rates of farm women to rural nonfarm women.[5] As we see in Table 16-5, rural farm men and women have substantially lower divorce rates than either rural nonfarm (small town) men and women or urban men and women. Is this because life on the farm is happier for men and women than

it is for urban people? While this possibility cannot be discounted out of hand, economics tends to look for explanations that have more to do with the existence of choices to individuals and the relative costs and benefits from those choices.

Department of Labor statistics indicate that about one-half of nonfarm women were in the labor force while about 30 percent of farm women were in the off-farm labor force. That is, women who lived on farms tended to specialize in household (including on-farm) work relative to nonfarm women. To the extent that specialized labor inputs by marriage partners increases the gains to marriage, the economic theory of marriage and divorce predicts that farm households would be more stable than nonfarm households.

You will note in Table 16-5 that the divorce rate for women living on farms is lower than that for men, whiel the opposite is true in urban areas—women have a higher divorce rate than men. What would explain this? People tend to migrate to where their best opportunities exist. When a farm marriage is dissolved, it is usually the case that the male retains farm ownership, and so stays on the farm to work, while the female moves to where her job opportunities will be better—urban areas.

Economic theory of marriage has predicted that the divorce rate increases as the earning ability of women increases. This prediction has been upheld in studies of urban women and of farm women. Farm women who have the lowest cost of learning of alternative uses for their labor are those who live on farms located in areas with relatively dense populations. That is, farm women in Massachusetts and New Jersey will have better knowledge of other opportunities, and less incentive to invest in farm-specific skills, than will farm women in sparsely populated states like Ne-

[4]For an overview, see Gary S. Becker, Elizabeth M. Landes, and Robert T. Michael, "An Economic Analysis of Marital Instability," *Journal of Political Economy*, December 1977, pp. 1141–1187.

[5]This analysis is drawn from: William Sander, "Women, Work, and Divorce," *American Economic Review*, June 1985, pp. 519–523.

TABLE 16-5		Divorce rates	
Percent of men and women ever married who were known to have been divorced, by place of residence (1970 data)	Location	Male	Female
	Urban	14.6	15.5
	Rural nonfarm	13.1	12.0
	Rural farm	7.4	6.6

vada and Wyoming. The differences between farm and nonfarm divorce rates is lowest in the densely populated states and greatest in the sparsely populated states. Hence, whether on the farm or in the city, the same economic factors affect divorce rates the same way—the more opportunities and the lower the cost of those opportunities, the more those opportunities will be explored.

Discrimination in the labor force: Theory and evidence

Economic models demonstrate that labor is paid its true market value—in the absence of any number of conditions that in the real world can prevent the true market wage from emerging. In some areas of the labor market there are restrictions, such as the minimum wage, that distorts the wage rate. In other areas there are legal prohibitions on competition, such as licensing requirements for lawyers, that affect the wage rate. Numerous studies have been done by labor economists to measure the consequences of distortions in the price of labor due to assorted factors. One factor that is difficult to quantify is discrimination. We know it exists, but what is the extent of it and what are the consequences in wage rate determination?

A MODEL OF DISCRIMINATION

Prejudice, which is revealed by discrimination, may affect the labor market directly in several ways. For simplicity, we will discuss discrimination only against women here, but the analysis is the same for any group that faces discrimination. Employers may be prejudiced. They may deny that men and women of equal talents have equal market values. This will lead to a bias in hiring, with discriminating employers hiring women only if they can pay them less than men for the same work. Employees may be prejudiced. Even if employers have no prejudice, if their employees are prejudiced it may be costly not to accept that prejudice. For example, an employer may attempt to hire a woman to work in an area previously dominated by males who resent the intrusion of a woman. To work with a woman the males may demand a wage premium or inflict costs on the employer that makes it cheaper to only hire men. Finally, even if employers and employees in an organization are not prejudiced, customers of the firm may be. Customers of a firm may not believe that a woman is capable of doing a certain job as well as a man could, and so may curtail businesss with the nondiscriminating firm. This would force the employer to employ discrimination in order to stay in business.

We can model discrimination in Figure 16-10. For simplicity we assume there are two groups of employers—discriminating employers and nondiscriminating employers. These employers hire employees from the same pool of people, which happens to be $\frac{2}{3}$ male and $\frac{1}{3}$ female. The men and women are assumed to have the same productivity, which is reflected in the market demand for labor curve, D_a for the discriminating employers; D_b for the non-discriminating employers. We will ignore the possibility of discrimination among employees or by customers and examine the impact of discrimination only by employers.

Initially we see that the labor force divides itself between the two groups of employers: S'_a and S'_b. In the absence of discrimination, the market wage is the same for both employers and groups of employees. Employees working for nondiscriminating employers earn W'_b, the market wage. But the discriminating employer will only pay that wage to his or her male employees, W'_m. The discriminating employers have a demand price for women that is lower, such as $D_a - C$, where C reflects the discrimination value. This discrimination may be due to a simple dislike of women as employees, regardless of ability, or may be due to a mistaken belief that women have lower productivity. In any event, the discriminating employer will pay women employees only W'_w.

FIGURE 16-10

Impact of discrimination by some employers

The labor market is divided into two sets of employers: discriminating and nondiscriminating. They hire men and women of similar ability and productive value, so employees are separated into the two sectors by the volumes S'_a and S'_b. Market wage is W'_b but since discriminating employers value women employees less (reflected by $D_a - C$) they will only pay men the market wage; they pay women W'_w. Women employees then migrate from discriminating employers to nondiscriminating employers, reducing supply of labor to S''_a for the former and increasing the supply of labor to S''_b for the latter. The wage rates then go to W''_b for all employees of the nondiscriminating employers, while the men working for the discriminating employer see their wage rise to W''_m. This causes men to shift to the discriminating employer, increasing the supply of labor and dropping the wage rate there, and decreasing the supply of labor and increasing the wage rate for the nondiscriminating employer, until wages become equal in both sectors for all employees.

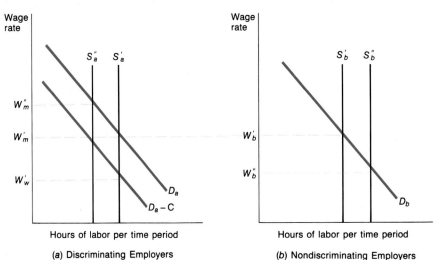

(a) Discriminating Employers

(b) Nondiscriminating Employers

Obviously this labor market is not in-equilibrium. Women working for discriminating employers can make themselves better off if they shift to nondiscriminating employers. The result of this will be an increase in the supply of workers for the nondiscriminating employers, to S_b'', and a decrease in the supply of workers for the discriminating employers, to S_a''. This shift has, as we see in the graphs, forced the equilibrium wage for men working for discriminating employers up to W_m'' and forced the equilibrium wage for men and women working for nondiscriminating employers down to W_b''. Since the market is still out of equilibrium, men working in the non-discriminating sector will shift to the discriminating sector, until wages between the two groups is equalized. In equilibrium, both employers will pay the same wage to men employees. Women working for nondiscriminating employers will be paid that wage too. Only women remaining with the discriminating employers would be paid less than the market wage. In the absence of any constraints, that would not happen, so that all discrimination in wages would be eliminated—even though discrimination still exists. The results of the analysis are the same regardless of the source of the discrimination—employers, employees, or customers.

REAL-WORLD PROBLEMS

While market forces are at work to push toward a nondiscrimination result as described above, we know that there are factors that inhibit the end of discrimination in wages. Since women comprise a substantial proportion of the labor force, there must be a sufficient number of nondiscriminating alternatives to absorb the women who would have to migrate away from discriminating employers. Women must also be free to be able to move to wherever the best job opportunity exists, but in fact mobility is often limited by family ties, geographical preferences, and other factors that outweigh the potential benefits of a better job opportunity in another location. As we noted previously, there are also legal barriers to competition in some labor markets and, since women tend to be newer entrants into these markets, they suffer disproportionally from the effects of such limitations on competition.

EMPIRICAL MEASURES OF DISCRIMINATION

A statistic that is frequently mentioned is the fact that women, on average, earn somewhere between 60 and 70 percent of the average wage of men. This is sometimes alleged to be due to discrimination in the labor force. Several empirical studies have been done to try to sort out the various factors at work to see how much of the "raw" wage differential between men and women is due to discrimination (or to other unexplained factors). Using data from different points in time, studies have estimated that anywhere from 31 to 100 percent of the raw wage differential can be explained by other factors than discrimination.[6]

Factors other than current prejudice in the labor market that have been estimated to explain part of the male-female wage differential include: differences in education and training (which may be due to past or current discrimination in what many people think is "proper" for women to study); marital status (unmarried women are not subject to the mobility constraints that may exist when two careers are at stake); and the number of children (which usually means that a woman has withdrawn from the labor market, sometimes for many years, which reduces years of work experience compared to males of the same age and educational background). The empirical studies, therefore, indicate that discrimination in the labor market is a real force but that its true measure is not the simple difference in raw wages between men and women. As usual, the real world is a complex place.

---

[6]A review of the studies and the model on which this presentation is based can be found in: Cotton M. Lindsay and Charles A. Shanor, "Economic and Legal Considerations for Resolving Sex-Based Wage Discrimination Cases," *Supreme Court Economic Review*, 1982, pp. 185–233.

SUMMARY

1   The marginal productivity theory of factor prices indicates that individuals are paid the value of their marginal products; this is, however, only the demand side. The wage rate is determined not only by the value of marginal product (or marginal revenue product) but also by the supply schedule of labor.

2   A worker gets paid an amount equivalent to the reduction in the firm's revenues if the worker quits. The value of the output that the worker generates, however, is equal to the marginal revenue of the output times each worker's *average* physical product, which exceeds the value of *marginal* product. The difference is available to remunerate other factors of production.

3   *Ceteris paribus*, wages will be higher in occupations that are less preferred. This phenomenon is called equalizing wage differences.

4   Wages can be expected to differ in proportion to relative marginal physical productivities.

5   The longer the time period for adjustment, the greater the elasticity of supply of any particular type of labor.

6   Apparent economic rents often are not rents at all but rather a necessary inducement to get enough individuals to enter an industry in the hope of "striking it rich" to drive the average wage rate down to the opportunity cost of potential entrance.

7   David Ricardo aggregated all uses of land and, therefore, assumed that land had no alternative use or opportunity cost; hence, all payment to land was considered by Ricardo to be a pure (economic) rent, which is now called a Ricardian rent.

8   Ricardian rent is demand-determined in the economy.

9   In the long run, if the factor of production is not paid its full opportunity cost, it will not be maintained or replaced.

10   The distribution of *money* income has not changed dramatically since World War II; if such in-kind transfers as food stamps are included, the lowest fifth of income earners have improved their relative share of *total* income by some 60 percent.

11   Income differences result from differences in (*a*) age, (*b*) inherited characteristics, (*c*) risk taking, (*d*) uncertainty and variance of income, (*e*) training, (*f*) inherited wealth, (*g*) market imperfections, and (*h*) discrimination.

12 Investment in human capital takes on such forms as (a) on-the-job training, (b) formal education, (c) informal education, (d) health maintenance and improvement activities, and (e) migration.

GLOSSARY

- **marginal productivity theory** A theory which relates the demand for an input to its marginal productivity. According to this theory, individuals are paid the value of their marginal product.
- **Ricardian (economic) rent** Another name for pure rent; a payment to a factor of production over and above what is necessary to keep a given quantity of the factor forever in existence in its current employment and quality.
- **quasi-rent** A payment over and above what is necessary to keep a factor of production in existence in the short run in its current quantity and quality; however, in the long run if the quasi-rent is inadequate, the factor of production will be allowed to depreciate and not be replaced. To be contrasted with a pure, or Ricardian, rent.
- **age-earnings profile** Income related to age; shows how real earnings rise with age, reach a peak between ages forty-five and fifty-five, and then fall (in real terms and disregarding changes in national productivity).
- **investment in human capital** Any activity that raises a worker's present or future marginal productivity: schooling, on-the-job training, etc.

QUESTIONS

(Answers to even-numbered questions are at back of text.)

1 According to the marginal productivity theory of factor pricing, how is a factor's price determined?
2 "If employers paid the VMP to each of their inputs, there would be no profits left over." Is this statement true or false, and why?
3 "Since all workers are not completely mobile, we should not expect to see wage differentials among firms or different regions of the country completely eliminated." Do you agree or disagree, and why?
4 Why do you think that many bank clerks earn less than many blue-collar workers having the same set of abilities? Assume in your answer that neither group is unionized.
5 Other things being equal, what might be the effect on regional wage differentials of the rising relative cost of energy?
6 Assuming that the work of a certified public accountant is no more or less pleasant than that of a supermarket checker and that neither group is organized, why would we expect to see the CPA's real wages higher in the long run?
7 What is the definition of economic rent? What is the difficulty in applying the concept to living resources?

8 "All revenue obtained by the Italian government from Renaissance art museums is economic rent." Is this statement true or false, and why?

9 What social function, if any, is served by economic rent?

10 How does a quasi-rent differ from pure economic rent?

11 Why must quasi-rents cover at least depreciation and the opportunity cost of the capital "tied up" in an asset, if the asset is to remain intact?

12 Why might we expect to find less sexual discrimination against employees in factories than in barber shops or restaurants?

13 If a proprietor is a racist and his or her customers are not, why will these preferences lower the earnings of the business?

14 "I know that racial discrimination in hiring is widespread. For that reason, if I ever open a light-manufacturing business, I'm going to hire black teenage women exclusively." What does the speaker have in mind?

15 "It would be inconsistent for a profit-maximizing entrepreneur whose customers and current employees carry no prejudices to discriminate in hiring on any basis other than that of productivity." Comment.

SELECTED REFERENCES

Cartter, Allan M., *Theory of Wages and Employment* (Homewood, Ill.: Irwin, 1959).

Dalton, Hugh, *The Inequality of Income,* 2d ed. (London: Routledge, 1925), part 4, pp. 239–353.

Dunlop, J.T., *The Theory of Wage Determination* (London: Macmillan, 1957).

Marshall, Alfred, *Principles of Economics,* 8th ed. (New York: Macmillan, 1949), book 5, chap. 10.

Pigou, A.C., *The Economics of Welfare,* 4th ed. (London: Macmillan, 1932), part 6, chap. 5.

Ricardo, David, *The Principles of Political Economy and Taxation* (New York: Dutton, 1962), especially chaps. 1–5.

Thurow, Lester C., *Poverty and Discrimination* (Washington, D.C.: The Brookings Institution, 1969).

Tobin, James, "On Limiting the Domain of Inequality," *The Journal of Law and Economics,* vol. 13, no. 2, October 1970, pp. 263–277.

General equilibrium analysis

*E*xcept on a few occasions, we have discussed individual markets as though they were completely isolated from the other markets in the economy. That is, we have taken into account only what happens in one particular market when, for example, a relative price changes, a tax is levied, a new law is passed, and so on. However, we are all aware that there are interrelations among the microeconomic units in our economy. At the very minimum, there are interrelations between the household sector and the business sector. In Figure 17-1, we portray the interrelations among the household sector, the credit sector, and the production sector. This is the so-called circular flow of income presented in Chapter 1. We have treated consumer decision making in some detail in Chapters 2 through 5. We looked into the credit and risk markets in Chapters 6 and 7, and then spent some time in Chapters 8 through 14 analyzing decision making by firms. Finally, household decision making with respect to supplying factors of production was taken care of in Chapters 15 and 16. What we would like to do in this chapter is put these sectors together into what is called **general equilibrium analysis**.

PARTIAL VERSUS GENERAL EQUILIBRIUM ANALYSIS

You have been presented almost exclusively with what is called **partial equilibrium analysis**. Partial equilibrium analysis can best be characterized by the Latin expression *ceteris paribus*, meaning "all other things being

FIGURE 17-1
The circular flow of income: money flows only
Here we show a general equilibrium model which includes saving and investment. In addition to the product and factor markets, we therefore show a credit market. A more complete general equilibrium system would include the government sector and the foreign sector. Note that only the money flows have been depicted; the "real" flows have been omitted for clarity.

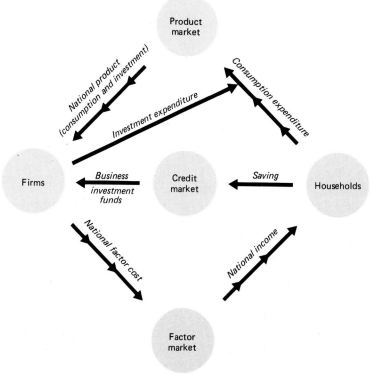

equal." In such an analysis, it is assumed that just about everything else is held constant. Not *all* other things are constant, because then there would be no change possible. In essence, partial equilibrium analysis allows us to focus on a single market and view it in isolation. For analytical purposes, the market is viewed as independent and self-contained; that is, it is independent of all other markets. We know, however, that markets *interact*. When we attempt to take account of these interactions among markets, we enter the realm of general equilibrium analysis.

General equilibrium analysis takes account of the interrelations among prices and quantities of various goods and services. Just as partial equilibrium analysis does not require that *all* other things be held constant, general equilibrium analysis does not allow *all* other things to vary. Something must be exogenous (determined outside the system) or "given" for us to start the analysis. General equilibrium analysis has been used to answer a question that has puzzled economists for some time: In a system of perfectly competitive markets, is there a set of prices that would allow all markets to be in equilibrium at the same time? Modern work by mathematical economists has resulted in an affirmative answer to this question. There does exist a set of relative prices that allows all markets to clear simultaneously if all markets are perfectly competitive. In this chapter, however, we will not analyze this question. Rather, we will present the rudiments of general equilibrium analysis in geometric form. By graphical necessity we are limited to two dimensions; accordingly, we will deal with a world in which there are two commodities and two factors of production. In order to generalize any further, we would have to employ a system of simultaneous equations. However, the following analysis does give the flavor of a larger model.

Limits to analysis

A note of warning: The distinction between general and partial equilibrium analysis is, in reality, one of degree. After all, there is a limit to how many markets can be taken into account in any analysis. That limit is set either by the cerebral limits of the economist doing the analysis or by the capabilities of the computer that he or she is utilizing. True general equilibrium analysis would require the setting up of an almost infinite set of simultaneous equations, and this is a task no one has yet undertaken. When economists talk of general equilibrium analysis in dealing with practical problems, they are referring to taking into account several markets and the relations among them. If the goal of the economist is to predict what will happen when the economic environment changes, his or her choice of partial or general equilibrium analysis depends on (1) the question being asked and (2) the degree to which the answer will change if more than one market is considered. Basically, it is a matter of what things can be "held" constant without invalidating the analysis.

We will now introduce the theory of exchange between two consumers. We will construct a tool to illustrate the interaction between two individuals with given endowments of two commodities.

EXCHANGE AND THE EDGEWORTH-BOWLEY BOX

To understand the origins of voluntary exchange, we consider a situation in which there are two individuals consuming two commodities whose total joint supply is absolutely fixed. Consider individual 1 and individual 2. Their respective commodity spaces are presented in panel (a) and panel (b) of Figure 17-2. The origin for the commodity space that pertains to individual 1 we label 0_1. 0_2 is the origin for individual 2's commodity space.

Now we wish to put these two commodity spaces together. We do this by rotating individual 2's commodity space 180° so that individual 2's origin, 0_2, is in the upper right-hand corner. We now see the two commodity spaces

■■■■■■■■■■

FIGURE 17-2
Two commodity spaces
Individual 1's commodity space for goods x and y is given in panel (a). Individual 2's commodity space for x and y is given in panel (b).

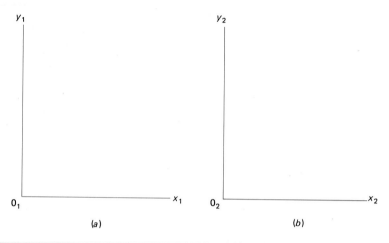

in the two panels of Figure 17-3. Panel (a) is the same, but panel (b) appears to be upside down; actually, it has been rotated.

We now wish to fit the two commodity spaces together. At first glance, it might appear that there is a problem involving the lengths of the horizontal and vertical axes. There is no problem, though, when we assume fixed supplies of commodity x and commodity y that must be shared by individual 1 and individual 2. That is, the amount of x consumed by individual 1 plus the amount of x consumed by individual 2 must equal the total available supply of x. The same is true for commodity y.

Thus, what we want to do is combine the commodity spaces in panels (a) and (b) in such a way that (1) the length of the line from 0_1 to x_1, representing the amount of x consumed by individual 1, plus the length of the line from 0_2 to x_2, representing the amount of x consumed by individual 2, equals the total fixed available quantity of x, and (2) the length 0_2y_1, representing the amount of y consumed by individual 1, plus the length 0_2y_2, representing the amount of y consumed by individual 2, equals the total fixed available quantity of y.

When we put the two panels together from Figure 17-3, we obtain Figure 17-4. This is called the **Edgeworth-Bowley box**, named after two English mathematical economists who contributed much to the early neoclassical revolution around the turn of the century. Any point, such as A, represents specifically how much of the available supply of commodity x and com-

FIGURE 17-3
Rotating individual 2's commodity space axes
We duplicate panel (a) from Figure 17-2; in panel (b), however, we rotate the origin of individual 2's commodity space 180°.

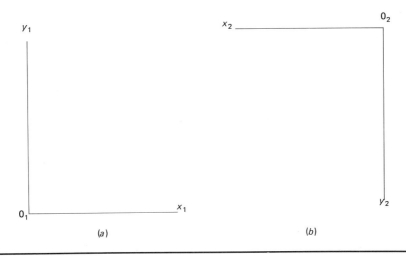

(a)   (b)

modity y is consumed by consumer 1 and consumer 2. Thus, from Figure 17-4, we see that $x_1 + x_2$ = total supply of x and that $y_1 + y_2$ = total supply of y.

Introducing indifference curves into the box

In Figure 17-5, we add two sets of indifference curves to the Edgeworth-Bowley box. Individual 1's indifference curves are labeled I_1, II_1, and III_1. Individual 2's indifference curves are labeled I_2, II_2, and III_2. Remember that the origin for the indifference curves for individual 2 is in the northeast corner (upper right-hand corner). It is labeled 0_2.

As always, the commodity spaces for both individuals 1 and 2 contain an infinite number of indifference curves. We have arbitrarily drawn in three for each individual.

Let us take an initial distribution of x and y allocated between individual 1 and individual 2 at point A in Figure 17-5. Individual 1 has x_1 of x; individual 2 has x_2 of x. Since there is a fixed amount of both x and y, $x_1 + x_2$ must equal the total amount of x available, or the horizontal dimension of the entire box. Similarly, the initial distribution of y is y_1 and y_2, with the sum being equal to the total fixed supply represented by the height of the box.

At the initial distribution point, A, individual 1 is on indifference curve II_1. Individual 2 is on indifference curve I_2. Given the definition of an indifference curve, individual 1 is indifferent among all combinations of x and

FIGURE 17-4
The Edgeworth-Bowley consumption box

x is measured on the horizontal axis; y on the vertical axis. Individual 1's origin is labeled 0_1; individual 2's origin is labeled 0_2. The dimensions of the box represent the total quantity of x and y available; thus, if we pick point A in the box, the quantity of x consumed by individual 1 is x_1, the quantity of x consumed by individual 2 is x_2, and x_1 plus x_2 is equal to total x available. The same is true for good y.

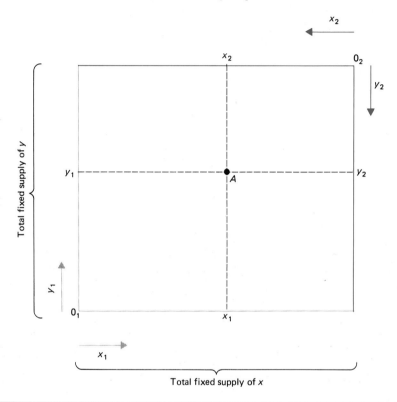

y which keep him or her on indifference curve II_1. We have drawn an arrow showing a movement of individual 1 along indifference curve II_1. The arrow goes from point A to point E'. Since individual 1 is indifferent anywhere on II_1, E' is just as preferred as A.

Gains from trade   However, notice what has happened to individual 2. At point A, individual 2 was originally on indifference curve I_1. At point E', though, individual 2 is on a higher indifference curve, II_2.[1] Looking at it from the origin 0_2 (you

---

[1]Of course, individual 1 would not gain from the movement from A to E'. Therefore, unless trading costs are zero and individual 1 receives utility from the trading process itself, he or she will not be willing to trade. For expository purposes, we ignore these considerations.

FIGURE 17-5
An Edgeworth-Bowley consumption box and exchange
This is in Figure 17-4 with indifference curves added. Note that the indifference curves for individual 1 are labeled with a subscript 1. The indifference curves for individual 2 are labeled with a subscript 2 and are convex to the origin at the northeast corner of the box. Thus, they look upside down; however, if you rotate the page 180°, they will appear right side up. Start out at point A, where individual 1 is on indifference curve II_1. Individual 2 is on indifference curve I_2. Clearly, it is possible to move from point A to point E' without reducing the level of individual 1. However, we will increase the level of utility of individual 2 because we will move him or her to indifference curve II_2, which is higher (relative to origin 0_2) than is I_2. Anywhere within the shaded area, or region of mutual advantage, one individual can be made better off without harming the other if there is a movement from A or B toward the middle. However, it is impossible to make a movement anywhere along the contract, or conflict, line CC without harming one individual in order to increase another's level of utility. Along CC, the marginal rate of substitution of x and y (MRS_{xy}) is the same for both individuals.

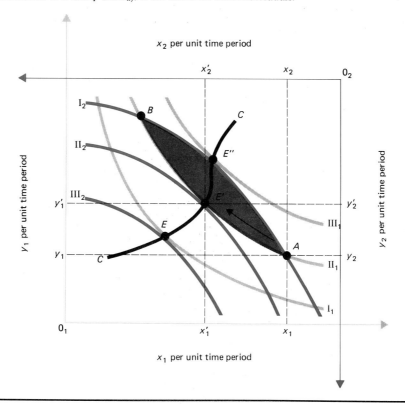

can do this by turning the book upside down), we can readily see that individual 2 is made better off by a movement from A to E', because distribution of goods represented by E' puts individual 2 on a higher indifference curve.

This is what the gains from trade are all about. Exchange of x and y between individuals 1 and 2 has increased the welfare of individual 2 without decreasing the welfare of individual 1. The new combinations for these two individuals (x_1' and y_1', x_2' and y_2') are "preferred" to the original combinations because someone has been moved to a higher indifference curve without anyone else having been moved to a lower one. Assume that the initial position is at point A. Given the indifference curves for individual 1 and individual 2 as drawn, we see that anywhere within the shaded region bounded by part of II_1 and I_2 in Figure 17-5, both individuals can be made better off relative to the starting position at point A (or alternative starting position B). It is because of this that the shaded region has been called the **region of mutual advantage**, which is specific to starting points A and B. If we had started at some other point, we would shade in a different region of mutual advantage.

Note that Figure 17-5 is usually just called an Edgeworth-Bowley box or just an Edgeworth box.

The contract curve

We assume that, with full knowledge and in the absence of transactions costs, two individuals will voluntarily exchange x and y until they reach a point such as E' where their indifference curves are tangent to each other, with the result that no further exchanges of mutual benefit can be made. We define such a situation as equilibrium for these two consumers. Thus, point E' is an equilibrium point. We have drawn in three such points, E, E', and E'', and have connected them by a curve CC. This curve is called the **contract curve**. The contract curve is defined as all the possible equilibrium combinations that *might* be obtained. Along the contract curve, one individual cannot be made better off without reducing the welfare of the other. Whenever the individuals' indifference curves are tangent to each other, we know that their marginal rates of substitution MRS_{xy} are equal. Therefore, we know that an *equilibrium in exchange* will obtain whenever the two individuals have the same marginal rates of substitution. Thus, for equilibrium,

$$MRS_{xy}^1 = MRS_{xy}^2 \qquad \qquad \textbf{(17-1)}$$

Along the contract curve, the marginal rate of substitution of individual 1 is equal to the marginal rate of substitution of individual 2. The contract curve is also called the **conflict curve** since movements along it lead to losses in utility by one party and gains in utility by the other. In other words, once two individuals have traded up to the point where they are on the contract, or conflict, curve CC, beyond this point any improvement in one individual's welfare implies a reduction in the other's; a movement to one individual's higher indifference curve necessarily means a movement to the other individual's lower indifference curve.

A summary of the consumption problem

We have what is called a consumption problem. There are two consumption goods, x and y. These goods are available in fixed amounts. We have two consumers (or two households) that will together consume all of x and all of y. We start off with each consumer in possession of a certain amount of x and a certain amount of y. The amount of x possessed by consumer 1 is represented by the distance from 0_1 to x_1 in Figure 17-6. Notice that consumer 1's endowments are measured from the southwest corner of the diagram. By assumption, consumer 2 has an initial endowment of x represented by the distance 0_2 to x_2 (as measured from the northeast corner of the diagram), which is equal to the amount of x not consumed by consumer 1.

Similarly, the initial endowment of consumption good y for consumer 1 is represented by the distance from 0_1 to y_1 (as measured from the southwest corner). Consumer 2 has initial endowment of good y equal to 0_2y_2. The starting point is at A.

Consumer 1's preferences are given by indifference curves I_1, II_1, and III_1, consumer 2's preferences by I_2, II_2, and III_2.

FIGURE 17-6

Equilibrium in exchange

Initial endowments are 0_1x_1, 0_1y_1, 0_2x_2, and 0_2y_2. At the initial endowment A, however, the marginal rates of substitution given by the slopes of tangents to indifference curves II_1 and I_2, T_1T_1 and T_2T_2, respectively, are not equal. Through exchange the consumers will move to somewhere between points $E'E''$. That is, they will move to a point on the contract curve CC where their marginal rates of substitution are equal.

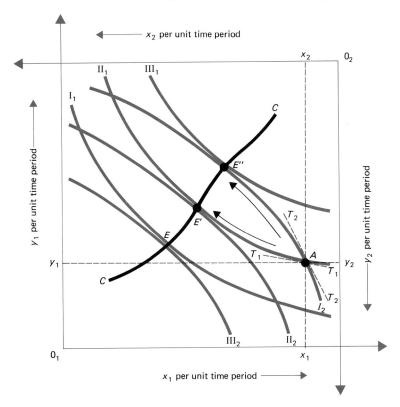

Initial utility levels

Given the initial endowment at point A, consumer 1 is situated on indifference curve II_1. Consumer 2 finds that indifference curve I_2 is being attained.

There is clearly a basis for exchange in this situation. The marginal rate of substitution of x for y for consumer 1 differs from the marginal rate of substitution of x for y for consumer 2. The two MRSs are given by the two tangents to the two respective indifference curves at the initial endowment point A. Those tangents are labeled T_1T_1 and T_2T_2. In other words, consumer 1 values the ratio of x to y differently, on the margin, than does consumer 2.

Exchange equilibrium

As long as these two individuals are free to trade, they will do so. Trade could move the individuals either to point E' or to point E'', or to any point on the contract curve between E' and E''. If trade moved them to point E', individual 1 would move to a higher indifference curve and individual 2 would remain on the same one. If they moved to point E'', individual 2 is the one who would move to a higher indifference curve and individual 1 would remain at the same level of satisfaction. Between E' and E'', they are both on higher indifference curves. Where they end up—closer to E' or to E''—depends on their relative bargaining abilities. We know, however, that they will move to somewhere between points E' and E'' before they cease exchanging.

The points between E' and E'' are all points at which the marginal rates of substitution are equal for both individuals, or $MRS^1_{xy} = MRS^2_{xy}$. When we connect all such points, represented by the line CC, we have a contract (or conflict) curve. It is the locus of points at which the two individuals' sets of indifference curves just touch each other. General equilibrium of exchange will always occur on the contract curve, for that is where the marginal rate of substitution for all parties consuming both goods is equal. Note that the general equilibrium is not unique; it can occur at any point along the contract curve.[2]

Now that we have looked at general equilibrium in exchange, let us go to the general equilibrium in production.

PRODUCTION GENERAL EQUILIBRIUM

We assume that consumer goods x and y are produced by two inputs: capital (K) and labor (L). For the purpose of this discussion, the total quantities of capital and labor available per unit time period are both fixed; we also assume that they are always fully employed.

Initial employment

In Figure 17-7, we show the initial employments of the inputs, capital and labor, in the production of goods x and y. Good x's use of capital and labor is measured from the origin labeled 0_x (southwest corner of the diagram).

[2]When we are dealing with more than two individuals, this would be called a contract hypersurface.

FIGURE 17-7
An Edgeworth-Bowley production box
This diagram is similar to the ones we have used, but we are now looking at an input space. If the two industries produce x and y, and initially employ capital and labor at D, the x industry will employ $0_x k_x$ of capital plus $0_x l_x$ of labor. The y industry will employ $0_y k_y$ and $0_y l_y$.

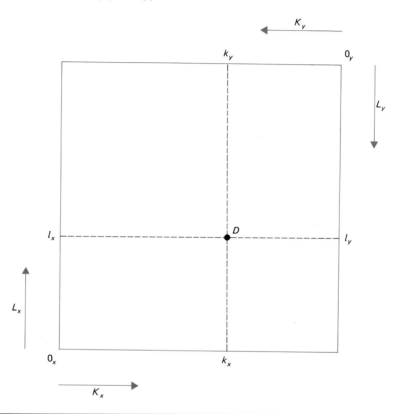

Good y's use of capital and labor is measured from the origin 0_y (northwest corner). By assumption, the use of capital in industry x and in industry y must equal the total amount of capital available; the same is true for labor. Thus, given an initial use of capital and labor represented by point D in Figure 17-7, we know that industry x uses k_x, industry y uses k_y, and $k_x + k_y = K$. With respect to labor, at point D industry x uses l_x of labor, industry y uses l_y, and $l_x + l_y = L$.

This is an Edgeworth-Bowley box diagram, but we are now using it to depict production.

Adding the production function

We assume that the production functions for both x and y are given and do not change. From these production functions, we construct normally shaped isoquants, represented in Figure 17-8 as Q_I^x through Q_{IV}^x for x and Q_i^y through

FIGURE 17-8

Equilibrium in production

If the initial input allocations are such that the x industry and the y industry find themselves at point D, the marginal rates of technical substitution as given by the slopes of the tangents ZZ and Z'Z' will not be equal. The interindustry resource allocation will change so that the industries move to some point on the production contract curve CC, between and including points E' and E".

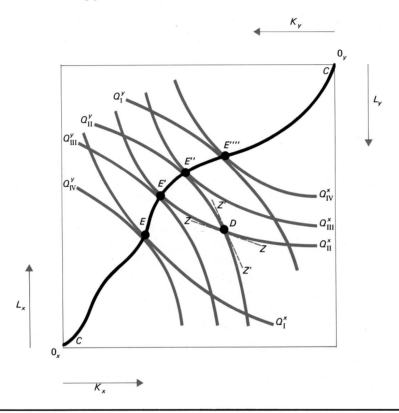

Q_{IV}^y for y. The initial allocation of inputs between the production of x and y is given by point D. The highest isoquant on which point D lies is Q_{II}^x for industry x and Q_{II}^y for industry y. The marginal rates of technical substitution in the two industries at point D are the respective slopes of the tangents to the two isoquants intersecting at that point. In other words, the marginal rate of technical substitution in industry x equals the slope of ZZ measured with respect to the origin 0_x, and the marginal rate of technical substitution in industry y is equal to the slope of Z'Z' measured with respect to the origin 0_y. These slopes differ and the marginal rates of technical substitution differ in the two industries.

Recall that $MRTS_{K:L} = MPP_L/MPP_K$. The diagram shows that $MRTS_{K:L}^x >$ $MRTS_{K:L}^y$. Thus in industry x, the marginal product of capital is low relative to the marginal product of labor. Production rate Q_{11}^x could be maintained by substituting a relatively small amount of labor for a relatively larger amount of capital. In other words, the marginal rate of technical substitution of capital for labor in producing x is relatively high. The opposite is true in industry y. There the marginal rate of technical substitution of capital for labor in producing y is relatively low.

Consider the possibility of the producer of x substituting one more unit of labor in exchange for several units less of capital. At the same time, the producer of y could take the several units of capital released from x's production and maintain output by substituting them for several units of labor. In other words, operating at point D, there could be input substitution by producers which would enable them to move either to point E' or to point E''. In either of these two cases, the output of one good would remain constant and the output of the other would increase. At point E' or point E'' the marginal rate of technical substitution of capital for labor is the same in industry x and industry y. The locus of points E' and E'' is represented by the heavily shaded line CC, the contract (or conflict) curve. It shows all input combinations that equalize the marginal rates of technical substitution. Along CC, $MRTS_{K:L}^x = MRTS_{K:L}^y$.

Production equilibrium

General equilibrium of production will occur whenever the marginal rate of technical substitution between each pair of inputs is the same for all producers who make use of those inputs. Just as the exchange equilibrium was not unique, this production equilibrium is not unique. It can occur anywhere along the contract, or conflict, curve.[3]

Note that the analysis of production equilibrium is analogous to exchange equilibrium analysis.

THE PRODUCTION POSSIBILITIES FRONTIER

Isoquants are drawn in an input space. The general equilibrium of production yields a contract curve that represents the locus of points in an input space where the marginal rates of technical substitution are the same for the production of two goods. What we do now is translate the production exchange represented by the contract curve CC to an *output space* which will show us the **production possibilities frontier**, also called the **transformation curve**. *The production possibilities frontier, or transformation curve, is defined as a curve showing the maximum attainable output combinations of two commodities when the initial endowments of the resources used in producing those commodities are given.*

---

[3]Note that a move from D to the contract curve is necessary but not sufficient for economic efficiency. Economic efficiency also requires a movement along the contract curve until the VMP of each input is the same and equal in each alternative use.

Mapping the contract curve

The way we obtain a transformation curve is to transfer the contract curve from the factor input space into a commodity output space. We look at the maximum combinations of x and y that can be obtained from a given set of capital and labor inputs. When we transfer these combinations from Figure 17-8, we arrive at Figure 17-9.

Two points, E' and E", are taken from Figure 17-8. E' represents less production of x than E". In other words, so long as resources remain fully employed, in order to obtain more of y, we must give us some x. The **marginal rate of transformation (MRT)** is the slope of the transformation curve TT in Figure 17-9.

Notice the concave-to-the-origin nature of the transformation curve. It is concave because the opportunity cost of shifting production from one good to another is increasing. If TT in Figure 17-9 were a straight line, the marginal rate of transformation would be constant. Were that the case, it would not matter, from an opportunity cost point of view, if society were already using all its resources producing x or very few producing x. To produce one more unit of y would require the same sacrifice in each case.

Since TT in Figure 17-9 is nothing more than a production possibilities frontier, its slope—the marginal rate of transformation (MRT)—must also be

---

FIGURE 17-9
The transformation, or production possibilities, curve
Transformation curve TT shows the maximum combinations of good x and good y that can be produced per unit time period with given resources and technology. Points E' and E" are taken from Figure 17-8. Point U represents underemployment of resources and is ruled out by assumption. Z is unattainable.

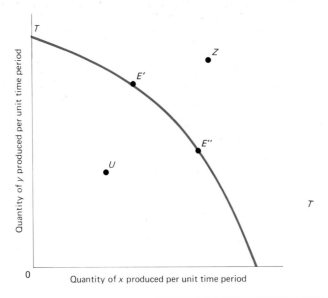

identically equal to the ratio of the marginal cost of commodity x to the marginal cost of commodity y. In other words,

$$MRT = MC_x/MC_y$$

Otherwise stated, the marginal rate of transformation tells you how much of one good you must sacrifice to get more of another.

Underemployment We rule out point U in Figure 17-9 because it is inside the transformation curve. Points inside the transformation curve indicate that society's resources are not being fully utilized.

A point such as point Z is outside the transformation curve. It is outside the production possibilities frontier, and hence it is physically unattainable at present. The maximum rate of production is represented by points such as E' and E". There is no way at this time for this economy to produce at point Z. Only if its endowments of factors of production were increased or technological change enabled them to be combined more effectively might Z be attained.

GENERAL EQUILIBRIUM FOR BOTH PRODUCTION AND EXCHANGE

We now put together the two previous sections. We deal with a world of two consumers, two commodities, and two factors of production. The input base is given by the initial available quantities of capital and labor shown in Figures 17-7 and 17-8. The utility functions of the consumers are given in Figure 17-6. They are represented by each of their indifference maps. The question now is, What will be the final equilibrium? How much of each good will be produced? How much will be consumed by each person?

Production and exchange on one diagram We transfer the transformation curve TT from Figure 17-9 to Figure 17-10 and start off at point R with that combination of good x and good y being produced. We then transfer the Edgeworth-Bowley box diagram from Figure 17-6 to Figure 17-10. The initial productions are $0x_0$ and $0y_0$. The question is, What will be the optimal distribution of x and y between consumers 1 and 2? We know that we will be somewhere on the contract curve CC. But where on CC is the question? We can find out where by realizing that for maximum consumer satisfaction the marginal rate of product transformation between x and y must be equal to the marginal rate of substitution in consumption between x and y. We therefore draw a tangent to point R on the product transformation curve. The slope of the tangent ZZ is the MRT_{xy} at point R. Now we go into the Edgeworth diagram and find a point along the contract curve where the tangency line drawn between the two tangent indifference curves has exactly the same slope as ZZ. This occurs at point E'. The slope of Z'Z' is equal to the slope of ZZ. At point E', then, $MRS_{xy} = MRT_{xy}$.

FIGURE 17-10
Equilibrium in production and exchange
Assume that we have an Edgeworth-Bowley box of the size 0_{y0} and 0_{x0}. Equilibrium will occur when both persons' marginal rates of substitution are equal to the marginal rate of transformation. This will happen when the tangent drawn to the point of equilibrium in exchange E' is parallel to the tangent drawn to point R on the transformation curve TT. To have a simultaneous equilibrium in both exchange and production, ZZ and $Z'Z'$ must be parallel.

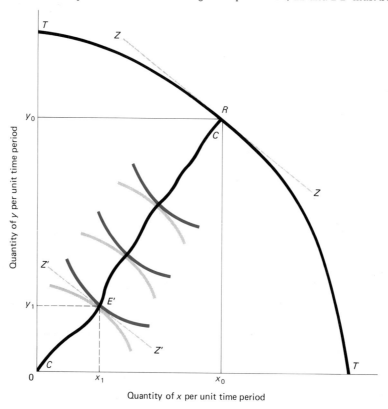

In final equilibrium, given that we started out at point R on TT, consumer 1 will consume $0y_1$ of y and consumer 2 will consume the rest, or the vertical distance between y_1 and y_0. Consumer 1 will consume $0x_1$ of x, and consumer 2 will consume the rest.

In terms of determining the amounts of capital and labor that are allocated to production of each commodity, we return to the Edgeworth-Bowley box diagram in Figure 17-8, which underlies the transformation curve in Figure 17-9 and Figure 17-10.

We have answered several questions: Given the amount of each good that is produced, we have shown how the output will be distributed between consumers. We also have shown how the available inputs would be distributed between industries when we assume maximum production and maximum consumer satisfaction. In Chapter 18, we will relax the assumption that the amount of each commodity produced is given. Note that the conditions given by point E' and the requirement that ZZ be parallel to $Z'Z'$ do not represent a unique solution. We still do not know how real income is distributed between individual 1 and individual 2, because $Z'Z'$ can be parallel to ZZ at any number of points on the contract curve. Basically, then, we have shown that at equilibrium $\text{MRS}_{xy} = \text{MRT}_{xy}$. We say nothing about what the distribution of income will actually be.

ISSUES AND APPLICATIONS

Be kind to your brother: The divide and choose problem

There is an old story that an elderly person was worried about how to divide his estate between two greedy children. This person worried that no matter how it was done, there would be endless bickering and bad feeling. A wise counsellor said there was a way to avoid the problem and to deter greed at the expense of each other. The counsellor said: "In your will you leave instructions that one of your children is to take your possessions and divide them into two groups. The other child then gets to pick whichever of the two groups of goods he or she wants. This way, if the first child, the divider of the goods, tries to be greedy, it will backfire as the second child, the chooser, gets to pick the more valuable pile of goods. This will insure a fair division. Neither child cannot say they did not have a choice."

Would you rather be the divider or the chooser in such a situation? Economic analysis tells us the answer. No matter what assumptions you make, you would rather be the divider. Here we examine one possible case. We assume that the two children, Divide (D) and Choose (C), know each other very well,

so they know the values the other would place on the goods to be inherited. They do not have identical preferences; they just know each others' preferences. To simplify the analysis, we assume there are only two types of goods to be divided. This will enable us to solve this problem within the confines of a two-dimensional Edgeworth-Bowley box.

THE PROBLEM IN A BOX

Looking at Figure 17-11 we see the basic problem. The will left a fixed endowment of two goods that we will call A and B. The measurement of these goods defines the borders of the box. D is responsible for dividing A and B into the two piles, such as at point Y, and allowing C to decide which of the two piles to take. Note that we show points Y and Y', where Y' is the mirror of Y. This allows us to see the alternative quantities D and C will get depending on which of the two piles C decides to take. That is, C can pick Y, which contains $55B$ and $100A$, or Y', which contains $25B$ and $200A$; D gets the leftover pile. As we see C's

■■■■■■■■■

FIGURE 17-11

Choice of bundles provided by divider

D has divided up the total endowment of goods A and B into two bundles. C now gets to pick the bundles. From the perspective of C, C picks the bundle represented by Y (55B and 100A) or the bundle represented by Y' (25B and 200A). Since D knows C's preferences, D picks a division that will lead C to pick bundle Y', which gives C more utility than bundle Y, which is just below the utility provided by Y' as we see from the indifference map of C.

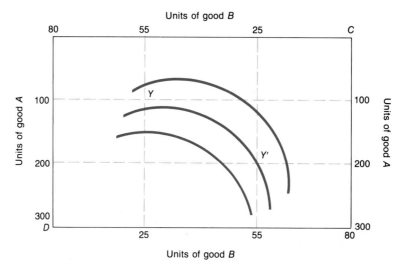

indifference map, we know C will be better off picking Y' over Y. Of course, D knew that C would prefer Y' over Y and deliberately combined the bundles of goods that way—so as to maximize what D gets out of the arrangement.

Looking at Figure 17-12 we see how D has benefited from being the divider. By rigging the piles of goods to account for C's preferences, D can offer a bundle that C will take that will put D on a higher level of utility than would be the case if C were to pick pile Y (or one just a bit to the south of point Y). If D knows C's preferences completely, and can arrange the piles of goods to maximize the outcome for D's benefit, the point that results may well be on the contract curve. That is, there will be no room for gains from trade after the piles are distributed. (What would happen if C engaged in strategic game-playing?)

A 50-50 DIVISION

Suppose that instead of trying to be clever, the elderly person had simply divided things 50-50, so that the goods were allocated in equal bundles: 150A each and 40B each. Now, greedy C and D could trade with one another to their mutual benefit—and one would not be able to take advantage of the other by being the divider. We see this in Figure 17-12, where the 50-50 allocation, point Z, leaves room for beneficial exchange, so that C and D will move to the contract curve, settling somewhere in the Z' range.

FIGURE 17-12
"Fairness" of equal division compared to divide and choose
When D is allowed to divide the goods, so that bundles Y and Y' are offered to C, if D has been careful, C will pick Y', which is far superior to point Y from D's perspective. This point will be on the contract curve, CC, if D knows C's preferences perfectly, leaving no room for gains from exchange after the bundles are chosen. If D and C were left an initial allocation that was equal, at point Z, they would trade toward the contract curve and settle in the range Z', which would be superior from C's perspective compared to the result that emerged from divide and choose.

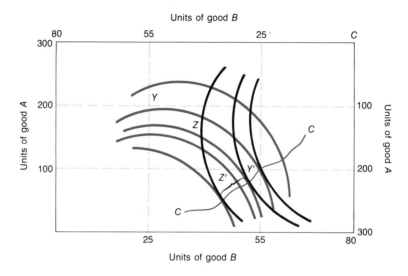

Expenditures on children—a general equilibrium model

Employing some simplifying assumptions, the family unit can be treated as a closed economy and analyzed within a general equilibrium framework. Such an approach was taken recently in modeling the expenditures made by parents on their children's education.[4] The basic question studied was how the family's resources are allocated among siblings when the children have different abilities and the

[4]Jere R. Behrman, Robert A. Pollak, and Paul Taubman, "Parental Preferences and Provision for Progeny," *Journal of Political Economy*, vol. 90, February 1982, pp. 52–73.

parents have an aversion to inequality in the distribution of their offsprings' lifetime earnings. Empirical estimates of the model's parameters using data on twins suggest that parents do indeed care about earnings inequality, and consequently spend more on the education of the less able child.

To introduce the model, assume that earnings are the sole determinant of an adult's economic well-being, and that expected lifetime earnings depend only on the individual's genetic makeup and the amount of education received as a child. Parents affect their children's subsequent economic status through the amount of resources they devote to education, and it is further assumed that parents provide all resources for their childrens' education. Parental expenditures on education, therefore, increase a child's expected lifetime earnings, but at a decreasing rate. In addition, assume that the family's total educational budget is determined independently of the parents' own consumption, parents do not give bequests or any other gifts to their children, and the price per year of schooling is the same for all children and independent of the level of education attained.

A given total of parental spending on education, along with the genetic endowments received by the offspring, determines a feasible set of expected lifetime earnings combination for the children. This opportunity set is illustrated in Figure 17-13 for a family with two children. As can be seen, the potential earnings of child 2 are higher than those of

child 1 because of different genetic makeup. Also displayed in Figure 17-13 is the parents' preference map. The indifference curves are drawn symmetrically around the 45° line to indicate equal concern for the children's economic well-being. That is, because the parents prefer equal expected lifetime earnings for their offspring, a given reduction in the expected earnings of one child must be compensated by an equal increase in the earnings of the other to keep the parents' utility at the same level.

Although equal concern rules out unequal treatment based on parental preferences which favor one child over the other, it does not guarantee equal expected earnings. Differences in genetic endowments may result in systematic differences in earnings among the children in a family. Figure 17-13 shows this possibility: Although the utility map is symmetric, the feasible set is not, and the optimal solution (at the tendency) yields different earnings for the two children.

FIGURE 17-13

Allocation of expected earnings of children

Given genetic endowments and the family's total educational budget, there is a feasible set of expected lifetime earnings combinations for the two children. The parental preference map is symmetric about the 45° line to show equal concern for the children's economic well-being. The parents maximize utility (at the tangency) by allocating funds to each child's education until the marginal returns to schooling for that child equal the market interest rate. If a greater genetic endowment implies higher (lower) marginal returns, then in equilibrium the parents spend more (less) on the education of child 2. Equal concern for their children's welfare does not imply that the parents will try to equalize their offsprings' expected incomes.

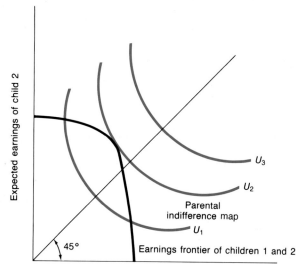

The optimum is attained. Out of the family's total educational budget, the parents allocate funds to each child's schooling until the marginal returns to education for that child equal the market rate of interest. (The market interest rate represents the opportunity cost of parental investments in education.) The amount spent on each child's schooling depends upon the relationship between genetic endowment and the returns of education. In particular, if a greater genetic endowment implies higher marginal returns to education, the parents will adopt a reinforcing strategy in which they devote more resources to the education of the abler child. On the other hand, if a greater genetic endowment yields smaller marginal returns to education, parents will spend more on schooling for the less able child. Only if genetic endowment and education are un-related will the parents divide the family educational budget equally among their children.

The main implication of the theoretical model is that parental aversion to earnings inequality leads them to devote different amounts of resources to each child's education. A sample of 914 white male fraternal twins born in the U.S. between 1917 and 1927 was used to test this hypothesis. The results suggested that distributional as well as investment considerations are important determinants of the allocation of resources within families. In general, the estimates implied that parents spend more on the education of their less able children. This indicates a fairly strong parental aversion to earnings inequality and indirectly suggest that schooling yields smaller returns for more able children.

SUMMARY

1 Voluntary exchange must, by definition, make both parties to the exchange better off.

2 When we consider a two-person exchange, if the two parties find themselves at a point in the combined commodity space (Edgeworth-Bowley box) where their respective indifference curves cross, gains from trade are possible. A movement along either's indifference curve does not harm that party and does move the other party onto a higher indifference curve.

3 No further gains from exchange can be obtained once the two parties reach the contract (or conflict) curve along which their respective indifference curves are tangent, i.e., along which the marginal rates of substitution for the two goods, x and y, are equal for both persons. Along the contract, or conflict, curve, there is an equilibrium in exchange.

4 Partial equilibrium analysis uses the *ceteris paribus* assumption. However, it is not true that *all* other things are held constant, because if they were, no change would be possible.

5 General equilibrium analysis takes into account interrelations among markets. Not *all* other things, however, are allowed to vary; something must be given or exogenous in order for us to begin such an analysis.

6 The choice of how many interrelations should be taken into account depends on the question being asked and the degree to which things can be assumed to be constant without invalidating the analysis.

7 Equilibrium in exchange requires that marginal rages of substitution between the same goods be equal for all individuals.

8 Equilibrium in production requires that the marginal rate of technical substitution between each pair of inputs be the same for all users of those inputs.

9 General equilibrium in both production and exchange requires that the common marginal rate of substitution for all consumers be equal to the common marginal rate of transformation for all producers. In a two-good, two-person, two-factor model, this would occur when the tangent drawn to the exchange equilibrium point on the contract curve has in the same slope—i.e., is parallel to—the tangent drawn to the output combination point on the transformation curve.

GLOSSARY

- **general equilibrium analysis** Economic analysis which takes into account the interrelations between markets; to be contrasted with partial equilibrium analysis.
- **partial equilibrium analysis** Analyzing a market in isolation without taking account of the interrelations among markets.
- **Edgeworth-Bowley box** A rectangular graph protraying two individual commodity spaces superimposed on each other with each individual's origin at a diagonally opposite corner of the box. Within the box we can draw two sets of indifference curves. The length of the box represents the total quantity of x available, and the height of the box the total quantity of y available. It is used to analyze exchange between two individuals.
- **region of mutual advantage** A region in an Edgeworth-Bowley box. An initial distribution of goods x and y is given. The indifference curves of the two individuals that intersect at that point form a "fisheye." Within this region, movements (exchanges) of the initial quantities can be made which benefit at least one of the parties without harming the other party.
- **contract curve** In an Edgeworth-Bowley box, the locus of all possible combinations; the marginal rate of substitution of one individual equals the marginal rate of substitution of the other individual. Any movement along the contract curve benefits one party and reduces the welfare of the other party.
- **conflict curve** Another name for the contract curve; once on the curve, the two parties are in conflict with each other.
- **production possibilities frontier** The locus of points showing the maximum technologically feasible rates of output of x and y with a given endowment of inputs.
- **transformation curve** Another name for a production possibilities frontier. A curve showing the maximum attainable output combinations from given initial

endowments of inputs. Otherwise stated, the transformation curve shows the rate of transformation of good x into good y when there is full employment of the initial endowment of inputs.

■ **marginal rate of transformation (MRT)** The slope on the transformation curve (production possibilities curve). MRT gives the rate at which one good can be "transformed" into another by reallocating existing fixed input quantities.

QUESTIONS

(Answers to even-numbered questions are at back of text.)

1 How does general equilibrium analysis differ from partial equilibrium analysis?
2 On the one hand, general equilibrium is said to encompass all markets; on the other hand, the analysis is typically presented for a world of two persons, two factors, and two goods. How can this be?
3 When would general equilibrium analysis be more appropriate than partial equilibrium analysis?
4 In a two-person, two-good world, what condition must exist for there to be a general equilibrium in exchange?
5 What is the "contract curve" and how is it related to general equilibrium in exchange?
6 "Given an initial distribution of the two goods, we can say only that exchanges will eventually redistribute the goods until some point on the contract curve is reached." Is this statement true or false, and why?
7 Suppose we did not know the initial distribution of the two goods between the two individuals. Can we say anything about those final distributions which will satisfy the conditions of general equilibrium in exchange?
8 Assume that the distribution of goods has reached a point on the contract curve. Now one or both of the persons' preferences change, for whatever reason. What must then occur?
9 In considering general equilibrium in production, are the initial endowments of productive resources stocks or flows? Explain.
10 Figure 17-7's rectangular dimensions represent the endowments of the two productive resources. What, then, is represented by D?
11 Could idleness of some labor or capital be shown on a diagram such as Figure 17-8? Explain.
12 What condition must be satisfied if there is to be a general equilibrium in production?
13 Point D in Figure 17-8 is clearly inefficient because the MRTs for goods x and y are unequal. What are the maximum gains to be realized from resource reallocation (a) measured in terms of additional output of good x? (b) measured in terms of additional output of good y?
14 Why must MRS and MRT be equal for all consumers and firms to achieve a general equilibrium in both consumption and production?
15 "The integration of general equilibrium in exchange with general equilibrium in production yields a unique distribution (satisfying the criterion of MRS equal to MRT) for any given output combination." Is this statement true or false, and why?

SELECTED REFERENCES

Barrett, Nancy Smith, *The Theory of Microeconomic Policy* (Lexington, Mass.: Heath, 1974).

Baumol, William J., *Economic Theory and Operations Analysis,* 3d ed. (Englewood Cliffs, N.J.: Prentice-Hall, 1972), chaps. 15 and 20.

Knight, Frank H., "A Suggestion for Simplifying the Statement of the General Theory of Price," *Journal of Political Economy,* vol. 36, June 1928, pp. 353–370.

Walras, Leon, *Elements of Pure Economics,* translated by William Jaffé (Homewood, Ill.: Irwin, 1954).

Zeuthen, F., *Economic Theory and Method* (Cambridge, Mass.: Harvard, 1955), chap. 11.

Welfare economics

CHAPTER 18

When the word "welfare" is mentioned, people generally think of programs to aid individuals with low incomes; also, some notion of well-being is implied. In economics, however, the term "welfare" has a specific meaning. Welfare refers simply to utility, and **welfare economics** is that part of the study of economics that explains how to identify and arrive at what are called *socially efficient* or *socially optimal allocations of resources*. The study of welfare economics concerns itself only with possible "best" solutions for resource allocation. What we have to do is determine what distinguishes the "best" or "optimum" among all the solutions available. However, since the term "best" is subjective, it is not within the province of scientific analysis to label one pattern of resource allocation as "better" than another. Even the term "optimal" is value-laden and hence we must be careful when talking about the optimal allocation of resources not to imply that we are talking about the "best" or preferred allocation of resources. Whenever the term "optimal" is used in this chapter and in Chapter 19, it does not carry with it this strictly valuative connotation; rather, it refers to maximizing the economic value of a given set of resources.

ASSUMPTIONS USED IN WELFARE ANALYSIS

In order to make welfare analysis operative and less arbitrary, some assumptions must be made explicitly at the onset. These assumptions are closely related to those used as the foundation for the theory of consumer behavior. Basically, there are three.[1]

[1] All basically are variations on the axiom of individual sovereignty, or competence.

1 The individual is the best judge of his or her own welfare.
2 If the individual prefers a to b, his or her welfare is greater with situation a than with situation b—that is, the individual is "better off" with situation a than with situation b.
3 The individual acts in accordance with his or her own preferences. The individual will choose that which he or she values more.

For welfare analysis to be meaningful, we must accept these assumptions, which, in themselves, could be considered as value judgments. Few economists will accept these value judgments without attaching a few of their own qualifications. For example, assumption 1 is generally not considered applicable to young children. Moreover, the state acts "in the best interests of the public" by preventing individuals from freely purchasing and consuming certain commodities which, it believes, should be allocated only by certified experts (prescription drugs, nuclear fuel, etc.).

Interpersonal utility comparisons

When we attempt to measure or establish levels of social welfare for groups of individuals, we immediately run into problems. If individual I is better off with situation a than with b, but individual II is better off with situation b rather than situation a, how do we measure the social welfare of individuals I and II? To do so would require interpersonal welfare comparisons, but there is no scientifically meaningful way to compare the utility levels of various individuals. Rather, all we are able to do is talk of utility rankings *by* an individual (but *not between* individuals).

If we cannot compare utility levels between individuals, we cannot say very much about one distribution of income as compared with another. If, for some reason, I receive 10 times as much income as you, there is no way to show that this is a worse distribution of income than if you receive 10 times as much as I.

EFFICIENCY AND THE PARETO CONDITION

Economists are uncomfortable, in general, with interpersonal utility comparisons. In modern welfare analysis they go as far as they can without making such interpersonal comparisons. This is done by focusing on the notion of economic efficiency. You remember that we made the distinction between technical efficiency and economic efficiency. Technical efficiency referred to the comparison of physical output to physical input; economic efficiency, on the other hand, related the value of output to the input or resource value used to produce this output. The measurement of economic efficiency requires that values be placed on commodities. In welfare analysis, the values placed on commodities are those which a competitive market presents to us.

The Pareto condition

The Italian economist Vilfredo Pareto specified a condition of optimal or efficient resource allocation, referred to as the **Pareto condition**. *We define the Pareto condition as an allocation of goods such that, when compared to any other allocation of goods, all parties are at least as well off and at least one of them is actually better off. Another way of defining the Pareto condition is as a situation in which it is impossible for some or all individuals to gain by further voluntary exchange.*

We will see that any economic organization that leads to all individuals in a society being at a point on the contract curve is a Pareto-optimal organization. (The term "Pareto optimality" is more in use than the terms "Pareto criterion" and "Pareto condition"; they all mean the same thing.)

It turns out that the Pareto condition is the common core of all social welfare functions, but it is indeed a weak core. It tells us only that a change that makes at least one individual better off and no one worse off is an "improvement" in social welfare. Conversely, a change that makes no one better off and someone worse off results in a reduction in social welfare. Nothing can be said by the Pareto criterion about a change that makes some better off and others worse off; that would require comparing the increased satisfaction of the gainers with the lost satisfaction of the losers. Because most policy changes are of this more complex kind, the Pareto condition or criterion is a weak one. A variety of more explicit welfare judgment methods have, therefore, been suggested to supplement the Pareto criterion. We will discuss several of these below.

Pareto versus efficiency criteria

It turns out that while the Pareto condition can be applied only to an economy with at least two individuals, the notion of economic efficiency can be applied to a one-person economy in which there are no property rights and no interaction problems. For most problems, though, the fulfillment of the Pareto condition coincides with maximum economic efficiency. In other words, for most purposes they are the same thing. Thus, failure to attain the Pareto condition generally implies economic inefficiency.

MARGINAL CONDITIONS FOR OPTIMAL ALLOCATION OF RESOURCES FOR SOCIAL WELFARE

We already have the tools for understanding the marginal conditions for Pareto optimality or optimal resource allocation. All you need remember is the definition of either a general equilibrium in exchange or in production. Equilibrium in Chapter 17 occurred somewhere on the contract curve. On the contract curve, it was impossible to make one trading partner better off without harming the other. However, off the contract curve, it was possible either to make one person better off without harming the other or to make both of them better off simultaneously. We know then that at any point on the contract curve, the Pareto condition is satisfied. This gives us the first marginal condition for social welfare.

Exchange optimality

The marginal condition for the *efficient allocation of goods* is stated simply as follows: The Pareto condition requires that the *marginal rate of substitution between any two consumer goods* must be the same for all individuals who consume both goods, or $MRS_{xy}^1 = MRS_{xy}^2 = \ldots = MRS_{xy}^n$ (where the superscript numbers indicate individual consumers and the x and y subscripts are the names of goods). This marginal condition for exchange must be satisfied or at least one individual would benefit from further exchange.[2]

Efficient factor usage

A second and similar marginal condition relates to the efficient use of factors of production.

The attainment of the Pareto criterion requires that the *marginal rate of technical substitution between any pair of factors* must be the same for all producers who use both factors, or $MRTS_{L:K}^x = MRTS_{L:K}^y$ (where the superscript letters name commodities being produced and the subscript letters name factors of production). If this condition did not hold, a reallocation of at least one input factor from one producer to another would increase total production without requiring the use of any additional input factors.

"Overall" optimality

The final condition required for Pareto optimality involves the interaction of the product and factor markets.

The Pareto condition is satisfied only when the *marginal rate of transformation in production equals the marginal rate of substitution in consumption* for every pair of commodities and for every individual, or $MRT_{xy} = MRS_{xy}$ for all individuals.

This can be seen most easily in a simplified example in which there is only one individual in the economy.[3]

The product transformation curve for the economy is given by TT in Figure 18-1. A tangent drawn to any point along that curve gives the marginal rate of product transformation between commodity x and commodity y. We now envision a set of indifference curves for goods x and y for our single consumer. The highest indifference curve that can be attained is labeled I. It is tangent to TT at point E. At point E, then, the marginal rate of product transformation (MRT) is just equal to the marginal rate of substitution (MRS) of x and y for this consumer. The optimal quantities of production and consumption are x_1 and y_1.

To further demonstrate that maximum consumer satisfaction requires

---

[2]Note, however, that Pareto optimality in exchange can occur with one person starving because he or she has so few resources with which to begin.

[3]This example cannot be used to demonstrate Pareto optimality in exchange, only economic efficiency.

FIGURE 18-1

Satisfying economic efficiency
We show a one-person economy. That person's
highest indifference curve I is tangent to the
transformation curve TT at E. Economic
efficiency requires output rates of $0x_1$ and $0y_1$
where the marginal rate of transformation is
equal to the marginal rate of substitution.

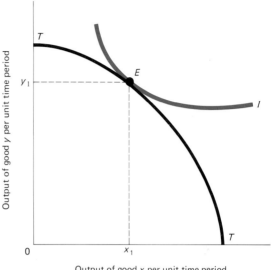

Output of good y per unit time period

Output of good x per unit time period

that MRS = MRT, we take an example. Assume now that MRS and MRT are
not equal. Consider the case:

$$\text{MRS}_{xy} = 1:1$$
$$\text{MRT}_{xy} = 1:2$$

(18-1)

Now assume that the amount of x produced is reduced by one unit, and
also assume that individual 1 wishes to reduce the consumption of x by one
unit. For individual 1 to maintain the same level of satisfaction, an additional
unit of y must be consumed in order to offset the loss of one unit of x.
Assume, then, that the production sector gives consumer 1 this extra unit
of y. How does it do this? By reducing the production of x. But notice, with
$\text{MRT}_{xy} = 1:2$, that the production sector, in giving up one unit of x, can shift
resources to the production of y and produce *two* more units of y. Therefore,
the production sector could satisfy consumer 1 by producing one less of x
and giving consumer 1 one more of y, but there would also be one unit of
y "left over." This one unit of y could be given to consumer 2. That is,
consumer 2 could be made better off without making consumer 1 worse off.
Consumer satisfaction therefore is not maximized if the marginal rate of
substitution between x and y is not exactly equal to the marginal rate of
transformation between x and y.

PERFECT COMPETITION AND
ECONOMIC EFFICIENCY

It turns out that the perfectly competitive price system examined in Chapter 10 has a very special quality. There is an exact correspondence between an allocation of resources that satisfies the Pareto condition and the allocation that results from a perfectly competitive price system. Every perfectly competitive allocation in long-run equilibrium satisfies the Pareto criterion, and every allocation that satisfies the Pareto criterion has associated with it a perfectly competitive set of prices.

Some caveats about the analysis

Before we show the equivalence of a perfectly competitive price system and an economically efficient system (one that satisfies the Pareto criterion), we must give a few warnings.

The first one is that *not every allocation that satisfies the Pareto condition is a social welfare optimum*, because the social welfare optimum depends on the social welfare function. A social welfare function tells us how to trade off gains to one person against losses to another. In the preceding example, there was only *one* possible social welfare maximum (even though there were a large number of possible allocations of resources that satisfied the Pareto condition) because there was only one person in the society.

Second, when we include a distributional criterion (the distribution of income) with which to judge the performance of an economic system, we *could* find that a competitive system satisfying the Pareto condition leads to an "inappropriate," even if efficient, allocation. For example, in some possible efficient allocations large numbers of individuals may receive very low incomes.

Third, even though we can show that a perfectly competitive system results in the satisfaction of the Pareto criterion, the real world seldom provides us with a perfectly competitive price system. Chapter 19 will show the many ways in which the competitive model is different from the real world.

The meaning of a perfectly competitive price system

To refresh the reader's memory, we will specify what is meant by a perfectly competitive price system. We assume that there are n well-defined homogeneous goods. These goods include producer capital goods, intermediate goods, and consumption goods. Each of the goods has an equilibrium price which is established by the interaction of supply and demand. (The price to which we are referring is, of course, *relative* price. *Absolute* price, or the price level, is of little concern when we are dealing with the allocation of resources.) Equilibrium prices clear each market; the quantities demanded and supplied of each good are equal. We further assume that transactions costs are zero and that firms and consumers have perfect information. Thus, each good has one and only one price; that is, the price per constant quality unit is uniform throughout the market.

Consumers take the prices of final goods and their budget constraints as givens, and adjust their behavior to maximize utility. In terms of firm behavior, we assume that there are a large number of firms and that each firm operates to maximize profits.

Now we are ready to show the relation between perfect competition and the satisfaction of the Pareto condition.

Perfect competition and satisfaction of the Pareto criterion

All we need to do is show that the marginal conditions for optimal resource allocation, discussed above, are satisfied in a perfectly competitive price system. We examine each of the three marginal conditions separately.

Exchange. To attain a Pareto optimum it is necessary that the marginal rate of substitution between any pair of consumer goods be the same for all individuals who consume both goods. In a perfectly competitive system, each consumer takes the price of each good as given. For utility maximization, each consumer must equate his or her marginal rate of substitution of x for y to the price ratio P_x/P_y. This was seen in the discussion of the consumer behavior in Chapter 3. In equilibrium, then, the consumer equates the rate at which he or she is *willing* to trade x for y to the rate at which x and y *can* in fact be traded in a competitive market. In other words the point at which an indifference curve is tangent to the budget contraint is the point of optimum allocation for the consumer. In perfect competition, each individual has an MRS equal to P_x/P_y; and, the marginal condition for exchange is satisfied. Otherwise stated, if $MRS^1_{xy} = P_x/P_y$ and then $MRS^2_{xy} = P_x/P_y$, then $MRS^1_{xy} = MRS^2_{xy}$.

Hence, *in perfect competition, no further exchanges could raise the welfare of one person without reducing another's.*

Factor substitution. To attain a Pareto optimum, the marginal rate of technical substitution (MRTS) between any two inputs must be the same for all producers who use both inputs. Again, this is seen to be the case in a perfectly competitive system. Producers take the prices of factor inputs as given. To maximize profits, subject to a budget constraint, they must operate where an isoquant is tangent to the isocost line. But the slope of the isocost line is the ratio of the prices of the two inputs which, like the prices of commodities in a perfectly competitive economy, are the same for all persons and uses. Hence, if all producers face the same input prices, they will all choose that combination of inputs are which the marginal rate of technical substitution between every pair of inputs is the same. In other words, if $MRTS^x_{L:K} = P_L/P_K$, and $MRTS^y_{L:K} = P_L/P_K$, then $MRTS^x_{L:K} = MRTS^y_{L:K}$.

Therefore, *in perfect competition, no alteration in the proportions of inputs used could increase the output of one good without reducing the output of another.*

Product substitution. A Pareto optimum requires that the marginal rate of transformation in production be equal to the marginal rate of substitution in consumption for each pair of commodities and for each individual who consumes those commodities. In other words, MRT must equal MRS. This can be shown to be satisfied in a perfectly competitive situation. The MRT is the slope of the transformation curve and is equal to the ratio of the marginal cost of x to that of y. We know, though, that each profit-maximizing firm in a perfectly competitive system will choose a rate of output at which marginal cost is equal to price. Therefore, for every firm, price equals marginal cost and hence $MC_x/MC_y = P_x/P_y$ for all firms, but P_x/P_y is also equal to the consumer's marginal rate of substitution of x for y. Hence, this third condition for a Pareto optimum is satisfied.

Therefore, *in perfect competition, no alteration in the mix of goods produced could increase welfare.*

Competitive markets satisfy all the marginal conditions for the attainment of a Pareto optimum. An important question is now brought to the fore. Given the equivalence of a perfect competition result and Pareto optimum, has anything been said that is important for policy purposes? Should the government be guided by this "equivalence theorem" and attempt to, say, break up monopolies? We will briefly examine this thorny issue in later sections of this chapter and in Chapter 19.

EXTENDING WELFARE ANALYSIS

Using the tools we have already examined, we can develop a model for welfare comparisons.[4] We have already developed an Edgeworth-Bowley box for exchange and an Edgeworth-Bowley box for production, and we have derived the production possibilities frontier, or transformation curve, from the production version of the Edgeworth-Bowley box. Now we derive a utility possibilities frontier from the contract curve of the Edgeworth-Bowley box.

A utility possibilities frontier

The contract curve in any exchange (Edgeworth-Bowley box) diagram, such as those in Figures 17-5, 17-6, and 17-10 in the last chapter, and as seen in Figure 18-2 here, represents the Pareto-optimal locus of exchange points. In other words, when we are on the contract curve, the Pareto criterion is satisfied. The marginal rate of substitution is equal for both consumers on the contract curve. We can transform this locus of equilibrium points (such as E, E', and E'' in Figure 18-2) from the commodity space of the exchange box to utility space, in order to obtain a **utility possibilities frontier**.

Each point in the Edgeworth-Bowley box represents a certain level of consumption and utility for each of the two individuals. We can pick any ordinal scale we want (such as the one we have here with values of 300, 400, and 500 for person 1 and values of 100, 130, and 175 for person 2) so long as higher indifference curves have a number attached to them that is higher than the number attached to lower indifference curves. We know that

---

[4]The presentation will largely follow Francis Bator, "The Simple Analytics of Welfare Maximization," *American Economic Review,* vol. 47, 1957, pp. 22–59, especially pp. 22–31.

FIGURE 18-2
Utility measures along the contract curve
The points of equilibrium in exchange, such as represented by points E, E', and E'', create the contract curve, CC. Each equilibrium point also represents a level of utility for each of the trading parties, 1 and 2. Associated with points E, E', and E'' are utilities of 300, 400, and 500 for person 1, and utilities of 175, 130, and 100 for person 2.

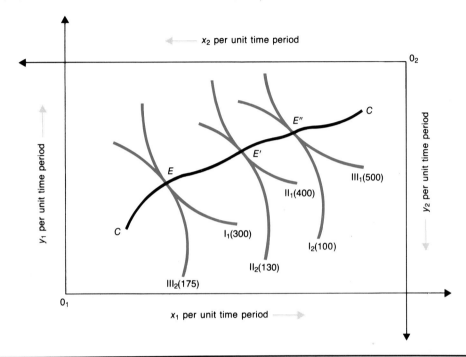

as we move from the left-hand side of the box to the right-hand side of the box along the contract curve, we are moving to higher indifference curves for individual 1 and to lower indifference curves for individual 2. At each point, then along the contract curve we have utilities for each of the two consumers. We translate these points to Figure 18-3. In that figure, consumer 2's utility is measured on the horizontal axis and consumer 1's utility is measured on the vertical axis. The resultant curve is a line such as UU. All the points on that curve are points on the contract curve. Note the similarity between the derivation of this utility possibilities frontier and the derivation of the product transformation curve, or production possibilities frontier.

The transfer of the contract curve to the utility possibilities curve is a transformation from output space to utility space. For production we had a transformation from input space to output space.

The curve UU in Figure 18-3 corresponds to only one Edgeworth-Bowley box. In this instance we derived it from the box of Figure 18-2. However,

FIGURE 18-3
Utility possibilities frontier
The curve *UU* is the utility possibilities frontier and is derived from Figure 18-2. It is a transformation of the contract curve from the output space to a utility space. We have to assign arbitrary ordinal rankings to the different indifference curves to obtain *UU*.

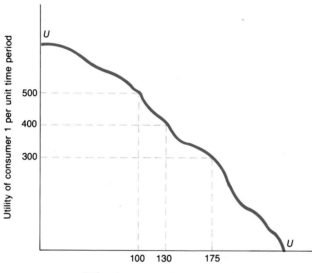

the curve in Figure 18-3 could correspond to the Edgeworth-Bowley box that would fit in the rectangle with vertical height $0y_1$ and horizontal width $0x_1$ in Figure 18-1. We know that there are a very large number of possible utility frontiers. There is one for each of the very large number of contract curves within the equally large number of Edgeworth-Bowley boxes that could be traced out from points along the product transformation curve *TT*. Each point along the product transformation curve results in a new utility possibilities frontier since each point corresponds to different total outputs of goods *x* and *y*. In Figure 18-4, we draw a number of utility possibilities frontiers. Each is associated with a different point along the product transformation curve or the production possibilities frontier and the exchange box from which it was constructed. These are labeled U_1U_1 through U_4U_4. Note that each utility possibilities frontier has a negative slope throughout. That is all we can say about its shape. What can we do with this essentially infinite set of utility possibilities frontiers? We can construct what is called a grand utility possibilities frontier.

A grand utility possibilities frontier

If we consider only those points on utility possibilities frontiers that are not inferior to any other point, we obtain a **grand utility possibilities frontier**. This is the heavily shaded "envelope" of *all* the utility possibilities frontiers,

FIGURE 18-4
Grand utility possibilities frontier
There are an infinite number of utility possibilities curves, such as U_1U_1 through U_4U_4 and each corresponds to different-sized Edgeworth-Bowley boxes drawn to different points on the production possibilities frontier. When we take the envelope of all such utility possibilities frontiers, we obtain the heavily shaded line which is called the grand utility possibilities frontier.

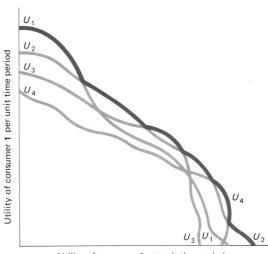

Utility of consumer 2 per unit time period

each of which is associated with a point on the production possibilities frontier. This makes sense because any point *within* the heavily shaded grand utility possibilities frontier is inferior to any point on the grand utility possibilities frontier. Interior points are inferior because the frontier points always yield higher utility for *both* consumer 1 and consumer 2.

To go further, we must be willing to assume a social welfare function that depends exclusively on the positions of consumer 1 and consumer 2 on their own preference scales. As we will see in the following section, the construction of a social utility function, even theoretically, is a difficult conceptual task. Nonetheless, we will assume that it is possible to derive such a social welfare function.

We have drawn the grand utility possibilities frontier as the heavily shaded, wavy line in Figure 18-5. It is taken from Figure 18-4. We have added four social welfare curves that are not dissimilar in their formal characteristics to individual indifference curves. *Maximum achievable welfare is attained at the tangency of the grand utility possibilities frontier to the highest attainable social welfare function.* This is welfare curve W_3W_3 in the figure. This tangency is at point E.

Bliss point

What we have done, then, is reduce a very large number of possible equilibria along the grand utilities possibility frontier UU to a single equilibrium point. The point E is called a **constrained bliss point** because it represents the one organization of exchange, production, and distribution that corresponds to maximum attainable social welfare. Society would, of course, be better off if it could attain W_4W_4, but that is impossible with its current resources and

FIGURE 18-5
A constrained bliss point
If we draw a set of social welfare functions such as W_1W_1 through W_4W_4, we can obtain a constrained bliss point at which the highest social welfare function just touches the grand utility possibilities frontier, UU, at point E.

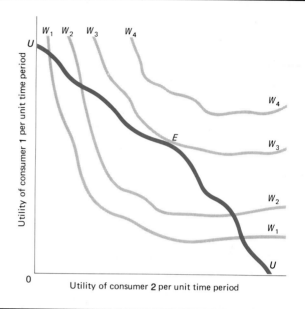

state of technology. Bliss point E is constrained by the available resources and the state of the art.

DISTRIBUTIONAL CRITERIA

Pareto optimality is one way to evaluate the performance of an economy. There are others, however, and we hinted at them when we discussed the construction of a social welfare function. Welfare discussions about the "best" distribution of income have taken on much importance in recent years. In fact, some economists argue that any welfare criterion that ignores distribution of income involves a contradiction in terms. After all, resource allocation involves, in addition to questions of what is produced and how it is produced, the question of to whom the output is distributed. Looking only at efficiency ignores the matter of income distribution. To be sure, the reason that economists have felt most comfortable with efficiency arguments is that value judgments are presumably eliminated from the discussion. However, distribution problems have been frequently interjected into economic policy questions. Discussions of income redistribution programs, in particular, often implicitly assume that the welfare of society is increased when income is redistributed from the relatively well-to-do to the relatively poor.

The Kaldor-Hicks criterion

In the 1930s a number of economists attempted to formulate distributive welfare criteria which they believed to be independent of value judgment considerations. In other words, value judgments of the relative importance

FIGURE 18-6
Kaldor-Hicks criterion
We draw in a utility possibilities frontier. If the economy is at point *A*, any move to any point between *B* and *D* is preferred, since no one is made worse off and someone is made better off; however, a movement to a point such as *E* would make consumer 1 better off and consumer 2 worse off. According to the Kaldor-Hicks criterion, since the gainer could and would be willing to compensate the loser for his or her loss, this move to *E* would be a preferred move.

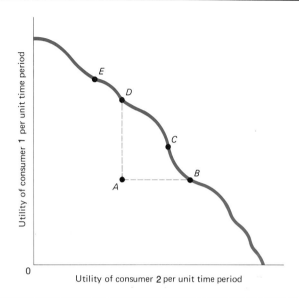

of different individuals' welfare were to be removed from the argument. The first attempt was made by two English economists, Nicholas Kaldor and John Hicks.[5]

We demonstrate the Kaldor-Hicks welfare criterion in Figure 18-6. We have drawn a standard utility possibilities frontier. All points on the frontier, of course, satisfy the Pareto condition. Any movement along the frontier involves a redistribution of wealth. A movement from point *E*, for example, to point *C* requires that consumer 1 lose and consumer 2 gain. In other words, along the utility possibilities frontier, any improvement in one consumer's welfare necessarily requires a reduction in the other consumer's welfare. Both Kaldor and Hicks assume that such redistributions can be affected by either *lump-sum transfers* of wealth or redirection of income flows.[6]

Now assume that the economy is at point *A*. A move to point *E* would not be an improvement according to the Pareto condition because it would involve a reduction in the welfare of consumer 2. However, a movement to point *B*, *C*, or *D* would result in welfare improvement for either consumer 2 or consumer 1 or both consumers. In fact, a movement to any point in the section bounded by *AD,AB*, and the utility possibilities frontier *between*

[5]Nicholas Kaldor, "Welfare Propositions in Economics and Interpersonal Comparisons of Utility," *Economics Journal*, vol. 49, September 1939, pp. 549–552; and J. R. Hicks, "The Foundations of Welfare Economics," *Economic Journal*, vol. 49, December 1939, pp. 696–712.

[6]A lump-sum transfer of income is done in such a way that there are no incentives for an individual to change behavior, whether they receive the income or are the source of it. Various schemes for making lump-sum transfers have been suggested, but none seems to be perfect.

points B and D would improve welfare for both. Everyone could be made better off by such a change.

Kaldor argued that a move from A to E could also be labeled an improvement, because when point E has been reached, we could redistribute income or wealth to move the economy to a point such as C at which everyone would be better off.[7]

Thus, by the Kaldor-Hicks criterion, any point on the utility possibilities frontier is preferred to any point below the frontier. The only assumption in the Kaldor-Hicks criterion is that consumer 1 *will* compensate consumer 2 for a loss in welfare by direct money payment. We should note, however, that both Hicks and Kaldor talked only of *potential* compensations. (It was shown later that unless compensation actually was paid the Kaldor-Hicks criterion could lead to paradoxical results.)

Hicks asked whether we could possibly get an agreement among consumers to go from A to E. Kaldor asked the question, If we are at E, could we ever get agreement to go back to A? Both assume that policymakers have knowledge of the utility functions and act as if to satisfy the Pareto condition.

THE THEORY OF SOCIAL CHANGE

We talked earlier about how to derive a social welfare function, but we really didn't indicate the full extent of the difficulties in deriving even the simplest welfare function. Work by Nobel Prize winner Kenneth Arrow showed that a social welfare function could not always be derived by allowing citizens to vote for different allocation outcomes. His main point was that a *consistent social welfare function often could not be obtained through voting even if individual preferences were consistent.*[8]

In investigating the formulation of social preferences, Arrow stated five axioms which he believes that social preference structures must satisfy to be minimally acceptable to the population. They are as follows:

- **Complete ordering.** *Social preferences must, like individual preferences, be completely ordered. They must satisfy the condition of transitivity. Thus, if α is preferred to b, then b is not preferred to α. Further, if α is preferred to b, and b is preferred to c, then α is preferred to c.*

- **Responsiveness to individual preferences.** *If situation α is socially preferred to situation b by a given set of individuals and if individual rankings change so that one or more individuals raise situation α to an even higher rank and no one lowers situation α in rank, then situation α must remain socially preferred to situation b.*

[7]Kaldor is stretching the point. The movement from A to B is not really an improvement in itself. Only the final outcome of his experiment, the movement from A to C, can be considered an improvement.

[8]See Kenneth Arrow, *Social Choice and Individual Values* (New York: Wiley, 1951).

- **Nonimposition.** *Social preferences cannot be imposed independently of individual preferences.*

- **Nondictatorship.** *Society must not prefer situation a to situation b just because one individual prefers a to b.*

- **Independence of irrelevant alternatives.** *Assume that there are three situations available, a, b, and c. Society prefers a to b and b to c. Consider the possibility of c disappearing. Society must still consider a preferable to b.*

Arrow impossibility theorem

The reason that we have the term **Arrow Impossibility Theorem** is that no *voting* system allows all of these five axioms to be satisfied. In fact, a simple model can show that the first axiom will not be satisfied even if individuals have consistent preferences. Consider three individuals. They are asked to rank situations *a*, *b*, and *c*. They vote by writing in the number 1 for their first choice, 2 for their second choice, and 3 for their third choice. Assume that the ranking or voting results are shown in Table 18-1. Each individual has consistent preferences.

Consider the choice between economic situation *a* and situation *b*. Individual I rates situation *a* higher than situation *b*. Individual III also rates situation *a* higher than situation *b* (because *a* is individual III's second choice and situation *b* is his or her third choice). Now consider the choice between *b* and *c*. Individual I prefers *b* to *c*; so, too, does individual II. You would think, then, that since two individuals prefer *a* to *b* and two individuals prefer *b* to *c*, consistency would require that *a* be preferred to *c*. This is not the case. The majority prefers *c* to *a*; individual II ranks *c* second and *a* third, and individual III ranks *c* first and *a* second. Thus, if we had majority voting to make a choice between *a* and *c*, the majority would choose situation *c* over situation *a*. Thus, preferences of the majority are inconsistent. Arrow's work indicates that the use of a democratic process of voting to formulate a social welfare function can produce contradictory welfare criteria.

Note that an important aspect of the Arrow Impossibility Theorem is the assumption of a majority voting system. He did not take up the possibility, for example, of a voting system that requires unanimity and permits the buying and selling of votes.

TABLE 18-1 *Voting for a, b, or c*	Economic situation		
Individual	*a*	*b*	*c*
I	1	2	3
II	3	1	2
III	2	3	1

FIGURE 18-7
Theory of second best
TT is a product transformation curve. W_1, W_2, and W_3 are social welfare functions. The welfare maximum occurs at point E. Assume, however, that only points on the line CC are attainable. The Pareto condition would require that we move to E' or E''' because that would put us back on the transformation curve TT. However, a move to point E'' would put us on a higher social welfare curve, W_2, than we would be on if we were either at E''' or at E'.

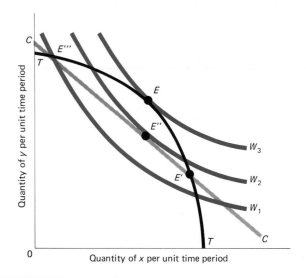

THE THEORY OF SECOND BEST

We have shown that satisfaction of the Pareto criterion results in an efficient allocation of resources. We showed in Figure 18-6, for example, that a movement from point A to a point on the utility possibilities frontier between B and D would improve social welfare measured by the efficiency or Pareto criterion.

However, it could occur that one or more of the Pareto conditions cannot be satisfied because of institutional restrictions such as monopoly, indivisibility of the product, or "externalities" (with which we will deal in Chapter 19). If the best or highest welfare position is unattainable, it then becomes relevant to ask whether a "second-best" position can be attained by satisfying the remaining Pareto marginal conditions. The so-called **theory of the second best** says it cannot necessarily be done. If one or more of the conditions for a Pareto optimum (i.e., the marginal conditions for optimal resource allocation) cannot, for whatever reason, be satisfied, then in general, it is neither necessary nor desirable to satisfy the remaining marginal conditions.

The formal proof of the second-best theorem is rather complicated.[9] We can demonstrate it on a much less technical level by using Figure 18-7. Here we show a product transformation curve TT. We know that a welfare maximum occurs when the social welfare function W_3 is tangent to the product

[9]See Kelvin Lancaster and R. G. Lipsey, "The General Theory of Second Best," *Review of Economic Studies*, vol. 24, 1956–1957, pp. 11–32.

transformation curve. This occurs at point E. (Note that we've drawn our social welfare function in the product space instead of in the utility space as we did before.) Assume for the moment that E is unattainable. Some institutional restraint or natural impediment reduces the attainable combinations to those along the line CC. If we wanted to satisfy the Pareto criterion, we might automatically say that a movement along the curve CC to point E''' would be called for because that would put us on the product transformation curve. However, that would put us on social welfare function W_1. If, instead, we move to point E'', we could attain a higher level of social welfare, W_2. Thus, in accordance with the theory of second best, it may be better when one of the marginal conditions for Pareto optimum is unattainable to violate some of the other marginal conditions in order to attain a welfare maximum.

The theory of the second best is intended as a warning against policy making that focuses too narrowly on the conditions in individual industries, without considering the broader general equilibrium implications for other industries. As we have seen, a policy of forcing perfectly competititve outcomes in Industry A may, in practice, undermine the competitive conditions or worsen existing noncompetitive conditions elsewhere in the economy.

MEASURING WELFARE COSTS

A topic related to the theory of welfare economics is how one can obtain actual measurements of what are called the welfare costs to market imperfections. In order to understand the concept of welfare cost, we must be willing to make a number of assumptions and to employ a measure which is called consumers' surplus.

Consumers' surplus

When you go into the store to buy a loaf of bread, the price you pay is, by definition, the market-clearing price. But the market-clearing price does not necessarily indicate the value that you place on the loaf of bread (unless you're indifferent between buying that loaf and not buying it). We do know that *if you buy the loaf of bread, the value you place on it cannot be less than the price of the loaf.* If the value you place on it were less than its value, you would not buy it. However, the value you place on it could be (and, indeed, many times is) higher than its price.

An experiment could show by how much the value you place on that loaf of bread exceeds the price you pay. It would be an *all-or-nothing* pricing experiment. Say you normally purchase 10 loaves of bread per month. If the store owner knows this, when you enter the store he or she could bargain with you for the maximum amount you would be willing to pay for the 10 loaves or go without.[10] The maximum you would pay would be the dollar

---

[10]In order for this experiment to work, the store owner would, of course, have to be a monopolist; otherwise, you would simply buy from another store.

value of the satisfaction you receive from having 10 loaves of bread rather than no bread at all. The difference between the maximum you are *willing* to pay for the 10 loaves of bread and what you would *have* to pay for them is **consumers' surplus**. *It is the amount over and above the market value of the commodity that consumers would pay rather than do without a specified quantity of that commodity.* Another way of looking at consumers' surplus is that it is the difference between total valuation of a specified quantity of the good in question and the market value of that commodity (price times quantity).

Graphically, consumers' surplus can be represented in Figure 18-8 as the area between the price line and the demand curve.

Consumers' surplus is a real part of economic welfare. It is not some fiction that we made up. Consider its definition. It is the amount of money income that you would pay, over and above what you have to pay, rather than do without the *quantity* of the commodity that you consume or actually purchase for consumption at the original price. Thus, if you were pressed, you would indeed give up more money in order to have that quantity of that commodity. Since the only way that you could pay more is to sacrifice the consumption of other less desired goods and services, consumers' surplus is an actual increase in real income. That is, the existence of consumers' surplus allows you to consume more of other commodities.

FIGURE 18-8
Consumers' surplus
Consumers' surplus is the area between the demand curve and the price line and equal to the triangle $P_eP_{max}E$. It represents the difference between total value and market value.

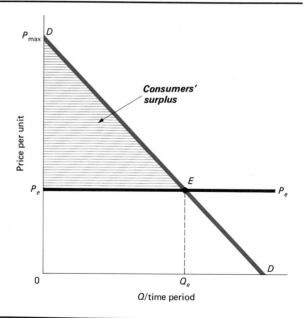

FIGURE 18-9
Producers' surplus or quasi-rents
The supply curve SS shows the minimum price at which given quantities will be forthcoming; and therefore, the amount of resources necessary to obtain given quantities. However, if price is P_e, the market value of quantity Q_e is equal to the rectangle $0P_eEQ_e$. The difference is the triangle $P_{min}P_eE$. The shaded triangle is producers' surplus; it equals the revenues received in excess of what is necessary to keep resources producing the quantity Q_e per unit time period.

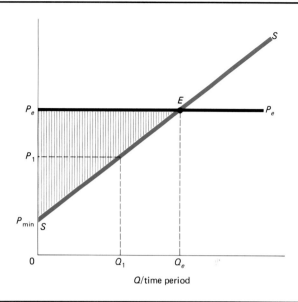

**Producers'
surplus**

A similar analysis can be made on the producers' side. In Figure 18-9, we show a typical upward-sloping supply curve, SS. We assume an equilibrium price P_e. The quantity produced is Q_e. Remember that the supply curve represents the locus of minimum prices at which different quantities are forthcoming. Thus, for example, for quantity Q_1, producers would be willing to supply that quantity at price P_1. At a market-clearing price P_e, Q_e is supplied. The difference, then, between the prices at which producers would be willing to sell their products and the prices they actually receive is economic rent. This particular economic rent is also called **producers' surplus** (to be symmetrical with the terminology for consumers). Actually, this economic rent is a short-run quasi-rent as explained in Chapter 16.

The shaded area in Figure 18-9 is our measure of economic rent. It is the quantity of money income over and above what is necessary to keep enough resources in the industry to produce quantity Q_e. Thus, the triangle $P_{min}P_eE$ is similar in nature to the shaded area in Figure 18-8.[11]

**Producers and
consumers
together**

When we put the supply and demand curves together, we can see that at any market-clearing price there is a consumers' surplus enjoyed by consumers and a quasi-rent enjoyed by producers. These are the two shaded triangles in Figure 18-10.

[11]E. J. Mishan, "What Is Producers' Surplus?" *American Economic Review*, vol. 58, no. 5, December 1968, pp. 1269–1282. Note that some economists question the existence of producers' surplus in the long run.

FIGURE 18-10
Putting consumers' and producers' surpluses together
At any given market-clearing price P_e, consumers' and producers' surpluses are the shaded triangles.

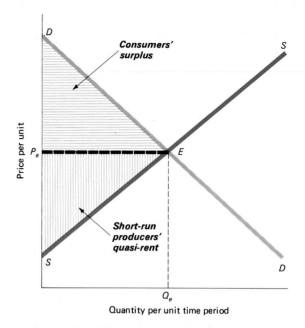

Welfare costs

We can obtain a geometric measure of the magnitude of the reduction in welfare that results from a market imperfection—taxes, subsidies, monopoly, etc.—by comparing the diagram in Figure 18-10 with a situation in which there is such an imperfection. What we do is look at the reductions in consumer surplus and in quasi-rents caused by the imperfection. We do this for a hypothetical output restriction in Figure 18-10; and in the Issues and Applications section we look at the application of welfare cost analysis to the measure of the social cost of monopoly and consider why there may be little incentive to end the welfare costs.

First consider Figure 18-11. In competitive equilibrium, the intersection of DD and SS is at E. The market-clearing price is P_e. The market-clearing quantity is Q_e. The consumers' surplus is the triangle $P_e P_{max} E$. The quasi-rent is represented by the triangle $P_e P_{min} E$. Now, a government authority imposes an output restriction that limits firms to producing no more than Q_R. Assume, for simplicity, that the output quotas are assigned to the least-cost firms so that the original supply schedule up to the restricted quantity is a part of the new supply schedule. The new supply schedule now becomes SA up to point A and then vertical to S'. The intersection of the new supply curve with the old demand curve is at point E'. The price at which Q_R will be sold is P_e'. *Note that there has been a reduction in consumers' surplus. The reduction in consumers' surplus is equal to $P_e P_e' E' E$.* The change in

FIGURE 18-11

The welfare cost of output restriction
If output is restricted to a maximum of Q_R, the supply curve becomes SAS'. (We assume that output quotas are given to the least-cost producers, so that we keep the same supply curve through the portion S to A.) The new equilibrium is at point E': The new market-clearing price is P_e'. The welfare loss will be the triangle $AE'E$.

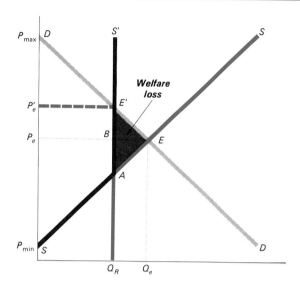

producers' surplus, or quasi-rents, is equal to the reduction given by the triangle ABE, plus an increase transferred from consumers to producers equal to the rectangle $P_eP_e'E'B$. Thus, not all the reduction in consumers' surplus is lost. The rectangle is transferred to the producer. That which is lost completely is the triangle left over, or $BE'E$. When we add this to the producers' surplus loss, or ABE, we obtain the welfare-loss triangle, or $AE'E$, due to an output restriction at Q_R. This **welfare loss** is also called welfare cost or deadweight loss.

WELFARE ECONOMICS AND SOCIAL ETHICS

Economists measure costs and make judgments in terms of alternatives foregone. Normative or welfare economics formulates judgments about the costs or benefits of alternative policies in terms of some "base point" or "initial state of the world." Most welfare analyses, and especially the Pareto criterion, select existing conditions as an appropriate base point for welfare comparisons. The choice of the status quo as the basis for all normative comparisons does not necessarily imply a bias in welfare economics. It is simply a reflection of the fact that, absent divine intervention, we must start from where we are. Nor should this selection of existing conditions imply any particular moral validation of these conditions. Welfare economics does not insist that those who are currently better off are somehow more virtuous than others or that they will inevitably remain better off. It merely notes that those with relatively more wealth, income, or political influence are not thereby deprived of any voice in social decision making.

The veil of ignorance

An alternative to the standard of normative social judgments arising from welfare economics is found in social ethics, as illustrated by the writings of John Rawls.[12] In *social ethics*, the central questions are: What policies are morally defensible? What principles may be referred to in order to distinguish morally preferable states of the world from morally inferior states? Following Rawls, many social ethicists would today answer these questions in terms of the choices made by a featureless individual behind the **veil of ignorance**. That is, they would maintain that the only legitimate judgments about social ethics are those untainted by any personal knowledge about people's existing traits or position in the social world.

Rawls's own conclusions from working through the exercise of making social choices behind a veil of ignorance are that many differences in conditions between individuals are morally unwarranted and should gradually be eliminated or compensated for. To arrive at this conclusion Rawls made rather stringent assumptions about the degree to which individuals suffer from being *relatively* worse off than those around them and about the impossibility of self-motivated achievement being able to benefit all individuals.

Concerns of ethics and economics

The most important difference between social ethics and welfare economics is not, however, in their relative conclusions. It is in their methodology and ultimate concerns. Social ethics is focused on what particular individuals merit. Social justice, which results from individuals receiving what they merit or deserve is a first necessary (if not entirely sufficient) characteristic of the "good society" according to the social ethicist. Welfare economics, on the other hand, is primarily concerned with the consequences of an individual's actions for his or her own utility and for the utility experienced by other individuals. In welfare analysis the primary question is not what is merited, but what are the utility consequences of particular social changes. Here the central questions are, Who gains and who loses? By how much? Can or will compensation be paid to the losers? If so, will the net gains be positive?

As we will see below, property rules are one way in which a society expresses judgments about whether to account for the utility losses to the individuals who occupy particular roles in that society. In competitive markets, for instance, the utility of consumers is paramount over any utility losses to unsuccessful competitive producers. Buggywhip makers may not have deserved or merited their falling incomes any more than plumbers have

[12]John Rawls, *A Theory of Justice* (Cambridge, Mass.: Harvard University Press, 1972).

merited their rising incomes. Such a distinction is not, however, very relevant to the economics of how to provide for or supply consumer wants.

OUTCOMES, CONSTITUTIONS, AND MARKETS

Traditional welfare economics is based upon an evaluation of alternative social outcomes or "states of the world." That is equally true whether the welfare criterion used follows the Pareto test, where the unanimous assent of each person concerned is required in order to adopt a given proposal, or a social welfare function, where social alternatives are "imposed from above."

The social choice between alternative economic institutions, systems of **property rights**, or economic constitutions (synonyms for our purpose) is not usually a choice between alternative social states with completely defined and known characteristics. Rather, it is a choice between certain types of uncertainties or risks and between incentives for particular types of behavior.

A tightly centralized economic structure, for instance, encourages relatively more investment in political scheming and maneuvering, relatively more concern over what will appeal to the particular tastes of one's superior, and relatively less concern about producing products desired by the broader masses of society. In a totally decentralized market situation, political maneuvering within a particular organization has little long-run payoff, while one could increase one's chances of success by developing skills or techniques that satisfy consumer wants at a lower cost. In both cases there is competition for scarce rewards and uncertainty in the payoffs from specific strategies for success.

The differences between economic systems rest upon the kinds of behaviors they encourage or inhibit and the kinds of risks that participants in the systems experience and must adjust to. No existing institutional system is characterized solely by changes involving the Pareto condition at the level of individual choice and experience. The fate of a market participant is determined not just by the decisions he or she makes, but also by changes in technology, consumer demands, and other market phenomena outside his or her control. Similarly, the fate of a participant in an "altruistic" command system is determined not just by his or her diligence in "serving society," but also by shifts in who determines and what is determined to be "social service."

Each of us would like to have full control over our environment, or at least have full knowledge of what that environment is like, but seldom, if ever, has anyone achieved that goal. A choice between economic systems based upon the resulting position of each individual is, thus, largely imaginary. At best we can choose institutions that increase the prevalence of certain desired behaviors and diminish the frequency of others that are undesirable.

▬▬▬▬▬▬▬▬

The welfare cost of monopoly

We are now in a position to estimate the social welfare cost of monopoly. Consider a hypothetical situation. We have a choice of either pure monopoly or pure competition. The cost curves are exactly the same in both cases. This is presented in Figure 18-12.

Assume, for simplicity, that marginal cost is constant. In a perfectly competitive situation, the curve labeled MC is also the supply curve and is the horizontal summation of all the individual firms' marginal cost curves.

The competitive solution is at the intersection of MC and *DD*, at point *E*. The competitive quantity would be Q_c and the competitive price would be P_c, because we assumed constant marginal costs. The amount of quasirent is zero. However, the amount of consumers' surplus at price P_c is the large triangular area $P_cP_{max}E$.

Now assume that the industry is monopolized and the cost curve remains exactly the same. The monopoly firm looks at the marginal revenue curve MR. It chooses the profit-maximizing quantity at the intersection of MR and MC at point E''. It then finds the price at which it can sell this quantity, Q_m, by consulting the demand curve *DD*. The product is sold at price P_m. Monopolization of the industry results in a higher price and a lower quantity produced and consumed. It also results in a reduction in consumers' surplus equal to the trapezoidal area P_cP_mAE. But the rectangle P_cP_mAE'' is transferred from consumers to the monopolist, leaving a deadweight loss equal

▬▬▬▬▬

FIGURE 18-12
The welfare cost of monopoly
Assume a constant marginal cost MC. Perfectly competitive equilibrium is found where the industry supply curve MC intersects the industry demand curve *DD*. Output would be Q_c. The price would be P_c. Assume now that a monopolist takes over and that there is no change in marginal costs. The monopolist sets output where marginal revenue equals marginal cost at point E''. The quantity sold will be Q_m. Price will be P_m. The reduction in consumer surplus is equal to P_cP_mAE. However, part of that reduction in consumer surplus is transferred to producers. This transfer or increase in producer surplus is equal to P_cP_mAE''. What is left is the shaded triangle $E''AE$, which is our measure of the welfare loss of monopoly.

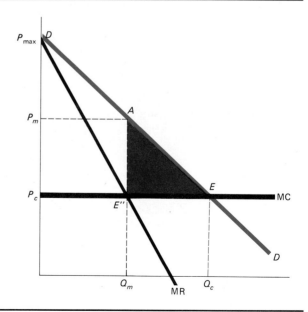

to the triangle $E''AE$. Note that we must further assume that the resources released from the monopolized industry go into other industries where they are fully employed and where they generate benefits just equal to their total cost of $Q_mE''EQ_c$. Then the welfare loss is the triangle $E''AE$.

MEASURING MONOPOLY POWER

In Chapter 12, we offered indexes of monopoly power. One often used is the Lerner Index, which is $(P - MC)/P$. We see from Figure 18-13, however, that the Lerner Index is not a reliable measure of the degree of welfare loss due to monopoly.

Consider two single-firm monopolies, I and II. Assume that the demand curve facing firm II is equal to one-half the demand curve facing firm I. They are selling in different markets, but they are both monopolies. The demand curve for the first monopolist is D_ID_I. The demand curve for the second monopolist is $D_{II}D_{II}$, which, it turns out, is also the marginal rev-

enue curve for the first monopolist because it is one-half of D_ID_I.[13] The marginal revenue curve for the second monopolist is the line MR_{II}. Both monopolists face demand curves which have identical price elasticities at every price. (Why?)

Each firm will produce quantities at which MR equals MC. We assume a common and constant MC. The first firm will produce quantity Q_I at the intersection of MR_I and MC, point E. The second firm will produce quantity Q_{II} where the marginal revenue curve MR_{II} intersects MC at point E'. Both firms will charge the identical price P_m. Their Lerner monopoly power indexes will be equal because $(P_I - MC_I)/P_I = (P_{II} - MC_{II})/P_{II}$.

However, the respective welfare costs, as represented by the shaded triangles I and II, are quite different. The welfare loss, or cost, to society (sometimes referred to as "deadweight loss") is much greater from monopoly

---

[13]See Chapter 5.

FIGURE 18-13
The welfare cost of two monopolies with equal Lerner Indexes
The two monopolists have the same marginal cost curves MC. One has one-half the demand of the other. They both sell at the same price P_m. The welfare cost of monopoly in the first case is the shaded triangle I; in the second case, it is the shaded triangle II. The former has a larger welfare cost than the latter, but they both have the same Lerner Index of monopoly power because the marginal cost and the price are the same.

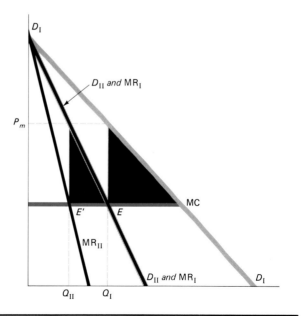

I than from monopoly II. Thus, the Lerner monopoly power index is seriously deficient in measuring the severity of the social welfare costs of monopoly.

FIGHTING TO KEEP A MONOPOLY

If a monopoly has been achieved, the monopolist may have incurred costs to obtain the monopoly. Moreover, in order to retain the monopoly profits, the monopolist most typically will incur further costs. On the other hand, consumers may, and indeed do in certain cases, spend resources in order to eliminate the monopoly or evade its effects. For example, if the monopoly arises because a law has been passed allowing only a limited number of companies to produce a product, consumers may band together to have legislation enacted which rescinds this policy.

Other producers will attempt to interfere with or infringe upon any monopoly that generates positive monopoly profits. Those profits are represented by the rectangle labeled P_cP_mAE'' in Figure 18-12. At the limit, that rectangle will be dissipated by the resources that go into maintaining and fighting the contrived monopoly. Thus, in a sense, the usual welfare triangle of monopoly is an underestimation of the deadweight loss associated with it.

EMPIRICAL ESTIMATES OF MONOPOLY EFFICIENCY LOSS

One of the first studies undertaken to estimate the actual welfare loss associated with monopoly in the United States was done by Professor Arnold C. Harberger. He looked at the period from 1924 to 1928. His assumptions were heroic: Marginal cost was assumed constant and the price elasticity of demand was assumed to be -1 in all industries. He identified monopolized industries by their relatively high average rates of return on assets. As can be seen from Table 18-2, he estimated the welfare loss to be 0.1 percent of national income.

Criticisms of Harberger's assumptions and analysis have been numerous. George J. Stigler[14] pointed out that the rational monopolist would operate only in the range where elasticity is equal to -1 if marginal cost were 0. Moreover, monopolists' reported (accounting) profit rates do not specify implicit monopoly returns and patent royalties. Finally, Stigler pointed out that such intangible items as goodwill are often counted as assets by monopoly firms so that their reported profit is shown to be a relatively small percent of total assets. This criticism, if relevant, would in-

[14]"The Statistics of Monopoly and Merger," *Journal of Political Economy*, vol. 64, February 1956.

TABLE 18-2
Measures of welfare loss to monopoly

*A. C. Harberger, "Monopoly and Resource Allocation," American Economic Review, vol. 54, May 1954.
†D. R. Kamerschen, "An Estimation of the Welfare Losses for Monopoly in the American Economy," Western Economic Journal, vol. 4, December 1966.
‡D. A. Worcester, Jr., "New Estimates of the Welfare Loss to Monopoly, United States, 1956–1969," Southern Economic Journal, vol. 40, October 1973.

Investigator	Assumed demand elasticity	Estimated welfare loss as a percentage of national income
Harberger*	-1.0	0.1
Kamerschen†	Various, averaging -2 to -3	6
Worcester‡	-2	0.5

dicate that Harberger defined too few firms as monopolists.

Stigler's objections were taken into account by other researchers. We find in Table 18-2 the results obtained by Kamerschen and by Worcester. The former's estimate is a relatively high 6 percent of national income. The latter's estimate, however, based on firm rather than industry data, is 0.5 percent of national

income and not much greater than Harberger's original estimate.

Even if these figures are accurate estimates of the welfare triangles or deadweight losses, they do not take account of the welfare losses associated with the dissipation of monopoly rents when resources are used to obtain, maintain, and protect those monopoly positions.

████████████

The disinterest in deregulation

As we have seen, the welfare cost of monopoly can be decomposed into two parts, the traditional deadweight loss triangle ($E''AE$) and any of the profit rectangle ($P_C P_M AE''$) dissipated by expenditures to obtain, defend, or eliminate the monopoly. In the limit, the rectangle of monopoly profits will be exactly dissipated by such expenditures so that the total welfare cost of monopoly is equal to the area of the trapezoid, $P_M AEP_C$, depicted in Figure 18-12. Empirical estimates by Harberger and others suggesting that the welfare loss due to monopoly in the economy is on the order of 0.1 to 0.5 percent of national income may, therefore, understate the true cost. However, this should not be taken to mean that the potential welfare gain from eliminating monopoly is large. On the contrary, the gains from deregulation may be smaller than they appear to be.[15]

The important point to keep in mind is that any resources used in the past to obtain or defend a monopoly position are *sunk*, and therefore cannot be recouped if the monopoly

is eliminated. These expenditures leave the economy permanently poorer, even if competition is restored to the monopolized sector. In contrast, the returns to preventing monopoly in the first place are relatively large. The implication is that if the rectangle of monopoly profits is exactly dissipated by rent-seeking expenditures, only a portion of the deadweight-loss triangle can be recaptured by deregulation of an existing monopoly.

Figure 18-14 compares the effects of monopolization with and without rent seeking. The production possibilities frontier P_1 represents the economy in the initial state. If both industries are competitive, the economy operates at a point such as 1, producing outputs Q_C^A and Q_C^B. Now suppose that Industry A is monopolized, but that no resources are used to obtain the monopoly right. In that case, the output restriction associated with monopolization moves the economy along P_1 to point 2, where output is higher in industry B because resources are shifted out of A. In the standard analysis, deregulation could conceivably move the economy back to point 1.

With rent seeking, however, monopolization of Industry A moves the economy from point 1 to point 2'. The production possibilities frontier shifts inward to P_2 as a function of the expenditures made to obtain the monopoly

[15]Based on Robert E. McCormick, William F. Shughart II, and Robert D. Tollison, "The Disinterest in Deregulation," *American Economic Review*, vol. 74, December 1984, pp. 1075–1079.

FIGURE 18-14
Reduction of production possibilities
A perfectly competitive economy operates at point 1 on the production possibilities frontier P_1, producing output Q_C^A and Q_C^B. If Industry A is monopolized but no resources are spent to obtain the monopoly right, output in Industry A falls to Q_M^A, and rises in industry B to $Q_C^{B'}$. The welfare loss is represented by the movement along P_1 to point 2. With rent seeking, however, the monopoly Industry A achieved is dissipated by unproductive activities. The production possibilities frontier shifts inward to P_2 and the economy ends up at point 2'. Efforts to deregulate can no longer restore the economy to point 1.

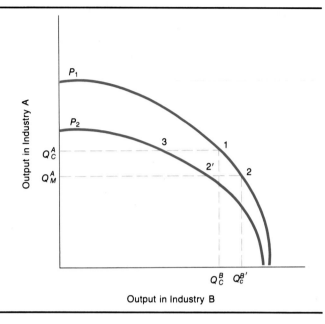

right. Efforts to deregulate Industry A can no longer restore the economy to point 1. At best, a return to the competitive output level in A requires a movement along P_2 to point 3. The impossibility of returning to point 1 is a reflection of the real resources consumed in rent seeking—the fixed costs of monopolization that are lost forever. Moreover, because specialized resources in A were used for rent seeking, it is now more costly (in terms of B) to produce output in A.

These increased costs are illustrated in Figure 18-15. The inward shift of the production possibilities frontier from P_1 to P_2 implies that the monopolized sector (Industry A) now has higher long-run marginal costs. The competitive long-run marginal cost schedule, LRMC_A, shifts to LRMC_A' (the MR curve intersects LRMC_A' at point M). Thus, a portion of the deadweight loss triangle (the shaded part) is lost to the economy along with the entire rectangle of monopoly profits. In other words, with exact dissipation of monopoly rents, the gross gain to the economy from deregulation is less than the area of the deadweight cost triangle. The competitive position in A retriev-

able through deregulation is $(P_C^{A'}, Q_C^{A'})$, not (P_C^A, Q_C^A).

RENT SEEKING COSTS

Expenditures made to obtain or defend a monopoly right deflect real resources from productive to unproductive activities. The act of rent seeking employs, for example, the best and brightest legal minds in the industry. This reduces the human capital stock of lawyers with knowledge of industry practices such as contract negotiation and enforcement when the industry is deregulated; marginal production costs are higher because lawyers are less efficient at providing services to the industry. The same point applies to other resources, especially managerial expertise. Managerial talents acquired under regulation—such as dealing with regulatory bureaucracies—lose their value in a deregulated environment.

The above analysis assumes exact dissipation of the monopoly profit rectangle. If this is not the case, or if the monopolist is required to spend resources periodically to protect the

FIGURE 18-15

Permanent loss from monpolization

The inward shift of the production possibilities frontier in Figure 18-14 causes the long-run marginal cost schedule in Industry A to shift upward from LRMC_A to LRMC'_A. The monopolist sets prices and output at (P^A_M, Q^A_M). Even if competition is restored later, price and output can be restored only to ($P^{A'}_C$, $Q^{A'}_C$), not to the premonopoly position at (P^A_C, Q^A_C). The shaded portion of the deadweight cost triangle cannot be recovered.

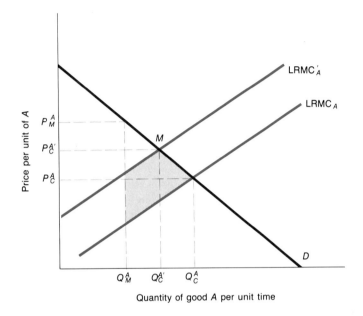

monopoly right, deregulation can retrieve the undissipated portion of the profit rectangle by saving the present value of the future resources that would have been used to defend the monopoly position. However, any resources already spent at the time of deregulation can never be recovered.

This helps to explain why deregulation is a rare event. There is simply little to be gained in welfare terms from eliminating an existing monopoly. Indeed, deregulation presents something of a paradox. Expenditures made to protect a monopoly position signify that the present value of the monopoly profits have not yet been completely dissipated. Therefore, the more resources currently being spent to maintain a monopoly (holding constant the monopoly rents), the more benefits deregulation will provide and the more likely deregulation will occur.

SUMMARY

1   In welfare economics we assume that (a) individuals are the best judges of their own welfare, (b) individuals who prefer situation a to situation b receive greater welfare from situation a than from situation b, and (c) individuals' choices reveal their preferences and, hence, their welfare.

2 Welfare economics attempts to analyze without comparing interpersonal utility levels.

3 The Pareto condition, or Pareto optimality, is generally synonymous with an economically efficient organization of resources.

4 The Pareto condition requires that marginal rates of substitution between goods be equal for all consumers, that the marginal rate of technical substitution between any pair of inputs be the same in all industries, and that the marginal rate of transformation for any two goods be equal to the marginal rate of substitution for those two goods.

5 We can derive the utility possibilities frontier by transforming the output space to a utility space. When we map all possible utility frontiers and obtain the envelope of the segments of the highest utility possibilities frontiers, we get a grand utility possibilities frontier.

6 If we had a social welfare function, we would find the constrained bliss point where one is tangent to the grand utility possibilities frontier.

7 The marginal conditions that satisfy the Pareto criterion are achieved when there is perfect competition and vice versa. In other words, there is an equivalence between perfect competition and the achievement of Pareto optimality.

8 The Kaldor-Hicks welfare criterion assumes that any movement from a point inside the utility possibilities frontier to a point on the utility possibilities frontier is an improvement because the consumer who is made worse off could be bribed by the consumer who is made better off. The Kaldor-Hicks criterion is based on potential and not on actual compensations.

9 In his theory of social choice, Kenneth Arrow presented five axioms he believes the social preference structure must satisfy to be minimally acceptable to the population: (a) complete ordering, (b) responsiveness to individual preferences, (c) nonimposition, (d) nondictatorship, and (e) independence of irrelevant alternatives.

10 Arrow showed that not even the first axiom would necessarily be satisfied in a democratic voting situation in which the majority rules. Thus we have the Arrow Impossibility Theorem, which states that no voting system can satisfy the five axioms.

11 In situations where not all the marginal conditions for Pareto optimality can be satisfied, the attempt to satisfy the remaining conditions will not necessarily improve social welfare. This is the theory of second best.

12 By using the concepts of consumers' surplus and producers' surplus, we can measure the welfare cost of distortions in the economy such as monopoly, taxes, subsidies, and output restrictions.

13 An important welfare cost in monopoly is the waste of the resources that are used to obtain, police, maintain, and fight monopolies.

14 Welfare economics that concerns policy prescriptions is normative if it is judgmental. If it only predicts the consequences of a policy, the analysis can remain positive.

15 Some economists advocate acceptance of a normative social ethic, such as Rawls's "veil of ignorance."

16 Analysis of social outcomes must consider the consequences of changes in the structure of property rights, or the "economic constitution." The analysis compares existing property rights structures to other institutional arrangements. It considers more than just the effects of changes within a given set of institutions.

GLOSSARY

- **welfare economics** The study of socially efficient solutions to the problem of resource allocation; involves eliminating solutions which can be shown to be "inferior" to other feasible solutions without the use of normative economics.
- **Pareto condition** A situation in which it is impossible for all individuals to gain from further exchange. In other words, if one individual is made better off, another must be made worse off. Also called the Pareto optimal allocation of resources, Pareto optimality, Pareto maximum, and Pareto criterion.
- **utility possibilities frontier** The transformation of the contract curve from an output space to a utility space; derived in a fashion similar to the derivation of the product transformation curve; gives the maximum combinations of utilities for consumer I and consumer II from given endowments of goods.
- **grand utility possibilities frontier** The envelope of the highest segments of all feasible utility possibilities frontiers. Each possible utility frontier is associated with a different point on the production possibilities frontier.
- **constrained bliss point** An organization of exchange, production, and distribution that leads to maximum attainable social welfare. The point on the grand utility possibilities frontier that is tangent to the highest social welfare function possible.
- **Arrow Impossibility Theorem** No democratic voting system can be used to obtain a social welfare function which satisfies the five minimal axioms Arrow specifies. In fact, the axiom of transitivity cannot be satisfied even if all individual preferences are transitive.
- **theory of second best** If one (or more) of the marginal conditions necessary for optimal resource allocation is not satisfied, it does not follow that welfare will be improved by satisfying the remaining marginal conditions.
- **consumers' surplus** The difference between what was actually paid for a particular quantity of a commodity and that which would have been willingly paid rather than do without the commodity entirely.
- **producers' surplus** The amount of revenues received by producers in excess of what is necessary to induce them to provide a specified quantity of a good.

- **welfare loss** The reduction in consumer and/or producer surplus from a distortion in the economy; also called welfare cost or deadweight loss.
- **veil of ignorance** A tool of policy analysis that assumes that no one knows what their position in society will be.
- **property rights** Institutional arrangements that assign various degrees of control over the uses of resources or goods to different decision makers (groups or individuals).

QUESTIONS

(Answers to even-numbered questions are at back of text.)

1 With what does welfare economics deal?
2 Is the optimal allocation of resources any "better" than any other? Explain.
3 What are the three basic assumptions of welfare analysis?
4 "Clearly a redistribution of $1 of Ted Kennedy's income or wealth to a very poor person would increase that person's well-being (utility) more than it would decrease Kennedy's. Consequently, the net effect of such a coerced transfer would be to increase social welfare." Is this statement demonstrably true or false? Explain.
5 "A government program which redistributes income through the coercion of taxation will decrease the nation's annual output from what it otherwise would have been." Is this statement demonstrably true or false? Explain.
6 What criterion was laid down by Vilfredo Pareto for an efficient allocation of resources?
7 What are some of the limitations of Pareto's condition?
8 Demonstrate graphically for a single-person economy the MRS-equal-to-MRT condition required for optimal allocation of resources.
9 In Figures 18-3 and 18-4, what is measured on the x and y axes? What are the units?
10 From what diagram is a utility possibilities frontier derived? How?
11 What is the "grand utility possibilities frontier" and how is it derived?
12 If a perfectly competitive economy will satisfy the Pareto criterion, does it follow that any move from a nation's existing market structures toward a perfectly competitive structure will necessarily increase social welfare?
13 According to the Kaldor-Hicks welfare criterion, any point on the utility possibilities frontier is preferred to any point below it. Why?
14 What does the Arrow Impossibility Theorem assert?
15 What is consumers' surplus and what does it have to do with economic welfare?
16 What is producers' surplus (short-run economic quasi-rent) and why does it not persist over time as consumers' surplus does?

SELECTED REFERENCES

Bohm, Peter, *Social Efficiency: A Concise Introduction to Welfare Economics* (New York: Wiley, 1973).

Baumol, William J., *Economic Theory and Operations Analysis*, 3d ed. (Englewood Cliffs, N.J.: Prentice-Hall, 1972), chap. 16.

Graff, J. de V., *Theoretical Welfare Economics* (London: Cambridge, 1957).

Little, I.M.D., *A Critique of Welfare Economics*, 2d ed. (Oxford: Oxford, 1957).

Scitovsky, T., *Welfare and Competition: The Theory of a Fully Employed Economy* (Homewood, Ill.: Irwin, 1951), chap. 7.

Externalities, public goods, and market failure

W e observed in Chapter 18 that a system of perfectly competitive markets would lead to attainment of a Pareto optimum. But perfect competition is not so "perfect" as it first seems. Unless demand and supply reflect, respectively, *all* the benefits and *all* the costs of producing and consuming a product, the prices that result from perfect competition will not be the "right" ones. If this be the case, maximum welfare will not be achieved by competitive adjustment to market prices. This is the result of externalities, about which we talked briefly earlier. This entire discussion falls under the heading of **market failure**. When the costs of barriers prevent markets from operating fully, a situation often described somewhat loosely as market failure exists and another approach to welfare maximization is required. In order to understand more clearly the concept of externality, we must first examine the concepts of social benefits and social costs.

SOCIAL BENEFITS AND SOCIAL COSTS

We dealt with true (opportunity) costs in Chapter 9. We pointed out that individual behavior is based on true—explicit plus implicit—costs. What we were talking about there was the concept of private costs or the costs to private individuals and firms.

But there is another concept that we must not overlook, and that is **social**, or full economic, **costs**. Social costs include all private costs incurred by the parties to a transaction, whether they be explicit or implicit, plus any additional costs visited on other individuals. A social cost thus includes private costs to persons in the same society *who are not parties to the transaction from which these costs emerge.* In order for these external costs of the transaction to remain external (not counted by the decision makers) there must be some barrier to negotiations or bargains between the external affected parties and those who are creating the externality. If such bargaining were possible, the external cost would be "internalized."

It is unlikely, if not impossible, that individual entrepreneurs will take into account all social costs. This is particularly so in a competitive market where, unless price is equal to marginal private costs, they will not maximize profits and will eventually go out of business.

If society's welfare is also to be at a maximum, however, marginal private costs must be equal to marginal social costs. To maximize profits, all activities of the individual firm must be carried to the point where marginal *private* revenue equals marginal private costs, or where marginal private benefits and costs are equated. But to maximize social welfare, marginal social benefits and costs are taken into account. Only then can we consider that a welfare maximum is being approached.

It is in the context of this terminology that the notions of external economies and diseconomies are discussed. An external economy is found when the marginal social cost of an activity is *less* than its marginal social benefit at an equilibrium of private marginal cost and marginal benefit. An external diseconomy occurs when marginal social cost is *greater* than marginal social benefit at an equilibrium of private marginal cost and marginal benefit. If either exists, the Pareto condition is not satisfied. That is, there is some rearrangement of production and/or consumption which would increase the total satisfaction of people in the economy. One of the leading articles[1] on "market failure" due to externalities distinguished between **technical** and **ownership externalities**. We will now examine each of these three in some detail.

TECHNICAL EXTERNALITIES

There are numerous technical externalities that impose costs upon or confer benefits (lower costs) upon others. In most cases, technical externalities do not share the problems of ownership externalities or public good externalities, so most economists do not view technical externalities as a problem that should be remedied.

Henry Ford made a lot of money for himself and the stockholders of the Ford Motor Company by his application of the assembly line and interchangeable parts to the production of automobiles. This improvement in technology imposed a technical externality (a diseconomy) on his competitor

---

[1]Francis M. Bator, "The Anatomy of Market Failure," *Quarterly Journal of Economics*, vol. 72, 1958, pp. 351–379.

firms, which suffered losses in sales and profits because of the shift in resources in favor of Ford. Obviously, the public benefited from this improvement in technology, but competitors within the industry were hurt. In some cases, improvements in technology confer technical externalities (an economy) on others. For example, the development of computer chips significantly reduced costs of production and improved the quality of various electronic consumer products, such as radios and stereos. The producers of those products were able to use these cheaper, higher-quality inputs to improve their positions in the market.

As we noted in our discussion of monopolies, it is possible that a natural monopoly will be created by increasing returns to scale for the dominant producer in the relevant range of production. Such a condition may develop because of a change in technology that allows the dominant firm to drive competitors out of the market because of declining marginal costs. The technical externality caused competitor firms to be eliminated. In almost all cases of technical externalities, the costs imposed upon other parties remain uncompensated.[2]

OWNERSHIP EXTERNALITIES

Often private costs differ from social costs because a resource that is being used or abused is not owned by the person inflicting damage on the resource. The classic cases of ownership externalities are pollution of air and of publicly owned bodies of water.

When private costs differ from social costs, we usually term the situation a problem of externalities because those making decisions bear less than the full costs of these decisions and those without the ability to influence these decisions bear some of the costs of them. Rather, some of these costs are external to the decision-making process. We review the problem in Figure 19-1. Here we have drawn a supply curve for product x. The supply curve, however, is equivalent to the horizontal summation of all the individual marginal cost curves and includes only internal, or private, costs. The intersection of the demand and supply curves will be at price P_e, and quantity Q_e. However, we will assume that the production of good x involves external costs which private businesses do not take into account. Those externalities could be air pollution, water pollution, "ugliness," or anything else along those lines.

In any event, we know that the social costs of producing x exceed the private costs. We can show this by drawing the supply curve $S'S'$, which is above the original supply curve SS. It is above that original curve because

---

[2]In recent years there has been increasing concern about technical externalities in domestic markets. Some state governments have considered imposing costs on firms that move a production facility out of the state because of lower production in other states.

FIGURE 19-1
Making private costs equal social costs
If firms take account of only private costs, the
supply curve is SS. The quantity demanded
and sold will be Q_e at a price P_e. However, if
social costs are taken into account, the supply
curve becomes S'S'. If a tax (equal to the
external costs per unit of output) were imposed
so that the price facing the consumer was P_1,
the quantity demanded and sold would be Q_1.
Consumers would then be paying for the full
social cost of their actions. (The pollution would
not necessarily be corrected; however, it would
be reduced because of lower levels of output.)

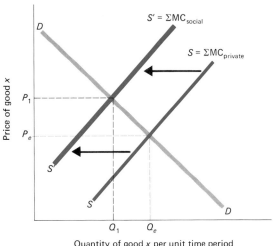

it includes both the externalities and the internal, or private, costs, together
comprising the full economic costs of producing the product. Now the "correct" market equilibrium price would be P_1 and the quantity supplied and
demanded would be Q_1. We see that the inclusion of external costs in the
decision-making process would lead to a higher price and a smaller quantity
of the product produced and consumed. We can say, therefore, that where
economic costs are not being fully borne by the creators of those costs, the
price is "too low" and the quantity produced "excessive."

**Correcting the
signals**

We can see here an "easy" method of reducing, at least to some extent, the
amount of pollution and environmental degradation. Somehow the signals
in the economy must be changed so that decision makers will take account
of all the costs of their actions. In the case of automobile pollution, we might
want to devise some method whereby motorists either are taxed according
to the amount of pollution they generate or are compensated for not generating it, depending on who "owned" the rights to clean air and, therefore,
who is in the position to "sell" those rights. In the case of a firm, we might
want to devise some system whereby businesses are taxed for the amount
of pollution for which they are responsible or are compensated *not* to pollute.
In both cases, they would have an incentive to install pollution-abatement
equipment.

When you think about it, however, it may not be appropriate to levy a
uniform tax on the physical quantities of pollution created. After all, we're
talking about social costs. The social costs of an action are not necessarily
the same everywhere in the United States. If you drive your smelly, fire-
belching car in the middle of the Mojave Desert, you probably will not inflict

significant damage on anyone. (We are notorious for ignoring the "preferences" of flora and fauna.) No one is there to complain; the natural cleansing action of the large body of air around you will eliminate the pollution you generate to such an extent that it results in little or no economic harm.

Essentially, we must measure the *economic damages* rather than the physical amount of pollution.[3] This point cannot be overemphasized. A coal-fed steam electric generator in New York City will cause more damage than the same equipment in, say, Helena, Montana. This is so because the concentration of people in New York City is much higher than it is in Helena. In addition, there are already heavy demands on the air in New York City, and additional pollution will not be naturally cleansed. Millions of people will breathe that smelly, sooty air and thereby incur the costs of sore throats, sickness, emphysema, and even premature death. There are many, many buildings that will become dirtier; cars and clothes will also become soiled much more quickly. A given quantity of pollution will cause more harm in concentrated urban environments than it will in less densely populated rural environments. If we were to establish some form of taxation to align social costs with private costs and force people to *internalize externalities*, we would need to have a measure of economic costs instead of merely physical quantities. Moreover, we would want to make sure that those who can decrease pollution at least cost do so; i.e., we want to minimize the *cost* of reducing pollution by any given amount.

SOCIAL COSTS AND PRIVATE COSTS

Now let's find out why there will be a difference between social costs and private costs. Why do certain situations create externalities while others do not? Consider, for example, some of the things you own. Suppose you own a bicycle. If someone slashes the tires or bends the spokes, you can, in principle, bring a civil action to recover damages. The damages you recover would be equal at least to the reduction in the market value of your bike. The same is true for a car. Anyone damaging your car is liable for those damages. The court will uphold your right to compensation (although *obtaining* compensation is far from a costless endeavor).

Common property

What if you live next to a stinky steel factory? That factory causes changes in the air around you, something that you use continuously. You may also be "changed" by breathing it. However, you more than likely have no right to stop the air pollution or to obtain compensation for the destruction of the air around you. This is so because you do not have property rights to the air surrounding you; nei-

---

[3]We are not, however, distinguishing between economic damage and other kinds of damage. Anything that a person would pay some amount to avoid or for which he or she would have to be compensated in order to endure (to maintain a constant level of utility) is "economic damage." The sum total of such payments is one measure of the amount of economic damage.

ther does anyone else. Air happens to be what is called a **common property** resource. Herein lies the crux of the problem. Whenever property rights are indefinite, nonexistent, or overly costly to enforce, social costs will differ from private costs. This is as you would expect. When no one owns a particular resource, its users have no incentive to consider their particular despoliation of that resource. In fact, a person would be wrong to assume that one individual's decision not to damage that resource will produce a significant effect on the total level of pollution. When one person decides not to pollute the ocean, there will still be about the same amount of ocean pollution, since the individual is a small part of the total number of polluters.

When property rights exist

When private property rights exist, individuals have legal recourse for any damages sustained through the unsanctioned use or abuse of their property. When property rights are well defined, the use of property—that is, the use of resources—will generally involve contracting by the owners of those resources with those potential users. If you owned land, you might contract with another person so that your land could be used for grazing cattle. The contract would most likely be written in the form of a lease agreement. We can predict that whenever contracting and/or enforcement of such agreements becomes exceedingly expensive or difficult, social and private costs will diverge. *Whenever contracting and enforcement of property rights are relatively costless, social costs and private costs will tend to be one and the same.* In fact, this is why externalities are problems only in certain areas of activity in our society. We don't worry about social and private costs in the majority of the activities that go on in our economy because almost all of what goes on involves contracting among individuals and the transference of property rights.

EFFICIENCY AND PROPERTY RIGHTS

Surprisingly enough, regardless of who has property rights, private costs can equal social costs; this is particularly true when transactions costs are minimal. In such situations, there is no misallocation of resources. Let's take a simple example. Suppose you live in a house with a nice view of a lake. The person living below you plants a tree. Over the years the tree grows larger and larger, and eventually it cuts off your view of the lake. In most areas, nobody has property rights to views, and therefore you usually cannot go to the courts for relief. You cannot file suit against your downhill neighbor for obstructing your view. That neighbor has the property right to grow a tree, and you have no right to your view.

Contracting to establish property rights

You do have an alternative, however. You can *contract* with your next-door neighbor to top the tree (to make it shorter). How large a payment would you offer? You could start out with a small money figure and increase the size of the offer either until your neighbor agrees or until you reach your limit. Your limit will be equal to the value you place on having an unobstructed view of the lake. The neighbor will be willing to top the tree if the payment is at least equal to the reduction in his or her property value due to a shorter tree. In this manner, you make your neighbors aware of the social cost of such action; you make explicit the social cost of growing a large tree which blocks your view and lowers the value of your property. But you do this in a rather odd way—by attempting to use bribery. Your neighbor is informed of the true cost of his or her actions. Alternatively, your neighbor could come to you and ask how much you would be willing to pay to have the tree topped.

Let's see whether things would be different if property rights were actually vested in views rather than in tree-growing. Let's say that the property rights to a view were vested in you. Therefore, anybody destroying the view would have to pay damages to you. In this particular case, the downhill landowner would have to bribe you for permission to block your view. The bribe to you would have to be at least equal to the reduction in the value of your property because of the obstructed view. (This bribe would also be a measure of the value of the view itself.) If the downhill landowner didn't offer a sufficient bribe, you would not accept, and the tree would have to be topped. The allocation of resource outcome is the same regardless of who owns the rights.

Opportunity costs

Now let's change the situation. Assume that your neighbor has the property right in *your* view. This is a strange situation indeed, but it is equivalent to the example in which no one had the view property right. If your neighbor has the property right in your view, will things be different compared to the situation in which you had the property right? If you think so, you're wrong. Just because your neighbor now owns "your" view does not mean that he or she will ignore the cost of its obstruction. After all, your neighbor would be giving up the opportunity of making some money in a deal with you by asking you how much you would be willing to pay to have the tree topped. If you were willing to pay enough, your neighbor would top it. If not, it would be left as is.

In other words, your neighbor would take account of the opportunity cost. This is the key to understanding why private costs will equal social costs in all three of the above situations. In the first instance, there were no property rights; in the second case, property rights were given to the uphill landowner; and in the third case, property rights were given to the downhill landowner. In each and every situation, opportunity costs exist and will be taken into account. The contracting involved is relatively simple. Only two parties are concerned, and verbal agreements could be made relatively easily. This particular example leads us to a strange, but nonetheless valid, conclusion.

When transactions costs are minimal, it does not matter who has the property rights in the resource under study, as long as somebody does (or even if *no one* does). The resource will be used in exactly the same way regardless of the property-right structure: Otherwise stated, *if transactions costs are small, the allocation of resources does not depend on who has property rights in those resources.*

The above statement is generally called the **Coase Theorem**, named after Ronald H. Coase. He demonstrated that in a world of zero transactions costs, the wealth-maximizing behavior of individuals takes account of external effects.[4]

Wealth distribution

Note that in reducing "externalities," the *distribution of wealth* will be affected and will depend on who, if anyone, has the property rights initially. The person who gets the property rights to some resource that was formerly common property will clearly be better off; the wealth of this individual will be increased. In the above example, if a large untopped tree is more valuable to its (downhill) owner than is the view to the uphill landowner, the tree will not be topped. Think about this. In the case where the uphill landowner has the property right in the view, he or she will accept a bribe from the downhill tree owner that is at least equal to the reduction in the uphill property value due to the obstructing tree. The downhill landowner will offer a sum that does not exceed the increase in his or her property value due to an untouched tree. If the view is more valuable than the untouched tree, the downhill owner will not succeed in bribing the uphill landowner but will have to top the tree.[5]

When transactions costs are high

Our example is pretty simple so far. It involves only two people, and the contracting or transactions costs are small. What about cases in which the transaction costs are not so small? Take the example of a factory polluting a city of several million people. It would be difficult for the several million people to get together to bribe the factory to reduce its pollution or for the factory to contract with them to acquire the right to pollute. The transactions costs here would be extremely high.[6] Therefore, we cannot predict that private costs will equal social costs for the factory. This is probably the case with many environmental problems.

Note that indefinite property rights in and of themselves do not lead to uncorrected externalities if contracting can be done cheaply. However, when large numbers of people are involved, contracting is difficult, and in many

---

[4]Ronald H. Coase, "The Problem of Social Costs," *Journal of Law and Economics,* October 1960, pp. 1–45.

[5]We ignore income effects on the demand curves for trees and for views. This makes the most sense when we are dealing with decisions made purely on a profit or loss basis. Due to differences in preferences and changes in income distribution, it may be the case that a reassignment of property rights would change demands, relative prices, and the output mix of an economy.

[6]It should be noted that the evolution of class action lawsuits in recent years has substantially lowered the transactions costs of legal proceedings in the environmental area.

instances the actual costs are difficult to measure and/or the creators of those costs are difficult to identify. If ships are spilling oil into the ocean, how do you find out which ones are doing it? The costs of finding out may be too high to justify the probable benefits of the undertaking. This discussion of property rights leads us to another possible solution to our environmental problems.

Assigning property rights

Instead of attempting to tax polluters in proportion to the economic damages caused by their pollution, we can define property rights more precisely; contracting would then have to take place between potential polluters and those whose environment is being polluted. In the case of the obstructing tree, it did not really matter who was endowed with property rights in the view. Property rights really were inconsequential to the outcome of the situation except, of course, for the wealth positions of the individuals. This is not the case with other environmental problems. For example, we might want to make factories liable for the pollution they create. When we do that, we are implicitly vesting the citizens of that community with the rights in the common property resources of water and air surrounding the factories; individuals living there will implicitly be the owners of the "public" air and water. The factory will therefore be liable for uses of water and air which impose costs on those persons.

In a sense, this is not really "fair." Customers and employees of and stockholders in that factory are made to bear the costs of pollution. After all, a common property resource is, by definition, owned by everyone. The problem is that when it is "owned by everyone," it is actually owned by no one. It would be arbitrary to assign rights in a common property resource to the local homeowners; it would be just as arbitrary to assign the property rights to the factory owners. But because it is less costly, administratively, to make the individual factory owners pay, we still might want to go ahead with an arbitrary assignment of property rights to the local homeowners. In essence, government decision makers will be acting on behalf of the homeowners when dealing with the polluting factory.

Governmental allocation of property rights

Government decision makers will somehow have to determine the value of the economic damages that the factory's pollution is causing and require that the factory make full compensation, install pollution-abatement equipment, or do some combination of the two. Any compensation would be distributed to the homeowners in a manner that approximated the economic cost sustained by each of them.[7] That, of course, is a difficult problem,

---

[7] Note how different this is from the usual suggestion of a tax on pollution without consideration of how the revenues are to be expended. The problem with a tax that is not paid to the damaged homeowners is that, although the factory adjusts its behavior to the full social costs of its actions, homeowners adjust their behavior to a "false" set of prices. Homeowners would, for instance, favor legislation to shut the factories down or to clean them up even when the marginal social value of doing so would be negative.

particularly since government decision makers are themselves unable to capture any increased benefits from "correctly" distributing the compensation. It might be simpler to use the "bribe" money to clean up some of the pollution caused by the factory instead of trying to compensate the losers (the individual homeowners). Note that here, as elsewhere, the optimal level of pollution is not zero.

The optimal level is that level at which the social benefits of further reducing pollution just equal the social costs of doing so. If the benefit to society is 90¢ for $1 more of resources devoted to pollution abatement, we've already gone too far.

PUBLIC GOODS

For the most part we have discussed goods that follow the **principle of exclusivity**. An apple has this characteristic. If I eat the apple, you cannot eat it. My use of the apple excludes your use of the apple. Thus, if at a price of 15¢ apiece I demand and get 10 apples per week, that means that there will be 10 fewer apples for anyone else to consume that week. If you demand and get 20 apples per week at that price, then altogether we will consume 30 apples per week that no one else will be able to consume.

There is a whole class of commodities for which the principle of exclusivity does *not* apply. Consider that when I turn on my television set, I do not subtract from your ability to watch the same television program at exactly the same time on your set. In other words, when I buy (if I could) a particular television signal and consume it fully, I do not prevent you from buying and consuming that exact same television signal. The same is true for national defense. My consumption of national defense does not in any way interfere with your consumption of national defense. National defense can be consumed simultaneously by individuals in the same geographic area without decreasing the consumption of it by anyone else in that area. Like it or not, we each get the same level of protection.

Lack of exclusivity

We call national defense and TV signals **public**, or **collective, goods**. These are defined as goods for which the principle of exclusivity does not apply. Once a public good is produced, the marginal cost that an additional user of the good imposes on society is effectively zero. We must be careful to distinguish two conditions here, although they are often found together. Some goods—such as national defense—have a *high exclusion cost*. Even someone who does not pay federal taxes receives the benefits from national defense. Similarly, we may charge a small fee to those who enter national forests or parks, but we find it difficult to enforce payment of the fee—some people will hike in where there are no tollbooths. The other condition that may exist is that of *zero marginal cost* for the additional consumer of a collective good. If 100,000 immigrants come into the United States this year, the cost of providing national defense for the nation as a whole, including those people, will not change.

Public good externality

The **public good externality** comes into play if the marginal social costs of sharing one more unit of consumption of the public good is zero and a price above zero is being charged; then we have violated the welfare-maximizing criterion of equating marginal social benefits and marginal social costs. Another way of looking at this is that in a system of perfect competition, there is an equality between the marginal rate of transformation of good x into good y and the marginal rates of substitution of good x for good y of, say, consumer I and consumer II. In the public situation, however, consumers I's consumption of good x does not restrict consumer II's consumption. Thus, the marginal rate of transformation should equal the *sum* of the two marginal rates of substitution. Perfect competition may lead, therefore, to underproduction and underconsumption of public goods.

Free-rider problem

With public goods, transactions costs are usually so high that it is difficult to monitor the intensity of consumer demands and charge for them. We run into what is known as the **free-** (or cheap) **rider problem**. Since it is difficult or impossible to exclude those who have not paid for the use of the public good, it is hard to get a sufficient number of individuals to reveal their true demands and then voluntarily agree to pay for the production of the public good. Bargaining between potential users and the potential suppliers of the public good is often costly.

Take the example of national defense. If everyone were asked to contribute voluntarily, we would probably devote a relatively small amount of resources to national defense. Each individual thinks that his or her contribution is an insignificant part of the total amount needed for national defense and that, therefore, it won't make any difference whether he or she does not contribute very much or any at all. That person may choose to be a free rider.

This problem is not always insurmountable with public goods. Many voluntary associations continue to exist even though the free-rider problem plagues them. Homeowners in a certain area may band together into a homeowners' association to which individuals voluntarily contribute dues each year in order to provide for trees on the perimeter of the development, special lights, and so on. Not everyone joins, and yet the association will continue to exist because a sufficient number of individuals will voluntarily pay their annual dues. Educational TV "subscriptions" would be another example. These examples indicate that public goods may be "underproduced" by markets rather than not produced at all.

Public goods that become private

We must be careful here, however, because the private market has a long history of entrepreneurs' attempts at converting public goods into private goods. This is exactly what putting a wall around a baseball field, a room around a movie screen, or cable television is all about. In this manner, private entrepreneurs can in fact provide what would otherwise not be provided if consumers were not charged for the right to see a baseball game, a movie, or some televised event. Indeed, even the history of the classic example of a public good that seemingly cannot be provided by the private sector shows how ingenious entrepreneurs can be.

This classic case of a public good is the lighthouse. Once a lighthouse is built, the marginal cost of providing the land-demarcation services to ships during storms is very close to zero, and it seems impossible to make ships pay for the use of the lighthouse because of the problems of identifying which ships go by it and of enforcing payment. A little historical investigation, however, reveals that in England lighthouses were private for many years. Lighthouse owners apparently were making profits on their lighthouses, because from 1700 to 1834 the number of private lighthouses increased. They obtained payment from shipowners by assessing the shipowners at the docks according to the tonnage of the ship. While it may seem that enforcement costs were high, apparently they were not high enough to prevent private entrepreneurs from collecting enough revenues to continue building more lighthouses. Usually only one ship was in sight of the lighthouse at any one time. If the ship (which displayed its flag) had not prearranged (prepaid) for the light, the light would not be shown.[8]

Public good benefits

Public goods are often seen as goods which generate positive externalities for which individuals "should" not have to pay because the marginal cost of providing those externalities is zero after the public good has been produced. The problem with this type of analysis is that it does not allow the individual members of the consuming public to be faced with their share of the total cost of producing the public good. Individuals react to signals. If the signal is nonexistent, i.e., if the price of consuming more of a public good is zero, the consumers will individually not take account of their combined actions. Thus, the amount of a public good produced by private market interactions among individuals may be less than these individuals would "really" want to pay for, if payment were required. Yet, we must be careful not to confuse publicly *provided* goods with public goods. Just because the government collects taxes to pay for the provision of a good does not mean that the good is public—as that term is used in economics. Similarly, as we have seen above, public goods are often provided by private parties, although often in less than "optimal" amounts.

[8]See Ronald H. Coase, "The Lighthouse in Economics," *Journal of Law and Economics*, vol. 18, no. 2, October 1974, pp. 357–376.

ISSUES AND APPLICATIONS

Honey bees and externalities

The classic case of ownership externalities occurs in the production of honey and apples. It turns out that the theory of this example, like that of the lighthouse, never fit reality; this can be seen if we examine it more carefully.

You can buy apple blossom honey, blueberry blossom honey, raspberry blossom honey, alfalfa honey, red clover honey, fireweed honey, mint honey, sage honey, orange honey, and even cabbage honey. We all know how honey is made. Bees extract the nectar of various blossoms and transform it, via one of nature's mysterious processes, into the honey you buy in the store. In many states there are large bee farms, with hives generally each consisting of one or two brood chambers, a queen excluder, and from zero to six supers. A brood chamber is a wooden box large enough to contain eight or ten movable frames. Each frame has a wax honeycomb built by the bees. It is in the hexagonal cells of the comb that the queen lays her eggs and the young bees, or brood, are raised. The bees store the nectar and pollen which they use for food. Honey usually is not extracted from this chamber but from the frames of a more shallow box, called a "super," placed above the brood chamber. The queen excluder is placed between the super, which is used only for honey, and the brood chamber, which is used only for raising young bees. The excluder prevents the queen from laying eggs in the upper section of the hive.

Beekeepers and bees work throughout the year. During part of the year, usually from spring to fall, the colonies of bees hatch continuously. The infants are raised on pollen, and they remain in the brood chamber for about 3 weeks of their working lives, helping to clean and repair the wax cells. For the remainder of their lives, usually 2 or 3 more weeks, they look for pollen and nectar.

Bees are at their busiest in the spring, when they are pollinating fruit trees and the infants must be fed with nectar and pollen. Fruit-tree owners benefit from having honey bees nearby; they enjoy a larger yield per acre because of the pollination services the bees provide. Here we have a classic situation that in economic literature has been labeled an "external benefit." In 1952 the economist J. E. Meade pointed out that applying more labor, land, and capital to apple farming will not only increase the output of apples but will also provide more food for the bees. Meade called this a case "of an unpaid factor, because the situation is due simply and solely to the fact that the apple farmer cannot charge the beekeeper for the bee's food."[9]

We can look at the situation from the other side of the coin. The apple trees may provide food for the bees, but the bees also fertilize the apple blossoms. If the beekeeper in the vicinity of the apple trees increases the size of the colony, he or she presumably foresees the increased benefit as the additional revenues received from selling a larger quantity of honey. At the same time, though, the apple farmer receives a benefit in the form of a higher pollination rate of his or her apple blossoms and, hence, a larger quantity of apples at the end of the season. Again we appear to have a situation of an unpaid factor or an externality.

There are benefits external to both the decision made by the apple farmer and the decision made by the beekeeper.

[9]J. E. Meade, "External Economies and Diseconomies in a Competitive Situation," *Economic Journal*, March 1952, pp. 56–57.

In economic analysis, an externality is associated with market failure. That is, the private market fails to allocate resources in an efficient manner. The apple and bee example has been used in economics for many years now as an example of an externality in which the government should step in and correct the relative prices by appropriate taxes and subsidies in order to take into account the benefits that the apple farmer and the beekeeper apparently do not perceive, or at least cannot charge for.

Only recently has someone taken the time to find out whether the quaint apple farmer–beekeeper example is real. Besides the fact that apple blossoms yield little or no honey, apparently both beekeepers and fruit growers do understand that bees provide valuable pollination services. Moreover, beekeepers and fruit growers realize that plants will provide valuable honey crops. Once it is understood by at least one of the parties in question that a valuable external benefit occurs as a result of one or the other's action, we would expect that some attempt would be made to take advantage of this knowledge. That attempt would translate itself into a contractual arrangement between the fruit grower and the beekeeper. Contracts are not a new invention; they have existed since the beginning of social relations among humans. We all know of certain types of contracts, e.g., the kind made with a bank in order to borrow money. But contracts are not limited to such obvious endeavors. In fact, contracts exist, either explicitly or implicitly, for an incredibly large number of economic and even noneconomic transactions. We can cite a marriage contract, an employment contract, and an educational contract; there are contracts for just about every action known. The beekeepers and the fruit and plant growers, therefore, might be expected to reach an agreement that would take account of the so-called externalities involved in each one's behavior.

We find conclusive evidence that both nectar and pollination services are indeed bought and sold in the marketplace. In many cases, all we have to do is look in the Yellow Pages. We find there an entry for "pollination services." Economists for many years thought that "the apple farmer cannot charge the beekeeper for the bees' food and the beekeeper cannot charge the apple farmer for the bees' pollination services," but this is not the case. Not only can the parties charge for the services they render each other, they actually do so; and some of them make a very good business of it. In a study in the state of Washington,[10] it was found that about 60 beekeepers each owned 100 or more colonies. During the peak season, the colonies' total strength was about 90,000. Beekeepers would relocate hives from farm to farm by truck. Beekeepers not only rendered pollination services to different fruit and plant owners at different times of the year but extracted different types of honey at different times of the year as well. On the average, each hive took care of more than two crops a year. Table 19-1 shows that beekeepers sometimes provided pollination services and sometimes didn't; plant owners sometimes provided honey services and sometimes didn't.

When we look at what beekeepers charge for pollination services, we find an interesting but not wholly unexpected phenomenon. The greater the expected honey yield, the smaller the pollination fee. Essentially, then, the beekeeper is paid partly in honey for the pollination services that are rendered to the plant owner. Moreover, the more effort per pint of honey the beekeeper puts into dispersing hives throughout the orchard, the more he or she charges for this service, because pollination improves with increased dispersal of hives.

Here we have a situation in which a seemingly elusive resource, a flying insect, renders services to the owner of another resource. A very specific type of contract has been drawn up for these circumstances in order to take account of any benefits obtained. These contracts take both oral and written forms. In the state of Washington, a printed one is issued

[10]Steven N. S. Cheung, "The Fable of the Bees: An Economic Investigation," *Journal of Law and Economics,* April 1973.

TABLE 19-1
Bee-related plants investigated in the state of Washington, 1971

*Soft fruits include pears, apricots, and peaches.
†Pollination services are rendered for alfalfa and the clovers if their seeds are intended to be harvested;
when they are grown only for hay, hives will still be employed for nectar extraction.
‡Sweet clover may also require pollination services, but such a case is not covered by this investigation.
§Pasture includes a mixture of plants, notably the legumes and other wild flowers such as dandelions.
Source: S. N. S. Cheung, "The Fable of the Bees: An Economic Investigation," Journal of Law and
Economics, April 1973, table 1.

Plants	Number of beekeepers	Pollination services rendered	Surplus honey expected	Approximate season	Number of hives per acre (range)
Fruits and nuts					
Apple and soft fruits*	7	Yes	No	Mid-April–Mid-May	0.4–2
Blueberry with maple)	1	Yes	Yes	May	2
Cherry (early)	1	Yes	No	March–Early April	0.5–2
Cherry	2	Yes	No	April	0.5–2
Cranberry	2	Yes	Negligible	June	1.5
Almond (Calif.)	2	Yes	No	February–March	2
Legumes					
Alfalfa	5	Yes and no†	Yes	June–September	0.3–3
Red clover	4	Yes and no	Yes	June–September	0.5–5
Sweet clover	1	No‡	Yes	June–September	0.5–1
Pasture§	4	No	Yes	Late May–September	0.3–1
Other plants					
Cabbage	1	Yes	Yes	Early April–May	1
Fireweed	2	No	Yes	July–September	n.a.
Mint	3	No	Yes	July–September	0.4–1

by the Association of Beekeepers. A contract need not be in writing, however, to be enforceable in a court of law. In any event, oral contracts are not generally broken when information about an alleged breach travels quickly. This is exactly the situation in the world of beekeepers and farmers, in which everyone knows everyone else's reputation. A glance at the written pollination contracts reveals stipulations concerning the number and strength of the colonies, delivery and removal times for the hives, what will be done to protect the bees from pesticides, how the hives should be placed, and the cost of the hives' services.

Whenever there are expected gains to be made from contracting among different parties in an economic system, and as long as the costs of making and enforcing the contract are less than the expected gains, we generally observe parties entering into written and oral contracts. This is true even where natural resources are concerned. Thus the economist's classic example of an externality turns out to have been largely internalized. It does provide us, though, with valuable clues to when and where externalities will exist. In the case of the bees, contracting was profitable for the parties concerned; in the cases of automobile pollution, destruction of scenic beauty, and "overfishing," the costs of negotiating and enforcing contracts clearly exceed the potential gains. This is so because we do not yet have any cheap (efficient) way to define, measure, and enforce property rights to clean air, scenic beauty, and the fish swimming in the ocean.

What happened to the blue whale?

Many problems concerned with the destruction and extinction of specific species lend themselves to an analysis of property rights. Let us set up a hypothetical situation in which whale-harvesting rights in the world's oceans are well defined. We depict the situation in Figure 19-2. On the horizontal axis we show the number of whalers per unit time period and on the vertical axis the whales caught per whaler (individuals who hunt whales, not whaling ships). Implicitly we are assuming that we are dealing with constant-quality units of whalers and constant-quality units of whales.

We have drawn the average physical product curve of whalers APP_w and marginal physical product curve MPP_w. Remember that the marginal physical product curve intersects the maximum point of the average physical product curve. Whenever the average physical product curve is rising, the marginal product curve is above it; whenever the average physical product curve is falling, the marginal physical product curve is below it. The relation between the marginal physical product of whalers and the average physical product of whalers is identical with the general case we provided previously in Eq. (8-3).

Let us add the opportunity cost of whaling to each whaler expressed in terms of whales caught per unit time expended. This opportunity cost is the alternative wage rate that

whalers could earn if they exited from the whaling industry. We will assume that it is the same for all whalers because they are measured in constant-quality units. This wage rate, or opportunity cost of whaling, is represented by the vertical distance $0S$. In other words, it is a wage rate expressed in whales per unit of time. The horizontal line SS', therefore, represents the opportunity cost of whalers. In some sense it can be considered the supply curve of the whalers also because they are presumably indifferent to whaling or not whaling at their opportunity cost.

WHEN NO ONE OWNS THE WHALES

When no one owns blue whales, we have a situation in theory that is very similar to what the facts have been in the whaling industry. We expect individuals to enter the whaling industry up to the point where it is no longer worthwhile. That occurs when the return from whaling just equals the opportunity cost of whaling. But the return from whaling is represented by the average physical product curve APP_w. In other words, a potential whaler assumes that it is possible to earn the industry average, but the industry average is merely the total physical product divided by the number of whalers, or APP_w. Therefore, we know that in the absence of property rights in blue

FIGURE 19-2
Productivity and whaling

We assume that all whalers are equally skillful. They are represented on the horizontal axis. The whales caught per whaler are represented on the vertical axis. The average physical produce curve APP_w first increases and then decreases. The curve marginal to it, MPP_w, intersects APP_w at point A. The opportunity cost of each whaler (expressed in terms of whales) is $0S$. The opportunity cost line is, therefore, SS'. It is also the supply curve of whalers. Without property rights in whales, entry into the industry would continue until there were W_3 whalers, each earning his or her opportunity cost of $0S$. However, at that point the marginal physical product of whalers is very low. If someone were to own all the whales, the maximum fee that could be charged would be the distance from A to B. If this were the fee expressed in terms of whales, W_1 whalers would be in the industry. That, however, is not the wealth-maximizing solution for the owners of whales. They would do better by charging CD. The number of whalers in the industry would be W_2, and each would be earning only $0S$, his or her opportunity cost.

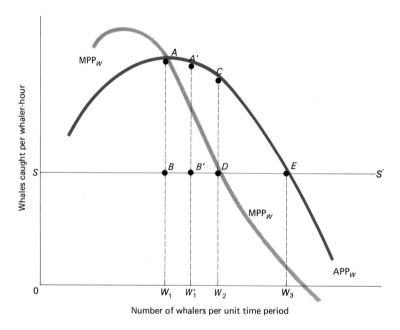

whales, the number of whalers working per unit time period can be determined analytically by the intersection of the average physical product curve APP_w and the opportunity cost line SS', or point E. The number of individuals who will be whaling will be at W_3. The number of whales caught per whaler will be equal to the vertical distance from the origin, 0, to S. The total number of whales caught would be equal to the area $0W_3ES$.

Notice one important thing here. In the absence of property rights in blue whales, it's possible that so many whalers engage in whaling that the marginal physical product in Figure 19-2 is negative.[11] In other words, we can operate in stage III, and this would never occur if an individual entrepreneur were "running the show." It can occur in this situation simply because no individual whaler can, even if he or she wants to, take account of his or her actions on productivity. If one whaler decides not to whale because of possible ex-

[11]Though this is not necessary.

tinction of the species, some other whaler will come in and harvest those whales that the previous whaler decided not to harvest. No individual whaler has any effect whatsoever on the total number of whales harvested. There will be whaling up to the point where the average wage rate, given in terms of whales, is equal to the opportunity cost.[12]

WHEN THE WHALES ARE OWNED

We now examine the situation in which the whales are owned by, let us say, one individual. That individual has the right to charge anyone who wishes to harvest the whales. The maximum fee that the owner of the whales could charge to each whaler is the difference between the opportunity cost of the whaler's time, $0S$, and the monetary value of the whales caught. Assume for a moment that the owner of the whales charges a price of AB for any and every person who engages in whaling. At this price, the maximum number of whalers would be $0W_1$. Why? Because given that number, the APP_w is equal to the vertical distance between W_1 and A. The owner of the whales takes away as a fee the vertical distance between B and A. What is left over is exactly equal to $0S$, or the opportunity cost to the whalers. No more than $0W_1$ individuals will enter this industry unless, however, the owner of the whales reduces the fee charged to each whaler.

It turns out that the maximum fee chargeable is AB because this is the maximum distance between the average physical product

[12]Contrary to what follows from this model, lack of property rights in blue whales—or any other hunted species—may not imply that all whalers earn exactly their opportunity costs. Some whalers are more efficient than others. See Stephen N. S. Cheung, "The Structure of a Contract and the Theory of a Non-Exclusive Resource," *The Journal of Law and Economics*, vol. 13(1), April 1970, pp. 49–70, and compare it with H. Scott Gordon, "The Economic Theory of a Common Property Resource: The Fishery," *Journal of Political Economy*, vol. 62, no. 1, 1954, pp. 124ff. Both are reprinted in H. G. Manne, *The Economics of Legal Relationship: Readings in the Theory of Property Rights* (St. Paul, Minn.: West, 1975).

curve and the opportunity cost to whalers. If $1 more were charged, no one would engage in whaling.

The other extreme would be to charge nothing. Then we are right back to the case where we began, in which no one owned the whales. We would end up with $0W_3$ of whalers, and they would each earn their opportunity costs.

In between these two extremes lies the optimal fee that the owner of the whales should charge each whaler. Let's start from the high end with a fee of AB.

We lower it a little bit to $A'B'$. More whalers would want to enter the industry than when the fee was AB because with only $0W_1$ whalers, they would be earning more than their opportunity costs. Thus more whalers enter the industry. As they do, average physical product falls because we are in the downward-sloping portion of that curve. The number of whalers that would ultimately stay in the industry at a fee of $A'B'$ (expressed in whales) would be $0W_1'$.

From the point of view of the owner of the whales, his or her total receipts have increased by the number of the additional whalers harvesting whales times the new fee $A'B'$ *less* the reduction in receipts due to the fact that the fee has been lowered to all those whalers, $0W_1$, who were previously paying AB. (We are assuming here that everyone is charged the same fee.) Thus, the owner of the whales must compare the additional revenues collected from the new whalers with the revenues lost from charging the old whalers a lower fee. It will be worthwhile for the owner of whales to continue lowering his or her fee and therefore attracting more whalers up to the point at which the increase in revenues due to the collection of fees from new whalers is just offset by the reduction in revenues that results from the lower fees charged to all the original whalers.

Thus, the owner will want to lower his or her fee up to the point where $MPP_w = 0S$. To reach that point, the owner will charge a fee of CD in Figure 19-2. There will be $0W_2$ whalers harvesting whales.

Notice that at point D, marginal physical product and the opportunity cost to whalers are equal. In the situation in which the whales are owned by an individual, that individual will force every whaler to take account of the impact that he or she has on the catch of the other whalers. What is that impact? It is the reduction in average physical product brought about by the addition of one whaler. We can find it by looking at the MPP_w curve in Figure 19-2, for that is the meaning of a marginal physical product curve—the change in total product brought about by the addition of one more unit of the variable factor of production.

When there are W_2 whalers harvesting whales, on the margin a whaler reduces the aggregate amount of physical product to everyone else by the distance between C and D. The owner of the whales charges each whaler this amount. The net income of each whaler, then, becomes equal to his or her marginal physical product. Total whale production equals $W_2 \cdot WC$, and this is less than the $0W_3ES$ total whales that are harvested when no one owns whales.

Our conclusion is that under private ownership, blue whales would not be harvested so intensively as when there is no ownership of whales.

Regulating market failures, or collecting rents?

Air and water are often treated as common property. When everyone is allowed to use a resource as if its price were zero there will be a misallocation of resources compared to the solution that would result if the property were allocated at market value. Environmental degradation is often cited as a classic case of the inability of the market to properly ration certain valuable resources. The result of a lack of property rights over air and water is their treatment as communal garbage dumps, which leads to calls for regulation.

ECONOMIC THEORY AND POLITICAL REALITY

Economists have written many articles and books concerning the relative merits of alternative regulatory schemes for common property such as air and water. Since these resources are, for the most part, not going to be sold to the private sector for marketing, schemes for efficient distribution by the government have been discussed. Most proposals advocated some kind of tax or emission fee that would be imposed on the users (polluters) of air and water, so they would reduce consumption to a level that produced acceptable environmental quality. The taxes or fees collected by the government could be used to repair past environmental damage or used as general revenue, so that all citizens would receive a form of payment for the sale of a public good.

While taxes or emission fees are regarded as leading to the most efficient allocation of resources, given public ownership of air and water, governments have generally not seen fit to adopt the economists' plans. Instead, Congress and the states have adopted a host of standards-based controls. That is, the laws impose standards or restrictions with respect to the levels of pollution that may be emitted, or technology-specific production requirements are imposed on producers.

ENVIRONMENTALISTS AS CARTEL BUILDERS?

What would explain the creation of environmental controls that achieve environmental protection in a manner less efficient than would occur if the prescriptions of economists were followed? One hypothesis is that industry co-operates with environmentalists in the political forum to structure the controls in a way that suits their joint interests—to the detriment of the consumer. Standards-based controls are imposed because they achieve the result desired by environmentalists—a reduction in pollution—and because they enable existing firms in the industry to shape the regulations in a manner that protects existing producers from potential competitors. For example, many regulations imposed by the Environmental Protection Agency imposed more stringent (and costly) pollution standards for new firms than they do for existing firms. The effect is to have the regulations restrict output for the industry as a whole, effectively cartelizing a previously competitive industry.

We can see how this would work by examining Figure 19-3. The firms in this competitive industry face a market demand curve D. A representative firm had cost curves AC and MC, leading to market price P_0, which meant the firm sold Q_0 units per period. The imposition of costly regulations increases the costs incurred by producers, so that the average firm now faces cost curves AC' and MC'. As price is increased to P_1 (and the firm begins to earn rents), quantity sold drops to Q_1. Obviously, consumers are the major losers. Can the situation persist? The costs imposed by the regulation may drive the least efficient producers from the market, benefiting the remaining firms. The regulations, which require even more costly controls be adopted by new producers, may serve to block entry into the industry so that above normal profits may be

FIGURE 19-3

Producer benefits from regulation

The representative firm in a competitive industry sold quantity Q_0 at price P_0 since it faced industry demand D. When a costly regulation was imposed, production costs increase to AC' and MC'. So long as the minimum cost point A lies to the left of the demand curve, the firm will be able to earn abnormal profits. How long these profits can persist will depend on the adjustment time in the industry.

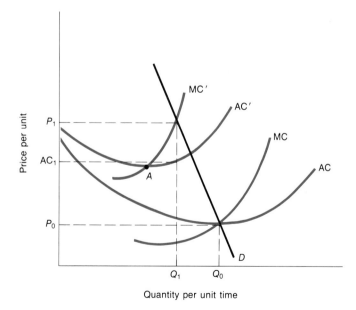

earned for some time period. The threat of foreign competition, not subject to the costly pollution controls, may have to be met with quotas or tariffs, but even without such protection, existing domestic producers may benefit from the controls.

EMPIRICAL EVIDENCE

Textile workers have always been subject to cotton dust. The seriousness of long-term exposure to cotton dust led the Occupational Safety and Health Administration (OSHA) to impose a cotton dust exposure standard. After the rule had been worked on for some time, in September 1974 the Department of Labor announced its intention to impose rigid restrictions on cotton dust exposure in textile mills. This was a technology-based standard that imposed substantial costs on producers. The impact of the rule can be measured on the firms in the industry by looking at the impact of the announcement of the cotton dust standard on stock prices. Stock prices reflect the expected future profits of firms, so if a regulation will serve to cartelize the industry, it will mean higher future profits, hence higher stock prices at the time the rule is announced. Holding constant other variables, a study of the stock prices of textile firms indicated that

their rate of return was 24 percent higher than what it would have been in the absence of the standard.[13] The producers of synthetic fibers also experience increases in stock prices, but the price increases were highest for the firms that had the greatest percentage of cotton fibers in their production process.

In the early 1970s the Environmental Protection Agency (EPA) was in the process of preparing standards to comply with the 1970 Clean Air Act. The rules finally imposed are called PSD rules (prevent significant deterioration). Their main impact was on pollutants emitted by copper, lead, and zinc smelters. The rules did little to existing smelters but restricted entry into the industry by requiring a lengthy EPA permit process for any new source of pollution (or any modification of existing sources)—which would have to employ costly pollution controls not required of existing smelters. An examination of the stock prices of firms with copper, lead, and zinc smelters indicated that their rate of return increased 44 percent when the impact of the impending rule became known.

[13]This analysis is drawn from Michael T. Maloney and Robert E. McCormick, "A Positive Theory of Environmental Quality Regulation," *Journal of Law and Economics*, April 1982, pp. 99–124.

SUMMARY

1   Whenever an unrestrained market leads to a violation of the marginal conditions for Pareto optimality, we have a market failure.

2   For a welfare maximum to be obtained, marginal social costs must equal marginal social benefits for all resource-using activities.

3   This maximum may not be achieved if there are technical, ownership, or public good externalities.

4   Technical externalities are the result of production functions that exhibit increasing returns to scale.

5   Ownership externalities result from the absence of well-defined ownership rights. In some cases, private costs can be made equal to social costs by taxation or subsidization.

6   It is necessary to estimate the economic damages rather than the physical damages of pollution-creating activities. The former will differ from the latter and will depend on the number of individuals affected by the same amount of physical damages.

7   We predict that common property will not be treated in the same way as property with well-defined rights assigned to someone or some group. In the case of common property, individuals will treat it as if they do not own it, and the result is pollution of air, water, etc.

8   In a world of zero transactions costs, the Coase Theorem indicates that a change in the property rights will not alter the allocation of resources. However, it will alter the distribution of wealth.

9   The key to understanding the Coase Theorem is to understand that an opportunity cost exists even when property rights do not exist. If my train emits sparks which set your cornfields on fire, I am suffering an opportunity cost equal to the amount of money you would give me to install spark arresters on the train (assuming, of course, that you would pay me more than the mere cost of the arresters).

10   The optimal level of pollution abatement occurs at that point at which marginal social benefits equal marginal social costs.

11   Public goods have marginal costs of zero only after they are produced. Prior to the production of the good, the production costs themselves represent a marginal cost to society.

12   Some goods are public goods because it is very costly to exclude someone (a free rider) from receiving the benefits of the good.

13   Individual wealth maximizers expend resources in order to convert public goods into private goods.

GLOSSARY

■ **market failure** A situation in which the market solution does not lead to a Pareto optimum.

■ **social costs** All private costs of an action, plus costs which are incurred by "innocent" third parties.

■ **technical externalities** Externalities which occur because of indivisibilities in the production process or returns to scale.

■ **ownership externalities** Externalities which occur because of ill-defined or nonexistent property rights—common property problems.

■ **common property** Property that is owned by all and therefore owned by no one.

■ **Coase Theorem** When transactions costs are zero, the assignment of property rights will not alter the allocation of resources.

■ **principle of exclusivity** The enjoyment by one individual of a commodity precludes its enjoyment by another. If you use the service of an auto mechanic, I cannot use those services at exactly the same time.

■ **public, or collective, goods** Goods for which the principle of exclusivity does not apply. Once a pubic good is produced, the additional cost that an additional user of the good imposes on society is effectively zero.

■ **public good externalities** Externalities which arise because of the nature of public goods; the cost of monitoring and charging for marginal units of the public good are prohibitively high.

■ **free-rider problem** Individuals may attempt to get a "free ride" on a commonly provided good by indicating that they do not want that good and therefore will not pay for it. They believe that enough others will indeed pay for the good so that it will be provided to them anyway. This is also known as the cheap-rider problem, because nothing is free.

QUESTIONS

(Answers to even-numbered questions are at back of text.)

1 Why do you think that economic discussions of external economies and diseconomies focus on *marginal* social costs and *marginal* social benefits rather than *total* social costs and *total* social benefits?

2 What is meant by the expression "market failure"?

3 How does a homeowner determine what quantity of resources to allocate in improving the outward apearance of his or her property? From a social point of view, in an urban or suburban area is the "right" amount of resources allocated to this task? Explain.

4 From a social standpoint, are too few, just the right amount, or too many resources allocated to the production and consumption of rooftop television antennas? Why?

5 In a given geographic area, might there exist technical externalities in the provision of fire fighting services? If so, why might there be an inefficient allocation of resources?

6 Construct a standard supply-demand diagram and show the initial equilibrium price and quantity. Assume that the good visits external costs on third parties (persons not involved in the transaction) and adjust the diagram to compensate for that fact. How does the "adjusted" situation compare with the original?

7 Now construct a second supply-demand diagram for any good and show the equilibrium price and quantity. Assuming that the good generates external benefits, modify the diagram to allow for them and show the new equilibrium price and quantity. How does the "adjusted" situation compare with the original?

8 What is the problem with common property resources?

9 Suppose you own a large piece of property in the center of which lies a lake. You locate a feedlot on the edge of the lake and begin fattening cattle. The feedlot runoff pollutes the lake and kills many of the fish. Are there any externalities here? Explain.

10 Do plants and animals have property rights?

11 Suppose you were contemplating a use of your property which would generate substantial external benefits for the property owners in the surrounding area. How might you go about capturing (internalizing) these benefits for yourself?

12 "Blockbusting" is a term used in recent years to describe the alleged profitability of certain approaches to racial integration of residential neighborhoods. Here is how it is supposed to work: A speculator places a family of a different race in a neighborhood that previously was racially homogeneous. This, it is argued, causes a panic on the part of the other residents, who fear that their property values will drop substantially on account of the integration. Now the speculator (Mr. or Ms. Blockbuster) reenters. He or she is the one who originally placed the "different" family in the homogeneous neighborhood. He or she now approaches the other owners and offers to buy their homes at rather low prices, which many accept because they think the bottom is yet to come. After buying most or all of the homes in the neighborhood, the speculator proceeds to sell the homes at nondepressed prices to members of the new racial or ethnic group who have wanted to live in the neighborhood for years but had somehow been unable to do so in the past. Analyze critically this "racism for fun and profit" theory with particular reference to externalities.

13 "Abate or compensate? That is the question." What does this statement have to do with external costs?

14 How much of an external diseconomy is socially optimal from the standpoint of an efficient allocation of resources? To what extent should society utilize its scarce resources in abating the nuisance?

15 Summarize the dilemma presented by public goods.

SELECTED REFERENCES

Bator, F.M., "The Anatomy of Market Failure," *Quarterly Journal of Economics,* vol. 72, August 1958, pp. 351–379.

Baumol, William, *Economic Theory and Operations Analysis* (Englewood Cliffs, N.J.: Prentice-Hall, 1965), pp. 368–371 and 375–380.

Buchanan, James M., and W.C. Stubblebine, "Externality," *Economica,* vol. 29, November 1962, pp. 371–384.

Chamberlin, E.H., "Proportionality, Divisibility and Economies of Scale," *Quarterly Journal of Economics,* vol. 62, February 1948, pp. 229–262.

Appendix A: Mathematical Derivations

Indifference curves

Consider a person's indifference curve for goods x and y. Let the utility function be

$$U = U(x,y) \qquad\qquad \text{(A-1)}$$

An indifference curve is defined as

$$U(x,y) = \overline{U} \qquad\qquad \text{(A-2)}$$

where $\overline{U}$ is a constant level of utility. Taking the total differential of (A-2) yields

$$dU = \frac{\partial U}{\partial x}dx + \frac{\partial U}{\partial y}dy = 0 \qquad\qquad \text{(A-3)}$$

Movements along an indifference curve leave utility unaffected. Since

$$\frac{\partial U}{\partial x}dx + \frac{\partial U}{\partial y}dy = 0 \qquad\qquad \text{(A-4)}$$

then

$$\frac{\partial U}{\partial x}dx = -\frac{\partial U}{\partial y}dy \qquad\qquad \text{(A-5)}$$

and therefore

$$\frac{dy}{dx} = -\frac{\partial U/\partial x}{\partial U/\partial y} = \text{MRS}_{xy} \qquad\qquad \text{(A-6)}$$

Equation (A-6) indicates that the slope of an indifference curve (dy/dx) is equal to the negative of the marginal rate of substitution of x for y. Earlier economists, who thought in terms of cardinal utility, would have referred to the right-hand side of Eq. (A-6) as the ratio of the marginal utility of x (that is, $\partial U/\partial x$) to the marginal utility of y (that is, $\partial U/\partial y$).

Utility maximization

We wish now to maximize utility $U = U(x,y)$, subject to a budget constraint. Assume that our consumer has a given money income M; the consumer's budget constraint is

$$M = p_x \cdot x + p_y \cdot y \qquad\qquad \text{(A-7)}$$

The task is to maximize $U = U(x,y)$ subject to the budget constraint $M = p_x \cdot x + p_y \cdot y$, a Lagrangian extremum problem. We construct

$$Z = U(x,y) - \lambda(p_x \cdot x + p_y \cdot y - M) \tag{A-8}$$

where λ is a Lagrangian multiplier.

First-order maximizing conditions require that both partial derivatives equal zero; that is, $\partial Z/\partial x = 0$ and $\partial Z/\partial y = 0$. Therefore

$$\frac{\partial Z}{\partial x} = \frac{\partial U}{\partial x} - \lambda p_x = 0 \quad \text{and} \quad \frac{\partial Z}{\partial y} = \frac{\partial U}{\partial y} - \lambda p_y = 0 \tag{A-9}$$

It follows that

$$\frac{\partial U}{\partial x} = \lambda p_x \quad \text{and} \quad \frac{\partial U}{\partial y} = \lambda p_y \tag{A-10}$$

Dividing yields

$$\frac{\partial U/\partial x}{\partial U/\partial y} = \frac{p_x}{p_y} \tag{A-11}$$

We interpret Eq. (A-11) as saying that at the utility maximization point the marginal rate of substitution of x for y equals the ratio of the price of x to the price of y. The slope of the indifference curve at that point is equal to the slope of the budget line. A necessary condition for utility maximization is that the budget line be tangent to an indifference curve.

Elasticity

We define *price elasticity of demand,* η, as the absolute value of the ratio of the relative change in quantity demanded, q, to a relative change in price, p. Thus

$$\eta = \left| \frac{\Delta q/q}{\Delta p/p} \right| = \left| \frac{\Delta q}{\Delta p} \cdot \frac{p}{q} \right| \tag{A-12}$$

when $q = f(p)$. In this appendix we discuss only point elasticities. Since by definition

$$\frac{dq}{dp} = \frac{\text{limit}}{\Delta p \to 0} \frac{\Delta q}{\Delta p} \tag{A-13}$$

$$\text{where} \quad \frac{\Delta q}{\Delta p} = \frac{f(p + \Delta p) - f(p)}{\Delta p} \tag{A-14}$$

we can denote point elasticity as

$$\left| \frac{dq}{dp} \cdot \frac{p}{q} \right| \tag{A-15}$$

If the demand curve is linear, then

$$\frac{dq}{dp} = \frac{\Delta q}{\Delta p} \tag{A-16}$$

since the slope of a (nonvertical) straight line is a constant. For example, given the linear demand curve

$$q = a - bp \qquad \text{(A-17)}$$

the derivative dq/dp is equal to $-b$; the value of the coefficient of elasticity becomes

$$\eta = \left| -b\frac{p}{q} \right| \qquad \text{(A-18)}$$

Note that η is calculated by multiplying a constant $(-b)$ by a ratio which varies along the straight-line demand curve; p/q is different for every "point."

On the other hand, consider a nonlinear demand curve, one form of which is the constant elasticity curve.

$$q = ap^{-b} \qquad \text{(A-19)}$$

The derivative of this curve is

$$\frac{dq}{dp} = -abp^{-b-1} \qquad \text{(A-20)}$$

It follows that

$$\eta = \left| -abp^{-b-1} \cdot \frac{p}{q} \right| = \left| \frac{-abp^{-b}}{q} \right| = \left| -b \right| \qquad \text{(A-21)}$$

since $q = ap^{-b}$. We conclude that the coefficient of price elasticity of demand for this (nonlinear) demand curve is the absolute value of the exponent of the price variable. Elasticity does *not* change along this demand curve.

Income elasticity of demand, μ, is defined as the ratio of the relative change in the quantity purchased, q, to a relative change in income, M, other things constant. Thus,

$$\mu = \frac{dq/q}{dM/M} = \frac{dq}{dM} \cdot \frac{M}{q} \qquad \text{(A-22)}$$

where $q = f(M)$.

Consider the linear income-demand function

$$q = a + cM \qquad \text{(A-23)}$$

where $c > 0$. The derivative of this function is

$$\frac{dq}{dM} = c \qquad \text{(A-24)}$$

Therefore, the coefficient of income elasticity can be written

$$\mu = c\frac{M}{q} \qquad \text{(A-25)}$$

Now consider the nonlinear income-demand function

$$q = aM^c \qquad \text{(A-26)}$$

The value of μ is a constant c, the exponent of the income variable, since

$$\frac{dq}{dM} = acM^{c-1} \qquad \text{and} \qquad \mu = acM^{c-1}\frac{M}{q} = \frac{aM^c}{q} \cdot c = c \qquad \text{(A-27)}$$

We now analyze *cross-elasticity of demand*, η_{xy}, which we define as the ratio of the relative change in the quantity demanded of commodity x, q_x, to a relative change in the price of commodity y, p_y. Thus

$$\eta_{xy} = \frac{dq_x/q_x}{dp_y/p_y} = \frac{dq_x}{dp_y} \cdot \frac{p_y}{q_x} \tag{A-28}$$

when

$$q_x = f(p_x, p_y) \tag{A-29}$$

Specifically, consider the linear demand function for commodity x:

$$q_x = a + bp_x + cp_y \tag{A-30}$$

The quantity demanded of commodity x depends on the price of commodity x and the price of commodity y. Taking the derivative of this function with respect to the price of commodity y yields

$$\frac{dq_x}{dp_y} = b\frac{dp_x}{dp_y} + c \tag{A-31}$$

If the price of commodity x is not changed when the price of commodity y changes, then

$$\frac{dp_x}{dp_y} = 0 \quad \text{and} \quad \frac{dq_x}{dp_y} = c \tag{A-32}$$

It follows that

$$\eta_{xy} = c\frac{p_y}{q_x} \tag{A-33}$$

for this function. If $\eta_{xy} > 0$, then x and y are substitutes. If $\eta_{xy} < 0$, then x and y are complements.

Finally, let us analyze *price elasticity of supply*, ε. We define it as the ratio of the relative change in quantity supplied, q_s, to a relative change in price, p. Thus

$$\varepsilon = \frac{dq_s/q_s}{dp/p} = \frac{dq_s}{dp} \cdot \frac{p}{q_s} \tag{A-34}$$

when $q_s = f(p)$. Note that supply curves are usually positively sloped; hence we do not take the absolute value of the ratio. Consider the linear supply curve

$$q_s = a + bp \tag{A-35}$$

The derivative of this function with respect to price yields

$$\frac{dq_s}{dp} = b \tag{A-36}$$

Therefore

$$\varepsilon = b\frac{p}{q_s} \tag{A-37}$$

But since $q_s = a + bp$,

$$\varepsilon = \frac{bp}{a + bp} \tag{A-38}$$

Thus if a (the y intercept) equals 0, then $\varepsilon = 1$; if the supply curve begins at the origin, it has an elasticity of unity throughout (regardless of price) regardless of the value of b (slope). Also, if $a > 0$, then $\varepsilon < 1$; if the supply curve cuts the quantity axis (quantity supplied exceeds zero at a zero price), then elasticity is less than unity—regardless of the slope. If $a < 0$, then $\varepsilon > 1$. Note that if a is nonzero, the value of the coefficient of elasticity *does* depend on price.

Isoquants

Assume that output Q is a function of capital K and labor L:

$$Q = Q(K,L) \tag{A-39}$$

The total differential of this function is

$$dQ = \frac{\partial Q}{\partial K}dK + \frac{\partial Q}{\partial L}dL \tag{A-40}$$

An isoquant is defined by the constant function

$$Q(K,L) = \overline{Q} \tag{A-41}$$

Output remains constant along a given isoquant. Setting the total differential equal to 0, therefore, implies that along an isoquant

$$\frac{\partial Q}{\partial K}dK + \frac{\partial Q}{\partial L}dL = 0 \tag{A-42}$$

Along an isoquant the marginal product of capital times the change in capital, plus the marginal product of labor times the change in labor, sums to zero. Rearranging this equation yields

$$\frac{\partial Q}{\partial K}dK = -\frac{\partial Q}{\partial L}dL \tag{A-43}$$

Thus

$$-\frac{dK}{dL} = \frac{\partial Q/\partial L}{\partial Q/\partial K} = \text{MRTS}_{KL} \tag{A-44}$$

That is, the negative of the slope of the isoquant equals the ratio of the marginal product of labor to the marginal product of capital. This ratio is also referred to as the marginal rate of technical substitution of labor for capital.

Cost minimization, given an isoquant

Given some output level, or some isoquant, what is the least-cost combination of inputs? Total cost is defined as

$$c = rK + wL \tag{A-45}$$

where r represents the unit rental price of capital and w represents unit wage rates. The problem is to minimize

$$c = rK + wL \tag{A-46}$$

subject to producing

$$\overline{Q} = Q(K, L) \tag{A-47}$$

units of output. We use the Lagrangian multiplier to construct a new function:

$$F = rK + wL - \lambda[Q(K, L) - \overline{Q}] \tag{A-48}$$

Taking the first partial derivatives and setting them equal to zero yields

$$\frac{\partial F}{\partial L} = w - \lambda\frac{\partial Q}{\partial L} = 0 \quad \text{and} \quad \frac{\partial F}{\partial K} = r - \lambda\frac{\partial Q}{\partial K} = 0 \tag{A-49}$$

Rearranging obtains

$$w = \lambda\frac{\partial Q}{\partial L} \quad \text{and} \quad r = \lambda\frac{\partial Q}{\partial K} \tag{A-50}$$

and dividing yields

$$\frac{w}{r} = \frac{\partial Q/\partial L}{\partial Q/\partial K} = \text{MRTS}_{KL} \tag{A-51}$$

We interpret this as follows: A firm can minimize the total cost of producing a given output by hiring inputs up to the point where the ratio of marginal products of the inputs is equal to the input price ratios. Alternately stated, total cost of producing a given output level is minimized when the isocost curve is tangent to the given isoquant; the slope of the isocost curve equals the slope of the isoquant at the cost minimization point. These, of course, are only the first-order conditions.

Profit maximization

The preceding section indicated how a given output level could be produced at least cost. We are now concerned with choosing the specific output level which maximizes total profits. We define profits Π as total revenue minus total cost; each is a function of q, output. Therefore we wish to maximize

$$\Pi = R - C \tag{A-52}$$

At the profit maximization output rate the first derivative of Π with respect to q is zero. Thus

$$\frac{d\Pi}{dq} = \frac{dR}{dq} - \frac{dC}{dq} = 0 \tag{A-53}$$

Note that

$$\frac{dR}{dq} = \frac{dC}{dq} \tag{A-54}$$

We interpret this last equation as follows: At the profit-maximization output rate, marginal revenue will equal marginal cost. This is a necessary condition; for ease of operation, we ignore second-order conditions.

Price determination under partial equilibrium

Quantity demanded, q_d, and quantity supplied, q_s, are both functions of price; q_d is inversely related to price, and q_s is directly related to price. Assume the linear demand function

$$q_d = a - bp \qquad a > 0, b > 0 \tag{A-55}$$

Further assume the linear supply function

$$q_s = cp - d \qquad d > 0, c > 0 \tag{A-56}$$

Note that the parameters b, a, c, and d can all represent different values. We have two equations and three variables (q_s, q_d, and p); as is usually the case in economics, the missing equation is supplied by the equilibrium condition. The equilibrium price is that at which $q_d = q_s$. Therefore

$$q_d = a - bp = cp - d = q_s \tag{A-57}$$

and since $a - bp = cp - d$, it follows that

$$a + d = cp + bp = p(c + b) \tag{A-58}$$

Therefore

$$p = \frac{a + d}{c + b} \tag{A-59}$$

Note that the unknown, the equilibrium price, is totally in terms of known constants (a, d, c, b) and we therefore have a solution to this simple system of simultaneous equations in a partial equilibrium situation.

The cobweb theorem

The cobweb theorem is a dynamic concept in that quantity supplied in the present is a function of last year's price—or this year's price determines next year's quantity supplied. That is,

$$q_{s_t} = cp_{t-1} - d \tag{A-60}$$

Quantity supplied in time period t is a function of price in the previous period, $t - 1$. Assuming the normal demand curve

$$q_{d_t} = a - bp_t \tag{A-61}$$

and that the equilibrium price in the present is established where $q_d = q_s$, we note that

$$q_d = a - bp_t = cp_{t-1} - d = q_s \tag{A-62}$$

Solving for p_t yields

$$p_t = \left(-\frac{c}{b}\right)p_{t-1} + \frac{d+a}{b} \tag{A-63}$$

From this equation we can infer price in period 1:

$$p_1 = \left(-\frac{c}{b}\right)p_0 + \frac{d+a}{b} \tag{A-64}$$

and price in period 2:

$$p_2 = \left(-\frac{c}{b}\right)p_1 + \frac{d+a}{b} \tag{A-65}$$

But we know p_1 from Eq. (A-64). Substituting this into the p_2 equation yields

$$p_2 = \left(-\frac{c}{b}\right)^2 p_0 + \left(-\frac{c}{b}\right)\frac{d+a}{b} + \frac{d+a}{b} \tag{A-66}$$

It can be demonstrated that the *general* solution for any time period t is

$$p_t = \left(-\frac{c}{b}\right)^t p_0 + \frac{d+a}{b+c}\left[1 - \left(-\frac{c}{b}\right)^t\right] \tag{A-67}$$

If the slope of the supply curve equals the absolute value of the slope of the demand curve ($c = |b|$), then

$$p_t = (-1)^t p_0 + \frac{d+a}{b+c}[1 - (-1)^t] \tag{A-68}$$

If t equals zero or any even number, then

$$p_t = p_0 + \frac{d+a}{b+c}[1 - 1] = p_0 \tag{A-69}$$

If t equals an *odd* number, then

$$p_t = -p_0 + \frac{d+a}{b+c}[1 + 1] = 2\frac{d+a}{b+c} - p_0 \tag{A-70}$$

It follows that if $c = b$, then price will perpetually oscillate between p_0 and $2[(d+a)/(b+c)] - p_0$ from even to odd years.

If $c < b$, then p_t approaches $(d+a)/(b+c)$ as t approaches infinity; oscillation is damped and approaches the value of price at the point of intersection of the supply and demand curves. If $c > b$, then p_t does not converge as t approaches infinity; $(-c/b)^t$ approaches infinity as t gets even larger. This last case is referred to as explosive oscillation; price and output changes get farther and farther away from equilibrium.

Price discrimination

Suppose that a monopolist is producing in one area and selling in two markets which can be segmented. Assume that price elasticity of demand is higher in market 1 than in market 2: $\eta_1 > \eta_2$. Let the subscripts 1 and 2 represent the different markets. Then R_1 is a function of q_1, R_2 is a function of q_2, and c is a function of $q_1 + q_2$. The monopolist's profit will then equal the difference between (a) the sum of total revenues from each market and (b) total costs. Mathematically,

$$\Pi = R_1 + R_2 - C \tag{A-71}$$

Taking the partial derivatives of this function with respect to q_1 and q_2 and setting them equal to zero yields

$$\frac{\partial \Pi}{\partial q_1} = \frac{\partial R_1}{\partial q_1} - \frac{\partial C}{\partial q_1} = 0 \quad \text{and} \quad \frac{\partial \Pi}{\partial q_2} = \frac{\partial R_2}{\partial q_2} - \frac{\partial C}{\partial q_2} = 0 \tag{A-72}$$

Rearranging indicates that at the profit-maximizing point the marginal revenues in each market are equated to the common marginal cost—and hence equal each other.

We can demonstrate that the monopolist will charge a higher price to those in the more price-inelastic market by recalling the relation between marginal revenue and the price elasticity of demand, η. Thus

$$\frac{\partial R_1}{\partial q_1} = p_1 \left(1 - \frac{1}{\eta_1} \right) \quad \text{and} \quad \frac{\partial R_2}{\partial q_2} = p_2 \left(1 - \frac{1}{\eta_2} \right) \tag{A-73}$$

Since the first-order conditions for profit maximization require that $\partial R_1/\partial q_1 = \partial R_2/\partial q_2$, and since we assume $|\eta_1| > |\eta_2|$, then remember,

$$\left(1 - \frac{1}{\eta_1} \right) > \left(1 - \frac{1}{\eta_2} \right) \tag{A-74}$$

It follows that to satisfy

$$p_1 \left(1 - \frac{1}{\eta_1} \right) = p_2 \left(1 - \frac{1}{\eta_2} \right) \tag{A-75}$$

p_2 must exceed p_1. That is, a higher price should be charged in market 2, where price elasticity of demand is lower.

Appendix B:
Linear programming

Students taking microeconomics and business people observing economists are sometimes critical of what they believe to be a lack of applicability of economic theory to the so-called real world. Linear programming is one area where the critics might be placated by witnessing economic principles in action in concrete situations. This form of analysis is much closer to the view that business people have of day-to-day production. Linear programming enables the analyst to isolate individual inputs in a production process and study the outputs of that production process. We can examine each output individually or look at a combination of outputs. The economist usually studies the production process in a generalized theoretical manner. Linear programming is merely a more detailed view of any production process.

A simple illustration

To get a rough idea of the type of problem that can be handled by linear programming, consider a simple example. Upon graduation, you are unable to bear leaving your alma mater, and you accept a position as head of food services for the school dormitories. Your instructions are simple: You must meet the minimum daily nutritional requirements of the students, you must do this with the foods available for this purpose, and you must minimize costs. There are three minimum daily nutritional requirments to be met: calories, protein, and vitamins. These three requirements must be met simultaneously, or the students may develop scurvy and other unpleasant diseases for which you will be held responsible. Not only must these minimum standards be met, but they have to be met with only two ingredients: meat and potatoes. This situation is pictured in Figure B-1. There the axes represent the quantities of the two foods you can order for the students you have to feed on a daily basis.

The lines within the quadrant display the alternative combinations of meat and potatoes that will fulfill the students' nutritional requirements, as defined by a dietetics handbook. AB shows that to provide the minimum number of calories required, it would take at least A pounds of meat or B pounds of potatoes, or any combination of the two along that line; i.e., AB represents all possible combinations of meat and potatoes that provide a given minimum number of calories. Similarly, CD displays the combinations of meat and potatoes that will just meet the minimum protein requirements, and EF shows those combinations satisfying the minimum vitamin requirements.

Examined individually, the lines EF, CD, and AB each represent a restriction on

██████

FIGURE B-1

Obtaining the feasible region
We assume that there are three nutritional
requirements given in nutritional handbooks;
vitamins, proteins, and calories. The lines *EF*,
CD, and *AB*, respectively, represent those
requirements. In order to meet all those
requirements simultaneously, you must be
along or above the line *EGHB*; it is labeled the
feasible region.

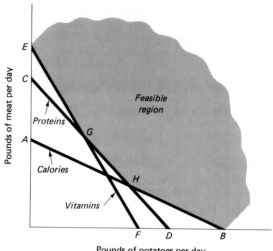

your choice of a menu. Taken together, these restrictions imply that your menu must lie somewhere along line *EGHB* or at some point above and to the right of that line. The entire area containing these points is labeled the feasible region in Figure B-1. The feasible region represents all possible combinations of meat and potatoes that satisfy (or more than satisfy) the three nutritional constraints.

There is likely to be only one point, among the multitude in the feasible region, that will also satisfy your instruction: to minimize costs. To meet that restriction, the relative prices of the foods purchased must be considered.

Contacting various food wholesalers reveals the best prices at which you can purchase meat and potatoes. Taking the two prices together, you can compute the price ratio; this ratio, when considered with the other restrictions, yields the solution to your problems. In Figure B-2, the price ratio has been added to the diagram to show the "lowest" (least costly) combination on the nutritional requirement boundary. Remember that the price ratio is the negative of the price of the commodity on the horizontal axis divided by the price of the commodity on the vertical axis. By shifting this line down through the quadrant until it just touches (is tangent to) the lowest point on the boundary of the feasible region (the point closest to the origin but still in the feasible region), the least-cost combination of meat and potatoes has been established. Thus you have determined that *I* pounds of meat per day and *K* pounds of potatoes per day will feed the students at the least cost and satisfy their nutritional needs.[1]

Some readers may have noticed the similarities between some parts of the example and some more general economic concepts. The line *EGHB* is somewhat akin to an isoquant, but it is composed of linear segments rather than being a smooth

[1]The rash assumption is made here that the students will in fact eat the food.

FIGURE B-2
Determining the least-cost solution
If we add a price line given by the relative price of the two foods, potatoes and meat, we can find where it just touches the boundary *EGHB* of the feasible region. This occurs at point *H*, so that 1 pound of meat per day and *K* pounds of potatoes per day would be chosen.

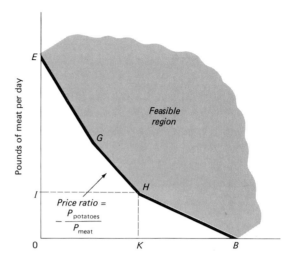

curve.[2] The line displays input combinations that can be used to produce a desired level of output, which is defined here with reference to three criteria. The price ratio line is like an isocost line and displays the various combinations of the inputs that may be purchased for a given level of expenditure. The point of tangency between an isoquant and an isocost yields the unique cost-minimizing point, just as here the junction of the segmented line and the price ratio yields the only cost-minimizing combination of the inputs.[3]

Basic concepts

The preceding example illustrates most of the major aspects of linear programming. This form of analysis concentrates on short-run choices of **production processes** and outputs.

A production process is a specific method of achieving a given output. There are always alternative processes which will produce the same result. In some instances there are a very large number of alternative processes available, but usually there are a small number of practical alternatives to be considered.

For example, in the production of a book such as this one, the alternatives might be having ten people set type by hand or having two people use an electronic typesetter. Such a trade-off would be between more capital (the use of an electronic typesetter) and more labor (eight typesetters' time). This is an example of a funda-

---

[2]This differs from the usual isoquant because it does not measure a specific volume or level of a product. However, since it "produces" a minimum nutrition requirement, it can be treated as effectively the same.

[3]The same would be true, of course, if this were a profit-maximizing example rather than a cost-minimizing one.

mental choice which was considered in more general terms in Chapter 8. The more production alternatives available, the closer the linear segment isoquant will come to looking like the smooth curve used to illustrate isoquants.

The production process alternatives considered in linear programming are usually short-run decisions and distinguish between fixed factors of production and variable factors of production. Fixed factors, such as the size of an existing factory building, are treated mathematically as having zero variable cost. The variable factors are treated as available in any desired amount at a constant unit cost, because each firm's decision makers assume that their short-run production decisions will not change input prices.

As the name suggests, the programming is linear. This is the simplest form of a more general analysis. **Linearity** is a simplifying assumption that keeps the problem in a form that can be handled easily and still illustrate the basic process. Linearity is the name of the mathematical relation between variables when variations in one variable are matched by proportional variations in another variable, the factor of proportions remaining constant. ($Y = aX$ is an example, where $a = Y/X$ and a is always constant.) In economic terms, linearity means constant returns and constant prices for inputs and outputs; that is, marginal and average products are identical and price lines are horizontal. This has the advantage of keeping the analysis manageable, yet it does not significantly affect the logic of the results.

Frequently, linear programming is used to solve for the minimization of costs or for the maximization of profits in a particular production situation. Technically, there is an **objective function** to solve. This function is merely an expression formalizing the basic problem at hand. For instance, in the meat-and-potatoes example just covered, the food-service manager was required to minimize food costs (the objective was cost minimization). Soon we will consider how such objectives can be expressed formally.

The objective function is subject to **constraints** which state certain conditions that must be surpassed or cannot be surpassed. For example, if a given machine requires at least four operators to function properly, there must be at least four operators, but there may be more (in mathematical notation, ≥4). Furthermore, the machine may be subject to the limitation that it cannot be operated more than 24 hours in a day, but it can always be run less than that (≤24).

After the constraints have been established, the range of **feasible solutions** can be considered. In the preceding example of the cafeteria food manager, there were many feasible solutions, but only one was revealed to be the **optimal solution;** it was the best, given the criterion of cost minimization, in the feasible region. This is usually the case, but occasionally there will be a number of optimal solutions. Then it is irrelevant which of those positions is chosen. For example, consider what would have happened in the example given above if the price ratio, as represented graphically by the price ratio line, had been parallel to and coincident with the line segment GH in Figure B-2. In that case, any of the points from G to H (including those two points) would have been equally acceptable and all would be optimal solutions.

Profit maximization

Using the concepts we've covered, let us now consider an example of profit maximization employing some simple algebra.

After a food riot in the dining hall, you have discreetly changed your occupation.

You went into business for yourself producing sailboats. After hiring some workers, producing some boats, and discovering the prices at which they would sell, you made the following observations. Each Swiftsail model (S) yields a profit of $520, and there is a $450 profit on each sale of a Rapidsail model (R). A Swiftsail requires 40 hours for assembly and 24 hours for finishing; each Rapidsail requires 25 hours for assembly and 30 hours for finishing. You have paid your workers for 1 month's labor. During the month you realize that, given the specialized nature of production, there are 400 hours of labor available for assembly work and 360 hours available for finishing work. Considering these data, which are summarized in Table B-1, how many of each boat should you produce each month, or should you produce only one of the two models?

Remembering your food-service days, you can solve the problem. Your objective functon is the maximization of total profits (Z) in the upcoming month. The function is stated like this:

$$Z = \$520S + \$450R$$

Multiplying the number of boats of each type to be produced by their respective profits yields total monthly profits. How many boats will be produced will be determined by the physical constraints you face. The following are the linear constraints confronting you:

$$40S + 25R \leq 400 \text{ (assembly)} \qquad \textbf{(B-1}a\textbf{)}$$

$$24S + 30R \leq 360 \text{ (finishing)} \qquad \textbf{(B-2}a\textbf{)}$$

You will have no more than 400 hours' assembly time available to be used in assembling the boats. Swiftsails and Rapidsails require 40 and 25 hours, respectively, for assembly. Similarly, you have up to 360 hours of finishing time. For that operation, Swiftsails and Rapidsails require 24 and 30 hours, respectively. For mathematical exactness there is also a nonnegativity condition that must be expressed; this condition does not enter into the calculations, but you cannot produce fewer than zero Rapidsails or Swiftsails: $R \geq 0$, $S \geq 0$.

The constraints can be graphed to show the feasible solutions by expressing the linear constraints in the form of equalities. Rearranging and simplifying Eq. (B-1a),

$$40S = 400 - 25R \qquad \textbf{(B-1}b\textbf{)}$$

$$S = 10 - \frac{5}{8}R \qquad \textbf{(B-1}c\textbf{)}$$

TABLE B-1		Hours required per Swiftsail	Hours required per Rapidsail	Hours available per month
Assembly hours		40	25	400
Finishing hours		24	30	360

$$30R = 360 - 24S \tag{B-2b}$$

$$R = 12 - \frac{4}{5}S \tag{B-2c}$$

Let's plot the linear constraints, Eqs. (B-1c) and (B-2c). Remember that in each equation the first number on the right-hand side is the vertical axis intercept and the second number is the slope. For Rapidsail, Eq. (B-2c), plot 12 as the intercept on the vertical axis (the R axis in this case). From that point, draw a line with the slope of $-\frac{4}{5}$ to the S axis, which will lead to a horizontal intercept at $S = 15$. To make Eq. (B-1c) consistent with the form of Eq. (B-2c), solve that constraint for R:

$$S = 10 - \frac{5}{8}R$$

$$\frac{5}{8}R = 10 - S$$

$$R = \frac{8}{5}(10) - \frac{8}{5}S \tag{B-1c}$$

$$= 16 - \frac{8}{5}S$$

Now draw Eq. (B-1c) in the same manner as Eq. (B-2c) is drawn. The result is seen in Figure B-3, where the constraints have outlined the feasible solutions, which are contained on the borders of and inside the shaded polygon. Note that the feasible region lies below or to the left of our constraints here, whereas in our previous example of menu selection it was above or to the right of the nutritional constraints. This is because our finishing and assembly constraints represent an upper bound on the labor resources available to produce sailboats, while the nutritional constraints represent a lower bound on the nutritional content of the menu.

FIGURE B-3
Solving a production problem
The two straight lines represent the technological production constraints for assembling and finishing Swiftsails and Rapidsails. We then find the feasible region.

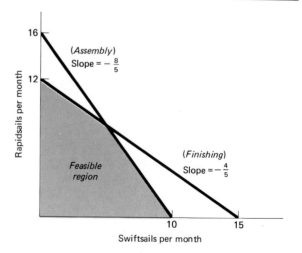

Through mathematics we can show that the optimal solution lies on the boundary of the feasible region. One possible candidate for the profit-maximizing solution is the point given by the intersection of the two constraints. This point lies on the boundary of the feasible region. To locate this intersection point we must solve the following two equations for R and S:

$$40S + 25R = 400 \qquad \text{(B-3a)}$$

$$24S + 30R = 360 \qquad \text{(B-4a)}$$

We can eliminate one of the variables by finding a common base and we can solve for the other. This can be done by multiplying Eq. (B-3a) by 3 and Eq. (B-4a) by -5 (-5 rather than 5 so that the equations can be added and one variable eliminated).[4] (Remember, multiplying both sides of any equation by a constant does not change its equality.)

$$120S + 75R = 1,200 \qquad \text{(B-3b)}$$

$$\underline{-120S - 150R = -1,800} \qquad \text{(B-4b)}$$

$$-75R = -600$$

$$R = 8$$

Adding the equations algebraically yields one variable and its unique solution. Substituting this value into either of the constraints [that is, into either Eq. (B-3a) or Eq. (B-4a)] yields the unique value for the other variable for the optimum solution.

$$40S + 25(8) = 400$$

$$40S = 200 \qquad \text{(B-3c)}$$

$$S = 5$$

This solution yields a profit of $Z = 5(\$520) + 8(\$450) = \$2,600 + \$3,600 = \$6,200$ per month. Before we can accept this as the maximum profit solution, we must examine other possible feasible solutions. In this case, we need only check the corners (except for the origin) of the polygon. These are the points ($S = 0$, $R = 1\ 2$) and ($S = 10$, $R = 0$). Substituting these into our objective function yields profits of $Z = \$5,400$ and $Z = \$5,200$ per month, respectively. Therefore we can be assured that our initial solution point ($S = 5$, $R = 8$) gives us the profit-maximizing combination of sailboats to produce. Figure B-4 displays the optimal solution graphically.

Applying linear programming

It is not difficult to realize that linear programming problems can quickly become large and complicated. When alternative methods of production are considered for a multiproduct firm which has many possible input combinations, the need for

---

[4]This is not the only way to get the solution. You can multiply the constraints by any numbers you can think of to help get one of the variables to the same coefficient in each equation. For instance, if Eq. (B-3a) had been multiplied by $-\frac{3}{5}$ [the negative of the ratio of S's in Eq. (B-3a) and Eq. (B-4a)], it would have also made possible the elimination of S so that we could solve for R.

FIGURE B-4

The optimum solution
We now subject Figure B-3 to profit
maximization. In this particular problem, it
occurs at a corner where the output rate is five
Swiftsails and eight Rapidsails per month.

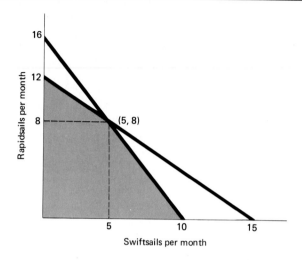

computers to solve the equations is obvious. Students interested in the more advanced
aspects of linear programming are referred to the references listed at the end of the
chapter. The purpose here is merely to give an overview of the use of linear programming in economics so that future encounters with the topic will not be totally
mystifying.

Some applications of linear programming have been in the areas of welfare
economics and advice to business people. Both these applications attempt to reveal
to the party concerned the most efficient manner of working toward his or her objectives. The following discussion examines the areas in which linear programming
is frequently applied.

Meeting minimum requirements. Like the first example considered in this appendix, contracts often include certain minimum specifications which a product
must meet. Such requirements are often self-imposed by manufacturers so that their
products maintain a certain level of quality. Feedlots often use linear programming
to calculate which diet will provide livestock with certain nutrient requirements for
optimal growth at the least cost. As relative feed prices change, so will the least-cost
diet. If the price of feed becomes too high relative to the market value of additional
heft on the livestock, that is, more pounds of meat per steer or hog, for example,
feeding will be stopped and the livestock slaughtered. This happened following a
year of poor crops combined with the Russian grain deal in 1973. If the market value
of the livestock is high and is expected to remain so, the diet may be increased to
make the animals grow faster. Hence, not only must relative input prices be considered, but also current and expected output prices.

Least-cost problems solved by linear programming have also included gasoline
blending, optimizing inventory levels, assigning personnel to jobs, and minimizing
waste of raw materials.

Optimal production processes. Firms are frequently constrained in the short run by factors such as plant size, the number of trained employees, and machine capacity. Given such short-run constraints, the firm must decide on the most efficient use of its scarce resources by considering the alternative outputs and their prices. The trade-offs that arise there are not difficult to imagine. One product might entail minimal use of personnel but require relatively large amounts of machine capacity. The other product might require much more labor input but less machine time. Coordination of all inputs in the most efficient manner, considering the relative profitability of alternative outputs, is the role of linear programming.

A building contractor may be faced with the problem of how to use laborers and machines most efficiently in erecting the walls of a brick building. Suppose that all the bricks and bricklayers are at the construction site (and have already been paid for) and that the contractor's problem is to decide how many machines to rent by the hour to hoist bricks and how many brick carriers to hire at a given hourly wage. This is a traditional labor-capital trade-off problem.

By experience the contractor knows it is "efficient" to use certain ratios of laborers to machines. These alternative ratios are displayed graphically as process rays in Figure B-5. The capital-intensive process is ray 0M. This process would use more machines per laborer, and the bricks would be delivered by machine close to each bricklayer. The labor-intensive process, ray 0L, would use fewer machines per laborer, and there would be more hand-carrying of bricks to the bricklayers.

FIGURE B-5
Choosing between capital- and labor-intensive processes
Along ray 0L more labor relative to capital will be used than along ray 0M. Line *ABDE* is a typical constant-output isoquant. The profit-maximizing point in this figure depends on the relative prices of capital and labor.

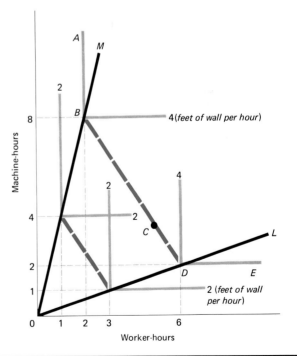

Assume that a tall building is under construction. The building is being constructed with bricks and is 100 feet long on each side. Progress is measured by the number of vertical feet per hour at which the 100-foot wall sections are built up. If there are enough bricks and bricklayers to build walls at the rate of 4 feet per hour, process 0M would require 2 human hours for every 8 machine hours. Process 0L requires 6 human hours for every 2 machine hours. Joining the same production level points on the two rays yields a kinked isoquant (one such isoquant is ABDE). The same can be done at the other production points on the process rays for isoquants displaying input combinations possible at different levels of output.

One can measure output along the process rays because the production function is assumed to be homogeneous of degree one. This type of production function exists when an increase of all inputs by some proportion increases the output by the same proportion. Hence, to increase the rate at which the wall is built from 2 to 4 feet per hour, the number of workers and machines used per hour must double (for example, from four machines and one worker to eight machines and two workers when the machine-intensive process is used).

The process that will be chosen will depend upon the relative price of labor and machine use per hour. As in the food-service example, the lowest point of tangency of the ratio of the input prices to the line ABDE will determine the minimum cost process for 4 feet of wall per hour. It is possible that an input combination as described by point C could emerge. For this to happen, the ratio of the prices of the inputs would be parallel and tangent to segment BD of the isoquant. Point C would have to be a technologically feasible combination for it to be chosen (which it is not here); otherwise, points B and D would do the same job at the same price, since any point from B to D would cost the same. The more processes that are available, the more kinks there will be in the production isoquant and the curve would begin to look more like the usual smooth isoquant. Such smooth isoquants, however, assume continuous substitutability between inputs; this rarely happens in the world faced by decision makers.

As in the food service problem considered previously, the applicability of the linear programming technique was displayed here. This tool permits complicated practical problems to be formulated and solved.

Transportation. Almost all goods have to be transported, and the shipment alone can be a major factor in the cost of production. A firm typically must ship inputs and outputs and maintain inventories of both. Careful planning of commodity shipments can produce important savings. A trucking firm must coordinate the use of trucks and the capacity of its transport facilities (warehouse space and truck service) and also plan the most efficient routing of the trucks in their pickup and delivery schedules. Complex rate structures further complicate transportation decisions.

Suppose a television manufacturer assembles television sets at plants in Atlanta and Chicago. To market the product, five distribution centers are maintained, in Atlanta, Chicago, Dallas, New York, and San Francisco. The plants could produce the televisions for their own market areas but would have to ship by truck to the other three distribution centers. The manufacturer would have to determine how many sets to ship from the two plants to the other three distribution centers to meet the given demands and, at the same time, minimize total shipping costs. This spatial problem is diagrammed in Figure B-6.

FIGURE B-6
A transportation problem: Minimizing total shipping costs
A television manufacturer assembles TV sets in both Atlanta and Chicago. It markets its product in both cities, plus New York, Dallas, and San Francisco. Its problem is to decide which plants should ship to which markets.

SHIPPING ROUTES: TWO PLANTS, FIVE DISTRIBUTION CENTERS

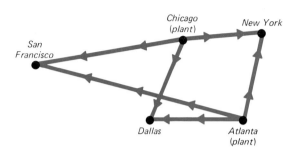

Linear programming could solve such a problem by taking into account various constraints (the respective production rates at the two plants, the demand for television sets in the separate market areas, seasonal variations in demand, and shipping costs). It may seem like common sense that the plant closest to a distribution center would supply it, but this may not be so. The result obtained by linear programming may confirm this notion or may reveal some other shipping pattern to be the cheapest. Instead of relying on seat-of-the-pants judgments or gut feelings, the linear programming technique involves the application of specific rules, based on the information used in the calculations, which guarantee that an optimal shipping pattern will be found.

The preceding introduction to some of the applications of linear programming is not intended to leave the impression that business decisions are based on the answers produced by programmed analyses. Just as economists use mathematics as a tool, linear programming is one of a number of tools used by decision makers in business. Often there are considerations which linear programming simply cannot handle that have to be taken into account. In such cases, linear programming analysis provides only one of the inputs into the decision-making process.

The primal and dual programs

In any linear programming problem there is an objective function to solve. Typically, this problem, called the *primal* program, is the maximization of profits. However, as noted before the primal program could be the minimization of costs or some other objective. Whatever the primal program, there is an analogous problem called the *dual* program. Very often, due to computational considerations, it is simpler to solve the dual program than the primal program. More important, the dual provides valuable economic insight into the problem under consideration, apart from the straightforward interpretation of the primal.

To illustrate the formulation and interpretation of the dual, let us return to the earlier example of producing two types of sailboats, Rapidsail and Swiftsail. The objective of the primal program was the maximization of profits. This primal problem was written as

Maximize $\qquad$ $Z = 520S + 450R$

subject to $\qquad$ $40S + 25R \leqslant 400$

$\qquad\qquad\qquad$ $24S + 30R \leqslant 360$

$\qquad\qquad\qquad$ $S \geqslant 0 \qquad R \geqslant 0$

The dual form (minimize cost Y) of this problem may be written

Minimize $\qquad$ $Y = 400A + 360F$

subject to $\qquad$ $40A + 24F \geqslant 520$

$\qquad\qquad\qquad$ $25A + 30F \geqslant 450$

$\qquad\qquad\qquad$ $A \geqslant 0 \qquad F \geqslant 0$

As can be seen, the dual is essentially the converse of the primal program. The inequalities of the constraints are reversed, the objective function is to be minimized instead of maximized, and the profit values for each sailboat have switched places with the assembly and finishing resource constraints. It is this symmetry that makes the dual analogous to the primal. In particular, a fundamental result in linear programming is that the objective functions in the primal and dual programs will reach the same value when the two problems are solved.

The fact that the two objective functions reach the same value at the optimum is important because it implies that the dual variables may be given a unit of measure. In the primal, Z denotes the profit earned from producing sailboats, as measured in dollars per unit time period. At the optimum, $Z = Y$, the objective function of the dual should also be measured in dollars. Examining the dual objective function, we see that the coefficient of A (400) represents the total hours available for assembly and the coefficient of F (360) represents the total hours available for finishing. Hence, if Y is to be measured in dollars, A and F must be expressed in dollars per unit of the assembly and finishing resources. That is to say, A and F will signify some valuation of our available resources. This valuation is an imputed one, often called the opportunity cost of utilizing these resources. The dual objective function thus may be viewed as one of minimizing the total opportunity cost of these resources.

In the present problem, we may solve the dual program for the opportunity costs of our assembly and finishing resources. The graph is left as an exercise for the student. The numerical solution may be found by checking the extreme points in the feasible region. This will reveal that Y is minimized at the points ($A = 8, F = 8.34$). Substitution reveals that at these points $Y = 6,200$, which is equal to the profit-maximizing value of Z in the primal program. The values of A and F here imply that the opportunity costs of our assembly and finishing resources are $8.00 and $8.34, respectively. These values indicate how much profit may be increased if the assembly and finishing constraints can be relaxed (over a given range). For example, if it were possible to obtain one more hour of assembly time, profit from sailboat production would increase by $8.00. Similarly, if it were possible to obtain one more hour of finishing time, profit would increase by $8.34. These relations are what make the dual interesting from an economic point of view. For a more complete development of the dual, the reader is urged to consult the reference materials listed at the end of this appendix.

Solving linear programming problems

Readers interested in more than the rudiments of linear programming provided in this appendix can work through some specific problems designed to illustrate the method of solution and the types of problems common to linear programming. Students are urged to diagram these three problems and solve them mathematically before reading the answers.

The oil refinery mix. The petroleum industry has made extensive use of linear programming to enhance efficiency in many phases of its complex operations. Consider the application of linear programming to a simplified refinery operation.

Assume that the following information is known. The refinery can store up to 5,000 barrels of gasoline G and up to 10,000 barrels of fuel oil F in each production period. The refining process uses 24,000 barrels of crude oil each period. Each barrel of gasoline produced requires 3 barrels of crude oil. Each barrel of fuel oil produced requires 2 barrels of crude oil. The profit from each barrel of gasoline is $8; each barrel of fuel yields a profit of $4.

The refinery operators must decide how much of its crude oil to devote to the production of gasoline and how much to fuel oil. The firm's objective is to maximize profits, Π. To solve, write the problem as follows:

Maximize $\Pi = 8G + 4F$

subject to $3G + 2F \leq 24,000$

$\qquad\qquad G \leq 5,000 \qquad F \leq 10,000$

$\qquad\qquad G \geq 0 \qquad\quad F \geq 0$

In Figure B-7, the problem can be visualized by defining the feasible region. The storage capacity constraints form two boundaries to the feasible region. The other

FIGURE B-7
A production problem

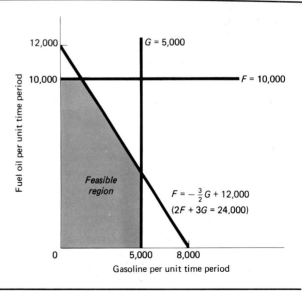

boundary is determined by the technological constraints of the production process. The optimal solution will lie on the boundary of the feasible region.

To determine the profit-maximizing solution, it is easiest to rewrite the profit function, $\Pi = 8G + 4F$, in the form $F = \Pi/4 + (-8/4)G = 1/4\Pi - 2G$. If profits were 0, the line defined by this equation would pass through the origin of Figure B-8 and have a slope of -2 (which equals $\frac{8}{4}$, the ratio of the two products' profitability). Since the highest profits possible are desired, move the line, called the isoprofit line, out from the origin to the farthest point still in the feasible region to which the isoprofit line is just tangent. This solution yields a value of $G = 5,000$. Substituting this value into the constraint yields the value of the other variable:

$$3G + 2F = 24,000$$
$$3(5,000) + 2F = 24,000$$
$$F = 4,500$$

The profit-maximizing production mix yields

$$\Pi = 8(5,000) = 4(4,500)$$
$$= 40,000 + 18,000$$
$$= \$58,000$$

The shipping crates. A company manufactures two types of wooden shipping crates. The profit on each type 1 crate is \$25, and the profit on each type 2 crate is \$20. Each crate must go through two production processes. In each production period,

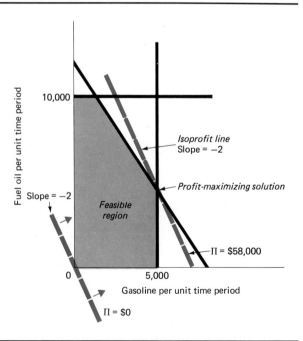

FIGURE B-8
Finding the profit-maximizing solution

a total of 100 hours is available on production line A and a total of 120 hours is available on production line B. Type 1 crates T_1 require 2 hours on line A and 4 hours on line B. Type 2 crates T_2 require 5 hours on line A and 3 hours on line B. Determine the number of crates of each type that should be produced in order to maximize profits. Solve the problem algebraically, rounding to the nearest whole number. (The diagram is left as an exercise; it is similar to the one in the boat-building example given previously.)

Set the problem up in this manner:

Maximize	$\Pi = 25T_1 + 20T_2$
subject to	$2T_1 + 5T_2 \leqslant 100$
	$4T_1 + 3T_2 \leqslant 120$
	$T_1 \geqslant 0 \qquad T_2 \geqslant 0$

Now, let us consider the solution point given by the intersection of our production constraints. (Remember that when you have two linearly independent equations and two unknown variables, you can solve for both variables, but first you have to solve for just one variable by adding the equations algebraically for the purpose of eliminating the other variable.)

Let us solve for one variable. If

$$T_1 + 5T_2 = 100$$

then multiplying by -2 yields

$$-4T_1 - 10T_2 = -200$$

Now add the other constraint

$$+4T_1 + 3T_2 = 120$$

which leaves one variable

$$-7T_2 = -80$$
$$T_2 = 11 \qquad \text{(approximately)}$$

Solve for the other variable by substitution

$$2T_1 + 5T_2 = 100$$
$$2T_1 + 5(11) = 100$$
$$2T_1 = 100 - 55$$
$$T_1 = 22 \qquad \text{(approximately)}$$

Substitute these values into the objective function to find profits

$$\Pi = 25T_1 + 20T_2$$
$$= 25(22) + 20(11)$$
$$= \$770 \text{ per unit time period}$$

The question now becomes one of whether this is a profit-maximizing solution. To ensure that this is the optimal solution we must check the other corner points of our feasible region. These are $(T_1 = 30, T_2 = 0)$ and $(T_1 = 0, T_2 = 20)$. Substituting these into our objective function gives profits of $\Pi = \$750$ and $\Pi = \$400$, respectively. Hence, we have found the profit-maximizing solution.

Labor contract restrictions. Suppose the manager of a widget-producing plant was told to manufacture 1,000 widgets of a certain quality per day at the lowest possible cost. With the existing machinery a widget can be produced by either $\frac{1}{5}$ unit higher-skilled labor H, or $\frac{1}{2}$ unit of lower-skilled labor L. This is expressed as $5H + 2L \geq 1,000$ to eliminate the fractions. Since 2 units of higher-skilled labor produce the same number of widgets as do 5 units of lower-skilled labor (i.e., 10 widgets), the labor productivity trade-off can be written in this manner. The plant has negotiated a contract with the labor union to pay the higher-skilled workers $80 per day and the lower-skilled workers $45 per day. The contract specifies that the plant must employ at least 300 lower-skilled workers, except that 2 higher-skilled workers can be substituted for every one lower-skilled worker released ($\frac{1}{2}H + L \geq 300$).

At the union hall there are 160 higher-skilled laborers available and 400 lower-skilled workers. Let's solve for the minimum wage cost within the restrictions of the labor contract.

Labor costs (the total wage bill, in this case) are to be minimized so that the objective function is

Minimize $\qquad\qquad\qquad W = 80H + 45L$

subject to $\qquad\qquad\qquad \frac{1}{2}H + L \geq 300$

$\qquad\qquad\qquad\qquad\quad 5H + 2L \geq 1,000$

$\qquad\qquad\qquad\qquad\quad H \leq 160 \qquad L \leq 400$

$\qquad\qquad\qquad\qquad\quad H \geq 2 \qquad\quad L \geq 1$

This set of constraints is diagrammed in Figure B-9. The feasible region is defined by both the labor union and technological constraints.

The optimal solution, where costs are minimized, is where the isocost line is just tangent to the feasible region. This line has a slope equal to the negative of the ratio of the wages ($-80/45$). Mathematically, the optimal values can be derived as follows. First, solve for one variable. If

$\frac{1}{2}H + L = 300$

multiplying by -10 yields

$-5H - 10L = -3,000$

adding the other constraint

$+5H + 2L = 1,000$

yields one variable

$-8L = -2,000$

$L = 250$

Solve for the other variable by substitution

$5H + 2L = 1,000$

$5H + 2(250) = 1,000$

$5H = 1,000 - 500$

$H = 100$

Solve the objective function for minimum cost

FIGURE B-9
An employment problem

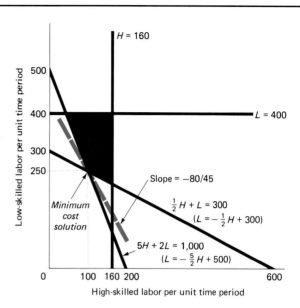

$$W = 80H + 45L$$
$$= 80(100) + 45(250)$$
$$= \$19,250$$

We leave as an exercise for you to check that this is the optimal solution.

Consider the change in solution that would emerge if the union were voted out by its members and the plant manager were free to hire whomever he or she wished. The constraint that the plant must hire at least 300 laborers, or 2 higher-skilled workers for every released lower-skilled worker, would no longer exist. The relative wages of the two classes of workers might change such that higher-skilled workers earned \$75 per day and lower-skilled workers \$25. In the short run, the number of higher-skilled laborers may be assumed to remain about the same as before with 160 still available. The number of lower-skilled laborers would probably expand (there was presumably an excess quantity supplied at $W = \$45/\text{day}$) and consequently there would be no constraint in the range of operation under consideration. (All changes are purely hypothetical.) Again, costs are to be minimized, taking into account the wages of the workers and the technological (i.e., labor productivity) constraints. The problem now looks like this:

Minimize $W = 75H + 25L$
subject to $5H + 2L \geqslant 1,000$
                       $160 \geqslant H \geqslant 0 \quad L \geqslant 0$

This situation is illustrated in Figure B-10, which displays the change in constraints and the broadened feasible range of positions.

As before, the optimal solution is where the isocost line just reaches the feasible

FIGURE B-10
Eliminating the union constraint.

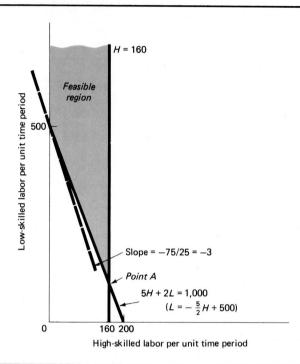

region. In this case, the slope of the line (the negative of the ratio of the wage rates) is $-75/25 = -3$, and the solution happens to be 500 lower-skilled workers and no higher-skilled workers. Solving the objective function for minimum costs yields

$$W = 75(0) + 25(500)$$
$$= \$12,500$$

This figure is considerably less than the \$19,250 figure arrived at previously. Note that if the lower-skilled workers' wages were to rise and/or the higher-skilled workers' wages were to fall so that the ratio of the relative wages fell below $\frac{5}{2}$, all the available higher-skilled workers would be hired and the employment of lower-skilled workers would drop by 80 percent.

Summary

1   Linear programming has developed since World War II and, to date, has been the most successful mathematical programming method. It enables business firms to make "better" decisions.

2   This technique allows decision makers to solve complex mathematical problems and to maximize or minimize key variables subject to actual or estimated constraints.

3   The most common applications involve the maximization of profits subject to certain technical cost and revenue constraints, the maximization of output subject to the constraint of limited resources, and the minimization of the costs of producing a predetermined rate of output.

4   A purely mathematical tool, linear programming can never do more than it is set up to do, nor can it be more accurate than the data and assumptions used in formulating the problem.

5   Feasible solutions are derived after the constraints have been established. Usually only one of the feasible solutions will be optimal when the objective function (which expresses whatever is required in mathematical terms) is maximized or minimized.

6   When linear programming analyses are portrayed geometrically, isoquants become kinked curves. When a corner on the isoquant is just touched by the isocost or price ratio line, a unique solution has been obtained.

7   The change in the value of a constraint or the addition of another constraint may or may not change the optimal solution.

Glossary

- **production process** Uses inputs to produce one or more outputs. In linear programming, each process is assumed to use inputs in fixed proportions.
- **linearity** A simplifying assumption that requires constant returns to scale and fixed prices for inputs and outputs.
- **objective function** A linear function to be maximized (or minimized) subject to certain constraints on the values of the variables.
- **constraints** Inequalities describing structural (capacity) limits (also called conditions).
- **feasible solutions** All possible combinations of the commodities that can be purchased, used, or produced, given the existing constraints.
- **optimum solution** The best of the feasible solutions; may be more than one.

Questions

(Answers to even-numbered questions are at back of text.)

1   Describe briefly the decision process of an analyst concerned with maximizing a firm's profits by using the linear programming method.

2   Construct a graph which shows labor and capital as inputs; draw three alternative process rays and connect them at the same output level, forming a kinked isoquant. (Essentially, by connecting the points with straight-line segments, we are assuming that there are no alternatives between the three process rays. See question 3.) Identify the most labor-intensive process ray and the most capital-intensive ray.

3   Sketch a "broken isoquant." Include on the graph several different groups of isocost curves. Find the optimal combination of inputs for those different groups by finding the point of "tangency."

a What is the relation between the isocost curves and the isoquant when there are many optimal solutions?

b What is the relation when there is only one optimal solution?

c Would the optimal solution be different if the isoquant was constructed by graphing only the corner points rather than including the line segments connecting them? (The discrete points represent a model in which the inputs are available only in discrete amounts; e.g., you can hire only 3 or 4 workers, not 3.14.)

For questions 4, 5, 6, and 7, use the following information: Suppose you are having a party and the only two inputs to go into producing drinks are 250 ounces of cola and 150 ounces of rum.

4 In a quandrant with the inputs measured on the two axes, graphically display the limits you face and the corresponding feasible region.

5 Suppose you hire a bartender who will (*a*) only mix drinks the same way all night, and (*b*) allow you only three choices for the proportions: 3 ounces of cola to 1 ounce of rum, 2 ounces of cola to 1 ounce of rum, or 1 ounce of cola to 1 ounce of rum. Display these production process rays in the graph drawn for question 4.

6 In the quadrant drawn for question 4, graph an isoquant corresponding to 30 drinks, where a drink is 1 ounce of rum mixed with the proportional amount of cola. If 30 drinks are to be consumed at the party, which process rays are feasible?

7 Same as question 6, but a drink is defined as 12 ounces of liquid mixed in the proper proportions.

Use the following information for questions 8, 9, and 10:

$$x_1 \geq 0$$

$$x_2 \geq 0$$

$$3x_1 + 2x_2 \leq 10$$

$$6x_1 + x_2 \leq 8$$

$$Z = 5x_1 + 2x_2$$

8 Which equation is the objective function? Which equations are the constraints?

9 Diagram the constraints and define the feasible region by shading.

10 Maximize the objective function subject to the constraints.

11 Noisy Records plans to use one of its record-making units to produce two different records. The profit is $2 for record 1 and $3 for record 2. Record 1 requires 4 minutes for pressing and 6 minutes for packaging. Record 2 requires 5 minutes for pressing and 3 minutes for packaging. There are 200 minutes per time period available for pressing and 210 minutes available for packaging. How many of each type of record should be produced to maximize profit for one time period, and what is that profit?

12 Solve question 11 if the profit for both records is $2.

13 Solve question 11 if the profit for record 1 is $2 and for record 2 is $1.

14 From the following information, diagram the constraints in the positive quandrant and define the feasible region. A beer factory makes both cases of beer *C* and kegs of beer *K*. Each case of beer contains 300 ounces, and each keg contains 3,000 ounces. The factory can produce up to 180,000 ounces of beer daily. The factory's packaging facility can handle 400 cases of 120 kegs per day, or any intermediate straight-line combination of the two. The factory's transportation facility can handle 1,000 cases or 50 kegs per day, or any combination. Do not solve the equations. In making the drawing, it will be helpful to know that the "corner" points of the feasible region are $K = 40$, $C = 200$, and $K = 30$, $C = 300$.

15 Given the diagram in the solution to question 14, if the profit from a case is $1 and from a keg is $6, what will be the profit-maximizing output combination of the factory? What if the profit from each is $3? (Draw in the profit ratios to determine the answers; do not solve mathematically but do substitute the corner points into the objective function to find the maximum profit.)

Selected references

Baumol, William J., "Activity Analysis in One Lesson," *American Economic Review*, vol. 48, December 1958, pp. 837–873.

————, *Economic Theory and Operations Analysis* (Englewood Cliffs, N.J.: Prentice-Hall, 1972).

Dorfman, Robert, "Mathematical, or 'Linear,' Programming: A Nonmathematical Exposition," *American Economic Review*, December 1953, pp. 797–825.

————, Paul Samuelson, and Robert Solow, *Linear Programming and Economic Analysis* (New York: McGraw-Hill, 1958).

Samuelson, Paul, "Professor Knight's Theorem on Linear Porgramming," *Zietschrift für Nationalökonomie*, vol. 18, 1958, pp. 310–317.

Wagner, Harvey, *Principles of Operations Research, with Applications to Managerial Decisions* (Englewood Cliffs, N.J.: Prentice-Hall, 1969).

Answers to even-numbered chapter questions

Chapter 1

2 No, it doesn't matter; what *does* matter is whether the model, taken as a whole, predicts well.

4 It went down; whereas a quart of tequila "cost" 10 liters of beer in 1974, by 1982 it could be "bought" for only 9 liters of beer.

6 Such a change in relative prices would make gas appliances somewhat less attractive in comparison with their electric counterparts because the former would have become relatively more expensive to operate. We would expect appliance manufacturers to adjust production accordingly.

8 What is important, you should point out, is that when the price of something rises, *some* of the users of the product decide to consume less than they had previously, and this results in a decreased quantity demanded. (One must make the distinction between marginal and average.)

10 It is meaningless to talk of the quantities that buyers would be willing to buy and sellers would be willing to sell, unless we have defined, at least conceptually, the product we have in mind. Unless consumers are indifferent between Hondas and Chevettes, and the relative successes of the two cars strongly suggest that they are not, we cannot meaningfully aggregate the two into something called the demand for "subcompact cars." Note that what is important is that potential buyers *perceive* the two products to be interchangeable; they need not actually be identical.

12 (a) Expected future clothes-washing services per year for n years, (b) expected future hours of sailing per year for n years, (c) expected future meals per unit time period for n time periods, (d) expected future dividends per year for n years, and (e) expected future consumption of goods and services per unit time period for n time periods.

14 (a) It does matter, particularly if you are desirous of bringing about a change in one of them. This lesson was learned, at immense cost, during the Great Depression of the 1930s. The Roosevelt administration felt that falling prices were causing the fall in production. On the basis of that theory, the National Recovery Administration (NRA) was created for the purpose of lessening wage and price competition. This, it was reasoned, would stop the fall in production and its corresponding layoffs. Its unconstitutionality aside, the program was an economic disaster; if anything, it aggravated the unemployment situation. The falling wages and prices were not the *cause* but rather, at least in part, the effect of declining production. Congress had the two reversed, and consequently, its NRA program was a dismal failure. (b) If changes in C are inducing changes in both A and B, then any effort to affect A via B, or vice versa, will be of no consequence.

Chapter 2

2 Such an institution (a "*barterplace*"?) would qualify as a market; however, by its very definition, the potential buyers and sellers are limited to those who either (a) have cows and want some pigs, or (b) have pigs and want some cows. The supply of, and demand for, pigs could be expressed as a function of their cow price [cow(s) per pig(s)]. Conversely, the supply of, and demand for, cows could be expressed as a function of their pig price [pig(s) per cow(s)]. The biggest potential problem in arriving at a mutually agreeable exchange, in the absence of the "lubricant," money, is the requirement that there be a "coincidence of wants." In this case, we have avoided that particular pitfall by assuming that the pig owners want some cows and the cow owners want some pigs. However, the problem of *divisibility* remains. If the haggling produces a price of $3\frac{1}{3}$ cows = 5 pigs, and if this price also reflects the absolute quantities that the traders wish to exchange, the liveness of the animals will frustrate the wishes of their owners.

4 This person is confusing *demand* with *quantity demanded*. When there is a change in the price of a good or service, the quantity demanded of that good or service changes. Only a change in any other of the *nonprice* variables affecting people's willingness to purchase will cause the *demand* to change (shift).

6 There are, of course, endless possible alternative assertions which might be made in an attempt to explain "the" reason for a rapid surge in the demand. One might hypothesize that the rising price of petroleum-fueled modes of transportation caused the demand for this particular substitute to increase. Alternatively, one could argue that an increasing awareness of the relationship between certain amounts of exercise and the state of one's health had increased the demand for roller skates. In most cases, careful scrutiny of the situation will suggest that a change in demand was not merely a spontaneous occurrence.

8 The suppliers are willing to supply their product in exchange for money; it is *money*—purchasing power over all goods and services—that they are, in effect, demanding. Perhaps this is easier to see in the case of barter, where the intermediary, money, is absent. In bartering rice for corn, the supply of rice *is* the demand for corn, and vice versa.

10 The equilibrium price is $4 per crate, and the equilibrium quantity is 50 million crates per year. At $2 per crate, the quantity demanded is 90 million crates per year and the quantity supplied is 10. This is called a shortage, or excess quantity demanded. The excess quantity demanded is 80 million crates per year. At $5 per crate, the quantity demanded is 20 million crates per year, and the quantity supplied is 80 million crates. This is called a surplus, or excess quantity supplied. The excess quantity supplied is 60 million crates per year.

12 There *is* no equilibrium price, nor is there an equilibrium quantity. Even at a price of *zero* there is a surplus, an excess quantity supplied. Not only is there no one willing to pay any positive price for any

rainfall in excess of that which naturally falls (200 centimeters per year), but that surplus of 50 centimeters per year, at a price of zero, represents an unwanted additional quantity which at least some people would presumably be willing to pay money to abate! You can get a feel for this by making a linear projection of the respective quantities demanded and supplied at a price of *minus* 10 cruzeiros per centimeter. The equilibrium "price" would be at a quantity of 175 centimeters per year (25 centimeters having been abated by the "rain takers"). Note that many "goods" become "bads" (nuisances) when they are supplied in sufficiently copious quantities.

14 While this person has learned well the definition of a surplus, one point has been overlooked. The "surpluses" which result from the above-equilibrium minimum prices *don't* go begging; the excess quantities supplied are in effect *purchased* by the Department of Agriculture. In that sense, they are not surpluses at all. When one *includes* the quantity which is demanded by the Department of Agriculture, along with the quantities being purchased by private purchasers at the support price, the quantity demanded *will* equal the quantity supplied, and there will be an equilibrium, of sorts.

Chapter 3

2 An indifference curve represents all the possible combinations of two goods which the consumer in question finds to be equally satisfying.

4 The difficulty is that such preferences are inconsistent. Since A is preferred to B, which is preferred to C, it should follow that A is also preferred to C. To assert the reverse is to be inconsistent. Note that the existence of some consumers who may in fact hold such preference patterns does not invalidate the theory. One does not empirically test the validity of a scientific model by examining the behavior of a single individual.

6 The MRS of f for d is 1:3 between 1f and 2f. Between 2f and 3f, the MRS of f for d is 1:5. Yes, the third f involved a greater sacrifice of d (5d) than did the second f (3d).

8 Since B is on both I and II, it would follow that all points on both I and II are equally satisfying. Comparing D with C, though, we note that both represent the same number of movies, but that D represents more concerts than C. This cannot be so unless the consumer finds both quantities of concerts equally satisfying, which violates our assumption that more is preferred to less. Therefore, the curves cannot cross.

10 Budget lines don't show levels of satisfaction, but merely attainable combinations of goods. Therefore, given the above information, there is no way of saying whether a consumer was made better off or worse off by the price changes. The addition of the indifference map of a particular consumer will enable us to answer the question. Draw two or three indifference curves on your diagram and you will see.

12 When more of a good is consumed, *total* utility derived from it increases (at least it does so until one reaches the point of "saturation," beyond which additional consumption actually decreases total utility). *Marginal* utility, on the other hand, decreases as more is consumed (it actually becomes negative beyond the point of saturation). Therefore, the only way to cause a good's marginal utility to increase is to cut down on its consumption. If this is still not clear, review Figure 3-9.

14 If we could measure levels of satisfaction in discrete units ("utils"), we could say, for instance, that I represented 55 utils and II represented 65 utils, and that the latter was 10 utils higher than the former. However, as the ordinalists have demonstrated, such "cardinal" measures of utility do not exist; consequently, we can only say that a consumer prefers those combinations of goods represented by II over those portrayed by I. We cannot say (nor can the consumer, for that matter), *how much* better off he or she is at the higher level of indifference represented by II.

Chapter 4

2 An inferior good is defined as one of which an individual purchases less when his or her income rises and more when his or her income falls. A normal good is defined as one of which an individual purchases more when his or her income increases and less when his or her income falls. Yes, the same good can be both. In fact, most goods are normal up to some level of income beyond which they become inferior. See the "backward-bending" Engel curve in Figure 4-6.

4 The price-consumption curve shows the different amounts of a good which a consumer will buy when faced with alternative prices for that good. One need only transfer the price and quantity combinations to a new graph where price is measured vertically and quantity horizontally.

6 In order to isolate the effect of a change in real income on the respective quantities of x and y purchased, the relative prices of the two goods must remain constant. If the relative prices are allowed to change, it is impossible to obtain an unambiguous measure of the change in income.

8 You would try to find a business that produced an inferior good. Why? Because when real incomes fall, the quantity of inferior goods demanded actually rises because of their negative income elasticity of demand.

10 If the good constitutes a very small proportion of one's budget (shoelaces, for example), the income effect can be set aside as insignificant. Even a doubling of the price of an item like shoelaces or toothpicks would have only a negligible effect on one's real income.

12 Unless the movie star really enjoys negotiating with merchants, we would expect him or her to spend less time searching. The time of a movie star probably is much more valuable than that of a police officer. Consequently, the "cost" of going from dealer to dealer, or even phoning them, is higher. If the cost is higher, we would expect less of it (information) to be consumed.

14 *System 1:* The family never gets off welfare but has the greatest incentive (of these three alternative systems, that is) to work since they can keep all their earnings.

System 2: The family will get off welfare if and when family earnings reach $300 per week. However, there is less incentive to work than under system 1 since the family gains only $2 for $3 earned.

System 3: The family will get off welfare when family earnings reach $100 per week. However, there is no incentive whatsoever to earn from $1 to $100 per week since welfare payments drop by $1 every time $1 is earned.

Chapter 5

2 We know that the $\Delta q/\Delta P$ term must remain constant, because it is merely the inverse of the slope, and a straight line's slope is, by definition, constant.

However, looking at the other term, because P and q are inversely related, we know that the ratio P/q will never be the same for two different prices; hence the product $(\Delta q/\Delta P)(P/q)$ must also change with every change in price (quantity).

4 At any given *price*, the steeper demand curve is less elastic (or more inelastic) than the other one. However, at any given quantity, their elasticities are identical.

6 No, it cannot. The household demand for table salt and the diabetic demand for insulin may have price elasticities near zero at their current prices. However, at sufficiently high prices, their respective demands must, of necessity, become elastic. After all, at any moment there is only a finite amount of real income with which to buy things.

8 The formula is $(\Delta q/\Delta P)(P/q)$. The second term is easy. You know the price P. Just "pick off" the corresponding quantity demanded, q, and you've got P/q. As for $\Delta q/\Delta P$, merely construct a tangent to the demand curve at point (q,P), measure its slope, $\Delta P/\Delta q$, invert it, and you have $\Delta q/\Delta P$. Now find the product of the two terms and you've got the point elasticity of demand at price P (quantity q).

10 (*a*) Negative (complements), (*b*) positive (substitutes), (*c*) positive (substitutes), (*d*) negative (complements), (*e*) negative (complements), (*f*) positive (assuming that they are substitutes; they well may be complements, at least for some people).

12 The problem is with the denominator, percentage change in P. Since the initial price was 0, any increase in price is of infinite percentage. However, if the arc-elasticity formula is used there will be no problem. The denominator of the denominator, P, will become the average of P_1 ($=0$) and P_2 ($=10$), or $(P_1 + P_2)/2$ ($=5$).

14 The statement is false. Economic theory makes no such prediction. The person making the statement is probably confusing the notion of search costs or transactions costs with elasticity. For example, we would expect persons whose time is less valuable to spend more of their time seeking bargains in the marketplace and looking for a longer time before deciding to buy. This does not prove, however, that their demand is more elastic, because we must include the value of their time spent shopping (search costs) in the prices they "pay." Note also that wealthier individuals often find it in their interest to hire others (agents, brokers, etc.) to examine the marketplace and maybe even make "minor" decisions on their behalf.

Chapter 6

2 The total price of golfing is the money price (club rental, green fees, etc.) *plus* the opportunity cost of time "consumed" playing and getting to and from the course. Consequently, as one's after-tax wages rise, it becomes more expensive to golf. Of course, this does not *necessarily* mean that you will golf less, because golfing may be a superior good (service) to you.

4 The person's preferences are consistent with a positive personal rate of discount. Our theory suggests that most persons are willing to pay more to consume something now rather than later. *How much* more they are willing to pay will determine when (if ever, since the person may *die* before the film gets to television) they see the movie in question. Note that watching a movie on TV is not free; it takes time, more time, in fact, because one must suffer through the commercials as well.

6 The present value of a future dollar is less than a dollar in hand, as long as there exists a positive interest rate. Put another way, a sum smaller than a dollar, invested today, at some positive interest rate, will grow until it becomes a dollar (or more) at some time in the future.

8 Originally, you would be willing to pay $20 for it because $1 per year is the "interest" on $20 at 5 percent per year. If the interest rate then fell to 2 percent per year, your perpetuity would be worth $50, because $1 per year interest on a $50 investment would yield 2 percent per year to its buyer.

10 For a 10 percent per year rate of return, the answer is $1,000. To earn 12 percent on your investment, you must pay no more than $887; to earn 8 percent per year, the bond must be bought for no more than $1,134.

Chapter 7

2 While stock in "blue chip" corporations (which Manville was once) and U.S. government bonds are relatively safe investments, portfolio diversification—spreading money over various assets—has been shown to be the least risky strategy. Since we cannot know the future of individual enterprises, how inflation may change, or other factors that will change the riskiness and rate of return on any one investment, diversification protects an individual's assets from falling victim to one unexpected change.

4 The annual premium would equal the expected annual claims divided by the number of participants, or 15 pregnancies × \$2,000 per pregnancy equals \$30,000, divided by 100 women equals \$300 per person per year. The first problem is that even though 15 pregnancies per 100 women may be the annual average, the figure would easily fluctuate from, say, 5 to 25 pregnancies and cause the \$30,000 per year to result in a surplus during some years and a deficit during other years. Second, and potentially much more disruptive of their scheme, is the likelihood of what insurance people call "adverse selection." The demand for the services of obstetricians and gynecologists slopes downward like any other demand curve; at a lower price, more will be demanded. Consequently, the quantity of deliveries demanded annually is greater at \$300 per year than it is at \$2,000 per year. Those women voluntarily joining this league are likely to conceive at well above the average rate of 15 per 100 per year.

6 A futures market "processes" information, both good and bad, affecting the future supply and demand for particular commodities. One way to make money trading in futures (some would say the only way to do so consistently) is to have better information than the other traders. In deciding how much to spend on weather information, one must weigh the present value of expected future benefits against the present value of expected future costs. It is unlikely that many speculators have their own weather service. The cost of producing reports which are better than those already available is, no doubt, very high.

8 It has been argued that all people are risk averse—if the size of the risk and the amount involved varies sufficiently to account for individual differences over smaller ranges. Many people are risk preferers for small amounts of their income or wealth. That is, they obtain pleasure from games of chance in which the odds are not in their favor (witness the rise in popularity of state-run lotteries which have a very low rate of return). But most people do not gamble with large fractions of wealth or income and we see

them buying insurance to protect against the consequences of large swings in wealth positions.

Chapter 8

2 It is indeed difficult to come up with any. While examples of "labor-intensive" pursuits (being a strawberry picker or bootblack) are numerous, examples of "labor-exclusive" production are far more difficult to think of. Perhaps personal services, the "oldest profession" being the most notorious, come the closest. Even there, however, some capital generally accompanies the labor input.

4 It is not only possible but not that uncommon. Many metropolitan transit companies don't own their own buses. Some taxi companies don't own the very tires their sedans roll on. This is accomplished by *leasing* the item (trucks, buses, tires) in question from a subcontractor of sorts (lessor). Why would a firm "job out" a task like the supplying of equipment? The entrepreneur has determined it (leasing) to be less costly than owning the equipment in question; it is more efficient.

6 The ability to *negotiate* is critical. There are many different outcomes realizable by exchanging with another person; that person may be a potential employee, supplier, customer, lender, or other business party. As will be seen later, since we do not live in a two-person world, competition will set limits on the range of prices at which goods and services will be exchanged. However, since information is a scarce commodity, the phenomenon of negotiation will always be with us. In each and every transaction, there are greater or smaller gains from voluntary exchange to be had by each party. Other things being equal, the larger gains will accrue to, and hence increase the wealth of, the better bargainer.

8 The problem, as was pointed out in the chapter, is one of cost. There is nearly always a trade-off between cost and time (or more accurately, expedience). At a higher cost one can get, say, a piece of equipment installed more quickly. How much a firm can justify spending to expedite a change in one of its "fixed" inputs will depend upon the present value of the contemplated additional input to the firm. Suffice it to say that, *ceteris paribus*, the lower the present value cost to change a "fixed" input, the sooner will "the" short run end and "the" long run begin.

10 You need to know the relative prices of the inputs you are using. A production function merely states the relationship between various combinations of inputs and output, in physical terms. In determining the cost-minimizing combination of labor and capital that will produce the desired output, you need to know the relative price of labor and capital.

12 Stage III is dispensed with most easily. Since total physical product actually declines as more of the variable input is added, it would clearly not be in a firm's interest to use more of that input, even if its marginal cost were zero. Stage I is equally unattractive because, over that range of outputs, the average physical product of the variable input is rising and causing the average variable cost (assuming the input can be hired at a constant unit price) to fall. For this reason, expansion of output beyond stage I is in order for a competitive firm.

14 A sufficient increase in total cost would shift tt' outward (upward) until Q_3 was attainable. Also, a sufficient decrease in either the price of capital (r) or the price of labor (w), or both, would rotate and/or shift tt' outward, making output Q_3 attainable. Note that we have assumed no change in technology. Such an improvement would shift Q_3 (and all other isoquants) toward the origin and make Q_3 attainable (if the advances were of sufficient magnitude) without any change in TC, r, or w.

16 The economic region of production for a fixed-proportions production function is made up of isoquants with sharp corners or "discontinuities." In the case of a single-proportion production function (one hammer head and one hammer handle equals one hammer), the isoquants will be right angles with the point of discontinuity lying along a straight-line ray from the origin, such as we see in Figure 8-10. The same pattern holds for fixed-proportions production functions with more than one feasible production combination. In the case of a two-combination or two-proportion production function, the isoquant map would look like the figure here.

The ray or rays from the origin always define the boundaries of the economic region of production. For the single-proportion production function the economic region is found *only* along the ray labeled A. For the two-proportions production function, it is the closed area bounded by the rays labeled A and B.

Note that the isoquants for a fixed-proportions pro-

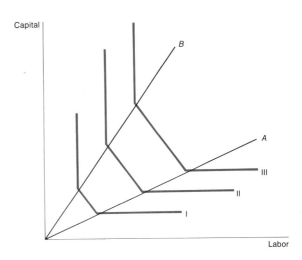

duction function become horizontal or vertical outside the economic region of production. This indicates that the marginal product of one factor (the one along the axis parallel to the isoquant) is zero. Typically, we assume that there is no uneconomic region of production for a fixed-proportions production function. (That is, there is no level of factor usage that will cause the marginal physical product or the factor to become negative. Thus, there is an economic region of production and a region where the MPP of a factor is zero, but no region where the MPP is negative.

This can be understood by reference to some common examples. The application of fertilizer to land in growing crops is a continuous-proportions production process. It is easy to imagine a case where applying too much fertilizer "burns" the crops and hence reduces the total yield. It is not so easy to imagine a case where too many hammer handles are joined to too few hammer heads in the production of hammers or a case where too many oxygen atoms are joined to too few hydrogen atoms in the production of water molecules.

Note that this does not mean that we can't have excess units of a factor of production—units that may have cost something to acquire. Nor does it mean that the disposal of such excess factor units is costless. We may be able to resell them only at a loss or we may have to pay someone to haul them away. Those questions, however, affect costs and values (reflected in the shape of the isocost line). They do not affect physical production processes, such as chemical reactions, as are reflected in the shape of isoquants.

Chapter 9

2 Despite the fact that the machine has long since been written off for tax-accounting purposes, it may still have a positive market value, which will be realized when the machine is sold or scrapped. The firm is still losing the interest that could be earned by selling the asset and investing the proceeds. Furthermore, even if the present scrap value is zero, there is an implicit cost of keeping it, equal to the rental value of the space it is taking up in the plant.

4 It is both. Pornography, like beauty, is in the eye of the beholder. Whether passersby find the video to be offensive (an external cost) or attractive (an external benefit) is a matter of individual preferences. Most communities would, no doubt, contain individuals holding both views.

6 Certainly most accountants would consider an existing long-term lease obligation, without rights to a sublet, to be a fixed cost. However, it is usually possible, through negotiation and possibly a lump-sum settlement, to get out of a lease. Consequently, this firm's short run may be terminable, at a cost, on fairly short notice.

8 You are not minimizing costs for output Q because, given the relative prices of capital and labor, you are using too much capital and not enough labor. By using less capital, its marginal product will rise; by using more labor, its marginal product will fall. This substitution of labor for capital should continue until the ratio of their marginal products is the same as that of their relative prices, or 10 to 1.

10 The "planning" or "envelope" (LAC) curve represents the locus of points that give the lease unit cost of producing any given rate of output. The concept is important when one must decide which scale of operations to adopt. Such a decision usually takes the form of deciding what size "plant" to construct.

12 You should increase output at plants 2 and 3, thereby raising MC at both, and decrease plant 1's output so as to decrease its MC. This should be continued until the MCs are all equal and will occur at an MC greater than $8 and less than $10.

If all sales occur at plant 1 the MC per unit of shipping output from plants 2 and 3 must be added into their costs of production to allow a relevant comparison across plants.

14 The authors of our Constitution may well have had something akin to our LAC concept in mind when they drafted the commerce clause. The effect of sufficiently high duties (taxes) levied by any state on the "exports" of another state would have been to limit the extent of the market, in which any one firm could sell, to its own state. This in turn would have prevented the realization of lower unit costs in those industries exhibiting substantial economies of scale, and consequently would have kept prices from being as low as they would have been otherwise. Note that those consumers in the states with the smallest populations would have had the most to lose.

Chapter 10

2 The industry demand curve is negatively sloped; it is relevant insofar as its interaction with the industry supply curve (ΣMC) determines the product price. The demand facing the individual firm, however, is infinitely elastic (horizontal) at the current market price.

4 There is no limit to the number of criteria one can dream up. Here are five which may or may not resemble the ones you selected:
(a) Queuing ("First come, first served.")
(b) By sex ("Ladies first.")
(c) By age ("Age before beauty.")
(d) By physical strength ("I'll fight you for it!")
(e) By income and/or wealth (a "means" test)

6 Sometimes profit maximization involves loss minimization—making the best out of a bad situation, so to speak. Since fixed costs are invariant to output in the short run, the decision whether to produce is based entirely on variable costs. As long as the going price is above average variable cost, it is better not to cease production entirely. The excess of revenues over variable costs can be used to defray part of the fixed costs which will have to be paid in any event.

8 Assuming that the business is not a corporation and that the year's "profits" included any salary that she drew for her own labor, the firm actually sustained an economic loss of $2,000 during the first year. Aside from the explicit accounting costs which have been deducted from revenues ("sales") in arriving at "profit," we must deduct the implicit costs of both the equity capital ($8,000 per year) and the owner's labor ($10,000 per year). Subtracting both of these from the $16,000 accounting profit yields an economic loss of $2,000 per year. Like many self-employed individuals, this person has "paid a price" to work for herself. Two other qualifications should be noted. In light of the risk typically involved in small businesses, an 8 percent per year opportunity cost of capital (that earned on a government-backed certificate of deposit) was far too low. Twelve to fifteen percent per year probably would have been more appropriate. Second, since most self-employed persons work very long hours, the $10,000 per year opportunity cost of her labor was also probably on the low side.

10 Equilibrium price means that the amount supplied equals the amount demanded. Of course, the sellers would prefer a higher price, while the buyers would prefer a lower one. Everybody is "happy" only in the sense that, given the price, each is able to buy or sell all he or she wishes. The problem with disequilibrium prices is that they cause frustration in the market. If the price is "too high" (greater than P_e), the amount supplied exceeds the amount demanded, causing frustration on the part of at least some of the sellers who are unable to "move" all the merchandise they would like to at that price. If the price is "too low" ($<P_e$), at least some buyers are frustrated by their inability to buy all they would like at that price. If that price were not permitted to rise, sellers would be forced to use some other rationing criterion or criteria besides money to decide who would get the less-than-equilibrium quantities of goods. The first situation ($P > P_e$) is often called a "buyers' market" and the second situation ($P < P_e$) a "sellers' market."

12 A nonscarce ("free") good is one of which, at a price of zero, the quantity demanded is less than or equal to the quantity supplied. Consequently, your graph should show a demand curve intercepting the horizontal (Q/t) axis at or to the left of where the corresponding supply curve intercepts that axis.

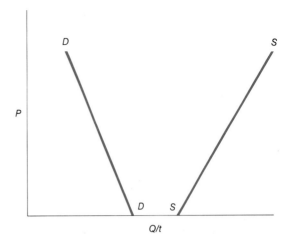

14 Apparently your friend, "Superentrepreneur," has a unique ability to combine resources more efficiently than others. One way to "handle" this is simply to assert that his or her opportunity cost is understated. Clearly, a sufficiently high opportunity cost assigned to the proprietor's time will shift up the firm's SAC until economic profits disappear.

Chapter 11

2 In addition to whatever humanitarian motives may be at work, whether expressed through organized charities or otherwise, this is one of many "disaster" scenarios which illustrate the signaling and incentive functions of a system of interrelated markets. Obviously, those stranded on rooftops would be willing to offer a higher price for boat services than is ordinarily paid for these services (demand has increased). This would cause owners of boats in other parts of Texas, and other parts of the nation, to hitch up their boats and bring them to Houston. An equilibrium is reached when the supply of boating services in Houston has expanded to the point where the prevailing market price just covers the marginal cost of bringing the last boat in from elsewhere. You might want to trace out the similar supply, demand, and price effects of the following: (1) a freeze of Florida citrus crops; (2) a hurricane which levels many homes and offices in Corpus Christi, Texas.

4 Just as markets provide incentives for invention, they also provide incentives for the distribution of valuable discoveries. There is a famous story about an American horticulturalist who stood in the town square and consumed a basket of tomatoes to demonstrate to his neighbors that "this was a harmless fruit." Such a demonstration would have had little effect, however, if tomatoes weren't also less expensive to produce (or otherwise "more available") than other food sources.

6 Primarily because of the development of new high-yield disease-resistant varieties of traditional crops. Strangely enough, the very nations which are benefitting the most from these privately produced new strains are now demanding that they be given the new developments free. The reasoning for this demand is that many of the new strains are hybrids of native varieties, the parent plants of which were originally obtained in the underdeveloped nations. What do you think would be the effect on future development of even more productive crops if the seed companies producing these new varieties were legally required to sell them at a price equal to that which they formerly received for ordinary seed grain?

8 Austrians believe that the economic world is in constant flux. Tastes change. New discoveries are made daily about production techniques and consumption alternatives. The essential feature of an economy is its ability to incorporate and utilize these changes, rather than suppressing or ignoring them. Planning, however, must proceed in terms of what is known when the plan is formulated. Continual revision of a plan simply means that there is no plan after all. Planning is thus possible only in a static, changeless world, a world different from the one we live in.

Chapter 12

2 If, at the price charged, the demand were inelastic, that would mean that total revenues could be increased and total costs decreased (if MC > 0) by raising the price and selling fewer units. Consequently, the profit-maximizing price must be a higher one. Trial and error would lead to further price increases until an elastic portion of the demand curve was reached. Then even further increases in price (decreases in output) would be in order as long as marginal cost exceeded marginal revenue.

4 If η is numerically greater than 1 (elastic), marginal revenue is positive; a decrease in price will result in more total revenues. If η is numerically equal to 1 (unitary elastic), marginal revenue is 0; a change in price will not affect total revenues at all. If η is numerically less than 1 (inelastic), marginal revenue is negative; a decrease in price will result in less total revenues.

6 Output Q is set at the level where MC = MR. The price charged is the maximum price at which that output Q can be sold, and can be "read" off the demand curve. Economic profits will exist if TR exceeds TC (where TR is equal to $P \times Q$ and TC is equal to ATC $\times$ Q). If TC exceeds TR, the monopoly is "reaping" economic losses.

8 To the extent that TR exceeds TC (economic costs, of course), the firm's market value will be higher by a multiple of those annual economic profits. The multiple is the inverse of the opportunity cost of capital. In effect, the stream of expected future economic profits is discounted to its present value as presented in Chapter 6, and that figure is included in the firm's market price, typically as "good will."

10 There are many possible reasons. Just because economic profits are being made doesn't necessarily mean that even higher profits aren't attainable. The demand schedule may have shifted since the last plant was set up. Technology may have changed. Relative input prices may have changed. Any one of these would alter the optimum scale of operations. Note how rare it is that firms ever purchase new equipment which is identical to the equipment which is being phased out.

12 A perfectly competitive firm, in long-run equilibrium, exhibits the following per unit cost and revenue relationships: P = MR = SMC = LMC = SAC = LAC. For the monopolist, the result is a bit different: SAC = LAC < P > MR = SMC = LMC. Note that if the monopoly profits are capitalized into the firm's value, SAC and LAC will *equal P*.

14 In both cases a sliding scale of prices is charged which results, in effect, in quantity discounts (lower unit prices when more is purchased). The difference is that while multipart pricing implies discrete variations in unit price according to quantity purchased, perfect price discrimination would capture all consumers' surplus from the buyers. Total revenues become the entire area under the demand curve up to the output being sold; and the last unit is sold for a price just equal to its MC. Note that the amount of information required to even approach perfect price discrimination would be astronomical.

16 People sitting in identical seats on an airplane may have paid significantly different amounts for their seats. The reason the prices are different is that even though the airline industry is competitive, the firms are able to price discriminate. The person who plans a trip months in advance can carefully shop for the best deal and will consider travel by car or bus, too. A business traveler or a person who has to go to a funeral usually cannot use any other means of transport, and will take whatever is available. To have the convenience of an empty seat being open at the last minute, a higher price will be charged and paid. This is simply market segmentation, as we see in Figure 12-12.

Chapter 13

2 The effect of tariffs is to penalize foreign producers when they sell in "our" market. This is, in effect, a barrier to those firms entering the United States market for goods. The reduction or elimination of tariffs increases competition and decreases any monopoly power that might have existed as a result of those tariffs. Note, though, that even with a tariff American producers must still compete. The tariff just means that they will produce at a higher MC, which causes a misallocation of resources on a global scale.

4 The possible criteria are many. The most obvious is money: auction off the rights to the highest bidder. Note that the form of competition will be directly related to the criterion or criteria established by the issuing authority. The "tune" of the bidding will be effectively "called" by the government. Whenever something of value is distributed, rivalry among potential recipients is bound to result.

6 The first problem is that, unless the government somehow controls production, an excess quantity supplied (a "glut" or surplus) will result. The quantity supplied will exceed the quantity demanded at the above-market-clearing price. Unless the government stands ready to buy unlimited quantities at that price, effectively pegging it at that level, a lower (black-market) price will develop. At this lower price, producers will be able to sell all their production, something which was not possible at the pegged price. Any program which attempts to subsidize producers by outlawing "low" prices, without getting a handle on supply, is doomed to failure. For this reason, "price support" programs are inevitably followed by (maximum) production quotas of one kind or another.

8 Cartel agreements are generally "out front." OPEC (the Organization of Petroleum Exporting Countries) holds periodic publicized meetings after which it typically announces what "the" price of crude oil will be. There is little pretense of secrecy. Other collusive agreements, executed in violation of the law, are typically characterized by secrecy and clandestine behavior in direct proportion to the penalties for being caught.

10 Is entry restricted? Yes. State bar examinations accomplish that. Is competition discouraged? Yes. "Recommended" minimum fee schedules discourage price cutting. In addition, advertising, perhaps the most common form of rivalry, is still restricted by the state bars. Are there sanctions for violating the "code of ethics"? Yes. In all states it is illegal to practice law without a license. Furthermore, transgressions of the rules by licensed attorneys (members of the bar) subject them to possible loss of license as a result of so-called disbarment proceedings.

12 A natural monopoly occurs in industries in which there are substantial economies of scale in relation to the market demand for the product. The relationship between LAC and DD is such that one firm can supply the entire market at lower unit costs than could two or more firms. For this reason, once one firm establishes a plant of sufficient size to take advantage of the economies of scale, there is no incentive whatsoever for another firm to enter.

14 Yes it does. For a firm that was highly "leveraged" (financed with borrowed money) the second method would be far more advantageous. Since the tax laws permit the deduction of interest payments as a cost of operation, chargeable against sales in arriving at profit, there would be a great incentive for a firm not only to buy new equipment frequently but to do so with borrowed money, *even if it had to pay an interest rate greater than 10 percent per year!* Note that this argument presupposes a demand of sufficient strength to generate revenues adequate to cover all these "costs" including the "permissible" rate of return on "investment."

Chapter 14

2 Recall that in a perfectly competitive market, in long-run equilibrium, $P = MR = SMC = SAC = LMC = LAC$. This outcome is shown graphically in Figure 10-10(b). In a monopolistically competitive market, the result is that $P = SAC = LAC > MR = LMC = SMC$. There exists "excess capacity," which, in Chamberlin's definition, is the price consumers pay for differentiated products.

4 The burden of proof rests on the person who seeks to demonstrate that a product difference is merely "artificial" or "superficial." Does the addition of carburetor-cleaning additives to gasoline amount to an "artificial" differentiation of the product? How about "service with a smile"? Is that not preferable to service with a frown? A better product, like beauty, is in the eye of the beholder. The fact that every day millions of people fork over the additional cost of these "mere frills" suggests that at least some consumers find them to be product-enhancing and therefore "real."

6 Marginal revenue in its usual sense refers to the change in total revenue attributable to a change in price of sufficient magnitude (a zero price change being sufficient in the case of an infinitely elastic demand schedule) to cause the quantity demanded to change by one unit. This involves a movement along a given demand schedule. In the case of advertising, however, "marginal revenue" results from a *shift* in the demand schedule which is the result of an advertising effort that enables (hopefully) more to be sold at each and every possible price.

8 If "MR" > MC, increased advertising outlays will further increase profits. Advertising outlays would be increased until "MR" = MC. More specifically, when MC$_{\text{advertising}}$ plus MC$_{\text{production}}$ equals "MR," advertising outlays are optimal from the standpoint of maximizing profits.

10 The distinction is not clear. Toothpaste, mouthwash, and deodorant ads are often informative only in the sense that they remind us of our inherent biological condition. Photographs of the Taj Mahal or Machu Picchu, which give potential tourists a glimpse of these tourist attractions, seem to be more informative. When the British Tourist Board beckons us to "Come home, America (to the United Kingdom), all is forgiven," we are reminded of our Anglo-Saxon heritage and, in some historical sense, are "informed" by the ad. Typewriter and car ads that focus on the product's performance would be classified as "informative" by nearly everyone.

12 The result is that each firm consistently overestimates the elasticity of its demand curve and makes decisions based upon an imaginary demand curve $d_f d_f$ and its associated marginal revenue curve mr$_f$.

14 If entry of new firms is not prevented, entry will occur in response to the existence of economic profits. As the number of firms, "n," increases, the proportional demand curve $d_p' d_p'$ will shift leftward (actually it will rotate clockwise about its price or vertical axis intercept). Eventually, economic profits will be completely dissipated by such entry and price will be equal to LAC. At this point, there are no economic profits and entry will cease.

16 Since entry is unrestricted, the potential for economic profits will result in entry, according to this simple model, so long as some segment of one of the proportionate demand curves lies above the LAC curve. Output can be more efficiently (cheaply) produced, in this case, by two firms rather than three; but three will, nonetheless, exist.

18 (a) Cournot assumed that perfect information would keep both firms' prices identical. He further assumed that each firm would behave as if the other would not change its output in response to any change in the other's output. (b) The long-run result was a price greater than MC (the competitive price) but less than the monopoly price.

20 In both models, both duopolists are assumed to continue to behave on the basis of assumptions about the rival's behavior that are repeatedly demonstrated to be false. They don't learn from their experiences. It is difficult to conceive of entrepreneurs so stubborn in their beliefs that they refuse to recognize overwhelming evidence that their reaction-function assumptions are inaccurate.

22 The kink arises from the assumptions of the model. Sweezy assumes that if any one firm raises its price, none of the others will follow. Consequently, a maverick firm's price increase will result in a drastic decrease in its total revenue. Conversely, the model assumes that any price decrease will be matched by all rivals. For this reason, the quantity demanded will probably not increase enough to cover increased costs and profit probably will be less. Under these assumptions, it is in no individual firm's interest to "rock the boat."

24 They are presumed to be completely passive and to behave as price takers. They act as though their individual demand curves were perfectly elastic at the price set by the dominant firm (which they "are" as long as the dominant firm permits the others to sell all they wish at that price), and they set their individual outputs at a level equating marginal cost with that price.

26 The consequences of an overt price war can be disastrous for oligopolistic firms. For that reason there are strong group pressures not to disturb the industry price structure. More subtle and less easily detectible means such as advertising and minor design variations are commonly used in an attempt to increase revenues and/or share of the market. Such revenue-increasing techniques are perceived by other firms to be less threatening and therefore more acceptable forms of competition.

Chapter 15

2 Their behavior was tantamount to killing the goose that laid the golden egg. Labor and capital are complementary inputs; each enhances the marginal productivity of the other. Higher-paid workers are typically the ones who work with such sophisticated equipment as giant punch presses, welding rigs, etc. Janitors, on the other hand, typically do their work with relatively unsophisticated tools such as brooms and mops; their substantially lower productivity is reflected in their lower wage rate.

4 By assumption, it does not. Generally, the quantity of labor hired by a single competitive firm is insignificant in relation to the overall demand for labor. However, the next chapter will deal with labor markets in which a firm *is* sufficiently large to affect prevailing wages by its own hiring and firing.

6 Just as a fall in the relative price of a commodity will induce consumers to substitute more of it in their consumption, entrepreneurs will make similar substitutions in response to a change in the relative price of an input. If the identical output is still to be produced, it will now be done with less capital and more labor in response to a fall in the relative price of labor.

8 In response to a fall in the price of labor, a firm will do more than just substitute labor for capital. In addition, it will go beyond merely increasing its labor purchases with the cost savings realized from a fall in the price of labor. Since the marginal product of capital has risen with the increased input of labor, the firm will actually increase its use of capital in attaining the new optimal input combination.

10 Suppose the demand for the output product is highly elastic. Even a relatively small increase in the price of the input factor, which correspondingly raises the price of the output product, will cause a large decrease in the quantity of output demanded, and therefore in the employment of the input.

12 The theory is not well suited to service industries because it is physically impossible for an entrepreneur to keep an inventory of, say, razor cuts. Services, by their very nature, are consumed as they are produced and are therefore not stockpileable. This is no doubt one of the reasons that barbershops seldom employ barbers on a straight salary. Part of the risk of idleness (and the corresponding reward of busyness) is thereby borne by the employee.

14 Two points need be made. First, the physical quantity of land *is* augmentable. The Dutch, by building elaborate systems of dikes and canals, have been pushing the ocean back for decades. Second, at sufficiently low rental rates, some land will be withdrawn from the land use market because the owner prefers to use it for hunting or picnics or just for the scenic beauty of its idleness.

16 It depends. If (a) Frisbees are manufactured in an area having a large labor force in relation to Whamo's employment demands, and (b) Whamo is not unionized, the example is apt. This assumes, of course, that you accept the characterization of Whamo as the monopoly seller of Frisbees.

18 The statement is false. It is true that in a competitive labor market the monopoly seller has no power to affect the wage rates it pays. However, exploitation refers to paying a worker less than his or her VMP. Monopolists don't hire *enough* of the resource in question; they cease hiring when the MRP equals the going wage. Since VMP always exceeds MRP for a monopolist, it must also exceed the going wage at the monopolist's profit-maximizing output. Consequently, there is exploitation, by definition.

20 Some examples would be Coors beer in Golden, Colorado; Bethlehem Steel in Bethlehem, Pennsylvania; Winnebago Corporation in Forest City, Iowa; and many coal mining towns in West Virginia. As long as your example is one of a dominant employer (dominant in its local labor market, that is) selling its product(s) in fairly competitive markets, you're correct.

22 This monopsony argument is not unlike the one in question 21. In the long run, if the wage level is unsatisfactory, some of these "specialists" will retrain. Similarly, students will choose not to go into the field; they will choose to acquire other skills. In the long run, the supply of labor faced by these monopsonists will be pretty flat.

24 The perfectly price (wage) discriminating firm never pays more than the opportunity cost of any unit of labor it hires. Under these circumstances, the MFC curve is the SS curve, and there is no reason for the firm to restrict its hiring. By assumption there is no problem of bidding up wages of existing employees in order to get an additional employee to come on board. If this is unclear, look again at Figure 15-12.

26 The nondiscussion of wages is consistent with price (wage) discrimination by employers. Keeping one's employees "in the dark" regarding each other's earnings facilitates the practice of unequal pay for "equal" work. Also, it is clearly in the interest of those employees who are better paid to stifle the flow of such information.

Chapter 16

2 The statement is false. Because a firm utilizes an input only to the point that the input's VMP or MRP is equal to its price, and marginal product is declining, it follows that all the inframarginal (up to the marginal) units are producing more value than they are being paid. This differential is used to compensate other factor inputs. The residual, if any, would be profits.

4 It is the nonpecuniary aspects of clerical and blue-collar jobs that account for much of the spread in pay. Aside from differences in "status," clerical workers typically don't have to dirty their hands or work around fumes and noise or out of doors. The probability of being killed or injured is much lower in an office than on a factory floor or construction site, and job security may also be greater.

6 Not only is a higher level of innate ability required, but the training of a CPA is substantially greater than that of a retail clerk. In the long run, CPA wages must reflect the costs of training in order that there be an incentive for additional workers to continue to train for that field.

8 The statement is false. Some of the revenue may indeed be rent. However, the buildings housing the art have to be maintained, guards hired, ticket takers paid, etc. Occasionally, ransoms on stolen paintings even have to be paid. All these costs are part of the cost of keeping the art objects intact, and these costs must be subtracted from revenues in arriving at the economic rent, if any.

10 Quasi-rent is a short-run concept. By definition, in the short run some inputs are fixed. In defining them as fixed, we are implying that their short-run opportunity cost is zero. Consequently, their supply to the firm is perfectly inelastic. The quasi-rent concept is applied primarily to specialized equipment which is costly to relocate. Bridges and hydroelectric dams would be good examples.

12 The consumers of factory products rarely meet or are even aware of the people who make the products. In service industries, however, the consumer typically meets the producer face to face. Those preferring to be served by a "this" or a "that" would presumably be willing to pay more to have that preference satisfied. Consequently, the incentives for the proprietor to discriminate in hiring are greater and more direct.

14 If the discrimination is noneconomic (not based upon productivity differences), the group being discriminated against ought to represent a bargain-basement pool of cheap labor. A manufacturer hiring that labor would have lower production costs than those of its discriminating competitors. Note that if enough firms caught on to this idea, their actions would cause the intergroup wage differentials to vanish. (Apply Figure 16-2 here.)

Chapter 17

2 Through the use of mathematics, general equilibrium analysis can handle multimarket economies. However, in order to present the concepts in two-dimensional (plane) geometry, we must restrict the number of consumers, inputs, and outputs to two each. Note that all the concepts developed are applicable to a multimarket reality.

4 The goods must be distributed in such a manner that the marginal rate of substitution between good x and good y is equal for both parties. If it were not equal, further voluntary exchange would benefit both individuals.

6 The statement is false because it is too broad. We can say a bit more about the final distribution once we know the initial allotments. Figure 17-6 shows that while it is true that trade will occur until the contract curve is reached, the final distribution will be limited to that portion of it which is between points E' and E". Study Figure 17-6 until you have satisfied yourself that, in the absence of coercion, it would be irrational for one of the consumers to move to a point on the contract curve outside of segment E' E".

8 A change in preferences will necessitate a reconstruction of the indifference maps. This will generate an entirely new contract curve. Now, additional exchanges will be necessary in order to enhance the well-being of both parties. These exchanges will cease when the new contract curve has been reached.

10 D portrays an initial allocation of the two resources to the production of goods x and y. In order to determine the respective outputs of goods x and y when resources are so allocated, we must look to the production isoquants for each good. These are shown in Figure 17-8. Q_{II}^x and Q_{II}^y correspond to specific rates of output for each good.

12 The marginal rate of technical substitution (MRTS) between each pair of inputs must be the same for all producers who make use of those inputs.

14 If the MRTs were not equal, resources could be reallocated in such a manner as to increase the production and consumption of one good without decreasing the production or consumption of the other. This would clearly increase the level of utility of either or both consumers (depending upon the distribution of the new output mix) without decreasing

the satisfaction of either one. If the MRSs of two or more consumers were unequal, additional utility could be generated for one or both by moving toward the contract curve (voluntary exchange).

Chapter 18

2 Positive economics is not designed to answer questions of good, bad, better, or worse. When we speak of an optimal allocation of resources, we are referring to an allocation which is socially efficient in the sense that no further voluntary exchange will occur.

4 Since interpersonal utility comparisons are impossible, there is no known way of proving or disproving such a statement. A "utilometer" device, cardinally quantifying persons' perceived utilities, has yet to be developed.

6 If the existing allocation of resources is such that no person can gain without another incurring a loss, the condition has been satisfied. This is just another way of saying that no further voluntary exchange will occur; the contract curve has been reached.

8 Your graph should look like the one in Figure 18-1. The highest attainable level of indifference is represented by the indifference curve which is tangent to the product transformation curve. The point of tangency shows the respective rates of production and consumption of the two goods; and the MRS is equal to MRT.

10 A utility possibilities frontier is another way of looking at a contract (or conflict) curve. Any movement along a contract curve will result in higher utility for one person and lower utility for the other (thus the notion of "conflict"). A number of those levels of indifference are ranked for each consumer. Those rankings become the ordinal units on the utility possibilities frontier.

12 No, it does not necessarily follow. The theory of second best suggests that such a partial movement toward perfectly competitive markets may actually lessen social welfare. This point has important implications for economic policy.

14 Arrow starts with five axioms which he believes that social preference structures must satisfy to be minimally acceptable to the population. He has found no majority voting system which satisfies all five criteria. This theorem has generated much critical reflection on the democratic process.

16 The producers' surplus obtained from producing and selling any particular unit of a good is the difference between what the producer would have been barely *willing* to accept for the unit and what he or she actually *did* receive for it. Free entry into an industry and/or expansion of existing firms will compete away short-run quasi-rents. In contrast, in the absence of perfect price discrimination, consumers' surplus will persist.

Chapter 19

2 Market failure refers to situations in which markets fail to allocate resources in a welfare-maximizing manner. By implication, some modification of the market outcome might succeed in improving the allocation of resources.

4 If we are in agreement that rooftop TV antennas detract from the appearance of a home and impose an eyesore cost (not to be confused with an isocost) on neighbors and passersby, then our nation over-allocates resources to production of such antennas. This is a situation of external diseconomies, because marginal social cost exceeds marginal social benefits.

6 Since the new supply schedule is to the left of the old (external costs have now been included) and the demand schedule remains unchanged, the new equilibrium price is higher, and the equilibrium quantity is smaller. Economic welfare would be increased by such a contraction of output and the associated increase in price.

8 Everyone owns them and nobody owns them. Consequently, there is no incentive for any user to be concerned with the future value of the resource in question. This is perhaps most clearly observable in the behavior of fishing boat owners. The goal of each boat owner is to harvest fish as long as marginal private cost is less than the going price of such fish. The opportunity cost of depleting the stock of fish does not affect the decisions of the proprietor. In light of the nonownership of the fish, any single boat operator would be foolish to behave otherwise.

10 In effect, much conservation legislation attempts to assign "rights" to plants and wild animals. Judges as well have been asked to define ecological rights. Historically, however, wild plants and animals have been "fair game" for Homo sapiens.

12 There is an implied assumption that some people would prefer to live in a racially and ethnically homogeneous neighborhood or, at least, that they think others hold such preferences. The whole notion of a "panic" rests upon such an assumption. More devastating to the theory, however, is the implied assumption that information costs are very high, at least in the short run. Even if the alleged decline in property values does occur, Mr. or Ms. Blockbuster will not be the only person seeking to buy on the downswing. To the extent that home-seeking persons, brokers, and speculators perceive the temporary nature of the decline, their bidding for homes will lessen, if not prevent entirely (in the case of perfect information), the decline in property values. This would remove Blockbuster's incentive for such an undertaking and prevent it from occurring. The theory fails.

14 Pollution should be further reduced as long as the marginal social benefit from such reduction exceeds the marginal social cost of doing so.

Appendix B

2

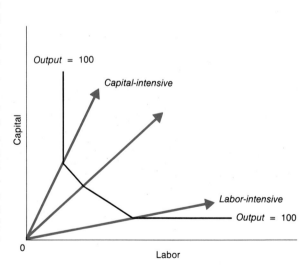

4

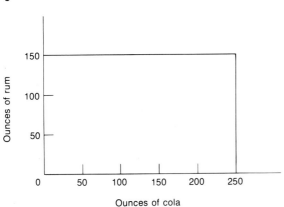

6

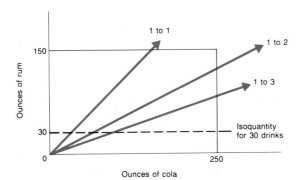

Note: The isoquantity is parallel to the constraint on rum because each drink requires 1 ounce of rum.
Answer: All process rays are feasible.

10

$$3x_1 + 2x_2 = 10$$
$$6x_1 + x_2 = 8$$

Multiplying the second by -2

$$3x_1 + 2x_2 = 10$$
$$-12x_1 - 2x_2 = -16$$

Adding, we obtain

$$-9x_1 = -6$$
$$x_1 = \tfrac{2}{3}$$

Substitution yields

$$3(\tfrac{2}{3}) + 2x_2 = 10$$
$$2x_2 = 10 - 2 = 8$$
$$x_2 = 4$$

Checking the corners, we have

$$z = 5(0) + 2(5) = 10$$
$$Optimal \rightarrow z = 5(\tfrac{2}{3}) + 2(4) = \tfrac{10}{3} + 8 = \tfrac{34}{3} = 11\tfrac{1}{3}$$
$$z = 5(\tfrac{4}{3}) + 2(0) = \tfrac{20}{3} = 6\tfrac{2}{3}$$

8

Objective function is $z = 5x_1 + 2x_2$

Constraints: $3x_1 + 2x_2 \le 10$
$6x_1 + x_2 \le 8$

Also $x_1 \ge 0$ and $x_2 \ge 0$ are called nonnegativity constraints. These correspond to real life in that products cannot be produced in negative quantities.

12

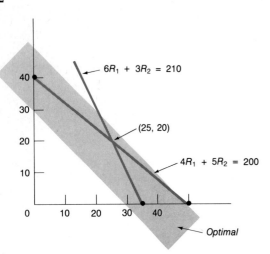

$6R_1 + 3R_2 = 210$

$(25, 20)$

$4R_1 + 5R_2 = 200$

Optimal

Checking corners:
$P(0, 40) = 1(0) + 1(40) = 40$
$P(25, 20) = 1(25) + 1(20) = 45 \leftarrow$ *Optimal*
$P(35, 0) = 1(35) + 1(0) = 35$

14

K = Number of kegs of beer @ 3,000 ounces
C = Number of cases of beer @ 300 ounces

$3,000\,K + 300\,C \leq 180,000$

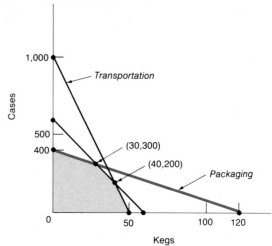

Cases

Transportation

$(30,300)$

$(40,200)$

Packaging

Kegs

Name Index

Subject Index

Index to Glossary Terms